SPEECH

FOR EFFECTIVE COMMUNICATION

SPEECH

FOR EFFECTIVE COMMUNICATION

Rudolph F. Verderber

 Harcourt Brace Jovanovich, Publishers

Orlando   San Diego   Chicago   Dallas

Rudolph F. Verderber (Ph.D. University of Missouri) is Chairman of the Department of Communication at the University of Cincinnati. In addition to teaching communication courses at the University of Cincinnati, he consults with high-school teachers and gives a variety of workshops for teachers and private organizations. He has served as parliamentarian for state and regional meetings of several national organizations and as Director of Forensics at the University of Cincinnati. He also has experience acting in theater productions. His publications include three best-selling college texts covering public speaking, interpersonal communication, and general speech communication skills; a manual on debate for high-school and college courses; and numerous articles. Professor Verderber is a member of the Speech Communication Association and the Central States Speech Association and is the recipient of the 1986 Distinguished Service Award from the Speech Communication Association of Ohio.

CRITICAL REVIEWERS

Elizabeth Bell
University Interscholastic League
University of Texas at Austin
Austin, Texas

Don M. Boileau
Director of Educational Services
Speech Communication Association
Annandale, Virginia

Ken Brooks
Morton East High School
Cicero, Illinois

Darcy Butrimas
Lake Highland Preparatory School
Orlando, Florida

David Chalfant
Walt Whitman High School
Bethesda, Maryland

Richard Dempsey
Evanston Township High School
Evanston, Illinois

Ronald Dodson
Westlake High School
Austin, Texas

Mary Fran Ferdinandt
Naperville Central High School
Naperville, Illinois

Carmendale Fernandes
Fremont High School
Sunnyvale, California

Merlyn Henry
Bennett High School
Bennett, Colorado

David J. Jecmen
John Marshall High School
Cleveland, Ohio

Kay Kalin Johnson
Amador High School
Pleasanton, California

Nan Kittel
Stafford High School
Stafford, Texas

Keith Kyker
Oak Ridge High School
Orlando, Florida

Luanne Pendorf
Lakewood High School
Lakewood, Colorado

Ronna Sloan
Sara J. Hale High School
Brooklyn, New York

Darla Wilshire
Altoona Area High School
Altoona, Pennsylvania

ACKNOWLEDGMENTS

For permission to reprint copyrighted material, grateful acknowledgment is made to the following sources:

American Forensic Association, James W. Pratt, Secretary: "American Forensic Association Debate Ballot."

Elizabeth Barnett, Literary Executor: Second stanza from "Recuerdo" in *Collected Poems* by Edna St. Vincent Millay. Copyright © 1922, 1950 by Edna St. Vincent Millay. Published by Harper & Row, Publishers, Inc.

Cambridge University Press: From "The Little Dog" in *Mountains and Molehills* by Frances Cornford. Published by Cambridge University Press, 1934.

CONTENTS

UNIT TWO: INTERPERSONAL RELATIONSHIPS

CHAPTER

7

CONVERSATION 137

UNIT THREE: PUBLIC SPEAKING

CHAPTER

10

UNIT FOUR: TYPES OF SPEECHES

CHAPTER

15

THE PROCESS SPEECH   355

CHAPTER

19

UNIT SIX: THE PERFORMING ARTS

CHAPTER

21

APPENDIX OF SPEECHES

QUICK REFERENCE GUIDE TO SPECIAL FEATURES

Profiles in Communication

Real-Life Speaking Situations

TO THE STUDENT

Until I was in the fifth grade, I took speaking for granted as a necessary activity—sometimes useful, sometimes fun, sometimes confusing and uncomfortable. Then I was chosen for a role in a local radio drama and discovered speaking as a performance, a skill I could learn, refine, and control. Before long, I was hooked on getting better at performing. I acted in plays, gave speeches, and joined in debates. I soon learned that "speech" was much more than talking; it was also listening and body language. When the time came to choose a career, I decided that I wanted to share all that I had learned about speech. In short, I decided to become a teacher.

Over the years that I have been teaching speech communication, I have given a great deal of thought to not only how people become better speakers but also *why* people might want or need to improve their speech skills. I have come up with at least four reasons: to become better citizens, to become more successful, to protect themselves, and to have more fun.

One of the main reasons for learning speech skills is to become a better citizen. All people who live in a democracy have a responsibility to participate in the running of their government. This means more than simply voting, as important as that is. It means discussing issues with other people, listening to speeches and debates, stating opinions, and taking stands on issues. Studying and practicing speech communication skills helps citizens to fulfill these responsibilities and take an active role in the democratic process.

Personal success is just as important as good citizenship. Being able to communicate well gives people control over their own lives. Sadly, too many people feel that life is a game they don't play very well; someone else makes the rules, and someone else always wins. As a high-school student, you may have felt that way sometimes. You may have wondered what to say or do to make friends, to get a job, or to let your parents and teachers know how you feel. By studying speech, you can learn how to talk to people easily, how to make a good impression in a job interview, and how to express your feelings more clearly. Being able to communicate effectively can help you win in the game of life, and the prize is success.

In addition to helping you control the course of your life, learning good communication skills helps you become aware of how other people attempt to control and manipulate you. Sharpening your critical listening ability enables you to protect yourself against propaganda that seeks to influence your thoughts and behavior. By applying critical listening skills, you can judge whether statements and ideas are true, sensible, and worthwhile, and you can defend yourself against those that are not.

Finally, the fourth reason for studying speech communication is to have more fun. Of course, talking to other people can be fun in itself if you feel confident in your ability to speak and listen well. But good speech skills also allow you to get involved in other enjoyable activities such as acting in skits and dramas, reading aloud to your friends and classmates, and appearing on radio or television programs.

As you proceed through this course, keep in mind that the way you communicate is not something you're stuck with like your height or shoe size. Speech communication is made up of a set of skills that are learned and can be changed or polished. The purpose of this book is to help you in doing just that. And even if you never plan to try out for a part in a radio play, as I did, remember that you are always on stage because to speak is to perform.

Rudolph F. Verderber

INTRODUCTION

SPEECH FOR EFFECTIVE COMMUNICATION is divided into 6 units, which are further divided into 22 chapters. Unit 1, containing Chapters 1–5, presents basic speech communication skills. Chapter 1 introduces the field of speech communication. Chapters 2 and 3 acquaint you with the concepts of verbal and nonverbal communication. Chapter 4 covers the vocalization process, and Chapter 5 introduces listening skills. Unit 2, containing Chapters 6–8, presents interpersonal communication skills, including making introductions, giving and receiving directions, using the telephone, engaging in conversations, and taking part in job and college interviews. Unit 3, containing Chapters 9–13, presents public speaking skills. Chapters 9–11 cover speech preparation skills; Chapter 12 discusses diction and effective word choice; and Chapter 13 introduces methods and skills for delivering speeches. Unit 4, containing Chapters 14–16, applies the information presented in Unit 3 to the development of three basic kinds of speeches: informative speech, process speech, and persuasive speech. Unit 5, containing Chapters 17–19, presents group communication skills. Chapter 17 covers group discussion; Chapter 18 introduces debate; and Chapter 19 discusses parliamentary procedure. Unit 6, containing Chapters 20–22, presents the performing arts, including oral interpretation, theater, and radio and television. Following these chapters are an appendix of speeches, a glossary of vocabulary terms, and the index.

Throughout this book you will find a number of special features designed to aid you in learning and mastering the information in each chapter.

Objectives.   The main skills and information that you should study are clearly listed at the beginning of each chapter.

Practical Approach.   The information in each lesson is first explained and then applied to specific cases and examples that show you how to use each skill or concept in actual situations you may encounter.

Key Terms.   The key terms that you need to know in each lesson are printed in boldfaced type so that you can recognize and find them easily. Each term is defined where it appears in boldface and is listed at the end of the chapter. All vocabulary terms, with their definitions, are collected in the glossary at the back of the book.

Examples.   Throughout each lesson numerous examples are given to demonstrate both correct and faulty applications of the skills and concepts being presented.

Illustrations. Photographs, charts, diagrams, and other visual aids are given in each lesson to help clarify the terms, concepts, and skills you are learning.

Activities. Every main section of each chapter contains at least one activity that gives you an opportunity to apply what you have learned. Additional activities are provided for key skills within some lessons and at the end of every chapter.

Guidelines. Each chapter contains at least one set of guideline questions you can ask yourself to ensure that you effectively practice the skills in that lesson.

Chapter Summary. At the end of each chapter you will find a concise summary that you can use to preview or review the information in that lesson.

Profiles in Communication. To help you recognize how communication skills play a part in everyday life, each chapter includes a full-page feature about an actual person who works in a field that requires the regular use of the skills covered in that chapter.

End-of-Chapter Questions. At the end of each chapter you will find a list of review questions and discussion questions, which you can use to check your understanding of the information in that chapter.

Real-Life Speaking Situations. On the last page of every lesson, you will find a pair of activities that give you practice in using communication skills in a personal and an occupational context.

Model Speeches. Throughout the book, selections from speeches that have been given by well-known speakers and by students are used to illustrate specific skills and concepts. In addition, twelve complete speeches are included in the appendix at the back of the book.

Glossary. All of the vocabulary words covered in the chapters are listed alphabetically, with their definitions, in the glossary found at the end of the book.

Index. To help you locate information quickly, a complete index is given on the last pages of the book.

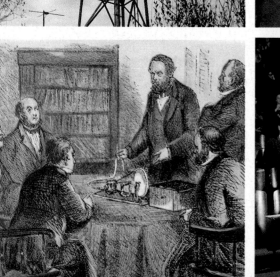

UNIT ONE
THE COMMUNICATION PROCESS

CHAPTER 1

FOUNDATIONS OF SPEECH

OBJECTIVES:

After studying this chapter, you should be able to

1. Define communication.

2. List the steps in the communication process.

3. Tell the difference between verbal communication and nonverbal communication.

4. Identify differences between formal and informal communication settings.

5. Explain what makes an effective communicator.

6. Tell how communication skills are important in your own life.

It's ten minutes before the first bell. Some students are at their lockers; others are standing in groups chatting; still others are making their way to their first class. The halls are echoing with the din of chatter. If you could listen in on all the conversations taking place, you would hear such things as:

> "Well, I thought I'd be able to finish my math homework before I had to get to soccer practice. Next time I'll make sure that . . ."

"How can you say they have a chance this year? They don't have a single good hitter in the lineup. Why, look at yesterday's game. If Walker had only . . ."

"Jane, I was wondering if, well, there's that dance Saturday night and I thought maybe . . ."

"That was a terrific paper you turned in, Melanie. It must have taken you hours just to find the information!"

"Jill, are we supposed to do *all* the problems in Part A?"

What you would hear are voices—explaining, arguing, hoping, praising, and questioning—all different, yet every one of them *communicating*.

Like the students in this photograph, you probably enjoy engaging in interpersonal communication with your friends nearly every day.

WHAT IS COMMUNICATION?

You communicate every day, and, if you are like most students, you take the seemingly simple process of communication for granted. However, in order to communicate to your best advantage, you need to take a closer look at how the communication process works.

Communication is the process of sharing information by using symbols to send and receive messages. Although it is possible to communicate with yourself, the type of communication you will study in this book is **interpersonal communication**—communication between two or more people.

Communication between people always involves sending and receiving a message. The person who sends the message is called the sender. The

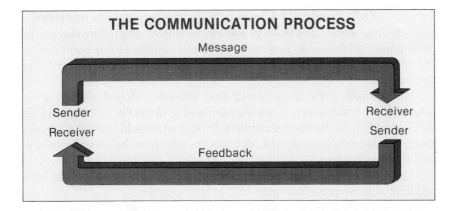

THE COMMUNICATION PROCESS

person who receives the message is called the receiver. Messages are carried by verbal and nonverbal symbols. Verbal symbols are words; nonverbal symbols include such things as gestures, facial expressions, and laughter.

Messages are always transmitted through channels. If you use verbal symbols to send a spoken message, the channel is sound waves. If you use nonverbal symbols to send a message, the channel is usually sound waves or light waves. To be effective, communication must also involve feedback—some indication that the message has been received.

Notice in the diagram of the communication process above that the sender and receiver exchange roles, depending on whether the message is being transmitted or feedback is being returned. Keep in mind that communication is not a one-way street but, instead, is a sharing, or exchange, of information.

To gain a better understanding of the communication process, listen further to the conversation between Jill and her friend Ben. Notice how the elements of the process work together in effective communication.

> Ben, with a look of panic, asks, "Jill, are we supposed to do *all* the problems in Part A?"
> "No," Jill replies, "just the odd-numbered ones."

This short exchange between Jill and Ben shows how the key elements of the communication process work together. The *sender* (Ben) uses *verbal and nonverbal symbols* (the words in his question accompanied by the look on his face) to send a *message* (his uncertainty and concern about the assignment) to the *receiver* (Jill). The message travels through two *channels* (sound waves and light waves). After Jill receives the message, she gives Ben *feedback* (her response).

Let's take a brief look at each of these key elements in the communication process.

People—Senders and Receivers

Human communication is the exchange of messages between two or more people. During the communication process, one person—the

sender—sends thoughts and feelings to another person—the **receiver**—who receives them. These roles are not exclusive and often change as communication proceeds. A person may be the sender at one point during the exchange of messages, while at another point the same person may be the receiver.

For example, in the short conversation between Ben and Jill, Ben is the sender of the first message ("Are we supposed to do *all* the problems in Part A?"). Yet when Jill, the receiver, answers, "No, just the odd-numbered ones," their roles become reversed. Jill becomes the sender of the second message and Ben the receiver.

The sending and the receiving processes work slightly differently. You will look at these processes more fully in later chapters.

Messages

People communicate by sending and receiving messages. **Messages**—the content of communication—are made up of ideas and feelings.

In our example, for instance, Ben sent a message to Jill. He thought he had heard the assignment accurately, but he was not certain. He asked Jill about it to make sure. This request for information was the idea part of Ben's message. In addition to an idea, Ben's message also included feelings. Ben was getting nervous about how much math homework he had, and his message communicated his nervousness.

Verbal and Nonverbal Symbols

Messages are carried between senders and receivers by verbal and nonverbal symbols. The **verbal symbols** are words. In our example, Ben's verbal message was "Are we supposed to do *all* the problems in Part A?"

What nonverbal message do you think the man sitting on the steps in this cartoon is sending?

Drawing by Koren. © 1985 by the New Yorker Magazine, Inc.

Do I detect a hint of depression?

Ben also used **nonverbal symbols,** which are any means used to communicate without words. The tone of his voice emphasized certain words, his facial expression communicated certain feelings, and his body actions added to his message by expressing his nervousness.

Your facial expression, your body movements, and the sound of your voice are all nonverbal transmitters in your communication. Even though you may be saying nothing verbally, your face and body may still be communicating messages to others. When Jill told Ben that the assignment included only the odd-numbered problems, Ben sent back a nonverbal message. The look on his face showed his relief.

The Channels of Communication

Channels are the means used to send messages. When talking with others, people send verbal messages through the air by sound waves. At the same time, they send nonverbal messages through the air by sound waves and by light waves. For example, when Ben asked Jill about their homework assignment, his question was sent on sound waves. At the same time, his "look of panic" was carried on light waves.

Feedback

When people attempt to communicate with others, they want responses to their messages. These responses, the verbal and nonverbal reactions to a message, are called **feedback.** Feedback tells the sender whether the message has been received and understood. In our example, Ben received feedback from Jill when she answered his question. Of course, feedback may also be nonverbal. People may simply nod their heads or shrug their shoulders in response to questions.

The ability to recognize and interpret feedback is vital to communication effectiveness. You probably have little difficulty recognizing feedback, although you may misinterpret it. For example, you may have trouble telling whether a smile someone gives you expresses a sincere feeling or is simply a social courtesy.

When you are giving a public speech or putting on a play, feedback is likely to be nearly all nonverbal. Very seldom does a member of an audience

ACTIVITY: Sending Nonverbal Messages

In everyday life you depend on gestures and facial expressions to communicate messages. Form a group of five students. Decide on a message to send using only nonverbal symbols. Some possible messages are "I don't know," "definitely not," "come here," and "keep away." Then choose a person to send the message nonverbally. Have the rest of the students try to guess the message.

These students are providing nonverbal feedback to a speaker. Most, but not all, are responding with obvious pleasure and interest.

break in with a comment. In a public setting, feedback may consist of nonverbal signs of restlessness: shuffling of papers, coughing, increased movement of chairs. Perhaps some people will smile and nod, while others may show pained expressions or may fall asleep. Whatever the form of feedback, to some extent your success depends on how well you can interpret it and respond to it.

In a mass communication setting such as a radio or television broadcast where there is no audience, a speaker has no idea of how the message is being received, of how the audience is reacting. Although cable companies are experimenting with "interactive" television in which viewers can communicate their reactions by pressing buttons, in most cases neither radio nor television allows for immediate feedback.

WHY IS COMMUNICATION ESSENTIAL?

Whether you are passing time with friends, participating in class, getting information, or selling tickets to the school game, nearly everything you do involves communication. Communication is a tool you use to accomplish goals and meet social and decision-making needs that affect every aspect of your life.

Social Needs

People have a number of social needs. For instance, we all need to receive affection, to show feelings, to be wanted, and to love. Through communication, we fulfill these needs. Let's look at a few of the ways in which communication helps us socially.

First, people communicate for pleasure. Think about it. You can probably recall many times just within the past day or two when you talked to people for no other reason than to pass time in an enjoyable way. When you come to class, you often strike up a conversation before the bell rings. *What* you say may be unimportant—it is the act of communicating that provides the pleasure.

Second, people communicate to show that they care about each other. Between classes, you might pass a friend in the hall and say, "What's happening?" You would not really expect the person to stop and recount the events of the day. What you would actually be saying is, "I recognize you. I want you to know that I recognize you and care." Think of days when you were feeling down. As people passed in the hall and said, "Hi" or "How're you doing?" or "What's happening?" didn't their greetings make you feel a little better?

Third, people communicate to build and maintain satisfying relationships. When you first meet people, you talk with them to find out what you have in common. You find answers to questions such as whether you enjoy the same kinds of foods and whether you think similarly about events and issues. If you find that you have much in common and that you enjoy each other's company, you become friends. In relationships that are well established, you communicate to maintain or deepen your friendship.

Since everyday social skills are so important, in later chapters you will practice developing speaking and listening skills that help you meet these social needs.

Decision-Making Needs

Just as communication is essential for fulfilling social needs, it is also necessary for making decisions. Every day you must make many personal decisions—some of them big, most of them small. Making many of these decisions involves communicating with others. For example, you make educational, social, and business decisions by talking with others to get information, to exchange ideas and feelings, and ultimately to decide what actions

For most people "small talk" is not small at all. We are social by nature, and everyday conversation brings us the pleasure of interacting informally with others.

to take. Since the best decisions are informed ones, you will find that how well you can give and ask for information is quite important. In later chapters you will learn how to give directions, to explain processes, and to exchange information effectively.

Decision making often involves influencing others. You may have made a good decision; however, if you cannot explain the merits of that decision to others, your decision may have no impact. Presenting your ideas persuasively and discussing them in a group are essential skills that can benefit you greatly. In later chapters you will study skills that will help you become a better decision maker and a more influential speaker.

WHEN DO YOU COMMUNICATE?

You spend a large percentage of your waking hours communicating. This communication takes place in both formal and informal settings.

Informal Settings

Most of your communication occurs in **informal settings,** which are casual, unstructured situations such as daily conversations with relatives, teachers, and friends. Other informal settings include conversations in which you introduce people, give directions, give and request information, and speak on the telephone. In these informal settings, communication is likely to be spontaneous, that is, largely unplanned. You think about what to say as you go along, and then you say it. Because these settings are so informal, you may forget that your effectiveness depends on how well you use such basic skills as expressing yourself clearly, describing your feelings, listening, and making appropriate responses. In this book you will study skills that will help you become even more effective in these informal settings.

ACTIVITY:
Recording and Analyzing Personal Communication Skills

To help you keep track of your progress, your discoveries, your questions, and other information in this class, keep a communication journal. For one week, use your communication journal to record instances in which your communication skills helped you achieve one of your goals. Also record instances in which you might have achieved your goal if you had been able to communicate more effectively. At the end of the week, share your journal entries with your classmates. Save your journal and add to it as you develop your communication skills.

Formal communication settings include (clockwise from top left): job and college interviews, group discussion, public speaking, debate, interpretative situations, and electronic communication.

Formal Settings

Although much less of your communication may take place in formal settings, it is in these situations that you will have a chance to affect the ideas and feelings of people in important positions or large numbers of people. **Formal settings** are those for which you can prepare your communication beforehand. The following situations are formal settings that you will study in this book.

Job and College Interviews. An interview is a form of communication in which the people involved ask and answer questions. Interviewing is usually a one-to-one form of communication. Although the actual number of interviews you take part in may be relatively small, your effectiveness in them can greatly influence your life. In this book you will learn how to ask and answer questions effectively and how to show yourself in the best light during job and college interviews.

Group Discussion. Group discussion is a face-to-face meeting among a small number of people who convey information, express their views, and reach conclusions. How well you can communicate within a group will affect the quality of decisions your group makes. The more effectively you and the other group members communicate, the more informed your decisions will likely be. When you study group discussion, you will learn formal methods of problem solving and decision making.

Public Speaking. In public speaking, one person speaks to an audience of many individuals to entertain, to inform, or to persuade them. Most people find speaking in public more difficult than speaking in informal situations or in small groups. Yet public speaking is very important. Many key decisions in our society are made on the basis of what we learn from and how we are influenced by public speakers. In this book you will learn how to prepare speeches and how to deliver them effectively. In addition, you will learn skills of information exchange and persuasion.

Debate and Parliamentary Procedure. Debate is a formal communication situation in which speakers take opposing sides on an issue and try to prove or disprove a statement about that issue. Parliamentary procedure is a set of rules for conducting orderly meetings. In this book you will study both of these essential ingredients of a democratic society.

Interpretive Situations. Some formal communication settings involve interpreting material. Oral reading is a performing art in which literature is read aloud and interpreted for an audience. Drama is a performing art in which characters in a play are presented by actors on a stage. In this book you will learn techniques for presenting interpretive and dramatic material to an audience.

Electronic Communication. Electronic communication includes radio and television, two of the most common and influential means of mass communication. Electronic communication provides opportunities for reaching an audience of thousands or even millions at one time. In this book you will look at some of the skills specifically related to radio and television performance.

ACTIVITY: **Analyzing Communication Situations**

In your communication journal, keep track of the different communication situations you take part in during an average day. How many are informal? How many are formal? What differences do you recognize between your informal and formal communication? Share your findings with your classmates.

STEPS IN THE COMMUNICATION PROCESS

The communication process consists of a series of interrelated steps. The progression of these steps varies according to the particular people, setting, and other circumstances involved. Steps may be repeated, may be in various orders, or may be combined in a number of ways. Nevertheless, to some extent, each of these steps comes into play whether you are talking with one person, participating in group discussion, or speaking before a large audience.

Let's take a brief look at each of these steps, which will be discussed more fully later in this book.

Finding Ideas

To communicate effectively, you need to have something to say. Finding good ideas is one key to your success. This step is especially important for formal speaking occasions such as group discussions and public speaking. In addition, even conversations with friends are more rewarding when the ideas being discussed are interesting. In choosing your ideas, you will need to consider your audience, the setting in which you will communicate, any time limit that has been set, and a number of other factors that will be covered in later chapters.

Ideas consist of topics and the development of those topics. You can get ideas from your own experience, from others, and from written sources. Usually you will begin with a general idea, or subject, and then narrow that subject to a specific topic that is adapted to your audience and to any special requirements that your speech must meet.

© 1983 by United Feature Syndicate, Inc. Reprinted by permission of United Feature Syndicate, Inc.

If you do not have anything to say, you will be left out while others are enjoying a discussion. Develop your own ideas, and join in.

Adapting to Your Audience

To communicate effectively, you must adapt to the needs of your **audience**—the listeners or spectators attending your presentation or performance. Adapting to an audience means directing the material to a specific person or group of people. To adapt to an audience, you must have some knowledge of its makeup. Depending on the situation, your audience may consist of one person or of millions of people. You can find information about your audience on a cultural level, a sociological level, or an individual level. This information will help you determine how you will send your message and how your audience will likely react to it.

When you examine your audience at a *cultural level,* you look at such things as age, race, and national background. In short, you determine whether you are speaking to a young black American or to a racially mixed audience of young and middle-aged Americans. Of course, this level of information provides you with only broad guidelines to follow. You will also need to tailor each of your messages to the individual listener as well.

When you examine your audience at a _sociological level,_ you look at such things as what groups members of your audience belong to and what affiliations they have. Based on what you discover, you can formulate some general ideas about your listeners. For example, if you knew that the members of an audience were football players, you could make generalizations about their levels of activity, physical fitness, and interest in sports.

When you examine your audience at an _individual level,_ you look at such things as a person's traits, interests, and plans. These items help you predict how the individual will respond to certain information. This level is particularly important in everyday conversation.

Encoding and Decoding

To communicate effectively, you must decide how to send each message. The process of turning ideas and feelings into verbal and nonverbal symbols is called **encoding.** In conversation the encoding process is nearly instantaneous. For instance, imagine that you are eating lunch and you decide to put salt on your sandwich, but the salt shaker is at the other end of the table. You would probably look at the person sitting at that end and say, "Will you please pass the salt?" You would not stop to say to yourself, "Hmm, I can't reach the salt. What words should I use to get someone to move the salt closer to me?" Instead, you would automatically encode your needs into words.

Whereas the encoding process is nearly instantaneous in a conversational setting, in public speaking it is quite different. Public speaking requires you to take time to plan how you want to state a particular idea. For a speech, you may try two or three different ways of stating the same idea before you are satisfied that you are phrasing it in the best way for that audience.

When information is encoded into electronic signals and broadcast from a radio station, a radio receiver will decode it. When it is keyed into a computer, a printer or a video screen will decode it.

Encoding is not just a matter of verbal communication. While you are verbalizing, you are likely to be sending nonverbal messages that affect how the receiver will respond. For example, it is possible to say "Will you please pass the salt?" in a tone of voice that sounds as if you are saying, "You took the salt five minutes ago, and now you're trying to keep it for your own personal use. How about sharing it!" Nonverbal communication involves your tone of voice, facial expressions, gestures, and movements. A great deal of confusion in communication results from contradictions between verbal messages and their accompanying nonverbal messages.

Communication does not end with the sending of a message. For communication to be complete, a receiver must decode that message.

Decoding means finding the meaning of verbal and nonverbal signals. Again, in conversation this process is usually instantaneous. A split second after you ask for the salt, someone is likely to pass it to you. However, if you have just come from chemistry class, you may decide to say, "Pat, will you please pass the sodium chloride?" The person you asked may very well look at you with a puzzled expression and ask, "The what?" After a second, he may answer, "Oh, the sodium chloride—the salt—sure." Pat would have translated *sodium chloride* into a meaning that made sense in the context of the lunchroom. He may have thought, "Oh, yes, *sodium chloride* is the chemical name for salt."

Encoding, then, is the process of turning messages into verbal and nonverbal symbols, and *decoding* is the process of interpreting these symbols. To a large extent, the words and other symbols you use depend on your understanding of the needs and abilities of your audience. For example, you would not use a term like *sodium chloride* if you did not know that Pat was also studying chemistry and could eventually understand you.

Interpreting Feedback

To communicate effectively, you must be able to interpret *feedback*. In conversation we expect people to talk with us. In other words, we expect them to respond to our messages by saying what they are thinking. In public speaking situations, audience responses are generally nonverbal, such as yawning or smiling. In both formal and informal settings, the more you know about your audience, the better able you will be to recognize and interpret the verbal or nonverbal feedback you receive.

Dealing with Interference

Interference is anything that interferes with, or gets in the way of, clear communication. One type of interference consists of **physical noise**—any sounds that prevent a person from being heard. For example, when you are giving a speech or acting in a play, people in the audience may interfere by whispering or cheering.

Another type of interference is **psychological noise**—the thoughts and feelings people have that interfere with what is being said. For example, members of an audience may not pay attention to a speaker because they are absorbed in their own thoughts. One person may be thinking about tomorrow's test, while another is worried about how much homework she has to do, and a third is dreaming of his date for Friday night. Psychological noise leads to inattention on the part of the audience.

A third type of interference is **semantic noise**—the interference caused by words that trigger strong negative feelings against the speaker or the content of the speech. For example, an audience of classmates might go along with you if you called your school football team "the underdog," but they might likely stop listening to you if you began calling the team "a loser." Semantic noise leads to misunderstanding.

Mastering techniques for dealing with each of these types of interference will help make your speech communication more enjoyable and more effective.

ACTIVITY: Dealing with Interference

Imagine that you are speaking in each of the following situations. For each case, tell the class how you would deal with interference.

1. You and a friend are discussing a problem. Three people at the other side of the room begin to talk so loudly that you cannot concentrate on what your friend is telling you.
2. You are leading a group discussion. One of the people in the back of the room is playing a radio loudly.
3. You are giving a report to your history class. The lights are making a very loud buzzing noise.
4. You are acting in a play. Suddenly a storm breaks out. Thunder drowns out your words.

HOW TO BE AN EFFECTIVE COMMUNICATOR

In this chapter you have looked at the communication process. The following guidelines list steps that you can take to become a more *effective* communicator.

1. *Care about your communication success.* Effective communication begins with caring. You must *care* about the people with whom you will be communicating and about what will happen as a result of your communication. Most of your communication has a purpose or goal. Whether that purpose is to transmit information, to change people's minds, or just to greet a friend, your effectiveness will depend on others' believing that you really care about them and about what you are saying. To be an effective communicator, you must want to succeed at sending and receiving messages.

2. *Know what you are talking about.* No doubt you have heard the expression "He talks to hear the sound of his own voice." Most people disregard those who need to talk but who do not really have anything worthwhile to say. On the other hand, people are likely to pay attention to someone who has the facts, is knowledgeable, and clearly understands the situation. To be an effective communicator, you must know what you are talking about.

3. *Be organized.* When people cannot follow what is being said, they lose interest and patience quickly. Organizing ideas before communicating them takes only a short time. However, this planning pays big dividends. To be an effective communicator, you must have your ideas well organized.

4. *Use language well.* People can enjoy listening for hours to a speaker who has a skillful command of language. Most successful speakers have taken the time to learn how to make their language clear and interesting. To be an effective communicator, you must take care in choosing your words and in putting them together.

5. *Control your nonverbal signals.* No speaker has complete control over all of his or her nonverbal behavior. However, speakers who look at their audience when talking, who use their voices to emphasize word meaning, who use gestures to describe and to stress points, and who know when to be quiet will have the most powerful effect. To be an effective communicator, you must have control over the nonverbal signals you send.

Learning to be an effective communicator will help you identify and achieve your goals.

6. *Listen effectively.* Sometimes the very best communicators are those who are good listeners. By listening, you can learn more and therefore be able to respond more appropriately. Careful listening will enable you to identify when and why your audience is not receiving your message and will help you decide how to communicate it more successfully. To be an effective communicator, you must be a good listener.

GUIDELINES FOR BECOMING AN EFFECTIVE COMMUNICATOR

- Do I care about the success of my communication?
- Do I know what I am talking about?
- Are my thoughts well organized?
- Have I selected my words carefully?
- Do I have control over my nonverbal behavior?
- Do I listen carefully to others?

Profiles in Communication

Wongnoi Pattranupravat, who came to the United States from Thailand in 1970, today works as a receptionist for her husband, a physician. She says, "Communication is important to me, most important, especially since I am in a service profession. I cannot be shy. If I do not understand what people say, I must ask. If they do not understand me, I must try to explain."

Mrs. Pattranupravat believes that listening and speaking well are particularly crucial for a receptionist because the employer's reputation may depend on her understanding each client's request or problem and then pleasantly, honestly, and clearly expressing herself.

When listening, Mrs. Pattranupravat always tries to look at the patients. She comments. "Paying attention helps to get their trust; they feel I understand and care about their problems. For example, one day a patient came to the office angry. She had not received her insurance check. I explained that we had filed her claim. Then I just listened to her and said, 'I understand how upset you are.'"

However, listening closely does not guarantee that Mrs. Pattranupravat can completely understand. Regional pronunciations, idioms, and common metaphors are frequently troublesome. Mrs. Pattranupravat laughs, "Once a woman told me her son had been sent home from school and that she thought he must have spring fever. The next day I asked her, 'Is your son feeling better? Is his fever lower today?'"

As for expressing herself, Mrs. Pattranupravat consciously controls her facial expressions and the way she speaks. When greeting a patient, she may either smile cheerfully and say "Hello" or with a sympathetic look ask "How are you today?" She always tries not to look or sound either bored or emotional.

She also feels that distinct enunciation and correct grammar are indispensable. She says, "Sometimes an unusual accent or word order acts as a barrier to understanding. Speaking clearly and correctly helps. Repeating what I have said in different words sometimes also helps."

For effective communication in any service profession, Wongnoi Pattranupravat advises both native and nonnative speakers to be professional, polite, unafraid to ask questions, and always willing to explain patiently.

SUMMARY

Communication is the process of using symbols to send and receive messages. People exchange messages by using verbal and nonverbal symbols.

Communication helps you meet both social and decision-making needs. You communicate with people to show them that you recognize them, to build and maintain relationships, and to make informed decisions.

Communication takes place in a variety of informal and formal settings. Some informal settings include daily conversations, telephone calls, and the giving and receiving of information. Some formal settings include job and college interviews, group discussions, public speaking, debate, oral interpretation and dramatics, and electronic communication.

Any communication involves several steps. You begin with an idea you want to communicate, and you adapt that idea to the cultural, sociological, and individual levels of your audience. You then communicate that idea to others by encoding and decoding it, using verbal and nonverbal symbols. As you communicate, you interpret feedback. Throughout the process you deal with any interference, including physical noise, psychological noise, and semantic noise.

To communicate effectively, you must care about succeeding in your communication; you must know what you are talking about; you must organize your thoughts; you must use language well; you must control your nonverbal communication; and you must be a good listener.

CHAPTER VOCABULARY

Look back through this chapter to find the meaning of each of the following words. Write each term and its meaning in your communication journal.

audience	✓ informal settings	physical noise
communication ✓	interference	psychological noise
decoding	✓ interpersonal communi-	✓ receiver
encoding	cation	semantic noise
feedback ✓	✓ messages	✓ sender
formal settings ✓	✓ nonverbal symbols	✓ verbal symbols

REVIEW QUESTIONS

1. What is meant by the term *communication?*

2. The communication process involves six key elements. One of these is the *message.* What are the other five?

3. Verbal communication uses words to communicate meaning. How does

nonverbal communication differ from verbal communication?

4. To a large extent, verbal messages are sent through the air by sound waves. What channel or channels are used to send most nonverbal messages?

5. Imagine that two people are having a conversation. What role does feedback play in ensuring that effective communication takes place?

6. Informal communication occurs in conversational settings. What are some of the settings in which formal communication takes place?

7. Regardless of the type of communication, a speaker must always *find ideas* to communicate. What are the other steps in the communication process?

8. To be effective, communicators need to adapt their speeches to suit their audiences. In addition to the cultural level, what are two other levels on which it is important to have information about an audience?

9. One type of interference a speaker faces is physical noise. What are two other types of interference?

10. What are the characteristics of an effective communicator?

DISCUSSION QUESTIONS

1. Imagine that your friend Jan says, "Getting that grade on my project really made my day!" What she means depends not only on her words but also on the way she says her words. Discuss how a listener could interpret Jan's words depending on *how* Jan says them.

2. Discuss the meaning of the following statement: Human beings are always communicating, whether they are conscious of it or not.

3. Imagine that you are to give a speech in support of a political candidate. Discuss the ways in which your knowledge of your audience would affect what you would say and how you would say it. For example, how would the speech you would give to a group that belongs to the same political party as your candidate differ from the speech you would give to a group that belongs to a different political party?

4. Bergen Evans, a critic and grammarian, once wrote: "Words are one of our chief means of adjusting to all the situations of life. The better control we have over words, the more successful our adjustment is likely to be." First discuss the meaning of this quotation. Then discuss how it relates to the encoding-decoding process.

5. The future holds many opportunities for you. In the near future, you are likely to play one or more of the following roles: a college student, a wife or a husband, a mother or a father, an employee or a boss. Discuss the value of developing communication skills in order to make the most of these roles.

1. Identifying Occupational Uses of Communication Skills

Conduct a survey of your fellow students' future plans. Then make a list of the occupations that these students plan to pursue. Under each occupation, indicate how communication skills will be an effective tool for advancement. For example, a nurse would need good communication skills to understand patients' needs and tell them about proposed methods of treatment. When your list is completed, share it with your classmates.

2. Interpreting Nonverbal Communication in Television Programs

A. Watch a television talk show. Make a list of the ways in which people communicate nonverbally during one conversation. Share your list with your classmates.

B. Watch a television program with the sound off. How much of the story are you able to follow? What nonverbal symbols help you to follow this much of the story? Share your findings with your classmates.

3. Identifying Learning Goals in a Speech Class

Work in a group of four or five students. Develop a list of ways in which you think this class will be different from other classes you are taking. What do you expect to learn in this class? How do you expect to use what you learn? After fifteen minutes, share your list with the class.

4. Diagraming Messages

Review the diagram of the communication process on page 5. Then, using this format, diagram four messages you sent and received today. Identify the sender and the receiver, and write brief summaries of the messages and feedback.

5. Analyzing Feedback

A. Prepare a short message. Deliver exactly the same message to five different people. Tell your class how the feedback you received differed from person to person.

B. In addition to acting as a sender of messages, you also act as a receiver. Report to your class on the feedback you gave to five different messages today.

Real-Life Speaking Situations

1. Throughout your life, your abilities and interests, and sometimes even blind luck, will make you eligible to win awards and prizes. Winners are often requested to speak publicly about how they won, their feelings about winning, the field in which they won, and other related topics. Picture yourself in such a situation—as the winner in sports or academic competition, as the winner of a blue ribbon for culinary or agricultural skills, as the winner at an art show or a car rally. Or, imagine yourself as the winner in some other situation involving one of your personal skills or simply a game of chance like a sweepstakes or a lottery. First, define the situation: What did you win? How did you win? Then, write a short speech (one or two pages long) of what you would say in such a situation. Be prepared to give your speech to the class.

2. Police officers need to call on their public speaking skills many times a day. They speak to the public in such diverse situations as issuing traffic citations, addressing groups like service clubs and committees, giving advice and directions, comforting injured people, and many others. Perhaps you have had a police officer speak to one of your classes in school or at a meeting of a club or organization you belong to. Imagine yourself in any two public speaking situations that a police officer would likely face. First, define each situation. Then, in a page or two for each, write what you would say. You can choose two entirely different situations, such as making an arrest and telling an elementary school class about your job, or you can choose similar situations viewed from different perspectives, such as issuing a speeding ticket to someone who almost hit a child and issuing a speeding ticket to a confused out-of-towner. Note the differences in your word choice, your nonverbal behavior, and other facets of communicating your message. Be prepared to deliver one or both of the talks to your class.

Poner los verbos en el tiempo
If I (be) you, I
By the time the
for three
Test Papers in English

SENDING VERBAL MESSAGES

OBJECTIVES:

After studying this chapter, you should be able to

1. Define language.

2. List and explain four characteristics of language.

3. Explain how language changes.

4. Define the connotation and the denotation of words.

5. Tell the difference between standard and nonstandard language.

6. Explain the appropriate use of jargon, slang, and dialect.

7. Explain what your language tells others about you.

8. Explain how to use language to present the best possible you.

"Hank, did you call Mr. Henderson about that job?" inquired Jayne.

"Yeah. But that there man don't want me in his office. He ain't givin' me no job."

"But I thought you were a shoo-in for the position. What went wrong?"

"You got me. I talked real nice to that guy on the phone, but he come back and told me the messenger's job was already full."

"What did you say to him?"

"Oh, I dunno," responded Hank. "When he answers the phone I said somethin' like, 'Hey, man, you know that summer job you got open for a messenger? My old man said talk to you about it. How about you and me get together?' "

Does this opening situation sound exaggerated? Perhaps you think no student would behave the way Hank did. However, recruiters in nearly every type of organization tell about people who sound a great deal like Hank—and who wonder why their job applications were not taken seriously.

Every day you use spoken language to send verbal messages. Since you have been sending verbal messages most of your life, the process seems very natural. However, unless you learn to control your language usage, it may say more about you than you want a receiver to hear. This chapter will introduce you to ways in which you can use language to your advantage.

WHAT IS LANGUAGE?

Language is a system of sounds and symbols used to communicate ideas and feelings. Let's examine the key features of language in more detail to get an appreciation of both its complexity and its importance.

Language Is a System

A **system** is a group of elements that work together. The English language system consists of three subsystems: sounds (phonology), words (morphology), and the way these sounds and words are arranged (syntax). None of these subsystems—sounds, words, arrangement—stands alone. All three must be blended together to create a language.

Language Is Symbolic

A **symbol** is something that stands for something else. Whenever you speak or write, words are the symbols you use to stand for ideas, actions,

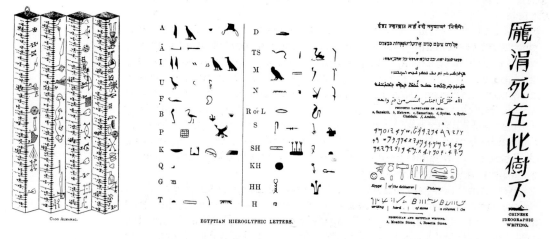

Different cultures have developed different symbolic systems for language.

objects, or feelings. For example, *book* is a word that stands for the object you are now reading from. The word *book* is not the object itself; instead, it represents the object.

a word = a symbol

Language Is Conventional

Conventional means "accepted by a large number of people." You write with an object called a pen or a pencil. The reason you are comfortable using the word *pen* or *pencil* to stand for that particular object is that after someone named the object for the first time, a large number of people accepted that name. If you wished, you could call your pen a *gork*. Calling a pen a *gork* would not change the pen itself, but since other people have never heard of the symbol *gork* standing for a pen, they would not know what you were talking about. The words in our language communicate meaning because large numbers of people who use the language accept and recognize particular meanings for particular symbols.

Most of the words you use daily are used by other people in the culture to mean about the same thing. If this were not true, then words would be of no help in communicating, since a person receiving a message could not be sure about what meaning the sender had intended for each word.

Language Is Learned

In order to communicate, each generation must learn the language it is going to use. This process of learning follows certain principles.

First, the learning of symbols goes from simple to complex. Children learn short words that can be used in a variety of situations. For instance, children learn *yes* and *no* at a very early age. Likewise, they learn specific words that stand for concrete things before they learn general or abstract words. For example, they learn specific words like *mama, daddy,* and *milk* before they learn general words like *parents* and *food* or abstract words like *love* and *friendship.*

Second, once children learn a rule of language, they are likely to overgeneralize. *Generalizing* means "drawing a general conclusion from specific cases and then applying that conclusion to other specific cases that are similar." For example, if you observed a chalkboard in each of several classrooms and then assumed that there would be a chalkboard in at least some other classrooms as well, you would be generalizing. *Overgeneralizing* means "applying a generalization to all specific cases, including those to which the generalization does not apply." If you insisted that because there was a chalkboard in some classrooms, there would be one in every other room in the school, you would be overgeneralizing.

How does overgeneralization relate to the learning of language? Since children first learn to form the past tense by adding *–ed* to verbs, they tend to add *–ed* to all verbs. They will say, "He *goed* home," "She *drinked* her milk," or "I *singed* a song." It takes time for them to learn the exceptions to this and other rules.

As you read the next page in this chapter, notice how many words you recognize and understand but rarely, if ever, use when speaking.

Third, we understand more symbols than we use. Most people have a reading vocabulary that is greater than their speaking vocabulary. Your *reading vocabulary* includes all the words you recognize and understand when you see them written. Your *speaking vocabulary* consists of only those words you feel comfortable using in oral communication. For example, when you read the sentence *Paul was imbued with qualities of goodness and high moral character,* you might know that *imbued* means something like "filled." However, even though you recognize this word when reading, you may feel uncomfortable using it when speaking.

So far in school, most of your effort has gone into learning written communication. In this class you will be concentrating on learning oral communication. Though the two are similar in some ways, they are also quite different. For instance, in writing English you use the twenty-six letters of the alphabet to form words; in speaking the language, you use forty-five speech sounds. Therefore, some letters must stand for more than one sound. The words *tough, thought, through,* and *although* are all spelled with the same four letters in the same order, yet in each word the letter group *ough* stands for a different vowel sound and in *tough* also includes the sound *f.* As a result, some words in English are spelled exactly the same but are pronounced differently. For example, "I have a *tear* (teer) in my eye because I have a *tear* (tair) in my shirt."

How else is oral language different from written language? In general, when you speak, you use shorter sentences than you do when you write. In speaking, you also use shorter words, more slang, and more repetition, and you tend to modify or correct your words as you go along.

Language Changes

Perhaps one of the most fascinating aspects of our language is that it is constantly changing. Although at times language may seem to be a system that is firmly established, it is actually a dynamic, constantly changing system that people control. Language is a tool that people form, reshape, and use however it will best help them communicate ideas and feelings.

Our control of language can be seen most clearly in how words change over a period of time. People create words to deal with current conditions. When conditions change, so does language.

One way people exercise control over language is in the selection of different words to represent objects that serve the same function. For example, some words replace others to represent newer versions of the same objects. Consider the following sentence: *Much to everyone's amazement, Angela put the victrola in the same room as the icebox.* Do you know what *victrola* and *icebox* mean? Today you would be more likely to say: *Much to everyone's amazement, Angela put the stereo in the same room as the refrigerator.* Who knows what people will say fifty years from now to communicate that same idea.

A second way people exercise control over language is by changing the meanings of words and by adding new meanings to words. For instance, during a six-hundred-year period the word *nice* has had a variety of meanings—"foolish, strange, lazy, coy, modest, refined, precise, subtle, critical, attentive, minutely accurate, dainty, appetizing, pleasant, and agreeable." Thus, at different points in history if someone had been referred to as *nice*, listeners would have thought that the person was foolish, modest, or lazy.

A third way people exercise control over language is by creating words for new objects and experiences. For instance, during the last twenty years of computer development, many new words have been created. Such words as *microchip, floppy disk, artificial intelligence, input,* and countless others have reshaped our vocabularies.

Are you curious about words and how they change? If you are, you should become familiar with the *Oxford English Dictionary.* The *Oxford English Dictionary* (or *OED,* as it is often called) gives definitions of words

1646 SIR T. BROWNE *Pseud. Ep.* IV. xii, Beside that computing by the medicall month. **1741-3** WESLEY *Jrnl.* 80 At Horseley upon Tyne, eight (computed) miles from Newcastle. **1849** MRS. SOMERVILLE *Connex. Phys. Sc.* xxxvii. 418 How far the computed ellipse agrees with the curve.
Computent, obs. form of COMPETENT.
Computer (kǒmpiū´tɔɪ). Also -or. [f. COMPUTE *v.* + -ER¹.] One who computes; a calculator, reckoner; *spec.* a person employed to make calculations in an observatory, in surveying, etc.
1646 SIR T. BROWNE *Pseud. Ep.* VI. vi. 289 The Calenders of these computers. **1704** SWIFT *T. Tub* vii, A very skilful computer. **1744** WALPOLE *Lett. H. Mann* 18 June, Told by some nice computors of national glory. **1855** BREWSTER *Newton* II. xviii. 162 To pay the expenses of a computer for reducing his observations.
Computist (kǒ`mpiutist). Forms: 4 compotyste, (5 competister), 6-7 compotist(e, 6- computist. [a. F. *compotiste, computiste,* med.L.

You may be surprised to find in this entry from the *Oxford English Dictionary* that the word *computer* dates back to the mid-1600's.

chronologically—that is, from the earliest to the most recent meanings of a word. For instance, the definition of the word *nice* runs for four columns to explain how the word has changed in meaning!

If language is always changing, why should anyone study vocabulary? The answer is that this change usually occurs very slowly. In addition, even though words grow in meaning and new words are created to stand for new versions of objects and for new objects and experiences, you need a good understanding of the meanings of words to communicate effectively. The more words and the more meanings you know, the more likely you will be to understand what another person is telling you and the more opportunity you will have to use words that another person will understand.

ACTIVITY: Exploring the Meanings of Words

In this section you have studied how the meanings of words change. For each of the following words, first discuss the meaning of the word with your classmates and agree upon a definition. Then check your definition against the dictionary you regularly use. Finally, consult the *Oxford English Dictionary* to find the earliest meaning of the word. Share your findings with your classmates.

amuse	fond	October
bread	forlorn	stew

THE HIDDEN MEANINGS OF WORDS

To understand language and to gain control over it, you need to realize that words may have many meanings, some of which are hidden. Moreover, these hidden, personal meanings often have the greatest effect on your communication. Meaning is communicated through both a word's denotation and its connotation.

The **denotation** of a word is its dictionary meaning, the meaning that most people in the culture give to it. For example, the denotation for the noun *pet* is "a domesticated animal such as a dog, cat, or bird kept for pleasure." Another denotative meaning for *pet* is "a favored person treated with unusual kindness or tenderness." Most words in English have more than one denotative meaning. In fact, for the five hundred most commonly used words, an average dictionary will list around fourteen thousand definitions.

The **connotation** of a word includes the feelings and associations aroused by the word. Connotations are the hidden meanings determined by the experiences a person has had with the concept the word symbolizes.

The girl in the cartoon hopes that the word *conceptualizing* will have a more positive connotation for her teacher than the word *daydreaming*.

Most of the words you use fit into one of three categories: those with positive connotations, those with negative connotations, and those that are neutral. Although the memories and associations a word arouses are generally personal, some words seem to arouse positive feelings in most people. For example, most people seem to get a positive feeling when they hear the word *pet*. They think of the love and companionship they have received from their own pets. Dogs are among America's favorite pets. When someone says "dog," most people feel warmth, love, and security. Therefore, we can say that the word *dog* usually has a positive connotation. However, *usually* does not mean *always*. Some people feel fear or hostility when they hear the word *dog*. Why the difference? The feelings that someone associates with a word depend to a large extent on the kinds of experiences that person has had with what that word represents. Although dogs are among America's favorite pets, some people hear the word *dog* and recall being barked at, chased, or bitten. For them, *dog* has a negative connotation.

Just as some words have positive connotations for most people, other words have negative connotations for most people. Consider the word *rat*. Its denotative meaning is "a member of the rodent family differing from mice by its considerably larger size and certain of its structural details." Despite this rather neutral denotation, for most people the word *rat* has a negative connotation. When they think of *rat*, they may frown, wince, or even shudder. However, words with generally negative connotations can have positive connotations for some individuals. For psychologists or laboratory scientists who depend on rats in research, the word *rat* may very well arouse positive feelings.

Many words you use are likely to be neutral; that is, they have neither a positive nor a negative connotation for most people. For example, the words *lamp* and *table* are likely to arouse neither good nor bad feelings.

Good communicators are able to choose words that will lead an audience to make certain associations. For instance, advertisers look for words such as *beauty, freshness, natural, homemade, fireplace,* and *healthy* that are likely to have pleasant connotations, which can influence people to buy particular products. Of course, you do not have to be an advertiser to make good use of connotation. You can learn to use the connotations of words to create the effects you want in your communications. In addition, you can communicate more effectively by becoming sensitive to the reactions your words arouse.

ACTIVITY: **Identifying Positive and Negative Connotation in Advertising**

Listen to commercials on television or on the radio. List the words advertisers use to arouse positive feelings toward their products. Then list the words they use to arouse negative feelings toward their competitors' products. Share your findings with your classmates.

SPECIAL SITUATIONS DEMAND SPECIAL LANGUAGE

Speakers adapt their language to the demands of different situations. For example, you probably would not speak in the same way to the principal of your school as you would to your friends. You probably would use different language at a sporting event than you would at a school council meeting. In formal situations you would use standard English. In informal situations you might use nonstandard English.

Standard and Nonstandard English

Standard English is language that is in keeping with established rules and conventions. It is language that follows the guidelines found in grammar and composition handbooks. These rules and guidelines cover such topics as agreement of subject and verb, correct use of tenses, and avoidance of double negatives. **Nonstandard English** is language that is not totally in keeping with, and in some cases even violates, those rules and conventions. Some situations demand standard English, while others do not. For example, if you were giving a formal speech before the entire school body, you would want to use standard English. In contrast, in a friendly chat with your friends you might use nonstandard English. You probably would use standard English in a job interview but might use nonstandard English while introducing one of your friends to another.

The language you use determines to some extent the impression that you make on others. For example, if a student, Tom, says to his job supervisor, Mr. Ortiz, "We ain't got no more napkins," Mr. Ortiz is likely to know exactly what Tom means. However, he is also likely to form an unfavorable impression of Tom based on his use of *ain't* and of the double negative. The problem is not so much that the language Tom uses is "wrong," but that it is inappropriate for the setting.

Appropriateness of language involves word choice. Let's examine some special types of words and then consider their appropriateness.

Sublanguages

Jargon, Slang, and Dialect

Jargon, slang, and dialect are all sublanguages. A **sublanguage** is a subsystem of an established language. Sublanguages provide a group of people with convenient words for ideas and objects that are of great importance to that group and that are spoken about frequently within the group.

One sublanguage is jargon. **Jargon** is language that is understood by people in a particular group or field but is not necessarily understood by those outside the group. Every academic discipline, every profession, and every trade has its own special jargon. For example, newspaper people speak of *slugs, cuts,* and *widows.* A *slug* is a two- or three-word heading at the top of each page of a news story identifying the subject of that story; *cut* refers to any art that appears in the printed material; *widows* are short lines at the end of a printed paragraph carried over to another column or another page. People not in the newspaper trade would likely be unfamiliar with these jargon meanings of *slug, cut,* and *widow.*

Of course, it is appropriate to use jargon when talking to people within the particular group or field that uses that jargon. Since they will understand the words as you mean them, your message will be clear. In fact, the use of jargon in such cases may even help in communicating with those people. However, it is not appropriate to use jargon outside that particular field. Unless you define terms carefully when you use them in an outside setting, jargon will only confuse the people you are speaking to, thereby making your message difficult, or even impossible, to understand. For example, when a journalist is talking to an audience of nonjournalists about how a newspaper is put together, the journalist should avoid using the words *slug, cut,* and *widow* unless he or she takes time to explain each word.

Another sublanguage is slang. **Slang** is language made up of newly coined words or figures of speech or old words used in new, often outrageous, ways. Many slang expressions start within one group and then spread

Slang words are often associated with a specific time period or group.

to the general population. In the early 1980's, young people in the valley around Los Angeles would describe something that was awful as *grody to the max.* This expression spread to other parts of the country, but it was still recognized as "Val talk." In the Navy, ships were once classified by letter and number. An *A-number-1* ship would be the fastest of all. Today that expression has spread to the general population, and anything that is considered the best is called *A-number-1.*

The words *bad, bread,* and *threads* are old words that have new slang meaning. *Bad* is a slang word for good, as in the sentence *That trumpet player is really bad! Bread* is a slang word for money, as in the sentence *You got any bread, man? Threads* is a slang word for clothes, as in the sentence *I just bought some new threads for the dance.* Because of its flexibility and its ease of change, slang has been called a made-to-order language. Much slang is limited to a particular time and place. It becomes popular for a while and then dies out. However, some slang expressions, such as *hike* and *handout,* eventually make their way into the language as standard expressions.

Generally, slang is inappropriate for formal situations. When speaking on formal occasions in which you want to create the best impression of yourself, take care to avoid all slang expressions in your language.

A **dialect** is a regional or cultural variety of language differing from standard English in pronunciation, sentence structure, and use of words. Speech that is rich in a particular dialect may be very effective when communicating with others who use that dialect, but it is not appropriate when speaking formally. For example, consider the following sentence: *He be havin' the time of his life.* This sentence is acceptable when speaking with people who share this dialect, but it is not acceptable when speaking in formal situations.

This wisest procedure to follow for anyone who speaks in a noticeable dialect is to continue using that dialect in informal conversation with friends and relatives but to use standard English for public speaking and formal conversation. If your speech is heavily influenced by a dialect, you may need to learn two "languages," not because one is necessarily better than the other, but because standard English will help you communicate effectively in a wider variety of situations.

What Does Your Language Tell Others About You?

Since language is a tool for communicating, you must be very conscious of the expectations and limitations of those with whom you are speaking. For instance, when you are chatting with your best friend about yesterday's game, about the movie you saw last night, or about tomorrow's history test, you have a great deal of flexibility in what you choose to say and how you choose to say it. Neither of you is likely to be very concerned with correctness of grammar, syntax, or vocabulary. You may be slightly aware of any major peculiarities of communication, but for the most part they go unnoticed and have very little effect on the meanings you share.

The less well you know people, the fewer meanings you share with them,

Cicero's speeches are masterpieces of literature. One reason that they have great impact is that he always wrote them out beforehand, considering every word carefully.

and the more they will rely on what you say and how you say it to draw conclusions about you as a person. Thus, when you are being interviewed for a job, you will find the interviewer paying close attention to every aspect of your speech to draw conclusions about your reliability, your sense of responsibility, your carefulness, and many other things that to you may seem unrelated to your use of language.

Language is a powerful tool. Use it carefully. If you want to be regarded as a reliable, hard-working student, make sure that your choice of language sends this message. If you want people to put faith in your words, make sure that your choice of language tells your listeners you are a responsible, trustworthy person.

To improve your language, study grammar and build your vocabulary. In addition, become sensitive to the way language is used by good speakers and good writers. Listen to people who speak well, and analyze what makes their speaking so effective. Read well-written fiction and nonfiction, and note the techniques that writers use. Practice writing. Never settle for your first draft. Edit and rewrite until you feel that your writing is as clear and correct as you can make it. You may be wondering what writing has to do with learning to speak more effectively. More than two thousand years ago, Cicero, one of the world's greatest speakers, taught that writing is the modeler, or shaper, of good speech.

Profiles in Communication

While communication skills play an important role in most businesses, communication skills *are* Paula Ludlow's business. Paula Ludlow is vice-president of Communispond, Inc., a major consulting firm that specializes in developing programs that teach executives in other companies how to sharpen their speaking, listening, and writing skills.

As an account executive, Ms. Ludlow creates and markets instructional programs tailored to meet the special needs of her clients. Often, she teaches the programs as well. Her programs and workshops have covered such skills as using visual aids, identifying problems, answering questions, dealing with nervousness, and being interviewed on television.

To succeed as a communication consultant, Ms. Ludlow must be a superior communicator herself. Perhaps the most important communication skill she needs, according to Ms. Ludlow, is listening. "Many times," she says, "executives aren't exactly sure what kinds of programs they need. Sometimes they talk about one kind of training when they really mean another. A good consultant must be able to listen closely to the needs described and identify the kind of program that will best meet those needs."

Interpersonal communication skills are also vitally important. "To sell, you must be good with people," Ms. Ludlow reports. "You must really like people. To be effective, a communication consultant needs to be sympathetic and sensitive." A consultant also must be assertive. For instance, when contacting a company, a consultant must be able to get an apppointment with a manager who has the authority to adopt a program. Getting such an appointment can be difficult. To succeed, the consultant must be persistent yet pleasant.

Ms. Ludlow suggests that a person interested in being a consultant should get hands-on experience in selling. An ideal way for high-school students to do this is to work for a department store, which affords opportunities to sharpen interpersonal and persuasive communication skills. Ms. Ludlow adds that doing volunteer work can also prove beneficial. "Although this will involve you in a great deal of 'gofer' work, it is through such experience that you learn."

For Paula Ludlow the stimulating field of communication consulting provides a rewarding challenge that she looks forward to meeting every day on her job.

Remember that language is a tool you can use to present the best possible you. It is a tool that you control. Think about the "you" that you are trying to present. Then begin to work on creating that "you" by adopting the language skills and habits suitable to your best image of yourself.

ACTIVITY: Analyzing Slang

Work in groups of five students. In each group, draw up a list of at least ten commonly used slang expressions. Then ask your parents for five slang expressions that they used when they were in school. Share your findings with your group and draw up a group list of slang expressions from the past. Then share your group's list with the entire class. Based on the class's findings, compile two new lists, one of common slang expressions popular today and one of common slang expressions from the past. Discuss with your classmates the differences between these two lists. What conclusion can you draw about the values and attitudes of the times from these lists? Are there any expressions that appear on both lists?

HOW TO USE LANGUAGE TO PRESENT THE BEST POSSIBLE YOU

In this chapter you have looked at language, the basis of all verbal messages. The following guidelines summarize the steps you can follow to use language to present the best possible you.

1. *Use words carefully.* Make sure you understand the meanings of the words you use. Do not be sloppy. If you are not sure of the meaning of a word, take time to look it up in your dictionary before you use it in speaking.
2. *Understand the connotations of words.* Know not only what a word means, but also what it suggests—the feelings and associations it arouses. Make sure you use words that call up the feelings you wish to stimulate in your listeners.
3. *Use language that is appropriate to the communication setting.* Know the expectations of your audience—the people to whom you are speaking. In formal settings, use standard English. In professional or occupational settings, you may use jargon judiciously. In informal settings, slang and dialect are acceptable.
4. *Improve your language.* Use your ears and your eyes to study the way effective speakers and writers communicate. Listen carefully—read widely—and write!

GUIDELINES FOR USING LANGUAGE EFFECTIVELY

- Do I understand the denotation of the words I use?
- Am I sensitive to the connotation of the words I use?
- Am I familiar with the difference between standard and non-standard English?
- Do I use jargon, slang, and dialect only in appropriate settings?
- Am I conscious of what my language tells others about me?
- Am I working to improve my language?

SUMMARY

Language is a complex system of sounds and symbols used to communicate ideas and feelings. This system consists of learned conventions that are slowly, but constantly, changing.

The denotation of a word is its dictionary meaning. The connotation of a word includes the associations and feelings it arouses. Words carry positive, negative, or neutral connotations.

Language is considered either standard or nonstandard. Language that is in keeping with the rules and conventions of English is standard. Language that ignores or violates these conventions is nonstandard. Three types of nonstandard language are jargon, slang, and dialect. The language you use should always be appropriate to the communication setting.

Your language reveals much about you. You can use your language to present the best possible you, and you can improve your language by studying, listening, reading, and writing.

CHAPTER VOCABULARY

Look back through this chapter to find the meaning of each of the following terms. Write each term and its meaning in your communication journal.

connotation	jargon	standard English
conventional	language	sublanguage
denotation	nonstandard English	symbol
dialect	slang	system

1. What is the definiton of *language*?

2. One characteristic of language is that it is conventional. What are three other characteristics?

3. What is one example of a word that has changed in meaning?

4. One principle of learning language is that such learning proceeds from simple to complex. What are two other principles?

5. What is the difference between the connotation and the denotation of a word?

6. How would you define *standard English*?

7. When is it appropriate to use nonstandard English?

8. When is it appropriate to use jargon?

9. How does your use of language affect the impression you make on people?

10. How can you improve your use of language?

DISCUSSION QUESTIONS

1. Imagine that you have discovered an object for which there is no name. Discuss what would have to happen for the name you give the object to become part of the language. Then do some research to find five words that have become part of the language within the past ten years. Share your findings with your classmates.

2. Many words you use have changed in meaning over the years. For example, this chapter pointed out that *nice* once meant "foolish," whereas now it means "pleasant, agreeable." Discuss how these changes in meaning affect your communication with others, particularly with older people.

3. Imagine that you know a person who is inclined to use nonstandard English in much of his or her conversation. Discuss what effect that use would have for the person in each of the following situations: (a) talking with a friend about a course in school; (b) talking with a teacher about a grade on an assignment; (c) talking with a parent about an increase in allowance; (d) talking with a prospective employer about a job.

4. Carl Sandburg once called slang "language that rolls up its sleeves, spits on its hands, and goes to work." What do you think Sandburg meant by this statement?

5. Roderick Nordell once wrote, "If only everyone talked the way we do in my household. I mean . . . if only everyone . . . like . . . talked . . . you know . . . the way we do . . . right? It would be so much . . . like . . . easier to . . . you know . . . understand . . . right?" What characteristic of modern speech is Nordell satirizing? How does this characteristic of modern speech affect our communication?

1. Analyzing the Methods Used by Effective Speakers

Make a list of effective speakers. Analyze their methods of speaking. What makes these people effective? Why did you include them in your list? Share your findings with your classmates. Then discuss with your class the factors that make a speaker effective.

2. Analyzing the Meanings of Words

A. List the five words you use most frequently to show your approval of something or someone. First, write the meaning you intend the words to have. Then look up the meaning of each word in your dictionary. Do the words mean exactly what you thought they meant? How many are dialect, slang, or some other form of nonstandard English? Share your findings with your classmates.

B. Prepare a list of five words that have a very positive connotation for you. Then prepare a list of five words that have a very negative connotation, that perhaps even make you angry when someone says them. Look up the meaning of each word in your dictionary. What parts of each word's definition contribute to its connotation? Compare your lists with those compiled by your classmates.

3. Defining Language

Many writers and thinkers have tried to define language. Use quotation books such as Bartlett's *Familiar Quotations* to compile a list of five particularly good quotations about language. Share your quotations with your classmates. Then compile a class list of quotations about language and copy this list in your communication journal.

4. Analyzing Cultural Differences in Communication

List five words that Americans use to express sounds animals make. Then find words from other languages that stand for these same animal sounds. Try to find a word from at least two other languages for each animal sound. How are the words from other languages like those we use? How are they different? What do these differences indicate about the ways that people from different cultures perceive their surroundings and communicate information?

5. Adjusting Language Usage to Different Audiences

Identify five different communication settings such as talking with your friends, with your teacher in class, with your parents, and with neighbors. How do you alter your words, your manner of speaking, and other facets of your speech from one communication setting to the next? When do you use slang, jargon, or dialect? Can you think of any ways that you can improve your use of language to present the best possible you?

Real-Life Speaking Situations

1. Understanding other people is difficult, even among friends, but it is this attempt at understanding one another that forms the basis of communication. Sometimes the lines of communication fail. Imagine that two good friends of yours have had a quarrel and are no longer speaking to each other. What could you do to bring them back together again? How would you try to ease the disagreement? Write a dialogue between the two estranged friends, with yourself as the message carrier—all communication has to go through you. What would you say to each friend to help the two of them reconcile their differences? Present your dialogue, along with what you would say, to the class. Ask for feedback on the effectiveness of your efforts at "mending the fences" in the dispute.

2. Eventually, in any field of work you choose, there will come a time when you want a raise in salary. To get your raise, you will likely have to ask for it. When you approach your supervisor, director, manager, or whoever is your boss, you will want to exhibit your best qualities. Imagine that you have decided to ask for a raise. The first thing to consider is whether you deserve it. Is asking for a raise a reasonable request? Make a list of reasons why you think you ought to have a raise. Examine your reasons. Are they convincing? Can you state them clearly and convincingly? Make sure that you know exactly what you want to say. Also consider how to approach the person you will ask. What will he or she say? Identify how you will tailor your request to make it particularly convincing to your boss. Prepare a one-page speech asking for a raise. Be sure to include all of your reasons why you deserve a raise and to tailor your request to suit your audience. Your message should be brief, concise, and very positive in tone. Be prepared to deliver your request to the class.

SENDING NONVERBAL MESSAGES

OBJECTIVES:

After studying this chapter, you should be able to

1. Define nonverbal communication.

2. List the four functions of nonverbal communication.

3. Explain how body language affects communication.

4. Explain how appearance affects communication.

5. Explain how paralanguage affects communication.

6. Explain how environment affects communication.

7. Check your understanding of another person's nonverbal message.

His eyes filled with anger, John looked at Susan as she took her books from the locker one by one. With a sneer on his lips, he said coldly, "I'm going to be late for class."

At the last possible moment, John let go of Susan's hand. A loving smile passed across his face as he looked at her and said, "I'm going to be late for class."

John laughed as Susan talked. Suddenly he looked at his watch, grabbed his books from his locker, and started to run. Looking over his shoulder, he shouted to her, "I'm going to be late for class."

In each of the situations involving John and Susan, John said the same words to Susan—"I'm going to be late for class." Yet each time he communicated a meaning beyond the words, and this nonverbal message was totally different in each situation.

WHAT IS NONVERBAL COMMUNICATION?

Nonverbal communication consists of all the elements of communication other than words. These elements include body language, appearance, the sound of the voice, and the communication environment.

How important is nonverbal communication? In your everyday communications, 50 to 90 percent of the messages you send are nonverbal.

Functions of Nonverbal Communication

Nonverbal communication serves at least four very important functions in communicating a message.

First, nonverbal communication may *complement* verbal communication. Nonverbal cues are complementary when they work with the verbal cues to communicate the message. For example, if you smile and laugh as you say "Jack, that's hilarious," the smile and the laughter—the nonverbal part of the message—go along with, or complement, what you say.

Second, nonverbal communication may *emphasize* verbal communication. Nonverbal cues add emphasis by giving special force to one word or to an entire message. For example, say that Mrs. Parker tells her daughter Pam, "I want this done now!" and, while saying the word *now,* pounds her left palm with her right fist. This gesture emphasizes that Mrs. Parker wants Pam to act immediately. Mrs. Parker may also give additional emphasis to the word *now* by saying it with greater force than she says the other words. Skilled speakers work very hard to learn how to emphasize ideas through gestures and voice.

Third, nonverbal communication may *replace* verbal communication. Such replacement occurs when nonverbal behavior takes the place of a verbal message. For example, you are reading and your brother leans over

Marvin by Tom Armstrong. © by and reprinted by permission of News America Syndicate.

Nonverbal signals may be sent on purpose, as Marvin is doing, but many are sent unconsciously, without thinking.

and asks, "Did you get the tickets?" In response, you nod your head. This nod communicates your message—"Yes, I got the tickets"—clearly without verbal symbols.

Fourth, <u>nonverbal communication may *contradict* verbal communication.</u> Nonverbal cues serve a contradictory function when they send a message opposite to that of the verbal message. In many ways, it is the contradictory function of nonverbal communication that is most important in learning to communicate effectively. For example, a teacher, Miss Gordon, wants to find out how far along her students are on their reports. She asks Paul, "Are you almost finished with your report?" and he responds "Yes." Miss Gordon may get a very good idea of whether Paul is telling the truth or not just by the way he says "yes." If Paul answers "yes" with a firm, relaxed tone of voice and looks directly at Miss Gordon when he speaks, Miss Gordon will likely believe him. If, on the other hand, he says "yes" hesitantly, if his tone is not firm, if he looks down or to the side as he speaks, Miss Gordon will be less likely to believe him.

Nonverbal cues can speak louder than words. For instance, if someone says to you, "You don't mind my barging in like this, do you?" and you answer, "No, of course not," your tone of voice will communicate more than your words. If your tone is light and friendly, the other person is likely to take your words at face value. If, on the other hand, your tone is hard or has a cutting sound to it, the other person is likely to take your response as negative regardless of your words.

Since nonverbal behavior can be difficult to control, contradiction is a common problem. While speakers usually plan or at least think about the words they say, they less frequently give thought to their nonverbal behavior. For example, say that two friends, Phil and Marge, are rushing through the mall, and Marge says to Phil, "I'm not walking too fast for you, am I?" Phil, who is a bit out of breath, takes a gulp of air and answers, "No, not at all." Although his words tell Marge not to slow her pace, his nonverbal behavior— taking a gulp of air—gives her the opposite message.

ACTIVITY:　　Observing and Analyzing Nonverbal Behavior

For one week, observe very closely the nonverbal behavior of your classmates, members of your family, and your teachers. In your communication journal, make notes on what you see. Then describe to your class your findings on how these people used nonverbal behavior to (1) emphasize a point, (2) illustrate a point, (3) take the place of words, and (4) contradict their words intentionally. Also, describe situations in which nonverbal behavior *un*intentionally contradicted a verbal message.

Sometimes, however, contradiction is intentional. For example, sarcasm is communicated by the sharp, planned contradiction between a verbal and a nonverbal message. If the girl sitting next to you in class uses an ironic tone of voice when she says, "Charlie's really smooth, isn't he?" she shows that she really thinks Charlie is a clod.

WHAT MESSAGE IS YOUR BODY LANGUAGE SENDING?

Body language is the use of facial expression, eye contact, gestures, posture, and movement to communicate. You use body language all the time, sometimes without even thinking about it. For example, when you feel nervous, you may find yourself biting your nails. When you feel frightened, quite unconsciously you may shut your eyes tightly and shudder. Although you may not make a sound, others can tell how you feel by simply looking at you.

Facial Expressions

People can tell much about you from the expression on your face. A person's face is capable of a nearly unlimited number of expressions. For example, the eyes can wink; the eyebrows can be raised; the mouth can be shaped into a smile, a frown, or a sneer. Many of these expressions communicate a clear meaning to others. For example, most people see wide-open eyes as an indication of wonder and squinting eyes as a signal of question or probe.

Audience members with folded arms are communicating, through body language, that they are not yet receptive to the speaker's message.

Usually, facial expressions are closely tied to the way a person is feeling. When something is funny, most people smile or laugh. When they are puzzled, they frown, often without even thinking about it.

It has often been said that the eyes are windows to the soul. In other words, people's eyes reveal what they feel. Eye behavior is a particularly noticeable aspect of facial expression. When you are embarrassed, you are likely to look away from a person. When someone has upset you, you may likely give him or her a piercing look.

Eye contact is an essential component of effective communication. In American society, a speaker and a listener generally look each other in the eye during much of a conversation. The ability to look someone squarely in the eye is taken as a sign of honesty and straightforwardness. The inability to do this is taken as a sign of untrustworthiness.

Even though most people do not have full conscious control over facial expression, they usually learn to mask their feelings at least some of the time. **Masking** means purposely using a facial expression normally associated with one feeling to disguise other, true feelings. For example, some people learn to mask their feelings of hurt or pain with a thin smile. Of course, masking can sometimes ease a social situation, but if used too frequently, it can get in the way of true communication.

Good communicators watch others' expressions closely and try to interpret them correctly. For example, suppose two friends, Todd and Anita, are chatting after class. When Todd smiles at something Anita has said, Anita may assume that Todd thinks her comment was humorous or agreeable. If Todd frowns, Anita may assume that Todd has found her comment puzzling or disagreeable. However, as you will see later in this chapter, the only way to be sure an interpretation of nonverbal behavior is correct is to do a verbal perception check.

Gestures

Gestures are the movements people make with their arms, hands, and fingers. Gestures serve three basic functions: they replace verbal language, emphasize points, and heighten description.

Gestures can take the place of verbal communication. No doubt you have learned many commonly understood gestures. You nod for *yes*, shrug your shoulders for *I don't know*, and show thumbs up for *we won*. From across the room, you can hold a brief conversation with a friend by using hand signals. Sports officials have to learn a number of gestures that represent violations, scoring, players' numbers, and the like. Sign language is a system of gestures that allows full communication between people without the use of words.

Gestures can emphasize. Pounding your fist, pointing your finger, and waving your hand all add emphasis to your words.

Gestures can describe. You can use gestures to show height, shape, thickness, and length while describing something. You can also use gestures to indicate number, position, intensity, and a wide variety of other thoughts and emotions.

Although the degree to which people "talk with their hands" varies, everyone uses some gestures. Gestures can be disruptive when they get so wild or so contrary to expectation that they either lose their meaning or create unintended meanings. Some people gesture so much that the gestures are distracting. To communicate effectively, you must learn to control your gestures, particularly when you are speaking in public. Effective speakers use gestures to emphasize and to describe, without causing distraction or confusion.

Posture and Movement

Posture is the position of a person's body. The way you hold your body when you walk, the way you sit in a chair, the way you recline—all of these postures tell others a great deal about you. For example, most people see someone who stands tall as sure and confident, whereas they see someone who stoops as uncertain or timid. They see someone who is slumped in a chair as bored or tired, while they perceive someone who sits up straight as eager and alert.

Movement is, quite simply, the way a person moves. Do you walk with a quick, sure step? Then you are likely to be seen as sure and confident. Do you move furtively, trying to escape notice? Then you may likely be perceived as sneaky or untrustworthy.

Learn to control your posture and your movement to create the effect you want. We have all been impressed by the person who walks into a room and immediately commands it. The effect this person creates is largely caused by his or her control of posture and movement.

Soldiers, cadets, and other military personnel are trained to use posture and movement to communicate pride, alertness, and confidence.

Work in groups of five or six students. Have each student in the group act out a situation in which he or she uses body language to express a strong emotion. The situation could be stubbing a toe, dropping a coin and watching it roll into a sewer, bringing home good (or bad) grades, or winning a prize at a fair. Write down the body language that each person uses to present the situation and to show emotions. After everyone has finished, discuss the different types of body language each student used.

WHAT MESSAGE IS YOUR APPEARANCE SENDING?

Another aspect of nonverbal communication is appearance. To some extent, you draw conclusions about others, and they draw conclusions about you, based on appearances. As you get to know people better and as they get to know you, appearance becomes less important in making judgments. Nevertheless, you have no doubt learned that first impressions do count and that a major part of a first impression is created by appearance. People use your appearance as a yardstick by which to measure you. What does appearance reveal?

People use your appearance as a key to who you are. For example, if you see a young woman dressed in a business suit and carrying an attaché case rush to catch a taxi, you may likely identify that person as a businesswoman. If you see someone wearing a ski jacket and ski cap and carrying a pair of skis, you probably will identify that person as a skier.

Sometimes people dress to fit into a group. For example, you may consciously dress so that everyone knows you are a cheerleader or a musician or a motorcyclist. You may wear special clothing and carry accessories such as dancing shoes or a gym bag to let people know you are a dancer or a gymnast.

People see appearance as a sign of a person's attitude toward another person or a situation. For example, imagine that a girl, Charlene, asks her friend Dan to join her for dinner with her parents at one of the town's better restaurants. Although Charlene does not say anything to Dan, she has expectations of how he will dress. It would be inappropriate for Dan to show up in blue jeans and a sweat shirt. Anything less than a tie and jacket would be taken as a sign of indifference toward the situation of meeting a friend's parents.

People also use appearance as a sign of a person's self-regard. For example, if you do not take care of your appearance, if you appear sloppy or slovenly, people will assume you think little of yourself. On the other hand, if you are always well groomed and appropriately dressed, people will

The turkey in this cartoon has craftily decided to alter its appearance in order to fit in with the group of hunters.

Drawing by Booth © 1971 by the New Yorker Magazine, Inc.

assume you have a good opinion of yourself. In many cases people base their opinions of you on what your opinion of yourself appears to be. In other words, if you treat yourself as someone special, others will tend to treat you that way too.

What guidelines should you follow in determining your appearance? First, consider the impression you want to create, the image you want to project. Second, consider the expectations of others and the demands of the situation. Then groom yourself and select your clothing to project the image you have chosen.

ACTIVITY: Analyzing Pictures for Nonverbal Clues

Select a magazine article or advertisement that features the photograph of one person and bring it to class. Join with four or five other students, into a group, and study the magazine items brought in by everyone in the group. For each item, jot down three to five adjectives, such as *lively, warm,* or *tender,* that you associate with the person in the magazine picture. Then compare your lists of adjectives with those compiled by the other members in the group. Discuss why each of you selected your particular adjectives for each person portrayed. If the lists include similar adjectives, discuss why these similar choices were made. If the lists contain major differences, discuss why these differences occurred.

HOW DOES PARALANGUAGE AFFECT COMMUNICATION?

The third aspect of nonverbal communication is paralanguage. **Paralanguage** is the use of voice variation and extraneous sounds to communicate. Paralanguage may be the most important part of nonverbal communication. Since the next chapter looks closely at the mechanics of voice, or vocalization, this section will simply identify three areas of paralanguage.

The sound of a person's voice is one area of paralanguage. Your voice is as flexible as any musical instrument. It can go up and down in scale (pitch). It can be loud or soft (volume). You can use your voice to talk quickly or slowly (rate). It can take on different tones (quality), so that you will seem to be happy, sad, sarcastic, warm, cold, loving, or feeling any other emotion that can be named. For example, when you say "I love you," it is the *tone* of your voice that indicates whether you really mean it and how much.

Cheerleaders are skilled at using voice variation to heighten the crowd's excitement and build their team's morale.

Use of pause is a second area of paralanguage. You can pause to indicate uncertainty or to create suspense. You can pause to emphasize an upcoming word. Notice how the pause works in the following sentence: *The winner of the scholarship is* (pause) *Hector Marin.*

Use of extraneous sounds or words to fill space in a sentence is a third area of paralanguage. Some of the sounds and words most commonly used are "uh," "well, uh," "um," and "you know."

Using Paralanguage to Communicate Meaning

Read the following short conversation:

"How are you?"
"Great, how about yourself?"
"Just fine."
"I've got to be going now."
"I'll catch you later."

Dramatize the above conversation in three ways. First, add paralanguage clues to the dialogue to show that the two people really like each other. Second, use another set of paralanguage clues to indicate that the two people are not particularly interested in each other but are merely being polite. Finally, use paralanguage clues to show that the two people do not like each other at all. After the dramatizations are completed, discuss the ways in which paralanguage affected the message in each situation.

HOW DOES ENVIRONMENT AFFECT COMMUNICATION?

The fourth aspect of nonverbal communication is **environment**, which is the immediate surroundings, including color, lighting, sound, and space. When you think of nonverbal communication, you may not think immediately of the effect of environment. Yet features of the environment can send very important messages.

What types of messages does the environment communicate? First, it sends messages that affect your behavior. For example, an amusement park with its rides, game booths, and food stands is set up the way it is in order to tell you to have fun. In contrast, a library with its tables, chairs, books, and hushed atmosphere tells you that it is a place to study and to learn.

Second, the environment sends messages that affect your feelings, or mood. For example, when you enter a shadowy room with half the light bulbs burned out, paint peeling from the walls, broken and ragged furniture, and junk strewn all over the floor, you are likely to feel sad, depressed, or blue. On the other hand, entering a room that is sunny, airy, freshly painted, and comfortably decorated, may likely lead you to feel cheerful, enthusiastic, or relaxed.

As a communicator, you must learn to use your environment to suit your purpose. Structure your environment so that it is in keeping with the type of behavior you want to encourage. For example, if you want people to listen carefully to what you say, make sure the environment sends that message instead of one telling your audience to feel free to talk among themselves. Control the message the environment is sending. For example, if you want people to feel comfortable and relaxed, use the elements of the environment—color, lighting, sound, and space—to create that mood.

Color

There is no doubt that people react to color. Some colors, such as reds, yellows, and oranges, have a stimulating effect and are seen as intense, full of vitality, and exciting. Others, such as blues, greens, and beiges, have a calming effect and are seen as cool, peaceful, or neutral. In general, black and brown have a depressing effect and are seen as sad, mysterious, or melancholy, while white has a joyous effect and is seen as light and innocent. Of course, since people are individuals, these generalizations about their reactions to colors do not always hold true.

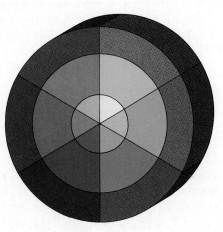

The mood of an audience is affected by the color of the speaking environment. A humorous speech may delight listeners in a yellow room but fall flat in a room painted a dark green or brown.

Lighting

Lighting also sends important environmental messages about the type of communication that is desired. In general, low lighting tends to create a relaxed, quiet atmosphere in which people want to linger. Bright lighting stimulates conversation and interaction, while extremely bright lighting causes fatigue and makes people want to leave an environment.

Sound

Sound has an obvious effect on communication, and it often complements lighting. For example, in a dimly lit restaurant you might expect and react positively to soft music. In a brightly lit restaurant, you might expect louder music.

Sound affects how you feel. When you are driving on a long trip, playing stimulating music on the radio can help keep you alert. When you are preparing for bed, playing soft, peaceful music can help put you in the mood for sleeping.

Loud noises, however, are almost always distracting. The lawn mower outside, a jet overhead, or the whining of a generator will make it very difficult to communicate. Wherever possible in speaking situations, try to control the noise level. Although soft music may go well with conversation, effective public communication requires a noise-free environment.

Space

Perhaps the most complicated element of environment is space. The space around you includes the relatively permanent structures that determine the limits of that space, the elements within a confined space that can be moved, and the area, or territory, itself.

The house you live in, the park down the street, and your school building are all relatively permanent structures that create a communication context. For example, a modern apartment creates a communication context very different from that of a massive two-story Victorian house. As a result, the type of place in which people choose to live communicates something about their ideas and feelings. You can draw conclusions about people based on the choices they make in their surroundings.

Every occasion for communication, whether formal or informal, requires that you observe an appropriate distance from your audience.

Yet even in permanent structures, people have the power to change the communication context by rearranging movable objects. Take a classroom as an example. In older school buildings all chairs and desks are usually bolted to the floor in rows so that little change is possible. However, in more modern buildings, desks can be easily moved about to change the environment. During class discussions, chairs can be arranged in a large circle to encourage the free exchange of ideas. When working in small groups, students can position their chairs to form small clusters. When there is a class demonstration, the chairs can be placed close to the wall to leave a large open space in the center.

Perhaps the most important aspect of space involves space itself—the distance between people which creates the area they call their "territory." Researchers have determined that most people have at least four different distances that have meaning for them—intimate space, personal space, social space, and public space. Of course, the more friendly you are with people, the more comfortable you feel having them close to you when talking. The less well you know people, the more distance you put between you and them when speaking.

Your **intimate space** consists of up to eighteen inches of space between you and other people. It is the distance at which you feel comfortable communicating with members of your family and people you like very much or know very well. Violation of intimate space by strangers causes friction. Most people will be nervous around, or will back away from, others who get within the eighteen-inch range if they are not close friends or relatives.

To some extent, the precise boundary of intimate space is dictated by custom. For example, most Americans feel a need for more distance between one another when talking than do people from southern Europe or the Middle East. When you strike up a conversation with a stranger, you must be careful not to violate that person's intimate space. Violation of intimate space is likely to make people uncomfortable and therefore will make communicating with them more difficult.

Your **personal space** consists of from eighteen inches to four feet between you and other people. It is the distance at which you conduct most conversations with acquaintances. You want people to be close enough so that you can hear and see each other easily, but not so close that either of you feels uncomfortable.

Your **social space** consists of from four to twelve feet between you and other people. It is the distance at which you carry on interviews and other fairly formal kinds of conversation. Your conversation with strangers at a party may be carried on at this distance.

Your **public space** consists of the area beyond twelve feet between you and other people. It is the distance at which you expect such types of communication as public speeches and oral readings to take place. Obviously, at this distance communication is impersonal.

Remember that people are likely to treat space as territory. How do you deal with a person who invades your territory, or space? If you overreact, you are likely to make everyone involved even more uncomfortable. Instead, try describing your feelings to the person. For instance, if someone sets some books near yours on a library table in a way that violates your space, try either to accept the situation or to explain your feelings. You might say something like "Could you move your books a little? Putting them there really makes me feel crowded."

How do you treat other people's space? If you are insensitive to others' territory, you are likely to make them behave defensively. A great deal of human conflict results from invasion of space.

ACTIVITY: Designing an Environment to Suit an Activity

Design a room. First, identify the kind of activity the room is being designed for. Is it a study room? a meeting room? a play room? Second, determine what color the room should be painted. Why is this color a good one for the type of activity you have chosen for the room? Third, determine the type of lighting you will use in this room. Why is this lighting appropriate for this type of room? Finally, determine the kinds of and the arrangement of furniture in the room. How are the furnishings and the arrangement appropriate for the activity? Share your design with your classmates. Listen to and respond to feedback from them.

CHECKING YOUR PERCEPTION OF THE MEANING OF THE MESSAGE

In many situations your ability to interpret nonverbal behavior accurately is vital. If you interpret incorrectly, your own response will be inappropriate. The only way to be certain that you have accurately interpreted nonverbal clues is to check verbally.

A **perception check** is a verbal response stating one person's understanding of someone else's nonverbal behavior. For example, consider the following situations:

Cheryl asks Paul if he liked the game. Paul looks up and says in a sarcastic tone, "Right, it was great." Cheryl does a perception check. She says, "It sounds as though you mean it was awful. What happened at the game?"

Marge, the most popular girl in school, has been talking to Charlie, a new boy in school. Because she has enjoyed their conversation, she says to him, "Would you like to come to the dance club with me after school?" Charlie, who is shy, sputters a bit and then simply shrugs his shoulders.

Marge thinks he means no. She does a perception check. She says, "I get the idea you don't want to come to the club. Am I reading you right?"

Harry comes into the house and walks past his brother without saying a word. His brother, remembering the argument they had that morning, first becomes defensive and then angry. He does a perception check. He says, "Harry, are you still mad about this morning? I thought we had settled that argument."

The famous psychiatrist Sigmund Freud (1856-1939) used perception checks to increase his patients' and his own understanding of their nonverbal behavior. Many psychiatrists today continue using this technique.

Although people do not always understand their own feelings, most of the time they can let you know whether your own interpretation is correct.

Why is a perception check so important? If you interpret a nonverbal message incorrectly, you may respond inappropriately. For example, in the third example above, if Harry's brother had not done a perception check, he might have started rehashing the morning's argument, when Harry had only walked past him because he was thinking about something else.

HOW TO USE NONVERBAL COMMUNICATION EFFECTIVELY

In this chapter you have looked at nonverbal communication. The following list summarizes the steps you can take to use nonverbal communication effectively.

1. *Make sure that your body language supplements what you are trying to say.* Consider your facial expressions, eye contact, gestures, posture, and movements. Change any that contradict your message.

2. *Make sure that your appearance is in keeping with what you want to accomplish.* Consider the image you wish to project, how it relates to the expectations of other people, and the demands of the situation.

3. *If possible, create an environment that is suitable for the kind of communication you want to have take place.* Use color, lighting, sound, and space to accomplish your purpose.

4. *Make sure that the sound of your voice is in keeping with your message.* Learn to control the pitch, volume, rate, and quality of your voice. Pay attention to your use of pauses and of extraneous sounds and words.

ACTIVITY: Making Appropriate Perception Checks for Different Situations

Respond to each of the following situations with a perception check.

1. Tom comes home from school with a pale face and slumped shoulders. Glancing at you with a sad look, he shrugs his shoulders. You say . . .

2. Mandy comes into your room, throws her books on the floor, and sits on the edge of a chair holding her head in her hands. You say . . .

3. Jill is reading a letter she received in the mail this morning. As she reads, she breaks into a big smile. You say . . .

4. Nick is waiting for a telephone call. He paces back and forth. He sits down and starts tapping his fingers against the table. Suddenly he jumps up and starts pacing again. You say . . .

GUIDELINES FOR EVALUATING NONVERBAL COMMUNICATION

- Does my body language complement my verbal message?
- Does my appearance project the image I wish to create?
- Is my appearance appropriate for the situation and the audience?
- Is the sound of my voice in keeping with my verbal message?
- Have I taken into account the nature of the environment?
- Do I check the accuracy of my perception of what other people's nonverbal behavior means?

Profiles in Communication

Angela Roth

Angela Roth is a professional nonverbal communicator. Watching people use sign language fascinated her as a child, and she renewed her interest years later when she and a friend helped another person with a hearing impairment learn sign language. Since then she has continued to study sign language and is now a teacher and nationally certified interpreter of both American sign language and manually coded English.

Ms. Roth draws upon her verbal background in English and Spanish to translate spoken Spanish to American sign language as well. As in using Spanish, she asserts, "it's not just a matter of using sign language, it's a matter of thinking in sign language. Learning a language is learning a culture, a way of thinking."

Like any language, sign language has its own rules. For example, facial expression is part of the grammar of sign language. "If you miss a facial expression," Ms. Roth says, "you may miss an adjective or adverb that is a key to the meaning of the sentence."

Sign language, however, is not mime, although according to Ms. Roth "it has elements of mime." Such dramatic use of gesture, facial expression, and other nonverbal cues often makes learning sign language difficult for Americans, who tend to be reserved when speaking. "Sign language is more expressive than spoken language," Ms. Roth says. "You need to be more open with your feelings." She comments that after learning a little sign language many Americans enjoy being able to express the emotional, subjective side of their messages so openly in signs. Many people, in fact, begin incorporating gestures more freely into their everyday communication.

For those interested in pursuing a career in teaching or translating sign language, Ms. Roth reports that the field is wide open. Many fields, such as psychology and business, are now looking for people fluent in sign language. Ms. Roth finds that the variety of her freelance jobs provides exciting opportunities to work with interesting people in many different fields. What she enjoys most about her work, however, is the sense of accomplishment and fulfillment she gets from helping people communicate through the fascinating nonverbal medium of sign language.

SUMMARY

Nonverbal communication is the communication that takes place beyond the use of words. Nonverbal communication involves body language, appearance, the sound of the speaker's voice, and environmental features.

Nonverbal communication serves four main functions: to complement, to emphasize, to replace, and to contradict verbal communication.

Much nonverbal communication is accomplished through body language. Body language includes facial expression, eye contact, gesture, posture, and movement.

People draw conclusions about others based on appearance. You have the power to use your appearance to create the kind of image you desire. However, you must make sure that your appearance is appropriate, that is, that it suits the situation and meets the expectations of others.

Paralanguage is the sound of a person's voice. Through pitch, volume, rate, and quality you alter the meaning of your words.

The only way to be sure that you are interpreting another person's nonverbal communication correctly is to do a perception check. A perception check is a statement or question that seeks to confirm one person's understanding of another person's nonverbal behavior.

CHAPTER VOCABULARY

Look back through this chapter to find the meaning of each of the following terms. Write each term and its meaning in your communication notebook.

body language	movement	posture
environment	nonverbal communication	public space
gestures	paralanguage	social space
intimate space	perception check	
masking	personal space	

REVIEW QUESTIONS

1. What is nonverbal communication?

2. Nonverbal communication may *complement* verbal communication. What are three other functions of nonverbal communication?

3. One way that body language communicates is through gestures. What are four other ways?

4. Why is eye contact important in communication?

5. An important key to using your appearance effectively is to dress appropriately. What does this mean?

6. How can you use your appearance to identify you as a member of a particular group?

7. What is paralanguage?

8. If you were painting your room to create a soothing, peaceful environment, what color would you paint it? Why?

9. Social space is one type of distance between people who are talking to each other. What are three other types?

10. Why are perception checks necessary?

DISCUSSION QUESTIONS

1. Eye contact is an important part of conversation. Discuss how you can use eye contact to (a) encourage people to talk, (b) show that you are listening, and (c) show that you would like the conversation to end.

2. Identify at least five different groups in your school, such as cheerleaders, band members, and basketball players. How does appearance help you identify the members of each of these groups?

3. Machiavelli once observed of human beings: "Men in general judge more from appearances than from reality. All men have eyes, but few have the gift of penetration." Analyze the meaning of this statement. Then discuss whether you agree with it or not.

4. Laughter is one way we communicate nonverbally. Josh Billings once wrote, "Laughter is the sensation of feeling good all over and showing it principally in one place." What do you think that this quotation means? Do you agree with this definition of laughter or not? How would you define laughter? How would you define its opposite, weeping?

5. Discuss the kinds of nonverbal communication you would use to show each of the following: anger, interest, surprise, self-confidence, happiness, boredom. Then discuss whether people from different cultures use basically the same nonverbal symbols to express particular attitudes and feelings.

1. Using Pantomime to Communicate Nonverbal Messages

Pantomime is a way of sending messages nonverbally. Use pantomime to convey each of the following messages.

a. I'm really glad to see you.
b. The room is down the hall.
c. Please may I have it?
d. Don't tell me any more!
e. Come a little closer.
f. I'm sorry.
g. Which way should we go?

2. Analyzing Nonverbal Communication in Silent Movies

Watch a silent movie. How do the performers in the movie communicate? Do any of the gestures they use seem to be standard? If so, which ones? Which gestures seem to be more effective? Present several of these gestures to an audience and describe how the gestures were used in the movie. Discuss how such gestures are used in everyday communication.

3. Giving an Oral Report on Nonverbal Factors Affecting Communication

Many self-help books have been published telling people how to achieve power or success through the way they dress, use body language, design an environment, or use color. Read one of these books and prepare an oral report on it for your class.

4. Exploring the Effect of Nonverbal Messages on Communication

A. Prepare a verbal message to send to a partner. Send the message verbally three times. Each time you repeat the message, vary your nonverbal message to convey a different meaning.

B. Working with a partner, act out a situation in which you use nonverbal communication to contradict a verbal message. Discuss with your partner the effects of sending such contradictory messages.

5. Analyzing Problems in Telephone Communication

Some people do not like to communicate important information by telephone because they think it difficult to send accurate messages through this medium. First discuss how the telephone may hamper communication. Then share instances when you misunderstood someone when talking on the phone.

Real-Life Speaking Situations

1. Many people secretly—or not so secretly—believe that they can talk their way out of almost anything. But sometimes talking does not work. Language can be a barrier in itself. For example, in communicating with someone who speaks only a little English, verbal communication is often much less effective than nonverbal communication. What other situations can you imagine in which spoken language is either a barrier or of little help in communicating? Identify two such situations. How could you use nonverbal clues to communicate your message in each of these situations? What types of nonverbal clues would be the most effective? Write a short speech (one to two pages long) explaining how you would use nonverbal clues to communicate in the two situations. Be prepared to discuss your nonverbal messages and to act them out for the class.

2. Receptionists, security guards, nurses, and people working in many other occupations greet customers and visitors every day. People who meet the public are expected to present a good appearance and to be helpful and courteous. Carrying out these job responsibilities requires the careful use of nonverbal communication. Customers and visitors are usually greeted with a smile by someone dressed neatly and appropriately. This person's tone of voice, actions, and general behavior should all be tailored to present a good impression of the company or institution to the public. Making a good impression requires different skills in different jobs. For example, a security guard greets the public differently from the way a nurse in a clinic does. Make a list of ten specific jobs whose regular duties include greeting the public. From this list, choose three jobs that interest you, and identify the nonverbal behavior that would be appropriate for greeting customers and visitors you would meet. Compare your lists with those of your classmates. Be prepared to discuss and exhibit the nonverbal behavior for the jobs you have chosen.

THE VOCALIZATION PROCESS

OBJECTIVES:

After studying this chapter, you should be able to

1. Explain how sound is generated.

2. Define resonance.

3. Identify three major cavity resonators.

4. Define articulation.

5. Identify the major articulators.

6. Define pitch.

7. Define vocal quality.

8. List four major vocalization problems.

9. List four common articulation problems.

"Ahm tryn ta figger watcha haf to do round here to ganywer!"

"Brian, if I've told you once, I've told you several times. You just can't expect others to understand you if you try to talk with your mouth full of gum. Now, get rid of that gum so that we can understand what it is that you want."

"Aw—"

"Come on, get rid of the gum!"

"Aw righ'!" Brian said as he wrapped the gum in a piece of paper and threw it in the wastebasket.

"Good. Now let's hear what you want to say."

"Ahm tryn ta figger watch haf ta do roun here to ganywer!"

Human speech, the ability to form sounds and use them to communicate ideas and feelings, is truly a miracle. However, as the opening situation illustrates, this miracle has its limits.

While the body has a respiratory system and a digestive system in which organs are dedicated specifically to breathing and digestion, the body has no "speech" system. The organs that we use for speech have other primary functions. For instance, the teeth and the tongue are for chewing food and moving it to the back of the mouth; the throat is for swallowing food and drink; and the lungs are for breathing. Yet in prehistoric times, human beings learned to use these organs and others to speak. Speaking requires coordination of parts of the body to *generate* sound, to *resonate* sound, and finally to *articulate* sound.

WHAT ARE THE GENERATORS OF SOUND?

You are probably familiar with the parts of the body that help you breathe. Although respiration is the main function of the breathing structure, it is not the only function. This structure also helps you generate, or produce, sounds for speech.

The primary generators of sound are the **vocal folds**—the muscles of the larynx. Sound is generated by pushing out air in such a way that the

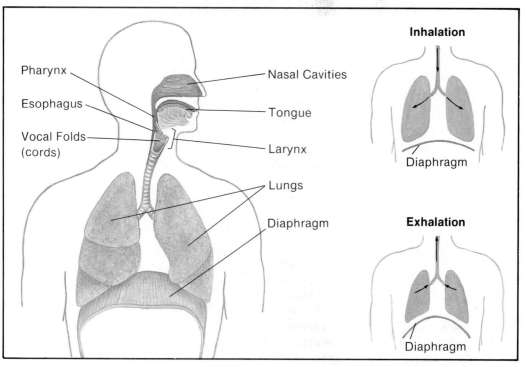

The generation of speech is a complex process that requires the interaction of many parts of the body.

vocal folds vibrate. To understand this process better, study the illustration on page 66.

Now consider regular breathing. To start the breathing process, the **diaphragm,** a dome-shaped muscle at the base of the lungs, contracts. As the diaphragm contracts, air is drawn in through the mouth or nose and down the throat. In the throat the air passes through the **larynx** (what most people call the voice box) and the **trachea** (what most people call the windpipe), and then is drawn into the lungs. As the diaphragm relaxes, the air in the lungs is pushed back up through the trachea and larynx, through the throat, and out through the mouth or nose. Since the same upper passageway is used for air, food, and drink, a valve in the larynx must open and close to make sure that food and drink go one way, while air goes another. The muscles that control this opening are called the *vocal folds.* Even though they are muscles and nothing at all like cords, you may know them by the more common term **vocal cords.**

To see how the process of breathing works, examine your own breathing. Notice that when you breathe, there is a regular cycle of intake and outflow of air. As you breathe in, watch how your chest and stomach expand. As you breathe out, watch how your chest and stomach deflate as air is expelled through the nose or mouth.

Now consider the slight changes in regular breathing that allow you to generate sound. First, to produce sound, you must take more air into the lungs than you do when you breathe regularly. For example, try saying the following sentence aloud:

> I like to sit by my bedroom window late at night and write,
> watching the stars twinkle in the sky above and the moon
> cast its icy spell upon the earth while I struggle to find
> the words to express my innermost thoughts.

Did you notice that as you read this sentence, you had to take in extra air to get to the end of it? Unless you learn to control the amount of air you take in when speaking, you find yourself "gulping air," or taking in large quantities of air quickly, in order to finish sentences.

Second, to form sounds, you push out air faster than in normal breathing, and you control this air flow. To speed up this flow of air, muscles in the abdominal and chest areas contract as the diaphragm relaxes, giving an extra push to the air. Put your hands on your waist so that your fingers are pressing on your stomach. Remember that your stomach is above your waist. Pretend that you are going to try to blow out all the candles on your birthday cake. Take a deep breath—and blow! When you took the deep breath, you felt pressure on your hands as the area near the stomach expanded. Then when you blew out, you felt a tight contraction of the stomach muscles. However, you made no sound other than the quiet whoosh of air as it rushed back through the larynx and the throat and out the mouth.

Now wrap your hands snugly around your neck so that your thumbs are pressing lightly at the front of your throat and your forefingers at the back. Take a deep breath and say "ah." Did you feel the vibration? Here is what happened. Instead of the vocal folds opening to allow air to rush out, the folds came very close together—so close, in fact, that when the air tried to get through them, the vocal folds began to vibrate, much in the way a guitar string vibrates when it is plucked. This vibration creates a weak sound, which can be enhanced and controlled to produce sounds that become speech. When you say "ah," your control of the air you exhale creates a slow and steady pressure in the diaphragm area. Examine the illustration below.

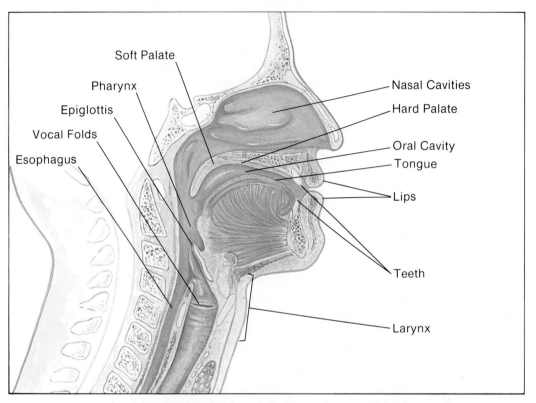

Sound created by forcing air between the vocal folds is modified by both the *resonators* and *articulators* before emerging as speech.

Now try another experiment. Put your hands back on your waist with your fingers pressing lightly on your stomach. This time, say "ah" as loud as you can. Notice that you can feel the same kind of stomach contraction that you felt when you were pretending to blow out the candles.

For regular breathing, then, air comes out at a steady rate as the diaphragm relaxes. However, to build power and to produce sound, stomach and chest muscles contract to give the air flow enough force to vibrate the vocal folds that have come close together. This vibration produces sound, which can then be turned into speech. But this sound is weak. To turn it into speech, the sound must be resonated.

Place the open palms of your hands tightly against your lower front ribs. Inhale slowly and deeply through both mouth and nose, feeling the push of the lower rib wall against your hands. Hold your breath for the count of five, noting that your ribs are held up and out. Now exhale slowly, pressing in with your hands but resisting this pressure by the slow lowering of the ribs. Turn your hands so that the tips of your fingers point toward your spine. Your open palms can now feel the rib movement of the side and back of the rib cage. Again, slowly inhale, hold, and exhale. Repeat this procedure until you are well aware of the movement of the rib cage.

WHAT ARE THE RESONATORS OF SOUND?

Before sound produced by exhaling air can be speech, it must be given **resonance,** or reinforcement produced by vibration. The **resonators** of sound for speech are the bones in the chest, neck, and head and the cavities of the throat, nose, and mouth. These two groups of resonators amplify sound in different ways.

Bones resonate by picking up vibrations of sound. To see how bone resonance works, grip a thick rubber band tightly in your two hands. Stretch the rubber band, place it near a board, and pluck it with your thumb. If the rubber band is the right length, its vibrations will cause the board to vibrate. However, since the board is thicker than the rubber band, the sound it produces will be greater and fuller than that produced by the rubber band. In a similar way, the bone resonators vibrate in tune with the vocal folds, creating louder, fuller speech sounds.

While the bones in the chest, neck, and head resonate some of the sounds generated by the vibration of the vocal folds, most resonance occurs in the cavities of the throat, the nose, and the mouth. A **cavity** is a partially enclosed area. Depending on its size, shape, and texture and the size of its opening, every cavity has a natural range of sounds it reinforces. Ordinarily, the larger the cavity, the lower the sounds it resonates, and the smaller the cavity, the higher the sounds it resonates. To remember this, think of cavity resonance in terms of musical instruments. The tuba, the largest of the wind instruments, resonates the deepest sounds. The piccolo, one of the smallest of the wind instruments, resonates the highest sounds. In addition, the texture of the walls of the cavity affects sound. The sound of a metal clarinet differs from that of a wooden clarinet.

The Throat, or Pharyngeal Cavity

Resonance begins in the throat, or **pharyngeal cavity.** Because of its size and the control that can be exercised over it, the throat greatly affects the sounds people make. For example, when your throat is tense, your voice is likely to sound harsh. When your throat is relaxed, your voice will usually sound mellow. This difference occurs because when your throat is tense, it resonates high pitches—metallic sounds. When it is relaxed, however, it resonates lower pitches—deep, rich, mellow sounds. You will learn more about the function of the throat in the section on vocal quality.

The Nose, or Nasal Cavity

The nose, or **nasal cavity,** has a direct effect on the three nasal sounds that you make—the [m] as in *make,* the [n] as in *now,* and the [ŋ] as in *sing.* When you produce each of these sounds, the front of your mouth is blocked by your teeth or your tongue, forcing the sound to come out your nose. To some extent, the nasal cavity affects the sound of all speech. For example, when people talk with their mouths rather closed, the nose resonates all their vowel sounds, and their speech has a twangy quality. In contrast, when someone has a cold, the nasal passages get blocked and the nose gives little resonance even in the [m], [n], and [ŋ] sounds. As a result, their speech has a dull quality.

The Mouth, or Oral Cavity

Of all the resonators, the mouth, or **oral cavity,** is the easiest to alter. You can change the size of the cavity and the shape of its opening. For example, you form the various vowel sounds by changing the size of the opening. You keep your mouth open wide to form the *o* in *hot,* while you keep your mouth more nearly closed to form the *ee* in *meet.*

ACTIVITY: Experimenting with Resonance

To experiment with oral resonance, take four twelve- or sixteen-ounce glass bottles. Fill each with a different amount of water. Now stretch a thick rubber band between your two hands, until it is tight. Hold the rubber band about one inch above one of the bottle openings and then pluck it with your thumb. Repeat this procedure for each of the bottles. In which case was the sound the loudest, or fullest? In which case was it the weakest?

Next experiment with different degrees of tightness. While plucking the rubber band, move your hands closer together and then farther apart. When you stretch the rubber band very tight, which bottle now resonates the sound—the one with the most or the one with the least water? You should find that the bottle with the most water (and thus the smallest air cavity) resonates the very tight rubber band, while the bottle with the least water (and the largest air cavity) resonates the less tight rubber band.

Also, moving the tongue, jaw, and lips contributes much variety to the sounds you make. For example, round your lips and say "oh," and hold it. While you are saying "oh," move your tongue forward in your mouth and then pull it back as far as you can. Did you notice the difference in the sound? Next, open your lips wide and then tighten them as you say "oh." Again, note the difference in the sound produced.

By changing the texture, size, and shape of the oral cavity, you can make an enormous difference in the sound of your voice. You will learn more about resonance when you study vocal quality.

WHAT ARE THE ARTICULATORS OF SOUND?

Articulation is the shaping of speech sounds into recognizable oral symbols that go together to make up a word. Many communication problems are caused by poor articulation.

©1987 ARCHIE COMIC PUB., INC.

Poor articulation can lead to misunderstandings, such as the one that has apparently occurred between Archie and Miss Grundy in this cartoon.

The major articulators of sound are in the mouth: the tongue, the hard and soft palates, the teeth, and the lips. Vowel sounds are formed by changing the size of the oral cavity and the shape of the opening. Consonant sounds are formed by moving the tongue to various parts of the mouth, by pointing, arching, or flattening the tongue, and by moving and shaping the lips. For example, while saying "ah," raise the tip of your tongue so that it touches the edge of the gum behind the two upper front teeth. Notice that the sound changes from "ah" to [l]. Now while saying "ah," bring your upper and lower lips together. Notice that the sound changes from "ah" to [m].

The Sounds of English

The English language uses forty-five different sounds, of which twenty are vowel sounds and twenty-five are consonant sounds. The grouping and accenting of these sounds is called **pronunciation.** Trying to represent the pronunciation of the sounds of English using the letters of the alphabet is very difficult because one letter sometimes stands for more than one sound. To solve this problem, dictionaries use a system of markings in which the sound of *a* in *back*, for example, is written as ă and the sound of *a* in *bake* is written as ā. No doubt you have run into this system when looking up a word in the dictionary and have used the pronunciation symbols to figure out the word's pronunciation. A more effective system for symbolizing sound is the International Phonetic Alphabet (IPA).

The International Phonetic Alphabet

Becoming familiar with the International Phonetic Alphabet makes a lot of sense for anyone who is trying to talk about or write about sounds. You will find it helpful to keep in mind the following points.

1. Each IPA symbol represents only one unit of sound.
2. When a sound is shown in a sentence, it is placed within brackets. For example: The sound [d] is one sound.
3. A consonant sound is pronounced by itself, without an accompanying vowel sound. For example, usually when asked to give the sound for the letter *d*, you say "dee." However, "dee" is two sounds—a [d] and an [i]. ([i] is the IPA symbol for the sound represented by the letters *ee*). The actual pronunciation of the sound produced by the letter *d* is simply [d].

IPA Symbols Frequently Used In Speech

Consonants

[b]	*boy*	[p]	*pie*	[d]	*dot*	[t]	*tap*
[g]	*got*	[k]	*cat*	[v]	*vim*	[f]	*fat*
[ð]	*then*	[θ]	*thin*	[z]	*zip*	[s]	*sat*
[ʒ]	*leisure*	[ʃ]	*ship*	[dʒ]	*jet*	[tʃ]	*chat*
[h]	*hot*	[m]	*map*	[n]	*nut*	[ŋ]	*ring*
[l]	*lit*	[r]	*rid*	[j]	*yet*	[w]	*wit*

Vowels

[i]	*me*	[I]	*it*	[e]	*bake*	[ɛ]	*pet*
[æ]	*back*	[a]	*bother*	[ɔ]	*caught*	[o]	*go*
[ʊ]	*took*	[u]	*moon*	[ʌ]	*hut*	[ə]	*above*
[ɝ]	*bird*	[ɚ]	*never*				

Diphthongs (combinations of vowel sounds)

[aI]	*ride*	[aʊ]	*cow*	[ɔI]	*toy*	[ju]	*cute*
[eI]	*may*	[oʊ]	*hoe*				

Classification of Sounds

Sounds are either voiced or voiceless. **Voiced** means that the vocal folds are vibrating when the sound is being made. **Voiceless** means that the vocal folds are held open so that air breathed out does not vibrate them. For example, say the word *view*. Notice that [v] is made by placing the lower lip against the inside of the upper front teeth. Now say the word *few*. Notice that [f] is made exactly the same way as [v]. However, [v] is voiced, that is, made with the vocal folds vibrating, while [f] is voiceless, made with the vocal folds held open.

Now place two of your fingers on that hard spot on the front of your throat that is sometimes called the "Adam's apple." Alternate saying *view* and *few*. When you say [v], you should feel a vibration; when you say [f], you should feel none.

Consonant sounds form four sound groups: plosives, fricatives, nasals, and glides. The **plosives** form a small explosion when you say them. The sounds [p] and [b], [t] and [d], and [k] and [g] are all plosives. The **fricatives** make a frictionlike noise. The fricatives are [f] and [v], [θ] and [ð], [s] and [z], [ʃ] and [ʒ], and [j]. The **nasals** are the three sounds resonated in the nasal cavity: [m], [n], and [ŋ]. Finally, the **glides** result from the gliding movement of the articulators: [l], [r], [w], and [j].

ACTIVITY: **Using the International Phonetic Alphabet**

Using the International Phonetic Alphabet (IPA), decipher each of the following statements.

hwaɪ mi?

hu tʊk ðə bɔl?

aɪ lʌv ju.

gɪv mi ə kɪs.

tek ə wɔk.

CORRECTING VOCALIZATION PROBLEMS

So far in this chapter you have looked at the way sound is formed and articulated. Now you will look at the aspects of voice that affect how you sound to others and at ways to correct specific vocalization problems. Your voice is a powerful tool for accomplishing your goals. You probably have encountered a person with a mellow voice you love to listen to. No doubt you have also run into someone whose voice destroys the effect his or her appearance creates—perhaps a football player with a high, squeaky voice or a businesswoman with a childlike, breathy voice. Do not let easy-to-cure vocalization problems stand in the way of your success.

Many vocalization problems are correctable. To help people overcome vocalization problems, speech therapists suggest exercises for improving pitch, rate, loudness, and quality.

Pitch

Pitch is the highness or lowness of the sound you make. Pitch, of course, varies from person to person. To understand pitch, think of the strings of a guitar or a violin. The longer, thicker, or looser the string, the lower the pitch. The shorter, thinner, or tighter the string, the higher the pitch. Take a long, thick rubber band and hold it between your hands. First, take a short section of it between your hands and stretch it, holding your palms about two or three inches apart. Now pluck the rubber band. Next, move your hands farther apart, increasing the tension on the rubber band. Continue to pluck the rubber band as you increase the distance between your hands. Note that the pitch of the sound gets higher as you move your hands farther apart.

Key is the average pitch at which you speak. One common problem of pitch is speaking in too high or too low a key. To correct this problem, find your **optimum pitch**—the pitch at which you speak with the least strain and with the very best resonance. For most people, their optimum pitch is approximately four notes above the lowest note at which they can speak comfortably.

Try this experiment. Start saying "ah" at a pitch that is comfortable for you. Then work your way down the scale, saying "ah" at each note. (If you have access to a piano, using it to help you hit the notes of the scale will make this exercise easier.) When you have moved as far down the scale as you can, move up the scale four full notes. Now say "ah" at this pitch. You should notice a firm, well-resonated sound that you can make with very little strain. This is your optimum pitch. Now speak a sentence or two at approximately this pitch. Although your voice should rise and fall within each sentence, your optimum pitch is the key that your voice should normally come back to.

A second common problem of pitch is speaking in a monotonous melody. **Melody** refers to the variations in pitch that help to give expression to a person's voice. A **monotone** is a melody pattern that consists of only one tone. If every sound you made were at your optimum pitch, your speaking would be monotonous. Of course, you do not speak that way. Instead, you vary the melody to help give meaning to what you say—to make your voice expressive. Flexibility and variation are shown through range and inflection.

Range is the spread between the lowest note you can speak comfortably and the highest. The greater your range, the more flexible your voice. If your voice is limited to a range of three notes or fewer, it will sound monotonous. If, on the other hand, it can cover ten tones, you have more room for variation. This enables your voice to be more expressive.

Inflection is the upward or downward glide of your pitch as you speak. Rising inflections communicate doubt, uncertainty, indecision, questioning, surprise, or an unfinished thought. Falling inflections communicate certainty, finality, or a completed thought. By altering your voice upward or downward, you express shades of meaning. For example, if you glide your voice upward on the word *home* in the following sentence, the upward glide indicates uncertainty: *Are you going home?* If you glide your voice downward on the word *home* in the next sentence, the downward glide indicates certainty: *I'm going home.* A **circumflex** is an up-and-down inflection. For example, suppose someone asks you what you are doing tomorrow, and you respond, "Tomorrow, hmm, I'm not sure." As you say the word *tomorrow*, it is likely that your voice will glide up and down the scale.

While inflections are gradual upward or downward glides, a **step** is an abrupt change in pitch. By abruptly changing your pitch, you emphasize a word in a sentence. For example, suppose a friend demands that you drop what you are doing and go with him. If you reply "I can't go," most likely you will abruptly change your pitch to emphasize the word *can't:*

can't

I   go.

Very few people talk in a true monotone, that is, with every word spoken at exactly the same pitch. However, many people approach a monotone when they are giving a speech or an oral reading or are trying to act. Remember that an effective speaking voice is flexible, using changes in pitch to express meaning and feeling. For example, try to say "Tom is the one who took the book" with every word on the same pitch. Now, note how different meanings can be expressed by changes in pitch. If you meant that it was *Tom,* not Charlie, who took the book, you would emphasize the word *Tom* by saying it at a higher pitch. Try it:

Tom
is the one who took the book.

On the other hand, if you were trying to communicate that it was the book Tom took and not the pencil, you would say the word *book* at a higher pitch. Try it:

book.
Tom is the one who took the

If you have problems with pitch, set up a program for improvement and practice at least three times a week. Ask a friend to listen to you read passages aloud and to tell you which words you read at a higher or lower pitch. When your friend recognizes changes in inflection or steps, you will know you are making progress.

Loudness

Loudness, or **volume,** is the intensity of sound. In speaking, loudness depends on the force exerted to produce the speech tone. When you breathe, the relaxation of the diaphragm forces air back out the mouth or nose. However, when you want to talk, you have to increase the pressure behind that column of air. The louder you want to talk, the more pressure you need.

Some people do not speak loud enough simply because they have gotten used to speaking softly. Having spoken softly for nearly as long as they can remember, they have become accustomed to how they sound. Therefore,

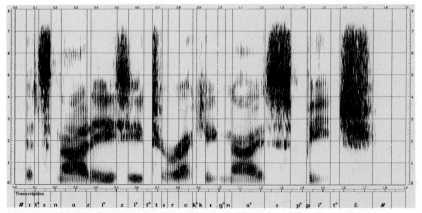

A *spectrogram* makes speech visible. This one shows the sound waves produced when a person says, "It's not easy to recognize speech."

they may think they are talking loud enough when they are not. The easiest way to test whether you speak loud enough is simply to ask other people.

Similarly, some people talk too loud. Again, they have become so used to the way they talk that it sounds just right to them. To identify this problem in your own speech, ask other people whether you speak too loud.

Another common problem with loudness is getting the power from the wrong source. To talk louder, you must exert pressure. If that pressure comes from muscles in your neck or upper chest, you will sound louder, but your voice will have an unpleasant, harsh, metallic sound. As a result, many people with ordinarily pleasant voices sound terrible when they try to speak louder, especially when they are under the pressure of giving a speech or of reading aloud. The source of pressure for increasing loudness should come from muscles in the stomach area or the lower chest, not from the throat.

Place your hands, like a belt, around your waist. In a normal voice say, "Get over here as fast as you can." You probably feel light pressure at the waist. Say the same sentence very loud. On at least three of the words, you should feel a sharp tensing of the stomach muscles. If you do, you are getting pressure from the right place. To identify power from the wrong source, again say the sentence very loud. This time, though, wrap your arms tightly around your waist to prevent use of your stomach muscles. You should feel tension in your throat area and should notice that your voice takes on an unpleasant quality.

By getting pressure from the right place—the stomach and lower chest—you can talk loud for quite a while without getting tired or hoarse. However, if you get pressure from the wrong place—the neck and upper chest—your throat will soon hurt, you will grow tired, and you will probably become hoarse.

Rate

Rate is the speed at which you talk. Although rate will vary a great deal depending on the circumstances and on what is being said, in general people tend to be either rather slow or rather fast speakers. Normal speed is anywhere from about 120 to about 160 words per minute. Actually, speed itself is not nearly as important as how distinctly a person speaks. Some rapid talkers can speak at rates of 200 to 300 words per minute and still be understood.

Just as you can alter the loudness of your speech, so too can you change its rate. To do so, first measure your speaking rate in conversation and in reading aloud. You need to measure both because these rates differ. The easiest way to do this is by using a tape recorder. First, with the permission of the person you are speaking to, record a conversation. Then record a few minutes of oral reading—perhaps an article in the newspaper or a passage of average difficulty from a book. Then, using a timer or a watch, count the number of words you spoke or read in one minute. If you find that your speech is outside the normal range, you can make a conscious effort to slow it down or to quicken it.

Timing Your Rate of Speech

Read through the following passage to familiarize yourself with it. Then read it aloud. By timing your reading, you will get a good idea of the rate at which you speak. If you finish before a minute is up, you are probably going too fast. If at the end of a minute you have not finished the first sentence of the third paragraph, you are going too slowly. As you read, try to give expression to your voice. In addition, try to read at an appropriate pitch and degree of loudness. Make sure also that your voice has a pleasant quality.

When you read factual material, you are likely to go much faster than when you speak to a friend. When you read, the words are already provided—you do not have to think about what is going to come next.

If what you read is simple material, your speech may get to the upper limits of normal, around 180 words per minute. Of course, as you get faster, there is greater chance for slurring words.

Usually your voice will reflect the emotion that is contained in the passage. For instance, if you are trying to create a mood of calmness, you are likely to read much more slowly than if you are trying to describe the final stages of a horse race. Changes in rate are normal—in fact, they are necessary because they help communicate the shades of meaning of your message.

If you read several passages aloud, you will notice both an overall reading rate, which represents your normal speed, and sudden bursts of speed or drawn out sentences to convey various moods, emotions, and shades of meaning in what you are reading.

Keep in mind that no rate is necessarily good or bad. Other factors such as variety of pitch and clarity of articulation also affect a listener's ability to understand you.

Quality

Quality is the tone of your voice. Your personal vocal quality is the tone that makes your voice identifiable as yours. Some people develop unpleasant qualities that can and should be changed. The most common quality problems are nasality, breathiness, hoarseness, and harshness.

Nasality is characterized by too much nasal resonance of all vocal sounds. It is caused by leaving the passage to the nasal cavity open too long.

Nasal resonance itself is not wrong. The three sounds [m], [n], and [ŋ] are supposed to be nasal. In addition, most people have a touch of nasal resonance in normal conversation. A problem arises when the nasal resonance is so pronounced that the voice sounds whiny or tinny.

To hear how a truly nasal voice sounds, try talking in a way that channels your speech "through your nose." To do this, raise the back of your tongue to the roof of your mouth so that the mouth is blocked and sound is directed into the nasal cavity. Now speak. Notice how unpleasant the sound is. While you are speaking, lower the back of the tongue so that sound is sent to the mouth. Notice how your voice changes. To correct a nasal voice, try to direct more sound through your oral cavity and less through your nasal cavity.

Breathiness results from too much unvoiced air escaping through the vocal folds as a person is speaking. Breathiness is caused by failing to bring the vocal folds close enough together. A breathy quality may be fine if you wish to sound that way. Some people even associate breathiness with softness or warmth. However, a problem occurs when the breathy quality is permanent. A major cause of breathiness is laziness. People get into the habit of letting air slip through the vocal folds, since speaking this way takes less energy. Another cause is growths on the vocal folds themselves, which prevent the vocal folds from coming together smoothly. If you have a problem with breathiness, you may want to consult a speech therapist to find out its cause. If the cause is simply laziness, you can correct it by doing vocal exercises.

Hoarseness is characterized by a thickness of sound or a muffled or rasping sound. Hoarseness is caused by speaking with excessive tension in the larynx area. Although a physical problem may lead to hoarseness, in many cases hoarseness is brought on by poor speech habits. For example, people often abuse their voices by yelling at athletic events or screaming at rock concerts. Fortunately, this kind of hoarseness is usually temporary and can be cured by resting the vocal folds.

Your vocal folds are muscles and, like other muscles, should not be strained. Shouting, screaming, and yelling, whether at a sporting event or in a machine shop, can cause hoarseness.

Harshness is characterized by an unpleasant, grating sound that may also be hard or metallic. Like hoarseness, harshness is caused by speaking with excessive tension in the larynx area. People who wrestle, play football, or engage in other activities that demand strong neck muscles may tend to keep their neck muscles tense all the time. To hear what harshness sounds like, tense your neck muscles as much as you can. Then try to talk for two minutes. Notice what happens to the sound of your voice after just two minutes. The obvious cure for harshness is to relax the neck muscles.

CORRECTING ARTICULATION PROBLEMS

To communicate effectively, you must speak so that people can understand you clearly and easily.

Four common articulation problems are: (1) substituting one sound for another; (2) leaving out a sound; (3) adding an extra sound; and (4) transposing sounds. (When interpreting the following information, refer back to the International Phonetic Alphabet on page 72.)

Irwin has made an error in substituting *ul* for *e*, or as his friend agrees, perhaps he hasn't in the case of Gaylord's poetry.

Substituting One Sound for Another

Regardless of your background, you have likely grown up substituting some sounds for others. Although these substitutions may not prevent your speech from being understood, particularly among family, friends, and neighbors, they may stand in the way of your success in the larger world.

Common Substitution Problems

[d] for [ð] (*da* for *the*, *radder* for *rather*, *dose* for *those*)
[t] for [θ] (*tink* for *think*, *anyting* for *anything*, *bot* for *both*).
[ks] for [s] (*excape* for *escape*, *expecially* for *especially*).
[f] for [θ] (*maf* for *math*, *bof* for *both*).
[n] for [ŋ] (*doin* for *doing*, *growin* for *growing*, *bein* for *being*)
[tʃ] for [dʒ] as in *judge* (*colletch* for *college*, *langwitch* for *language*)
[I] for [ɛ] (*git* for *get*, *pin* for *pen*)
[I] for [ʌ] (*jist* for *just*)

Leaving Out a Sound (Omission)

Although some shortcutting is normal when speaking, excessive shortcutting is considered an articulation problem.

Common Omission Problems

dropping [d] (*wount* for *wouldn't, frien* for *friend*)
dropping [t] (*mos* for *most, jus* for *just*)
dropping [l] (*hep* for *help, sef* for *self*)
dropping initial [h] after other words (*see 'um* for *see him, gave 'er* for *gave her*)
dropping [ə] (along with an accompanying consonant sound) in the middle of a word (*probly* for *probably*)

Adding an Extra Sound

Adding a sound that does not occur in a word is another common articulation problem. Sometimes this problem consists of pronouncing a letter that should be silent. Sometimes it consists of adding a sound to make a word easier to say.

Common Problems With Added Sounds

adding [t] in words where *t* is silent (*soften* for *sofen, hasten* for *hasen*)
adding [ə] (*filum* for *film, athaletic* for *athletic*)
adding [r] to ends of words (*idear* for *idea, drawr* for *draw*)

Transposing Sounds

Transposing sounds refers to the switching, or reversing, of the order in which sounds are spoken.

Common Problems With Transposing Sounds

[ks] for [sk] (*aks* for *ask*)
[ɚd] for [rɛd] (*hunderd* for *hundred*)
[pɚ] for [pri] (*perscribe* for *prescribe, perfer* for *prefer*)
[ɚn] for [rɛn] or [rɛn] for [ɚn] (*childern* for *children, modren* for *modern*)

ACTIVITY: Correcting Articulation Problems

Identify any problems you have with substituting, omitting, adding, or transposing sounds. To do this, read aloud the words used as examples in the four parts of this section. Practice the correct pronunciation of any sounds that you mispronounce. At first, the correct pronunciation may sound strange to you and be difficult for you to form. After you have pronounced the sounds correctly for a while, though, they will replace incorrect pronunciations and become a natural part of your speech.

HOW TO SEND EFFECTIVE VOCAL MESSAGES

In this chapter you have looked at the process of vocalization. This process affects your social success as well as your success in school, at work, and elsewhere. The following list summarizes the steps you can take to make your vocal messages effective.

1. *Breathe properly.* Breathing properly helps you get the air necessary to generate speech. It also provides the force to allow you to talk without excessive strain on your neck and chest muscles.
2. *Use your resonators effectively.* Proper use of the throat, the nose, and the mouth helps you to shape the vowel sounds necessary for clear speech. Using resonators effectively also helps you produce a strong, rich tone free of excessive breathiness, nasality, harshness, or hoarseness.
3. *Articulate clearly.* Good articulation enables you to form clear consonant sounds and to deliver your words so that your listeners can understand you.
4. *Try for vocal variation and emphasis.* Vocal variation and emphasis allow you to give the precise meaning you intend to your words and sentences. Moreover, your use of proper pitch, loudness, and rate allows you to speak in a way that is both expressive and pleasant to listen to over long periods of time.

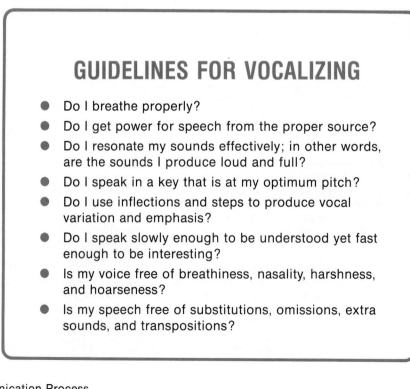

GUIDELINES FOR VOCALIZING

- Do I breathe properly?
- Do I get power for speech from the proper source?
- Do I resonate my sounds effectively; in other words, are the sounds I produce loud and full?
- Do I speak in a key that is at my optimum pitch?
- Do I use inflections and steps to produce vocal variation and emphasis?
- Do I speak slowly enough to be understood yet fast enough to be interesting?
- Is my voice free of breathiness, nasality, harshness, and hoarseness?
- Is my speech free of substitutions, omissions, extra sounds, and transpositions?

Profiles in Communication

Mary Ellen Wall

Puppets have entertained people for generations, but they come to life in a special way for Mary Ellen Wall, a speech pathologist in a large school district. To help her clients overcome vocalization problems, she uses a variety of props, including puppets and peanut butter. Ms. Wall sews tongues in the puppets so that they can be used to demonstrate where to place the articulators in the mouth to form sounds correctly. The peanut butter serves the same purpose. She dabs it in the client's mouth as a target for the tongue to hit.

Equally important to puppets and peanut butter in a therapy session is Ms. Wall's modeling of effective communication skills, especially clear articulation and appropriate syntax. "Modeling alone cannot correct a disorder, but it is one more strategy I can use in the session to help a client learn the pattern he or she needs to develop." In a more subtle way, Ms. Wall uses nonverbal communication skills, such as eye contact, facial expression, and tone of voice, to establish a climate in which clients feel cared about and motivated to improve their vocalization.

Ms. Wall sees clients between the ages of three and eighteen whose disorders range from language problems, such as significantly immature sentence structure, to speech disorders, such as articulating *s* to sound like *th*. Whatever the condition, an accurate diagnosis of it is the prerequisite to designing an appropriate therapy program. Ms. Wall determines a client's status by evaluating his or her development in terms of established norms for people of that age. According to Ms. Wall, "What is normal for a child of four can be a problem that will not correct itself in, say, an eight-year-old child."

In observing the speech habits of the general population, Ms. Wall notices many people who unknowingly risk "vocal abuse" by screaming themselves hoarse in everyday situations, such as playing games and cheering at sporting events. Sustained yelling pounds the vocal cords together, often causing nodules to develop on them. Complete vocal rest repairs some cords. Yet Ms. Wall cautions that stubborn cases require surgery to remove the nodules and restore the individual's natural vocal quality.

Ms. Wall is dedicated to helping her clients, and she feels deep satisfaction in their triumphs. When progress is slow, she patiently helps them meet the challenge to make steady progress in improving their vocalization skills.

SUMMARY

The primary generators of sound are the vocal folds—the muscles of the larynx. A speaker generates sound by pushing air past the vocal folds when they are drawn close enough together to vibrate.

This weak sound needs to be built up—to be resonated. The major resonators are the cavities of the throat, the nose, and the mouth.

After sound is resonated, it is articulated. Articulation is the shaping of speech sounds into recognizable oral symbols that go together to make a word. Twenty vowel sounds and twenty-five consonant sounds are used in the English language.

Vocalization has many characteristics. Pitch is the highness or lowness of sound. The pattern in which we arrange high and low sounds is called melody. The elements of melody are: key—the average pitch at which someone speaks; inflection—glides from one pitch to another; steps—sharp moves from one pitch to another; and range—the distance between the highest and the lowest notes a person can make comfortably. One of the major problems speakers have with melody is monotone—talking on roughly the same pitch at all times.

Loudness is the force exerted to produce the speech tone. To maintain a pleasant voice quality while increasing loudness, you should contract the muscles in the stomach area, not those in the neck and throat.

Rate is the speed at which a person speaks. A normal rate is anywhere from 120 to 160 words per minute.

Quality refers to the tone of a voice. Problems concerning quality include nasality, which is caused by excessive resonance in the nasal cavity of non-nasal sounds; breathiness, which is usually caused by laziness in closing the vocal folds; and hoarseness and harshness, which are caused by tension in the neck and chest.

Voice and articulation are important tools for creating a positive image.

CHAPTER VOCABULARY

Look back through this chapter and find the meaning for each of the following terms. Write each term and its meaning in your communication journal.

articulation	loudness	quality
breathiness	melody	range
cavity	monotone	rate
circumflex	nasal cavity	resonance
diaphragm	nasality	resonators
fricatives	nasals	step
glides	optimum pitch	trachea
harshness	oral cavity	vocal folds (vocal cords)
hoarseness	pharyngeal cavity	voiced
inflection	pitch	voiceless
key	plosives	volume
larynx	pronunciation	

1. Regular breathing involves the diaphragm's contracting to draw air into the lungs and then relaxing to push the air out again. What is the basic difference between this process and the breathing process used by a person who is speaking?

2. The bones in the chest, neck, and head help to amplify sound. How is bone resonance different from cavity resonance?

3. One major cavity resonator is the throat, or pharyngeal cavity. What are two others?

4. The major articulators are located in the mouth. What are they?

5. People who study speech or who deal with speech problems usually use the International Phonetic Alphabet. Why is this alphabet more effective for their purposes than the regular alphabet?

6. Pitch is the highness and the lowness of the sounds that you make. What is the difference between steps and inflections?

7. Loudness is the force exerted to produce the speech tone. What common problem do speakers have in getting the power to exert this force?

8. One of the four major vocalization problems is harshness. What are the other three?

9. One of the four major articulation problems is omitting a sound. What are the other three?

10. The nasal cavity plays an important role in speech. What is the difference between nasal resonance and nasality?

DISCUSSION QUESTIONS

1. Discuss how learning to control pitch, rate, and volume can contribute to the expressiveness of your voice. How can these aspects of your voice be used to emphasize key ideas?

2. Suppose you are giving a speech in a large room with no public address system. To be heard by everyone in the room, you have to use a loud voice to deliver the speech. Discuss the ways in which you can assure yourself that you are generating loudness from the proper source.

3. Consider a wide range of people in the public eye. Do you think that having an effective voice is particularly useful for these people? Why or why not? Which of these people in the public eye have particularly effective voices? What makes their voices so effective?

4. The movie *My Fair Lady* is based on George Bernard Shaw's play *Pygmalion*. In the play, Professor Higgins claims that he can pass off a flower peddler as a cultured person simply by teaching her how to speak properly. Discuss with your class whether or not such a feat is possible.

1. Practicing Breath Control

With your open palms against your ribs, inhale quickly through your mouth, purse your lips, and blow a steady, forceful stream of air, as if you were trying to blow out a candle some distance from you. Continue blowing until most of your breath is exhausted. Feel the inward movement of the abdominal wall and the gradual lowering of the ribs. Try this also with an actual candle in front of you, this time blowing evenly, with little force, so that the flame merely bends steadily away from you but does not go out and does not waver.

2. Opening the Throat to Gain Resonance

The throat works best as a resonator when it is open and relaxed. To open and relax your throat, begin by yawning. Feel the tongue as it is lowered in the back. Your throat is now open. With the aid of a mirror explore as much as can be seen of your mouth and throat during this exercise. Note the position of the tongue when the throat opens. Then with your throat open, read the following phrases aloud to hear how opening your throat affects the sound of your voice.

Who are you?
Over the rolling waters go
Up, up and away
Our other operator

3. Practicing Vowel Sounds

The formation of vowel sounds is dependent on how the mouth opening is formed. Say "ah," "aw," "o," "oo," "ee." Note how your mouth moves from open to closed. Now say the following words separately: *cow, taught, nose, who, me.* Now say them as if they were a sentence. Note the opening of your mouth and the changes in that opening as you go through all the words.

4. Practicing Pronunciation and Articulation

Say each of the following lines aloud three times in succession. Try to pronounce each word as carefully as you can.

The sea ceaseth and sufficeth us.
The sixth sheik's sixth sheep is sick.
She sells sea shells by the seashore.
The pitcher chided the churlish catcher for changing his signals.

Ruby rented rubber baby-buggy bumpers.
Three-sixths equals six-twelfths.
Theosphilus Thistle, the successful thistle sifter, in shifting a sieve full of unsifted thistles, thrust three thousand thistles through the thick of his thumb.

Real-Life Speaking Situations

1. You are no doubt well aware that dealing successfully with different people and different situations requires different methods of communication. People need to be versatile in switching roles and in changing their manner of speaking to suit a variety of circumstances. How do you act and speak at school? at work? at home? at a gathering of your friends? In each of these cases, you are likely to know how to adapt yourself to meet the expectations of others. Sometimes, however, you have to adapt quickly to unexpected or changing circumstances. For example, imagine that your car had been hit in the back at a stop-light. As you look in your rearview mirror, you see a huge man, hollering at the top of his voice, get out of his car and stomp down the lane toward you. How would you address this irate driver? A few minutes later, a police officer arrives on the scene to investigate the accident. How would you address the officer? How would you approach witnesses to get their statements? Outline a short scenario indicating how you would use communication skills to deal with these different people. Be prepared to present your scenario in class and to discuss how and why you varied your communication to meet each situation.

2. In most communities people share information in a number of different ways—through public addresses, through radio and television announcements, through all sorts of printed matter, and through various other means. To relay this information, journalists and others involved in public communication must master different forms of language. Imagine that you are working for a company that needs to make a public announcement about a new development in its field. You have been called upon to deliver the announcement in short public addresses to business and service groups and on television and radio. First, define an imaginary development in a field in which you have had some experience—perhaps mechanics, food preparation, computers, or child care. Next, define your audience. Choose a specific group and a specific radio station. Tailor your announcements to suit these audiences. Finally, prepare your announcements and present one or both of them in class. Ask for feedback on the effectiveness and clarity of your presentation.

CHAPTER **5**

LISTENING EFFECTIVELY

OBJECTIVES:

After studying this chapter, you should be able to

1. Explain the difference between hearing and listening.

2. List and explain four reasons why listening is important.

3. Discuss five factors that affect listening.

4. Discuss five guidelines for listening critically.

5. Recognize the main idea of what you hear.

6. Identify five forms of faulty reasoning.

7. Identify six propaganda techniques.

8. List five guidelines for becoming a more effective listener.

Tom truly enjoyed geometry class. He liked working with forms and concrete problems. He had a ready grasp of sizes, shapes, angles, and the like. Today's class looked like a particularly good one. Ms. Jackson was going to introduce theorems relating to angles. She began writing on the chalkboard, but try as he might, Tom just couldn't stop thinking about the final inning of the game the night before. Who would have thought it would end as it had? The Cougars were five runs behind; there were two outs and no one on base. Then steadily, one at a time, the Cougars got base hit after base hit until they trailed by only one run. With Brewster up, the pitcher threw two quick strikes. Brewster then fouled off the next two pitches before

Listening Effectively   **89**

the pitcher made his big mistake—he hurled a fastball straight down the middle. The minute bat met ball everyone in the park knew—

"Tom, *Tom!*" Ms. Jackson was standing right in front of him, looking him squarely in the face. "Tom, go to the board and write the proof we just covered!"

Tom slowly sank down in his chair. He had just struck out!

Have you ever found yourself in a situation like this? Unless you are very different from most people, something like this has probably happened to you more often than you would like to admit. Listening seems to be such an easy thing to do, but good listening can be one of the most difficult of all communication skills to master.

HOW IS LISTENING DIFFERENT FROM HEARING?

Hearing means being able to detect sounds. Unless you have a physical problem that affects your hearing, you are capable of detecting sound. However, having normal hearing is not the same thing as being good at listening. **Listening** means getting meaning from sounds that are heard. For example, although Tom, the student daydreaming in geometry class, did not realize it, he had *heard* Ms. Jackson's explanation. In other words, his ears had received the sounds of her voice. However, he could not go to the board and write the proof because he had not *listened*—he had not gotten the meaning of what she had said.

Tom's experience is not at all unusual. Researchers report that most people listen with only about a 25 to 40 percent efficiency. That means that somewhere between a quarter and a half of what most people hear is lost.

Norman has made the common mistake of not listening to all of a speaker's message. Listen carefully to make sure you understand fully.

Why Is Listening Important?

What difference does it make if you do not listen well? Certainly everything you hear is not worth your undivided attention. However, in far more situations than you likely realize, good listening is very important.

Practice etiquette. To begin, listening is a matter of etiquette. **Etiquette** is good manners, a pattern of behavior that should be observed in social and public life. The key to good manners is treating others as you want to be treated. Just as you want others to listen to you, so others want you to listen to them. Others regard how well you listen to them as a sign of how much you care about them. Even if there were no other reason, developing good listening habits would be important to you for social reasons alone.

Increase enjoyment. Good listening helps you increase your enjoyment of what you hear. You never know beforehand when another person's words or ideas might give you pleasure. To take advantage of these unexpected enjoyable moments, you have to be listening when they occur. In addition, a great deal of the enjoyment you get stems from your involvement in the situation. Listening carefully increases your involvement.

Listening attentively not only shows your regard for others but also increases your enjoyment when you participate in conversation.

Comprehend and evaluate ideas and information. Good listening helps you to comprehend better and evaluate more critically. Some of the nation's best leaders were not avid readers, but they were excellent listeners. By listening carefully to people with ideas and information, they learned what they needed to know to make good decisions. As you improve your listening skills, you will find that you understand more than you ever did before.

Become a better student. Good listeners are likely to be among the best students in a class. Why? First, careful listening can help you complete your homework more efficiently. Have you ever noticed that when you listen carefully in class that homework seems easier? Teachers usually lay the groundwork in class for the material they assign as homework. By listening in class, you build the foundation for understanding your assignment.

In addition, good listening can help you get better grades on your tests. Even though you may read the books and other materials you are assigned, reading alone is not enough for most students. In class, teachers go over the material with you, especially the material they intend to include on tests. They clarify important points; they emphasize key ideas; and they dramatize hard-to-picture concepts. In addition, teachers add information that comes from their own research or experience, information that may not be in the reading material. In other words, teachers are invaluable resources. By listening carefully to them, you can increase your mastery of the material on which you will be tested.

ACTIVITY: **Analyzing Listening Skills Practiced on Talk Shows**

An important characteristic of a talk-show host is the ability to listen carefully to what the guests are saying. Who do you think are the best listeners among television and radio talk-show hosts? How does being a good listener go along with being a good talk-show host? Discuss your findings with your classmates. Use specific examples from talk shows you have seen or heard.

WHAT FACTORS AFFECT YOUR ABILITY TO LISTEN?

Your ability to listen depends on many factors. As you read over the following discussion of these factors, keep in mind that you can learn to control almost all of them.

Lack of Rest

It is hard to listen well if you are tired. Everyone needs a certain amount of rest to do his or her best. Of course, the number of hours of sleep needed varies from person to person. However, if you do not get the amount of sleep you need, your ability to perform will decrease—and nowhere will this be more apparent than in your ability to listen.

Poor Nutrition

Good listening requires energy. If you look closely at a person who is listening carefully, you will see that this person is actively involved in the communication process. If you do not eat healthful foods, your energy level will be down, and your ability to listen well will be impaired.

Did this drowsy man skip breakfast this morning? Did he stay up half the night? Or does he just automatically doze off when he thinks the speaker will be boring?

"But I see you're having difficulty following my argument."

Lack of Interest

Poor listeners often choose not to listen because they lack personal interest in the topic. However, personal interest has very little to do with the potential value of what is being said. Good listeners start with the assumption that a speaker has something valuable to share. They learn that by paying attention they can become interested in a speaker's topic, no matter what it is. One way to increase your interest is to try to imagine circumstances in which the information being presented might be of value to you now or in the future.

Personality of Speaker

Some people base their willingness to listen on how well they respond to the personality of the speaker. Personality involves a person's traits, attitudes, and habits. How often have you "tuned out" speakers because some mannerism or quirk of theirs bothered you? Although not all speakers have sparkling personalities, you cannot afford not to listen to a particular speaker simply because you find that speaker's personality boring or annoying. If you do this, you may miss much of what you can learn. Although good listeners prefer to hear dynamic speakers, they listen well to any speaker, regardless of that speaker's personality.

Environment

A listening environment is made up of heating, lighting, seating, and other physical features that affect your ability to listen. Negative features of the environment include temperatures that are too high or too low, lighting that is too bright or too dim, and seats that are uncomfortable or are placed too far from the speaker or at a bad angle—all of these factors get in the way of listening. However, good listeners try to overcome the effects of a poor listening environment and take steps to improve that environment whenever they can. For example, if the room is too warm, they turn down the temperature. If the lighting is too dim, they turn up the lights. Although you may not be able to control *every* aspect of an environment, you may be able to improve enough of it to make listening comfortable for you.

To provide us with the best listening environment, architects design auditoriums with tiered seating and special acoustical features.

ACTIVITY: Analyzing Your Listening Habits

In your communication journal, note your listening habits for one week. Record any occasions during which you listened particularly attentively. What factors helped you to listen so well? Record any occasions when you had trouble listening. What factors hindered your listening? Were you able to change these factors so that you could listen more effectively? Did you do so? After the week is over, share your findings with your classmates.

DO YOU LISTEN CRITICALLY?

Critical listening means not only trying to understand what is being said but also testing the strength of any ideas that are being presented. Work on listening critically in any situation in which a speaker is presenting information that is unfamiliar to you or that is intended to change your beliefs or your behavior.

Identify the Speaker's Goal

A speaker's **goal** is the reason he or she has for speaking. A speaker has both a *general goal* and a *specific goal*. The general goal might be, for example, to amuse, to share information, or to try to influence others' beliefs or behavior. The specific goal might be, for example, to tell about the night that Mother dressed up as Santa Claus, to explain the steps in proving a geometry theorem, or to motivate people to go to see a movie. Often speakers state their goals in an introduction. For instance, a speaker might say: "My goal in speaking to you today is to convince you of the benefits of using solar energy." In addition, speakers often restate their goals in a conclusion. For example, a speaker might say, "After examining each of my points, you can reach no conclusion but that the advantages of using solar energy far outweigh the disadvantages."

Good listeners take care to identify a speaker's specific goal so that they can examine the main ideas and supporting details that the speaker uses to achieve that goal. When you are listening to a speaker, either write down the goal as you understand it or make a mental note of it.

Identify Main Ideas

To listen critically, you must identify the main ideas that help a speaker accomplish his or her goal. **Main ideas are the most important points that the speaker presents.** For example, if a speaker's goal is to convince listeners of the benefits of using solar energy, one main idea that the speaker might present is that solar energy is inexpensive. Another is that solar energy is clean.

Some speakers state their main ideas quite clearly. Others, though, simply imply their main ideas or refer to them vaguely. When main ideas are left unclear, you will have to analyze the information given by the speaker to identify what you believe the main ideas to be. (In Chapter 11 you will learn more about main ideas.)

Identify Supporting Details

Supporting details are the items a speaker uses to back up main ideas. Supporting details may take the form of examples, facts, statistics, reasons, or incidents. For example, imagine that a speaker presents the idea that solar energy is inexpensive. One way the speaker can support this idea is by using facts or statistics. The speaker can show that out of a sample of five hundred families living in Vermont, those who heated their houses with solar energy spent 50 percent less on heating during one winter than did those who heated their houses with oil.

Identifying supporting details helps you to determine the basis for a speaker's main ideas and to evaluate whether the speaker has backed up the main ideas successfully.

These students are taking notes to make sure that they remember their teacher's main points and supporting details.

Use Context Clues

Speakers may use words that are unfamiliar to you. However, these speakers will often provide enough clues, called **context clues,** in the same sentence or in surrounding sentences so that you can figure out the meanings of the unfamiliar words on your own. A good listener knows how to use context clues to discover the meaning of an unfamiliar word. For example, consider the following sentence:

> We must be more pragmatic, less idealistic, when dealing with this situation.

Perhaps you do not know the meaning of the word *pragmatic*. However, look at the context clues. The sentence contrasts *pragmatic* with *idealistic*. In other words, it tells you that *pragmatic* is the opposite of *idealistic*. Therefore, you could determine that *pragmatic* likely means "not idealistic; practical."

Now look at the next two sentences, and see if you can figure out the meaning of the word *precarious* from the context clues.

> Before the outbreak of World War I, the world maintained a precarious peace. However, this uncertain peace was shattered forever with the assassination of Archduke Ferdinand, Crown Prince of Austria.

The first sentence gives you a clue to the meaning of *precarious*. It tells you that the world was at peace, but that this type of peace was followed by war. On the basis of this sentence, you could conclude that a *precarious* peace is not a very stable peace. The second sentence provides you with a synonym for *precarious—uncertain*. On the basis of these context clues, you can make a pretty good guess that *precarious* means "risky; insecure; dependent on circumstances."

Take Advantage of Nonverbal Clues

As you have learned in Chapter 3, *nonverbal clues* include the sound of the voice; appearance; facial expressions, hand gestures, and other body language; and the communication environment. Since nonverbal clues provide as much as 85 percent of the social meaning of communication, effective listeners are sensitive to such clues and weigh them against what is being said. For many good listeners, paying attention to nonverbal clues, especially to those that emphasize or contradict a speaker's words, is an unconscious part of their behavior. Poor listeners, on the other hand, often ignore even the most obvious nonverbal clues.

A good listener asks: In what ways are nonverbal clues emphasizing what is being said? Once you recognize which words or points are being stressed, you have a key to understanding the message. For example, suppose some pencils are missing and one suspect, Charlie, says, "I didn't *steal* the pencils." His emphasis on the word *steal* suggests that Charlie might be prepared to admit that he took the pencils but that he does not consider his action stealing. By paying attention to emphasis, a good listener can respond appropriately.

Equally important, a good listener asks: Do the nonverbal clues contradict what the person has said? For example, if as Charlie says "I did not steal the pencils" you notice tension in his voice, sudden perspiration on his upper lip, or shifty eye contact, you may sense that he is not telling the truth. As in the case with emphasis, a good listener can learn much about a speaker's true thoughts by paying attention to whether nonverbal clues confirm or contradict the words spoken.

To avoid misunderstandings, good listeners check their interpretations of nonverbal clues by asking questions. For example, suppose that you are discussing the next political election with a friend. On the basis of nonverbal clues, you sense that your friend is bothered by the fact that the two of you disagree. You might say, "I sense that my opinions disturb you. Is that right?" If your friend confirms your interpretation as correct, you might suggest that you both cool off before continuing the discussion. If your friend tells you that your interpretation was not correct, you can continue the discussion, knowing that your disagreement does not bother him or her.

Nonverbal Clues

Eye contact—where the speaker is looking; whether eye contact is constant

Paralanguage—the sound of the voice; the variations in pitch, rate, volume, and emphasis

Gestures—what the speaker's arm and hand movements are saying

Posture—how the speaker's body is positioned

Movement—what the speaker's body movements communicate

Facial expression—how the speaker's face looks when speaking

Silence—what the speaker does not say

CAN YOU SPOT FAULTY REASONING?

Faulty reasoning is a mistake in the reasoning process. Even when supporting details are precise and accurate, the conclusions drawn from them may be meaningless or illogical. Good listeners are able to identify several types of faulty reasoning.

Hasty Generalizations

Generalizations are general conclusions or opinions drawn from particular observations. Everyone makes generalizations all the time. For example, suppose that you are on vacation for a month and spend every other day fishing on the lake. Each day you catch at least two or three fish. On the basis of fifteen different observations, you could reasonably make the generalization that fishing is good in the lake. Drawing valid generalizations is a sign of good thinking.

Hasty generalizations are general conclusions or opinions that are drawn from very few—perhaps only one or two—observations. For example, if a student, John, turns in his paper late today, a person may draw the hasty generalization that John never turns in his work on time. However, this may be the *only* time John has turned in a paper late. Basing a conclusion on only one or two observations is a sign of faulty thinking.

A good listener examines a speaker's generalizations to make sure that they are based on an adequate number of observations.

Begging the Question

Begging the question means assuming the truth of a statement before it is proven. For example, imagine a speaker says, "Whole wheat bread is more nutritious than the plastic white bread they make today. Therefore, you should eliminate white bread from your diet and eat only whole wheat bread." The speaker has given no proof to show either that whole wheat bread is more nutritious or that white bread is "plastic" or nonnutritious. Therefore, the speaker is begging the question. As a listener, you should carefully analyze assumptions expressed in the wording of a statement and should not accept the truth of a statement without proof.

Using Irrelevant Evidence

Irrelevant evidence is information that has nothing to do with the argument being made. Some evidence may sound impressive, but unless it is related to the point at hand, you should ignore it. For example, imagine that a speaker says, "The merchandise in Blue Chip Department Store is top quality. Why, the manager has clothes shipped in from all over the world." The supporting detail that the clothes come from all over the world has nothing to do with the conclusion that the merchandise is top quality. The store could be looking all over the world for the cheapest merchandise available, with no regard for quality.

Good listeners must pay close attention to make sure there are logical relationships between the evidence a speaker presents and any conclusions the speaker draws from that evidence.

Reasoning from False Premises

A **premise,** which is a stated or an implied starting point for an argument, is assumed to be true. A **false premise** is a premise that is untrue or distorted. Suppose that Eric, a football player, says "We're bound to have a winning team this year. Five of our starters are back." Eric's statement is built on the premise that experienced players can ensure that the team will win. Since experience is not necessarily related to success (the five returning players may all be mediocre), Eric is reasoning from a false premise.

Look at the following argument: "The salesperson says I look terrific in this jacket, so I think I'll buy it." The premise of this argument is that the salesperson's views are valuable to someone making clothing decisions. Since some salespeople may falsely compliment a customer to make a sale, basing a decision to purchase something on what a salesperson says is an example of reasoning from a false premise.

The Greek philosopher Aristotle (384-322 B.C.), shown here talking with his students, was the originator of the science of logic.

All arguments are based on premises. Good listeners examine premises very carefully to see whether or not they are true before accepting conclusions drawn from them.

False Analogies

Analogy is a form of reasoning by comparison. While a good analogy draws valid conclusions from items that can be logically compared, a **false analogy** draws invalid conclusions from weak or often farfetched comparisons. Suppose that a band member, Norm, wants to persuade Tom to learn to play the saxophone so that Tom can join the marching band. Norm says, "I wish you'd think about learning to play the saxophone. Since you play the violin so well, I'm sure that you could learn the sax easily, and we need more saxophone players in the marching band." Norm's reasoning is based on an implied analogy that is false. He is comparing two things, playing the saxophone and playing the violin, that are alike in some ways but are significantly different in others. Although a saxophone and a violin are both musical instruments, the skills needed to play one differ considerably from the skills needed to play the other. Playing a saxophone requires breath control and good lip and tongue control. Playing a violin requires strength in the left hand, good bow technique, and a knowledge of the strings.

ACTIVITY: Identifying Faulty Reasoning

Read each of the items below. Identify each item as an example of one of the following types of faulty reasoning: hasty generalization, begging the question, using irrelevant evidence, reasoning from false premises, or false analogy.

1. Even though he's a pitcher, Paul ought to be a very good hitter. After all, Marv is a pitcher, and he's a good hitter.
2. I saw Jackson play basketball once. He didn't make any baskets. He's a very poor player.
3. Did you see that no-good Wilson vote for Andover?
4. We're sure to win against Hamilton High. Their team has three new players.
5. We've had plenty of rain, the temperature has been normal, and workers have been available. Food prices are sure to drop tremendously this year.

Then, spend one week listening for faulty reasoning. In your communication journal, write down every instance you hear of making a hasty generalization, begging the question, using irrelevant evidence, reasoning from false premises, and making false analogies. At the end of the week, share your findings with your classmates.

Although it is possible that Tom could, in fact, learn to play the saxophone, his experience with the violin is not analogous.

Speakers often use analogies to support their arguments. Good listeners make sure that any analogy the speaker uses can stand up to two tests: (1) the two subjects being compared are similar in enough important ways to support the speaker's point and (2) the two subjects being compared are not different in ways that weaken the analogy.

CAN YOU SPOT PROPAGANDA TECHNIQUES?

Persuasion is the attempt to convince others to do something or to change a personal conviction or belief of their own free will. **Propaganda** is a particular form of persuasion that tries to convince people to accept an idea or a belief without thinking for themselves. Speakers who use propaganda techniques try to get their listeners to think automatically. At their worst, propagandists rely on one-sided or deliberately distorted arguments. As a good listener, you must examine any persuasive statement closely.

In the 1950's, a group called the Institute for Propaganda Analysis gave various propaganda techniques some catchy labels. These labels have survived even though the institute has not. The following techniques are among those that were identified.

In some countries the public is barraged with the government's propaganda and is given no access to other points of view.

Transfer

Transfer is a method of building a connection between things that are not logically connected. In advertising, this connection is built between a product and a positive value. For example, an advertisement may show a picture of a prosperous, happy, loving family drinking a certain brand of milk. The goal of the transfer technique is to get the viewer to associate, or connect, the brand of milk with prosperity, happiness, and love.

A speaker will often try to build a positive connection between some desirable value and a product, a person, an organization, or an idea. Good listeners demand that the link between these things be supported by evidence. In the example just given, a good listener would ask whether prosperity, happiness, and love were truly a product of drinking a particular brand of milk.

Bandwagon

The **bandwagon** technique encourages people to act because "everyone else is doing it." When the bandwagon appeal substitutes for reason or when it is intended to keep its audience from thinking, it is propaganda. For example, imagine someone says that you should vote for a person because all your friends are voting for that person. As a good listener, you should ask why the person is worth supporting. If you vote unthinkingly for a candidate just because your friends may be voting for that person, you are a victim of propaganda. When you hear a bandwagon appeal, you should insist that the speaker draw conclusions based on relevant evidence, not on what "everyone else" is doing.

Name-calling

Name-calling is a form of labeling in which words are used in a manner intended to arouse powerful negative feelings. Its purpose is to show a particular person or group as inferior or bad without providing any evidence to support that claim. For example, a speaker might ask you to vote against a person because the person is "a dupe," "an egghead," "a warmonger," or "a bleeding heart." A good listener looks beyond labels such as these and demands evidence to back up the speaker's position.

Card-stacking

Card-stacking means presenting only partial information so as to leave an inaccurate impression. Card-stacking is based on half-truths. For example, a speaker may refer to a person who has amassed a fortune through intimidation and illegal means as "a good breadwinner." This phrase tells only part of the story, since it ignores the negative methods the person used to become "a good breadwinner."

Naturally, speakers emphasize information that supports their viewpoint. However, good listeners withhold judgment until they hear the supporting details or the case for the other side.

In addition to these four traditional propaganda techniques, there are at least three other techniques of which you should be aware.

Stereotypes

A **stereotype** is a biased belief or attitude about a whole group of people based upon insufficient or irrelevant evidence. A stereotype ignores the individual. For example, imagine a large manufacturing plant in which employees are divided into two groups—management and labor. In this plant, management holds stereotyped views of labor as untrustworthy, irresponsible, and interested only in high pay for little work. Therefore, whenever a worker raises an objection about a job, a member of management sees the worker as lazy or irresponsible. In other words, the manager does not hear the objection of an individual, because the manager's mind is clouded by the stereotype of the group. In this same plant, labor holds stereotyped views of management as aloof from the workers, overpaid, and interested only in profit. Therefore, whenever a manager urges a worker to be more efficient, the worker sees the manager as interested only in profit.

Stereotypes are dangerous because they get in the way of true communication. A good listener rejects stereotypes and demands specific information about specific people and specific organizations.

Emotional Appeals

Emotional appeals are statements used to arouse an emotional reaction. For example, imagine a speaker wants you to contribute money to improve health conditions in a certain part of the country. To arouse your emotions, the speaker may likely tell you many moving stories of children who died for want of better medical care.

Many speakers use emotional appeals to get you to act on their proposals. However, emotional appeals become a propaganda device when their use is so extensive that logic or reason is ignored. The good listener will respond to emotional appeals but will also demand support for any conclusion presented.

Loaded Words

Loaded words are words that evoke very strong positive or negative attitudes toward a particular person or group. How many times have you heard people describe the same behavior in different ways depending on who is acting? For example, in talking about similar instances of assertive behavior, Nan might describe herself as "confident," Chris as "pushy," and Rita as "a braggart." Although the behavior described may be exactly the same, the use of loaded words—*confident* versus *pushy* versus *a braggart*— makes Nan's behavior seem positive, Chris's behavior seem negative, and Rita's behavior seem the worst of all. Good listeners form their own attitudes based on clear, unbiased statements about the people, things, or behaviors being described.

Identifying Propaganda Techniques

Identify each of the following items as an example of one of the prop-aganda techniques discussed in this chapter.

1. Folks, it's going to be a landslide. Garver is carrying the entire West Side. Join the ground swell of support for Garver. He's going to win it all.
2. Don't vote for Hanover. She's over sixty. You all know that old people are not healthy enough to stand the pressures of this job.
3. Goodlook clothing is the brand to buy. You'll always see Goodlook clothes on happy, fashionable, good-looking people.
4. Wilson must be a gangster; he comes from a family of gangsters. A vote for Wilson will put the criminals in control.
5. They're trying to call Wilson a mouthpiece of organized crime. But would a criminal treat his family the way Wilson does? His wife and his children are everything to him. He is a devoted husband and father. Vote for Wilson.
6. At night, these refugees go to sleep with no food or shelter. In the morning, they wake up to face another day of hunger. Do not ignore the plight of these helpless people. Send money to feed them now.
7. I'm an extrovert, but that Kelly is nothing but a big show-off.

HOW TO BE AN EFFECTIVE LISTENER

In this chapter you have looked closely at listening skills that affect every aspect of your life. The following list summarizes the steps you can take to become a more effective listener.

1. *Get ready physically to listen.* Adjust your position so that you are ready to listen. For example, some people find that they listen better if they sit up straight in a chair, lean slightly forward, or even rivet their eyes on the speaker.

2. *Pay attention to the speaker.* To listen effectively, you must give a speaker your complete attention. Poor listeners daydream or let their minds wander while listening to others. Good listeners make a conscious attempt to concentrate on what a speaker is saying.

3. *Practice listening critically.* Listening critically means identifying the speaker's goals, main ideas, and supporting details. Critical listeners also use context clues to figure out the meaning of unfamiliar words, and they use nonverbal clues to interpret the meaning of a message.

4. *Identify faulty reasoning and propaganda techniques.* Good listeners spot hasty generalizations, begging the question, irrelevant evidence, false premises, and false analogies. They are alert to propaganda techniques such as transfer, bandwagon, name-calling, and card-stacking. They do not form judgments based on stereotypes, emotional appeals, or loaded words.

5. _Do not jump to conclusions._ One habit that contributes to poor listening is anticipating what the speaker will say and then not listening closely to what the speaker actually does say. Poor listeners often listen until they are "sure" of the direction a speaker is taking. Then they "tune out" until the speaker moves on to another point. Even when you think you know what is coming next, listen carefully. After a speaker has finished a point, you can weigh and evaluate it. However, you cannot fairly evaluate a point until you have heard a speaker out.

6. _Listen actively._ Good listeners take an active part in listening. They mentally summarize main ideas and supporting details. As they listen, they ask themselves questions about what the speaker has said and pay attention for answers to their questions as the speaker continues talking.

Good listeners use associations and mnemonics to remember what a speaker has said. **Association** is tying a behavior to some vivid mental image. For example, if a speaker is discussing the importance of giving solid evidence to support a point, a good listener may create an association of a bridge standing on supporting pylons. The bridge stands for the point, and each of the pylons stands for one of the kinds of evidence presented. **Mnemonic devices** are rhymes, acronyms, and other verbal forms created to help people remember information. An acronym, for instance, is a mnemonic device in which the first letter of each word in a series is used to form a new word. For example, a speaker talking about three purposes for speaking might mention entertaining, informing, and persuading. To remember these purposes, you could form the word _pie_ using the first letter of each purpose.

Developing effective listening skills will help you be able to understand and remember information more easily.

Profiles in Communication

Family practice physician Dr. Manuel Galceran says that although he had no formal medical school course in listening skills, the importance of good listening habits was emphasized throughout his medical training. "Listening is vital in the practice of medicine," he states. "It is part of observation, and it can help in making a diagnosis."

However, Dr. Galceran believes that listening involves more than just hearing and understanding the words a patient says. It includes paying attention to the patient's tone of voice, manner of speech, gestures, facial expressions, and posture. It also means asking the right questions in the right way, getting the patient to open up and talk.

Teenagers can sometimes present special listening difficulties. Dr. Galceran observes, "It can be harder to get teens to open up because they try to play down their problems, especially emotional problems. With them, I don't dismiss subtleties."

Teenagers and some special cases, such as patients who either resist treatment or feel that treatment is hopeless, need to be drawn into discussing their symptoms and problems through careful questioning. Dr. Galceran recommends four useful questioning techniques: (1) rephrase sensitive questions or those that receive little or no response; (2) drop a sensitive question and come back to it later; (3) phrase questions in tactful ways; (4) when the patient is most comfortable, bluntly "come straight out with a question." To avoid leading uncertain or untalkative patients into giving incorrect descriptions of symptoms, he offers them two or more options, such as identifying a pain as either "a burning pain or a sharp pain."

Dr. Galceran also believes that nonverbal behavior is extremely important. He lets the patient know he is interested and concerned by making eye contact, taking his time and not rushing or fidgeting, taking notes in front of the patient, looking up when he has finished a note, and staying on the subject. He is especially careful "never to yawn, because it shows a lack of interest."

Dr. Galceran puts his communication skills to use every day in his busy practice. While he regards his speaking ability as crucial, he feels that "one cannot be a good speaker without being a good listener."

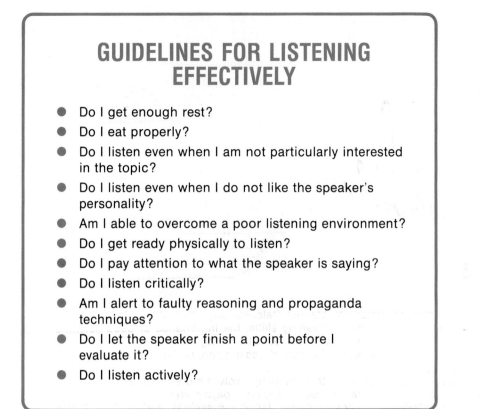

GUIDELINES FOR LISTENING EFFECTIVELY

- Do I get enough rest?
- Do I eat properly?
- Do I listen even when I am not particularly interested in the topic?
- Do I listen even when I do not like the speaker's personality?
- Am I able to overcome a poor listening environment?
- Do I get ready physically to listen?
- Do I pay attention to what the speaker is saying?
- Do I listen critically?
- Am I alert to faulty reasoning and propaganda techniques?
- Do I let the speaker finish a point before I evaluate it?
- Do I listen actively?

SUMMARY

Hearing means simply receiving sounds; listening means getting meaning from what you hear. Listening is a critical communication skill for several reasons. In addition to showing good manners, listening will help you to increase your enjoyment of what you hear, to comprehend information better, and to become a better student.

Many people fail to listen well because they have not gotten enough sleep, they are hungry, or they are physically uncomfortable. In addition, they fail to listen because they lack interest in the subject or react negatively to the personality of the speaker.

Good listeners are critical listeners. They examine information and test the strength of the ideas being presented. They identify a speaker's goals, main ideas, and supporting details. In addition, they take advantage of context clues and nonverbal clues to get the maximum meaning from what is said.

Good listeners are alert to faulty thinking and propaganda techniques. They do not accept information immediately but, instead, ask questions and demand evidence of a speaker's conclusions.

Good listeners prepare themselves physically and mentally to listen. They do not jump to conclusions but take an active part in listening.

CHAPTER VOCABULARY

Look back through this chapter to find the meaning of each of the following terms. Write each term and its meaning in your communication journal.

analogy
association
bandwagon
begging the question
card-stacking
context clues
critical listening
emotional appeals
etiquette
false analogy

false premise
faulty reasoning
generalizations
goal
hasty generalizations
hearing
irrelevant evidence
listening
loaded words
main ideas

mnemonic devices
name-calling
persuasion
premise
propaganda
stereotype
supporting details
transfer

REVIEW QUESTIONS

1. How is listening different from hearing?

2. One reason for developing good listening skills is etiquette. What are three other reasons?

3. One factor that affects your ability to listen is lack of sleep. What are four other factors?

4. A speaker's goal is the reason that he or she has for speaking. What are main ideas and supporting details?

5. One aspect of critical listening is using nonverbal clues. In what two very important ways can nonverbal clues affect the meaning of the message?

6. Another aspect of critical listening is using context clues. How can context clues affect your ability to comprehend a message?

7. One type of logical fallacy is making hasty generalizations. What are four other types?

8. One type of propaganda technique is transfer. What is transfer?

9. What are at least three other propaganda techniques?

10. How can you prepare yourself physically and mentally to listen?

DISCUSSION QUESTIONS

1. Discuss the difference between average listening and critical listening.

2. Imagine that you are in a class that is reviewing information for a test. Discuss the kinds of negative factors that are likely to interfere with good listening. Then discuss specific kinds of behavior that can help you overcome these factors.

3. Some feel that one of the major problems people face is the inability to listen to each other—to give each other

a fair hearing. John Kenneth Galbraith wrote, "Faced with the choice between changing one's mind and proving that there is no need to do so, almost everyone gets busy on the proof." Discuss the meaning of Galbraith's words. Then discuss whether you agree with him or not.

4. William A. Orton wrote, "If you keep your mind sufficiently open, people will throw a lot of rubbish into it." Discuss the difference between critical and uncritical listening. How does this difference relate to Orton's words? How can uncritical listening be dangerous?

5. Edward R. Murrow once wrote,

To be persuasive, we must be believable,
To be believable, we must be credible,
To be credible, we must be truthful.

Discuss the meaning of Murrow's words. Then discuss how this quotation reveals the difference between persuasion and propaganda.

ACTIVITIES

1. Observing and Analyzing Listening Behavior

As you talk with people, you are likely to be conscious of those who really listen and those who do not. The next time you are talking to a group, take particular notice of who is truly listening and who is not. What specific behavior indicates that a person is listening carefully? Also notice the effect, if any, that your listeners' attention or inattention has on you as a speaker. Share your findings with your class.

2. Identifying Mnemonic Devices and Analyzing Their Usefulness

Make a list of mnemonic devices you use to remember things. For example, a common mnemonic device used by many students to remember the names of the Great Lakes is HOMES—Lake Huron, Lake Ontario, Lake Michigan, Lake Erie, and Lake Superior. Share your list with your classmates, and compile a class list. Which mnemonic devices are most useful to you? Discuss in class what makes some mnemonic devices more useful than others.

3. Practicing Listening Skills to Gather Information

A. Talk with three or four people who have lived in your neighborhood or nearby for at least twenty years. Ask them to tell you what the area was like when they first lived there. Make no notes while they talk, but listen attentively. After each session, write down the important facts you remember. Share your findings with your classmates.

B. Working with a partner, listen to a five-minute segment of a radio news broadcast. Then write down everything you remember hearing. Compare your notes with your partner's.

4. Recognizing Propaganda Techniques

Spend a week listening and looking for propaganda techniques. Listen to speeches, sit in on discussion groups, watch television news and talk shows, read editorials in the newspaper, and study advertisements and commercials. In your communication journal, record any examples you find of the following propaganda techniques: transfer, bandwagon, name-calling, card-stacking, stereotypes, emotional appeals, and loaded words. At the end of the week, share your findings with your classmates.

5. Identifying Negative Listening Habits

A. The following statements identify negative listening habits. Do any of these statements represent your behavior? For each statement that does, think of ways that will help you change your behavior.

1. I tend to blow up at anyone who criticizes me.
2. There are several people I just can't listen to, no matter what they have to say.
3. When someone's voice irritates me, I just stop listening.
4. I get so tense when we talk about tests that I just can't listen.
5. When I go to the dentist, I worry so much that I don't listen to what the dentist tells me.

B. Read the following statements; then indicate whether each statement applies to you *often, seldom,* or *never.* Give yourself three points for each statement that applies to you often, two points for each statement that applies to you seldom, and one point for each statement that applies to you never. If you score twenty points or more, you need to work on your listening behavior.

1. I never let a person complete more than a few sentences before I interrupt.
2. I like to finish people's sentences for them.
3. I often clean my fingernails or fiddle with a pen or pencil or gaze out the window rather than look at the person who is speaking.
4. I tend to accept whatever anyone tells me.
5. I seldom try to summarize the key points that a person has made.
6. I tend to slouch in a chair and to get sleepy when someone is speaking.
7. When a pleasant thought pops into my mind, I tend to think about it rather than listen to what a speaker is saying.
8. If a speaker uses a word or expresses an opinion that angers me, I quit listening.
9. I seldom check with people to make sure I have understood what they have said.
10. I get bored when I have to listen for a long period of time.

Real-Life Speaking Situations

1. Listening skills are a vital part of the communication process. Nowhere is this fact more evident than in communication between parents and their teenage sons and daughters. Teenagers often complain that their parents do not listen to them, and parents commonly have the same complaint about teenagers. Imagine that you are the parent and that you are in a discussion with your teenage son or daughter about improving his or her performance in school. How can you get your point across without causing a standoff or a disagreement? What kinds of questions should you ask? What kinds of statements should you make? How should you respond to the answers and statements that your son or daughter makes? Should you directly confront the situation or should you use a sideways approach? When should you talk and when should you listen? Write a short dialogue of the discussion between you and your teenager. Be prepared to present your dialogue in class and to discuss ways for using listening skills to make communication between parents and teenagers more effective.

2. Counseling is one occupation in which listening skills are of critical importance. Counselors must listen carefully to each client in order to help that client recognize causes of and discover solutions to problems. Imagine that you are a counselor trying to help someone identify and solve a problem that he or she is having. First, who is your client? Write a brief description of your client's main characteristics. Next, define the hypothetical situation. Why has this client come to you? Finally, determine how you will counsel your client. What clues should you listen for to help your client recognize and solve his or her problem? How should you respond to what your client tells you? Write a case analysis of your client's problem and how you tried to help solve it. Read your analysis to the class and discuss the effectiveness of your communication skills in counseling your client.

UNIT TWO
INTERPERSONAL RELATIONSHIPS

SPEAKING INFORMALLY

OBJECTIVES:

After studying this chapter, you should be able to

1. Introduce yourself to others.

2. Introduce other people to each other.

3. Give clear directions.

4. Understand directions you receive from others.

5. Make and receive social telephone calls.

6. Make business telephone calls.

Jill walked into her first class at West High School, after transferring there during the summer break. She had left behind many friends at her old school, and she missed them greatly. Before starting her first day, she had said to herself, "I've got to try to make new friends," but she was worried about how she would be received. Her first class was English. She walked in and took a seat next to a girl who was looking through some papers. "Hi, I'm Jill Norman," she said. "I moved here during the summer, and this is my first day at West High. What's it like?"

In this situation, Jill was attempting to deal with one of the many kinds of informal communication settings in which we all find ourselves. Even though these situations are informal, they are, nevertheless, very important. Whether you are introducing yourself, introducing others, giving or receiving directions, or making or receiving telephone calls, how you act in each of these informal situations can have a major effect on your life. Whether others accept you, like you, or are willing to do business with you is, to a large extent, related to how well you deal with these informal situations.

MAKING INTRODUCTIONS

When you meet people you do not know, or when you find yourself with people who do not know each other, you will want to make introductions. An **introduction** is the presentation of one person to another or to a group. The ability to make introductions smoothly tells others something about you. It marks you as a confident, take-charge person who is able to handle situations with ease. Even if this is not the way you actually feel in some situations, isn't it the image you would like to project? Although many people shy away from making introductions, you will be able to make them easily by mastering a few basic guidelines.

How to Introduce Yourself to Others

Sometimes when you meet others, there will be no one to introduce you, and you will need to introduce yourself. Such introductions are called **self-introductions.** One type of self-introduction is a social self-introduction. Although you may prefer to wait for someone else to introduce you, you can do yourself and others a service by taking the initiative. Introducing yourself is an effective way to break the ice in a social situation. In the situation Jill faced in the beginning of this chapter, she could have walked into class, sat by herself, and waited to be "discovered." Instead, she broke the ice by taking the initiative and introducing herself.

Jill's situation illustrates the steps involved in making a self-introduction. First, she greeted the other person. In Jill's case, she said, "Hi." Second, she gave her name by saying, "I'm Jill Norman." Third, she said something about herself that was meant to encourage the other person to respond—"I moved here during the summer, and this is my first day at West High. What's it like?"

For Better or For Worse®   **by Lynn Johnston**

Have you ever felt the way the young students in the last panel of this comic strip do?

If making introductions is so easy, why do people have trouble introducing themselves to others in social situations? Often, people feel shy about making a self-introduction. They are uncertain of how others will respond and so do not say anything. If shyness prevents you from introducing yourself, try to remember that often the other person feels just as ill at ease as you do. By taking charge of the situation, you can make both of you feel more comfortable.

A second type of introduction is the business self-introduction. A business self-introduction is similar to a social self-introduction. You greet the person, give your name, and state something about yourself. However, with the business self-introduction, you also state your purpose. For example, imagine that a classmate, Paul Phillips, wants to apply for a summer job at a certain company. As he approaches the company's receptionist, he might say, "Hello. My name is Paul Phillips. I'm a student at West High School and I would like to apply for a summer job here." Notice that the greeting is more formal than with a social self-introduction. Instead of saying "Hi" as Jill did, Paul says, "Hello." He might also have said, "How do you do?"

A good self-introduction is especially important for success in business. You will not be able to get information you need, to present an idea, or to sell a product if you cannot introduce yourself. People respond well to others who are willing to take the first step and introduce themselves.

How to Introduce Others

Even though the opportunity to introduce people to each other comes up frequently, most people feel rather uncomfortable about how they should go about it. Years ago, many people were schooled in formal etiquette and learned set ways for behaving in social settings. Today, there is much less stress on rules of behavior. People are encouraged to act casually in social situations. Yet by not following some very simple guidelines, you can risk hurting a person's feelings or causing embarrassment. On the other hand, by following these guidelines, you show sensitivity to other people's feelings.

The two main problems with introductions concern the order of names and the wording of the introduction.

Order of Names. Order of names refers to the order in which people are presented to each other. The person named first is the person to whom the other is being introduced. For example, in the following simple introduction, Jeff is being introduced to Amy: "Amy Riveras, I'd like you to meet Jeff Conway." What rules govern who is named first in an introduction? Tradition provides three guidelines for answering this question.

1. *Name the person of higher status first.* Although we in the United States do not have inherited titles, we do recognize earned status to some extent. In other words, we recognize achievements people have made, and we show this recognition by naming the person of higher earned status first. For example:

Ms. Parker [the school principal], I'd like you to meet a new student, George Anderson.

Mr. Tenley [the manager of a business], I'd like you to meet Tim Glo-wacki, a salesman for Hernway.

Dr. Esposito, this is a new patient, Sheila Weinberg.

An exception to the rule of status occurs when a family member is introduced. Tradition calls for naming the family member last. For example:

Mr. Chin, I'd like you to meet my mother, Mrs. Robey.

Mrs. Simpson, I'd like to introduce my father, Mr. Johnson.

Heidi, this is my sister, Bess.

2. *When the status of the people is the same, name the older person first.* In other words, introduce the younger person to the older person. For example:

Mr. Henderson, I'd like you to meet my classmate, Jayne Lee.

Mrs. Rosenberg, I'd like you to meet a member of our school band, Melissa Browne.

Bill Crenshaw [a senior], I'd like you to meet Tom Karas [a ninth-grader].

At school, in business, and in social settings, you will feel comfortable making introductions if you learn a few simple guidelines.

3. *When status and age are the same, name the woman first.* Traditionally, the male is presented to the female. For example:

Betty Donnelly, I'd like you to meet my old friend Harry Doyle.

Donna, I'd like to introduce Chip.

Mrs. Carter, I'd like you to meet my father, Mr. Basehart.

4. *If the rules for status, age, and gender do not seem to apply, simply present the person you know better to the other person.* For example:

Howie, this is my good friend Nick.

Gene, I'd like you to meet my roommate Michelle.

Lee, I want to introduce my next-door neighbor Sarah.

With a little practice, you will soon find yourself making introductions automatically in such a way that everyone involved feels good about how you handled the situation.

Wording of the Introduction. Just as some people have trouble deciding who to introduce to whom, so others are stumped by the wording of the introduction. They cannot decide how formal to make the wording and when to use first names. There are many acceptable variations of wording you can use to introduce one person to another. However, formal situations require somewhat formal wording, as well as the use of last names and titles. For example:

Professor Martin, I would like to introduce Chip Jones.

Felicity Brosnan, I would like you to meet Howard Spencer.

Dr. Klein, may I present my friend Anita Reyes.

In informal situations, you may use more informal, or casual, wording for your introductions. In addition, you may omit titles, and, if you are the same age as or older than the people you are introducing, you may introduce them by their first names. For example:

Maria, do you know Mike?

Karen, this is Jerome.

Paula, have you met Hank?

Of course, in the most informal of situations, you may say something as simple as, "Chris, Harry."

How to Respond to an Introduction

An introduction paves the way for comfortable social conversation. The simplest response to an introduction is to politely acknowledge your pleasure at meeting the other person. Therefore, if your friend Brian says to you, "I'd like you to meet my brother Matt," your simplest response would be, "Glad to meet you, Matt."

Of course, Brian may have added some information to the introduction to help get a conversation started. For example, he may have said, "I'd like you to meet my brother Matt. He's on the school baseball team." In such a case, your best tactic would be to follow up with a question to get a conversation started. For example, you might say, "Glad to meet you, Matt. I enjoy watching baseball games. How do you think the team will do this year?" Or, Brian may have told you something about his brother beforehand.

The handshake, once a courtesy between knights proving that they held no weapons, is still used to communicate good will when people meet.

In that case, you might say, "Glad to meet you, Matt. Brian tells me that you're on the school baseball team. What position do you play?" Of course, if Matt answers, "Third base," it would be rude for you to pass his answer off with "How nice," and then turn to Brian and change the subject.

The purpose of good manners is to help social situations run smoothly. To a large extent, good manners are simply good sense. For example, you may wonder whether to shake hands with someone to whom you are introduced. In the United States, men usually shake hands when they are introduced. Women often choose to do so, too. When a man is introduced to a woman, the woman may extend her hand or not. Boys and girls should shake hands when they are introduced to adults. However, if shaking hands is inconvenient or would cause disruption, it makes good sense to ignore

ACTIVITY: Making Introductions

Explain what you would say in each of the following situations.

1. You are at a party at which you know no one except the host, who is busy at the moment. You walk over to a person who also seems a bit lost. To introduce yourself, you say: . . .
2. You have an appointment to see Ms. Koriyama at the Parker Stenciling Company. You walk up to the receptionist and say: . . .
3. You wish to introduce your mother to your math teacher, Mr. Parkhurst. You say: . . .
4. You invite a new girl in school to dinner at your house. To introduce her to your parents, you say: . . .
5. You wish to introduce your friend Anne to your brother George. You say: . . .

the custom. For example, imagine you are at a large party and are holding food in one hand and a beverage in the other. If you are introduced to someone whose hands are also full, it makes better sense simply to nod and smile in greeting rather than try to put everything down and shake hands. Of course, no matter what the situation, if someone offers a hand to you, it would be impolite not to shake hands.

Good sense also governs whether you should stand up. Standing up is considered a sign of respect. However, if standing up is awkward, as it might be in a car or on a bus, it makes better sense to overlook this courtesy.

GIVING AND RECEIVING DIRECTIONS

Heather did not think of the city as being very large, but there was no doubt about it, she was lost. She pulled her car to the curb and called to a man who was standing outside a store. "Excuse me, sir," she said, "Can you tell me how to get to the town hall?" For several seconds he thought about her question, and then he began shaking his head. "Sorry, miss," he said, "but as far as I can figure out, you can't get there from here."

You may well have found yourself in situations similar to Heather's. Sometimes when you are either giving or receiving directions, the route seems so complicated that you almost come to believe that "you can't get there from here." However, with practice, you will be able to avoid such predicaments.

How to Give Directions

Directions are instructions for finding a particular place. Give directions only if you are sure of the way. No matter how helpful you are trying to be, if you give incorrect directions, you are only making the situation worse for the person requesting help. Determine whether the directions demand a long answer or a short answer. For example, directions to a restaurant on the other side of town might require you to spend a few minutes framing your reply, while directions to the soup shelf in a supermarket might require you merely to point. In addition, determine whether the destination is a general area or a specific spot. When the directions are for a specific spot, you will have to make them much more precise. With these points in mind, use the following guidelines to frame clear and accurate directions.

1. *Select the simplest route.* Do not think of directions in terms of the way you would go, but instead the way that a stranger would find it *easiest* to go. Everyone knows shortcuts that save a few minutes here and there. However, shortcuts often involve complex routes and tricky directions. It is safest to give directions for the most uncomplicated route, even if the person has to go extra distance and take extra time.

2. *Give directions chronologically.* The person asking for directions needs to know what to do first, what to do second, and so on. For example, if someone were looking for a local shop, the following directions would be quite helpful:

Continue in the direction you're headed until the first stoplight. Turn left at that light, and the shop you are looking for is the third or fourth one on the right-hand side of the street.

Note that these directions give three steps in order: (1) to continue to the stoplight, (2) to turn left, and (3) to locate the shop on the right-hand side.

Notice how the boldly featured landmarks on the map in this photograph provide clear visual references for people to follow.

3. *Use visual terms when possible.* Most people are more comfortable with such terms as *right* and *left* than with *north* or *south*. Directions telling someone to "go three blocks *north*, one block *east*, and two additional blocks *north*" can be hard to visualize. On the other hand, directions telling someone to "go *straight ahead* for three blocks, then turn *right* and go for one block, and finally turn *left* and go three more blocks" are usually much easier to follow.

Similarly, people are much more likely to understand concrete references than conceptual ones. Directions naming places and landmarks are easier to follow than directions using feet or yards or miles. Most people would likely be able to understand the following directions with little difficulty:

Go straight ahead until you reach the third traffic light. There you will see a fork in the road. Take the right fork and travel until you come to an intersection with Parker's Gas Station on the right and the YMCA on the left. The building you are looking for is about half a block down the street from the gas station.

Note how much less visual the following directions are:

Go straight ahead for 150 yards, veer east, and go two and a quarter miles.

4. *Repeat directions.* If the directions are at all complicated, repeat them. When you do, use language as close to your original wording as possible, or else the person is likely to hear your repetition as a separate set of directions. In addition, you may want to ask the person to repeat the directions back to you.

5. *Give the directions fluently.* Nothing is more difficult to follow than directions interrupted by many "uh's," "well, uh's," and "mm's." To prevent this, stop for a minute to gather your thoughts before you give directions.

6. *Consider drawing a map.* If the directions are long and complicated, you may want to draw a map. A good map includes only those details that are necessary to help someone find the way. For example, if you are directing a person across town and the first part of the journey is made all on one street, there is no need to draw in all the streets along the way. Similarly, it is not necessary to keep the map to scale, but if you use a short line to stand for a long distance, make a note of this inconsistency on the map. Use arrows to show the person's path. When you get to parts of the directions that are more complicated, make sure you include all the necessary details.

When someone with a map asks you for directions, use the map to *show* them their current location and the best route for them to take.

How to Receive Directions

How many times have you asked for directions, received them, and then walked or ridden away as confused as ever? Just as there are guidelines for giving directions, so too there are guidelines for receiving directions.

1. *Ask for directions clearly.* Frame your request so that the person you have asked for directions can clearly understand what you want to know. Be specific. For example, instead of saying, "Where's the Methodist

Church?" try saying, "I'm looking for the Methodist Church on Adams Street. Can you tell me how to get there? I'm going to a wedding and I'm unfamiliar with the area." Notice that in the second request, you have told the listener two very important things: first, that you want the Methodist Church *on Adams Street* and, second, that you do not know the area. This information will help the listener frame a helpful response.

2. *Listen carefully.* By listening carefully, you can make sure you do not miss an important step. If you have paper and pencil and the directions are complicated, take notes.

Listening carefully is courteous. No one likes to take the time to think through a set of directions, state them carefully, and then have the person who requested the directions give the impression that he or she is not really interested.

3. *Repeat directions carefully.* It is always wise to repeat directions to make sure that you got them right. A short statement such as the following one checks your understanding and may save you time later.

> Let's see if I have this right. I go straight for three blocks, then right for one, and left for two. The gallery is on the right-hand side of the street at the intersection. Is that right?

4. *Thank the person.* Regardless of how well someone has given you directions, thank that person for helping. If some of the directions were not clear enough for you to follow, go part of the way and ask someone else for directions.

ACTIVITY: Giving and Receiving Directions

Improvisation is the act of inventing or composing without preparation. Work with a partner to improvise the following situations. For each situation, take turns playing the role of the person giving directions and the person receiving directions. After each situation, listen to feedback from your classmates.

1. This is your first day at your school. You need to find your way to the lunchroom.
2. In your math class, you strike up a conversation with the person sitting behind you. You invite this person to come to your house after school, and you have to tell the person how to get there.
3. Your class is having a picnic at the lake. Instead of taking the school bus, you are going to drive up with some friends. You ask a teacher for directions to the lake.
4. For the holidays, the school singing club is putting on a concert at a local hospital. As president of the club, you need to give directions for using public transportation to get from school to the hospital.

SPEAKING ON THE TELEPHONE

The telephone has become a powerful instrument for accomplishing goals and simplifying life. It is the major means of both "keeping in touch" with people who live across the country and cementing relations with people who live nearby. It gives quick and easy access to a wealth of sources of information. Since most people have been using the telephone since childhood, they are likely to take making and answering telephone calls for granted. Nevertheless, a careful review of effective telephone behavior can pay big dividends for you. Your skill in making social calls will affect your relationships with others. Your skill in making business calls will affect your success in getting a job, getting information, and obtaining goods and services.

How many telephone calls (and headaches) could Norman have saved by placing his first call at an appropriate time?

How to Make a Social Call

A **social call** is a telephone call made for pleasure or for help in solving a personal problem. Unfortunately, the telephone is often abused in social situations. Here are several guidelines for good telephone use.

1. *Call at appropriate times.* Many people grab the phone any time they have an urge to talk to another person. Unless your call is urgent, make it at a time that seems appropriate for the other person. Early in the morning, late at night, and at mealtimes are usually very poor times to call. If you are calling someone who lives in another time zone, make sure that you try to reach that person at a time that is appropriate in that time zone. Charts of the different time zones are available in most telephone books.

2. *Dial correctly.* With any type of phone, and especially with the touch phone, it is easy to make a mistake when dialing. Dial slowly. If you think you dialed incorrectly, hang up before the phone rings and start again. Always make sure you know the correct number. Mistakes in dialing can occur no matter how careful you try to be, but you can keep such mistakes to a minimum.

3. *Let the phone ring.* Let the phone ring at least six times and as many as ten times before you hang up. Six rings gives the person only about eighteen seconds to get to the phone. Remember your own frustration when you have dropped what you were doing, rushed to the phone, and found that the person had hung up after only three or four rings. Always let the phone ring long enough to give the person a chance to answer it.

4. *Identify yourself and state your purpose.* When a person answers the phone, identify yourself, state the name of the person you wish to speak to, and, when appropriate, give your reason for calling. For instance, "Hello, this is Scott Lewis. May I speak to Nancy Phillips?" If you recognize the voice answering the phone as Nancy's, you might simply say, "Hello, Nancy? This is Scott Lewis. I'm calling to see what you thought of the show."

Never assume that a person will recognize your voice. Simply saying "Hi" or "Hello" or "Good morning" can throw a person off guard. Since obscene phone calls, crank calls, and joke calls are not uncommon, many people can become a little anxious when they answer a call and the caller does not give his or her name.

5. *Use your best voice and articulation skills.* Be careful not to talk too slowly or too quickly, or to slur words. It is much harder to distinguish between certain sounds, such as *v*'s, *b*'s, and *d*'s, on the phone than it is in person. Moreover, background noise can hinder hearing and understanding. Therefore, speak clearly, enunciate carefully, and use changes in pitch, loudness, and rate to help emphasize points.

6. *Keep calls to a reasonable length.* Perhaps the worst telephone abuse is talking for too long a time. Dominating the phone affects other members of your family who may have calls to make or who may be expecting calls from others. Lengthy phone calls also show a lack of consideration for the person you are speaking to, since that person may have other things to do. Try to limit calls to five or ten minutes.

How to Receive a Social Call

Just as there are guidelines for making social calls, so too there are guidelines for receiving social calls.

1. *Answer appropriately.* The best way to answer the telephone is simply to say "Hello." Telephone etiquette used to suggest using such statements as "Hello, this is the Ricardo residence" or "Hello, this is Bob Ricardo." However, because of the many abuses made of the telephone, people are becoming more cautious.

You may want to wait until you identify who is calling and what the person wants before you give your name. If after you say "Hello" the caller does not give a name, you have two choices. If you think you recognize the voice, you might use the person's name to check who it is; for example, "Is this Jack?" If you do not recognize the voice, you will probably want to ask for the person's name; for example, "Who is this speaking, please?"

2. *Never tell a stranger your number.* If the caller seems confused about whether he or she has dialed correctly, ask, "What number are you dialing?"

If the person dialed incorrectly, you can say so. If the person dialed correctly, you can ask him or her to call directory assistance for the appropriate number. 3. *Be honest.* If you are short of time or are expecting another call, explain this to the caller. If you do not explain your reasons for wanting to get off the phone, the caller might simply think you are being rude. You might say, "John, I'm in the midst of a project. Can you call back in about an hour?" or "John, I'm in the midst of a project. May I call you back when I'm done?" 4. *Handle unpredictable situations smoothly.* What do you do if you pick up the phone and it's a wrong number? When it becomes apparent that the person has dialed incorrectly, try to accept the situation gracefully. Everyone makes mistakes.

What do you do if the call is for another member of the family? Do not ask, "Who's calling?" or "What do you want?" If the person the call is for is nearby, a better tack would be to ask, "May I say who's calling?" If the person is not there, you might ask, "May I take a message?" When there is a message, record it clearly and post it in a place where it can be seen.

How to Make a Business Call

A **business call** is a telephone call made to conduct business, to request information from a business or an organization, or to pursue some other

A place of business is *busy*. When you call a business, plan what you are going to say, be brief, and be patient if you are placed on hold.

official matter. The telephone is vital for contacting businesses or agencies for information or help and for making a complaint. In most cases, the same rules apply to making business calls as to making social calls, except that business calls require you to be more formal. In addition to giving your name as soon as the phone is answered, you should also give your organization, if you represent one, and the purpose of your call. For example:

> Hello, my name is Dale. I'm with North High School. May I speak with Mr. Helmsley? He asked me to call as soon as we completed our schedule of summer workshops.

Just as with personal calls, you have to be able to handle unpredictable occurrences smoothly. What should you do if you are cut off? Always make sure you know to whom you are speaking. This is particularly important when you need to be transferred. Then, if you are disconnected, you can simply redial and ask to speak to that person again.

What do you do if you are put on hold? If the call is important, you should wait patiently. If a long time goes by, hang up and dial again. Sometimes you are put on hold and are forgotten or disconnected.

What do you do when someone new comes on the line? In such cases, give your name again and repeat your purpose.

Two important types of business calls you will be making are requests for information or help and complaints.

Requests for Information or Help. By far, the greatest number of business calls you make will be requests for information or help. Using the following guidelines will help you to make these calls more effectively.

1. *Select the company or agency most likely to have the information.* For example, if you need information about returning overdue books, you would call the public library. If you suspect that your little brother has drunk some perfume, you would call the local police, a hospital, or the Poison Control Center. In an emergency, if you do not know the exact agency to call, dial your city's emergency number or the operator (O).

2. *Be specific about what you want.* Before making a call, pause for a moment to get a clear idea of exactly what you want and what you will say. State your request clearly and directly. For example:

> Hello, my name is Eileen Cheng. I'm calling to see whether you carry $9\frac{1}{2}$- by 6-inch spiral notebooks with college-ruled paper.

3. *Make sure the person understands your request.* If the person repeats your request incorrectly or in some other way shows a lack of understanding, stop the person and repeat your request.

4. *Listen carefully to the response.* To understand the response to your request, you have to concentrate on what the person tells you. You may want to repeat the information to make sure you understand it correctly.

Complaints. The second type of business call you are likely to make is a complaint call. When you have a problem with a product or a service, you may likely want to make sure that the company or agency responsible knows of your dissatisfaction. Follow the same guidelines for complaints as for calls for information or help, but when making a complaint, you should have two additional concerns.

1. *Make sure you are talking to the right person.* Many businesses have a department that hears complaints. It does you no good to complain to the first person who answers the phone. You must talk with the proper person. To reach the proper person you might say:

> Hello. This is Ryan Maricanos. I'm having a problem with a product I bought from your company recently. To whom should I talk?

2. *When you are connected to the proper person, state your name, your complaint, and what you expect to happen.* Remember that no matter how angry you are, it is useless to be nasty, belligerent, or rude. You will get much better results by simply stating your complaint clearly and firmly. For example:

> Hello. This is Barbara Rose. Recently I purchased a tool kit from your West Side store. The first time I used the hammer, it broke. What do I have to do to get the hammer replaced or to get my money back?

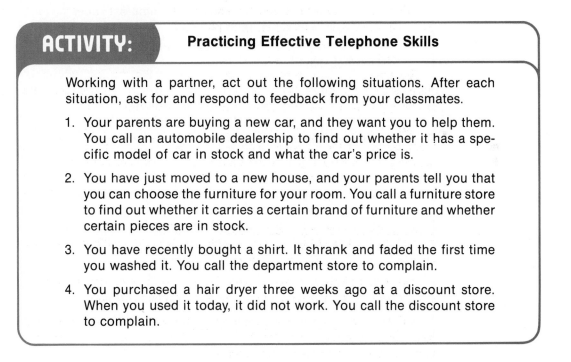

ACTIVITY: **Practicing Effective Telephone Skills**

Working with a partner, act out the following situations. After each situation, ask for and respond to feedback from your classmates.

1. Your parents are buying a new car, and they want you to help them. You call an automobile dealership to find out whether it has a specific model of car in stock and what the car's price is.

2. You have just moved to a new house, and your parents tell you that you can choose the furniture for your room. You call a furniture store to find out whether it carries a certain brand of furniture and whether certain pieces are in stock.

3. You have recently bought a shirt. It shrank and faded the first time you washed it. You call the department store to complain.

4. You purchased a hair dryer three weeks ago at a discount store. When you used it today, it did not work. You call the discount store to complain.

GUIDELINES FOR SPEAKING INFORMALLY

- When I introduce myself to others, do I greet the person, give my name, and say something about myself?
- When I introduce myself in a business setting, do I follow the procedure for social situations and also state my purpose?
- When I introduce people to one another, do I first state the name of any person of higher status, of any older person, or of any woman who is present?
- When I give directions, do I first determine whether the directions need be detailed or simple and whether the destination is a general area or a specific spot?
- When I give directions, do I select the simplest route and explain it in visual terms?
- Do I give directions chronologically and repeat them when necessary?
- Do I give directions fluently?
- Do I consider drawing a map if the directions are complicated?
- Do I ask for directions clearly and listen carefully when they are given, repeating them when necessary?
- Am I courteous when asking for directions?
- When I make a social telephone call, am I considerate of the other person?
- When I make a social telephone call, do I identify myself and state my purpose?
- When I receive a telephone call, do I answer appropriately?
- When I make a business call, do I state the purpose of my call and make sure that I am speaking to the right person?

Profiles in Communication

In the five years Gary Todd has been a directory assistance operator, systems and practices have changed greatly. When Mr. Todd went to work for Southwestern Bell, the ARS, their Audio Response System, had not been installed. "Then we looked up and read the number to the customer," he reflects. "That took longer than keying in. And sometimes as I started to read the number, the customer would have to look for a pencil or paper." Now, with the ARS, operators are able to process calls much more quickly.

Mr. Todd explains that directory assistance operators are evaluated in three areas: productivity, accuracy, and customer effectiveness, or satisfaction. Productivity is determined by their AWT, average time per call. The ARS has lowered operators' AWT; however, this increased speed may affect an operator's accuracy and customer effectiveness. Mr. Todd says, "We are trained to be courteous and patient, but if a directory assistance operator is ever brusque with you, it might be because the operator is concerned with meeting overall efficiency requirements.

One change in practices involves the polite responses operators give to callers. Mr. Todd notes, "We used to have to say 'Thank you' no matter what the customer had said. If he said, 'Could you give me Joe Smith's number?' I had to say, 'Thank you.' Now I can say something more appropriate like, 'I'll be glad to.' "

Mr. Todd says difficulties in communication arise when people think of modern directory assistance as the old "Information," with its local operator and the services that name implied. Today he locates numbers in all of the 214 area code, consisting of over eight hundred cities, towns, and communities. To do this, he must know the city or town, the complete name of the person being called, and sometimes the street name. "One woman wanted 'Mr. Jones on Elm St.' When I asked for the city, she said, 'Well, here.' People ask me where to get tags for their cars and if they have to wear seat belts. One man asked for the number of a business that was 'something like Maggie's Gone Mad.' He was lucky; I just happened to know the correct name was Katie's Off Her Rocker."

Even though directory assistance has changed over the years, Gary Todd still believes that both directory assistance operators and customers should be courteous, speak slowly and distinctly, and be willing to clarify what they have said when necessary.

SUMMARY

Daily communication often involves making introductions, giving and receiving directions, and making telephone calls.

When you introduce yourself socially or greet a person or group, give your name and say something that will encourage the other person to respond. When you introduce yourself in a business situation, state your purpose as well as follow the etiquette of a social call.

When you are with people who have not met, introduce one of them to the other (or others) by name. The person you name first is the person to whom the other is being introduced. Try to name first any person of higher status, any older person, or any woman who is present. Wordings such as "I'd like you to meet" and "I'd like to introduce" are appropriate.

When you give directions, determine whether they need to be simple or detailed and whether they are for a general area or a specific spot. Select the simplest route, give the directions chronologically, use visual terms, repeat the directions slowly, speak fluently, and draw a map if necessary.

When you receive directions, ask for the directions clearly, listen carefully, be courteous, repeat the directions, and thank the person for giving you directions.

The telephone is a major means of keeping in touch and of gaining access to information. When making a social call, call at appropriate times, dial correctly, let the phone ring six to ten times, identify yourself and state whom and what you want, use your best voice and articulation, and keep calls to a reasonable length. When answering the phone, answer appropriately, never tell a stranger your number, be honest, and handle unpredictable situations smoothly.

When making business calls, follow many of the same rules that apply to social calls. To request information or help, select the company or agency most likely to have the information, be specific about what you want, make sure that the person understands what you want, and listen carefully. When making a complaint, be sure you are speaking to the proper person. In addition, state your name, the situation, and what you expect to happen. Assert yourself, but do not be rude or belligerent.

CHAPTER VOCABULARY

Look back through this chapter to find the meaning of each of the following terms. Write each term and its meaning in your communication journal.

business call   introduction   social call
directions   self-introductions

1. The first step in introducing yourself to another person is to greet the person. What are the other two steps?

2. Introducing yourself in a business setting begins with the same three steps as introducing yourself in a social setting. However, business introductions require one additional step. What is that step?

3. According to tradition, when you introduce one person to another, you should name the person of higher status first. What are two other guidelines for determining who should be named first?

4. "Mr. Carter, I'd like you to meet Mr. Jones" is one appropriate wording for introducing one person to another. What are two other appropriate wordings?

5. One guideline for giving clear directions is to select the simplest route. What are three other guidelines?

6. One guideline for receiving directions is to repeat them after they have been given to you. Why is repeating directions important?

7. When you are making a social call, you should let the phone ring long enough to give the other person a chance to answer it. How many times should you let the phone ring before you hang up?

8. Many people abuse the telephone by talking too long. What is a reasonable length of time for a social phone call?

9. One reason you might make a business call is to request information or help. What is another important reason?

10. When you are making a business call, you should make sure you know to whom you are speaking. How will this knowledge help you if you are cut off?

DISCUSSION QUESTIONS

1. Discuss in which situations you think it would be appropriate to introduce people by using only their first names. How do these situations differ from those requiring you to introduce people by their full names?

2. Discuss under what circumstances drawing a map would be appropriate when you are giving directions. Give examples of directions that would make drawing a map necessary.

3. Etiquette is simply a series of behaviors that help you handle situations smoothly. Discuss in what types of situations knowing exactly what is expected of you would help you communicate.

4. Sometimes people who have no trouble talking to others face to face have difficulty talking on the telephone. Discuss why this might be so.

5. Like many modern inventions, the telephone has affected the quality of life both positively and negatively. Discuss the benefits of the telephone. For example, it lets you keep in touch with people who live far away. Then discuss its drawbacks. For example, a ringing telephone can interrupt a good dinner conversation.

1. Practicing Self-Introduction

A. Make a list of five situations in which you have to introduce yourself to others. Then, working with a partner, act out each of these situations.

B. Working with other members of your class, act out self-introductions for the following situations:

   1. You are at a party where you know very few people. You see a boy (or girl) you would like to meet. Walk up to this person and introduce yourself.
   2. You are trying out for the softball team. While in the locker room, you notice another student who seems as nervous as you feel. You go up to this student and introduce yourself.

2. Practicing Introductions

A. Make a list of five situations in which you have to introduce people to each other. Then, working with a partner, act out each of these situations.

B. Working with other members of your class, act out introductions for the following situations:

   1. While you and your mother are browsing through a department store, you see a friend of yours from school.
   2. While you and a friend are standing in line at the store, you meet your family doctor.
   3. While you and your father are at the hardware store, you meet your science teacher.

3. Practicing Giving Directions

A. Make a list of five common situations in which you have to give clear directions. Then, working with a partner, act out each of these situations.

B. Imagine that someone has asked for directions to a place that is on the other side of town. Select such a place in your community. Then, working with other members of your class, draw a map (or maps) giving a good picture of the directions.

4. Practicing Making Telephone Calls

A. Make a list of five people you might talk to on the telephone—for example, a friend, your grandmother, a cousin. Work with a partner. Have your partner pretend to be each of these people. Act out identifying yourself and stating your purpose to each of these people.

B. Make a list of three common situations in which you have to make a business call. Be sure that one of these situations involves making a complaint. Working with a partner, act out each of these situations.

Real-Life Speaking Situations

1. At one time or another, you may likely own an automobile, and if you do come to own one, sooner or later you will probably want to get rid of it. Instead of trading your car in on a new one, you may decide to sell it yourself. To do so, you will likely place advertisements requesting that interested buyers call you. When potential buyers do call, you will need to give clear directions to your home or wherever they can see your car. Imagine that you have placed advertisements to sell your car and that you are expecting phone calls from people interested in buying it. When they call, what will you tell them about your car? How will you describe it? How will you handle discussing its price? If someone wants to see your car, what directions will you give? Outline your description of your car and other information about it. Write a complete set of directions that interested parties can follow to find the location where they can see your car. Be prepared to present the information in your outline as if you were speaking to an interested buyer. Be ready also to read your set of directions aloud.

2. Office assistants play a vital role in many businesses. As part of their regular duties, office assistants often make introductions, handle phone calls, and give directions for finding objects and locations. Imagine that you are working as an assistant in an office, a shop, or some other business and an angry client calls on the phone. The client wants to return something recently purchased from your company. Working with a classmate, present an imaginary dialogue between this caller and you. Begin by identifying your company and the product the customer wants to return. Then decide how your partner will portray the customer—angry, disappointed, demanding, businesslike. Finally, write a simple script for both of you. End the dialogue by giving the caller directions to find your office. Be prepared to discuss how you would handle introducing the customer to your supervisor, manager, or whoever is in charge.

CHAPTER 7

CONVERSATION

OBJECTIVES:

After studying this chapter, you should be able to

1. Define conversation.

2. Define a good relationship.

3. Explain the factors necessary for good conversation.

4. Ask well-phrased questions.

5. Paraphrase.

6. Discuss ways of coping with disagreement.

7. Present guidelines for discussing disagreement.

"Jay, I heard you had a new job after school. How's it going?"
"OK, Paula."
"So, what is it you do?"
"Oh, whatever they want."
"I see. Well, uh, the first day can always be kind of tough to figure out."
"Naw, it wasn't bad."
"Did they explain what you were supposed to be doing?"
"Yeah."
"What was the best part of the day?"
"You can guess that one, Paula—going home!"
"Right—well, Jay, see you around."

Have you ever had an experience like Paula's? You try to have a conversation with someone, and that someone is as communicative as a stone. Some of the greatest pleasures you can have, and some of the most vivid disappointments, come from communicating with others. When people are talkative, witty, cheerful, and knowledgeable, you look forward to conversations with them. When they appear terse, sullen, dull, or uninformed, you are likely to avoid them. Becoming a good conversationalist takes work—but the results are well worth the effort.

WHAT IS CONVERSATION?

Conversation is the informal exchange of thoughts and feelings by two or more people. Carrying on a good conversation is a polished art. Saying that a person is a good conversationalist is one of the finest compliments you can pay someone. Like most people you probably want to be a good conversationalist for many reasons. Among these reasons are to increase your pleasure in talking with others, to help you develop new relationships, to help you cement old relationships, and to influence others.

"The best of life is conversation, and the greatest success is confidence, or perfect understanding between sincere people."

—RALPH WALDO EMERSON

Increase Pleasure in Talking to Others

Most people are social beings. They enjoy talking with each other. Two people can sit for hours talking just for the fun of it. The better a conversationalist you are, the more people are going to enjoy talking with you, and the more you will enjoy talking with them.

Develop New Relationships

Conversation is the starting point for developing new relationships. A *good* relationship is any mutually satisfying interaction between people. You probably have many different kinds of good relationships with people. These relationships can usually be grouped under three basic categories—acquaintances, casual friends, and close friends.

Acquaintances are the many people you know by name and talk with when you run into them. Most people have both social and business or school acquaintances. Casual friends are the people you like and who like you. You look forward to your conversations with them because you enjoy their company. Close friends are the people with whom you share your deepest feelings. Close friendships are built on trust and require a personal commitment to the maintenance of the friendship.

Through conversation, you make acquaintances that often lead to friendships. In the course of your daily activities, you meet people you do not know. By having conversations with them, you get to know them. Throughout your teen years you will develop hundreds of acquaintances and a smaller number of casual friendships that will make your life more enjoyable. With some of these people, your relationships will turn into deep friendships that will last for a lifetime.

Cement Old Relationships

Just as conversation helps you to develop new relationships, so too it allows you to maintain and strengthen old relationships. Whatever kind of relationship you have with a person, you must work to maintain it. Good conversation is the best sign of your effort to keep a relationship going. If you enjoy talking with another person and that person enjoys talking with you, that is a sign of a relationship that is strong. On the other hand, if a person avoids talking to you, you are likely to see this loss of interest in conversation as a sign of a weakening in that friendship.

The kinds of conversations you have are likely to differ depending on the depth of the relationship. With acquaintances, you may talk about the weather, school, or a sports team. With casual friends, you are likely to share more information about your thoughts and feelings. However, discussions of the most important matters affecting you are likely to occur only with your closest friends.

ACTIVITY: **Analyzing Personal Relationships and Their Influence on Conversation**

Think about the people you know. Estimate what percentage you would classify as acquaintances, as casual friends, and as close friends. Discuss what you see as the differences in these relationships. Then make three lists. In the first, list the types of things you are likely to talk about with acquaintances. In the second, list the types of things you are likely to talk about with casual friends. In the third, list the types of things you are likely to talk about with close friends. Share your lists with your classmates.

Influence Others

Through your conversations, you share information and affect attitudes and behaviors. First, conversation provides an excellent opportunity to explain processes, to describe things you have done or seen, and to share facts. Good conversationalists are excellent sources of information. If you have something to say, people will listen to you. Second, conversation is thought provoking. Through conversation, you express your own ideas and encourage people to react to those ideas. If your ideas are interesting, clear, and well thought out, people will be likely to believe and to act upon what you say.

WHAT MAKES A GOOD CONVERSATIONALIST?

Your decision to spend time with some people rather than others is likely to depend on how much you value their conversation. Consider some of the qualities that make a good conversationalist.

Knowledgeable

Good conversationalists are knowledgeable. They can talk intelligently on a number of topics. Have you noticed how you are likely to seek out people who can speak on several topics and how you tire of people who seem to be limited to *only* sports, cars, cooking, or some other single topic? Although good conversationalists do not know everything there is to know, they are likely to have interesting information and insights on several topics. Knowledge is an essential ingredient of lively conversation. The greater the

A good conversationalist always draws others out, listens carefully, and responds with interest.

amount of information that each person brings to a conversation, the more interesting that conversation can be. Therefore, if someone begins to talk about the bakery where he or she works part-time, a good conversationalist is able to enter into the conversation by talking about bakeries, baked goods, part-time jobs, or simply working.

Empathic

Good conversationalists are empathic. **Empathizing** means being sensitive to the feelings of others. Whether people are talking about their joy in receiving a prize or winning a game or their disappointment in getting a low grade or losing a friendship, an empathic person recognizes their feelings and shows understanding. To empathize, you have to care about others.

Caring is shown by focusing conversation on the other person's point of view as much as on your own. Instead of always talking about themselves— how great they are, what good fortune they've had, what they want to do, what they value—caring people show a sincere interest in the other person's needs, problems, and interests. Likewise, when empathic conversationalists see that their words are embarrassing others, they either stop discussing that point or change the way they are discussing it. Good conversationalists do not belittle others, act sarcastically, or say things just to "get a rise" out of someone.

Some people only pretend to care about others. However, pretending seldom works because most people soon see through the pretense. To be a good conversationalist, you must have a sincere interest in other people.

Able to Draw People Out

A good conversationalist is able to get people to talk about themselves and their experiences. Many people are shy and need encouragement to discuss their ideas and feelings. A good conversationalist asks open questions that help other people share their thoughts and experiences. (In the next section you will look at how to ask questions effectively.) Often, just getting people to start talking is enough to spark a good conversation. Usually, the quickest way to get someone talking is to ask about an experience or activity that is important to that person. For example, if a shy girl has a part-time job in a restaurant, a good conversationalist will ask questions that will get her to talk about her experiences at the job and, perhaps, even about the restaurant business in general.

Natural

Good conversationalists are natural. They do not try to put on airs or act like big shots. You enjoy talking to people for what they are, not for what they pretend to be. People who are natural talk about those things that interest them, and they find ways to talk about things that interest others. They do not try to impress others with big words or big ideas.

Flexible

Good conversationalists are likely to be flexible. Flexible people weigh and evaluate what another person is saying. They listen to the views of others, and if these views differ from their own, they may well change their minds. Being flexible is not the same as being wishy-washy. Flexible people may still take a strong position on a subject. However, they keep their minds open, and when they are persuaded otherwise, they are willing to change their views.

Good Listener

Good conversationalists are also good listeners. Since effective communication involves both speaking and listening, a good conversationalist knows when to listen and how to listen well. In fact, there are times when a person needs a listener far more than someone to listen to. For example, if one of your friends, Carla, were talking about her part in the school play, it would be rude of you to break in to tell her about the time you had acted in a play. To be a good conversationalist, you would listen carefully to Carla and would share in her excitement about the part. Good listeners do not try to dominate the conversation, nor do they interrupt another person before that person has finished. (To sharpen your listening skills, you may want to review the information covered in chapter 5.)

To prevent your conversations from "going nowhere," be sure that everyone has an opportunity to talk.

THE LOCKHORNS

"OF COURSE THIS CONVERSATION'S GETTING US NOWHERE! YOU'RE DOING ALL THE TALKING!"

Reprinted with special permission of King Features Syndicate, Inc.

DEVELOPING GOOD CONVERSATIONAL HABITS

Much of your *effectiveness* in conversation depends on your verbal skills. Asking good questions, paraphrasing others' ideas, talking in clear, vivid language, using nonverbal clues, and practicing will all help you develop your conversational ability.

List the qualities that make a good conversationalist. Then rank these qualities, beginning with the most important, followed by the next in importance, and so on. Discuss your rankings with your classmates. On the basis of these characteristics, how do you rate yourself as a conversationalist? In which areas are you strong? In which are you weak?

Ask Good Questions

You have been asking questions since you learned to talk. Generally, you ask questions to find out information. In conversation, questions also show your interest and your grasp of what others are saying. Mastering the following principles for asking good questions will help you gather information and build enjoyable, rewarding conversations. (You may also want to review pages 140–42.)

1. *Ask open rather than closed questions.* **Open questions** are those that must be answered with an explanation. **Closed questions** are those that can be answered with *yes* or *no* or with only one or two words. "How do you feel about being elected to the student council?" is an open question. To answer it, the person would have to talk about his or her feelings. "Were you happy to be elected to the student council?" is a closed question. Once the person answers yes or no, the conversation has ended.

2. *Ask follow-up questions for responses that need further explanation.* **Follow-up questions** are related to the subject matter of an earlier question. Whether you can keep a conversation going often depends on the quality of your follow-up questions. For example, imagine that in answer to the question "What have you been doing?" your friend George answers, "I've been running at least three miles a day." One good way to respond to his answer is to ask a follow-up question that will encourage him to continue talking on that subject. You might ask, "Where have you been running?" or "How long does it take you?"

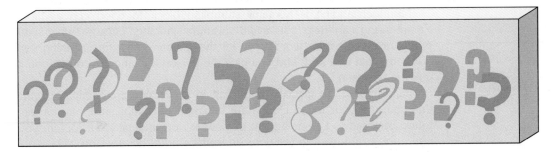

3. *Ask questions in a nonthreatening way.* For example, imagine that Barbara, who sits next to you in math class, says, "I can't believe it. I got a D on the test." If you reply, "Wow, didn't you bother studying?" she is going to feel threatened by your question. However, if you say, "Did you have a chance to talk with Miss Solomon about it?" Barbara will likely interpret your question as an indication of your concern and will continue the conversation.

4. *Ask questions that relate to a person's interests.* To encourage people to talk, ask questions about topics that are likely to trigger mutual interest. One of the most common topics for starting a conversation is the weather. For example, you might start a conversation by saying, "This is the warmest May we've seen in years." Then you would ask a question relating this common topic to the person's interests. For example, "How does the warm weather affect your tennis game?"

When you want to strike up a conversation with someone you do not know, you can ask questions that relate to the situation you are both in. For example, to start up a conversation while standing at the bus stop with a new boy in school, you might ask, "Is it my imagination or have all the buses been running late recently?" The boy would probably take this question as an invitation to talk. If he wanted to accept the invitation, he would respond with a friendly comment such as, "It's gotten to the point where I never depend on the schedule." With such encouragement, you might keep the conversation going. If, on the other hand, he merely said something like "Beats me" and then buried his nose in a book, you would know that he was not interested in talking. You would have lost nothing, since you would be no worse off now than you were before, but at least you would have made an attempt.

Paraphrase

A second good conversational habit is to paraphrase. **Paraphrasing** means putting into your own words your understanding of another person's ideas. After a person has talked for a while, you can show your understanding of what he or she has said by paraphrasing. For example, imagine that your sister Deanne has said, "I had a really great party. Mom put out plenty of snacks; people talked and danced and had a great time. I can't understand why Phyllis and Gena seemed so unhappy." To paraphrase Deanne's thoughts, you might say, "So, you're puzzled about Phyllis's and Gena's behavior last night, since you thought the party was really great."

Misunderstanding is a major stumbling block to good conversation. Paraphrasing can help you avoid misunderstanding, because when you paraphrase someone's words, you let that person know the meaning you got from what was said, and you give the person a chance to correct you if you are mistaken.

Paraphrasing is especially important in preventing arguments. Imagine that you and your friend Donna are having a discussion and that you are totally opposed to Donna's point of view as you understand it. Before you reply, you might want to test your understanding of her position. You might say, "Let me make sure I really understand your point. I take it that you are saying. . . ." You may find, after paraphrasing, that you have misunderstood at least part of what the person has said. For example, Donna might reply, "Well, you sort of have the idea, but you're missing the key point." Without your paraphrasing, Donna wouldn't have known that you had not understood her, and she could not have corrected your misunderstanding. Therefore, you might have gotten into a disagreement over nothing.

By occasionally paraphrasing what others say to you, you can be sure that you are receiving the messages they are trying to communicate.

Create Clear, Vivid Word Pictures

Good conversation is both clear and vivid. As you will study in more detail in Chapter 12, specific and concrete words are clearer than general and abstract words. The more specific and concrete your word selection, the more interesting your conversation will be. Poor conversationalists tend to rely on overused words and expressions that are almost meaningless. They might start a conversation with the sentence "We're planning some neat things for the picnic." What are "neat things"? Contrast that sentence with the following conversation opener: "We're planning a horseshoe tournament, volleyball challenge games, and a softball game for the picnic." Likewise, a poor conversationalist might say, "I'm kind of bummed out by things." What exactly does the person mean by "bummed out"? By what particular things is the person "bummed out"? Contrast that wording with this conversational opener: "I'm really disappointed that Mr. Nichols won't let me organize the dance this year." Because the wording of the second example is more specific, it is far clearer than that of the first and should make for a far more interesting conversation.

Good conversation is likely to be vivid. Conversation is fun when it is lively. In addition to stating ideas clearly, you need to use words that appeal to the senses. The key to being vivid is being able to relive the experiences you are explaining and then using words that capture the feelings and sensations you had.

A good conversationalist would never stop with a statement such as "Hank's play was really terrific yesterday," because the image of "terrific" is neither very clear nor very vivid. A good conversationalist would expand the idea of "terrific" by saying something such as "Hank made a super play to end the game. The Panthers had two runners on in the ninth inning with only one out, when Carson hit a hard shot over second. Hank dived for the ball and slid three feet on his stomach before grabbing Carson's line drive on the first hop. Still lying on the ground, Hank flipped it back to Parker at second, and Parker tossed it to first for a double play and the last out."

Use Appropriate Nonverbal Clues

As you may likely recall from Chapter 3, the nonverbal elements of your conversation are every bit as important as the verbal in communicating ideas clearly and vividly.

Nonverbal signals, such as gestures, facial expressions, and vocal variation, help make communication more lively.

Use body language to describe and emphasize. Good conversationalists are often lively. Their use of gestures, facial expressions, and movements give added meaning and emphasis to their words. For example, in telling about subjects such as Hank's great play, good conversationalists would use their hands to show the way Hank flipped the ball backhanded. Such actions help bring words to life, thereby making communication more effective.

Use paralanguage to emphasize and to heighten interest. Varying the pitch, intonation, and other aspects of your voice can add power to your conversation. The more expressive your voice, the more enjoyable you will be to listen to. Practically no one wants to listen to even an exciting story delivered in a monotone. When good conversationalists talk about subjects like Hank's play, for example, they change their voices at appropriate points to emphasize key words and to create a tone of excitement.

Speak fluently. Good conversationalists do not fill every pause with "you know," "well, uh," or a popular slang word. Not only do they seem to have interesting information to share, they also have the vocabulary to present that information in highly arresting language.

Practice

The only way you can improve your conversational skills is by practicing. You may be reluctant to work at conversational skills with someone else

ACTIVITY: Practicing Conversation Skills

Working with a partner, act out each of the following situations. For each situation, first construct a question that will get you more information—in other words, that will get the conversation started. Then once your partner has responded, continue the conversation until it reaches its natural conclusion. Remember to take time every now and then to paraphrase—to test your understanding by briefly reviewing your partner's statements. In addition, use clear and vivid language to make your conversation exciting. (You may change the name of any character in a situation to fit you or your partner.) After each conversation, ask for and respond to feedback from your classmates.

1. Clayton has said that he has just gotten a job at the library.
2. Charlene is working to improve her test-taking ability, since she hopes to win a scholarship for college. She seems to be having trouble with multiple-choice questions.
3. Gloria is going on a date with Don, but she doesn't know what to wear.
4. Bill is feeling glum because basketball practice went very poorly today.
5. Melissa is trying out for the school softball team.

because you do not want to risk sounding foolish or looking dull and awkward. Yet every day you find yourself in situations where you can make friends and learn about yourself and others if you just take the initiative. Since the best way to get better at nearly anything is through practice, the next time you have an opportunity to strike up a conversation, take it. Even if the conversation does not work out, you can learn from the experience. You will find that with each conversation you are likely to grow more relaxed and confident.

DEALING WITH DISAGREEMENT

Disagreements are situations in which two or more people do not share the same view on something. Since disagreements are a necessary part of living, good conversationalists learn to handle disagreements constructively. The following section covers three ways that people commonly deal with disagreement and then gives guidelines for handling disagreements so that they will not diminish relationships.

Withdrawal

Withdrawal is the physical or psychological removal of yourself from a disagreement. For example, suppose two friends, Pete and Rick, are working together and Pete says to Rick, "I have a date tonight, so I'm not going to be able to finish my part of this job." In response, Rick turns to him and says, "I covered for you last time. You're always cutting out and leaving me with the work." Pete replies, "Well, this is important—I can't break the date." Rick becomes very angry with Pete, but instead of saying any more, Rick walks to his locker. Rick's behavior is an example of withdrawal. Although withdrawal is a common way of reacting to disagreement, it does little to

Drawing by Modell. © 1985 by the New Yorker Magazine, Inc.

"One thing about Martin, he doesn't mince words."

Martin's injuries indicate that he apparently has never learned the most effective way to handle a disagreement: discussion.

settle the problem. If Rick withdraws each time he gets angry with Pete, most likely he and Pete will continue to have problems working together.

Use of Force

Perhaps equally as common as withdrawal is the use of force. Let's continue with Pete and Rick's disagreement over work. Pete says, "Well, this is important—I can't break the date." Rick takes Pete by the shoulders and says, "If you take off and leave me with all the work, I'm going to punch you out." As in the case of withdrawal, the use of force will likely lead to further disagreements. If Rick and Pete do get into a physical fight, the only thing the fight will show is who can beat the other that day. If Pete wins, he will go on the date, and Rick will still be angry. If Rick wins and Pete gives in, Pete will very likely resent missing the date and will be angry with Rick. In either case, the fight will be a poor way of dealing with the disagreement.

Discussion

A third method of dealing with disagreement is discussion. Discussion is by far the most effective method because it is the only one that stands a chance of providing mutually satisfactory results. In other words, it is the only method that allows both parties to get some satisfaction. Discussion may not completely solve the problem, but it will give both parties a better understanding of the issues involved and of the other person's thinking.

Discussion means talking through a disagreement by following the problem-solving method. The **problem-solving method** involves identifying the problem, determining its nature and causes, talking about possible ways of solving the problem, and selecting the best choice. For example, consider Rick and Pete's conflict. Rick has said that he is angry about doing Pete's work. At this point, Pete is the one who will have to start a discussion. He might try to do so by saying, "Rick, I know you think I'm letting you down, but let me explain why this date is so important to me."

Discussion requires the participation of at least two people. At this stage of the disagreement, Rick could choose to become part of the discussion or not. Rick might say, "Pete, there is no sense in talking about it—that's it." However, if Rick values the relationship and wishes to resolve the problem on friendly terms, he could indicate his willingness to take part in the discussion by saying, "Okay, I'll listen to you." Once two parties have agreed to discuss their differences, then all the aspects of the situation can be brought out and a mutually satisfying solution may be reached.

How to Use the Problem-Solving Method to Manage Disagreements

You can settle disagreements on friendly terms by applying the problem-solving method to discussion.

1. *Identify the problem.* You cannot begin to resolve a disagreement until you at least know what you are arguing about. For example, Pete could

have tried to clarify the problem by saying, "Rick, what is it that bothers you—that I'm not doing my share of the work or that I leave work early more often than you do?" In this case, Rick's answer would help identify the problem that is causing the disagreement.

2. *Focus on the specific disagreement.* Disagreements have a way of spreading to areas that are not related to the issue at hand. When people broaden the area of disagreement, they lessen their chances of resolving the problem satisfactorily. For example, imagine that after Pete had asked Rick to finish up for him, Rick had replied, "Pete, this is just another instance of your being unreliable." Pete might likely have responded, "What do you mean 'unreliable'? Explain yourself, fellah." Then the two would have argued about instances of unreliability instead of discussing the specific work problem.

ACTIVITY: Using the Problem-Solving Method to Settle Disagreements

Working with a partner, act out each of the following situations. In each situation, settle the disagreement by using the problem-solving method in discussion. After each situation is settled, discuss your feelings during the disagreement. Then have the class evaluate how successfully the disagreement was handled and make suggestions for resolving it more effectively.

1. You and your younger brother share a room. You try to keep your side of the room neat, while he not only keeps his side a mess but also throws his clothing and belongings onto your side.

2. For the last three months, you have been working after school at a store on Main Street. Two other students work with you. You believe that the manager gives you many more tasks than she gives the other two students.

3. Together, you and your best friend, Anita, organized and ran the school drive to raise money to feed victims of a recent flood in your area. The drive was a huge success, but you believe that Anita has taken all the credit.

4. You are in a group of five students writing a committee report for your history class. You believe that the head of the committee has assigned you the worst topic.

5. You and your sister are saving to buy your parents a special anniversary present. You just found out that your sister has used the savings to buy herself a new sweater.

3. *Describe your feelings.* When you are angry with someone, you are likely to lash out in a way that may make you feel better but that hurts the other person. For example, imagine that Rick had reacted to Pete's news about leaving early by saying, "You're so selfish. You never think about anyone but yourself." Pete would not only be hurt and insulted by the outburst, but he also might likely not understand the reason for it. It would be much more effective for Rick to say, "Pete, your leaving early makes me angry. I feel I am being asked to do more than my share of the work."

4. *Verbalize the other person's position.* Before you can discuss opposing views, you must be sure you accurately understand the other person's position. For example, Pete might say to Rick, "If I understand you correctly, you feel that I'm trying to push all the work off on you while I go out and have fun." Now Rick can agree or disagree on whether or not that is his position. If he agrees, both parties know where they stand. If he disagrees, he can explain exactly what his position is.

5. *Do not let the disagreement become a battle of egos.* People may well be willing to be reasonable, but if they feel that they are backed into a corner, they are likely to respond defensively. No one likes to "lose face" at any time. Both parties should try to approach a problem in such a way that the other will not feel that his or her value as a person would be undermined by looking at the problem from a new perspective. Pete might say, "Rick, I'm not trying to take advantage of you. I can see why my leaving early would make you angry. But look at things from my side for a moment."

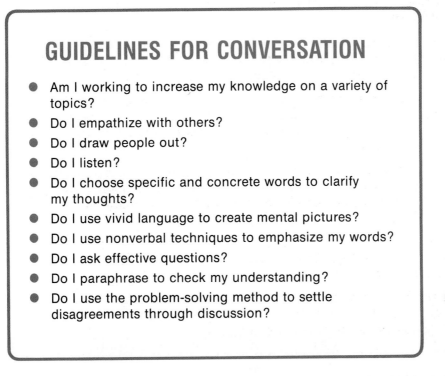

GUIDELINES FOR CONVERSATION

- Am I working to increase my knowledge on a variety of topics?
- Do I empathize with others?
- Do I draw people out?
- Do I listen?
- Do I choose specific and concrete words to clarify my thoughts?
- Do I use vivid language to create mental pictures?
- Do I use nonverbal techniques to emphasize my words?
- Do I ask effective questions?
- Do I paraphrase to check my understanding?
- Do I use the problem-solving method to settle disagreements through discussion?

Profiles in Communication

Lynda Chaney

No one would ever suspect that Lynda Chaney, owner of the successful Scissor Magic Beauty Salon, once considered herself too shy to talk to strangers. "I had to force myself to join in conversations when I was younger—make myself meet and talk to new people. But it's not so hard; I've learned that the main thing I have to do is just listen."

Mrs. Chaney believes that conversation skills and a sincere interest in people are indispensable in her business because hair styling is a highly personal activity. Patrons want a relaxing experience, and pleasant conversation that centers around their interests, builds trust, and puts them at ease.

She is convinced that the atmosphere of the salon is important in making quiet conversation possible. She says, "The salon should be attractive, cheerful, clean, and peaceful." Mrs. Chaney's salon, with its large windows, crisp curtains, and pots of lush, green plants, certainly fits that description.

To begin a conversation with a new patron, Mrs. Chaney asks about his or her work, family, or home. If the client is a child, she asks about school or a favorite teacher, book, or toy. However, she says, "I want children to feel at ease, but I can't get too friendly with them. If I do, they wiggle."

Two topics of conversation Mrs. Chaney strictly avoids are religion and politics. "It's easy to get into arguments when you start talking about emotionally charged subjects, and one rule we have here is never to argue with the patrons."

Mrs. Chaney feels that if an entrepreneur wants an enterprise to thrive, a policy of "the customer is always right" works best. "Sometimes it is hard not to argue—especially when you know you're right," she admits. "For instance, a new client said I had told her we had a certain brand of permanent. I knew I hadn't said we stocked it; we didn't. But I didn't get angry or argue. I listened to her and then explained what permanents we did have. She stayed to get her permanent and has become a regular customer now."

Lynda Chaney adds that being able to talk pleasantly and comfortably with people isn't just good for business; it's important in daily life. For success in business and life, she says, "Don't be shy. Join in conversations. Think about other people and ask them about themselves. Get to know them."

Conversation is the informal sharing of ideas and feelings by two or more people. Improving your conversational skills will help you to increase your pleasure in talking with others, to develop new relationships, to cement old relationships, and to influence others.

A good relationship is mutually satisfying. Relationships can generally be grouped under three categories: acquaintances, casual friends, and close friends. In new relationships, people use conversation to learn about others and to begin friendships. In established relationships, people use conversation to keep their friendships active.

Effective conversation requires knowledge, empathy, the ability to draw people out, naturalness, flexibility, and the ability to listen. A person can develop good conversational habits by asking good questions, using appropriate nonverbal clues, and practicing.

An important aspect of interpersonal communication is dealing with disagreement. Although some people handle disagreement by withdrawal or by using physical force, the best method is by discussion. Effective discussion involves identifying the problem, focusing on the specific disagreement, describing your feelings, stating the other person's position, and not letting the disagreement become a battle of egos.

CHAPTER VOCABULARY

Look back through this chapter and find the meaning of each of the following terms. Write each term and its meaning in your communication journal.

closed questions	discussion	paraphrasing
conversation	empathizing	problem-solving method
disagreements	follow-up questions	withdrawal
	open questions	

REVIEW QUESTIONS

1. Early on, a baby learns how to talk. How is mere talking different from conversation?

2. One purpose of good conversation is to increase your pleasure in talking with other people. What are three other purposes?

3. A good conversationalist can speak on a number of subjects. What are at least three other characteristics of a good conversationalist?

4. Empathy is the ability to put yourself in another person's shoes so that you can better understand that person's thoughts and feelings. Why is empathy important for good conversation?

5. Two types of questions are open questions and closed questions. How does an open question differ from a closed question?

6. What are follow-up questions?

7. Questions are effective when they are honest requests for information. How can questions be threatening?

8. A good method for preventing arguments is paraphrasing. What is paraphrasing?

9. Some people withdraw from a disagreement rather than try to resolve it. What is withdrawal?

10. Besides withdrawal, disagreements can be settled by resorting to violence or by engaging in discussion. How is the problem-solving method used in discussing a disagreement?

DISCUSSION QUESTIONS

1. Discuss the role of conversation in building and maintaining relationships. How can being a good conversationalist win you new friends? How can it be a key to popularity? What are the qualities of a poor conversationalist? Does being a poor conversationalist contribute to making a person boring? Why or why not?

2. Discuss methods you have used up until now for dealing with disagreements. Which of these methods seemed the most effective? Which seemed the least effective? Can you think of a better method of dealing with disagreements in the future?

3. Dorothy Nevill once wrote, "The real art of conversation is not only to say the right thing in the right place but to leave unsaid the wrong thing at the tempting moment." Discuss the meaning of this quotation. How does it relate to the ability of a good conversationalist to empathize with the person with whom he or she is speaking?

4. Richard Armour wrote, "It's all right to hold a conversation, but you should be part of it now and then." Discuss the meaning of this quotation. How does it relate to the ability of a good conversationalist to listen?

5. A Chinese proverb states, "The man who strikes first admits that his ideas have given out." What is the meaning of this proverb? How does this proverb relate to what you have learned about dealing with disagreement?

ACTIVITIES

1. Making Up Proverbs About Conversation

Proverbs are short statements that record the wisdom of a certain time. Make up one- or two-sentence proverbs for our time concerning conversation. Can you think of any clever or ironic insights about conversation? What do people get out of engaging in conversations? When and where do conversations take place? How are conversations conducted?

2. Identifying Suitable Topics for Conversations

A. List five topics that you believe you can talk about easily in conversation with others. Then list five current topics about which you do not know enough to carry on a conversation. Compare your lists with those of your classmates. Then discuss ways in which you can increase your knowledge of the topics from your second list.

B. Write down at least two topics that you might use to start a conversation with each of the people in the following list. Then compare your topics with those of your classmates. Be prepared to give your reasons for choosing the topics that you did.

1. Your friends at a party
2. A cousin that you do not know very well who is visiting your home for the first time
3. A boy starting his first day at your school
4. Your mother's boss, who is having dinner at your house
5. A new member of your school volleyball team

C. Imagine you have been invited to a party at a new friend's house. You will not know anyone there except your new friend. List at least five topics you could use for making conversation with the other people at the party.

3. Writing Paraphrases

For each of the following statements, write a paraphrase that shows your understanding of the meaning of the statement.

a. Kelley says, "Three times I got ground balls hit right at me, and every time I made an error. Yet when I went either left or right, I had no problem."

b. Malcolm says, "I've been playing piano for eight years, and this is the first time anyone has asked me to perform."

c. Calvin says, "The car's not running right. It doesn't have much pep, and it keeps stalling at lights. It really bugs me."

d. Gayle says, "I asked him if he had a good time, but all he ever did was shrug his shoulders. I just can't seem to get him to say anything more."

e. Caroline says, "I did want to go to that party, but since I didn't receive an invitation until just a day before, I decided to stay home."

f. Pat says, "My dog and my cat always got along well with each other until we moved to our new house. Now they get into fights almost every day."

g. Chris says, "I've always gotten good grades in math, but English has always given me trouble. My English teacher suggested that I consider hiring a tutor."

4. Asking Questions to Become Better Acquainted with Someone

When you have just met a person and are sincerely interested in getting to know him or her, you are likely to ask that person questions to become better acquainted. Two skills you will want to develop in order to ask questions effectively are phrasing questions in a non-threatening manner and delivering them in a friendly tone of voice. You will want your words and your tone to communicate friendliness without appearing to be prying into someone's life. Working with a partner, write a list of questions that might fit into a conversation with the following specific individuals upon meeting them.

a. a new employee at the supermarket where you work fifteen hours per week

b. a student who was transferred into your science class

c. a neighbor who is new in town and who will attend your high school

d. an adult who has hired you to do household chores each Saturday morning

e. an eight-year-old child for whom you will baby-sit once each week

5. Dealing with Disagreement

Using specific techniques to solve problems can help you in settling disagreements you have with others. Working with a partner, plan a situation in which two friends strongly disagree about whether or not they should cover up for a third friend who cheated on a test. Plan enough specific details of the disagreement to establish what exactly is at issue in the argument. Use the problem-solving method to settle the dispute. As you plan, you might actually write key lines of dialogue between the two friends. Act out your disagreement and its settlement as an improvisation, with your classmates as the audience.

Real-Life Speaking Situations

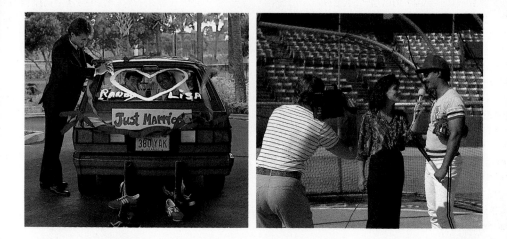

1. Have you ever thought about getting married? If you are like most students in high school, you have probably given marriage a good deal of thought. As in most close relationships, being able to settle disagreements through discussion is vital to a successful marriage. Suppose that you have been married for six months. The two of you had gotten along fine until last week when a disagreement arose concerning finances. How can you and your spouse use effective conversation skills to settle this disagreement? Begin by defining a specific problem. For example, you disagree on how much to spend for an apartment or a car, or you disagree on how much to put in savings and how much to spend on recreation. What would you do to try to reach some sort of agreement? Identify your and your spouse's points of view. Then try to find a common ground that can be used for resolving the conflict in a compromise. Create a dialogue between you and your spouse in which the two of you use the problem-solving method to resolve your disagreement. Be prepared to present your dialogue to the class for comment and discussion.

2. Sports heroes need to be proficient not only at athletics but also at on-the-spot conversation. How many times have you seen interviews featuring athletes immediately following a ball game or some other sporting event? Even though they may be tired, disappointed, or jubilant, professional athletes have to be ready to discuss a wide range of topics. Imagine yourself as an athlete competing in an event in the Olympics or as a member of a team competing for the championship in your favorite sport. The event or the game has just ended, and you are heading for the showers when a sports reporter stops you for an interview. What questions can you expect to be asked? Make a list of five likely questions. How will your victory or loss affect your communication skills? Prepare a short dialogue in which you answer your questions as if you were being interviewed. Present your dialogue in class and ask for additional questions from your classmates.

THE INTERVIEW

OBJECTIVES:

After studying this chapter, you should be able to

1. Define interviewing.

2. Identify the differences between a job interview and a college interview.

3. Anticipate what interviewers look for in an applicant.

4. Anticipate what kinds of questions interviewers ask.

5. Prepare for an interview.

6. Write a résumé.

7. Handle yourself during an interview.

8. Follow up an interview effectively.

"Terry, I got the job!"

"Angie, that's wonderful! When did you hear?"

"I got a call last evening."

"Were you surprised?"

"Well, I think that he saw I really wanted the job and that I would work like crazy at it. He said he had interviewed several people but that I was the one who impressed him the most."

"Great. When do you start, Angie?"

"Monday morning."

Like most people looking for a job, Angie had to go to an interview. Unlike some people, Angie was able to make the most of her interview. By presenting herself in the best possible light, she got the job.

WHAT IS AN INTERVIEW?

An **interview** is a form of communication in which people obtain information by asking questions. Usually, an interview is conducted one-on-one and face-to-face. The **interviewer** is the person who conducts the interview. The **interviewee** is the person being interviewed. The interviewer asks questions to find out whether the interviewee meets set criteria for employment by a firm, for acceptance by a college, or for some other opportunity. The interviewee responds by describing his or her qualifications and experiences. However, an interview is not a one-way form of communication. The interviewee can also ask questions to find out if the firm, the college, or whatever meets his or her own criteria.

Although interviews can be conducted for a number of purposes, this chapter focuses on the two types of interviews most likely to have a major impact on your life—the job interview and the college interview. (In Chapter 10 you will study how to interview others to gather information.)

The Job Interview

When you apply for a job, you are likely to have to take part in a **job interview**. In some companies job interviews are conducted by the head of each department. For example, Angela Thompson, the girl in the short dialogue at the beginning of this chapter, was interviewed by Richard Parker, the director of the marketing division of Generic Products. In small companies, job interviews may be conducted by the head of the company. Large companies usually have personnel departments in which there may be several people responsible for interviewing and hiring.

The job market is highly competitive. Good grooming, appropriate dress, and good manners will give you a very important edge.

The College Interview

If you apply to a college, most likely you will find a **college interview** to be part of the application process. Although many two-year and four-year colleges base acceptance on applicants' high-school grades and test scores alone, some colleges and most professional schools, such as law schools and medical schools, use the interview as a major determinant in their selection process. College interviews are generally conducted by people from the admissions office of the college. A large university made up of several colleges and graduate schools is likely to have an admissions office for each of them.

ACTIVITY: Reporting an Interview Experience

Have you ever been interviewed for a job or for admission to a professional school or college? If so, tell your class about your experience. If not, talk with someone who has been interviewed and tell your class about this person's experience. Identify the job or school and the purpose of the interview. Then tell who the interviewer was, what the interviewer's position was, and what the result of the interview was. If you were the interviewee, also review anything that you did then that you would do differently now.

PREPARING FOR AN INTERVIEW

Since you can expect to face a number of interviews that will be important to you, you will want to be very well prepared for them. The following steps will help you get ready for an interview.

Read the Advertisement Carefully

When reading a job advertisement, you must make sure you understand two things: (1) the type of job being advertised and (2) the qualifications for that job. Here is the ad that Angela Thompson replied to:

RECEPTIONIST

Summer Replacement

Generic Products is looking for a person with a good phone voice to handle our six incoming phone lines. Person must be a good typist. We will train on CRT. Applications will be taken on Wed. and Fri. Apply 2693 Spring Ave. Write for interview.

The two qualifications for this job are a good telephone voice and good typing skills. Angela thought that she met these qualifications, so she filled out an application and wrote a business letter requesting an interview.

In that same newspaper, Southern Ohio College was advertising for people to apply for its summer business program. In the ad, the college listed the courses that would be offered during the summer and the degrees to which these courses could be applied. By reading the ad, a person could tell before applying to Southern Ohio College whether the college was offering a course the person wanted and whether that course led to the degree the person sought.

Determine the Purpose of the Interview

Whether you are interviewing for a job or for college admission, the interview will have several purposes. The primary purposes are to make sure that you have the qualifications for the job or college and that you are the kind of person the company hires or the school admits.

However, a job or college interview may have other purposes as well. For example, it may be a preliminary screening interview that is the first step in a much longer selection process. In a screening interview, the interviewer will not be making the final decision but instead only recommending whether or not you should be allowed to proceed through the other steps of the process. In other cases, an interview may be conducted not to make any decision at all but solely to gather additional information about you. Try to learn the purpose of an interview beforehand so that you can carefully prepare yourself for it.

Find Information About the Company or College

You will be in a much better position to anticipate and answer questions if you have some knowledge of the company or the college holding the interview. The interviewer will likely ask what you know about the business or college to which you are applying, and if you answer "Nothing" or "Not much," your chances of getting that job or being admitted to that college will diminish markedly. Interviewers see your knowledge of the company or college as a sign of interest, initiative, and responsibility. By communicating what you know and feel about the company or college, you can also help the interviewer see where or how you would fit in. Therefore, before you go on the interview, make sure you read carefully any available brochures and catalogues. If the business or college has recently been in the news, read the news articles about it. Other sources of information may also be available in the library or the career counseling office at your school.

Know What You Want to Say

What do you want the interviewer to remember about you? Whether you are on a job interview or a college interview, make sure that you have the following types of information about yourself at your fingertips.

Your success at a college or job interview may change the course of your future. You owe it to yourself to prepare thoughtfully.

Qualifications. What is it about your education or experience that makes you a good candidate for this job or for this college? You will want to list both your *general qualifications,* those that you would use for all interviews, and your *specific qualifications,* those that apply only to the particular job or college.

Goals. What is it that you hope to achieve with this job or at this college? Just as with your qualifications, you will want to list both general and specific goals. Your general goals will be much the same for any job or college. For example, your general goal may be to find yourself a career that will provide challenging work and will be rewarding to you. Specific goals apply solely to a particular job or college. For example, when applying to a restaurant, you may have a specific goal of being the grill operator, the top-selling counterperson, or the restaurant manager.

Interests. Because an interviewer will likely want to know how you spend your time when you are not working or going to school, prepare a list of hobbies, sports, and other interests. Put special emphasis on interests that relate to the job or college. For example, if you are applying for a sales job, an interviewer may see your interest in competitive sports as a sign of good preparation for selling. Likewise, if you are applying to a college as a computer-science major, your membership in a computer club may likely be seen as a sign of personal interest and commitment in the field.

Prepare a Résumé

A **résumé** is a brief account of personal data. When applying for some jobs, you have to mail a cover letter and a résumé before you will be asked for an interview. Whether you have sent a résumé ahead or not, bring an extra copy with you to the interview. The résumé provides the interviewer with a quick overview of data that is relevant to the position. After the interview is over, the interviewer will have facts in hand to remind him or her of your qualifications.

A résumé is seldom more than one page long. It should include such items as your name, address, and telephone number; your education, including any honors and special features of that education; and your previous work experience. Below is an example of the kind of résumé you should prepare.

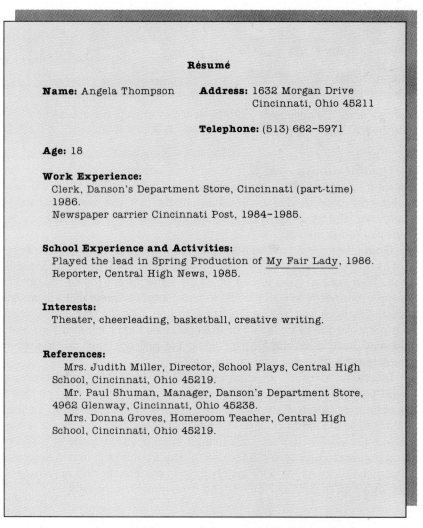

Résumé

Name: Angela Thompson   **Address:** 1632 Morgan Drive
                                               Cincinnati, Ohio 45211

Telephone: (513) 662-5971

Age: 18

Work Experience:
Clerk, Danson's Department Store, Cincinnati (part-time) 1986.
Newspaper carrier Cincinnati Post, 1984-1985.

School Experience and Activities:
Played the lead in Spring Production of My Fair Lady, 1986.
Reporter, Central High News, 1985.

Interests:
Theater, cheerleading, basketball, creative writing.

References:
    Mrs. Judith Miller, Director, School Plays, Central High School, Cincinnati, Ohio 45219.
    Mr. Paul Shuman, Manager, Danson's Department Store, 4962 Glenway, Cincinnati, Ohio 45238.
    Mrs. Donna Groves, Homeroom Teacher, Central High School, Cincinnati, Ohio 45219.

Notice not only the information contained in this sample résumé, but also the form in which it is presented. Make sure that the format you use in your résumé presents your information clearly and concisely.

Know What to Ask

Remember that an interview is not a one-way form of communication. Although its main focus is on finding out how well you meet the needs, goals, and requirements of the company or college, an interview also gives you the opportunity to gather information that can help you determine if you will be happy with the company or at the college. The interviewer's answers to your questions help you decide whether you will take the job if you are offered it or will enroll in that school if you are accepted there.

Prepare a list of questions. The answers to most of your questions will probably come out during the course of the interview. However, if there is information that you need to consider in making your decision to take the job or attend the college, request a few moments to ask questions. The following questions are some of the ones you may want to ask.

Job

What will be my specific duties?

If I have questions, whom should I ask?

What kinds of clothes are required? If uniforms are required, who pays for them?

Is there a union?

Will I be expected [or will I have the opportunity] to work overtime?

College

How many credits am I expected to handle [or am I allowed to take] each semester?

What is the balance between required courses and electives?

Are there any work-study programs?

Besides books, tuition, and dorm fees, what other expenses can I expect?

How can I apply for financial aid and for scholarships?

Schedule an Appointment

Usually the personnel director of the company or the admissions officer of the college will schedule the interview for a specific time. However, if you are asking for an interview, you will be responsible for setting up a time with the interviewer or his or her assistant. Volunteering to just "show up anytime" will be seen not as a sign of enthusiasm but as a lack of understanding of business etiquette. Always make an appointment.

Rehearse the Interview

Your final step in thorough preparation is to rehearse the interview. Even though you cannot anticipate every question you may be asked, rehearsing answers to possible questions will still be very helpful. You may think that you are comfortable with your knowledge of your qualifications, goals, and interests, yet in the heat of an actual interview, it is easy to get upset. If you have not practiced, you may get tongue-tied, lose confidence, and even forget what you know. The more important the interview, the greater your need for careful practice.

Get a classmate or one of your parents to play the role of interviewer and ask you all the questions you have anticipated. Try to give your answers just as you will have to in the actual interview. Simply going over the answers in your head is not enough. You need the practice of stating answers to the questions aloud. After you have finished, you and the person who helped you can then go back over your answers to see whether they were clear and concise. You may want two or three practice sessions before the interview.

ACTIVITY: Writing a Résumé and Preparing for an Interview

In your newspaper, find an advertisement for a job that appeals to you and for which you are qualified. Using the format on page 164, write a résumé that you could use if you were applying for this job. Then prepare a list of your qualifications and a list of questions you would ask the interviewer. Finally, rehearse the interview with a classmate.

WHAT DO INTERVIEWERS LOOK FOR?

During the interview, the interviewer will be looking for information about your knowledge, your interests, and your attitudes. In addition, the interviewer will be watching for signs that indicate you are an attractive candidate.

Promptness

Be prompt. Arriving at an interview on time is seen as a sign of how you will perform in school or on the job. If you are late for an interview, an employer will assume that you will be tardy for work or class. Because you can never predict what occurrences may affect your travel to the interview (car trouble, traffic conditions, and so forth), it makes sense to give yourself more time than you really need to get there. Further, you are less likely to be nervous if you are not rushed. Take a book or a magazine with you. Then, if you are a little early, you can read for a while. Remember: it is better to be fifteen minutes early than five minutes late. If you are late, you

The humor in this cartoon derives from its clash with reality. If responsible positions were filled on managers' whims, the business world would be in chaos.

"Miss Adamson, pluck someone from nowhere and put him in a position of responsibility."

Drawing by Stevenson. © 1985 by the New Yorker Magazine, Inc.

better have a very good excuse. If illness, an accident, or some other major mishap prevents or delays you from getting to the interview, be sure to call before the time of your appointment to let the interviewer know that you will not be there on time.

Appearance

Dress appropriately and groom yourself well. You want to impress the interviewer as a person who is ready to do business or attend classes rather than as one who is on his or her way to play tennis, lounge in front of a television set, or go hiking. If your appearance is far below the interviewer's expectations, you are likely to have a mark against you before you even get a chance to talk.

Poise

Poise complements appearance. **Poise** is your composure, your assurance of manner, your confidence in handling the situation. Show poise during the interview. Some interviewers may try to make you uncomfortable, believing that if you can maintain an assured, confident manner under the stress of the interview, you will be able to maintain your poise as well under the stress of a demanding job or course of study. Of course, during the interview you are apt to feel somewhat nervous. However, the more you have practiced interview skills, the more poised you are likely to be. To deal with nervousness, focus on the content of the questions rather than on the

This applicant's explanation does not outweigh the bad impresson he is making. Always do all you can to make a good first impression on the interviewer.

Drawing by Stan Hunt. © 1983 by the New Yorker Magazine, Inc.

"I'd just like to say, sir, that I always make a bad first impression."

situation itself. Keep your mind on your answers to the questions, and take the questions one at a time. As you answer each of them, you will become more confident and poised.

Flexibility

Interviewers look for flexibility. They want people who can adapt to the many kinds of problems that arise in business or college. Do not create the impression of a rigid, dogmatic, inflexible person; interviewers expect that this type of person is likely to have difficulty in any job or at any school. Give answers that show you are able to adapt to new situations.

Honesty

Be honest. If you don't know the answer to a question, say so. No business or college can afford to take a chance on applicants who appear to be afraid to admit they do not know something. Successful people do not have ready answers for every question. What they do know is how to find answers to difficult questions.

Initiative

During the interview, look for opportunities to show initiative. The success of a company is directly related to the productivity of its employees. Employees who show initiative are often among the most productive. Likewise, a good education is likely to be put to use best by someone who is willing to take on new tasks and enterprises.

Communication Skills

Employers and colleges greatly value people who possess good written and oral communication skills. Even at the lowest levels within a company, people must be able to communicate with their fellow employees and take direction from supervisors. Doing these things requires at least basic interpersonal competence. At higher levels, communication skills become even more important to success. In college, the ability to communicate with teachers and other students is essential, as is the ability to express thoughts in writing.

ACTIVITY: **Playing the Role of a Job Interviewer**

Imagine that you are hiring someone for a job. First, write the advertisement telling about the job responsibilities and requirements. Then discuss with your class which characteristics mentioned in this chapter you would consider the most important in a person applying for this job. Also explain your reasons for selecting these characteristics.

TYPES OF QUESTIONS

Interviewers obtain information by asking questions. Although no two interviewers will ask exactly the same questions, you can anticipate the types of questions they will ask.

Questions That Request Information

Questions that request information are designed to reveal personal data. Because one important function of an interview is to provide the interviewer with information about the interviewee, the majority of questions you will be asked will be of this type. Answer all questions fully. Avoid answering simply "yes" or "no" or giving only one- or two-word answers. However, don't ramble. Instead, keep to the point. Listen carefully to each entire question. Do not lose track of what the interviewer is saying as you formulate your answers. Answer each question directly and avoid going into long explanations or off on a tangent.

You can expect to be asked questions concerning the following categories: current status, background, interests, and goals.

Current Status. Current-status questions are aimed at finding out where you stand at the moment in school and on your current job. Such questions include

What grade are you in now?
What kind of program are you taking in school?
What are your duties on your current job?

If you are well-prepared for your job interview, you can be confident that the interviewer's questions will not take you by surprise.

Background. Background questions deal with previous work and school experience, places you have lived, and things you have done. Through these questions, interviewers find out about your preparation and qualifications. Background questions give you a chance to emphasize those reasons that you feel make you well suited to the job or school. The kinds of questions an interviewer may ask are

What kinds of experiences have you had that might prepare you for this job?
What courses have you taken that might prepare you for this program?
What are some of the things you are particularly good at?

Interests. Questions about your interests deal with how you spend your time. Your answers to questions such as those that follow tell a great deal about the kind of person you are.

What do you do in your spare time?
What are your hobbies?
What places would you like to visit?

Goals. Interviewers ask questions about your goals to find out your hopes and plans for your future. You may be asked

If you are hired, how long would you expect to work for this company?

In five years, what position would you like to hold?

After you graduate, what do you see yourself doing?

Questions That Probe Deeper

Questions that probe deeper seek to find out more about your answers to other questions. They are used to challenge statements you make and to find reasons for actions. Answer probing questions as honestly as you can. However, be careful to frame your answers so that you present yourself in the best possible light.

The following questions are examples of those asked by interviewers to probe deeper.

You say you quit your newspaper delivery job after three weeks. Why?

You say math is your favorite subject. What in particular do you like about math?

It says here that you failed economics the first time you took it. Why?

Questions That Check Understanding

Questions that check understanding are questions asked by an interviewer to make sure that he or she accurately understands what you have said. Listen carefully to such questions because they often reflect the perception the interviewer has of you. These questions give you the opportunity to correct any inaccuracies or misperceptions. Questions that check understanding are also likely to give you hints about what the interviewer thinks is important. Your answers to them may well make the difference between making a good impression and making a poor impression.

The following questions are examples of those that an interviewer might ask to check understanding.

Are you saying that you took typing, but you are not sure that you really have a good grasp of letter-format rules?

Are you saying that your grades in math do not accurately reflect your understanding of mathematical principles?

Why do you think that you would be able to handle dictation if you have not had a course in shorthand?

Questions That Require You to Take a Stand

Questions that require you to take a stand are designed to get you to respond under pressure. Once again, answer these questions honestly and carefully. Do not be afraid to take a few moments to frame your response. However, keep in mind that in recent years the Equal Employment Opportunities Commission has written guidelines for the kinds of questions that may and may not be asked. For example, questions directed to a woman about her plans for marriage or children are not allowed. Questions about marital status, family, race, physical characteristics, age, education, and social

Taking tests in school has helped prepare you for handling high-pressure situations in job interviews and in the workplace.

security are also not allowed unless they directly bear on an occupational qualification.

The following questions are some that would require you to take a stand.

Why do you want to work for this company?
Why do you want to attend this school?
What kind of pay are you expecting?

ACTIVITY: Planning and Conducting a Job Interview

Look again at the advertisement you wrote for a job. Write at least ten questions you would ask an applicant for that job. Then working with a partner—one of you playing the interviewer and the other the interviewee—use your questions to conduct an interview. Finally, discuss the interview with your classmates. Have them determine the strengths and weaknesses of the interview and suggest ways in which the interviewer's questions and the interviewee's responses could have been improved.

FOLLOWING UP THE INTERVIEW

After the interview, you should write a short thank-you note to thank the interviewer for taking the time to talk with you. In the note, indicate that you look forward to hearing from the company or college as soon as possible. For an example of a follow-up letter, look at Angela Thompson's, which is shown below.

702 Oak Street
Cincinnati, OH 45227
June 4, 1987

Mr. Richard Parker
Director
Marketing Division
Generic Products
2847 Spring Avenue
Cincinnati, OH 45227

Dear Mr. Parker:

Thank you for taking the time to talk with me about the opening in the Marketing Division of Generic Products. I look forward to hearing from you about my application.

Sincerely yours,

Angela Thompson

Angela Thompson

Writing a Follow-up Letter

For the second activity in this chapter, you selected an advertisement in the newspaper. Imagine that you went on an interview for the advertised job. Write a follow-up letter to the interviewer.

GUIDELINES FOR BEING INTERVIEWED

- Do I have a résumé to give the interviewer?
- Have I allowed enough time to get to the interview?
- Have I dressed appropriately for the interview?
- Am I relaxed and confident?
- Do I speak clearly?
- Am I enthusiastic?
- Am I prepared to answer questions clearly, honestly, and carefully?
- Do I have questions to ask the interviewer?

Profiles in Communication

Wanda E. Snowton

   In searching for a job, the first place that many people go is the local office of the state employment commission. And when they do, the person they talk to may be an employment counselor like Wanda Snowton.

   Ms. Snowton says that her job in her state's employment commission gives her a chance to work in both of the fields she studied in college: business and sociology. Her business training helps her not only in recognizing the qualities and skills sought by employers but also in filling out the required forms for the employment commission. Her sociology training helps her to better understand and advise clients from different cultures and backgrounds.

   Ms. Snowton may spend about an hour interviewing new clients to learn what their work experience is, why they are currently unemployed, what type of job they are seeking, and whether they want to file for unemployment compensation. Ms. Snowton observes, "Some people come into the office worried and discouraged because they're out of work, some are cheerful, even joking, happy to be looking for a new job and confident about getting one." She adapts her tone and approach to the client, being sympathetic with those who are discouraged and optimistic with those who are in good spirits.

   "Most of the time," Ms. Snowton states, "I'm primarily concerned about the tone of voice I use. It's my tone that lets people know my feelings and attitudes. That and my expressions." Because of the importance of tone and facial expressions, she tries never to become angry or impatient. "Sometimes I have several deadlines or a heavy work load, but I continue to show my concern by sounding and looking pleasant."

   Ms. Snowton advises individuals who are being interviewed for employment to be careful, to state facts rather than opinions, to arrange for child care and transportation to work beforehand, and to be honest.

   For young people interested in a career as an employment counselor, Ms. Snowton suggests that they develop their communication skills, get a college degree, and work in a busy retail business for a year. She says, "I write reports and talk to people every day. My degree helped prepare me for my job. But the best training I had was working at a busy restaurant. There I learned to have the attitude that 'the customer is always right.' "

SUMMARY

An interview is a form of communication in which people obtain information by asking questions. The interviewer conducts the interview; the interviewee is the person being interviewed. Although there are many types of interviews, two that are particularly important to you are the job interview and the college interview.

Always be well prepared for an interview. Thorough preparation involves reading the advertisement for the job or college carefully, determining the purpose of the interview, finding information about the company or college, knowing what you want to tell the interviewer about yourself, knowing what kinds of information you want the interviewer to tell you, preparing a résumé, scheduling an appointment, and rehearsing the interview.

Interviewers will be alert for anything you might reveal about yourself that will help them decide whether or not they should make you a job offer or accept you for their college. Among the characteristics they look for are promptness, good appearance, poise, flexibility, honesty, initiative, and good communication skills.

An interviewer is likely to ask you four kinds of questions: those that request information, those that probe more deeply, those that check understanding, and those that require you to take a stand.

After the interview you should show your appreciation for the interview by following up with a short note of thanks.

CHAPTER VOCABULARY

Look back through this chapter and find the meaning of each of the following terms. Write each term and its meaning in your communication journal.

college interview	interviewer	poise
interview	job interview	résumé
interviewee		

REVIEW QUESTIONS

1. An interview is a form of communication in which people obtain information by asking questions. How is an interview different from a question-and-answer session in which students ask questions of a guest speaker?

2. The person conducting the interview is called the interviewer. What is the person being interviewed called?

3. Reading the advertisement for the job or college carefully is the first step in preparing for an interview. What are three other steps?

4. What is the difference between general qualifications and specific qualifications?

5. A résumé is a brief account of your experience. In general, what information should you include in your résumé?

6. Interviewers look for promptness in an applicant. What are five other qualities they look for?

7. Why must you be careful to dress appropriately for an interview?

8. You may be asked four types of questions during an interview. What are they?

9. An interview is not a one-way form of communication. What types of questions should you ask the interviewer?

10. You want to leave the interviewer with a favorable impression of you. How should you follow up an interview?

DISCUSSION QUESTIONS

1. Imagine that you are interviewing for a job selling clothing at a department store. Discuss the importance of good appearance in interviewing for that job.

2. The Equal Employment Opportunity Commission does not allow questions that deal with plans for marriage, religious preference, racial background, and other personal matters. Discuss with your classmates what you think are the reasons for disallowing such questions.

3. Horace Mann once wrote, "Unfaithfulness in the keeping of an appointment is an act of clear dishonesty. You may as well borrow a person's money as his time." Discuss the meaning of this quotation. Do you agree or disagree with it? Why? Discuss what advice you think Mann would give to a person preparing for an interview.

4. The French philosopher Voltaire suggested, "Judge a man by his questions rather than by his answers." Discuss the meaning of this quotation with your classmates. Then discuss what the interviewee can learn from the questions the interviewer asks. Finally, discuss what the interviewer can learn from the questions the interviewee asks.

5. Interviewers look for honesty in applicants. Discuss with your classmates why this trait is so important and what an applicant can do to establish his or her honesty. Then discuss the meaning of the following quotation by Archbishop Richard Whately and its relation to interviewing: " 'Honesty is the best policy,' but he who acts on that principle is not an honest man."

1. Analyzing Interviewing Skills

Watch an interview on television and report to your class on it. What kinds of questions did the interviewer ask? How effective were these questions in getting the interviewee to talk? How could the questions have been made more effective?

2. Gathering Information from Others About Interviews

Ask your parents or an older friend to describe a job interview. In this person's eyes, was the interview a success or a failure? Why? Report your findings to your classmates.

3. Preparing for and Practicing a College Interview

A. Choose a two- or four-year college in which you are interested. Write questions that you would ask an interviewer from that college. Then write your answers to these questions. Compare your questions and answers with those of your classmates.

B. Write a letter to the college of your choice asking for an interview.

C. Working with a partner, conduct a college interview. Have one person act as the interviewer and the other as the interviewee. After the interview, invite and respond to feedback from your classmates.

4. Preparing for and Practicing a Job Interview

A. Imagine you are going to interview for a summer job. List the questions you would expect an interviewer to ask you. Then list your answers to these questions. Compare your questions and answers to those of your classmates.

B. Working with a partner, conduct an interview for a summer job. Have one person act as the interviewer and the other as the interviewee. After the interview, listen to and respond to feedback from your classmates.

5. Identifying Techniques for Reducing Nervousness

Discuss with your classmates techniques you can use to help reduce your nervousness before an interview. Compile a class list of these techniques and copy the list in your communication journal.

Real-Life Speaking Situations

1. When you hunt for a job, you want to make every effort to land one that is right for you. Giving a positive impression of yourself during an interview can determine your success in obtaining the job you want. Imagine that you see an ad in the newspaper for a job that you think would suit you perfectly. Stop for a minute and identify such a job. Imagine further that you meet the qualifications listed in the ad. Write a résumé, giving your personal data and qualifications, just as you would if you were actually replying to the ad. Make sure that your résumé is complete and shows that you meet the requirements for the job. If you were invited to interview for this job, how would you go about making a favorable impression on the interviewer? What would you wear? What would you present as your strongest qualifications for the job? At an interview for this job, the interviewer might likely ask why you want the job and why you think you should be hired for it. Construct a brief answer to these questions. Be prepared to discuss your answer in class.

2. Interviewers need to have a strong command of verbal and nonverbal skills. They must be able to ask questions that will encourage an interviewee to open up and give informative answers. Along with verbal and nonverbal skills, interviewers also need to have a number of personal qualities that enable them to deal effectively with applicants. What are some of these qualities? Make a list of the five most important personal qualities that an interviewer needs. Now show how these qualities come into play by applying them in the following interview situation. You are an interviewer asking questions of an applicant for a summer job. So far, the applicant has given only very short answers, and you want the person to become more at ease and more talkative because you feel that he or she would be a good candidate for the job. Write a short dialogue that you can present in three or four minutes, showing how you would draw out this applicant. Be prepared to give your dialogue in class and, following your dialogue, to conduct a short question-and-answer session in which you discuss the personal qualities that you feel are necessary for an interviewer to have.

UNIT THREE
PUBLIC SPEAKING

GETTING READY

OBJECTIVES:

After studying this chapter, you should be able to

1. List possible topics for a speech.

2. Identify qualities that make a topic a good one to use.

3. Select a suitable topic for a speech.

4. Identify major speech purposes.

5. Tell the difference between a general purpose and a specific purpose.

6. Write a thesis statement.

7. List data about members of your audience and draw conclusions about their knowledge, their interests, and their attitudes.

8. Determine how the occasion will affect your speech.

9. Differentiate between fact and opinion.

10. Identify five other kinds of information that are useful in preparing a speech.

Joel Foster looked forward to giving his first speech. "I'm really excited," he thought. "I know I'll knock their socks off with it. It will be the best speech in the whole class." As he closed his eyes, he could hear the applause. "No doubt about it. It'll be the greatest!" Suddenly Joel remembered one nagging problem. "Uh oh, just one thing. I don't have any idea what I'll talk about—and the speech is due tomorrow morning!"

Have you ever been in a situation like Joel's? Some people behave just as he did. They spend their time daydreaming about their success and do not sit down to begin preparing their speech until the night before it is due. In a panic, they pick the first topic that comes to mind. Then they rush to an encyclopedia to find something to say and try desperately to complete their speech on time. Few speakers who follow such a course achieve their dreams of success.

The key to making a successful speech is thoughtful preparation. Since getting started can often be difficult, this chapter presents steps that you can follow to make sure that you start off on the right track.

GATHERING IDEAS FOR YOUR TOPIC

Very soon you will give your first formal speech in class. What will its topic be? There are many topics that you can develop into a good speech, if only you take the time to give the matter some thought. Speech topics in subject areas that you are interested in and that you already know something about will be your best choices. A good way to begin identifying a topic for your speech is to list a subject area that interests you under each of the following headings.

Vocational Knowledge and Interests

Do you have a part-time job after school or on weekends? If so, that job should give you an interesting subject area for a speech. For instance, Joel Foster has been working part-time for nearly two years at a nursery that specializes in lawn and garden care. He works in the greenhouses during the winter and with a lawn maintenance crew during the summer. Under *Vocational Knowledge and Interests,* Joel would write "lawn and garden care."

Whatever activity you are involved in, you know many interesting things about it. For instance, if your hobby is painting, you might choose to talk about the materials you use, how to mix colors, or a famous work of art you especially admire.

Some people have already made tentative decisions about what they want to do after they graduate from high school. If you have already decided on a vocation, such as being a doctor, a beautician, an accountant, a pharmacist, or a computer scientist, write the name of that vocation under this heading.

Hobbies and Activities

No doubt you have several hobbies or activities that you enjoy. Perhaps you collect stamps, play a musical instrument, dance, participate in sports, or play chess. If you have several hobbies, write the one that interests you most under this heading. Joel Foster's choice was easy. This year he joined the school football team. Although he has had only a few minutes of playing time so far, he loves the sport. Football tops his list under this heading.

Past Events

Perhaps something that happened in the past has really captured your interest. For example, a few weeks ago Joel Foster watched a television program about the sinking of the *Titanic,* and he has since read several books about this event. He would write "the sinking of the *Titanic*" under this heading.

Current Issues

Every day issues that affect us all are discussed in newspapers, magazines, and other news sources. On the international level, Joel Foster is concerned about the Arab-Israeli conflict and terrorist activities. On the local level, he is worried that budget cutbacks will cause his local library to close earlier, making it difficult for him to study at night. He would write one of these issues under this heading.

Places

Either from personal experience or from reading, you may have discovered a place that especially appeals to you. Joel spent a week last summer at Myrtle Beach, and he hopes to visit Hawaii some day. He would list one of these places under this heading.

Processes

No doubt, you are familiar with many processes. You know how to do certain things, how to make certain things, and how certain things work. Joel helps his father tune the family automobile, and he knows how to build model cars. He could list one of these processes under this heading.

People

You may have a relative or may know someone whose courage, skill, integrity, or thoughtfulness impresses you. In addition, you probably admire at least one famous person because of that person's effect on history, culture, sports, or entertainment. Joel's special heroes are his grandfather, who is a firefighter who has been decorated twice for bravery, and Bill Cosby. He would list one of these people under this heading.

ACTIVITY: **Choosing Subjects for Speeches**

Write the seven headings for subjects on a piece of paper, placing each heading on a separate line. After each heading, list one subject area that is of particular interest to you. Then from the seven subject areas you listed, select three that interest you most.

CHOOSING THE TOPIC

A subject area is too broad to use as a topic because it cannot be covered effectively in one speech. Whereas a **subject area** is a general area, like football, a **topic** suitable for a speech is a specific category within a subject area. How can you break down a subject area into a speech topic? A good way is to list as many specific ideas as you can under the subject area.

Brainstorming

Brainstorming means listing whatever comes into your mind as you think about a subject. When you brainstorm, you make your list quickly without stopping to evaluate what you write. By applying brainstorming to a subject area, you can compile a list of possible topics for your speech.

When you *brainstorm,* each topic idea you think of will suggest others, and you will soon have a substantial list.

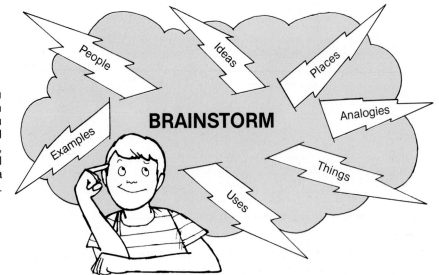

For example, Joel Foster decided to brainstorm the subject area *football* to discover possibilities for a specific topic for his speech. In just a few minutes, he was able to list all the following items:

Football

players	offense	defense	passing
tackling	plays	calling plays	stadiums
rules	injuries	equipment	stretching
zones	positions	cheerleaders	coaching
practice	strategy	numbers	the ball
placekicking	punting	blocking	pass patterns

Brainstorming provides you with choices. It is much easier to select a topic from a list of specific possibilities than to try to think of a topic without such a list. After Joel had compiled his list, he read through it and selected the three topics that interested him most: calling plays, pass patterns, and placekicking. Any one of these would make a good topic for Joel's speech. Because Joel liked placekicking best, he chose this as his topic.

Limiting Your Topic

Limit your topic enough so that you can cover it effectively in one speech. Limiting a topic is much the same as limiting a subject area. Narrow your topic by focusing on specific aspects, examples, parts, uses, and other features of it. For example, another student in Joel's class, Kim, limited her topic, *types of games*, in the following way.

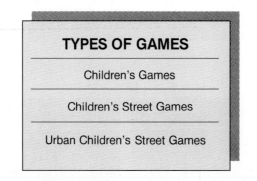

TYPES OF GAMES

Children's Games

Children's Street Games

Urban Children's Street Games

Joel's topic, *placekicking,* is still too broad to be covered effectively in one speech because there are so many different aspects of placekicking— the use of placekicking in football strategy, famous plays involving placekicking, the two different styles of placekicking, and many more. For his speech Joel further limited his topic to *soccer-style placekicking.*

Notice where Joel now stands in his speech preparation:

Subject Area: football
Topic (his favorite item on the list under football): placekicking
Limited Topic: soccer-style placekicking

Choosing a Subject and Limiting It to a Topic for a Speech

Compile a list similar to Joel's for each of your three subject areas. Brainstorm one list at a time. Write down as many ideas about your subject area as come to mind. When you run out of ideas, put your list aside. Then return to it later. See if you can add to your list so that you have at least thirty items.

After you have completed your three lists, read each list again. On each list, check the three items that interest you most. Next, consider these three items, keeping in mind that preparation for your speech will take more than one day. Which of these items would you be most willing to spend some time developing? Which would you be most willing to research? For each list, select the item that interests you more than the others. This item is your speech topic for this subject area. Finally, limit each of these topics so that it can be covered effectively in one speech.

KNOWING YOUR PURPOSE

Your **purpose** is what you intend to achieve in your speech. You will have both a general purpose and a specific purpose.

General Purpose

Your **general purpose** is the overall intent of your speech. Speeches may be given for several different general purposes. For example, in many

A person telling a humorous story speaks to *entertain;* a tour guide at a historical site speaks to *inform;* a person making a proposal at a city council meeting speaks to *persuade.*

social situations, the general purpose of a speech may be simply to **entertain an audience**—to amuse the audience or even just to make its members laugh. For the speeches you give in school, your general purpose will likely be either to entertain, to inform, or to persuade.

A speech to **inform** is given to present new information to an audience or to give new insights into information that an audience has. Speeches to inform are given in many situations. For example, experts give public lectures, salespeople demonstrate products, and supervisors explain procedures. On page 598 you will find a speech to inform.

A speech to **persuade** is given to stimulate interest in a topic, to change an attitude or a belief, or to move an audience to action. For example, politicians try to persuade voters to support them, religious leaders try to get followers for the teachings of their churches or temples, and salespeople try to persuade consumers to buy products. On page 603 you will find a speech to persuade.

In speech communication classes, teachers usually assign speeches according to general purpose. Therefore, at this stage of preparation, you will know whether your speech is supposed to entertain, to inform, or to persuade. Joel Foster's assignment was to prepare a speech to inform.

Specific Purpose

Once you know your general purpose, you must define your specific purpose. The **specific purpose** of a speech is its specific goal, which is stated in one complete sentence. If the general purpose of a speech is to inform, then the specific purpose will be a statement of what particular information the speaker intends to present to the audience. For example, for his speech to inform, Joel may want to show the class the steps in learning soccer-style placekicking. Another student in Joel's class may have the specific purpose of explaining how a printing press works. Other specific purposes may include

explaining how the United Nations was formed;
convincing an audience to vote for a particular candidate for class president;
motivating a class to see a school play.

Each of these examples is an idea for a specific purpose. You will want to express your idea for your specific purpose in a complete sentence, which will likely need careful revision before you go much further with your preparation.

The following guidelines will help you write your specific purpose.

1. *Express the specific purpose as a complete sentence.* Joel Foster wants to talk about soccer-style placekicking. Soccer-style placekicking is a topic, but it is not yet a complete thought. "The steps in soccer-style placekicking" is moving closer to the goal. A complete sentence would be, "I want to explain the steps in soccer-style placekicking."

2. *Make the specific purpose as precise as possible.* Joel's specific purpose, "I want to explain the steps in soccer-style placekicking," is still not precise enough. How many steps are there in the process? If you can get your sentence down to a number of steps, points, parts, stages, or reasons, the specific purpose will be much more precise. Therefore, Joel would rewrite his specific purpose, "I want to explain the four steps in soccer-style placekicking."

A football player always has a specific goal, or purpose, in each play in a game. This player's goal, for example, is to carry the ball into the end zone. Like this player, make sure you know your specific purpose in each speech you give.

3. *Make sure the specific purpose contains only one idea.* Suppose Joel had decided on the specific purpose, "I want to explain the four steps in soccer-style placekicking and the three steps in punting." The sentence is not a good choice as a specific purpose because it includes two separate ideas: (1) the steps in soccer-style placekicking, and (2) the steps in punting. Each idea might be good for a speech purpose, but both purposes should not be used in the same speech.

4. *Write the specific purpose sentence as a declarative sentence.* "How do you placekick?" is a good question, but it is not a good specific speech purpose because it does not state an idea. "Today's Placekicking" might be a good title, but it does not give any idea of what you will say in the speech. "I want to explain the four steps in soccer-style placekicking" is a complete declarative sentence that fully states the specific purpose of the speech.

5. *Include a word in the speech purpose that shows your intent.* The words that show your intent should be in keeping with the general purpose of the speech. If the general purpose is to inform, you would use such words as *explain, show,* or *give.* If the general purpose is to persuade, you would use such words as *prove, convince,* or *motivate.* Joel used the words *to explain* to show his intent to inform.

Notice how far Joel has come in his speech preparation:

Subject Area: football
Topic: placekicking
Limited Topic: soccer-style placekicking
General Purpose: to inform
Specific Purpose: I want to explain the four steps in soccer-style placekicking.

ACTIVITY: Writing Specific Purposes for Speeches

For each of the limited topics you selected for the Activity on page 188, write a specific speech purpose. Be prepared to show your classmates how each specific purpose follows the guidelines for a statement of specific purpose.

WRITING A THESIS STATEMENT

Writing a thesis statement is the final step in stating your topic. A **thesis statement** expresses the overall concern of the speech. In other words, it expresses the most important idea a speaker wishes to tell an audience about a topic. Just as a topic sentence guides the development of a paragraph, a thesis statement guides the development of a speech. Expressed as a complete sentence, the thesis statement clarifies a speaker's purpose by stating the key point of the speech. Therefore, if your specific purpose were stated "I want to explain that the federal government is divided into three branches," your thesis statement would give your audience more information about your key points. Your thesis statement might be "The federal government is divided into the executive branch, the legislative branch, and the judicial branch." If your purpose were stated "I want to explain the characteristics of the six major classifications of show dogs," your thesis statement might be "Show dogs are classified according to their characteristics as hounds, terriers, working dogs, toys, sporting dogs, and nonsporting dogs."

If you already know a great deal about your topic, you can write your thesis statement at this stage of your planning. For most of your speeches, however, you will have to complete some or all of your research before you can write the thesis statement. For example, if your purpose were to explain how the United Nations was formed, you might need to wait until you have done some research before you could state the number of steps in the formation and what those steps were.

Since Joel knows the steps involved in soccer-style placekicking, he would be able to complete his thesis statement at this stage of preparation. Joel's preparation has now come this far:

Subject Area: football
Topic: placekicking
Limited Topic: soccer-style placekicking
General Topic: to inform
Specific Purpose: I want to explain the four steps in soccer-style placekicking.
Thesis Statement: The four steps in soccer-style placekicking are to spot the ball, to mark off the steps, to approach the ball, and to kick the ball.

ACTIVITY: Writing and Identifying Thesis Statements for Speeches

Write a thesis statement for each of the purpose sentences you developed for the Activity on page 191. Then identify each of the following sentences as either a specific purpose sentence or a thesis statement. Be prepared to discuss your basis for making each identification.

1. The four main components of a computer are the central processing unit, the disk drive, the keyboard, and the monitor.

2. I want to inform the class about the three major causes of juvenile delinquency.

3. I want to convince the class of the value of vocational education.

4. People should donate to United Appeal because one gift covers many charities and because almost all of the money donated goes to the charities themselves.

5. The powers of the presidency are held in check by the legislative and judicial branches of government.

KNOWING YOUR AUDIENCE

The people who will hear your speech are your **audience**. Your speech will not be effective if your audience does not have or cannot develop some interest in your topic. By knowing your audience, you can figure out what you will need to do to get that audience to follow and respond to what you have to say.

Notice how attentive these listeners are. This speaker obviously knows his audience and therefore knows how to reach them.

First, you need to ask two groups of questions about your audience. One group of questions gives you specific **demographic data,** or information about the characteristics of a population. This information includes such things as the average age, the living environment, the educational background, the economic conditions, and the gender of the audience you will be facing. Demographic questions include

1. Will the audience be all male, all female, or mixed?
2. Will the audience be composed of teenage students, middle-aged working people, or elderly retirees?
3. Are most members of the audience from an urban, a suburban, or a rural environment?

The other group of questions provides insight into the audience's general attitudes and opinions. The answers to these questions will help you determine how much the members know and are concerned about the topic and what their feelings and beliefs are about it. Questions under this category include

1. Will the audience know a great deal, a little, or very little about this topic?
2. Will the audience be very interested, somewhat interested, or uninterested in this topic?
3. Will the audience's attitude toward this topic be positive, neutral, or negative?

As you answer questions such as these, you may be able to determine in what ways the members of the audience are alike and in what ways they differ. Answering these questions can also help prepare you for problems you may face when you talk on your topic. For instance, if Joel Foster found that the members of his audience had no knowledge of soccer-style place-kicking, he would proceed differently than he would if he found that his audience was familiar with soccer-style placekicking.

The final wording of your speech purpose and the selection of the material you use in the speech are often determined by the conclusions you draw from your study of the audience. For example, imagine that Joel is going to present his speech on soccer-style placekicking to the Northside Parents Club. Keeping his audience in mind, he will adapt the emphasis of his speech to parents' interests. Therefore, he will want to select supporting material that parents will find interesting and convincing. For example, he may use the steps in soccer-style placekicking to illustrate the pressures that a placekicker faces. In speaking on the same topic to his classmates, Joel may emphasize instructions that would help classmates actually learn how to placekick.

Knowing your audience may not alter your topic selection, but such knowledge certainly will alter the examples, details, and other supporting information you will use to develop that topic.

For Better or For Worse®   **by Lynn Johnston**

In most speaking situations you will have to suit your speech to your audience—not find an audience that suits your speech.

ACTIVITY: Analyzing an Audience

Consider your classmates as your audience. With your classmates in mind, apply the two sets of questions discussed in this section to the topic you chose in the Activity on page 188. Then explain what effect, if any, the answers to those questions will have on the emphasis of your speech and on the material you will use to present your topic.

KNOWING YOUR OCCASION

Every speech that you prepare will be given for some **occasion,** which includes the time, the place, and various other conditions that help define the setting in which the speech will be given. Knowing the occasion will help you decide how appropriate your topic is and how you should proceed with it. For each speech you give, ask yourself the following questions regarding the occasion.

1. *When will the speech be given?* The answer to this question should include both the date and the time of day. The date your speech is given may be the reason for the speech. For example, you might be asked to give a speech about Martin Luther King, Jr., on his birthdate or one about patriotism on the Fourth of July.

If your speech happens to be given on or close to some significant date but is not about the person or event that made that date significant, try referring to the significance of the date in your speech. For example, if you were giving a speech on December 7 about increasing military spending, referring to the date as the anniversary of the surprise attack on Pearl Harbor might alert the audience to the need for readiness.

The time of day also affects your speech. For example, imagine that you were to give your speech early in the morning. You would probably be safe in assuming that some members of your audience would still be sleepy. Therefore, you might want to include some audience participation in your speech. You probably would not want to turn the lights out and show slides for fifteen minutes.

2. *Where will the speech be given?* The size of the room, the seating arrangement, the presence of a speaker's stand, and other features of the location where you will give the speech may all affect your presentation and,

If you are asked to speak at a special occasion, such as a graduation ceremony, tailor your speech to what is special about that occasion.

to some extent, the content of the speech. For example, if the room were very large, you would need to prepare different types of visual aids from those you would use if the room were very small.

3. *What are the restrictions for the speech?* Restrictions that are placed on your speech are very important to your preparation. Do you have a time limit? A time limit certainly affects the amount of material you can use. Are you allowed to use notes? Whether or not you may use notes affects the way you will deliver your speech.

ACTIVITY: **Determining the Effect of Occasion on a Speech**

Apply to your own speech each of the questions presented in this section concerning occasion. Then discuss what effect, if any, this information will have on the emphasis of your speech and on the kind of material you will use.

SUPPORTING YOUR THESIS STATEMENT

You now have a topic and a purpose for your speech, and you have identified your audience and your speaking environment. However, whether you plan to entertain, to inform, or to persuade, you will need to find information to back up, or support, your main idea expressed by your thesis statement. The support you choose must be logical, that is, it must follow the rules and principles of correct reasoning discussed in Chapter 5. Your

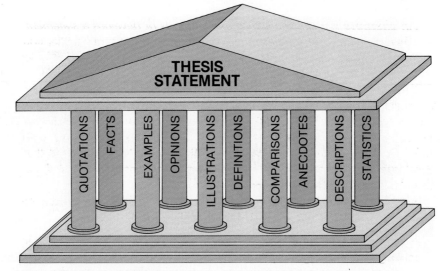

Many different kinds of information can be used to support your thesis statement. You will probably never use all of them in one speech.

support must also be ethical—conforming to accepted standards of right and wrong. At times, your support may be emotional, arousing strong feelings in your audience.

Facts and Opinions

Usually the best material for your speech is fact. Statements of **fact** contain information that can be proved, or verified, by testing, by observing, or by consulting reference material. That iron weighs more than aluminum, that robins can fly, and that triangles are three-sided figures are all facts. You can weigh equally sized pieces of iron and aluminum; you can observe robins flying; and you can consult a dictionary for a definition of a triangle.

Statements of **opinion** express personal beliefs or attitudes. Such statements contain information that cannot be proved. That roses are more beautiful than tulips, that spaghetti with pesto sauce tastes better than spaghetti with clam sauce, and that the Dodgers will win tomorrow's game against the Braves are all opinions. Beauty and taste are matters of personal likes and dislikes. Predictions about the future, such as who will win a game, cannot be proved in the present and are, therefore, always opinions.

In some situations, you may seek expert opinion. An **expert opinion** is a statement of belief about a subject from a person who is recognized as an authority on that subject. For example, an opinion from a publisher on how the market for nonfiction will continue to grow, from a coach on how the level of football talent in the district will be seen by college recruiters, and from a chef on how cooking with lighter sauces will change the look of gourmet foods are all expert opinions. In addition to opinions, experts can also supply facts. For instance, a high-school coach can report on how many college recruiters have visited players on the team.

Examples and Illustrations

An **example** is a single instance that supports or develops a statement. An **illustration** is a detailed example. When you are not sure whether you understand someone, you often ask, "Can you give me an example?" Just as you look for examples from others, so people look for examples from you. In planning his speech, Joel Foster looked for examples to support the statement that soccer-style placekickers are often much smaller than other players on the team. While reading, he found that Chris and Matt Bahr, the brothers who kick for Los Angeles and Cleveland, respectively, are both under six feet tall and weigh less than 180 pounds. Joel also found that placekicker Jim Breech, who is 5'7" and 165 pounds, was the smallest player on the Cincinnati Bengals in 1985.

Had Joel's speech been longer, or had he cared to do so, he could have expanded the Jim Breech example into the following illustration:

Many people who are relatively small are aware that their chances of making it as a college or professional football player are very slim. The only position where this is not true is placekicker. Today placekickers are the smallest players on the team. For example, look at Jim Breech of the

Cincinnati Bengals. When the players are in street clothes, Jim looks more like a mascot or a trainer than like one of the players. Standing only 5′7″ tall and weighing only 165 pounds, he was by far the smallest player on the team's 1985 roster.

Anecdotes

An **anecdote** is a brief, often amusing, story. Do your ears perk up when someone says, "That reminds me of a story"? In many cases you can gain your audience's interest and can aid understanding by telling a story. The purpose of an anecdote is to give information in a form that an audience will remember. Therefore, when Joel recalled a humorous incident that had happened to him the first time he kicked off in a game, he used that story as part of his speech introduction:

I wanted to do my very best that first game. We opened the game kicking off, and I had visions of kicking the ball all the way into the end zone where no one could run it back. The whistle blew and all eyes were on me as I moved toward the ball. Just as I was into the kick itself, a gust of wind blew the ball off the kicking tee. I kicked at the ball, missed it entirely, and fell flat on my back. Luckily, the referee had blown his whistle just as the ball was falling off the tee, so I got to try again. But I was never so embarrassed in my life.

Statistics

Statistics are numerical facts. Saying that "only six out of every ten registered voters voted in the last school election" or that "unemployment dropped $1\frac{1}{2}$ percent" gives useful information in a short statement. Keep in mind that citing a few statistics may help you make the speech more informative. However, giving too many statistics can be boring and distracting. Look for statistics that are particularly impressive or that make some point clearly. In his speech on placekicking, Joel made the following statement using statistics to show what a large percentage of college kickers use the soccer style: "In the last year, more than 85 percent—that's more than eight out of every ten placekickers on major college teams—kicked soccer style."

Comparisons

A **comparison** is a statement that shows the similarities between objects, people, or ideas. Comparisons are used in speeches to help listeners relate new ideas to ideas that are more familiar to them.

Comparisons may be figurative or literal. A **figurative comparison** shows the similarities between things that are essentially unalike. For example, you may speak of a person as being "as slow as molasses in the wintertime." In this comparison, you are comparing a person to a thick syrup. How are they alike? They both move slowly. A **literal comparison** shows the similarities between things that are essentially alike. For example, *Tom runs slower than Mike* is a literal comparison.

Dagwood has mistaken the cook's statement for a *figurative comparison;* however, the cook is actually making a *literal comparison.*

Occasionally, a comparison is phrased as a **contrast,** which shows the differences between two things. For instance, the following statement is a contrast: "Unlike last year's team, on which most of the starters were seniors, this year's team is made up mostly of sophomores."

Definitions

A **definition** explains what a word or a concept means. Whenever you use words and concepts that may not be understood by everyone in your audience, you will want to define them carefully. For example, in Joel Foster's speech on football, he defined *soccer-style* in the following way: "*Soccer-style* means approaching the ball at an angle and kicking the ball with the instep as the leg crosses the body."

Descriptions

A **description** is a word picture of a person, place, thing, or event. In your research, you may find a good, clear description of some aspect of your topic. Accurate descriptions help an audience to see and hold a mental picture that corresponds to the actual thing described. For example, when Joel was explaining the importance of posture in getting ready to kick, he said, "Before kicking the ball, kickers stand with their arms swinging freely at their sides, their weight on their left foot, which is placed slightly ahead of the right, their shoulders square to the ground, and their eyes fixed on the point where the ball is placed."

Quotations

A **quotation** contains the exact words of another person. Most of the time, you will express your ideas in your own words. However, in some cases you will find that someone has said something so well that you want to use those exact words. For example, to sum up the importance of sportsmanship in football, Joel might have used the following quote by Grantland Rice in *Alumnus Football:* "For when the One Great Scorer comes to write against your name,/He marks—not what you won or lost—but how you played the game."

Profiles in Communication

"In the auction business, you have to know your product," says auctioneer Dave Manor, "because in an auction you introduce an item, set the price, and sell it in minutes."

Even though Dave Manor sometimes goes to great lengths to learn about a product he is going to sell, he refrains from talking too specifically about items during a sale because he feels he cannot be a specialist in everything. "You need to know enough about a product to answer customers' questions," he comments, "but, of course, you can't hope to be a master of all trades."

However, one thing Mr. Manor, championship chanter, is master of is the auctioneer's rapid-fire delivery. He says the reason auctioneers use the traditional rapid chant, which includes about one-half filler words plus repeated numbers, is both that people expect it and that it keeps the action going and the excitement high. To learn the chant, he went to auction school and practiced a great deal.

Besides chanting, Mr. Manor's training included nonverbal communication, such as holding out his hand to the audience to mean "I want something from you," always standing not too far above the audience, establishing eye contact, and dressing to suit the audience.

Since the auctioneer is an arbitrator between the buyer and the seller, Mr. Manor believes it is vital to gain the trust of the audience in a short time. He says, "First I tell a personal story to make the people feel comfortable, like we're old friends. I also try to put myself in the other person's place and have compassion. Most people react differently in situations they're unaccustomed to. I try to take that into account."

Mr. Manor uses phrases that help create good will by making the buyer and the seller more comfortable. For example, he will say "conditions have changed" for a client rather than the client "went broke." In addition, to make sure the buyers are satisfied when the sale is over, he begins by explaining the formal conditions of the sale.

To those who are interested in selling a product, Dave Manor advises, "Know your product, know your customer, tell the truth, advertise, and, as Davy Crockett said, 'Be sure you're right; then go ahead.' "

Vivid quotations can help make your speeches especially interesting. However, you must limit the number and the length of quotations you use. After all, you want the speech to be yours, not just a collection of other people's words and ideas.

When you do use quotations, of course, you must give credit to the source from which the words were taken. You will learn how to credit material in the next chapter.

ACTIVITY: Recognizing Different Kinds of Supporting Information

Read the editorial page of your newspaper every day for a week. Find examples, illustrations, anecdotes, statistics, comparisons, definitions, descriptions, and quotations that writers use to support main points or to clarify ideas. Share your findings with your classmates.

GUIDELINES FOR GETTING STARTED

- Have I chosen a topic that interests me?
- Have I thought about my own knowledge of this topic?
- Do I know my general purpose?
- Have I clearly identified my specific purpose?
- Do I have a well-worded thesis statement?
- Have I considered my audience's interest, knowledge, and point of view concerning my topic?
- Have I considered the occasion of the speech?
- Have I considered the types of information I will need to support my main point?

SUMMARY

Getting ready to give a speech involves a systematic approach to topic selection. First, identify subject areas in which you are interested and about which you already have some knowledge. When given a choice of subject area, select one from the following categories: vocational knowledge and interest, hobbies and activities, past events, current issues, places, processes, and people.

Second, you need to determine your topic. To do this, brainstorm your subject area to compile a list of specific topics. From this list, choose one topic and limit it further to a manageable size.

Third, you need to know your purpose. The general purpose of a speech is either to entertain, to inform, or to persuade. The specific purpose is the specific goal you want to achieve in your speech. A well-written specific purpose should be a complete declarative sentence that is as definite as possible. It should contain only one idea and should include wording that shows your intent.

After you know your purpose, you need to write a thesis statement. Your thesis statement expresses the most important idea you wish to get across to your audience. You may need to conduct some or all of your research before you can complete this step.

The final wording of your thesis statement and the selection of your supporting material will likely depend on the makeup of your audience. To draw conclusions about your audience, you need to know both your audience's demographic features and your audience's opinions, knowledge, and attitude about your subject.

Nearly every speech is given for some occasion. Determine the significance of when and where the speech will be given, and make sure that you know any restrictions that apply to your speech.

Good speechmaking depends upon the quality of the information used to develop the thesis statement. Support must be logical and ethical. At times, it will be emotional. Information can take the form of facts and opinions, examples and illustrations, anecdotes, statistics, comparisons, definitions, descriptions, and quotations.

CHAPTER VOCABULARY

Look back through this chapter to find the meaning of each of the following terms. Write each term and its meaning in your communication journal.

anecdote	example	opinion
audience	expert opinion	persuade
brainstorming	fact	purpose
comparison	figurative comparison	quotation
contrast	general purpose	specific purpose
definition	illustration	statistics
demographic data	inform	subject area
description	literal comparison	thesis statement
entertain	occasion	topic

REVIEW QUESTIONS

1. One source of ideas for speech topics is vocational knowledge and interest. What are five other sources?

2. Brainstorming can help you list topics under a subject area. After you choose one of these topics, why should you limit it?

3. One general purpose for giving a speech is to entertain. What are two other general purposes?

4. For every speech, you will have both a general purpose and a specific purpose. What is the difference between a general purpose and a specific purpose?

5. After you have identified your specific purpose, you need to make your thesis statement. How does the specific purpose differ from the thesis statement?

6. Demographic data provides you with information about the makeup of an audience. What other information do you need about your audience?

7. The occasion of a speech affects how you will give that speech. What are three questions you should ask yourself about the occasion?

8. A statement of fact contains information that can be proved. How does a statement of opinion differ from a statement of fact?

9. An example is a single instance that supports or develops a statement. How does an illustration differ from an example?

10. A figurative comparison shows the similarities between basically unlike things. How does a literal comparison differ from a figurative comparison?

DISCUSSION QUESTIONS

1. Discuss with your classmates why it is important to find a topic that interests you and that you know something about. Then discuss the seven headings for subject areas included in this chapter. Would you add any headings to this list? If so, what are they? Tell your class why you would add these headings.

2. Discuss why brainstorming is likely to produce better topics for your speeches than just sitting down and trying to come up with a topic. What were the results of your brainstorming sessions? How could you have made these sessions more productive?

3. Imagine that you are giving a speech on soccer-style placekicking. Discuss the ways in which the makeup of each of the following audiences would affect either your specific purpose or your approach in such a speech.

   a. An audience of boys ages 9–14 who are very interested in soccer-style placekicking but who have very little knowledge of the subject

b. An audience of senior citizens who are not very interested in soccer-style placekicking but who have some knowledge of football

c. An audience of exchange students from China who have little direct knowledge of football but are very interested in learning about the game

d. An audience of male and female high-school students who are somewhat interested in learning about soccer-style placekicking and have some knowledge of football

4. Bertrand Russell once wrote, "The degree of one's emotion varies inversely with one's knowledge of the facts—the less you know the hotter you get." First, discuss the meaning of this quotation. Then discuss how the quotation relates to the need to use facts in your speech.

5. Ralph Waldo Emerson advised, "Stay at home in your mind. Don't recite other people's opinions. I hate quotations. Tell me what you know." First, discuss the meaning of this quotation. Then discuss why Emerson would have advised this. Finally, discuss when and where you think quotations can be used effectively in a speech.

ACTIVITIES

1. Identifying Facts and Opinions

Identify the following statements as fact or opinion. If an opinion is an expert opinion, explain why it qualifies as an expert opinion.

a. Ronald Reagan first took office as President on January 20, 1981.

b. The mechanic at the garage told my father that our truck needs a new fuel pump.

c. Cheerleading is an enormously enjoyable high-school activity.

d. Over 60 percent of the students who take speech in our school go on to college.

e. In this school, athletes must maintain a B average to play on teams.

f. As soon as photoelectric cells become more efficient, auto manufacturers will begin building many more electric-powered cars.

g. The decision to lower taxes was a bad one.

h. According to the almanac, we had a record rainfall last year.

i. That comic strip is very funny.

j. My uncle, who repairs electronic office equipment, predicts that voice-operated typewriters will be on the market before the middle of the next decade.

2. Limiting a Topic and Developing It Into a Thesis Statement

A. Choose one of the following subject areas: basketball, cars, school dances, mountains, dogs, or college. Work together with a group of students who have chosen the same subject area. Brainstorm. Bounce ideas off each other until you come up with a list of twenty-five to thirty topics. Then choose one topic from the list and limit it. Compare your limited topic with those of your classmates.

B. For the limited topic you selected in part A of this activity, write a purpose statement. Then turn your purpose statement into a thesis statement. Finally, compile a list of quotations you might use in a speech about this topic. Share your list with your classmates.

3. Analyzing the Use of Statistics in an Article

Read an article about a local sports team's most recent game. Underline all the statistics used in the article. Could any of the points in the article have been made without statistics? If so, identify which ones.

4. Identifying Figurative and Literal Comparisons

Read the following list of comparisons. Identify each as either figurative or literal. Explain your reason(s) for classifying each comparison as you did.

a. The cheerleading squad worked as smoothly as a well-oiled machine.

b. Tom Daniels, Central High's center, was about the same size as Miller High's center.

c. A basketball is slightly larger than a soccer ball.

d. Derrick Williams was a tiger on defense during the entire game.

e. The crowd at game time was larger than any other crowd that had attended a Central High game in more than a year.

5. Using Description Effectively

Play the following game with your classmates. Pretend you are an inanimate object: for example, a baseball, a coffee pot, a Christmas tree, or a rock. Do not tell the class directly what you are, but describe yourself very carefully. If your description is so clear that someone can guess the object you are, you get five points and the person who made the guess gets five points. Every student should have a turn at being an object. The student with the most points wins the game.

6. Planning a Speech on a Personal Topic

A. Take a personal inventory and choose a speech topic from the information you gather on your inventory. Completing the following statements may help you discover a suitable topic.

1. On a Saturday afternoon, I most like to. . . .
2. You can always count on me to tell you my opinion about. . . .
3. My friends think I'm a whiz when it comes to. . . .
4. If I could be anything I want, I would be. . . .
5. I will read almost any book about. . . .
6. My dream is to one day. . . .
7. I spend most of my spare time. . . .
8. My favorite school subject is. . . .
9. When I go to the movies, I most like to see. . . .
10. If I could tell you only one thing about me, it would be that I. . . .

B. Imagine that your general purpose for your speech is to inform your listeners about this topic. Brainstorm your topic and decide upon a specific purpose for your speech.

C. Using the specific purpose you wrote for Part B of this Activity, write your thesis statement and list five facts you would use in your speech to support this thesis statement. Also, list five opinions you would use.

Real-Life Speaking Situations

1. In the course of conversation, people often tell amusing personal anecdotes and secondhand stories about the escapades of others. At a party and in other group situations, someone skilled in storytelling often becomes the center of attention, using a range of verbal abilities to entertain appreciative listeners. Imagine that you are standing outside class with a group of friends, and you want to give them a laugh by telling them about something that has happened to you. Who is your audience? Which friends are you with? What story will you tell them? (Pick a story that will be suitable for telling in class.) Why did you choose that particular story? Why do you think that this story will amuse these specific friends? Practice telling your story, and be prepared to present it in class. Also be ready to take part in a group discussion on how you and your classmates planned your stories to suit your purpose (to amuse), your audience, and the occasion (a class activity).

2. A teacher is usually aware of two things: (1) who is in the "audience" in the classroom and (2) what style of speech is needed to communicate with that audience. Having attended school for a number of years, perhaps you have thought about how you would teach a class. Imagine that you have been asked to teach a class on a subject that interests you and that you are knowledgeable about. What subject would you choose? It need not be a school subject; you can choose a hobby, a vocational skill, a process, or any other area of interest that you feel you could teach to others. Who will be your audience—high-school students? adults taking a community education course? children at a summer camp? Write a short outline of what you would say to your class. Then, based on your outline, prepare a three- to five-minute speech summarizing

   (1) what you would teach (your subject);
   (2) what you would say (what you would teach your students about your subject);
   (3) what approach you would take to teach your students (how you would tailor your speech to communicate with your particular students).

After giving your speech, ask for feedback on your plan for teaching your class.

RETURN
BOOKS HERE

CHAPTER 10

GATHERING INFORMATION

OBJECTIVES:

After studying this chapter, you should be able to

1. Select information from your own experience for speeches.

2. Learn from your observations.

3. Observe more accurately.

4. Conduct an interview.

5. Conduct a survey.

6. Locate a book in the library.

7. Select and use appropriate reference books.

8. Locate newspaper and magazine articles in the library.

9. Use the vertical file.

10. Prepare note cards for speeches.

11. Cite sources in your speech.

Cathy Jackson walked to the front of the room, paused, and then began her speech with a humorous anecdote about her first cheerleading experience. In the body of her speech, she told the class how the idea of cheerleading originated; she discussed how organized cheerleading squads developed; and finally, she commented on the roles of today's cheerleaders. She then summarized her points and concluded with another humorous personal experience. After she finished, Bill, one of the school's cheerleaders, turned to his friend and said, "I didn't think she was going to tell us anything I didn't already know, but I really learned a lot. Cathy was well organized, and she really knew her stuff."

Bill's comment puts speechmaking in perspective: Good speakers are well organized, and even more important, they "really know their stuff." In the next chapter, you will look at how to organize a speech. In this chapter, you will study how to find information for your speech.

YOUR FIRST SOURCE OF INFORMATION—YOURSELF

Start your search for information with yourself. Your own experiences and observations will usually provide you with details to include in your speech.

Personal Experience

Before you look anywhere else, think about what information your own experience can provide about your topic. Remember, you chose your topic because you were interested in it and because you already knew something

If this boy decided to give a speech on music or one of his other interests, he would begin gathering information by reviewing his own knowledge.

about it. Cathy Jackson decided to talk about cheerleading because she had been a cheerleader since eighth grade. As Cathy thought about her cheerleading experience, she realized that she already had information about types of cheers, tumbling routines, cheerleaders' practice, game routines, crowd response, and much more. In fact, her personal experience and knowledge could provide most of the information needed to build her speech.

Everyone has gained knowledge from experience. This knowledge can be used in gathering information for a speech. For example, animal lovers have special knowledge about types of animals, about animal care, and about animal training; automobile enthusiasts know about types of automobile engines, fuels, and automotive design; dancers know about dance steps, choreography, and dance studios.

An important reason for taking the time to gather information from your own experience is that audiences will listen more carefully to speakers who can give firsthand information, that is, information based on personal experience.

For speech assignments asking you to talk about something that happened to you or to demonstrate a product or a procedure, your personal experience *alone* may provide all the information you need to prepare your speech. However, even for topics that require you to get additional information, your own experience provides an excellent starting point for preparation.

Observation

Using yourself as a source does not stop with thinking about your own experience. You also can gain information from planned observation.

Think again about Cathy Jackson's experience in preparing for her speech. Cathy knew that the rival Miller High School cheerleading squad had an excellent reputation for putting on creative routines. By attending a football game at which they were cheering and by carefully observing their behavior, Cathy learned a great deal about how important personality is to a cheerleader. For instance, she saw that none of the cheers used by the Miller High cheerleaders were really much different from those her squad used, nor were their stunts really very difficult. However, every cheerleader's facial expression, gestures, and movements were perfectly in tune with the routine. The cheerleaders showed that they enjoyed what they were doing, and the crowd responded to the cheerleaders' enthusiasm as well as to their words and stunts.

You may find that you can learn a great deal about a topic by observing, especially if your topic requires a how-to approach. Examples of such topics include

printing a newspaper	preparing foods
directing traffic at rush hour	word processing
taking care of an infant	painting cars
training dogs	coaching sports
paving streets	bowling

Giving an accurate description of something is not as easy as it might seem. However, you can improve your powers of observation by using the following guidelines and by practicing.

1. *Make a conscious effort to "see" and not just "look."* Looking means focusing your eyes on some part of the area around you; *seeing*, on the other hand, requires being consciously aware of specific parts of that area. What is the difference? Your eyes record nearly everything that comes before them, but you exert control over what you pay attention to. For example, when you walk down a busy street and come to an intersection, you have trained yourself to look at the color of the traffic light and then to look each way to see whether cars are coming or have stopped. Yet, on that same walk you may pass many shops that you have looked at but are totally unaware of. By concentrating, you can *see* and *remember* a great deal more about things around you. In walking that same busy street, you can train yourself to *see* every store—where exactly each one is, which are busy or not busy, which advertise sales in their windows, and any other information you choose to focus on.

2. *Put what you observe into words.* By saying aloud what you see, you help reinforce the images. For example, look at what is around you. If you take the time to *name* and *describe* aloud everything in your surroundings, you will sharpen your focus, and as a result, you will remember more accurately. In addition, by putting what you see into words, you prompt yourself to notice objects and aspects of those objects that you might miss otherwise. For example, when you say "shoe store" aloud, you are likely to see the kinds of shoes being featured, how they are displayed, and which are on sale.

3. *Recognize whether anything is different or unusual about a person, a setting, or an object.* Do you remember those children's puzzles that ask, "What's wrong with this picture"? The solutions to those puzzles are often obvious: A person in the picture may be wearing two different shoes; a cow may be on top of a house; a police officer may be wearing a uniform with missing buttons. Applying this game to your surroundings can help you sharpen your powers of observation. If you concentrate on a setting, you can determine what is different or unusual. Once you have identified different or unusual features, you are likely to remember them.

4. *Take notes on your observations.* When newspaper reporters go to the scene of a news event to gather information, they always have a tape recorder or a pad and pen or pencil handy. They never trust their observations to memory. Instead, they take quick notes to remind themselves of what they have observed. They ask "Who?" "What?" "Where" "When?" "Why?" and "How?" You can adapt this method of note taking to your circumstances by asking questions that organize your observations into categories. For example, when Cathy visited Miller High, she carried a tally sheet for noting any information that might help her answer such questions as (1) Who were the best cheerleaders? (2) Why did Miller High have such an outstanding cheerleading squad? (3) What kinds of equipment did they use? (4) Where

Personal observation provides reliable information, but only if you can remember what you have seen. Take careful notes as you observe.

did the Miller High cheerleaders make mistakes? (5) When did the cheerleaders practice and for how long? (6) How were practice sessions conducted? As you take notes, be as objective as possible. It is very easy to let your own feelings affect the notes you take. Try to stay with the facts as they occur.

ACTIVITY: Drawing Information from Your Own Experience and from Observation

List three topics that you can talk about almost totally from your own experience. For one of these topics, list six facts that you know but think your classmates may not know. Then see how much more you can learn about your topic from planned observation. Observe carefully over a two- to three-day period. Take notes on your observations. Report to your class what additional information you gained from your observations. Ask for and respond to comments from them on how you might have improved your observations.

YOUR SECOND SOURCE OF INFORMATION—OTHERS

The effective speaker's motto might well be "I've never met a person I couldn't learn something from." In addition to gaining information from your own experience and from your observations, you can also obtain information by asking questions of others. In preparing her cheerleading speech, Cathy Jackson knew from her own experience that certain cheers were easier to learn than others, that some were enjoyable to perform, and that some seemed to appeal to the crowd more than others. However, to find out what other cheerleaders thought, Janet asked questions. First, she talked with Diane Meyers, a college cheerleading advisor who ran a summer cheerleading camp. Later, she questioned her own squad members. In her preparation, Cathy used the two most popular forms of questioning others for information: the interview and the survey.

The Interview

For almost any topic, you can get valuable information by interviewing. An **interview** is a form of communication in which people gain information by asking questions. In Chapter 8 you studied how to be interviewed. In this chapter you will look at how to interview others.

Good interviews do not just happen. To get the most from interviewing someone, you will need to consider setting up the interview, preparing questions, conducting the interview, and recording information during the interview.

Setting Up the Interview. Your first step in setting up an interview is choosing the person you will interview. For any topic, you can likely find several people who can provide you with good information. Start by making a list of the three or four people who might help you the most. Cathy Jackson thought about interviewing Judy Sanchez, Miller High School's cheerleading squad captain whom Cathy knew from cheerleading camp; Diane Meyers, the university cheerleading advisor who ran a successful summer cheerleading camp; and Pat Marshall and Andrea LaSalle, both of whom were highly regarded cheerleading advisors at local high schools.

How should you determine which people on your list to interview? There are three important tests:

1. Is the person knowledgeable about the information you want?
2. Is the person a reliable source?
3. Is the person a primary source or a secondary source? That is, is the source's information firsthand or secondhand?

A **knowledgeable source** is a person who is likely to have the knowledge you want. For information about teaching cheerleading, Cathy selected Diane Meyers because of Diane's experience running a camp. If, on the other hand, Cathy had wanted information on high-school training programs for cheerleaders, she would have been more likely to consider one of the two high-school advisors.

A **reliable source** is a person who can be depended upon to give accurate information. You may know enough about potential interviewees to determine their reliability. Sometimes, however, you just have to assume that because people hold certain positions, they will be likely to give accurate information. Cathy thought that being an advisor to a college squad and managing a well-known summer camp qualified Diane Meyers as a reliable source.

There are at least three aspects of reliability that you should consider carefully. The first is the age of the source. An older person is likely to have had more experience than a younger person has and is therefore often perceived as a more reliable source. The second is memory. As a rule, the longer ago an event took place, the less reliable information about that event will be. The third is bias. Even the most reliable of sources will usually have a point of view that may affect the accuracy of what he or she is reporting.

A **primary source** can give you firsthand information. A **secondary source** can give you only secondhand information. *Firsthand* means that the information comes from a person's direct experience. *Secondhand* means that a person got the information from another source. For example, if chef Pierre tells you how *he* prepares his famous soufflé, he is a primary source giving you firsthand information. If, on the other hand, Pierre tells you how another chef says she prepares the soufflé, he is a secondary source giving you secondhand information. Cathy Jackson chose sources who could all give her firsthand information.

Your second step in setting up an interview is making an appointment with the person you want to interview. You cannot expect to visit someone unannounced and to have that person drop everything to answer your questions. Call or write the person. Explain why you would like an interview and what you hope to gain from the interview.

Displaying a friendly, interested attitude will help you draw out your interviewee and make the interview enjoyable for both of you.

Most of the time you should try for an in-person interview. However, if the person lives far away or if the person's schedule does not permit a face-to-face visit, you may have to conduct the interview by telephone. Telephone interviews are also useful for getting or verifying information quickly. For example, you might call a store to find out if they stock a particular product, or you might call a government official to verify changes in regulations or public needs. The principles for conducting both types of interviews are essentially the same.

Preparing Questions. To prepare intelligent questions, you need to know something about both the information you are seeking and the person you are interviewing. Since Cathy Jackson was herself a cheerleader, she knew enough about cheerleading to phrase good questions. However, she knew only that Diane Meyers was a cheerleading advisor, so Cathy looked up Diane's name in the college directory to get background knowledge of Diane's rank, title, duties, and cheerleading experience. Having some knowledge about the topic and the interviewee before conducting the interview will enable you to ask better questions. In addition, if you display evidence of some preparation, the person will be encouraged to talk more openly to you.

You can phrase the questions in an interview two ways, depending on the information you want. You can ask *open questions,* those that let a person talk at some length, or *closed questions,* those that can be answered with yes or no, or with only a few words. In Cathy Jackson's interview with Diane Meyers, she asked, "How did you first get interested in cheerleading?" This is an open question. She could have asked, "At what age did you actually start cheerleading?" This would have been a closed question. Use open questions when you want to give a person a chance to share feelings and impressions. Use closed questions when you want specific information quickly. Most interviews will include both open and closed questions.

No matter how well you have planned your questions, you are likely to find points in the interview where you need more information about a previous question. In these cases, ask **follow-up questions** to probe for additional information. For example, in answer to Cathy's question, "How did you first get interested in cheerleading?" Diane Meyers gave the short comment, "Oh, I guess I just always thought it would be fun." Since Cathy wanted more information, she quickly followed up with another question: "What was it about the cheerleaders you watched that made you think being one would be fun?" Diane responded, "Well, all the cheerleaders seemed to be enjoying themselves so much. Even when they weren't actually doing a cheer, you could tell that they were just excited about being there." During an interview, you might have to ask several follow-up questions before moving on to your next planned question.

Try to be as objective as possible. Ask questions that are neutral rather than leading. **Neutral questions** give the interviewee no hint of what particular answer you want. **Leading questions** suggest the answer you expect or desire. An example of a neutral question Cathy might ask would be, "How do you feel when the crowd doesn't react to your cheers?" A leading question on the same subject might be, "Doesn't it really make you upset when a crowd doesn't react to your cheers?" By asking neutral questions, you encourage people to contribute their own thoughts rather than giving you answers that they think you want to hear.

Once you have a list of questions, you will want to organize them into the best possible order. An interview should always have a beginning, a middle, and an end. Begin an interview by trying to relieve any tension the person may have about answering your questions. The beginning is a good time to ask easy-to-answer open questions to help the interviewee get going. For example, Cathy Jackson's question "How did you first get interested in cheerleading?" gave Diane Meyers a chance to talk freely about her background.

The body of the interview includes the questions that are meant to provide the greatest amount of specific information. For example, one of the questions that Cathy Jackson asked Diane Meyers was "Do you have any special ways of getting your squad ready for a game?" Usually interviewers ask easy-to-answer questions first and then move on to more difficult ones.

At the conclusion of an interview, thank the interviewee for taking time to answer your questions and give him or her a chance to make any additional comments. A good final question is "Is there anything else you think I should know about this topic?"

Prepare your questions ahead of time. The interviewee will appreciate the advance work you have done and will be more likely to give you an organized set of answers.

Here is a list of the questions that Cathy Jackson prepared to ask Diane Meyers.

Opening questions:
How did you first get interested in cheerleading?
What are some of your most memorable experiences?

Body:

Do you have any special ways of getting your squad ready for a game?

Do your cheerleaders have a plan for what cheers they will use and when they will use them? Or do they wait to see what is happening?

How often do you want the squad to cheer?

Is there a difference between the kinds of cheers the squad does from the sidelines and the kinds they do when they take the field during time-outs?

How much does the squad practice?

What does your squad do if a cheerleader cannot be at a game?

What makes a cheerleader really good?

How important are gymnastics to good cheerleading?

What do you think is the advisor's role in cheerleading?

Is cheerleading really of any value?

Closing:

Thanks for taking the time. Is there anything else you'd like to tell me about cheerleading?

Conducting the Interview. By following some simple advice, you will be able to turn your careful planning into an excellent interview.

First, be courteous during the interview. The person who is taking the time to talk with you is not getting paid to do so. Show patience and encouragement. Show respect for the person regardless of his or her answers.

Second, listen very carefully. At various points in the interview, paraphrase what the person has told you, especially when you have doubts as to the person's meaning. *Paraphrasing* means stating in your own words the idea or feeling you get from another person's words. For example, in answer to Cathy Jackson's question about how often the squad should cheer, Diane Meyers said, "Well, we don't have any set number of times. A squad has to be in tune with the action, so that when the game seems to be building to a climax or when the team especially needs a lot of vocal support, the squad should pick up on it." To make sure she understood, Cathy accurately paraphrased Diane's statement by saying, "From what you're saying, I'm getting the idea that when to cheer is something that a good squad begins to get a feel for—that certain stages of the game are just right for a cheer."

Third, make sure that your nonverbal reactions—your facial expressions and your gestures—are in keeping with the tone you want to convey. Keep good eye contact with the person. Nod to show understanding. Smile occasionally to maintain the friendliness of the interview. How you look and act is likely to determine whether the person will give you a good interview.

Recording Answers. The interview will not do you much good if you cannot remember what the person told you or if you distort what the person said. To prevent such flaws, keep a record of each interview. One way to do this is to tape-record the interview. If you plan to record an interview, ask the interviewee's permission. Some people are very concerned about having their words taped and may refuse permission. In such cases, of course, you would not use a tape recorder. However, if the interviewee does give you permission, take a minute to make sure the recorder is working properly and then proceed.

A second way of keeping a record is to take careful notes. Leave enough space between the questions you have prepared so that you can write in brief answers. If the information is very sensitive—for example, if you are interviewing your principal about a new school policy—you might even want to have the interviewee check the accuracy of your notes.

The Survey

When you take a **survey,** you question, or canvas, people selected at random or by quota in order to obtain information from them. For example, suppose that you wished to determine what kind of jeans students at your high school prefer. One way to find out would be to survey a number of your classmates about their preferences.

The survey is a widely used tool for measuring attitudes and opinions. You are probably already familiar with such professional surveys as the Gallup Poll, the Harris poll, and various other public-opinion polls. These professional polls survey such things as whom the public favors for a particular office or what a community thinks about nuclear power, gun control, or other controversial issues.

People are often pleased to contribute information about their attitudes or opinions when they are asked to participate in a survey.

The value of a survey is that it allows you to get an impression of attitudes very quickly. The problem with surveys is that when they are conducted in ways that violate surveying rules, the results can be inaccurate, misleading, or just plain wrong. Today, professional pollsters follow very detailed guidelines. To take a reasonably accurate informal survey, make sure to follow these guidelines.

1. *Phrase questions clearly and concisely.* Imagine that you are surveying students in your school to find out what kind of jeans they prefer. The question "What kind of clothes do you like to wear?" would be too vague to reveal useful information. The question "What kind of jeans do you wear?" might sound fine, but the words "what kind" might get answers like "designer" or "work" instead of brand names. In addition, the words "do you wear" could cause some students to wonder "When?" "What brand names of jeans do you buy?" would be a good question if you were looking for information on purchased jeans. However, this question does not account for gifts. Moreover, there may be times when you buy jeans different from those you prefer. "What brand name of jeans do you prefer to wear?" is by far the best phrasing if you are seeking information about brand preference. As you can see, you will want to use precise words and phrases in constructing your survey questions.

2. *Ask enough people.* Since there is neither time nor opportunity to ask everyone about his or her preference, you can usually ask only a portion of the total population. Suppose you ask three of your male friends in your grade which brand of jeans they prefer. Your polling method would be faulty because you have not asked enough people. If your school has five hundred students, how many should you poll? In a formal poll such as the Gallup, mathematical tables provide this data. However, in an informal poll such as the ones you will conduct, five to ten percent of the student body—that is, twenty-five to fifty students out of a population of five hundred—would be enough.

ACTIVITY: Gathering Information from Others

Imagine that you are going to give a speech on the popularity of a certain sport, a certain television show, or a certain place to eat. First, choose one of these topics. Then list three people who would be likely to give you the most information on your topic. Which one of these people would you choose to interview? Why? Next, write six questions that you would ask this person. Organize these questions into the most effective order.

Finally, survey the student body in your school, using these same questions. Tell your class how many people you surveyed and how you conducted the poll. Report your findings. Ask for and respond to your classmates' evaluations of your survey.

3. *Survey your group at random.* Another problem with a survey that includes only three male friends in the same grade would be that your three friends were not randomly chosen to be in your survey. Ideally, a survey canvases a sample that has all the main characteristics of the entire group on which you are gathering information. In theory, a **random sample** is one in which every member of a group has the same chance of being selected. One way of getting a random sample is to assign a number to every person in a group, put all the numbers into a container, draw fifty numbers, and then ask those fifty people questions. Another method, called the *fixed-interval method,* is to station yourself at the school entrance and ask your questions of every fifth person who enters (or every eighth or tenth, whatever you decide).

After you have finished your survey, tally the results. Then in your speech, support points you are making with data from your survey.

YOUR THIRD SOURCE OF INFORMATION—THE LIBRARY

Some speeches can be based solely on information found through thinking, observing, and asking questions. However, for most informative or persuasive speeches, you will also need to read about your topic. Through reading, you verify facts you have already discovered and, more important,

The library is the place to go to find detailed factual information that will add substance and power to your speech.

find new information that gives your speech depth. Recall Bill's reaction to Cathy Jackson's speech: "She really knew her stuff!" After thinking, observing, and asking questions, Cathy went to her local library to find more information on her topic. It was through her reading that Cathy found much of the material about the origins of cheerleading and about how and why cheerleading has grown in popularity.

To get an idea of how to find information in a library, follow Cathy Jackson as she does her library work at the Midtown Public Library.

Cathy knew that her topic was cheerleading, and she had already done some library research. Before continuing her research, she decided to talk with the librarian to make sure she would not miss anything. To avoid wasting the librarian's and her own time, Cathy prepared a list of specific questions she wanted answered. Then she asked the librarian for the kinds of sources that might give information to answer those questions. For example, Cathy was curious about when cheerleading originated, how it had evolved, and what the newest trends were in cheerleader training and performance. The librarian advised Cathy to consult the card catalog, key reference works, and recent newspaper and magazine articles on cheerleading.

The Card Catalog

There is always a chance that you may find a gem of a book in the library just by browsing. However, a much more effective method for researching is to use the **card catalog,** which lists all the books contained in a particular library. In the card catalog, cards providing information on books are filed alphabetically in three different ways: by subject, by author, and by title. You will probably start your research as Cathy did, by looking for books under the subject heading. That subject might be cheerleading, computers, architecture, baseball, musical instruments, or any other category.

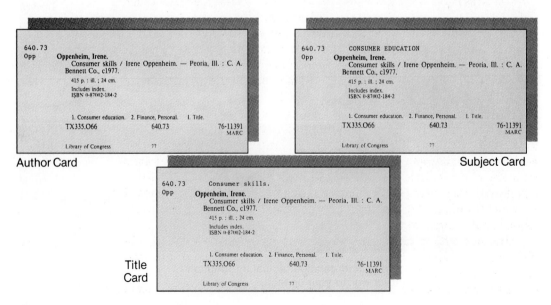

Author Card

Subject Card

Title Card

Of course, if you know the name of an author or the title of a specific book, you would consult the author or title card. For example, you may be a fan of Robert Ludlum, the popular suspense writer. By looking under Ludlum, Robert, you can determine which of his books, if any, your library has. If you are looking specifically for Ludlum's *The Bourne Identity,* you would look under the B's for *Bourne* (the articles "The" and "A" at the start of a title are ignored).

Cathy Jackson went to her card catalog and looked up the subject *cheerleading.* Under that heading, she found cards for seven books. One of the cards listed the book *The Official Cheerleader's Handbook,* by Randy Neil. Note the information given on the subject card, author card, and title card shown on page 223 for *The Official Cheerleader's Handbook.*

The key to being able to use a card to find a book on the shelves is the call number in the upper left-hand corner of the card. **Call numbers** are the numbers, which sometimes include letters, that are used to organize books in the library. Note that all three cards show the number 371.89/Nei. Looking on the shelves numbered 350 to 400, Cathy quickly located *The Official Cheerleader's Handbook.* All nonfiction books are organized by number, following either the Dewey Decimal System or the Library of Congress System. Books of fiction are arranged according to the last name of the author.

Reference Books

Reference books are prime sources of useful facts and information. Because they are for ready reference in the library, many reference books are noncirculating, which means that they cannot be checked out. The following reference books are useful sources for general information.

Encyclopedias. Encyclopedias contain information on a wide range of subjects. This information is written in articles arranged in alphabetical order. Although most encyclopedias cover all branches of knowledge, some are specialized, covering only one field, such as encyclopedias of slang and of baseball. Encyclopedias are a good starting point for research. Most libraries have several different encyclopedias. Among the most useful are the *Encyclopaedia Britannica,* the *Encyclopedia Americana,* and the *World Book Encyclopedia.*

You may find, however, that an encyclopedia is not always a good source of information. Some subjects are not covered. For example, Cathy Jackson found that neither the *World Book* nor the *Encyclopedia Americana* had entries on cheerleading. In addition, encyclopedias are usually anywhere from one to three years out of date. Even when a new edition comes out, a particular article may not have been updated. Some articles go unchanged for years. Consequently, an encyclopedia may not be the best source for researching a current topic.

Almanacs. Almanacs are annual publications containing statistical, tabular, and other general information about the previous year. For example, an almanac would likely be the best source for such information as the capitals of the countries of the world, recent historical events, birth and death dates of famous people, population figures, Academy Award winners since the beginning of the awards, and other such facts. Two of the most popular almanacs are the *World Almanac and Book of Facts* and the *Statistical Abstract*.

Atlases. Atlases are bound collections of maps, charts, and plates. If you want information about the roads, mountains, lakes, rivers, or major cities in a state or country, consult an atlas. Large atlases also provide additional historical, geographical, and other facts about such places. Two useful atlases are the *Hammond Contemporary World Atlas* and the *New York Times Geographic Atlas of the World*.

Biographical Sources. Biographical sources give information about well-known people. This information may be presented in thumbnail sketches, articles, or long essays. *Who's Who* (short sketches of British citizens) and *Who's Who in America* (short sketches of American citizens) are two popular biographical sources.

Books of Quotations. Books of quotations are filled with famous sayings. Bartlett's *Familiar Quotations* and Palmer's *Quotations in History* are two popular sources of quotations.

Dictionaries. Dictionaries contain a wealth of information about words: definitions, guides to pronunciation, etymologies, synonyms, and more. Always keep a dictionary beside you as you work on your speeches. Whenever you are not certain about how a word is spelled, pronounced, or used, look it up. The definitions and discussions of words in a dictionary can also give you ideas about how to approach a topic.

Dictionaries range in size from pocket-sized dictionaries to complete, unabridged dictionaries. In addition, many fields and areas of interest, such as medicine, electronics, fishing, and slang, have special dictionaries. The kind of dictionary that you ought to keep on hand is a college dictionary.

Familiarize yourself with standard reference works. Some will supply the information you need; others will tell you exactly where to find it.

Three useful college dictionaries are *The American Heritage Dictionary of the English Language, Webster's New World Dictionary of the American Language,* and *Webster's Ninth New Collegiate Dictionary.*

Newspaper and Magazine Articles

For current topics, the best sources of information are likely to be newspapers and magazines. Your local library probably has an index of articles appearing in the nearest major daily newspaper and an index of articles appearing in the *New York Times.* Even if your library does not carry back issues of the *New York Times,* you will find that when the *Times* index refers to an article on a particular subject, your local paper may likely have an article on that subject appearing that same day.

Your library probably carries both current and back issues of popular magazines. To find the specific magazines that contain articles on your topic, consult the appropriate index. All the articles in over 170 popular magazines and journals are indexed in the *Readers' Guide to Periodical Literature.* The *Readers' Guide* (as it is called for short) gives complete reference information for articles in magazines such as *Time, Newsweek, Ebony, Sports Illustrated, Reader's Digest,* and *U.S. News and World Report.* The *Readers' Guide* comes out yearly with indexes for articles from magazines and journals published the previous year. For each year in progress, the *Readers' Guide* prepares monthly and quarterly indexes. When Cathy Jackson looked through the 1979–1980 volume of the *Readers' Guide,* she found the following articles listed under the subject *cheerleading.*

```
CHEERLEADING
Keep smiling!  pompom girls.  L. Hall and L. Tintera.  il Seventeen 38:108
   Ag'79
Some wild and crazy guys:  oddball mascots or cheerleaders. B. Newman.  il
   Sports Illus 51:62-6+ S 17 '79
Three cheers for the Shout-It-Out winners, il Teen 23:56 J1 '79
```

Note that the entries give the title, author, magazine, volume, page, month, and year. The entry for the article "Keep Smiling!" tells you that it can be found in the August 1979 issue of *Seventeen* magazine, volume 38, page 108.

A second excellent index of magazine articles is the *Magazine Index,* which lists articles for nearly 350 magazines. The *Magazine Index* is kept on microfilm. If your library carries the *Magazine Index,* you will want to use it, since it covers more magazines than the *Readers' Guide* does. In addition, as a service to students, each month the editors of the *Magazine Index* feature a number of "hot topics." These are arranged in a looseleaf binder and are kept near the microfilm machine.

Two Specialty Sources

Microfilm. To save room, many libraries put as many newspapers and magazines as they can on microfilm. Microfilm is photographic film bearing a reduced-scale record of printed or pictorial material. Microfilm usually comes on a spool holding what looks like a film strip. This spool is placed in a microfilm reader, which magnifies the picture to about the size of half a newspaper page. The reader allows you to go forward or backward through the spool. If you do not know how to use a microfilm reader, ask your librarian for help.

Vertical File. The vertical file is a collection of pamphlets and clippings maintained by the library to answer brief questions or to provide information that is not easily located. These materials are not catalogued and are kept in vertical filing cabinets. For example, a library is likely to have a vertical file of folders containing pamphlets and other odd-sized and odd-shaped material about vacation places. Cathy found that her library had pamphlets, fliers, and other promotional material under a file titled "Cheerleading Camps." Again, ask your librarian whether your library has a vertical file and how to use it.

ACTIVITY: **Finding Information in a Library**

At the top of a sheet of paper, write the topic for your first speech. If your library is organized by the Dewey Decimal System, write on this sheet of paper the number or numbers for books on your topic. If your library is organized according to the Library of Congress System, write the letter or letters for books on your topic. Then use the card catalog to find five books that your library has on your topic. For each book, write the call number, title, author, and date of publication. Next, use the *Readers' Guide* or the *Magazine Index* to find articles about your topic. On your sheet of paper, list five articles that you think will contain information you can use. Finally, consult the *Encyclopaedia Britannica,* the *Encyclopedia Americana,* and the *World Book* (or three encyclopedias found in your school or local library). If any of these have articles on your topic, list the articles under the name of the encyclopedia.

RECORDING YOUR INFORMATION

As you find information that you can use in your speech, you will need to record it. A simple way to do this is to make **note cards** on which you copy the information (or a summary of it) and the source in which you found it. Note cards give you flexibility in sorting and arranging information. Remember, though, that you will probably not use all the information you have recorded on your note cards. Before you write your speech, you will select from your note cards only the specific information that is most useful.

One of Cathy Jackson's note cards looked like this:

```
Famous people who were cheerleaders

Former President Dwight D. Eisenhower,
Jimmy Stewart, Cheryl Ladd, and former Miss
America Phyllis George were all
cheerleaders.

Randy Neil, Official Cheerleaders Handbook,
p. 16
```

When you make your note cards, be sure to write neatly so that you will have no difficulty reading them later.

Use 4- × 6-inch cards. On each card, note the name of the source, the author, if one is given, and the page number. How many sources should you use for a speech? Certainly never fewer than three. One-source speeches often lead to plagiarism, the copying of another person's words or ideas. In addition, one or two sources would not give you a broad enough view to speak authoritatively on your topic.

As you read about your topic, record each fact or idea on a separate index card. Later, you can easily organize your information by rearranging the cards.

Of course, the information you use from various sources needs to be credited. You do not need to credit general information—information that is widely known or that can be found in any number of sources. However, you do need to credit exact quotations and information gained from the research or insight of others.

A statement giving credit to the source of quoted material is called a **citation.** In a speech you can credit a source by using a short citation. Here are some typical wordings for citations.

> According to an article about interest rates in last week's *Newsweek*, . . .
>
> In a speech before the National Association of Manufacturers, Vice President Bush said . . .
>
> Martina Browne, in her interesting book on parrots, presents the idea that . . .
>
> Jim Hawkins, in his book entitled *Cheerleading Is for Me*, suggests that . . .

ACTIVITY: **Preparing Note Cards and Source Citations for Information**

Consult the sources you listed for the last activity. Prepare a note card for three items of information you have found in these sources. Then imagine that you are going to use this information in your speech. Write an appropriate introductory citation for each source.

GUIDELINES FOR GATHERING INFORMATION

- Have I called upon my personal experiences for information?
- Have I gained information from my own observations?
- Have I interviewed others to gain information?
- Have I conducted surveys as a way of gathering information?
- Have I used the library effectively?
- Have I recorded information on note cards?
- Do I know how to cite information in my speech?

Profiles in Communication

Jo Wiefering

Jo Wiefering's occupation? Interviewer for B&B Market Research. When organizations want to find out how people are behaving or what people think, they call in professional marketing firms like B&B Market Research, which hire both full-time and part-time employees to conduct surveys and interviews.

Jo Wiefering is regarded as B&B's top interviewer. She conducts all types of interviews, from finding data on political preferences to in-depth analyses of attitudes about new products. She conducts some interviews over the telephone, others in large public places like shopping centers, and still others through door-to-door canvassing. Her interviews run from just a few questions for a political preference poll to thirty or forty-five minutes of questioning for an in-depth interview. Ms. Wiefering comments that she is always surprised "how nice people are, and how they're willing to give up so much of their time."

Ms. Wiefering says that researching is an excellent job that has a great future. "Twenty years ago few people knew about market research, but now, more and more companies conduct research to survive. A young worker can do very well."

When asked what guidelines she would give a person who was interested in pursuing a career in market research, Ms. Wiefering focussed on four points: (1) Look and act professional—dress and act in a way that encourages people to talk. (2) Relate to people of all races, religions, ages, and economic levels—really show an interest in people as individuals. (3) Be diplomatic—be courteous at all times and take a serious approach to sensitive topics. (4) Have drive and self-discipline—be willing to work hard on your own even when hours are long and when it is raining or cold, or conditions are less than ideal.

Jo Wiefering enjoys her work and plans to be asking questions for a long time to come.

SUMMARY

Good speechmaking begins with reliable information. Your first source of information is yourself. By thinking about your own experiences, you can find material that will form the basis of your speech. Using yourself as a source also means observing. You can improve your powers of observation by making a conscious effort to "see," not just to "look"; by putting what you observe into words; by recognizing what is different or unusual about what you observe; and by taking notes.

Your second source of information is other people. You can gain information from others by asking questions. One form of questioning is the interview. Good interviewing procedures involve setting up an interview, preparing questions to ask, conducting an interview, and recording answers. A second form of questioning is the survey. Good surveying procedures involve asking clear and concise questions, asking enough people, and asking a random sample of people.

Your third source of information for your speech is the library. To find books in the library, you must look through the card catalog and find the call numbers of books you should consult and of sections of the library where books on your subject are likely to be. Books are listed in the card catalog by subject, by author, and by title.

Effective research also includes checking key reference books. Encyclopedias contain information on all branches of knowledge. They range from one-volume works to multi-volume sets. Other useful reference books are almanacs, which contain statistical information; atlases, which contain maps and charts; biographical works, which have essays about people; books of quotations; and dictionaries.

Especially for recent topics, you are likely to get a great deal of information from newspapers and magazines. Looking in the *New York Times Index* will help you find newspaper articles on your topic. Although your library may not carry the *New York Times,* you may find that your local paper carried stories on the same topics and on the same days that similar stories appeared in the *New York Times.* Looking in *The Readers' Guide to Periodical Literature* and the *Magazine Index* will help you find magazine or journal articles on your topic.

As you are researching, record your information on 4- × 6-inch index cards, and in your speech, give credit to your sources.

CHAPTER VOCABULARY

Look back through this chapter to find the meaning of each of the following terms. Write each term and its meaning in your communication journal.

call numbers	knowledgeable source	random sample
card catalog	leading questions	reliable source
citation	neutral questions	secondary source
follow-up questions	note cards	survey
interview	primary source	

1. You can use yourself as a source of information by drawing upon your own experiences and observing things for yourself. When you observe, what is the difference between seeing and looking?

2. A carpenter tells you how she made a cabinet. Is she giving you first-hand or secondhand information?

3. If you were taking a survey, you would want to question a random sample. What are two methods for taking a random sample?

4. One way that books are listed in the card catalog is by author. What are two other ways?

5. Encyclopedias have many strengths as sources of information for speeches. What weaknesses do encyclopedias have?

6. Another useful reference book is the almanac. When would you use an almanac as a source of information for your speech?

7. If your speech were on a topic that had recently been in the news, you would want to look in the newspaper for articles containing information you could use. What index would you make sure to consult?

8. Magazine articles are also excellent sources for current topics. What are the titles of two indexes of magazine articles?

9. When you gather information in the library, you will want to be sure to check all sources. In addition to books, magazines, and newspapers, what two other sources of information are found in many libraries?

10. When giving your speech, you do not need to give credit for information that is commonly known. When do you need to give credit?

DISCUSSION QUESTIONS

1. Suppose that you are giving a speech on one of the following subjects: mechanics, computer games, bicycling, cooking, homework, or dancing. First choose one of these subjects and limit it to a specific topic. Then discuss why you yourself would or would not be an excellent source of information.

2. Imagine that you want to learn as much as you can from observing fire fighters extinguish a fire, telephone workers install a telephone, or painters paint a house. Discuss what you should do to become a better or more accurate observer.

3. Suggest several topics on which you could conduct a survey to gather useful information for a speech. Discuss how you would go about conducting a survey on one of these topics. Be sure to mention whom you would survey, the types of questions you would ask, and the number of people you would question.

4. Otto Kleppner once said, "The purpose of all higher education is to make men aware of what was and what is; to incite them to probe into what may be. It seeks to teach them to understand, to evaluate, to communicate." First discuss the meaning of this quotation. Then discuss how its values are fulfilled when you gather information for a speech.

5. A Ph.D. thesis is a type of long and detailed research paper a student has to write in order to receive a doctorate degree. J. Frank Dobie once wrote, "The average Ph.D. thesis is nothing but a transference of bones from one graveyard to another." First discuss the meaning of this quotation. What is Dobie criticizing? Then discuss ways in which you can make a speech based on your own research, rather than have the speech be simply a summary of other people's thoughts.

ACTIVITIES

1. Practicing Observations

Take a minute to look around the classroom. Then cover your eyes and describe a particular part of the room—for instance, the teacher's desk, the back wall, or the area by the doorway. Report your observations carefully. Then open your eyes and compare what you reported with what you can now see.

2. Using Library Sources to Find Information

Working alone or with a partner (whichever your teacher directs), consult reference sources in the library to find the answers to the following questions. All of the answers can be found in sources discussed in this chapter. Be prepared to present the answer to each question and to identify the source in which you found that answer.

a. What is the average rainfall in San Francisco, California; Miami, Florida; and Chicago, Illinois?
b. What is the origin of the word *tantalize*?
c. What are the titles of three books by Ernest Hemingway?
d. When did Arizona become a state?

e. Who was the twelfth president of the United States?
f. How is coal mined?
g. What are the names of Teddy Roosevelt's mother and father?
h. What is the motto for the state of Texas?
i. What movie won the Academy Award for best director in 1983?
j. Where is the only place in the United States where four states touch at one point?

3. Identifying Sources to Interview to Gather Information

Find out the name and position of a person you could interview locally to obtain information about each of the following topics:

a. Public television programming
b. History of your city
c. Location and special features of your city's public parks
d. Scheduling of local functions such as concerts and speeches
e. Athletic activities for high-school students
f. Consumer information about local businesses
g. Obedience training and health care for pets
h. Employment counseling
i. Fishing regulations
j. Soil and climate conditions for growing a garden

4. Conducting a Telephone Interview to Gather Information

Conduct a telephone interview with the manager of a local retail store to determine what changes in pricing are likely to occur during the next few months. Find out which products are likely to go up in price, which are likely to go down. Ask for the manager's opinion of why he or she thinks the prices on those particular products will change. Based on the answers you receive, ask at least one follow-up question to clarify your understanding or to gather more information.

Be sure that you take notes during the interview. Record each of your questions followed by the manager's answer. Report on your interview to the class, and ask your classmates for feedback on the effectiveness of your interviewing techniques.

5. Conducting a Survey to Gather Information

Conduct a survey to find out which rock group is most popular with students in your school. To make your survey as accurate as possible, be sure to ask a large random sample of both male and female students from different grade levels. Share your findings with your classmates.

A. Imagine you are preparing an informative speech for your history class. Think about events from 1970 to the present. Select a topic and narrow it. Then list the information you could supply about this topic from your own experience.

B. Think again about the topic you selected for Part A of this activity. List two to five people who could provide you with information for your speech.

C. List five to ten questions you would include in a survey to gather information for your speech.

D. Consult the card catalog in your library. List the titles, authors, and call numbers of five to ten books you would consult for information for your speech.

E. Consult the *Readers' Guide to Periodical Literature.* List five to ten articles you would read for information for your speech.

F. Using the books and periodicals you chose above, create note cards for three items of information from three different books and three items of information from articles found in three different periodicals. On each card, write a general category at the top, a note or quotation in the center, and a source citation at the bottom, including the author's name, the title of the book or article (also the title of the periodical when citing an article), and the page number.

   After your teacher has checked your note cards, make photocopies of them (three to a page). Keep the copies in your communication journal to use as models when you make up note cards for your speeches.

Real-Life Speaking Situations

1. You never know when you will need to call upon your skills of observation. Many times a day, you come into contact with people, places, things, and events that you want to be able to recall accurately. Sometimes the accuracy of your observations can be of critical importance. For example, imagine that you are at the scene of an accident on the highway and that the police have asked you to report what you saw. Using the details of an actual accident or of an imaginary one, write a one- or two-page account of your observations. How will you begin your report? What details will you include? In what order will you present your details? What opinions or comments of your own will you give? Read your report aloud to the class and invite feedback on the accuracy and completeness of your observations.

2. You may have seen people at shopping malls asking questions of shoppers and then recording the responses. You may even have been asked yourself about your opinion on a particular topic. The people asking these questions are opinion pollsters. Opinion polls are conducted to determine people's thoughts and feelings about an issue, a product, a candidate, or some other topic. No matter what the topic, opinion pollsters must carefully choose what questions they will ask and which people they will survey. Imagine that you are taking an opinion poll. Begin by identifying a specific topic on which you will ask your questions. Next, determine exactly what questions you will ask people to discover their stand on your topic. Also identify a specific group of people whose opinions you want, such as registered voters, teenage male shoppers, retirees, or mothers with young children. Write four questions on the topic you have chosen and survey ten people from your target group. Compile the results of your opinion survey and share them with the class. Conduct a question-and-answer session on (1) the questions you asked, (2) the group of people you chose to ask, and (3) the effect that these choices had on the accuracy of your survey.

CHAPTER 11

PREPARING YOUR SPEECH

OBJECTIVES:

After studying this chapter, you should be able to

1. List the three parts of a speech.

2. Determine the main points of a speech.

3. List three common organizations for main points of a speech.

4. List and explain the goals of a speech introduction.

5. Give examples of six types of speech introductions.

6. List and explain the goals of a speech conclusion.

7. Give examples of three types of speech conclusions.

8. Use transitional devices.

9. Outline a speech.

10. List the steps in rehearsing a speech.

11. Prepare speech notes.

Todd walked to the front of the class, paused for a moment, and then began his speech:

> The building was filled with smoke. The father led his wife and children into the yard—everyone was gasping for breath. As smoke cleared from his eyes, he looked around only to discover that something had happened to Julie, his five-year-old daughter.

Just as he was about to rush back into the house, he saw Kelly, the family German Shepherd, pull Julie through the door.

Is this just a story? No, it's a true occurrence—the kind of occurrence that happens several times every year. Such feats as these are just one of the ways that dogs have shown themselves to be our friends. Today I want to talk with you about the ways in which dogs have earned their place as our "best friends."

In the rest of his speech Todd presented the following points: (1) dogs work with people to accomplish tasks; (2) dogs protect people and their property; and (3) dogs bring warmth and devotion to human beings. He concluded with a quotation that reinforced the point that dogs are truly our "best friends."

A well-prepared speech has three parts: an introduction, a body, and a conclusion. Each of these three parts is prepared separately. Then the parts are put together, according to a complete outline.

To see how a speech is constructed, follow Todd through the various stages of preparing his speech.

ORGANIZING THE BODY OF YOUR SPEECH

After Todd had selected a topic, written a specific purpose, analyzed his audience and occasion, and gathered information (for a review of these activities look back at the last two chapters), he began to prepare his speech. Todd set to work organizing the body of his speech first. You might wonder why he did not begin at the beginning—with the introduction. Although the introduction is the first part of the speech that an audience will hear, it is usually easier to prepare after you know exactly how the speech will develop.

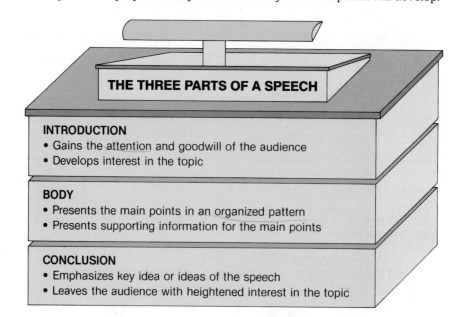

THE THREE PARTS OF A SPEECH

INTRODUCTION
- Gains the attention and goodwill of the audience
- Develops interest in the topic

BODY
- Presents the main points in an organized pattern
- Presents supporting information for the main points

CONCLUSION
- Emphasizes key idea or ideas of the speech
- Leaves the audience with heightened interest in the topic

The portion of a speech in which the main points are developed is called the **body** of the speech. Organizing the body of the speech involves (1) determining the main points, (2) organizing the main points in a consistent pattern, and (3) outlining all the material you plan to use in the speech.

Determining the Main Points

The **main points** of a speech are the main ideas under which supporting information is organized. If you have already composed a well-written specific purpose (or preferably a clear thesis statement), then determining the main points of your speech should be fairly easy. For instance, Todd's specific purpose was "I want to explain the three ways that dogs have earned their place as our 'best friends.'" The main points of Todd's speech would be the three ways that dogs have earned this place. Therefore, the specific purpose alone would determine the main points in Todd's speech. Here is how Todd worded his thesis statement: "Dogs have shown themselves to be our best friends by working with people, by protecting people and their property, and by showing love and devotion to people." Notice how both the specific purpose and the thesis statement lead to the wording of the main points:

Specific purpose: I want to explain the three ways that dogs have shown themselves to be our "best friends."

Thesis statement: Dogs have earned their place as our "best friends" by working with people, by protecting people and their property, and by showing love and devotion to people.

Main points:
I. Dogs work with people.
II. Dogs protect people and their property.
III. Dogs show love and devotion to people.

What would be the main points for the following two purpose sentences?

1. I want to show how the federal government is divided into three branches.
2. I want to describe the four main components of a computer.

The main points for the first purpose sentence would be each of the three branches of the federal government, and the main points for the second one would be each of the four components of a computer.

Specific purpose: I want to show how the federal government is divided into three branches.

Thesis statement: The three branches of the federal government are the executive branch, the legislative branch, and the judicial branch.

Main points:
I. One branch is the executive.
II. A second branch is the legislative.
III. The third branch is the judicial.

Specific purpose: I want to describe the four components of a computer.

Thesis statement: Computers are composed of four main components: the central processing unit, the disk drive(s), the monitor, and the keyboard.

Main points:

I. One component is the central processing unit.

II. A second part is the disk drive(s).

III. A third part is the monitor.

IV. A fourth part is the keyboard.

As you saw earlier in the discussion of writing the specific purpose, putting a number in your specific purpose will help you identify your main points.

Types of Organizational Patterns

The main points of your speech may be organized in any of a number of logical patterns.

Chronological Order. Chronological order is the order in which events happen in time. In many speeches information must be presented in chronological order for the audience to understand it. For example, giving directions, showing how things are made, and explaining the history of something are three types of informative speeches that require chronological order.

A speech organized in chronological order presents information according to how it is related in time. The total time span may be very short (seconds or minutes), very long (centuries or millenia), or somewhere in between (hours, days, weeks, months, or years).

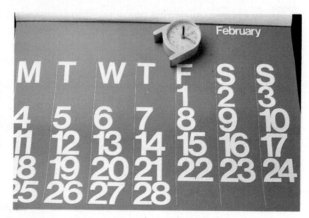

The following organization for a speech uses chronological order to present the history of bicycles.

Specific Purpose: I want to explain the five stages in the evolution of the bicycle.

I. The first stage is the origin.

II. The second stage is the development of a steering device.

III. The third stage is the attachment of pedals to the front wheel.

IV. The fourth stage is the addition of chain drive.

V. The fifth stage is the development of modern safety features.

Spatial Order. Spatial order is the organization of things according to their position in space. The information in some speeches, usually those involving description, is particularly well suited to arrangement in a pattern that represents what a person would see. For example, a description of a building is best visualized when main points are presented in spatial order. The following organization for a speech describing a building shows how spatial order is used to arrange main points, moving from bottom to top.

Specific purpose: I want to describe the three levels of the University Center.

    I. The basement contains various recreational facilities.
    II. The main floor contains restaurants and administrative offices.
    III. The second floor contains the auditorium, smaller meeting rooms, and the president's dining room.

Topical Order. Topical order is a pattern of organization in which a topic is broken down into parts that are rearranged in an order determined by the speaker. In speeches arranged this way, the main points are statements of the categories used by the speaker to organize information about the topic.

For example, the outline of the speech on the branches of the federal government (see page 239) is an example of topical order. The main points do not occur in any time sequence, nor do they represent any visual pattern. Another example would be a speech on the strength of the Soviet Union as a world power.

Specific purpose: I want to discuss three measures of the Soviet Union's strength as a world power.

    I. One measure of the Soviet Union's strength is its natural resources.
    II. A second measure of the Soviet Union's strength is its military.
    III. A third measure of the Soviet Union's strength is its technology.

Other Organizational Patterns

When you prepare complicated informative speeches and persuasive speeches, you will need to consider additional organizational patterns. In Chapter 14, on the informative speech, in addition to reviewing chronological order, spatial order, and topical order, you will look at climactic order, cause and effect, and comparison and contrast. In Chapter 16, on the persuasive speech, you will look at deductive approach, inductive approach, statement of reasons, problem/solution, comparative advantage, criteria satisfaction, negative method, and Monroe's Motivated Sequence.

Developing the Main Points

Once you have determined the main points of your speech and have outlined them appropriately, you can continue the preparation process by arranging your supporting information under appropriate headings. What do you do with the material that does not seem to fit under any of the headings?

Set it aside. You may be able to use it later as you revise your speech or at some other time. Having spent time and effort researching your topic, you may be anxious to use all of your information. However, if you find yourself thinking, "I worked hard gathering this information; I'm going to fit it in," stop and calm yourself down. Your goal is to prepare an effective speech. If the speech will be better organized by leaving some material out, then that is what you should do.

Composing your speech only of material that relates to your topic gives your speech **unity.** That is, a speech is unified when all its parts fit together to make a whole. A speech cannot have unity when information, even very interesting information, is irrelevant to the specific purpose of the speech. The best way to test for unity is to prepare an outline. Any information that does not fit under one of the main ideas in the outline does not belong in the speech.

As you study your informal outline, you may also find that you do not have developmental material for one or more of your main points. In such cases you will need to determine whether that point is necessary to carrying out the main purpose of the speech. If it is, you will need to find more information to develop that point.

ACTIVITY: **Writing the Specific Purpose and Organizing the Main Points for a Speech**

Write a specific purpose for a speech that you might give this term. Under it, organize the main points for the speech. Are the main points you have written in chronological, spatial, or topical order? Is the organizational pattern you have used appropriate for the material? Discuss your answers with your classmates.

ORGANIZING THE INTRODUCTION

The several sentences that make up the beginning of your speech are its **introduction.** Having a good introduction is crucial. The effectiveness of your introduction often determines how much attention your audience will pay to your speech. The introduction, which can be as short as a few sentences but should seldom be longer than 10 percent of the speech, serves three very important purposes. It helps you (1) get the attention of the audience, (2) gain the good will of the audience, and (3) develop interest in the subject.

Attention means more than just momentary attentiveness; it involves sustained regard, or interest. For instance, blowing a whistle at the start of the speech would get the audience's attention. However, this action would not necessarily hold that attention. You have to find a way to focus the

This speaker has succeeded in getting his audience's undivided attention. His listeners are definitely interested in hearing what he has to say.

audience's attention on the subject matter of your speech. Then, when you get into the body of the speech, the audience will continue to listen.

In addition, you need to get the audience's attention in a way that builds good will. **Good will** is the audience's respect or positive feeling for the speaker as a person. If your opening remarks cause members of the audience to dislike or distrust you, they will likely be suspicious of anything you say throughout the speech. Often, the way in which you present the introduction—your tone, your inflection, and other nonverbal signals—can establish a bond of good will between you and your audience. In short, a pleasant, sincere voice can do more to create good will than any of the words you say.

The third primary purpose of your introduction is to develop interest in the topic of the speech. **Interest** refers to the involvement, or concern, your audience shows in your topic. Developing interest in your topic will require you to present facts, examples, and other information that will hold your audience's attention.

How you get attention, build good will, and develop interest in a topic is a matter of your own ingenuity. Of the dozens of ways of beginning a speech, there are several methods favored by professional speakers. These methods are favorites because they work. Here are the most effective types of speech introductions. Notice that the emphasis of each is on getting attention and developing interest in the topic of the speech.

Startling Statement

A **startling statement** is a one- to three-sentence speech introduction that catches the audience's attention. For instance, Todd could start his speech on dogs by saying

There are an estimated 30 million dogs in the United States. That's roughly one for every two families in the country. In my speech today, I want to look at the ways dogs have become our "best friends."

Preparing Your Speech   **243**

One of the strongest features of this kind of introduction is that it quickly focuses the attention of the audience on the topic.

Question

Asking a question in an introduction is another way to get an audience interested in your speech. Sometimes with as little as one question you can both get audience attention and lead into the subject matter of the speech. Todd might have begun his speech in the following way:

Why is it that roughly one out of every two families in the United States has a pet dog? What is it about dogs that make them far and away the leading pet and our "best friends"? Today . . .

Story

Another method for starting a speech is with a short story, or anecdote. The strength of this type of introduction is that it always gets attention. The problem is that you can run into difficulty finding stories that are relevant to your topic and are short enough to use in short speeches. If you look back at the opening of this chapter, you will see that Todd began his speech with a short story.

Quotation

Often, you can find a quotation that is just right for the opening of your speech. Your library contains many collections that you can use to locate

ROTHCO

"—And now, I take great pleasure in introducing the surprise speaker . . ."

This "surprise speaker" did not have an exciting opening for his speech, so instead, he has decided to make a startling entrance.

famous quotations. In Bartlett's *Familiar Quotations,* Todd found a quotation from the fifth stanza of a poem entitled "Vagabond's House" by Don Blanding. He considered using it for his speech because it comes so close to describing most people's feelings for dogs.

> There are times when only a dog will do
> For a friend—when you're beaten, sick and blue,
> And the world's all wrong; for he won't care
> If you break and cry, or grouch and swear;
> For he'll let you know as he licks your hands
> That he's downright sorry—and understands.

Personal Reference

By giving a **personal reference** in the introduction the speaker relates the speech topic directly to the audience's experience. Using a personal reference can be an excellent method for building good will. Todd could have started his speech by using the following personal reference:

> I'm sure many of you have a pet—perhaps it's a cat or a parakeet. Maybe some of you may go in for more exotic pets like monkeys, snakes, or rare tropical fish. But unless I miss my guess, more of you own a dog than own any other kind of family pet. Today I want . . .

Audiovisual Material

Another way of starting a speech is with audiovisual material. Although audiovisual material is seldom used alone, it can be a key attention-getting

ACTIVITY: **Analyzing Speech Introductions and Presenting Your Own Speech Introduction**

Obtain a copy of *Vital Speeches of the Day. Vital Speeches* is a bimonthly magazine containing approximately ten major speeches given recently for various occasions. Select one speech introduction from those included and read it to the class. Then discuss with your classmates how the speech's introduction gains the audience's attention.

Next, identify the kinds of introductions that were used in the speeches in that issue of *Vital Speeches.* Label each introduction as *startling statement, question, story, quotation, personal reference,* or *audiovisual.* Which kind of introduction was used most often?

Finally, prepare an introduction that you can use for a speech. Present it to the class. After everyone has given his or her introduction, have the class vote on which introductions best captured attention, gained good will, and developed interest in the topic of the speech.

device for your speech. For instance, Todd could have begun his speech by saying "Think about these pictures for a moment." Then he could have showed four or five pictures of dogs helping people get work done.

ORGANIZING SPEECH CONCLUSIONS

The force of many a speech has been lost by a speaker's not knowing how to finish. The **conclusion** is a very short ending of the speech, seldom more than a few sentences, but it is very important. Its goals are (1) to emphasize the key idea or ideas of the speech and (2) to leave the attention of the audience on a high note.

Bring your speech to a conclusion as soon as you have covered the main points. Unorganized speakers make the mistake of concluding their speeches and then adding more to them. They finish their main points and say, "So, in conclusion, . . ." However, before they actually conclude, they think of something they left out or something they could add, then they start discussing this new material. When they have finished with this extra information, they say something like "So, in final conclusion, . . ." In cases such as this, the speaker's disorganization can alienate the audience, causing them to lose all interest in the message.

Just as there are dozens of ways of starting a speech, so, too, there are many ways of concluding. The following methods are three of the most effective.

Summary

The shortest, easiest, and often most informative way of ending a speech is with a summary. A **summary** is a short restatement of the key information in a longer work. Todd could very well have ended his speech with the sentence "So we can see that by working together with people, by protecting people and their property, and by showing unparalleled love and devotion to people, dogs have earned their place as our 'best friends.' "

Recommendation

Although a summary is usually appropriate, there are times when you will want to give more information in your conclusion. Especially in a persuasive speech, you may want to make a recommendation. A **recommendation** is a short statement that tells the audience the specific behavior you want them to follow. For example, in a speech on the reasons why Mary Johnson would make an excellent class president, you might end with the recommendation "Tomorrow, when you go to the polls, be sure to vote for Mary Johnson."

Stirring Ending

One of the goals of a conclusion is to leave a speech on a high point, that is, to stir emotions. A **stirring ending** is one that helps you intensify the emotion, or feeling, you want the audience to experience. To do this, you might use a vivid quotation, tell a story, give an illustration, or relate a personal experience. Whatever ending you choose, however, your aim is to intensify your audience's emotional reaction to the topic. For example, to tie together the idea that dogs are our "best friends," Todd might have ended his speech with the following quotation:

I have a little dog and my dog was very small
He licked me in the face, and he answered to my call
Of all the treasures that were mine, I loved him most of all.

The aim of this quotation would be to stir the emotions of the audience to create a warm feeling toward dogs.

The ending of a speech is as critical as the finish of a race. Put forth an extra burst of effort in your conclusion to drive home your main points and ensure that your audience will remember them.

ACTIVITY: Analyzing Speech Conclusions and Presenting Your Own Speech Conclusion

Select a conclusion from one of the speeches that you used to analyze speech introductions for the Activity on page 245. Read the conclusion to your class. Then show how the speaker summarized key points and ended the speech on a high note.

Next, label the conclusions of the other speeches that appear in the same issue. Identify each conclusion as *a summary, a recommendation,* or *a stirring ending.* Which kind of conclusion was used most often?

Finally, prepare a conclusion that you could use for a speech. Present it to the class. After everyone has given his or her conclusion, have the class vote on which conclusions best summarized the key ideas and best left the attention of the audience on a high note.

USING TRANSITIONAL DEVICES

A final part of the organizational process is to consider the transitional devices you will use between the various parts of the speech. **Transitional devices** are bridges between ideas. They connect parts of a speech and help emphasize points you are making.

By using transitional devices, you lead the audience from one part of the speech to another. For example, between the opening and the body of his speech, Todd might say, "First, let's look at ways that dogs help people." Between the first and second point, he might say, "Now that we have seen how dogs work with people, let's move on to our second point." In these examples the words *first* and *now* are transitions that help the audience follow the speaker's discussion.

Transitional devices help you emphasize ideas. For example, at some point in your speech you might say, "Here is a point I want to stress," or "The key point here is . . ." Transitional statements such as these help your audience recognize the information that you think is most important or striking.

Your teacher may want you to indicate transitions on your speech outline. Notice the transitions in parentheses at the appropriate points in the outline on pages 251–52.

ACTIVITY: Analyzing the Use of Transitions in a Speech

Analyze the use of transitions in the speech you selected for the previous Activity on page 247. How exactly do these transitions help the audience move from one point or part of the speech to another or help the audience recognize important points? Share your findings with your classmates.

OUTLINING

Written in complete sentences, a **formal outline** is a short skeleton of the speech. It helps you to test the strength of your organization. No doubt you are familiar with preparing outlines for papers that you write. Here you will look at preparing outlines for speeches that you give.

Why Should You Outline?

For most of the speeches you give in class, you will have to prepare and turn in a formal speech outline. To create a formal outline, take the informal outline that you have been preparing and revise it into a formal outline.

The first reason for writing a formal outline is to test the structure of the speech. Many times, ideas for main points and supporting material sound good when you first think of them but then seem weak or inappropriate on reconsideration.

The only way to be certain that your main points are well stated, that your material supports the main points, and that the main points support your specific purpose is to test the structure. An outline is the best device for making such a test. As you study your outline, you can see not only how ideas are related but also which ideas are complete and which need more work. Every stage of the preparation process—writing a specific purpose, determining main points, arranging main points, and developing the main points—has all been done through outlining.

The second reason for writing an outline is that a good outline helps organize your information so that your audience can follow your speech better. If your speech does not have a clear, solid structure and good transitions, the audience's understanding of what you say is likely to be garbled and confused. When your speech is well organized, you make it easier for your audience to understand and remember. Clear organization assures that your audience will be able to recognize your main points and follow your development of them.

The third reason for writing an outline is that a good outline can help you rehearse your speech. The final section of this chapter focuses on the rehearsal process and on the role of the outline in that process.

The fourth reason for writing an outline is to provide a base for good speaker notes. You can reduce the sentences in your formal outline to words or phrases in a shorter outline that you can use as speaker notes when giving your speech.

Just as steel beams form a building's skeleton, your formal outline provides a strong skeleton upon which to build your speech.

How to Outline

Even though you have had experience outlining, you will find it useful to review a few guidelines for preparing your formal outline.

1. Use Roman numerals to indicate the main points of your speech. Use capital letters to indicate major subdivisions of main points. Use Arabic numerals to indicate the next level of subdivisions and use small letters for further subdivision. Although you can designate still more subdivisions with Arabic numbers in parentheses and then small letters in parentheses, you are unlikely to go beyond the four levels of headings shown in the following example.

I.

    A.

        1.

        2.

    B.

II.

    A.

    B.

        1.

            a.

            b.

        2.

2. Write all points in complete sentences. Complete sentences help you understand relationships between ideas.
3. Write main points in parallel language. This means that each of the main points should start with the same grammatical structure. Notice that in Todd's speech each of his three main points began noun/verb: "Dogs work," "Dogs protect," and "Dogs bring." (See page 239.)
4. Make sure that each main point and each subdivision contains only one idea.

    Incorrect: Dogs work with people and protect them.
    Correct: Dogs work with people.
               Dogs protect people.

5. Try to have no more than five main points. Occasionally you have no choice about the number of headings. For instance, with the specific purpose "I want to explain the characteristics of the six classifications of show dogs," you must have six points. Most of the time, however, if you have more than five points, you should group points under broader headings. (For more on grouping main points, see Chapter 11.)

Study the sample outline that follows to improve your grasp of the parts and features of a complete outline.

Speech Outline

Specific Purpose: I want to explain three ways that dogs have become our "best friends."

Speech purpose at top of page

INTRODUCTION

I. Telling the true story of Kelly's rescuing a five-year-old girl from a fire.

Introduction separated from body

II. Thesis Statement: Dogs have shown themselves to be our best friends by working with people, by protecting people and property, and by showing devotion to people. (Now let's look at each of these main points.)

Transition in parentheses

BODY

I. Dogs work with people.
   A. Some dogs are specialists at herding.
      1. Collies have been used on small farms and large ranches for centuries.
      2. Many other kinds of dogs can be trained to herd.
   B. Some dogs are specialists at hunting.
      1. Hounds have been hunting-companions for humans throughout history.
      2. A good dog can track game, can point its quarry, and later can locate the fallen animal or retrieve it.
      (In addition to working with people, dogs can be vital to our well-being.)

Main points are complete sentences.

Transition in parentheses

II. Dogs protect people.
   A. Dogs will keep potential intruders away.
      1. Dogs will bark when they hear a strange noise.
      2. Dogs will show where the noise is coming from.
   B. Dogs will intervene when their masters are attacked.

Main points in topical order

Each of these five subdivisions develops the idea of protection.

1. Dogs will attack if someone is harming a member of the family.
2. Dogs will hold an attacker off until their masters can get away.
C. Dogs can find people who commit crimes.
   1. Dogs have a remarkable sense of smell that enables them to track people.
   2. Dogs remember a scent for a long time.
D. Dogs can rescue people in danger.
   1. Stories of dogs' heroic sacrifices are well documented.
   2. The opening story about Kelly was a good example of such a feat.
E. Dogs can guide the handicapped.
   1. Dogs are used by the blind.
   2. Dogs are used by the deaf.
      (Finally, there is one more way, perhaps the most important way, that dogs are our best friends.) — Transition in parentheses

III. Dogs give people unquestioning love and devotion. — Main point
   A. Dogs will greet their owners joyfully.
   B. Dogs will sit on their masters' laps or at their masters' feet for an entire evening.
   C. Dogs will play with members of the family for hours.
   D. Dogs may provide our best key to mental health.
      1. People with dogs as pets are basically better adjusted.
      2. Disturbed people who get dogs for pets improve in mental health.

CONCLUSION

I. So we can see that dogs work with people, dogs protect people and property, and dogs show love and devotion to people. — Conclusion separated from body
II. Final quotation.

ACTIVITY: Creating a Speech Outline

Review your response to each Activity you have completed so far in this chapter. Then use these responses to create a complete outline for your speech.

TRANSLATING YOUR OUTLINE INTO A SPEECH

At this stage of your preparation, you have a complete outline that contains enough information to make up one-third to one-half of your speech. As you practice your speech, you flesh out this skeleton. The best way to do this is to deliver the speech in a number of practice sessions, or **rehearsals.**

Setting the Stage for Speech Rehearsal

Complete your outline at least two days before you plan to deliver the speech. The sooner you complete the outline, the more time you will have to work on the speech itself.

You should begin a rehearsal by creating a situation that is as much like the actual speech situation as possible. For example, since you are going to give your speech standing up, you should stand up when you rehearse. If you are going to be speaking from a speaker's stand, you should rehearse with a speaker's stand or something like one. Pretend that objects around the room are members of the audience and practice maintaining eye contact. (The next two chapters closely examine elements of language and delivery.)

Before you begin your rehearsal, read your speech outline over once or twice to refresh your memory of the key ideas. Then check your watch to see the exact time that you begin. Present the speech just as you hope to deliver it to your audience. Go through the entire speech. When you have finished, check your watch again. Write down exactly how long you took to deliver your speech. Evaluate your performance. What were the weaknesses of your speech? What were the strengths?

A tape recorder can be a valuable tool during rehearsal. After each session, you can play the tape back and analyze your delivery to determine how you can improve it.

Your first rehearsal may likely be much shorter than the minimum time limit for the speech. In this first rehearsal, you will probably forget portions of the speech. In addition, although you will talk too long on some points, you are more likely not to talk long enough on others. Analyze your speech. Which parts seemed to go well? Which parts need more development? What could you say that you did not say during the first rehearsal?

Now you are ready for a second rehearsal. It is usually a good idea to rehearse at least twice during one session so that ideas are fresh in your mind. Your second rehearsal is likely to be both longer and better than the first. Compare your rehearsals. Where did you improve? Were there any parts that did not go as well as the first time? Put the speech aside for several hours—or even until the next day. Give your subconscious a chance to work on your speech. Many speakers rehearse once just before going to bed so that while they are asleep their minds can work on the speech. Professional speakers find that the time between practices is just as valuable to the preparation process as the rehearsals themselves.

How many rehearsals will you need? Only you can determine that. Some speakers do better with just two or three rehearsals. Others need more. The point is that no beginning speaker and very few experienced speakers can do a good job without rehearsing. Do not try to give a speech in class without at least two rehearsals over a two-day period.

The Role of Notes in Rehearsal

Depending on the kind of speech you are giving, its length, and your teacher's instructions, you may be allowed to use notes when you give your speech. Regardless of what you will do in the speech, you will probably feel safer using notes during practice. Your formal outline will not work as speaker notes because it is too long. If you try to use your formal outline, you could

Dogs are our best friends.
   Work with people
      Herd
      Hunt

Dogs protect people and property.
   Keep out intruders
   Attack aggressors
   Find aggressors
   Rescue people
   Guide people

Dogs show love and devotion.
   Happy to see you
   Keep company
   Play
   Improve mental health

end up practically reading your speech. The handiest way to manage your notes is with note cards composed of a series of single words or phrases in outline form. The examples shown at the bottom of page 254 would be acceptable note cards for the outline on pages 251–52.

Avoid Memorization

Try not to memorize your speech. When you give a speech, you want to appear natural. Memorization can make you seem wooden and inflexible. In addition, memorization can prevent you from adapting to the audience's moods, from making necessary changes in your development of ideas, or from recovering smoothly when you forget a word or point. However, many speakers fall into a trap of memorizing without even knowing it. If you try to say key ideas exactly the same way each time you rehearse, you will begin to memorize the entire speech even if you are not trying to do so.

You need to develop a method of practice that will help you master your speech without memorizing it. Each time you rehearse, try to say various parts of the speech in different words. Your outline contains the information that must be included in your speech—it gives you the structure of the speech. The words you use to present this information may well differ from practice to practice. Remember that your goal is to know your speech, not to memorize it.

What's the difference between knowing a speech and memorizing it? Do you have a pencil handy? Look at it closely—it is probably much like mine. Mine has a six-sided shaft of wood encasing a solid cylinder of graphite. It has an eraser attached by a metal band. These elements (shaft, graphite, eraser, and band) are what would appear in my outline if I were going to give a speech describing my pencil. A description of each of these four elements would be included in every practice and in the speech itself. However, every time I practice the description, I would talk about the elements slightly differently. For example, my first practice might go like this:

Let's take a look at the common pencil. My pencil consists of a wooden shaft with six sides that has a cylinder of graphite running the length of its center. An eraser is attached to one end of the shaft with a brass band. The other end of the shaft is sharpened to a point.

My second practice might look like this:

Have you ever looked closely at a pencil? Most pencils are very similar. Mine consists of a six-sided wooden shaft encasing a piece of graphite that's about $\frac{1}{16}$ of an inch in diameter. At one end of the shaft is a slightly worn eraser that is attached to the shaft with a brass band. At the other end, the shaft is sharpened to a point.

Both examples contain the same key points, but the way they are expressed is slightly different. By changing your wording, you are likely to improve it with each practice. If you practice this way, your speech will steadily improve, and you will not fall into the rut of memorization.

Profiles in Communication

Sandra A. Stelmach

Listen in on one of Coach Sandra Stelmach's speeches to the team and you hear a skillfully designed message aimed at motivating every player to be the best she can be. Ms. Stelmach has been steadily developing her style during the fifteen years she has been coaching winning girls' volleyball teams at a large Midwest high school.

Clear communication is essential in coaching, according to Ms. Stelmach, and she plans her messages carefully. She sets aside forty minutes each day to gather her thoughts and outline the message her players will hear at practice. After jotting down every detail she wants to discuss, Coach Stelmach organizes the details under specific topic headings. Finally, she settles on an overall order for the main topics. "The decision here is guided by the effect I want the day's speech to have on the girls," Coach Stelmach says. "Sometimes I end with an area or plan of improvement for them to ponder. Other times I plan to end so that the team leaves relishing the joy of a recent success."

An outline attached to her clipboard is Coach Stelmach's insurance against forgetting important points. While her delivery is definitely extemporaneous, she knows how easy it is to lose a thought. Consequently, she always speaks with the security of having her outlined notes at hand.

Coach Stelmach often prepares visual aids to help illustrate her message. She finds that the clearest way to teach a formation, for example, is to hand out a printed diagram of the pattern to the players. She then has the team watch a demonstration of the maneuver while she explains how it is executed. In this way, Coach Stelmach uses verbal and nonverbal communication to help her players fully understand the information she is presenting.

Perceiving nonverbal cues from the players is another top communication priority for Coach Stelmach. She "listens" with her eyes from the moment the girls arrive in the locker room. "I notice nonverbal signals all the time. Who comes in together? What expressions are on their faces? Are they quiet or noisy? I look for indicators to help me adjust my message to their mood."

Experience has convinced Sandra Stelmach that "cooperative team spirit is grounded in an environment of clear, open communication." For Coach Stelmach and her players, such communication has proven to be the game plan for victory.

Make note cards from your formal outline. Using these note cards, rehearse your speech at least three times. To avoid memorization, work on improving your wording in each rehearsal.

GUIDELINES FOR PREPARING YOUR SPEECH

- Is my specific purpose clear?
- Does my introduction get attention and lead into the speech?
- Are my main points clearly stated?
- Do my points follow a consistent pattern?
- Are each of my points developed with supporting material?
- Does my conclusion summarize and leave the audience with heightened interest in the topic?
- Have I practiced the speech enough to be familiar with the main ideas and supporting information?

SUMMARY

A speech has an introduction, a body, and a conclusion. The body of the speech should be prepared first. The first step in preparing the body is to determine the main points. The main points of the speech are established by the specific purpose. If the specific purpose is well written, the main points will be easy to identify.

The second step is to make sure that the main points follow a consistent pattern. Most speeches are organized in chronological order, spatial order, or topical order.

The third step is to complete an outline of all the material you plan to use in the speech.

A speech introduction gets the audience's attention, develops interest in the topic, and gains the good will of the audience. Among the most effective kinds of speech introductions are startling statements, questions, stories, quotations, personal references, and audiovisual materials.

A speech conclusion emphasizes the key idea or ideas of a speech and leaves the audience with heightened interest in the topic. Three of the most effective kinds of conclusions are the summary, the recommendation, and the stirring ending.

After you have your speech roughly organized, the next step is to write a formal outline. You can use your outline to test the logical structure of the speech, to provide an organization that the audience can follow, to help you in your practice, and to provide a base for speaker notes.

An effective speech outline uses a standard set of symbols to represent major and minor points, is written in complete sentences, has main points written in parallel language, has each subdivision relate to the point it supports, has only one idea in each main point and subdivision, and contains a maximum of five points.

You translate your outline into a speech through rehearsal. You should rehearse in the same way that you will give the speech. In each rehearsal, time the speech, go through the speech in its entirety, and analyze what you have done. If you use notes, they should be short words or phrases. To avoid memorizing your speech, focus on key ideas and change the wording of your speech each time you rehearse.

CHAPTER VOCABULARY

Look back through this chapter to find the meaning of each of the following terms. Write each term and its meaning in your communication journal.

attention	introduction	startling statement
body	main points	stirring ending
chronological order	personal reference	summary
conclusion	recommendation	topical order
formal outline	rehearsal	transitional devices
good will	spatial order	unity
interest		

REVIEW QUESTIONS

1. One part of the speech is the body, which contains all the main ideas and supporting information for the topic. What are the other two parts of a speech, and what do they contain?

2. Chronological order is one common organizational pattern for speeches. What are two others?

3. Gaining good will is one goal of the speech introduction. What are two other goals?

4. One way to begin your speech is with a quotation. What are four other effective methods?

5. A recommendation is one kind of speech conclusion. What are two other effective conclusions?

6. Transitional devices are important elements in a speech. What are the two main purposes of transitional devices?

7. One rule for making a formal outline is to write all points in complete sentences. What are two other rules?

8. One reason for outlining has to do with organization. How does a speech outline help you organize your speech?

9. Rehearsing your speech is an essential part of preparation. How is knowing a speech different from memorizing it?

10. How much rehearsal should a speaker have before delivering a speech?

DISCUSSION QUESTIONS

1. Discuss with your classmates why the body of the speech should be prepared before the introduction and conclusion. Then discuss which of these sections of a speech is likely to be most difficult to prepare. Give the reasons for your choice.

2. Discuss which kind of speech introduction you would choose for a short speech. What kind would you choose for a longer speech? Give the reasons for your choice.

3. In *Fundamentals of Good Writing,* Robert Penn Warren writes, ". . . one begins a piece of writing by asking himself what kind of treatment is natural to the subject and what kind of effect he wants to work on the reader." Although his comment is directed toward writers, it could easily be applied to speakers. First discuss the meaning of the quotation. Then discuss how it applies to people preparing speeches.

4. Nicholas Boileau once wrote, "Whatever we conceive well we express clearly." First discuss the meaning of the quotation. Then discuss whether or not you agree with it. Finally discuss how it relates to the need to outline your speech.

5. Ralph Waldo Emerson once wrote, "Practice is nine-tenths [of the job]." First discuss whether you agree with this quotation or not. Then discuss how it relates to the need to rehearse your speech.

ACTIVITIES

1. Identifying Different Organizational Patterns for Speeches

Identify the following speech patterns as *chronological order, spatial order,* or *topical order.*

a. Blue is on top.
   Pink is in the middle.
   Green is on the bottom.

b. One feature is hitting.
   A second is running.
   A third is throwing.

c. First dig a furrow in the ground.
   Then plant the seeds.
   Finally water the seeds.

d. The Greeks established the basis of law.
   The Romans codified laws.
   Modern societies have reworked laws.

2. Identifying Kinds of Speech Introductions

Identify the following speech introductions as *startling statement, question, quotation,* or *personal reference.*

a. What do you do when you get home from school each afternoon?

b. Twenty-two great civilizations have risen and disappeared during the course of history.

c. I think I feel much the same way you do about having to make that long climb up to the fourth floor for art. We're all huffing and puffing long before we get there.

d. Sybil Marshall wrote, "Education must have an end in view, for it is not an end in itself."

3. Identifying Different Types of Speech Conclusions

Identify the following speech conclusions as *summary, recommendation,* or *stirring ending.*

a. As you have seen, the three main skills are hitting, running, and throwing.

b. Therefore, tomorrow morning, take the bus to school.

c. He looked at us and said, "It's not the color of the balloon that matters; it's what it's made of."

d. If you are going to take up a sport, try racquetball.

4. Preparing a Speech

A. Choose a topic you know very well and for which your main source of information would be your own experience—for example, getting along with a kid sister, choosing a particular college, or planning the perfect weekend vacation. Write your specific purpose and your thesis statement for a speech on this topic. Write a startling statement you would use to begin this speech.

B. Think again about your topic from Part A. Write a question you could use to begin your speech.

C. Jot down the information you would include in this speech. Arrange this information in chronological order, spatial order, or topical order.

D. Write a summary that you could use to conclude your speech.

E. Write a stirring ending you could use to conclude your speech.

F. Find five quotations you could use to end your speech.

Real-Life Speaking Situations

1. How many oral reports do you remember giving in school? You have probably delivered reports on countries, famous people, historical events, books, and a number of other subjects over the years. The need to give such reports usually does not end when you leave school. On many jobs and in many social situations, informational reports are an important part of group communication. Think of the occupation and the social activities you intend to pursue after you have finished your schooling. What kinds of reports would you need to give in those pursuits? Imagine that you belong to a service club, a political committee, or another social group and that you have an idea about what the group should do concerning a project, a recent controversy, or some other subject. First, identify the group and the subject of your report. How do other members of the group feel toward this subject? How much do they know about it? What are the main points you will need to present? How will you introduce the subject? Write an outline for a three- to four-minute oral report on your subject. Be prepared to deliver your report in class.

2. When you buy, sell, or rent a place to live, you are likely to hire the services of a real estate agent. In helping clients, real estate agents give reports on property; present deals to buyers, sellers, and renters; conduct meetings and discussions; and engage in many other activities that require verbal communication skills. Imagine that you are a real estate agent and that you have been hired to sell a house or an apartment exactly like the one in which you are now living. How would you present that house or apartment to prospective buyers? What would you say about it? How would you bring up price? How would you point out weaknesses and flaws in the property? (Remember that real estate agents are bound by ethical standards to be honest and forthright in presenting a property.) Make an outline of what you would say, and be prepared to use your outline to deliver a short presentation in class as if you were showing the property to a prospective buyer. When you have finished, conduct a question-and-answer session in which your classmates ask questions from a prospective buyer's point of view.

CHAPTER **12**

USING APPROPRIATE LANGUAGE

OBJECTIVES:

After studying this chapter, you should be able to

1. List the differences between good speaking and good writing.

2. Choose the words that most clearly express your thoughts.

3. Explain the difference between specific and general words.

4. Explain the difference between concrete and abstract words.

5. List ways of making language more vivid.

6. Define and give examples of simile and metaphor.

7. Define and give examples of exaggeration, understatement, and irony.

8. List and use ways to emphasize ideas.

9. Identify and use appropriate tone.

10. Adjust language to suit an audience.

Alice was helping Donna with her speech on Camp Hudson. Donna began, "Camp Hudson, it's like a really cool place."

"Wait a minute, Donna," Alice broke in. "Before you praise it, describe it for me."

"OK. Well, this camp is in the woods—it's something else."

"You say it's 'in the woods.' Can you be more specific?"

"Well there's this mountain. And at the bottom there's this lake. And the camp is sort of between them, like at the bottom of the mountain—but still in the woods."

"Let's see if I'm getting this. Camp Hudson is at the foot of a mountain nestled in a woody area between the mountain and a lake."

"Right! Just like I said."

Donna is facing the same problem everyone faces when giving a speech. She has material that is vivid to her, and she wants to share it with her friend Alice. How well Alice appreciates and understands Donna's speech will depend to a large extent on the language Donna uses to express her thoughts.

In the last chapter, you learned about rehearsing your speech. As you continue rehearsing, you will need to focus on two separate but interrelated parts of presentation: language and delivery. In this chapter you will explore language, and in the next chapter you will look at delivery.

HOW GOOD SPEAKING DIFFERS FROM GOOD WRITING

Although good speaking and good writing are similar, they differ in many important ways. The basis for the difference is that spoken language is meant for the ear, while written language is meant for the eye. Spoken language must be understandable immediately, since listeners cannot go back to look at a sentence, a paragraph, or a page the way readers can. Yet, despite this drawback, speakers do have one major advantage over writers. In addition to words, speakers have facial expressions, gestures, and tone of voice to help them clarify meaning.

While good writing and good speaking differ, most effective speakers, such as the famous journalist Edward R. Murrow (1908-1965), write and then carefully revise their speeches before delivering them.

Spoken language generally relies on fewer words than written language does. In other words, good speaking does not require as large a vocabulary as good writing does. In addition, speakers rely more heavily than writers do on familiar words and on short words.

Spoken sentences tend to be slightly shorter than written sentences. Especially when listening rather than reading, it is difficult to follow the train of thought in a long sentence.

Spoken language also tends to contain more qualifiers than does written language. Speakers often use such expressions as *I think, it seems to me, that is to say,* and *the point I want to make.* The reason for this abundance of qualifiers is that a reader can go back over a sentence several times to wring *every* ounce of meaning from it, but a listener has only one shot at the meaning. Knowing this difference, good speakers help listeners by providing verbal clues that are unnecessary in writing.

Good speaking allows more use of personal words than does good writing. Good speeches often contain many personal pronouns, such as *I, you, we, us,* and *our.* In addition, spoken language generally has more references to family members and relationships than does written language.

Spoken language is usually more repetitive than written language. A speaker may say the same thing two or three times to make sure the audience understands. Usually, a writer need say something only once.

Spoken language allows the use of more slang and informal constructions than does written language. Perhaps the most important sign of informality is the use of contractions. Good speaking allows for the use of contractions to a far greater extent than good writing does.

ACTIVITY: Analyzing a Speaker's Presentation

Listen closely to a public speech such as a sermon or a campaign speech. Analyze the speaker's use of distinctive spoken-language characteristics in the following areas: vocabulary, sentence length, use of qualifiers, repetition, and use of personal words, contractions, and slang. Share your findings with your classmates.

CHOOSING THE RIGHT WORD

To be understood by listeners, speakers must be careful to choose the right words—the words that most clearly and exactly express their thoughts. Using precisely the right words will give you the greatest chance of communicating your meaning to your audience. Too often, in both informal conversation and in public speaking, people make statements that are simply not clear. How often have you heard someone say something like "I'm going to that place where they have those things I need for class" instead of "I'm going to that business supply store that carries notebook paper and erasers."

Clarity, the clearness of your language, is a matter of choosing the right words. Although you never know whether a word is truly the right one for every member of the audience, you increase your chances of communicating clearly when you use simple words, precise words, specific words, and concrete words.

Simple Words

Your ideas will be easier to understand if you use simple words. **Simple words** are familiar words, usually words of one or two syllables. Difficult words are words known to a much smaller number of people. Difficult words are often based on Latin and often have three syllables or more.

English gives us a wide range of words that can be used to express various shades of meaning. In some circumstances, you may believe that you need to use a difficult word to be accurate. For instance, you may wish to express the idea that your brother's hardheaded behavior only exacerbated a problem he was having with his boss. *Exacerbate* is a perfectly good word for expressing the meaning "to increase something's severity." However, would you need to use that word? Wouldn't it be clearer to say that your brother's hardheaded behavior only *aggravated* the problem he was having with his boss? Or you could say that your brother's hardheaded behavior only made the problem he was having with his boss worse.

Too often, speakers use difficult or fancy words for no particular reason. Unless you have some good reason for doing otherwise, select the simplest, most commonly used word that will accurately express your meaning. In doing so, you will make your speech appear much less stilted and will aid your audience in understanding what you are saying.

"Stockworth," reprinted by permission of Sterling & Selesnick, Inc.

Like any good speaker, Stockworth has no use for a speech, or a speech writer, that does not use simple words.

In the "Stockworth" cartoon shown above, Stockworth's message is that whoever confuses or misunderstands the importance of basic change in industry is in danger of being set aside or replaced. However, Stockworth realizes that his speechwriter has chosen pretentious words that will probably prevent most people in the audience from understanding the message of the speech.

Of course, sometimes a less well known word is so accurate or so expressive that no simpler word can be substituted for it. However, most of the time the less well known word is pretentious, stuffy, not as clear, or simply not necessary. English has grown by borrowing words from other languages. As a result, it contains many words that are very close in meaning. When words have nearly the same meaning, choose the simpler word whenever possible.

Here is a brief list of simple words that are better to use in speaking than their more pretentious equivalents, which follow them.

death	*for*	demise	wedding	*for*	nuptials
avoid	*for*	eschew	home	*for*	residence
view	*for*	vista	begin	*for*	commence
drink	*for*	quaff	use	*for*	utilize

Precise Words

You will make your ideas easier to understand if the words you use to state them are precise. **Precise words** express your thoughts and feelings accurately, or exactly. To choose precise words, you must (1) have a large enough speaking vocabulary to give you choices and (2) be sensitive to differences in meaning.

The larger your speaking vocabulary, the greater the number of choices you will have. For example, imagine that you went to a party and did not have a good time. In speaking about the party, you might say, "That was a bad party." The word *bad* is vague because it does not give a precise picture of what was wrong with the party. Rather than saying *bad,* you could express your reaction more accurately by saying that the party was *slow, boring, noisy, uninteresting,* or *humdrum.* If you have choices and are sensitive to differences between words, you can often come up with a word that more clearly and accurately communicates your point.

When you rehearse your speech, think about your choices in wording and decide whether you have used the most precise word. If you are not sure, consult a dictionary or a thesaurus (a book of synonyms) to help stimulate your thinking. The thesaurus will give you choices, while the dictionary will help you develop an understanding of precise differences in words that seem quite similar.

Even slight differences can be important. For example, suppose that you were giving a speech on football and were trying to explain that one lineman's frequent success in breaking up the opposing team's plays was due primarily to his speed. As you are rehearsing, you discover that you have a choice of referring to the lineman as very *fast* or very *quick.* Even though the two words are similar, they say something quite different. *Fast* means that a runner can cover a distance in a short period of time; *quick* means that a runner can move or react immediately. It may be that the lineman runs no faster than his teammates. However, since he can move forward as soon as the ball is snapped and before opposing players can react, he is quick. Thus, for the lineman, how quickly he can move is really more important than how fast he can run over a distance.

Specific Words

Your ideas will be easier to understand if you use words that are specific rather than general. **Specific words** focus on the items within a category; **general words** refer to an entire category. The word *building,* for example, is a common general word for referring to different kinds of structures. *House, apartment, hotel,* and *condominium* are all specific types of buildings. Therefore, to make your idea clearer, instead of saying, "Magda's company just finished construction of a *building,*" you might say, "Magda's company just finished construction of a *condominium.*"

Almost any concept can be made more general or more specific by the words you use to express it. The more specific you are, the more control you have over what your audience visualizes. For example, if you say "pet," some people in your audience may visualize dogs, some cats, some parakeets, some fish, and some even snakes. If you are more specific and say "cat," the pictures still will vary somewhat. One person may think of a tabby, another a Siamese, another an Angora, and another a pure black cat. If you become even more specific and say "blue point Siamese," the members of your audience are likely to picture in their minds the specific image you want them to see.

The following pairs of sentences show the contrast between general and specific words. The first sentence in each pair uses a general word; the second sentence uses a more specific word.

A *bird* was at the feeder.
A *robin* was at the feeder.

He sat reading a *book.*
He sat reading a *paperback novel.*

Carmen drove by in her *automobile.*
Carmen drove by in her *convertible sports car.*

She brought them several *things.*
She brought them *pencils, paper, and crayons.*

Concrete Words

In your speech, use more concrete words than abstract words. **Concrete words** name things that can be perceived by the five senses. For example, *desk, peanut butter, photograph,* and *record* are all concrete words. **Abstract words** name things that cannot be perceived by the five senses;

instead they name such things as ideas, values, and beliefs. For example, the words *beautiful, freedom, fairness,* and *justice* are abstract words. The more concrete the words you use, the easier your speech will be to understand.

Of course, you need at least some abstract words in your speech to name the categories and ideas you are using to organize your concrete words and examples. Be careful, though, that you always illustrate the meaning of any abstract word with concrete words. Note in the following paragraph that the abstract word *democracy* is illustrated with several concrete examples.

> We are fighting for democracy. We are fighting for the man and woman at the voting booth. We are fighting for the worker demanding the right to negotiate, the student speaking freely against a proposed law, the tenant demanding protection by the police.

ACTIVITY: **Analyzing Word Choice in a Speech and Finding Specific Words and Expressions**

Listen to a speech. It may be a sermon, an editorial delivered on television or on the radio, a political address, or any other address. Note the key word in each sentence. Is each key word precise? Would you have used another word? If so, what word would you have used? Does the speech contain more specific words than general words? Does it contain more concrete words than abstract words? Report your findings to your class.

Finally, using a dictionary, a book of synonyms, or your own creativity, find a more specific word or expression for each of the following terms: *car, office furniture, wearing apparel, cutlery, kitchen utensil, crime, animal, flower.*

USING VIVID LANGUAGE

Sometimes ideas are clear, but they lack punch—they are not memorable. Clarity is important in increasing understanding, but vividness gives language punch. **Vividness** is the quality of being full of life—of being vigorous or exciting. Vivid language captures the imagination, appeals to the senses, and creates mental pictures.

Sensory Words

One way to make your speech vivid is to use sensory words. **Sensory words** appeal to one or more of the five senses. To find sensory words, look in either a dictionary or a book of synonyms for words that have roughly the same meaning as the word you intend to use but that create a vivid picture. For example, in each of the following pairs of sentences, the first sentence is bland. Notice how each sensory word in the second sentence creates a more vivid picture.

Al *walked* out of the room.
Al *stomped* out of the room.

The snake *moved* through the grass.
The snake *slithered* through the grass.

The *noise* was *loud.*
The *explosion* was *deafening.*

Figurative Language

Another way of expressing an idea vividly is by using figurative language. **Figurative language** contains words and phrases that are not literally true, but that create a new, sharp meaning all their own. For example, have you ever heard an announcer say that a show or a game held people ''riveted to their seats''? Of course, the announcer did not mean those words literally. The cartoon shown below is funny because these words are used in their literal, not their figurative, meaning.

Drawing by Lorenz. © 1985 by The New Yorker Magazine, Inc.

''E-242 and 243 in the mezzanine! A couple riveted to their seats!''

Here are some of the types of figurative language that you can use to create vivid images in your speeches.

Simile. A **simile** is a comparison between essentially unlike things. In similes, the comparison is introduced by *like, as,* or a similar word (*seem* or *appear,* for example). The effectiveness of a simile depends on the vividness of the picture it creates.

Notice how the similes in the following examples create vivid images.

Paul's mind was like a patio rotisserie. It kept turning at the same slow rate, no matter what was on it.

Mike can't make up his mind which girl he wants to dance with. He's like a bee going from flower to flower.

Vicky's criticism was as sharp as a knife edge.

For some reason, good news always comes like a herd of snails, while bad news comes rushing like a stampede of elephants.

Her embrace was as warm as a down comforter.

Metaphor. A **metaphor** is also a comparison between essentially unlike things. Unlike a simile, a metaphor does not contain the words *like* or *as.* For example, "The ship went through the water like a plow" is a simile; "The ship plowed through the water" is a metaphor. Here are some other examples of metaphors.

The veteran base stealer regretted that his wheels weren't what they once had been.

The snow blanketed the ground.

Jack is a tiger when he competes.

Nancy will be a guinea pig for the new project.

Our offensive line is a wall.

Hit it to Pete; his hands are sieves.

Exaggeration. Exaggeration, or **hyperbole,** is a form of figurative language when it is used to emphasize or to enlarge, but not to deceive. In its simplest form, exaggeration involves selecting words that go beyond the accuracy of the situation. For example, when you are hungry, you may say that you're starved. A person may express embarrassment by saying, "I thought I'd die." In anger, someone may tell a friend that she won't talk to her again "in a hundred years."

Exaggeration is often used as a source of popular and literary humor. Many people enjoy getting together and trying to top each other's stories with even greater exaggerations. Some places even hold "tall tale" contests.

Understatement. Understatement is just the opposite of exaggeration. By stating an idea in terms that are less than what could be used, you can create a vivid image of an idea, an event, or a thing. For instance, when a batter strikes out five times in one game, a writer may comment, "Jones didn't distinguish himself today." After hiking through the Rocky Mountains for a month, someone might remark, "I just thought I'd go for a bit of a stroll in those hills there." A father might say of his son, "Bernie just had a little snack—five sandwiches and a quart of milk."

Irony. Irony is the use of words to imply that something is considerably different, perhaps even the opposite, from what is actually said. A student may be speaking ironically when he or she says, "I just love to prepare speeches," or "Alex just happened to be in the hall when Mary Harper walked by on her way to class."

When irony becomes cutting, biting, or bitter, it is called **sarcasm.** For example, when one diver does a belly flop into the pool, another diver may make the sarcastic remark, "There's the team's ace diver. That sure was a great performance." Seeing a friend give a small tip at a restaurant, a companion may comment, "Marie's very generous—she always leaves the waiter at least a nickel." After a boring play, someone leaving the theater may sarcastically say, "That was really an exciting performance. In the middle of the second act, the lady behind me accidentally hit me with her program and woke me up."

ACTIVITY: Analyzing Sensory Words and Identifying Different Kinds of Figurative Language

First, find a paragraph that you think is particularly vivid because of its use of sensory words. Analyze these words to identify the senses that they appeal to. Share your findings with your class. Then identify each of the following uses of figurative language as *simile, metaphor, exaggeration, understatement,* or *irony*.

1. The peace was like the eye of a hurricane.
2. Tilly is so strong that she could knock Jupiter out of its orbit.
3. We had a little breeze the day before yesterday—I think it was called a tornado.
4. When he's boxing, his arms are pistons.
5. Don took a little nap after dinner. I woke him up to go to work this morning.

Finally, change the following similes into metaphors (the first one has been done for you).
Simile: Howie moved like a cat to get to the ground ball.
Metaphor: Howie was a cat as he pounced on the ground ball.

1. He sleeps as soundly as a bear in the dead of winter.
2. The icy hill in front of school was like glass. People kept slipping and sliding.
3. The bright green spotlight made Donna look like a frog standing on a lily pad.
4. The baby's cry was like a siren in the night.
5. Her thoughts ran as deep as mountain canyons.

EMPHASIS

Emphasis is the force or special attention given to a particular word or point. Through emphasis, you can signal to your audience exactly what you want them to remember.

In Chapter 3 you learned how emphasis can be achieved through your gestures and the sound of your voice. Now you will look at how emphasis can also be achieved through repetition and announcement.

What message do you think this coach is emphasizing by making this gesture with his arm and hand?

Repetition

By far the easiest and most common means of showing emphasis is repetition. **Repetition** is saying the same thing again. If you said to someone, "Charlene got A's on every one of her physics tests—imagine that, A's on every one of her physics tests" you would be drawing special attention to Charlene's grade by repeating it. Repetition tells an audience, "Pay attention—this is really important." Used sparingly and appropriately, repetition is a powerful device.

Another form of repetition is restatement. **Restatement** is the repetition of an idea but not necessarily in the same words. Suppose you were to say, "Charlene got A's on every one of her physics tests. Imagine that! On all seven tests during this term, Charlene got an A." With restatement, the idea is repeated, but the language is different.

Repetition can be used to emphasize one single bit of information, or it can be used to build a series of related ideas. One of the masters of the use of repetition was Dr. Martin Luther King, Jr. In many of his speeches, he used word repetition to add power to his statements. His speech "I Have a Dream," which is included in full on page 608, contains many examples of repetition. In the following passage from that speech, notice the power of a particular kind of repetition called **parallelism,** in which a word or phrase is repeated in the same form to emphasize an idea, a mood, or some other feature in a work. In this example of parallelism, the same word or words are repeated at the start of each sentence to give Dr. King's words added force.

There are those who are asking the devotees of civil rights, "When will you be satisfied?" We can never be satisfied as long as the Negro is the victim of the unspeakable horrors of police brutality. We can never be satisfied as long as our bodies, heavy with the fatigue of travel, cannot gain lodging in the motels of the highways and the hotels of the cities. We cannot be satisfied as long as the Negro's basic mobility is from a smaller ghetto to a larger one. We can never be satisfied as long as a

Negro in Mississippi cannot vote and a Negro in New York believes he has nothing for which to vote.

Since repetition is such a powerful device, it should be used sparingly. If you overuse it, an audience can no longer tell what is being stressed. Too much repetition leads to no emphasis at all.

Announcement

A second way of emphasizing a point is to precede what you intend to say with an **announcement** that states your feelings about that point. For instance, you might use any of the following statements as an announcement.

Now I come to what I consider my most important point.
This second idea is the key to understanding the material.
Pay close attention to the steps of this process. They are a little tricky to follow.
The formula I am about to give you is the one that you will use most in this entire unit.

ACTIVITY: Identifying and Applying Methods for Achieving Emphasis

Read each of the following items. For each item, tell whether it achieves emphasis through repetition, restatement, or announcement.

1. Three new cases of this deadly disease are reported each week—that's 156 new cases a year!
2. Everyone was amazed by Casper's margin of two million votes—that's two million votes.
3. Jack hit .287 last year, just about .300!
4. The United States Coast Guard traces its history back to 1790—that means it is almost as old as this country.
5. Pay attention to this next step. It is crucial to the success of your project.

Now rewrite each of the following sentences in three different ways. First, rewrite it using restatement. Second, rewrite it using repetition. Third, rewrite it using announcement.

1. The ship is 1,100 feet long.
2. Martinez climbed the mountain in a record two hours and fifteen minutes.
3. Unless we cut back on spending now, the city will be out of money by September.
4. The war dragged on for another three years.
5. A record fourteen inches of snow fell yesterday.

TONE

Tone indicates the speaker's attitude toward the subject and the audience. No doubt, you are most familiar with tone expressed through the sound of a speaker's voice. Choosing the appropriate tone is essential. For example, using an encouraging tone to deliver a speech about the need to help keep school grounds clean will have a greater appeal to an audience than giving the same speech in a nagging tone.

CONFUSION.

Pater (fuming). "Don't Look at Me, Sir, with—ah—in that Tone of Voice, Sir!"
Filius. "I never uttered a——"
Pater (waxing). "Then don't let me See—ah—another Syllable, Sir!"
[*Exeunt.*

Tone is often associated with nonverbal behavior. In this 1884 cartoon from the British Magazine *Punch*, the father is interpreting his son's nonverbal message as if it were a verbal one.

Tone is also expressed through the speaker's choice of language. The most obvious differences in tone are set by the level of formality or informality of the language. At one end is the dignified, polished tone of a manuscript speech on a very serious, solemn, or formal occasion. At the other end is the chatty, personal tone used in conversation with close friends. Although different occasions call for slight differences in tone, you will generally want to avoid extremes. A very formal, pompous tone will fail to ring true to an audience. Likewise, excessively informal, slangy speech is too casual for most public speaking situations.

Consider the following two sentences:

The esteemed police officers of our community need, nay, merit the total support of every committed citizen in order to preserve the very essence of legal standards.

Face it man, we've got to support the cops or we're dead!

Setting aside any other considerations, the tone in each of these sentences makes them inappropriate for a speech on the role of the police in a community.

Certain tones can turn an audience off. Avoid sarcasm and condescension. For example, if your friend got a D on a test you would not say, "Wow, that's great! Donna got a D." Donna might likely interpret your remark as sarcasm. Likewise, you would not say, "You should feel good about the D. After all, Donna, you're not that good a writer, you know." Such a statement has a condescending tone, which would also insult Donna.

This does not mean, of course, that only one tone should be used for all occasions. A report given to the principal's advisory board should be delivered in a tone that differs from a report on the same information given to fellow members of a student committee at an informal meeting.

For formal speaking occasions, use your best vocabulary, grammar, and syntax. Formal language is not stuffy or unnatural, but it is more careful and exact. Informal speaking occasions allow for the use of some slang and colloquial expressions. Informal language also contains many more personal references to the speaker and to members of the audience.

ACTIVITY: Adjusting Tone for Different Audiences

Prepare a short statement describing how you get ready for a speech. First, prepare this statement assuming that your audience is your teacher. Second, prepare this statement assuming that your audience is your best friend. Then tell your class how the tone of each statement differs.

ADJUSTING YOUR LANGUAGE TO YOUR AUDIENCE

Like all groups of people, audiences differ from one to another. In Chapter 9 you looked at essential information you must learn about your audience when you are preparing your speech. Here you will look at how to adjust your vocabulary to your audience and how to use personal pronouns and rhetorical questions to make your speech more audience-centered.

Vocabulary Level

Adjust your vocabulary level to suit your audience. You must use a level of vocabulary that your audience will understand and find appropriate. Obviously, the words you use in a speech given to kindergarten students will differ from those you use in a speech given to members of the city council. Choosing a word that is accurate, specific, and vivid will not matter if your audience does not understand that word.

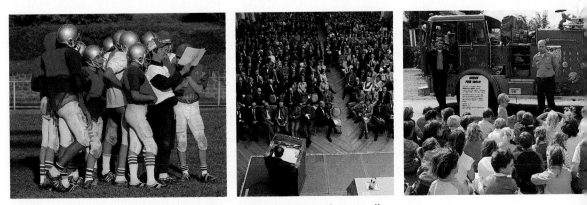

If you were giving a speech on the same subject to these three audiences, how would you vary your language to suit each group of listeners?

Audience-Centered Material

Whenever you have a choice, use material that is most closely related to your audience's experience. For instance, if you could use one of two examples—driving a car or flying an airplane—in a speech to your classmates, you would usually want to use driving a car because that example relates more closely to your audience's experience.

At times, you have to create ways to relate your material to your audience's experience. Two ways of creating such relationships are by using personal pronouns and by asking rhetorical questions.

Personal Pronouns. Using personal pronouns helps to involve your audience in your speech. You give each speech to a specific audience—not to some general or unknown group, but to the one that is sitting right there in front of you. It is important for that audience to see you as talking with them. One of the ways to do this is to use the personal pronouns *you* and *we* freely. The pronoun *you* will make the audience feel that you are talking directly to them. The pronoun *we* will make them feel that they are joining with you for some shared purpose. Therefore, instead of saying *"One* will always want to make sure that . . . ," say, *"You* will always want to make sure that . . ." Instead of saying *"People* often find that . . . ," say, *"We* often find that . . ."

Rhetorical Questions. A **rhetorical question** is one that is not meant to be answered but is asked only for effect. You can make your points in a speech by posing them in the form of rhetorical questions. Using rhetorical questions helps to involve your audience by getting them to think actively. Audiences remember more about a speech and like it better when the speech involves them. An excellent device for inviting audience involvement is the rhetorical question.

For example:

Across the country, parents are telling their children to turn off the TV set. Did you know that television can actually help your children to learn?

You say that you think cars are unreliable. Do you know that 40 to 45 percent of cars are still on the road after ten years of operation?

"Don't worry," you say. "We've experienced hurricanes before." Did you know that in 1970 Hurricane Celia cost Texans $453.8 million in damage?

Say that you are practicing a speech on the history of the bicycle. Instead of beginning "The bicycle originated in about . . . ," you might try the following phrasing: "Do you know when the first bicycle was built? Can you come up with a specific date? If you thought during the 1800's—you're absolutely right!"

These rhetorical questions get the point across in a way that involves the audience. As a result, the audience will likely remember information better and find that information more interesting than if you simply began by telling it to them.

ACTIVITY: Adjusting Language to Suit an Audience

Rewrite the following sentences so that they relate better to an audience of your classmates.

1. One should always brush one's teeth at least twice a day.
2. Athletic programs can build school morale.
3. Driving a car to school can be frustrating.
4. Students should take courses that will benefit them.
5. Some say that the only truly American art form is jazz.

Then listen to a speech. Listen carefully to the speaker's language. Was it well suited to the audience? Write down five specific examples of words or phrases that were particularly suitable. If the speaker used any unsuitable language, write down changes that would adapt that language to the audience. Be prepared to report your findings and changes to your class.

COMMON PROBLEMS

There are several common problems with language that can make your speech less interesting. As a rule, you will want to avoid using jargon, clichés, euphemisms, slang, and words that have unintended meanings.

Jargon

Jargon, you will remember from page 33, is language that is used by people in a particular group or field but is not necessarily understood by those outside that group or field. When you give a speech, you usually select a topic that is familiar to you. In so doing, you may be tempted to use vocabulary that is familiar only to those who share your grasp of your topic. For example, in giving a speech on baseball to an audience of non-baseball-fans, if you mentioned that hitters strive for *frozen ropes* and *taters* (for line drives and home runs), you would very likely lose the attention of many members of your audience.

Baseball, cooking, sailing, woodworking, and most activities each have a unique language that outsiders do not readily understand.

Clichés

A **cliché** is a figurative expression that has been used so often that it has lost its power. The expressions "smooth as silk," "to last through thick and thin," and "do your own thing" may still have meaning, but they do not have the ability to arouse audience attention. In fact, overuse of clichés is likely to cause an audience to lose interest in what you have to say. If you want to use figurative language to make your speech more vivid, try to create original phrases and avoid worn-out clichés.

The following phrases are some common clichés.

Slow as molasses	Tried and true
Eats like a bear	Calm, cool, and collected
Cold as ice	Selling like hotcakes

Euphemisms

Euphemisms are words or phrases that are not very expressive or vivid but are used in place of words that are thought to be unpleasant or distasteful. Of course, euphemisms have their place in speech. They help you avoid offending people or hurting their feelings. However, using too many euphemisms can make your writing dull.

Common euphemisms include

sanitary engineer	*for*	janitor
passed away	*for*	died
preowned car	*for*	used car

Slang

Slang is highly informal language that is formed by creating new words and by giving common words new meanings. Much slang is related to a particular time and place. For example, in the 1960's, students often described anything good as "groovy" and anything serious as "heavy." New slang expressions tend to last a short while and then die out. A few pass into the mainstream of language.

Slang is generally out of place in most public speaking, except in very informal speeches and when you want to create a particular effect. Regular or repeated use of slang can make your speech seem unconventional, unreliable, and dated.

Unintended Meanings

Connotations are the emotions and associations that are suggested by certain words. (See Chapter 2 for more on connotation.) Because the connotations of a word can differ from person to person, you always run the risk of unintended meanings creeping into your speech.

However, by listening carefully during your practice sessions you can weed out a great deal of unintentionally offensive language. For instance, it does not take much audience sensitivity to recognize the offensiveness of words that ridicule a person or belittle someone's sex, race, or religion. Avoid all words and images that stereotype people or that assign qualities to individuals without regard to individual differences between people. As you rehearse your speech, listen for meanings that your words may have for your listeners, not just for the meaning you intend your words to have.

ACTIVITY: **Identifying Common Language Problems in Speeches**

Choose a partner with whom to rehearse your speech. After you have given your speech, identify any jargon, clichés, euphemisms, slang, or unintended meanings that should be removed from it. Then have your partner tell you whether he or she spotted any other revisions in language that you should make.

Reverse roles, and note any jargon, clichés, euphemisms, slang, or unintended meanings in your partner's speech. Share your findings with your partner.

Profiles in Communication

Olga Bichachi

While many people have difficulty choosing the right words in one language, Olga Bichachi has to choose the right words in two languages! As a community relations coordinator for a large public school system, Ms. Bichachi uses her multilingual communication skills to perform tasks ranging from interpreting at international student conferences to translating musical lyrics.

To interpret messages accurately, Ms. Bichachi needs to understand the cultural context of the languages she is interpreting. As Ms. Bichachi states, "Every language has its own idiosyncrasies." She feels that it is important to live in a country for some time to get acquainted with the culture before trying to tackle these idiosyncrasies.

Understanding a culture involves understanding the patterns of thought that members of the culture share. According to Ms. Bichachi, "You don't think language, you think thoughts." A trained interpreter's grasp of cultural thought patterns enables him or her to translate quickly—almost automatically. Ms. Bichachi feels, however, that no one is a born interpreter and says that "the only way to develop the skills is to practice." Ms. Bichachi recommends tape-recording a passage from the newspaper and then playing it back, interpreting the words into another language as quickly as possible.

In addition to having learned several languages, Ms. Bichachi has also earned a master's degree in applied linguistics. She is convinced that an interpreter must study a language scientifically, taking it apart and analyzing its grammar and vocabulary. This detailed study gives the interpreter an understanding of the language that can then be applied to particular situations. For example, just as each language has specific characteristics, every profession has its own set of words, or jargon. When translating messages between people in a profession, an interpreter must be familiar with these specific terms in both languages.

Ms. Bichachi notes that effective communication skills can make a person more self-confident and more eligible for many kinds of jobs. However, the most important benefit of having these skills, according to Ms. Bichachi, is that they "can give you an awareness of the world that makes you better appreciate and accept different cultures and behaviors."

SUMMARY

In your speech rehearsals, work to develop appropriate language.

Although good speaking and good writing are similar, they differ in several important ways. Spoken language uses a smaller vocabulary; uses shorter words and sentences, more qualifiers, and more personal words; is more repetitive; and allows for more informal constructions.

How well you communicate depends on your choosing the right words. Select the most precise words you can. Look for specific and concrete words to replace general and abstract words whenever possible. Select simple rather than difficult or fancy words. Choose vivid, sensory words rather than plain words, and use figurative language when appropriate.

Emphasize ideas to help your audience remember them. Emphasis is achieved through repetition, restatement, and announcement.

Choose a tone that is appropriate for both the audience and the occasion. Adjust your language to the audience. When you have a choice of material, base your selection on how well it relates to your audience. When your material does not relate well to the audience, create ways to relate it. To promote your audience's involvement in your speech, use the personal pronouns *you* and *we* and rhetorical questions.

Avoid the common problems of overusing jargon, clichés, euphemisms, and slang. Be careful that the words you choose do not carry any unintended meanings.

CHAPTER VOCABULARY

Look back through this chapter to find the meaning of each of the following terms. Write each term and its meaning in your communication journal.

abstract words
announcement
clarity
cliché
concrete words
connotation
emphasis
euphemism
exaggeration
figurative language

general words
hyperbole
irony
jargon
metaphor
parallelism
precise words
repetition
restatement
rhetorical question

sarcasm
sensory words
simile
simple words
slang
specific words
tone
understatement
vividness

REVIEW QUESTIONS

1. List four ways spoken language differs from written language.

2. To convey your meaning clearly, your words must be precise. When is a word considered precise?

3. The word *sports* is somewhat general. List ten specific words that can replace the general term *sports*.

4. The word *shoes* is concrete, since it names something that can be perceived by the senses. What is an example of an abstract word?

5. Vivid language creates strong, clear mental pictures. One way to make your language vivid is to use sensory words. What are sensory words?

6. Two types of figurative language are similes and metaphors. How does a simile differ from a metaphor?

7. Two other types of figurative language are exaggeration and understatement. How does exaggeration differ from understatement?

8. How does irony differ from sarcasm?

9. Repetition can help you emphasize points. How does repetition differ from restatement?

10. One way to make your speech audience-centered is to use rhetorical questions. What is another way?

DISCUSSION QUESTIONS

1. Figurative language helps make your writing vivid. However, a speech filled with too much figurative language appears "flowery." Discuss with your classmates the use of figurative language. Try to set up guidelines for determining how much is too much.

2. Many good speakers are witty, or able to use language in a sharp or amusing way. However, wit can often deteriorate into sarcasm. Discuss the difference between wit and sarcasm.

3. George Orwell once wrote, "The inflated style is itself a kind of euphemism. A mass of Latin words falls upon the facts like soft snow, blurring the outlines and covering up the details. The great enemy of clear language is insincerity." By "inflated style" Orwell means a style that uses many long, difficult words based on Latin. First discuss the meaning of Orwell's statement. Then discuss how it relates to your need to keep your language simple in your speech.

4. A Yiddish proverb says, "Words should be weighed and not counted." First discuss the meaning of this quotation. Then discuss how it relates to the use of language in your speech.

5. The power of language has been recognized throughout the ages. The following advice is found in the *Maxims of Ptahhotep* of ancient Egypt: "Be a craftsman in speech that thou mayest be strong, for the strength of one is the tongue, and speech is mightier than all fighting." First discuss the meaning of this maxim. Then discuss how it relates to using appropriate language in your speeches.

ACTIVITIES

1. Identifying Elements That Make a Speech Effective

Some speakers are known for eloquence, or exquisite use of language. One such speaker was Sir Winston Churchill. In the library, find a speech by Churchill. Pay special attention to the words and figures of speech that Churchill used. What specific, concrete words in the speech help to increase the audience's interest and understanding? Identify any metaphors and similes and examples of exaggeration, understatement, and irony. Analyze how these figures of speech contribute to the effect that Churchill was trying to have on his listeners. Also identify and analyze the methods Churchill used to emphasize particular ideas. How do these methods affect the tone of the speech? Do they make it dramatic? forceful? dignified? solemn? pompous? Carefully choose several words that state precisely your impression of the tone of the speech. Record your responses to these questions in your communication journal.

2. Revising Sentences to Make Word Choice More Precise

The following sentences contain vague words. Rewrite each sentence by replacing vague words with precise ones to make the meaning of the sentence clearer.

a. A little girl was happily playing with a toy.

b. An irritated police officer was trying to give directions to people.

c. The music of the South is interesting.

d. I got lots of stuff for Christmas.

e. Just go down the road a way and then turn.

3. Defining Differences Between Synonyms, and Identifying Vivid, Exact Synonyms

A. Immediately following these instructions are lists of several synonyms for the words *best, angry,* and *walk.* First, write a definition for each of the synonyms. Make sure that the definition you give for each word describes the special meaning that makes that word different from the other synonyms. Then, study the sentences following the synonyms, and replace the italicized word in each sentence with the synonym of that word that you think creates the most vivid image.

best—supreme, maximum, inimitable, peerless, superior
angry—irate, irascible, fuming, indignant, fierce
walk—march, pace, trudge, stalk, strut

1. What do you think is the *best* price we can get for this?

2. When she found that she had been overcharged for her prom dress, Erin was very *angry.*

3. When he saw that Sal was making fun of him, Scott *walked* out of the room.

4. Scott felt *angry* because he had thought that Sal was his friend.

5. When we saw Jan *walk* to the podium, we could tell that she thought that her speech would be the *best* one.

B. Using either a dictionary or a book of synonyms, list five words that you think would be good, vivid choices to replace the following words:

happy   said   ran   hit   friend

4. Analyzing the Language in a Political Speech

Many politicians are effective speakers. They have to be effective to win elections. Listen to a political speech. Analyze the speaker's use of language. How does the speaker use language effectively? Can you find any weaknesses in the speaker's use of language? If so, identify those weaknesses. Share your findings with your classmates.

5. Analyzing a Newscaster's Use of Language

News stories on television can be considered short informative speeches. Listen to your favorite newscaster. In what ways does the newscaster use language effectively? In what ways does he or she use language ineffectively? What advice would you give this person on improving his or her use of language? Share your advice with your classmates.

6. Completing Similes

Complete each of the following similes by creating an original comparison. Avoid writing clichés, such as "as sound as a dollar" for the first item.

a. The economy of a nation needs to be as sound as . . .

b. She was a great woman, as courageous as a . . .

c. A tall man, he looked like a . . .

d. Reading a book is like . . .

e. After the war, the peace between the two nations was as fragile as . . .

f. After helping clean up the house all day, I was as tired as . . .

g. That old car he bought looks like . . .

h. When the sun comes out after several days of rain, I feel as . . . as . . .

i. The waves washing up on the loose sand sounded like . . .

j. The light, cool breeze felt like . . .

7. Analyzing Methods for Achieving Emphasis

Analyze the methods used to achieve emphasis in two of the student speeches included in the Speech Appendix on pages 598–617. Begin by copying the specific words that the speakers use. Then identify whether these words achieve emphasis through repetition or announcement. Next, briefly state the idea or ideas that are being emphasized in each case. Finally, evaluate the effectiveness of each speaker's use of emphasis and compare how emphasis was used in the two speeches to communicate the speaker's ideas to the audience.

Record all this information in your communication journal and be prepared to share your findings in class discussion.

Real-Life Speaking Situations

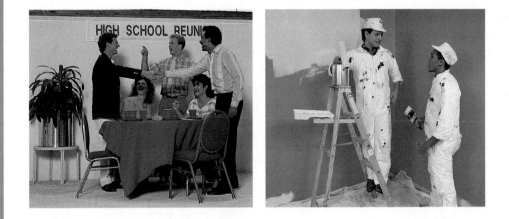

1. After you graduate, you will probably lose track of many of your high-school friends. However, in the course of your business and personal pursuits, you may likely run into some of these friends over the years. One common experience that brings old friends together is a high-school reunion. Imagine that you have just arrived at the ten-year reunion of your graduating class. As you look around, you notice many people who seem familiar, but they have changed in appearance— some are heavier, others are balding, and still others are in better physical shape than you remember. Despite these changes you still recognize the familiar voices and speech patterns of friends you haven't seen for a long while. What would those voices and speech patterns sound like? Which friends would you recognize by tone of voice? by word choice? by other distinctive speech characteristics? Using the speech characteristics of two of your friends, write a two-page dialogue depicting the three of you meeting at your ten-year reunion. Be prepared to present your dialogue in class and to respond to your classmates' feedback on how well you have captured your two friends' speech patterns.

2. Nearly all occupations have their own particular jargon. Because jargon terms often have other, more common, meanings, people not familiar with the jargon meaning of a term may be puzzled or misled by the jargon usage of that term. For example, you may be surprised to hear housepainters complain about holidays. Do painters enjoy their work so much that they don't like to take vacations? No, painters look forward to their time off, just as most people do. The situation becomes clear when you learn that *holiday* is painters' jargon for a spot that has been left uncovered on a painted surface. Think of jargon terms you know for various occupations, such as food preparation, mechanics, teaching, or retail sales. Identify five jargon terms used in a particular occupation. Find the definitions for these terms, and determine what relationship, if any, the jargon meaning has to a more common meaning of each term. Be prepared to give a report to your classmates on the five terms you chose and on how these jargon terms help people within the occupation communicate more efficiently and precisely.

PRESENTING YOUR SPEECH

OBJECTIVES:

After studying this chapter, you should be able to

1. Compare and contrast methods of giving a speech.

2. Cope with stage fright.

3. Use nonverbal behavior to your best advantage when presenting your speech.

4. Use vocal clues to your best advantage when presenting your speech.

5. Use appropriate language and grammar in your speech.

6. Understand how timing affects your speech.

7. Respond to feedback.

8. Anticipate distractions and respond with poise when the unexpected occurs.

9. Use audiovisual aids in your speech.

10. Evaluate your delivery.

Jenny Brown walked to the front of the class, set her notes on the speaker's stand, paused, looked at her audience, and then launched into her speech. Jack Collins was especially impressed by her poise. She seemed genuinely enthusiastic. She looked at members of the class throughout her presentation. Not only was her speech interesting, but her use of voice, gestures, and movement added significantly to the quality of her presentation. As she walked back to her seat, Jack leaned over and said, "Jenny— that was great."

"Oh, Jack," she said as she collapsed into her seat, "I thought I was going to die. At the start I could feel the butterflies in my stomach, and my knees were shaky."

Jack looked at her as if she were kidding. "You could have fooled me," he said.

Was Jenny kidding? Was Jack insensitive to her behavior? Did he miss something? It is likely that Jenny *was* nervous. What is equally likely is that her preparations for giving the speech helped her manage her nervousness so that it was not noticeable to anyone in class.

In this chapter you will look closely at speech presentation to see how to cope with the very real nervousness that people often feel when faced with giving a speech. To begin, you will study the four methods for delivering speeches.

METHODS OF DELIVERY

Jenny learned that a speech can be delivered in any one of four ways: impromptu, manuscript, memorized, or extemporaneous. Although Jenny's effectiveness was largely due to her mastering the most usable method— extemporaneous speaking—each of the four methods of delivery is appropriate for certain circumstances.

Impromptu

An **impromptu speech** is one that is given on the spur of the moment with no direct preparation. When a visiting dignitary is stopped by reporters and asked to comment on a particular issue, the remarks the dignitary makes are delivered impromptu. In other words, the dignitary does not read from a prepared statement or follow a prepared outline but instead delivers the words as they come to mind.

Almost all of your ordinary conversation is impromptu. When your parents ask, "What happened at school today?" you are not likely to reply, "I need five minutes to think out what I want to say on that topic." Instead, you give them an impromptu answer immediately.

Impromptu delivery can often sound very natural, but it can also seem disorganized, since most people are not used to phrasing clear responses on the spur of the moment. Nevertheless, impromptu speaking is necessary in some public-speaking situations and in conversation. It is also useful as a classroom exercise, because it forces you to think on your feet and to speak clearly without much preparation time. Most formal speeches, on the other hand, require careful preparation and are not suited to impromptu delivery.

Though he speaks impromptu on many occasions, President Reagan reads major speeches from manuscript to minimize the chance of error.

Manuscript

A **manuscript speech** is one that is written out completely and read to the audience. The advantages of this type of delivery are that you can revise your wording until it is exactly right and that you can make sure you present your speech without leaving out a point.

Most presidential speeches you hear are manuscript speeches. By using a manuscript, a president avoids the risk of making blunders that might have major repercussions. This method of delivery also enables a president to show the careful thought that has been given to every aspect of the speech.

A manuscript speech has the additional benefit of allowing a speaker to know the exact amount of time the speech will take. Since the speaker does not deviate from the prepared speech, the amount of time the delivery takes during rehearsal should be the same as the actual presentation time. This advantage is especially important for a speech given on radio or television.

Although many speakers, especially beginners, favor delivering a speech from manuscript, this method is usually not best for the beginner. First, very few people can read a manuscript in a way that sounds natural and interesting. Second, in many cases a person does not have time to write and revise a complete manuscript. Third, and perhaps most important, the manuscript method does not teach you the skills necessary for most of the public speaking you are likely to do in real-life settings.

Memorized

A **memorized speech** is one that is written out completely and remembered word for word. Actually, a memorized speech is just a manuscript speech committed to memory and, as a result, presents some of the same problems. Just as few people can read a manuscript in a natural and interesting manner, so too can few people memorize well enough to make their speeches sound real. Listening to a speaker struggle to remember what words come next is even worse than listening to a person read poorly. Memorization also usually takes a long while and, like reading, does not teach you many of the public-speaking skills you will need. Although memorization may seem like an ideal method for controlling your delivery, this method can greatly increase your difficulty in making your speech appealing to your audience.

Extemporaneous

An **extemporaneous speech** is one that is fully prepared but not memorized. The extemporaneous method is preferred by most professional speakers for several reasons. First, since it is outlined and practiced, the extemporaneous speech gives a speaker greater control than does the impromptu speech. However, because the exact wording is left until the speech is given to an audience, the speaker's delivery maintains the freshness of an impromptu speech. Second, although prepared beforehand, the extemporaneous speech allows for far more audience adaptation and spur-of-the-moment change than does a manuscript speech or a memorized speech. Third, the skills of extemporaneous speaking can be used in nearly any speaking format, including group discussion, debate, and legislative speaking.

Since the extemporaneous method is usually the most effective, the remainder of this chapter deals with presenting a speech extemporaneously from an outline.

ACTIVITY: Analyzing Methods of Delivery

In your communication journal, keep a record of all the speeches you hear. Identify the method that you think was used in delivering each speech: manuscript, memorized, impromptu, or extemporaneous. Which of the speeches are the most effective? What relationships do you notice between effectiveness and method of delivery? Discuss your findings with your classmates.

STAGE FRIGHT

When you ask people how they feel about speaking in public, most will confess that they suffer from stage fright. **Stage fright** is the nervousness that speakers feel before and during the presentation of their speeches. Even though this nervousness, or stage fright, is real, you can learn to manage it and even to use it to your advantage.

Are you nervous about giving your speech? A review of what other people have learned about the effects of stage fright may help you put the problem into its proper perspective.

First of all, nearly everyone experiences nervousness. Whether you are a beginner or a very experienced speaker, you are likely to feel stage fright.

Can you imagine experienced speakers such as Abraham Lincoln or Franklin Delano Roosevelt feeling nervous before giving a speech? According to their own accounts, they were. Like many experienced speakers, they learned to accept this nervousness. Instead of thinking about how they felt, they put their minds on the content of the speech and on the audience. Experienced speakers find that some nervousness actually is beneficial, since people who are a little nervous are more likely to be alert and ready to do their best.

Second, your audience is not likely to notice your nervousness. You may think that everyone in the audience can actually see you shake. In fact, though, most of the time audiences are concentrating on the speech itself and are not aware of the speaker's nervousness. After having finished your speech, were you to confide in a friend that you had been very nervous, that person would likely say, "I didn't notice it. You didn't seem nervous at all."

For Better or For Worse®   **by Lynn Johnston**

Your nervousness is almost always more apparent to you than to your audience. Concentrate on your speech, and it will usually subside.

Third, the more often you speak, the better you will be able to cope with nervousness. For this reason, it is important to take advantage of every opportunity you have to speak. You are bound to make mistakes in your first few speeches, but with each speech you will make fewer and fewer mistakes, and your confidence will grow.

Knowing that stage fright does not spell disaster is one thing. Controlling your own stage fright is quite another. The following techniques will help you reduce your nervousness even in your very first speech.

Before the Speech

1. *Prepare for your speech carefully and completely.* Nervousness is directly related to preparation. If you know you are poorly prepared (or not prepared at all), you are likely to be very nervous. If, on the other hand, you have a good topic and have carefully worked through the steps of speech preparation, your nervousness is likely to be less intense.

Being prepared also means taking time for complete rehearsal. If you are scheduled for a speech on Wednesday, you cannot afford to wait until

Tuesday night to begin working on your presentation. Even if you have chosen a good topic, found plenty of information on it, and written an excellent outline, you will still not have enough time to practice your delivery. It is the confidence gained through practice that helps you handle your nervousness. Make sure that you leave yourself one or two days just for rehearsal. As you practice during that time, even the breaks between rehearsals will help you. Your mind will be working on your speech even when you are not conscious of it.

2. *If you can choose the order in which you will speak (first, second, last), schedule your speech to your own advantage.* Know what makes you most comfortable. If you need to "get it over with," then try to be one of the first to speak. If you do better by waiting, then schedule your speech nearer the end of the day.

3. *Look your best.* Dress in a way that gives you the greatest confidence. As a rule, the better you look, the better you will feel. Being appropriately dressed, well groomed, and enthusiastic when you give your speech will help boost your assurance and lessen your nervousness.

4. *Learn to relax tense muscles.* Tension is likely to reach its highest point shortly before you speak. During the speech immediately before yours, work on relaxing. While you are sitting at your seat, go through the steps in the chart below at least once.

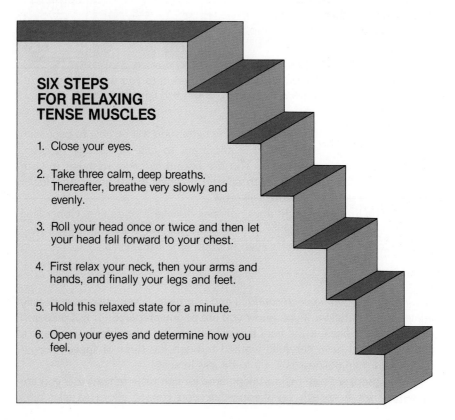

SIX STEPS FOR RELAXING TENSE MUSCLES

1. Close your eyes.

2. Take three calm, deep breaths. Thereafter, breathe very slowly and evenly.

3. Roll your head once or twice and then let your head fall forward to your chest.

4. First relax your neck, then your arms and hands, and finally your legs and feet.

5. Hold this relaxed state for a minute.

6. Open your eyes and determine how you feel.

5. *Give yourself a pep talk.* Immediately before the speech, remind yourself that you are well prepared and that the audience is going to profit from what you have to say. This reassurance will help you realize that even a mistake will not override the value of the speech.

6. *Walk to the speaker's stand confidently.* Let your movements and posture tell your audience that you are sure of yourself. Pause a few seconds before you begin speaking. Take a deep breath. Then start. Remember that you will survive regardless of what happens. No one is going to throw anything at you. If you forget some of your speech, you will not be disgraced.

During the Speech

Regardless of how well you are prepared, you may still experience the kinds of feelings and reactions that speakers often report. Take a minute to consider some of the most common sensations, which are given in the following list. Remember that each of these is a perfectly normal response shared by many other people.

Queasy feeling, butterflies, sweaty palms, general weakness. These are typical symptoms of nervousness, but given the right behavior, they will go away. As strong as these symptoms feel when you begin speaking, they lessen quickly once you get into your speech. Do not let your mind dwell on them. Remember that they really have no direct effect on your delivery. Ignore these sensations and concentrate on your content and your audience.

Dry mouth. Once you are in front of your audience, you cannot stop to get a drink. Licking your lips and swallowing will not help either, and doing so will detract greatly from your appearance. Start your speech slowly—and again, concentrate on what you are saying. As you talk, your lubricating system will return to normal.

Stumbling over words at the start. Stumbling is often a result of trying to say an idea exactly as you wrote it. Practice saying the opening lines several different ways so that you do not try to memorize only one opening.

Perspiration, squeaky voice, slight trembling. These reactions are generally beyond your control. They hurt your speech only if you start worrying about them. If you ignore them and get down to business, your body will likely return to normal.

Strong desire to quit. Resist quitting. The worst thing you can do is to give up before you have finished. Stopping will make giving a speech even more difficult the next time. Finish your speech no matter how painful the experience seems at the moment. When you are done, no doubt you will find that the audience did not think that the speech was as bad as you thought it was. In addition, you will build your confidence by proving to yourself that you can finish.

When any of these normal reactions continue throughout the speech, remind yourself that with each speech you will get a little more accustomed to speaking in public. The more speech experience you get, the more readily your body will return to normal before you get very far into your speech.

ACTIVITY: Managing Nervousness

Practice the relaxation techniques discussed in this section. Go through them immediately before class. Then tell your classmates whether or not you find them helpful.

In your communication journal, keep a record of the kinds of nervousness you experience before and during your speeches. Which of the suggestions related to stage fright help you most in managing your nervousness? Share your findings with your classmates.

REFINING NONVERBAL BEHAVIOR

Wise speakers know that their nonverbal behavior has as much, if not more, effect on achieving their goals as do the words they speak. If you give your speech with a "deadpan" face or with a scowl, if you shuffle about nervously, or if you look at the floor or at the ceiling, your audience is not going to trust you. Make sure that your nonverbal presentation sends the appropriate message.

Appearance

Wise speakers do everything they can to increase their chances of giving the best speech possible. Although there are some aspects of speechmaking over which you may have little control, you have a great deal of control over your appearance. Your *appearance* is how you look to your audience. Two key features of your appearance are your clothing and your grooming.

You may not realize the importance of appearance to your effectiveness in public speaking. You know that in daily conversations, good friends are likely to listen to you regardless of how you look. However, when you become a public speaker, even friends will look for clues to determine whether or not they should pay attention to you. Whether they should or not, audiences are going to draw conclusions about you and your speech based on how you look.

Good appearance is not going to guarantee a good speech, but poor appearance can destroy nearly any chance you have of achieving your goal. Proper appearance depends on the situation of the speech. For instance, official occasions require formal dress. Dress for classroom speeches, however, may be informal, but it should still be neat. You should be clean, well groomed, and your clothes should look neat and tidy. A good rule of thumb is that you should always be dressed as well as the best-dressed people in your audience. For some audiences and occasions, jeans are appropriate.

Most of the time a dress shirt and slacks for men and a dress or a skirt and blouse for women are appropriate. For more formal occasions, appropriate dress is a suit or sport coat and slacks for men and a suit, a dress, or a blazer and skirt or slacks for women.

In addition, you will want to avoid wearing anything that will be distracting to your audience. You should avoid loud colors, bright stripes or plaids, and clothing that could be called faddish. You should also avoid jewelry that will distract. Long necklaces or earrings that dangle or make noise when you move, flashy rings, ornate broaches, and the like will call attention to themselves and will distract your audience from your speech.

Eye Contact

A second nonverbal behavior that is essential to your effectiveness is eye contact. **Eye contact** refers to the way you look at members of your audience. Establishing eye contact helps to create a bond of communication. When a speaker looks at the audience, the audience looks back. When an audience looks at a speaker, there is a good chance that the audience is paying attention to that speaker. When a speaker refuses to make eye contact with members of the audience, the audience's attention drifts, and soon the bond of communication is broken.

To have good eye contact with an audience, give every person in it the impression you are speaking to him or her personally. Note the word *impression*. If you really tried to look one person in the eye throughout the entire speech, you would make that person very nervous and would lose everyone else's attention. Good speakers look randomly at individuals and groups of individuals throughout the entire audience. For instance, for just a second or two you may be talking to people on the left side of the front row. For the next few seconds you may be talking to people in the right rear of the audience. By moving from group to group, at random, you develop a bond with the entire audience. The key is to be looking at someone or some group at all times.

Facial Expression

Your audience will use your facial expression as a clue to the content of your speech. When you are being humorous, an audience expects a smile. When you are being serious, an audience expects a sincere, serious expression. Although controlling facial expression can be difficult, there are two common facial behaviors that you can learn to identify and to avoid: the "deadpan" and the conflicting expression.

Deadpan. A **deadpan** is an expressionless facial appearance that never changes, regardless of what is being said. Fear sometimes makes people lose all facial expression. However, if you are thinking actively about your content, your face will likely reflect your feelings.

Conflicting Expression. A **conflicting expression** is a facial appearance that does not agree with a speaker's words or feelings. For example, some people have developed the habit of smiling when they are angry or scared. Therefore, if they are a little nervous at the start of a speech, they may start smiling regardless of what they are saying. This conflict between verbal expression and facial expression can have a devastating effect on the speech.

To correct this problem, concentrate on your speech and on your audience, not on your fear. If you really are thinking about your material, your face is likely to reflect the appropriate feeling.

Gestures

Beginning speakers are always worried about what to do with their hands. When you are standing in front of an audience, you may get the impression that no matter what you do with your hands, you look strange. During a speech you should use the same natural gestures that you use in conversation.

Since nervousness may affect your gestures, make sure that you start your speech with your hands in a neutral position at your sides or resting palms up on the speaker's stand. Then as you start to talk, your hands will be free to move normally. If you start your speech with your hands clasped behind your back, gripping the speaker's stand, or in your pockets, you will not be able to make natural gestures. You do not think of what to do with your hands during conversation. Likewise, unless your teacher points out that you are doing something wrong, you should not think of what to do with your hands during your speech.

Some people "talk with their hands" more than others do. Unless you gesture so much that people pay more attention to your gestures than to your ideas, you should not worry about how much you gesture. However, do pay close attention to how appropriate your gestures are to what you

Your hand gestures will be natural and unstudied if you can avoid worrying about them before and during your speech.

say. For example, if you point to your audience as you say, "I want you to think about this," your gesture appropriately directs your words to your audience. Since gestures should seem natural, it is seldom a good idea to practice all of your gestures. Gestures that are practiced can tend to look artificial.

Posture

Good posture creates an impression of confidence and authority. Do not lean on a table, the wall, or the speaker's stand. At the start of your speech, stand up straight with both feet firmly on the ground. As you speak, you will shift position, but you should never slump, slouch, or look sloppy.

ACTIVITY: Evaluating Nonverbal Behavior

Rehearse your speech once again in front of your partner. This time, have your partner evaluate your nonverbal behavior. Discuss your partner's findings and ask for suggestions for improving your nonverbal behavior.

REFINING VOCAL SKILLS

The sound of your voice plays a major role in your success as a speaker. If you deliver your speech with enthusiasm, your audience will likely share your positive feelings. Conversely, if you are hesitant and seem uncertain, your audience will share your doubt and discomfort. Always do your best to promote a positive attitude in your speeches and to eliminate negative influences.

Enthusiasm

Show enthusiasm through your voice. *Enthusiasm* is the strong positive feeling speakers show for their topics. Almost all studies conclude that enthusiasm is the most important factor determining how much confidence an audience has in a speaker. Listeners who believe that a speaker is truly enthusiastic will become enthusiastic themselves about the speech and about the speaker.

The best way to achieve enthusiasm is to believe in your speech. If you really think your topic is a good one, if you really think you have found excellent material, and if you really think the material will interest your audience, you will be enthusiastic about giving your speech. Picture the following situation. Ken has hit three home runs in a playoff game to beat the other team virtually single-handedly. When he rushes home to tell his family about the game, he will sound enthusiastic even if as a rule he rarely gets very excited. His enthusiasm grows naturally out of his excitement about his topic and about telling his audience about that topic. In giving a speech, you need to generate the same excitement about giving your speech that Ken had in his report of his batting feats. Therefore, the key to enthusiasm is your attitude. Build a positive attitude, and the sound of your voice will take care of itself.

Vocalized Pauses

One aspect of voice that can destroy your effectiveness as a speaker is the vocalized pause. **Vocalized pauses** are the meaningless speech sounds that speakers use to fill time. The most common vocalized pauses are *uh, well uh, um,* and the ever-popular *you know.* Everyone uses these fillers at one time or another in conversation. When you are searching for the right word, when you are flustered or embarrassed, when you are rushing, you are likely to slip in one or more vocalized pauses. However, while vocalized pauses may be acceptable in conversation, they are not acceptable in public speeches.

Most of us do not hear our vocalized pauses. Because vocalized pauses are not related to content, our minds do not pay attention to them. As a result, some speakers are totally unaware that their constant use of vocalized pauses is driving their listeners to distraction.

The following program is a three-step method for identifying and moderating the use of vocalized pauses.

First, find out whether you overuse vocalized pauses. (Note that you should focus on overuse, not on the informal slips that nearly everyone makes now and then.) You are overusing vocalized pauses when your audience becomes aware of them because they call attention to themselves. One way to learn if you are overusing them is to ask people (including your teacher) whether they notice your vocalized pauses. You might ask, "When I talk are you aware of my use of *uh*'s, *well uh*'s, *um*'s, or *you know*'s?" If they say they are, then you need to work on limiting your use of vocalized pauses.

For Better or For Worse®   **by Lynn Johnston**

This speaker probably never noticed her use of vocalized pauses, but they were quite obvious to her listeners.

Second, train your ear to hear vocalized pauses when they occur. One way to do this is to have a person listen to you talk in practice sessions and raise one hand whenever he or she hears a vocalized pause. By having someone call attention to your vocalized pauses, you will begin to tune your ear to them. After a while you will hear vocalized pauses even before the listener signals you. At that point you will know that your ear has become trained to hear vocalized pauses.

Third, once you begin to hear yourself using vocalized pauses, you can start to limit their use through practice sessions. As you become more successful at limiting them during rehearsals, you will start to recognize them and limit them in your regular speaking.

Articulation, Pronunciation, and Enunciation

In public speaking more than in any other setting, you must be very careful of your articulation and pronunciation. As you learned in Chapter 4, *articulation* is the shaping of speech sounds into recognizable oral symbols that go together to make up a word. *Pronunciation* is the grouping and accenting of the sounds. (If you have problems with articulation and pronunciation, review the exercises in Chapter 4.)

If you are unsure of the pronunciation of a word, look it up in a dictionary. If you have a persistent problem of distorting, omitting, substituting, or adding sounds, you may want to work closely with a speech therapist. If you have the common faults of slurring sounds and leaving off word endings, you can help yourself with both problems. Take ten to fifteen minutes a day to read

THE FAR SIDE   By GARY LARSON

© 1985 Universal Press Syndicate

Trouble with pronunciation is seldom a life-threatening problem, as it is in this cartoon, but it can be an embarrassing one. Look up the difficult words in your speech, and practice saying them.

"Look out, Thak! It's a ... a ... Dang! Never can pronounce those things!"

passages aloud, trying to overaccentuate each of the sounds that give you difficulty.

When you deliver your speech, do your best to enunciate clearly. **Enunciation** refers to the distinctness of the sounds you make. Good enunciation is clear and precise. Many people suffer from sloppy enunciation. For example, they say *gotcha* for *got you*, *gimme* for *give me*, *commere* for *come here*, *liberry* for *library*, and *gunna* for *going to*. Although such sloppiness may sometimes be acceptable in casual conversation, it is not acceptable when delivering a formal speech.

Specific Vocalization Problems

Before delivering your speech, you may want to review the section on correcting vocalization problems in Chapter 4. Remember that pitch is the highness or lowness of the sounds you make. To speak effectively, you must speak at your *optimum pitch*, the pitch at which you feel the least strain and have the best resonance. Speaking at your optimum pitch will help you avoid using a monotone, a melody pattern that consists of only one tone. You must also show inflections—upward or downward glides of your pitch that communicate feelings.

Loudness, or *volume*, is the intensity of the speech tone, which is determined by the force exerted to produce it. When you deliver your speech, you must speak loud enough to be heard in the back of the room, but not so loud as to upset the people in the front of the room. A good way to determine whether you are speaking loud enough is to look at your audience. Do the people in the back of the room seem comfortable, or are they straining

Audiences generally expect an auctioneer to speak at a volume and rate that are greater than normal. Your listeners will likely not expect these same vocal traits from you. Always adapt your vocalization to suit your audience.

to hear you? Do the people in the front of the room look agitated, as if you were shouting at them? The more practice you gain speaking, the more easily you will be able to determine the appropriate degree of loudness for your speech.

Rate is the speed at which you speak. You must not speak so quickly that your audience cannot follow your points or so slowly as to bore them. Once again, the best test of your rate is your audience. By looking at their responses, you should be able to determine whether you are speaking at an appropriate rate.

ACTIVITY: Evaluating Vocal Skills

Working in groups of five, have each person stand and talk to the group for two minutes about his or her favorite class. Every time the person says *uh, well uh, you know,* or some other vocalized pause, each of the other people in the group should raise one hand. Can anyone get through the entire two minutes without a vocalized pause? Have the group evaluate each speaker's enthusiasm, articulation, pronunciation, pitch, volume, and rate.

REFINING VERBAL MESSAGES

A verbal message consists not only of the meaning of its words but also of the words themselves and their arrangement in sentences. (You may want to review Chapter 2 before delivering your speech.)

Diction

Diction refers to the words you choose to send your messages. As you recall from Chapter 12, your words should be precise, specific, concrete,

BLOOM COUNTY   **by Berke Breathed**

Choose simple words that will not seem pompous or pretentious. Your audience should be focused on your message, not on your vocabulary.

and simple. They also should be vivid and should place emphasis on appropriate points. In addition, they should be fresh, avoiding clichés and overuse of euphemisms and slang.

Grammar

Grammar refers to the rules and conventions for speaking and writing English. When you deliver a formal speech, use your best grammar. Work on mastering the following standard English forms, which commonly cause problems in speaking.

1. Use the nominative case for pronouns used as subjects.
   NONSTANDARD   *Him* and *me* saw an accident.
   STANDARD   *He* and *I* saw an accident.

2. Use the objective case for a pronoun used as the object of a preposition.
   NONSTANDARD   The problem is between Jim and *I*.
   STANDARD   The problem is between Jim and *me*.

3. Make sure that a verb agrees with its subject in number.
   NONSTANDARD   One of the books *are* missing.
   STANDARD   One of the books *is* missing.

4. Avoid confusing similar words.
   NONSTANDARD   I *set* down for a while.
   STANDARD   I *sat* down for a while.

5. Use adjectives to modify nouns and pronouns; use adverbs to modify verbs, adjectives, and adverbs.
   NONSTANDARD   He was doing *real good*.
   STANDARD   He was doing *really well*.

ACTIVITY: Evaluating a Speaker's Diction

Watch an effective public speaker giving a speech. Concentrate on the speaker's diction and grammar. Does the speaker use standard or nonstandard English? If you notice any nonstandard usages, do you think that the speaker used them for effect or in error? How did the speaker's words and grammar affect the message of the speech? Share your findings with your classmates.

OTHER FACTORS AFFECTING DELIVERY

Once you have coped with your stage fright and have refined your nonverbal, vocal, and verbal messages, you are ready to deal with other factors affecting your delivery. These factors are timing, feedback, distractions, and unexpected events.

Timing

As you gain experience in public speaking, you will also gain a sense of timing. **Timing** is the controlled pacing of a speech so that it fits within a time limit. To sharpen your timing, you need to develop a mental clock that helps you gauge the delivery of your speech so that you always know how much time you have left.

Your rehearsal periods give you an opportunity to develop this mental clock. During your rehearsals, you will get a sense of the length of your speech. Of course, this is only an approximate sense. Most people behave somewhat differently when actually giving a speech rather than when rehearsing it. Consequently, the time it takes to deliver your speech will probably vary somewhat. Experience will help you judge whether the actual delivery of your speech is likely to take more or less time than rehearsals take.

During your speech your teacher or a classmate may keep time with time cards so that you can see how you are doing. If not, you can set a watch on the lectern so that you can glance at it occasionally.

Timing also means pacing material to achieve maximum effect. Consider Henny Youngman's old one-line joke, "Take my wife—please." As many times as he tells this joke, it still gets a laugh because of his timing, the way he pauses before he says "please." As you gain experience, you will learn how to time the delivery of key sentences to get the most out of them. Timing comes with experience. The more you speak, the more you will develop this delicate sense.

Feedback

The test of effective speech delivery is how well the speaker reacts to audience feedback. Effective speakers know when to repeat an idea, to talk louder or softer, to speed up a point, and to add to a point. These decisions should be based on how an audience is reacting to a speech as it is being delivered. You cannot make these decisions during rehearsal because you are not practicing in front of the audience that will hear the speech.

Most speakers find that in their first speeches they concentrate primarily on getting through the material in the way they had rehearsed. However, with more experience, they begin to be able to use the audience as a monitor of how they are doing. A good speaker enjoys using feedback to interact with an audience.

Distractions

Many aspects of the speech setting can become distractions. In the middle of a speech, a speaker's stand, a microphone, or some other piece of equipment can draw attention away from your speech. Members of the audience may become hecklers. Here are some hints about how to handle these common distractions.

Speaker's Stand. A **speaker's stand,** or **lectern,** is a piece of furniture designed to hold a speaker's materials. Sometimes the lectern resembles a metal music stand. Sometimes it is an elaborate structure made out of wood. Sometimes it is a portable boxlike object that sits on a table. In any case, the top is slightly tilted so that materials can be seen easily by the speaker while being kept out of sight of the audience.

In most speaking situations you can expect a speaker's stand to be available. However, just when you take for granted that one will be there, it is not. Consequently, when you rehearse your speech, try not to rely on a speaker's stand. Then, when you give your speech, you will feel free to use the stand if one is available and free to speak without it if one is not.

This speaker is using a large lectern that stands on the floor.
Another common style is smaller and is placed on a tabletop.

A lectern can be a great help to you. First, it is a place where you can rest notes and other materials without your audience seeing them. Second, it provides a focal point for your audience's attention. Third, it represents a kind of "home base." During the speech you may walk away from the stand, and it will mark the place to which you will return.

When a stand is present, it can be a distraction if you do not use it well. A lectern is not a leaning post. Nor is it to be clutched as a drowning person might clutch a life preserver. Nor should you hide behind it during the entire speech. A lectern is an aid and should be treated as such. If you are allowed notes, rest them on the stand. Use them when you need to, but do not appear to be reading from them. In fact, even when a stand is present, many good speakers prefer to hold note cards in one hand while they speak so that they have freedom of movement. Once the speech has begun, feel free to stand behind it, beside it, or in front of it. The only way to learn to use the stand properly is to practice with one until it becomes an aid, not a crutch.

What should you do if no lectern is available? Stand in front of your audience naturally. Perhaps the most important question is what to do with your hands when you have no stand to rest them on. Begin with your hands at your sides or with one arm slightly bent at the elbow so that the arm is parallel to your waist. Then, as you get into the speech, your hands will be free to move to illustrate or emphasize your points. When you are not gesturing, rest your hands at your sides.

The only time you will be inconvenienced by the lack of a stand is when you are planning to read from a manuscript. If that is your intention, then it is up to you to make sure that some kind of stand is there.

Microphone. When speaking to a large audience or in a large auditorium, you will likely want to use a **microphone,** which is simply an electronic device for broadcasting sound. In class you may be asked to use a microphone for one of your speeches just for the practice.

Microphones are of two basic types: the **standing microphone,** either standing on the floor or attached to the lectern, and the **lavaliere microphone,** which is a type of portable microphone that hangs around your neck. Although standing microphones are much improved, you still have to speak directly into them for them to work. Ordinarily you will want to be eight to twelve inches from the microphone. However, the only way you can be sure of your distance and angle is to practice with a microphone for some time before giving your speech. A standing microphone can become a distraction, since it severely limits your movement. If you are used to moving around freely when delivering a speech, you will need several practice sessions to master using a standing microphone.

A lavaliere microphone is much easier to use because it is attached to you in such a way that it remains at the same distance from your mouth and at the same angle. Therefore, once you have it properly adjusted, you will have considerable freedom of movement. The distraction of the lavaliere microphone is that it will be attached by a cord. If you are not careful you can trip over the cord or get the cord caught around some other object and end up looking rather foolish.

With any microphone you will need to take care with plosives (*p, b, d, t, k,* and *g*). The *p* and *b* sounds especially can pop and be quite distorted by a microphone. Also, you will need to take special care not to talk too loud or raise your pitch or volume too much to emphasize a single point.

Hecklers. Once in a while in a public speech you will encounter a **heckler,** a person who tries purposely to disturb you while you are speaking. Even though a heckler can be extremely annoying, you can learn to cope with heckling rather easily. First, keep in mind that the audience came to hear you and therefore will likely not be very sympathetic to a heckler. In fact, in many situations an audience quiets a heckler without your having to do anything. If a heckler persists, try to ignore the disruption. A heckler wants recognition. When it becomes obvious that you are not going to give up the floor, the heckler will usually stop. When a heckler is really persistent, you may want to stop and announce that you will take questions after the speech but that until then you are the speaker. Do not get excited, and do not get into a battle with the heckler. Making you lose your composure is just what the heckler wants. Often you can say, "I'm not going to continue until you are quiet." After such a statement the audience or an usher is likely to deal with the heckler.

Unexpected Events

Murphy's Law states that anything that can go wrong will go wrong. Nowhere is this "law" more true than in public speaking. As a result, a well-prepared speaker leaves nothing to chance and never acts as if everything will go as expected. Although you cannot anticipate all the infuriating things that can happen, you should consider what you would do in case of the following unexpected events.

Dropping Material. Whether you drop two or three note cards or a stack of papers, the advice is the same: If you can go on with the speech as if nothing had happened, do so. If you must retrieve the material, do so as gracefully as possible. When you have gathered everything, continue as if nothing had happened. There is a good chance that after the speech is over,

On October 14, 1912, intrepid speaker Theodore Roosevelt persevered in the face of a serious unexpected event—he was shot. Despite his pain he insisted on giving his speech, which had been pierced by two bullets.

the audience will have forgotten the incident. At any rate, dropping material is likely to be more bothersome to you than to the audience—so long as you do not make an issue of it.

Noise. Especially in a classroom you may likely face a buzzing light, a lawn mower, interruptions from an intercom, or some other distracting noise. If you think that the noise is going to last through much of your speech, you will have to deal with it. For instance, if a buzzing light is not too loud, ignore it. If a lawn mower is right outside the window, you will have to close the window or talk louder.

If the distraction is momentary, pause until it subsides and then go on as if nothing had happened. If you anticipate that a distraction will last more than a few seconds, announce that you are going to pause until it lessens. Most of the time, you will be able to pick up right where you left off. Sometimes you may find it useful to summarize the point you were making before the pause and then go on.

Speaking Without Key Material. After starting your speech, you may realize that you do not have with you an important bit of material you need for your speech. If it is at your desk and is a necessary part of your speech, then as gracefully as possible walk to your desk, get it, return to the lectern, and go on as if nothing had happened. If it is elsewhere, do not tell the class that you had some great material but do not have it with you. It is much better either to skip reference to it or to think of a way to present the same information in some other way. If it was a visual aid, for instance, you might substitute an accurate description of what you would have shown for the material itself.

Forgetting a Key Point. Anyone is likely to forget some part of a speech. Unless what you forget is vital to your audience's understanding of the speech, go on without it. If something is vital, then you need to make a comment such as, "I forgot to mention a very important point. Let me go over it with you, tell you where it fits, and then go on." This is likely to affect the quality of your speech, but if the point is truly important, you have to

ACTIVITY: Using a Lectern and Microphones

Practice all or a portion of your speech in a classroom that has a lectern. Determine how you will stand at the beginning of your speech. Practice moving away from the lectern and then moving back to it.

If your school has either a standing or a lavaliere microphone or both, practice all or a part of your speech using one or both. For a standing mike, determine how close to it you have to be to get the best projection. Find out how much you can move without losing the necessary projection. For a lavaliere microphone, determine how close to your mouth it must be to give you the best projection. Walk around with it. Does movement affect your ability to project?

bring it up. If you can do so without getting flustered, the harm to your speech is likely to be minimal.

If you can face unexpected events with a sense of humor, you can overcome them. We're all human—we all make mistakes. If you are a likable person, if your speech is interesting, your audience will put up with a small amount of distraction with no harm.

AUDIOVISUAL AIDS

Audiovisual aids are materials that a speaker uses to clarify or add to the verbal presentation of a speech. Audio aids are external materials that an audience can hear, such as phonograph records or cassette tapes. Visual aids are external materials that an audience can see, such as slides, pictures, or films.

You can use audiovisual aids to heighten the appeal of your speech, to stimulate interest and increase attention, to present or to explain information, and to help your listeners remember points. You may want to bring in a person to give a demonstration or to dress for a particular role. You may find it effective to use records and tapes to create a mood, to illustrate a style, or to recapture an event. You may choose to use pictures and photographs to help your listeners visualize your points. In addition, you may use charts, diagrams, graphs, and maps to reinforce and clarify certain information.

You may be able to draw many of your visual aids. You do not have to be an artist to create effective drawings if you keep the following guidelines

Sometimes you will be lucky enough to find the perfect visual aid ready-made, but most of the time you will have to create your own.

in mind. Lettering on your visual aids must be block style and be large enough for your audience to see at a distance. The colors you use should contrast nicely, making the details easy to recognize.

To use visual aids effectively, you must show them in such a way that everyone in the audience can see them. Do not reveal a visual aid unless you want your audience to be looking at it. If you display all your visual aids at the beginning of your speech, or if you pass them around during the speech, the audience is likely to look at the aids and not listen attentively to you.

Carefully consider the number of visual aids you will use. You should have enough visual aids to portray necessary information in your speech clearly and vividly—but no more.

ACTIVITY: Analyzing a Speaker's Use of Audiovisual Aids

Watch a television broadcast or a speech in which the speaker uses audiovisual aids. Determine whether the aids are appropriate for the speech. Are they well prepared? Are they used effectively? Would the speech have been as effective or less effective without the aids? How does the speaker use the aids—to create interest, to explain, to give examples, or to achieve some other purpose(s)? Share your findings with your classmates.

EVALUATING YOUR DELIVERY

After you finish giving your speech, you should evaluate your delivery. What were your strengths? What were your weaknesses? Use the Guidelines for Delivering a Speech on page 313 as a basis for your evaluation. You may want to have one or two of your classmates help you with your analysis. Of course, your teacher will give you oral or written comments that you can use too.

ACTIVITY: Evaluating Delivery of an Extemporaneous Speech

Using the extemporaneous method, deliver a formal speech to your class. Use the Guidelines for Delivering a Speech (see page 313) to evaluate your delivery. Have the members of your audience evaluate your delivery also.

Profiles in Communication

Sundai Brown

How would you like to present several speeches a day, every day, on your job? Working as a tour guide at Sea World, Sundai Brown does exactly that as she introduces visitors to the marine park's shows and exhibits.

Enthusiastic and creative, Ms. Brown regards her presentations more as performances than as speeches. Using factual information provided by Sea World's education department, she tailors her talks to her audience "so that young people can understand them, while adults find them interesting." Audience interaction is also important. "I always chat with people and encourage their questions," Ms. Brown says. "My aim is always to be informative, yet entertaining, too."

To accomplish this goal, Ms. Brown practices a variety of communication skills. "The most important communication skill on this job," she reports, "is clarity. Guests must be able to understand what you are saying." To ensure that her talks are clear, Ms. Brown pays close attention to her enunciation and her grammar. Although she uses "a little bit of informality on tours," she avoids doing so when speaking to larger groups from a podium, and she rarely uses "slanguage."

In addition, she brings into play many gestures, facial expressions, and other nonverbal cues. By displaying a smile and a variety of animated expressions, Ms. Brown makes visitors feel welcome and encourages them to have a good time. She also takes care not to speak in a monotone, which could quickly dampen her listeners' enjoyment. In some cases, gestures help both to entertain and to inform, such as her use of her open hand to illustrate the movement of a shark's or a dolphin's dorsal fin through water.

Based on her experience conducting tours, Ms. Brown offers the following advice about giving talks that are both interesting and informative: (1) At all times, speak clearly and practice good language skills; (2) Take advantage of training available in speech classes and theater groups; (3) Get involved with groups who use speech, such as service clubs and, again, theater groups; (4) Practice writing to get yourself in the habit of "thinking about what you are going to say"; and, finally, (5) "Take your time when you speak, and think about every syllable."

SUMMARY

Effective delivery is vital to the success of your speech. An impromptu speech is delivered on the spur of the moment. A manuscript speech is a written speech that is read to an audience. A memorized speech is a manuscript speech that has been committed to memory. An extemporaneous speech is fully planned, usually in outline form, and is given with the aid of notes.

You may be concerned about experiencing stage fright. Keep in mind that nearly all speakers are nervous, that audiences are seldom aware of nervousness, and that the more speaking experience you get, the better you will learn to control nervousness. Moreover, you can take steps to help you prevent stage fright. Plan your speech carefully, practice it several times, work out your speech strategy, relax yourself, give yourself a pep talk, and walk confidently to the stand. During the speech you may experience queasiness, dry mouth, perspiration, and other symptoms of nervousness. If you understand that these reactions are quite normal and that they will not bother you if you ignore them, you will cope quite well. Whatever you do, do not quit.

Nonverbal communication plays a key role in delivery. Make sure that you present a good appearance. Keep eye contact with the audience by looking at individuals and at groups at random throughout the speech. Keep your facial expression in tune with the material. Use gestures that are appropriate to what you say and that describe and emphasize naturally.

The effectiveness of your delivery also depends on your vocal and verbal messages. Show enthusiasm through the sound of your voice. Work to eliminate vocalized pauses. Refine your articulation, pronunciation, and enunciation. Make sure that your volume, rate, and pitch are appropriate. In addition to the content of your speech, pay attention to your diction and grammar.

Good speakers have a keen sense of timing. Develop an accurate sense for how long you speak, and learn to use pauses effectively.

Feedback gives you clues about your audience's reaction to your speech. As you gain experience, you will learn to adjust your delivery to respond to feedback from your audience.

Speakers need to learn to anticipate distractions and unexpected events. Become familiar with using the lectern and the microphone, and master ways of dealing with hecklers. Dropping material, noise disturbances, forgetting material, and forgetting a point are all irritants, but none should destroy your speech.

Wherever appropriate, use audiovisual aids to emphasize ideas, to stimulate interest and increase attention, to help clarify key points, and to help your audience remember.

After giving a speech, always evaluate your delivery.

CHAPTER VOCABULARY

Look back through this chapter to find the meaning of each of the following terms. Write each term and its meaning in your communication journal.

audiovisual aids	grammar	microphone
conflicting expression	heckler	speaker's stand
deadpan	impromptu speech	stage fright
diction	lavaliere microphone	standing microphone
enunciation	lectern	timing
extemporaneous speech	manuscript speech	vocalized pauses
eye contact	memorized speech	

1. One way of delivering a speech is the impromptu method. What are three other ways?

2. Which of the ways of delivering a speech requires careful preparation but allows for the most adaptation to the audience?

3. What are the five kinds of nervous behavior that most speakers experience in their first few public speeches?

4. Being well prepared is one way to reduce nervousness before the speech is given. What are four other ways?

5. One aspect of nonverbal behavior that has a crucial effect on your speech is your appearance. Why is appearance so important?

6. Facial expression is also important. What is meant by "conflicting expression"?

7. One positive aspect of your vocal message is enthusiasm. What is the effect of excessive vocalized pauses in a speech?

8. Beginning speakers often have trouble deciding what to do with their hands when they are speaking. If you do not have a speaker's stand, what should you do with your hands as you begin your speech?

9. Microphones help you to be heard clearly; however, they can also cause problems. How can the lavaliere microphone cause a distraction?

10. One type of audiovisual aid is people. What are two ways in which people can serve as audiovisual aids?

DISCUSSION QUESTIONS

1. Do you believe that most people are nervous about speaking in public? Why do people feel the way they do about public speaking? Working in groups of five, share your opinions. On what do you base those opinions?

2. Discuss the kinds of behavior you find most annoying in public speakers. Why are these kinds of behavior so annoying?

3. Discuss the kinds of behavior that impress you most in a speaker. Why do they impress you?

4. Discuss what you should do in the following situations when giving a speech: (a) you drop material; (b) a loud noise occurs outside; (c) you discover that you have left material at home; (d) you forget a point.

5. Ralph Waldo Emerson wrote, "There are men whose language is strong and defying enough, yet their eyes and their actions ask leave of other men to live." First discuss the meaning of the quotation. Then discuss how it relates to delivering your speech.

ACTIVITIES

1. Identifying Ways of Coping with Nervousness

Talk with people who give speeches as part of their jobs. Are they nervous before they speak? If so, under what circumstances? How do they cope with that nervousness? Compile a class list of ways to cope with nervousness. Copy this list in your communication journal.

2. Analyzing Others' Delivery

While others are giving speeches in class, make notes on their delivery. After everyone has given a speech, review your notes. Identify specific behavior that helped each speaker be more effective and specific behavior that caused the speaker to be less effective. Share your findings with your classmates.

3. Analyzing Your Own Delivery

A. After you have given your speech, use the Guidelines for Delivering a Speech (page 313) to analyze your delivery. Identify your strengths and your weaknesses. Once you have arrived at conclusions about your delivery, ask at least three other students from your class to comment on your conclusions.

B. If your school has videotape equipment, videotape all or a part of one of your final practice sessions or of your actual delivery to the class. Use the Guidelines for Delivering a Speech (page 313) to analyze your delivery. Discuss your conclusions with classmates who saw your delivery.

4. Giving an Impromptu Speech

Think about current topics in the news. Select one of these topics and write it on a piece of paper. Fold your paper and drop it into a hat holding your classmates' choices. Once the hat is shaken to mix up the slips of paper, select one and give a two-minute impromptu speech on the topic you pick.

5. Analyzing a Professional Speaker's Delivery

A. Watch a professional speaker deliver a speech. Make a list of any nonverbal behavior that interferes with or adds to the speaker's effectiveness. Share your findings with your classmates.

B. Watch a professional speaker deliver a speech. Make a list of any vocal or verbal behavior that interferes with or particularly adds to the speaker's effectiveness. Share your findings with your classmates.

Real-Life Speaking Situations

1. Outside of school, when was the last time you had to speak before a group of people? How many times have you been in such speaking situations? How did you feel as you stood before the group? If you are like most people, you probably felt rather nervous. What did you do to keep your nervousness under control? Imagine that you have been asked to speak before a group that you belong to—perhaps a scout troop, a sports team, a hobby club, or a family reunion. What could you do to control your nervousness? Write a one-page talk that you might give to that group in an actual situation, such as an award ceremony, a victory party, a meeting, or a special occasion. First, deliver your talk to your classmates as if you did not have your nervousness very well under control. Then deliver your talk with your nervousness under control. Discuss with your classmates the differences between your two talks and the effectiveness of the methods you used to control your nervousness.

2. Many people are needed to staff the thousands of hotels and motels that provide lodging for travelers. Being in unfamiliar surroundings, travelers often need to call upon staff members for explanations, directions, and other information. All staff members are expected to give helpful, courteous replies to guests' inquiries. Moreover, giving such replies is one of the surest ways that a staff member has of earning generous tips from grateful guests. Imagine that you are working in a hotel, and a harried guest stops you in the hall to ask for assistance. You are in a hurry yourself because you must be in a staff meeting in the manager's office in less than five minutes. How will you respond to the guest so that your reply is courteous and helpful, yet also brief? Define such a situation. What is the guest's inquiry? Is the guest young? middle-aged? alone? with his or her family? What time is it? Are you already late for the manager's meeting? Write a one- or two-page dialogue of your exchange with the guest. Be prepared to present your dialogue to your class (don't forget to include appropriate nonverbal behavior). Ask your classmates for feedback on how well you handled the situation. Perhaps you might ask how much of a tip each of them would have given you if he or she had been the guest.

UNIT FOUR

TYPES OF SPEECHES

CHAPTER **14**

THE INFORMATIVE SPEECH

OBJECTIVES:

After studying this chapter, you should be able to

1. Define informative speaking.

2. Identify the goals of an informative speech.

3. List five methods of presenting information.

4. Explain the importance of speaker credibility.

5. Open an informative speech effectively.

6. List and use six types of organizational patterns for an informative speech.

7. Close an informative speech effectively.

8. Adapt information to an audience.

9. Know when to use audiovisual aids.

10. Conduct a question-and-answer period.

11. Analyze and evaluate an informative speech.

I was just finishing my assigned homework the other night. I was about to put everything away and go watch a television show I wanted to see when something inside me said that I had better go over the story we were studying in English class. Something told me that we were going to have a pop quiz the next day, and I hadn't really read the story that closely. Sure enough, first thing in English class the next day Mr. Coughlin said, "Take out a piece of paper—we're going to have a quiz."

Have you ever had a similar feeling that something was going to happen, and then, to your surprise, it did? It might have been wishful thinking or perhaps a coincidence. Or it might have been ESP.

Gwen Jones had begun her informative speech on extrasensory perception. Her introduction certainly got her audience interested in her topic.

WHAT IS AN INFORMATIVE SPEECH?

An **informative speech** is one that provides information. It helps an audience understand a topic and remember details about it. Although teaching something to another person can be difficult, information can be presented in ways that help the other person learn.

Giving informative speeches in class will prepare you for important speaking situations you may encounter later in life.

Understanding

The first goal of an informative speech is to help the audience understand the information that is being presented. *Understanding* means "grasping the meaning of information." People *understand* when they are able to apply what they have learned. For example, suppose that Gwen Jones had said, "Extrasensory perception is knowing about something without seeing it, hearing it, tasting it, smelling it, or feeling it." Imagine that you said afterward, "According to Gwen, some people seem to be able to know things without direct sensory experience of those things. Gwen told a story about how she had had a feeling that there would be a pop quiz in English the next day and there was!" By associating Gwen's statement with her example, you would be showing your understanding of the information.

Listening to people talk does not ensure that you understand what they say. In fact, you are likely to understand only a part of much of the information you hear. Think of the number of times you thought you understood what a person was saying only to find out later that you really had not understood at all.

Effective speakers can present information in ways that increase audience understanding considerably. In preparing her speech, Gwen devised ways to make the abstract concepts she was explaining understandable to her classmates.

ACTIVITY: Understanding and Remembering Information

How good are you at understanding and remembering? Read the following paragraphs as many times as you need to in order to form a visual picture of the house that is being described.

You are looking directly at the front of a house that has the shape of a rectangle standing on its shorter side. The vertical side (the longer side) is about twice as long as the horizontal side.

The lower half of this rectangle represents the first floor of the house. Directly in the middle of this lower half is a door. To the right of the door is a picture window centered in the space between the door and the side of the house. The top of the window is at the same level as the top of the door.

The upper half of the rectangle represents the second floor of the house. In this upper half there are three windows, all the same size, evenly spaced across the front of the second floor. The roof of the house is like a triangle sitting on the rectangle. Halfway up the left side of the triangle that represents the roof is a chimney.

Now cover the paragraph and draw the house you see. After you finish, go back and reread the paragraph once more. Did you get it right?

Remembering

The second goal of an informative speech is to help the audience remember the material. *To remember* means "to think of again; to keep in mind." Because people encounter a lot of information every day, they cannot keep it all in mind. By the end of a normal school day, you have been exposed to a great deal of information. By the next day, you probably have forgotten a great deal of the information you received the day before. By the end of a week, you probably have forgotten at least half—and maybe most—of what you heard days earlier. This inability to remember information is why review is so essential.

Effective speakers learn to present information in ways that increase a listener's ability to remember that information not only the next day but even weeks later. For her speech, Gwen had to think of ways to explain aspects of extrasensory perception so that her classmates would be likely to remember them.

In this chapter you will look at types of informative speeches, at the preparation of those speeches, and at means of helping audiences both understand and remember information.

METHODS OF PRESENTING INFORMATION

At least five different methods are used to present information in informative speeches. Each of these methods can be used to develop either a part of a speech or an entire speech.

Narration

A **narration** is an account of the details of a story or an event. The information you use to develop a narration is usually obtained through direct personal experience.

Your first experience in giving an informative speech before an audience was probably during "show and tell" in elementary school.

You can likely give narrations on such experiences as searching for a part-time job, changing a tire in a storm, shopping for new school clothes, getting lost in the woods, or learning how to take care of a pet. In preparing for an informative speech, you will need to select your experience with care so that your speech will inform, and not simply entertain, your audience.

A narration can be used as an entire speech or as just one part of an informative speech. For instance, Gwen might use the following narration on ESP as her entire speech or as a part of a longer speech.

Is seeing believing? If so, then I'm a believer. I dropped in to visit my friend Stephanie the other evening just to chat. At one point, while we were talking about the impressions that clothes can create, Stephanie suddenly grew quiet. A peculiar look came over her face, and for a moment she got very pale. When I asked her what was wrong, she said, "Just for an instant I had a sudden, empty feeling—I really can't seem to explain it, but it gave me a real chill." About ten minutes later the doorbell rang. It was a neighbor. He said that he had been driving down the end of the street when Biff, Stephanie's dog, dashed into the street. It had happened so quickly that he couldn't stop. His car had struck Biff and killed him instantly. Biff had been hit precisely at the moment that Stephanie had experienced that unexplained feeling. What had caused her to feel the way she had at the exact time Biff was killed? Those who study psychic phenomena would say that Stephanie had experienced extrasensory perception. Whatever it was, I saw it happen.

This example illustrates several common aspects of narration. First, a narration usually has some point, a climax, that the details build up to. Second, a narration includes the details needed to build up to the climax. Third, a narration is usually told in a way that keeps the audience in suspense. The audience may have an idea of the point of the story, but the climax is always a bit of a surprise. Finally, a narration often includes dialogue.

Description

A **description** gives a vivid word picture of something, such as a build-ing, a place, an object, an animal, or a person. In other words, a description tells what something looks like. For instance, suppose two friends, Danielle and Gloria, are discussing what they plan to wear to a party. Danielle might say to Gloria, "I bought a new dress that I think you will really like. It's a three-quarter-length cocktail dress in black velvet." Danielle's information about the dress is a description. Her words give Gloria a mental picture of what the dress looks like.

A description can include details such as size, weight, shape, color, age, condition, and arrangement (the way various parts fit together). To prepare to give a description, you have to be a good observer: you need a good eye for detail and a good memory.

In her speech on extrasensory perception, Gwen might describe the physical layout of an ESP test. Notice that the following description includes size, shape, and arrangement.

The other day I watched Stephanie being tested for ESP. She sat at a brown table that was the size of a regular card table, with seats on opposite sides. Across the middle of the table, there was a wooden partition about one inch thick that spanned the width of the table and stood about two feet high—high enough so that neither Stephanie nor the person seated at the opposite side of the table could see the other person or what the other person was doing.

In this description, Gwen included the sizes of the table and the partition, the shape of the table, and the way the parts—table, partition, seats, and participants—work together.

Most subjects for descriptive speeches can be listed under the following five categories:

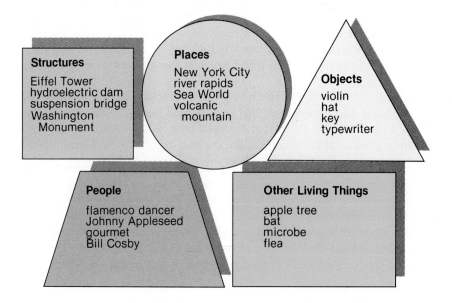

Structures
Eiffel Tower
hydroelectric dam
suspension bridge
Washington
    Monument

Places
New York City
river rapids
Sea World
volcanic
    mountain

Objects
violin
hat
key
typewriter

People
flamenco dancer
Johnny Appleseed
gourmet
Bill Cosby

Other Living Things
apple tree
bat
microbe
flea

No matter what item you choose under any of these categories, keep in mind that the key to good description is specific sensory detail.

Definition

A **definition** gives the meaning of a word or an idea. The more abstract a word is, the more skill you need to make its definition clear. Abstract words such as *knowledge, love, courage,* and *enthusiasm* can prove difficult to define because they refer to ideas that cannot be directly perceived by the senses. Concrete words such as *lion, kiss, computer,* and *dentist* can be easier to define, because you can use sensory details.

One very common way to define is to classify, which means to arrange or organize according to class or category. The class or category is determined by the individual characteristics of the word or concept. For example, Gwen might define telepathy as "a form of extrasensory perception in which information is communicated between minds without using the five senses of seeing, hearing, tasting, feeling, or smelling."

Another common way of defining is to provide a *synonym*—a word or term that has a similar meaning. For example, in her speech Gwen might say, "Another term for *extrasensory perception* is *the sixth sense*."

A third common way of defining is to show a word's function or to explain the scope of a word or an idea. For example, Gwen might define extrasensory perception in terms of its scope by saying that it involves telepathy, clairvoyance, and precognition.

Process

A **process speech** explains how to do something, how to make something, or how something works. Gwen could develop her information into a process speech by showing how an extrasensory-perception test is conducted. Since process speeches are common and are important to your development as a speaker, Chapter 15 will focus on them.

Report

A **report** is a detailed factual account based on research. In a report, you put together information that you have found in several different sources. Gwen could turn her informative speech on extrasensory perception into an oral report by talking about studies conducted at Duke University under the direction of J. B. Rhine. She would get information for her report from books and research articles listed under the heading "extrasensory perception" in the card catalog, the *Readers' Guide to Periodical Literature,* and the *Magazine Index.*

The following list gives typical examples of subjects that can be developed into good oral reports:

Eruption of Mount St. Helens	Education of women in colonial
The Forty-Niners	America
African influences on jazz	Organic foods
History of prison reform	Traditions of the Sioux
American cartoon strips	Pop art

ACTIVITY: Analyzing and Presenting Information

Think of information you have heard presented during the last few days. Which material came in the form of narration, description, definition, process, or report? Think of an experience you have had within the past week. Tell the class about it. Make sure that your presentation is informative and has a point. Choose details that help build up to the point. If possible, use dialogue in your talk.

PREPARING TO SPEAK

To make sure that you present your information clearly, work through the following steps as you prepare an informative speech.

Choosing a Topic

In Chapter 9 you learned that when you choose a subject, you should find one in which you are interested and about which you already know something. Do you have an interest in and some knowledge about sports? stamp collecting? current events? historical oddities? other cultures? automobiles? If so, any of these can be a subject you can limit to a topic for an informative speech. Since Gwen Jones was particularly interested in psychic phenomena, the topic of extrasensory perception was an excellent choice for her.

Gathering Information

Gathering solid information helps you establish your credibility. The more convincingly you can show your listeners that you know what you are talking about, the more likely they are to pay attention to and remember what you say.

Review briefly the key sources of information discussed in Chapter 10. You can begin your search for information by thinking of what you already know about the topic. Then you can consider interviewing one person or surveying a group of people to collect more of the information you need. Finally, you can use your library. By looking through the card catalog, the *Readers' Guide to Periodical Literature,* the *Magazine Index,* and other reference works, you can find books and magazine articles that contain additional information for your speech.

To get ready for her speech, Gwen Jones read the section on parapsychology in two different encyclopedias. She also found several articles on psychic phenomena in the *Readers' Guide,* and she checked out from her public library three books on extrasensory perception.

Preparing Your Introduction

Introductions for informative speeches range from very short ones (in some cases, even none at all) to quite long ones, depending on the topic and the interest and knowledge of the audience. The goals of the introduction in an informative speech are to get attention, to focus attention on the subject, and to gain the good will of the audience.

To gain good will, you may want to explain to your audience how your background and experience qualify you to speak on your topic. Any of the common methods for beginning a speech—a startling statement, a question, a quotation, a story, or a personal reference—can work well for you in an informative speech. (See Chapter 11 for a discussion of these methods.)

In addition, you may want to use humor. Through the use of humor, you can gain the audience's acceptance and put the audience in a receptive frame of mind to remember the information. However, humor can backfire. If you do use humor, make sure it is appropriate for the audience and the occasion. For example, most members of your audience would probably find it improper for you to tell a joke at the start of a funeral oration. Do not tell ethnic or off-color jokes, and avoid any topics that would offend your audience. Finally, consider whether or not you are the type of person who can tell jokes well. If your jokes usually fall flat, if your friends rarely laugh at your punch lines, do not chance telling a joke during your speech introduction.

"Stockworth," reprinted by permission of Sterling & Selesnick, Inc.

An audience may be required to hear your speech, but it is up to you to generate interest in your topic.

Organizing the Body of the Informative Speech

The body of the informative speech can be organized in many different ways. The following methods, which include three of those discussed in Chapter 11, are the most common.

Chronological Order. Chronological order is a pattern that arranges details or events according to the order in which they occurred in time. Consider using chronological order when you present a process (how something is done, how something is made, or how something works) or when you present a history of something. For instance, in the following outline, chronological order is used to organize information for a speech giving a brief history of the computer.

Specific Purpose: I want to explain the three major steps in the evolution of the computer.
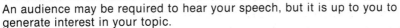
  I. The first electronic computers used vacuum tubes and took up an entire room.
  II. The second generation of computers used transistors and were considerably smaller than earlier computers.
  III. The third generation of computers uses microchips and has been further reduced in size.

Spatial Order. **Spatial order** is a pattern of organization in which items are arranged according to their position in space. You are likely to use spatial order for any description. For instance, spatial order is used in the following outline to arrange information for a speech describing the essential parts of a word processor.

Specific Purpose: I want to explain what a typical word processing unit looks like.

    I. Immediately in front of the operator is a standard keyboard.
    II. Directly above the keyboard is a screen.
    III. Below or to the side of the keyboard is a disk drive.

Topical Order. **Topical order** is a pattern of organization in which a topic is broken down into parts that are arranged in an order determined by the speaker and stated in the specific purpose. Topical order is the most common pattern for informative speeches. For example, the following topical outline would work well for Gwen in her speech on ESP.

Specific Purpose: I want to explain the three major types of extrasensory perception.

    I. One type is telepathy.
    II. A second type is clairvoyance.
    III. A third type is precognition.

Climactic Order. **Climactic order** arranges items according to their order of importance. Climactic order usually starts with the least important

Make sure that your audience can clearly follow the organizational pattern of your speech.

information and ends with the most important. The following outline using climactic order would work well for a speech on coaching.

Specific Purpose: I want to explain three requirements for being a good coach.
  I. A good coach must have an eye for talent.
  II. More important, a good coach must understand the mechanics of the sport.
  III. Most important, a good coach must be able to motivate players to do their best.

Cause-and-Effect Order. In **cause-and-effect order,** information is arranged to show causes or conditions and the effects or results of those causes or conditions. For example, high interest rates for consumers can help cause a recession. The following cause-and-effect outline would work well for a speech showing the relationship between high interest rates for consumers and recession.

Specific Purpose: I want to explain the relationship between high interest rates for consumers and the onset of recession.
  I. High interest rates for consumers drive down consumer demand for financing to make purchases.
  II. A reduction in purchases calls for less production, which causes more unemployment.
  III. The result is recession.

Comparison-and-Contrast Order. In **comparison-and-contrast order,** items of information are organized to show similarities and differences between the items. The following comparison-and-contrast outline would work well for a speech on pets.

Specific Purpose: As pets, dogs and cats are similar in one way but are quite different in two others.
  I. Dogs and cats can both be affectionate pets.
  II. Dogs show more devotion to owners than most cats show.
  III. Cats generally show more independence than dogs show.

Preparing Your Conclusion

The conclusion for an informative speech usually includes a summary of the main points. For instance, Gwen could have ended her speech on extrasensory perception by saying, "So, we can see that extrasensory perception includes telepathy, clairvoyance, and precognition."

Many speakers also look for material such as illustrations or quotations to help make their summaries more memorable. Gwen might have ended her speech with another interesting story about extrasensory perception.

Adapting Your Speech to Your Audience

Keep in mind that an *effective informative speech* helps your audience understand and remember the information you present. Whether your speech achieves these two goals depends to some extent on how well you adapt, or adjust, it to your audience. To adapt your speech successfully to your audience, you must have information about the members of your audience. You would want to analyze such things as their average age, gender, occupation, interests, and attitudes. For example, you would make the speech you give to a group of professionals different from the speech you give to a group of students. You would make the speech you give to ten-year-olds different from the speech you give to fifty-year-olds. To make sure that you have carefully considered your listeners, use the following five categories to adapt your speech to your audience.

Experience. Relate the speech to your audience's experience. Your classmates are not likely to listen to your information for very long if they cannot figure out what your information has to do with them. Some topics are very easy to relate to an audience. For instance, if you were planning to give a speech to college-track high-school seniors on how to improve their SAT scores, the information would directly relate to your audience's needs.

However, sometimes your topic may not seem to have much of a direct relationship to your audience. For example, imagine that you want to talk about the building of the Egyptian pyramids. One way that you can relate such a topic to your audience would be to compare ancient building methods with today's methods.

Familiarity. Recognize that your audience is not likely to be familiar with the information you present. New speakers often are afraid that their audience will already know everything they are talking about, yet this is very unlikely. Moreover, even if a few individuals are familiar with some of your information, they are not likely to be familiar with all the details.

For example, one of Gwen's classmates, Todd, had an experience that illustrates this point and shows what you can do to double-check your audience's knowledge. Todd had decided to give his speech on dogs. From the time that Todd was very young, he had traveled with his parents to dog shows all over the state and had learned much about show dogs. Because Todd was so familiar with show dogs, he assumed that everyone in class knew that dogs were classified into six groups: working dogs, terriers, sporting dogs, nonsporting dogs, hounds, and toys. However, just to make sure, he asked several classmates whether they knew the classifications of dogs. He was amazed to find that none of the people he asked could name all six groups correctly. Moreover, several people gave answers that were way off the mark. After discovering his audience's lack of familiarity with his subject, Todd made sure that he included more background information in his speech than he had originally planned to provide.

You can proceed on the assumption that very few people are going to be familiar with the specific information that you are planning to present. If you want to check, though, talk to some members of your audience a few days before the speech to find out the extent of their knowledge on your topic.

Technicality. Avoid making your explanations too technical. *Technicality* refers to the use of detail and language that is meaningful only to a

Know your audience. As you plan your speech, consider how familiar your listeners are with your topic so that you can adapt your use of detail and language to suit them.

specialist. If you are speaking to an audience of specialists in a field, technical terms and details are suitable. However, most of your audiences will probably not be filled with specialists in any one field. Always adapt the level of technical language in your speech to your audience's level of technical understanding. For example, if you were speaking to a group of electronic hobbyists, you would use technical terms to explain how a picture is formed on a television screen. However, if you were speaking to an average audience composed mostly of nonspecialists in electronics, you might simply say that a television picture tube shoots beams of light onto the screen in such a way that they create pictures.

Here is another example: Suppose that you were trying to explain the law of supply and demand. You could say,

> The law of supply and demand is a basic economic principle predicated on the belief that the production of and the final price of consumer goods is directly related to the willingness of a producer to make available various quantities of an item at various prices and the willingness of consumers to purchase those quantities of the item at each price level.

Although a student of economics may understand this explanation, most people are likely to find it difficult to grasp. Notice how simplifying the language and giving examples make the explanation more understandable to a nonspecialist in economics.

> The law of supply and demand is an economic principle that is supposed to determine how the price of a product is related to the interrelationship of supply (the number or amount available) and demand (the desire of the public for the product). Let's see how this interrelation-

ship works. During the winter many people consider buying new coats. If the winter is cold enough, and if the cold lasts long enough, all stores can sell their stock at regular prices because the demand for the product will be high. However, if the winter is mild, stores will end up putting winter coats on sale because the supply of the product will exceed the demand of the public.

It will generally take longer to explain ideas in nontechnical language. However, keep in mind that your goal is to inform your audience. Make time in your speech to present your information in language that is clear to your audience.

Mnemonic Devices. Mnemonic devices are memory aids that work on the principle of association. Mnemonic devices are formed in various ways. One common way is by rhyming. For example: *In fourteen hundred ninety-two / Columbus sailed the ocean blue.* Another common way is by using the first letter of each important word in a group of words to create a single new word, such as *scuba* for self-contained underwater breathing apparatus.

Often you can create a special mnemonic device for an audience. Suppose that you were giving a speech on the Great Lakes and you wanted the audience to remember the names of the five lakes. By taking the first letter of the name of each lake, you could create the mnemonic device *HOMES*: Huron, Ontario, Michigan, Erie, Superior. The audience could then use the one-word mnemonic device HOMES to help them remember the names of all five lakes.

Audiovisual Aids. Audiovisual aids are materials that a speaker uses to clarify or add to the verbal presentation of a speech. Remember that an audience will understand material better and remember it longer if they can use more than one channel of communication to receive it. Since good audiovisual aids often take some time to prepare, here are several key questions you can ask yourself to help you decide whether or not to use audiovisual aids.

Can I use an audiovisual aid to save time? In preparing your first speech, it may seem that even the shortest time limit is too long to fill. However, you will soon discover that staying within the time limit is a real challenge. For many speeches you will need to present large amounts of information in a small amount of time. If using an audiovisual aid will save you time, then use it. Even though no visual aid can be shown without a spoken explanation, a visual aid may still save you many words.

Can I use an audiovisual aid to help clarify a point? If such an aid will, use it. Some ideas are easily explained verbally. Others require visual help. You must be the judge of how much clearer you can be with a visual aid.

Can I use an audiovisual aid to help the audience remember a point? Although audiovisual aids almost always help people remember, if you used audiovisual aids for every point in your speech, their power to aid recall would diminish considerably. You have to decide which points will be most clearly and economically emphasized by audiovisual aids.

Sometimes you can find audiovisual aids already prepared. By looking

(continued on page 338)

AUDIOVISUAL MATERIALS

CHARTS

Informational Chart of the Average Weight of Americans by Height and Age

MEN

HEIGHT	AGE					
	20-24	25-29	30-39	40-49	50-59	60-69
5'2"	130	134	138	140	141	140
5'3"	136	140	143	144	145	144
5'4"	139	143	147	149	150	149
5'5"	143	147	151	154	155	153
5'6"	148	152	156	158	159	158
5'7"	153	156	160	163	164	163
5'8"	157	161	165	167	168	167
5'9"	163	166	170	172	173	172
5'10"	167	171	174	176	177	176
5'11"	171	175	179	181	182	181
6'0"	176	181	184	186	187	186
6'1"	182	186	190	192	193	191
6'2"	187	191	195	197	198	196
6'3"	193	197	201	203	204	200
6'4"	198	202	206	208	209	207

WOMEN

HEIGHT	AGE					
	20-24	25-29	30-39	40-49	50-59	60-69
4'10"	105	110	113	118	121	123
4'11"	110	112	115	121	125	127
5'0"	112	114	118	123	127	130
5'1"	116	119	121	127	131	133
5'2"	120	121	124	129	133	136
5'3"	124	125	128	133	137	140
5'4"	127	128	131	136	141	143
5'5"	130	132	134	139	144	147
5'6"	133	134	137	143	147	150
5'7"	137	138	141	147	152	155
5'8"	141	142	145	150	156	158
5'9"	146	148	150	155	159	161
5'10"	149	150	153	158	162	163
5'11"	155	156	159	162	166	167
6'0"	157	159	164	168	171	172

Flow Chart of Placing an Order over the Telephone

Line-Staff Chart of Personnel in a Team-Teacher Plan

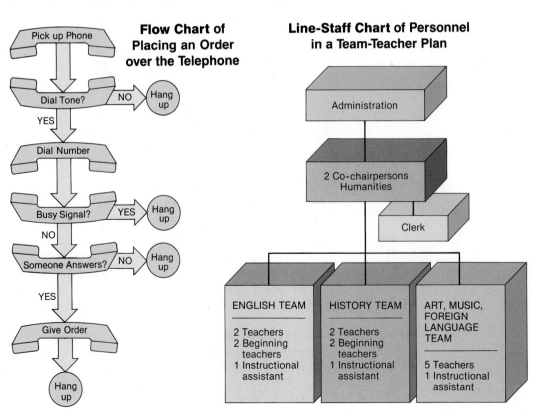

Pick up Phone

Dial Tone? — NO → Hang up

YES

Dial Number

Busy Signal? — YES → Hang up

NO

Someone Answers? — NO → Hang up

YES

Give Order

Hang up

Administration

2 Co-chairpersons Humanities

Clerk

ENGLISH TEAM
2 Teachers
2 Beginning teachers
1 Instructional assistant

HISTORY TEAM
2 Teachers
2 Beginning teachers
1 Instructional assistant

ART, MUSIC, FOREIGN LANGUAGE TEAM
5 Teachers
1 Instructional assistant

GRAPHS

Line Graph of Average Male and Female Teenage Growth in Weight

Bar Graph of Average Male and Female Teenage Growth in Height

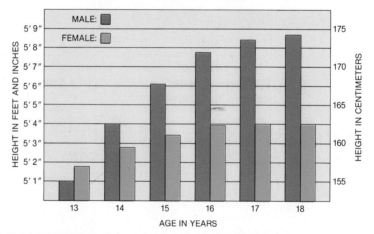

Pie Graphs of Methods Used by Students to Travel from Home to School

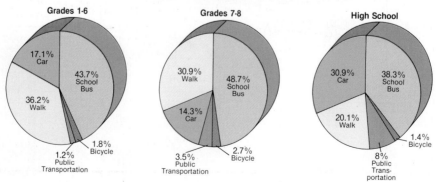

DIAGRAMS

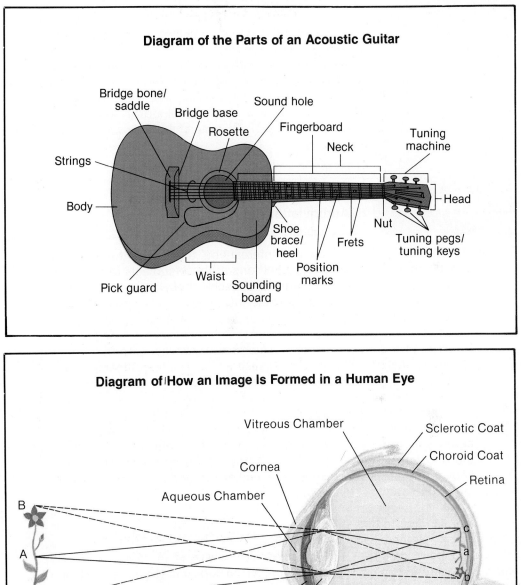

Diagram of the Parts of an Acoustic Guitar

Bridge bone/saddle
Bridge base
Sound hole
Rosette
Fingerboard
Neck
Tuning machine
Strings
Head
Body
Nut
Shoe brace/heel
Frets
Tuning pegs/tuning keys
Pick guard
Waist
Sounding board
Position marks

Diagram of How an Image Is Formed in a Human Eye

Vitreous Chamber
Sclerotic Coat
Choroid Coat
Cornea
Retina
Aqueous Chamber
B
A
C
c
a
b
Iris
Lens
Ciliary Muscles
Optic Nerve
Muscles to Eyeball

through newspapers and magazines, the students in Gwen's class found photographs, diagrams, charts, graphs, maps, and many other kinds of visual aids to use in their speeches. A **diagram** gives a visual representation of details and ideas, such as the steps in putting something together. A **chart** is a visual aid that gives information in words or in tabular form. A **graph** is a special type of drawing that shows comparative information. A *line graph* shows this information through a series of points connected by lines. A *bar graph* shows this information through bars of differing lengths. A *pie graph* represents items being compared as parts of a circle. The diagrams, charts, and graphs on pages 335–37 are some of the audiovisual aids that Gwen's classmates used.

ACTIVITY: Planning a Speech and Creating Audiovisual Aids

Make a list of five subjects that interest you, and check the three you already know the most about. Limit one of these subjects to a specific topic that you will develop into a speech. Then list the sources of material that you can use to provide information for a speech on this topic. What is likely to be the major source of information for your speech?

Write your specific purpose. Which organizational pattern (chronological, spatial, topical, climactic, cause-and-effect, or comparison-and-contrast) do you think would work best to develop the specific purpose you have written?

Next, prepare three or four questions about the most important information you are planning to give in your speech. During the week before you give the speech, ask various people in your school to answer the questions. How many people know all the answers? How many know none? Was your experience similar to Todd's? Share your findings with your classmates.

As you work on your speech, identify the technical language you are planning to use. Are there other ways you can express those ideas that would be clearer to a general audience?

Finally, create or find audiovisual aids to use in your speech. Be prepared to explain how these audiovisual aids add to your speech and help you present information more effectively than you could with words alone.

DELIVERING YOUR SPEECH

Any speech will be more effective if it is well delivered. In preparing for your informative speeches, keep in mind the guidelines discussed in Chapter 11.

Ethos

Ethos refers to the distinguishing character, attitudes, beliefs, and nature of the speaker. When you deliver your speech, you must establish yourself as a speaker whom the audience can trust to give accurate information about your topic. One way to do this is to tell the audience a little bit about your background. What makes you qualified to talk about your topic? Another way is to be honest. Be thoroughly prepared, but if you do not know something, or if a point is still being debated, freely admit this.

Charlie Brown cannot convince others to believe in him simply by telling them to do so. To establish himself as trustworthy, he needs to give his listeners good reasons to put their faith in him.

© 1956 by United Feature Syndicate, Inc. Reprinted by permission of United Feature Syndicate, Inc.

Enthusiasm

Be enthusiastic about your topic. If you do not sound enthusiastic, your audience certainly will not become so. The more enthusiasm you show, the more likely you are to get and hold attention.

Eye Contact

Establish eye contact with your audience. If you look at the members of your audience, they will look at you. If you fail to establish eye contact, the members of the audience will let their eyes wander around the room or take on a vacant stare, and you will have lost your listeners' attention. To be an effective speaker, you need the bond of communication that is begun with good eye contact.

Vocal Variety and Emphasis

Show vocal variety, and use your vocal skills to emphasize key points. Vary your tone, rate, volume, pitch, and other vocal qualities to make your speech more interesting. A speech that is delivered with an expressive voice will be listened to. A speech that is delivered in a dry monotone will be tuned out.

Clear Articulation and Enunciation

Speak clearly. When words are slurred and run together, audiences find it very difficult to understand a speaker. One of your main goals as a speaker is to make listening to your message easy and enjoyable for your audience.

Good Pronunciation

Know how to pronounce the words you use. Nothing hurts your credibility more than mispronouncing key words in your speech. Consider for yourself: How much faith do you think you would have in a speaker who does not even know how to pronounce the words in his or her own speech?

ACTIVITY: Evaluating the Delivery of an Informative Speech

Record a rehearsal of your informative speech. (If you are unable to record it, have someone listen to your rehearsal.) Rate yourself (or have your partner rate you) on enthusiasm, vocal variety and emphasis, articulation and enunciation, and pronunciation. Use 1 as the lowest score and 5 as the highest.

CONDUCTING A QUESTION-AND-ANSWER PERIOD

Regardless of how well you prepare and present your speech, it is likely that some people in the audience will have questions. For this reason, question-and-answer periods are often scheduled to follow an informative speech. Allot one third to one half of your time to questions and answers. Therefore, if you are instructed to give a thirty-minute speech, reserve ten to fifteen minutes for questions.

Since people are sometimes reluctant to ask questions, you must let the audience know that you truly are interested in answering questions. At the end of your speech introduction, you might say, "As I'm going along, make note of any places where I haven't been clear, or where you would like more detail—and I'll answer your questions at the end." Or you might say, "I think that what I have to say may raise many questions. I'm planning to leave time at the end for you to ask them."

Too often speakers wait until the end of the speech and say something such as "Are there any questions" in a tone of voice that tells listeners "I really don't want to answer any." Audiences will usually sense a speaker's lack of sincerity and will not bother to ask questions. A more appropriate way to stimulate audience questions at the end of a speech is to say, "What I've said may have gotten you thinking about some aspects of the topic that either I didn't cover or you need explained further. I'll be happy to answer any questions you have."

Conducting a question-and-answer session following your speech will help you ensure that your audience understands your message and will provide feedback on the effectiveness of your presentation.

Once you get the audience asking questions, you will need to keep a few guidelines in mind.

1. *See to it that people ask questions, not give speeches.* If someone starts talking and no question comes forth within the first few sentences, you should interrupt to make sure that the person has a question.

2. *Call upon people from all parts of the audience.* Avoid the tendency to call only on those in the middle of the audience seated in the first few rows. Do not call on anyone to ask a second question until everyone else who has a question has been called on.

3. *Try to answer all questions briefly.* Remember that you have a time limit and that you want to give as many people as possible a chance to ask their questions.

4. *If you cannot answer a question, feel free to say so.* It is much better to say something like "I'm sorry, I really don't have an answer for that" than it is to hem and haw and end up saying something you might regret later.

Practice Answering Questions from Your Audience

After you rehearse your speech, rehearse answers to potential questions. Either ask yourself questions or have a friend listen to your speech and then ask you questions.

RESPONDING TO FEEDBACK

Since you are trying to reach as many people as possible with your information, watch for signs of audience inattention or lack of understanding. In any audience, there will be people whose minds will wander or who will fail to understand you. By being alert to feedback from your audience, you can determine where and how to adjust your speech to regain attention or to clarify your presentation.

The major signs of audience inattention are yawning, rustling of papers, shuffling of feet, and coughing. If you see more and more people adopting these behaviors, you can assume that you are losing the audience's interest. Begin at once thinking of ways to recapture your listeners' attention, such as varying your voice or increasing your movements and gestures.

Beginning speakers will often be unaware of how an audience is behaving. As you gain experience, you will become more aware of audience behavior. The mark of a truly effective speaker is the ability to adapt to these signs and regain the audience's interest.

Evaluating Your Response to Feedback

When you speak, how aware are you of what your audience is doing? When your next speech is over, write down some of the behavior that you observed during your speech. What kind, if any, affected your delivery? How did you keep or regain audience attention?

ANALYZING AND EVALUATING INFORMATIVE SPEECHES

After each of your classmates has presented his or her speech, you will likely be called upon to give an oral or a written critique of the speaker's effectiveness. A **critique** is an analysis and evaluation. A critique of an informative speech focuses on what the speaker did to help the audience understand and remember information. In addition, the critique comments on the speaker's organization, content, language, and delivery.

The Oral Critique

Oral critiques provide a valuable learning tool, since everyone in class can profit from analyses of the successes and mistakes of others. Many teachers set aside time at the end of each class period to hear oral critiques of the speeches given that day. Keep the following guidelines in mind when you give an oral critique.

1. *Praise one or two things that were done well in the speech.* An effective critique should contain positive as well as negative comments. Everyone needs positive reinforcement. For example, if you thought that a speaker used excellent examples and an especially good introduction, begin your critique with these comments.

2. *Include only one or two negative comments.* Too often critics try to identify every little thing that went wrong. However, most people have difficulty dealing with more than a few specific criticisms. For example, suppose that you found the following things wrong with Gwen's speech: She said "uh" and "well" with almost every sentence; she tended to look at only one side of the class; she used unfamiliar words without defining them; she did not provide clear transitions between points; and she had a relatively poor conclusion. Instead of mentioning all these points, your critique would be more helpful if you concentrated on the two most serious criticisms.

3. *When making negative comments, mention what the speaker could do to improve.* For example, if you were criticizing Gwen's use of transitions, you could suggest, "After you finished your first point, Gwen, you might have said, 'Now that we have seen how telepathy works, let's define *clairvoyance* and see how it differs.' "

Just as athletes do, speakers striving for excellence need feedback to identify which areas of their performance are solid and which need more work.

4. *Be specific.* For example, you might evaluate Gwen's speech introduction by saying, "Gwen did a good job of opening her speech. Not only was the material interesting, but it also focused on the purpose of her speech."

One last point to keep in mind: The purpose of an oral critique is not to show how wonderful the critic is. It is to help the speaker understand what went right and what went wrong in the speech.

The Written Critique

A written critique, or evaluation, usually takes a more complete look at the speech than an oral critique does. The most common form is based on a checklist. Use the checklist on page 345 as the basis for your written critiques.

Learning to write a good critique is as important as learning to give a good speech. On the following pages, you will see how the checklist on page 345 could be used in writing a critique of "A Profile of the Successful High-Tech Salesperson," a speech included in the Appendix on pages 598-602.

Organization. Start your critique by analyzing the organization of the speech. Once you get a sense of the structure of the speech, you will find it easier to determine whether the content was sufficient to achieve the speech's purpose. Evaluate the clarity of the statement of the purpose for the speech. For example, early in her speech on being a successful high-tech salesperson, Jeanne Greenberg said, "So, I hope that by taking out a psychological pen and drawing a profile for you of this new breed of successful high-tech salesperson, that all of you, regardless of the product or service you are selling, will be able to assimilate some aspect of these findings into your sales management experience." This statement specifies her purpose clearly and in detail.

Next, determine whether the key points were easy to identify. In her speech, Jeanne Greenberg organized her material around five questions: What is high-tech? What is unique about a high-tech salesperson? What are the necessary characteristics of a high-tech salesperson? Where are high-tech salespersons found? How can these lessons about high-tech salespeople be applied to other specific situations?

Decide whether the speaker used good transitions to help clarify the key points. Jeanne Greenberg did. At one point she moved from one idea to another by saying, "Now, I have just described a unique individual for you. . . . I told you that by getting a clearer understanding of what it takes to succeed on the leading edge of new developments, there would be lessons for all of us in sales."

Finally, look at the introduction and the conclusion. Ms. Greenberg's introduction created interest in her speech by showing its immediate importance to her listeners. In addition, her introduction clarified her purpose. Her conclusion summarized her key points (or lessons) and showed how members of the audience could apply them to their own situations.

Content. Examine the content of the speech. Throughout her speech, Jeanne Greenberg used specific examples and quotations to help explain her points. Often, she drew from her experience to specify and dramatize

Evaluation Checklist for Informative Speeches

Organization:
Was the purpose of the speech clear?
Did the introduction gain attention? Did it clarify the purpose?
Was each of the main ideas clearly identifiable?
Did the main ideas follow a consistent pattern?
Did the speaker use good transitions?
Did the conclusion summarize the key ideas? Did it close the speech on a high point?

Content:
Did the speaker seem to have a solid understanding of the topic?
Did the speaker appear to consider the audience's interest, knowledge, and attitude?
Was there enough information to make the key ideas of the speech understandable?
Were materials selected that would help the audience remember the key ideas of the speech?

Language:
Was the language precise?
Were the words specific and concrete?
Did the speaker use words that the audience could understand?
Did the speaker emphasize key ideas?
Was the tone appropriate for the audience and the occasion?

Delivery:
Did the speaker seem confident?
Was the speaker's appearance appropriate?
Did the speaker show enthusiasm?
Did the speaker look at the audience during the speech?
Were facial expressions, gestures, and movements natural?
Were articulation, enunciation, and pronunciation correct?

Additional Comments:

Evaluation:

points. Notice how she moved from the general to the specific in the following passage:

> Our research findings underscore that people who excel in high-tech sales are excellent communicators—both verbally and in writing. They must have the ability to compose letters, proposals and reports clearly, concisely and convincingly.

In addition, Ms. Greenberg appeared to know her audience well and to be able to make her speech meaningful to them. At one point she said, "What these new technologies do is create or realign markets and demands. And that affects all of us."

Language. Look at the language of the speech. What is probably most important in an informative speech is that the language is specific. In her speech Jeanne Greenberg used language that is clear, accurate, and simple. She emphasized points well, and several of her points were stated quite vividly. For example, early in the speech she said,

> So, the first salesperson of an abacus had a more difficult task than those around him who were peddling sandals. His marketplace was limited, its uses difficult to comprehend at first, and the need had to be explained—if not created.

> Centuries later, the pocket calculator posed a similar dilemma. They were initially expensive, really too large to fit into anyone's pocket, and only used by a rare few. Now, banks give them away along with toasters as incentives for opening an account.

Delivery. Finally, evaluate the delivery of the speech. Of course, when you are writing a critique of a written representation of a speech, you cannot comment on delivery.

Keeping in mind content, organization, and language, a critical listener should conclude that Jeanne Greenberg's speech was a well-organized, clear statement of the profile of a successful high-tech salesperson.

ACTIVITY: Giving an Oral and a Written Critique of an Informative Speech

Working with a partner, find an informative speech in an issue of *Vital Speeches of the Day.* Have your partner deliver this speech. Then, using the guidelines discussed in this section, give an oral critique of it. Finally, provide a written critique of it.

Profiles in Communication

After completing his eighteen weeks of training at the Texas Highway Patrol Academy in 1983, Officer Herman Ward's public speaking responsibilities began almost immediately. He had been on the job less than three months when he was asked to speak to the Lions Club about the Highway Patrol's training program.

Since that time, giving both formal and impromptu public information speeches has been an important and integral part of Officer Ward's professional duties. He is frequently asked to talk to a variety of audiences: students; members of public service, business, and social organizations; and church groups.

Usually his audiences are fairly uniform in age and interests; however, one church asked him to speak to a group of Sunday school classes that included both children and adults. "That was a challenge," Officer Ward recalls. "I had to talk to the kids and keep their interest while not losing the adults' attention." To hold children's interest, he uses gimmicks, audience participation, a lively pace, and repetition. "But I like talking to children best *because* it's challenging, and surprising," he says with a smile. "One time I gave a speech on seat belts at an elementary school. I told them that every time I said 'seat belt' they were all supposed to yell 'Buckle up!' Well, after a while I had forgotten all about it. I was talking along and happened to say 'seat belt.' To my surprise, suddenly everybody in the auditorium yelled 'Buckle up!' "

Some audiences request that Officer Ward speak on a specific topic such as radar operations or accident investigation; others leave the topic selection up to him. Once he has a definite topic, he reviews the information he wants to present, writes an outline, decides "when to show and when to tell," and practices fitting the presentation into the time frame he has been given. Sometimes, however, he is asked to speak at the last minute and has no time for formal preparation. In such cases, he speaks extemporaneously, taking a lead on a topic from an initial question-and-answer period.

"I was lucky," he says. "Before I ever chose a career in law enforcement, I took a speech course in college. It gave me a chance to practice public speaking first in front of people I knew." What is Officer Ward's advice for giving good informative speeches? Be sensitive to the concerns of the public, be willing to learn and to share information, and take a speech class.

GUIDELINES FOR GIVING AN INFORMATIVE SPEECH

- Have I selected a good topic?
- Have I written a clear specific purpose?
- Have I gathered information from a variety of sources?
- Does my topic relate to my audience's experience?
- Is my material well organized?
- Does my introduction spark my audience's interest in learning more about my topic?
- Is the information new, or does it offer new insights?
- Can I use humor to make my delivery more effective?
- Can I use audiovisual aids to help my audience understand and remember information?

SUMMARY

An informative speech is one that helps an audience understand and remember the material presented.

Informative speeches can be developed in several ways. A narrative speech presents a personal experience and gives information in story form. A descriptive speech provides information by creating word pictures that give size, weight, shape, color, age, and condition. A definition speech explains words or concepts through classification, synonym, or function. A process speech explains how to do something, how to make something, or how something works. A report uses research material to discuss past or present events.

The criteria for choosing a topic for an informative speech are the same as for any other kind of speech. Your topic should be something that you are interested in and that you know something about.

Obtain information from a variety of sources. You can gather information from your own experience and observations, from others in interviews or surveys, and from written sources.

A good informative speech has an introduction, a body, and a conclusion. The introduction should focus attention on the topic and should interest the audience in knowing more about it. An introduction should also establish a bond of mutual respect between the audience and the speaker. Material for an informative speech can be organized in chronological order, spatial order, topical order, climactic order, cause-and-effect order, or comparison-and-contrast order. The conclusion for an informative speech should summarize the key information.

Relate your material to the audience. Always adapt your speech to the specific skills, interests, and needs of your audience.

Deliver your speech forcefully. If possible, use audiovisual aids. The tests for deciding whether to use an audiovisual aid are whether the aid will save you time, whether it will help clarify a point, and whether it will help emphasize a point.

Always try to leave time following an informative speech for a question-and-answer period. Answer questions carefully and fully. Throughout the speech you should be conscious of audience feedback and should respond to it as much as possible.

A critique is an analysis and evaluation of a speech. A critique of an informative speech focuses on what the speaker did to help the audience understand and remember the information.

An oral critique of an informative speech consists of comments made directly to the speaker. In giving an oral critique, you will want to praise one or two things that were done well and to criticize one or two things that could have been done better. In both cases, you will want to be specific.

A written critique usually takes a more complete look at the speech than an oral critique does. Most written critiques are based on a checklist composed of questions directed toward speech organization, content, language, and delivery.

CHAPTER VOCABULARY

Look back through this chapter to find the meaning of each of the following terms. Write each term and its meaning in your communication journal.

- audiovisual aids
- cause-and-effect order
- chart
- chronological order
- climactic order
- comparison-and-contrast order
- critique

- definition
- description
- diagram
- ethos
- graph
- informative speech
- mnemonic devices

- narration
- process speech
- report
- spatial order
- topical order

1. An informative speech provides information. What are the two major goals of an informative speech?

2. Narration is one method for presenting information in an informative speech. What are four others?

3. A good speech introduction should spark the audience's interest in the topic. What else should the introduction accomplish?

4. One way of organizing the body of the speech is according to chronological order. In what cases would this be a good organizational pattern to use?

5. Another way of organizing the body of an informative speech is through comparison and contrast. In what cases would this be a good organizational pattern to use?

6. Suppose you wanted to show the causes leading up to certain events. What organizational pattern would be the best one to use?

7. Suppose you wanted to save your most important point for last. What organizational pattern would you use?

8. What does the conclusion of an informative speech accomplish?

9. When should audiovisual aids be used in an informative speech?

10. "Call upon people from all parts of the audience" is one guideline for handling the question period following a speech. What are three other guidelines?

1. Suppose you were giving a speech on a subject that interested you greatly but that you thought might not appeal to your audience. Discuss with your classmates how you would introduce this speech to arouse audience interest.

2. Discuss the factors involved in deciding which method to use in presenting information in an informative speech.

3. Discuss the reasons for including a summary as part of a conclusion in an informative speech.

4. Samuel Johnson once wrote, "Knowledge is of two kinds. We know a subject ourselves, or we know where we can find information upon it." First discuss the meaning of this quotation. Then discuss how you can use both kinds of knowledge in an informative speech.

5. Albert Szent-Györgyi wrote, "Research is to see what everybody else has seen, and to think what nobody else has thought." First discuss the meaning of this quotation. Then discuss how it relates to the informative speech.

1. Testing Your Memory

A. Read the following paragraph as many times as you think you need to in order to remember it.

Go straight until you come to a fork in the road. Then turn left and keep going until you see the third four-way stop. Now turn right and go until you come to an overpass. Turn right again at the street immediately before the overpass. Continue for three stop signs and you will see a church with a steeple. You want the white building directly across from the church.

Now cover the paragraph and write the directions as you remember them. After you finish, check your version of the directions against the paragraph.

B. Work with a partner. Listen to a newscast on the radio. After it is over, jot down everything you remember from it while your partner does the same. Finally, share your notes with your partner.

2. Giving an Informative Speech—Narration

List five topics that would be good ones for you to develop in a narration. Then list the organizational pattern you would use for three of these topics. Choose one of these topics and write a specific purpose and a thesis statement for it. Develop your information into a short narration. Present your narration to your class. After your speech, hold a question-and-answer period and respond to your listeners' feedback. Ask for feedback on these items in particular: your enthusiasm, eye contact, vocal variety and emphasis, articulation, pronunciation, and nonverbal behavior.

3. Giving an Informative Speech—Description

Present a short, impromptu description of a thimble, a chair, a book, a lamp, a pencil, a ruler, a paper clip, or a window. Try to keep your description to one hundred words or less. Ask your classmates to use the "Evaluation Checklist for Informative Speeches" (page 345) to evaluate how effective your description was.

4. Giving an Informative Speech—Definition

Choose a common object in your classroom, such as an eraser, a wastebasket, or a window, or choose an idea or emotion, such as courage, equality, or anger, and write a short definition of it. Define the topic you choose by classifying it, by explaining its use or function, or by describing its scope or what it includes. Present your definition to your class. Ask your listeners to use the "Evaluation Checklist for Informative Speeches" (page 345) to evaluate your delivery. Conduct a question-and-answer session following your speech, and respond to your listeners' feedback.

5. Giving an Informative Speech—Report

Choose a topic that you are studying in another class, such as the use of different drill speeds and bits when drilling different materials (industrial arts), the development of manufacturing in the Midwest during the nineteenth century (American history or economics), or the discovery of radioactive elements by the Curies (chemistry or world history). Research this topic by consulting three different sources. Using your notes from your research, prepare a brief extemporaneous report on your topic. Include citations for at least two of your sources. Present your report in class. Ask your listeners to use the guidelines for giving an oral critique (pages 343–44).

6. Giving an Oral Critique of an Informative Speech

Using the "Evaluation Checklist for Informative Speeches" (page 345), prepare a careful critique of an informative speech delivered by one of your classmates. Present your critique orally in class. Ask your classmates to evaluate your critique, and respond to the feedback they give you.

7. Giving a Written Critique of an Informative Speech

Using the "Evaluation Checklist for Informative Speeches" (page 345), write a critique of an informative speech delivered by one of your classmates. Give at least two "additional comments" that specify what you thought were strong points in the speech and include only one or two comments on negative points. In stating your evaluation, be sure that you cite specific examples from the speech to support your opinions.

1. Whenever you get or do something new or different, don't you often ask your friends for their opinions of what you have gotten or done? Although everyone welcomes favorable critiques, you probably want more than simple flattery from your friends. Instead, you look to them for honest evaluations and helpful criticism. One of the best ways to ensure that you get thoughtful critiques is to be able to give such critiques yourself. Imagine that your best friend has just gotten or made something and has asked your opinion of it. Your reaction is generally favorable, but you see some flaws. What will you say to your friend? First, identify the situation. Which of your friends has asked your opinion? What have you been asked to critique—a bike, a hairdo, a musical recording, an idea, a decision? What specifically is good about it? What is flawed? How will you express your overall favorable impression and your reservations as well? Write a one- or two-page critique giving your opinion. Be prepared to present your critique in class. Ask your classmates for feedback on the helpfulness and tactfulness of your comments.

2. Engineers often need to present complex information in a readily understandable form. To explain the features of a machine, a road plan, or any other engineering product, an engineer must be able to translate technical data so that it can be understood by nonspecialists, such as company and government officials, machinists, and media reporters. While you are not an engineer, you probably have specialized technical knowledge about some device or procedure. Perhaps you can describe the features of an internal-combustion engine or a computer disk drive, or can define the differences between types of cloth or water purification systems. Imagine that you have to report on your specialized knowledge to an audience of nonspecialists. Begin by identifying your topic and your audience. Adapt your language and the complexity of your report to your listeners. Write a one- to two-page report on your topic and be prepared to present your report to your classmates. Following your report, conduct a question-and-answer session on the effectiveness of your presentation.

THE PROCESS SPEECH

OBJECTIVES:

After you have studied this chapter, you should be able to

1. Give directions on how to do something.

2. Give directions on how to make something.

3. Explain how something works.

4. Choose a topic for a process speech.

5. Use chronological order to organize information in a process speech.

6. Use topical order to organize information in a process speech.

7. Demonstrate a process.

8. Analyze and evaluate a process speech.

"Susan, where in the world did you learn to fold napkins that way?" Gloria asked.

"At the restaurant. Remember when I worked part time at The Oak Inn for a while? Part of my job was getting the place settings ready, and that included folding the napkins."

"How do you do it?"

"It's really easy once you get the hang of it. Here, let me show you. First, fold the napkin in half. You have to make sure that it's even. Then . . ."

Susan may not know it, but she is explaining a process to Gloria. Telling someone how to do something, how to make something, or how something works is a common experience. Nearly every day in conversations or in formal presentations, you are likely to explain to others a process you are familiar with.

WHAT IS A PROCESS SPEECH?

A **process speech** explains how to do something, how to make something, or how something works. In the opening situation, Susan is explaining how to do something, specifically, how to fold napkins for special occasions.

In this book the process speech is discussed as a separate speech because of its many possible applications. For example, a process speech can be a type of informative speech, or it can be a part of a sales speech. Because of the importance of process explanations, learning how to present them clearly and dramatically is very useful.

Process speeches are given for at least three reasons. First, a process speech may be given to enable the audience to perform a process. In such a speech the emphasis is on learning the process. "How to throw a knuckle ball" and "How to make a doghouse" are two speeches that would be given for this reason. Second, a process speech may be given to enable the audience to understand a process better. A speech on how a candidate is chosen in a national political convention or how a car's catalytic converter works would be given for this reason. Third, a process speech may be given to demonstrate the value of a product in order to motivate a person to buy the product. A speech showing how a vacuum cleaner or a sewing machine works would be given for this reason.

ACTIVITY: Identifying Topics for a Process Speech

Think about all the processes you know well enough to explain. Carefully review the steps of each process. How many processes can you explain completely from start to finish so that someone following your explanation could complete the process successfully? On a piece of paper, list the processes that you can fully explain. Share your findings with your classmates. Insert your list in your communication journal so that you can consult it later to choose a topic for the process speech you will develop in later activities in this chapter.

TYPES OF PROCESS SPEECHES

Most process speeches can be classified according to purpose into one of three categories: giving directions on how to do something, giving directions on how to make something, and explaining how something works.

Giving Directions on How to Do Something

The purpose of some process speeches is to give directions on how to do something. In these speeches the emphasis is on presenting the steps of the process clearly enough so that each member of the audience is able to accomplish the process.

Before you can *explain* how to do something, you have to *know* how to do it. Maybe a kind librarian will forward Norman's letter.

The following topics are examples of processes that would be suitable for how-to-do-it speeches:

How to use a compass	How to design a dress
How to study for tests	How to paint a car
How to placekick	How to shop for shoes
How to write a business letter	How to water-ski
How to play racquetball	How to fold napkins

Giving Directions on How to Make Something

Another common purpose of process speeches is to give directions on how to make something. In these speeches the emphasis is on presenting the steps of the process clearly enough so that each member of the audience is able to make the object. The following topics are examples of processes that would be suitable for how-to-make-it speeches:

How to make whole-wheat bread	How to make pottery
How to build a doghouse	How to tie fishing flies
How to make paper flowers	How to build a patio
How to build a theater set	How to build a dollhouse
How to build a bookcase	How to make a canoe

Explaining How Something Works

A third purpose of process speeches is to explain how something works. In these speeches the emphasis is on presenting the steps of a process clearly enough so that the members of the audience can understand how the process works even though they might not be able to complete the steps themselves. For example, a speech on how jet propulsion works is not given so that the members of the audience can build a jet engine, but so that they will better understand what is involved in jet propulsion. The following topics are examples of processes that would be suitable for how-it-works speeches:

How a washing machine works	How a telephone works
How a computer works	How a television works
How a helicopter works	How a radio works
How a camera works	How a drawbridge works
How a cuckoo clock works	How a sewing machine works

ACTIVITY: **Analyzing and Identifying Topics for Process Explanations**

List six processes that have been explained to you recently. Classify each as how to do something, how to make something, or how something works. Then list topics that you would be able to use to show how to do something, how to make something, or how something works.

PREPARING TO SPEAK

Preparing for your process speech involves choosing a topic, preparing an introduction, organizing the body of the speech, and preparing a conclusion.

Choosing a Topic

When you choose a topic for a process speech, select a process that you know well. When Susan needed to decide on a topic for her process speech, she chose how to fold napkins because she had performed the process often and was very familiar with it. One of Susan's classmates, Nicholas, decided to explain how an automobile engine works, since he had taken courses in automotive mechanics and had worked on cars as a hobby.

Preparing Your Introduction

You will recall that a speech introduction is designed to get the audience's attention, to focus that attention on the topic, and to gain good will for the

Choosing a Topic for a Process Speech

Look at the list of topics you wrote for the activities on pages 356 and 358. You may be able to develop one of these into a good process speech. If so, select the topic that you feel you can best explain. If not, go back to work on your lists. Add to them until you discover a topic that you feel you can present effectively in a process speech.

speaker. As with other speeches, you should start your process speech with an attention-getting statement, a question, a story, or a personal reference.

Your introduction will succeed if it motivates your audience to want to learn more about your topic. Before listeners will concentrate on how to do something, how to make something, or how something works, they must have some personal interest in doing so.

As Susan worked on her process speech, she asked herself how she was going to interest people in folding napkins. She thought of two approaches for her opening. One was based on an appeal to people's natural curiosity: People may have wondered how the napkins at fancy restaurants are folded so attractively. The other was based on the common desire to please family members: For special occasions people may want to surprise members of their families by creating fancy place settings. Using these two approaches, Susan constructed two possible introductions for her speech:

> Have you ever admired the special ways napkins are folded at fancy restaurants? Have you ever had the urge to get the waiter to show you how to do it? Actually, napkin folding is not as difficult as it may seem. In the next few minutes, I will show you two of the most attractive ways of folding napkins.

> Think of the times your family was preparing a special meal for your mother's or your father's birthday, and you wondered what you could do to give that meal a special touch. One way is to do what they do in expensive restaurants—fold the napkins in some unique, formal manner.

Now that Susan has tried two introductions, she can choose the one that she thinks will most appeal to her audience.

Organizing the Body of a Process Speech

Most process speeches are organized around the steps involved in completing the process. Therefore, most process speeches present information in either chronological order or topical order.

Chronological Order. You will recall that **chronological order** is a pattern for arranging items in the order in which they happen in time. If you were giving a process speech on how to repaint a section of a car, the following chronological order of main steps would work for you.

Using a diagram or a flow chart to show the chronological order of steps in a process can help your audience understand them better.

Specific Purpose: I want to explain the steps in repainting a section of a car.

    I. Sand the area that is to be repainted.
   II. Apply two coats of primer.
  III. Apply two coats of finish.

Topical Order. You will recall that **topical order** is a pattern of organization in which a topic is broken down into parts that are arranged in an order determined by the speaker and stated in the specific purpose. When you are explaining a single process such as repainting a section of a car, you should organize the main points so that they follow chronological order. However, suppose you were giving a speech on folding napkins and you wanted to explain how to make both the fan and the turtle. In this case, the organization of the speech would have two main points (making the fan and making the turtle) with the subdivisions of each main point arranged according to chronological order.

Specific Purpose: I want to explain two simple but attractive ways of folding napkins.

    I. One way is the fan.
       A. The first step is . . .
       B. The second step is . . .
       C. The third step is . . .
   II. A second way is the turtle.
       A. The first step is . . .

B. The second step is . . .

C. The third step is . . .

Grouping Steps. One of the greatest problems you are likely to have with a process speech is identifying the key steps in the process. A process speech should seldom have more than five main points, since a person listening to a speech will have difficulty trying to remember more than five steps. Yet, many processes appear to have seven, ten, or even fifteen steps. To make remembering easier for your audience, group the steps under broader headings. Members of an audience can remember four main points with four subdivisions each much better than they can remember sixteen main points.

Here are two outlines for a speech on soccer-style placekicking. The specific purpose is to explain the steps in a soccer-style placekick.

Poor (twelve separate steps)	*Better (four separate steps)*
I. Spot the ball on the tee.	I. Spot the ball on the tee.
II. Face the goal posts.	II. Mark off steps.
III. Take three steps back.	A. Face goal posts.
IV. Take two steps left.	B. Take three steps back and two to the left.
V. Take three steps into the ball.	C. Stand facing right goal post.
VI. Stand facing right goal post.	III. Step toward the ball.
VII. Contact ground on left heel.	A. Take three steps beginning with left foot.
VIII. Swing right leg through.	B. On third step, contact ground with left heel.
IX. Keep toe pointed.	IV. Kick the ball.
X. Lock knee.	A. Swing right leg through.
XI. Strike ball at a spot one-third up from ground.	B. Keep toe pointed.
XII. Kick with instep.	C. Lock knee.
	D. Strike ball at a spot one-third up from ground.
	E. Kick with instep.

Preparing Your Conclusion

Because the primary aim of a process speech is to have the audience master the key steps of the process, an effective conclusion for a process speech often includes a summary of those steps. Therefore, the following paragraph would make a good conclusion for Susan's process speech on folding napkins.

By following the steps I have presented, you can add a little special something—attractively folded napkins—to your next dinner party. Let me quickly review those steps. First, fold the napkin into a rectangle. Then accordion-fold it in two-inch strips, tuck the center of the edge into the center of the fold, and stand one napkin on each plate.

It may also be useful to go through the process again quickly as you summarize.

ACTIVITY: Determining the Specific Purpose and the Steps of a Process Speech

For the topic you choose for your process speech, write a specific purpose. Then decide whether your main points will follow chronological order or topical order. Be prepared to explain your decision.

Finally, list all the steps in the process you are planning to explain. If your list has more than five steps, group the steps into no more than five categories.

DELIVERING YOUR SPEECH

Once you put yourself in the proper frame of mind, you may enjoy delivering your process speech because you will be talking about something you know how to do well. As with any other speech, you must make sure that your audience trusts you and that you deliver your speech with enthusiasm. Use your vocal skills to show variety and emphasis and, of course, speak clearly and precisely. However, when giving a process speech, slow the rate of your delivery during the explanation. Since your goal is to help your audience learn the process, you must take them through the steps slowly and carefully.

When you are giving a process speech, you are a *teacher*. You know how a thing is done or how something works, but your listeners do not. Go over every step of the process with them patiently.

Adapting Your Speech to Your Audience

In Chapter 14 you learned that *adapting* to your audience means presenting your information in a way that relates it directly to the attitudes, knowledge, and interests of the particular audience you are addressing. Do not overestimate your audience's knowledge—avoid making your explanations technical. In addition, use mnemonic devices and visual aids when possible.

In this section you will consider additional ways to adapt your process speech to your audience so that your delivery will be more effective.

Details. Include sufficient details to clarify the process. Since the members of your audience do not know how to accomplish the process, do not assume that they can or will supply missing details. For example, here is a first explanation of how to check the oil level in a car:

> You should regularly check your car's oil level. Remove the dipstick, wipe it clean, reinsert it, and remove it again. The oil will leave a line on the dipstick. If the line is near the "Full" mark, you have no problem. If it is near the "Add" mark, you will have to add oil.

Although the explanation is clear, it glosses over two very important pieces of information needed to complete the process: (1) what a dipstick is and (2) how you find it. Although most people in the audience are likely to know what a dipstick is, some may not. In addition, some members of the audience may have trouble finding the dipstick in their own cars. The following revised version begins with preliminary details and then moves on to the explanation:

> You should regularly check your car's oil level. To do this, you have to find and remove the dipstick. The dipstick is a long, thin piece of metal with a handle (usually a loop). The dipstick goes into the engine itself. In many models it is in plain view, but in some you must look for it. Remove the dipstick. Wipe it clean, reinsert it, and remove it again. The oil will leave a line on the dipstick. If the line is near the "Full" mark, you have no problem. If it is near the "Add" mark, you will have to add oil.

Essential Steps. Focus on the essential steps of the process. Your audience will not be able to follow a speech in which you include every detail related to the process. To determine what is essential, ask the question, "What could be left out and still allow the listener to understand the process?" For example, a speech on how to bowl could be based on the following information:

> Hold the ball in front of you in your right hand. As you take a short, sliding step with your right foot, push the ball out in front of you. On your second step, begin a pendulum swing. By your third step, the ball should have swung behind you. On your fourth and last step, swing the ball forward and slide on your left foot. Release the ball as it passes your leg. Bring your arm straight up in your follow-through.

This explanation focuses on the essentials. What a bowler does with his or her left arm during the swing is a nonessential detail. If you tried to include in your speech every aspect of every part of the bowler's body, you would confuse your listeners more than you would help them.

Familiar Objects and Processes. Use familiar objects and processes for comparisons. People understand material better when it is related to information that is already familiar to them. Suppose you wanted your audience to visualize a computer keyboard. An easy way to help your audience see it would be to talk about it in terms of a typewriter.

Imagine a typewriter keyboard. A computer keyboard has the same keys. The difference between the two is that the computer has additional keys. Often these are set off to the side of the regular keyboard. Also, some of the standard typing keys have additional functions.

The better you know your listeners, the better able you will be to relate information in your speech to knowledge they already have.

Appropriate Language. Especially in a process speech, you must pay particular care to your language. Look for specific, concrete, and vivid words to explain the process. Avoid using difficult or technical words that are familiar to you but may not be familiar to those who are learning the process. Note the wording of the following excerpt from a speech on how to be a more effective leader in public meetings.

Make sure that you require people to move the previous question when they want to end debate. If you are not very careful about this, you can get into real trouble.

To someone who has been the chairperson of many groups, the concept of "moving the previous question" is self-explanatory. Yet many people in a general audience may not know what the phrase means. The excerpt could be revised in the following way to adapt it to an average audience.

> Make sure that when a person is trying to get you to stop discussion, he or she makes a statement in the form of a motion. The person might say, "I move we stop discussion and take a vote."

Although for a student of parliamentary procedure, this wording may not be quite as precise as the previous wording, it is likely to be a great deal clearer to a general audience.

Demonstrating the Process

If possible, demonstrate the process. Demonstrations can be especially helpful when you are talking about how to do something or how to make something.

Demonstration. A **demonstration** is a procedure in which the speaker goes through the actual steps of the process. For example, when you visit the kitchenware department of a retail store, you may see demonstrators showing people how various products work. Watching a demonstrator complete a process helps members of an audience understand the process and learn how to perform it themselves. Demonstrations of processes work very well when the process is relatively simple, when the demonstrator is able to complete the demonstration smoothly, and when the audience can see everything that is being done.

When you deliver a process speech, you can give a demonstration yourself, or you can invite a well-qualified person to give a demonstration. For example, if you were presenting a speech on giving artificial respiration, you could ask a paramedic, a nurse, or some other qualified specialist to demonstrate the process.

Partial Demonstration. You may decide that a complete demonstration of a process would not be suitable for your speech because

1. the process is too complicated for you to demonstrate it fully;
2. the parts of the process are too small for all members of the audience to see well;
3. you are too nervous to be able to do the demonstration perfectly.

Under one or more of these circumstances, you might want to consider doing a partial demonstration.

In a **partial demonstration** either some of the parts of the demonstration are already completed or the size of items is exaggerated so that the audience will be able to see them clearly.

How to patch a hole in plaster or plasterboard is a topic for which a partial demonstration would work quite well. Suppose that you were planning to mix water with dry plaster to form wet plaster patch. In the first place, you might have difficulty measuring the amounts needed to mix the patch perfectly. Second, you would need a few minutes for the patch to set up, or harden. During your speech, you would not want to ask the audience to wait a few minutes before you continue. You could avoid such a delay by

Giving a demonstration often enables an audience to get a better grasp of a process, like cooking, that would take thousands of words to explain.

completing some of the steps before giving your demonstration. You could bring two containers—one containing water and one holding the dry plaster—and mix the water with the dry plaster. While you were talking about how long to stir the mixture, how to test its consistency, and how much time it needed to set up, you could bring out a third container that had the proper mixture ready for use. Then you could go on to the next step in the demonstration.

Imagine that you were going to give a speech on how to sew a button on a coat. For a partial demonstration of this process, you would want to exaggerate the size of your tools. You could make a cardboard button about the diameter of a dinner plate and could use a sharpened pencil for a needle, with string tied to the end for the thread. Then, as you were going through the process, everyone in the audience could easily see what you were doing.

Responding to Feedback

When giving a process speech, you have to be very sensitive to audience feedback. If your speech allows you to involve the audience directly in going through the process, then you can monitor members of the audience to make sure that they understand.

Otherwise, you need to be sensitive to such clues as people frowning, shaking their heads, and showing puzzled expressions, since these clues indicate that the audience does not understand what you are saying.

ACTIVITY: **Delivering a Process Speech**

Give a process speech to your class. Prepare a two- to five-minute speech showing how to do something, how to make something, or how something works. If appropriate, demonstrate the process.

Complete an outline for the speech and submit it to your teacher before you begin. Your teacher will be looking for how well you have organized the speech.

As you give your speech, make a mental note about how people are behaving while you speak. Be prepared to explain your response to your audience's feedback.

ANALYZING AND EVALUATING THE PROCESS SPEECH

A critique of a process speech is based on the same criteria that are used for evaluating any informative speech. The focus of the critique is on the organization of the stages of the process and on the use of visual aids to increase understanding of the process.

The Oral Critique

Use the following guidelines to prepare an oral critique.

1. *Praise one or two things that were done well in the speech.* Try to focus on those elements that are particularly relevant to an explanation of the process: demonstration, visual aids, and organization. For example, imagine that you were critiquing Susan's speech. If you were particularly impressed with her ability to fold napkins while she was talking and her ability to impress the entire class with the attractiveness of folded napkins, you would want to start your oral critique by mentioning these items.

2. *Include only one or two negative comments.* Regardless of how many mistakes a speaker made, you should limit your criticism to only one or two of them. For example, you might have thought that Susan's enunciation was sometimes unclear, that she used too many vocalized pauses, and that her demonstration could not be seen clearly by all of the audience. Instead of making all three criticisms, you would want to bring up only the most serious one or two. In this case, you might choose the third point because it deals with the flaw that would most hinder audience understanding.

3. *Suggest ways that the speaker could have improved the speech.* For example, if you criticized Susan for not demonstrating in a way that everyone could see, you might explain or actually show her how she could have done the demonstration so that everyone could have seen it.

4. *Be specific.* If the speaker cannot tell what you mean, your critique will not be useful. Telling Susan that her demonstration was "no good" would not be useful criticism. Instead, you would want to specify what was wrong—that all of the audience could not see the demonstration.

Evaluation Checklist for Process Speeches

Organization:

Was the purpose of the speech clear?

Did the introduction gain attention? Did it clarify the purpose?

Was each of the main points clearly identifiable?

Did the main points follow chronological or topical order?

Were the steps of the process grouped so that there were no more than five main groups?

Did the speaker use good transitions?

Did the conclusion summarize the key ideas? Did it leave the speech on a high point?

Content:

Did the speaker appear to understand the topic?

Did the speaker appear to consider the audience's interest, knowledge, and attitude?

Was there enough specific information to make the key points of the speech understandable?

Was the demonstration clear?

Were audiovisual aids used effectively? Were the visual aids large enough? Were they clear enough? Were they well drawn?

Were materials selected that would help the audience remember the key ideas of the speech?

Language:

Was the language precise?

Were the words specific and concrete?

Did the speaker use words that the audience could understand?

Did the speaker emphasize key ideas?

Was the tone appropriate for the audience and the occasion?

Delivery:

Did the speaker seem confident?

Was the speaker's appearance appropriate?

Did the speaker show enthusiasm?

Did the speaker look at the audience during the speech?

Were the speaker's facial expressions, gestures, and movements natural?

Were the speaker's articulation, enunciation, and pronunciation correct?

Additional Comments:

Evaluation:

The Written Critique

The written critique of a process speech takes a more complete look at the elements of the speech than the oral critique does. Use the checklist on page 368 to help you identify information to include in your written critiques of process speeches.

Now look at how the checklist on page 368 provides a basis for a written critique of Monica Seebohm's speech, "The Half-Time Show," which is included in the Appendix of Speeches.

When you receive written critiques of your speech, carefully review each comment to identify the strengths and weaknesses of your presentation.

Organization. Start your critique by analyzing the organization of the speech. Monica Seebohm's goal, to explain the steps in producing a half-time show, is clearly stated in the introduction. The information in her speech is organized in chronological order with each of the five steps (planning, teaching squad leaders, teaching the sections, coordinating and practicing, and putting on the show) clearly stated. Her opening effectively focuses attention on her topic. Her conclusion ends her speech on a high note. In fact, her speech is a very well organized explanation of a process.

Content. Analyze and evaluate the content of the speech. In a process speech, the emphasis should be on the clarity of the explanations and on the use of visual aids. Each of Monica Seebohm's explanations is made clearer by her visual aids. In the speech she uses five different visual aids, and two of them are used more than once. As she proceeds through each step, the audience can easily follow the process.

Language. Look at the language of the speech. Explanation of a process demands especially accurate, specific, and simple language. Clarity is a necessity. If the language is also vivid and emphatic, the speech is even better. Throughout her speech, Monica Seebohm uses simple language, yet her choice of words is consistently precise and specific. She does a particularly effective job of picking up a point she began in the introduction and finishing it with this sentence in the conclusion: "Next time you're at a football game and the half-time whistle blows, skip the snacks and enjoy the performance."

Delivery. When you hear a speech, you will want to include in your critique an analysis and evaluation of the way it was delivered. However, since you are only reading Monica Seebohm's speech, you can have no idea of how effective her delivery was. Therefore, in your written critique, you would focus on the speech's organization, content, and language.

In preparing a written critique of a process speech, or of any speech, pay close attention to your grammar and usage. Be sure that you proofread your critique carefully to correct mistakes, and copy it over before handing it in.

ACTIVITY: **Preparing a Written Critique of a Process Speech**

Prepare a written critique of a process speech delivered in class. Use the checklist on page 368 to make sure that you cover all important points. Pay strict attention to your grammar and usage and to the mechanics of your writing—spelling, punctuation, and capitalization.

GUIDELINES FOR DELIVERING A PROCESS SPEECH

- Have I selected a process that interests me and that I know how to perform?
- Have I written a clear specific purpose?
- Have I organized my speech carefully?
- Will my presentation help the audience visualize the process?
- Have I adapted the speech to my audience?
- Can I deliver the speech confidently?
- Can I respond appropriately to audience feedback?

Profiles in Communication

"It's fun—it's just so much fun," Jay Hebert says of his job as County Extension Agent for a state university's Institute of Food and Agricultural Sciences. His favorite part of the job is teaching young 4-H Club members how to become winning horse judges.

After carefully analyzing the process of horse judging, Mr. Hebert devised a system for his teenage judges to follow. First, he teaches them to establish priorities and to use key terms. "Don't make it complicated," he advises. "Know what's most important to your audience, and give your explanation in language your audience understands."

He has his novice judges write out their explanations and read them in group sessions as practice. "I encourage them to sell me and the group on each point," Mr. Hebert explains, "to help them build self-confidence and sharpen their speaking skills."

As they practice, the student judges use fewer and fewer notes until they can present their evaluations extemporaneously. Mr. Hebert insists on "no canned speeches." Continual rehearsal plays a key role in his students' mastery of extemporaneous delivery. Mr. Hebert has his student judges "train every week for months to bring them along step by step."

In teaching these skills Mr. Hebert uses a variety of audiovisual aids, including live horses, photographs, slides, and sheet transparencies. He points out that visual aids should be used only to reinforce what the speaker is saying and should not be explained at great length. "Any time you leave a slide on for over three seconds, that's too long," Mr. Hebert says. "Your audience will concentrate on the picture and will tune you out." He advises keeping the speech moving and referring to visual aids only to demonstrate specific points in the process that is being explained.

Jay Hebert wouldn't trade his job for any other. "When those young people can stand in front of a judge at a competition and express themselves with confidence, that's what it's all about."

SUMMARY

A process speech is one that gives directions on how to do something or how to make something or that explains how something works.

To begin, choose a topic that interests you and that you already know something about. In addition, try to choose a topic that you would feel comfortable demonstrating.

Most process speeches are organized by chronological order since they focus on the steps of the process. Sometimes a speech contains two or three related processes. In this case, the main points will generally be in topical order, and the subpoints of each process will be organized in chronological order.

You need to adapt your speech to your audience by including important details, concentrating on essentials, relating information to your audience's existing knowledge, and using appropriate language. In addition, demonstrating the process when possible can make your delivery more effective. With a process speech, perhaps more than with any other type, you have to be sensitive to audience feedback.

An oral critique of a process speech consists of comments made directly to the speaker. Begin an oral critique by praising one or two things that were done well. Then criticize one or two things that could have been done better and give suggestions for making improvements. In all cases, be specific. Focus on the organization and the use of visual aids—elements that are of key importance in a process speech.

A written critique takes a more complete look at a speech than the oral critique does. Base your written critique on your answers to a checklist of questions about a speech's organization, content, language, and delivery.

CHAPTER VOCABULARY

Look back through this chapter to find the meaning of each of the following terms. Write each term and its meaning in your communication journal.

chronological order
demonstration

partial demonstration
process speech

topical order

REVIEW QUESTIONS

1. One type of process speech explains how to do something. What are two other types?

2. Two reasons for giving a process speech are to enable the audience to perform the process and to enable the audience to understand a process better. What is a third reason?

3. What is the best source of topics for a process speech?

4. Chronological order is the most common organizational pattern for a process speech. When is topical order more appropriate?

5. In organizing your speech, you may find you have as many as fifteen steps. What should you do in this case?

6. One way to adapt your speech to your audience is to include all important details. What are three other ways?

7. For which two types of speeches would you be most likely to include a demonstration?

8. What is the difference between a demonstration and a partial demonstration?

9. What is the difference in focus between a critique of a process speech and a critique of a general information speech?

10. Why do you begin a written critique with an evaluation of the organization of the speech?

DISCUSSION QUESTIONS

1. Suppose you were planning a speech that you believed had eleven steps. How could you organize the speech to meet the guidelines of having no more than five steps? Discuss your answer with your classmates.

2. Suppose you were giving a speech on how to make something. How could you demonstrate it without taking the time to go through every detail? Discuss your answer with your classmates.

3. Have you ever seen a demonstration in a department store? If so, tell your class about it. What made it effective? How could it have been improved?

4. Think of the courses you take in school. In which of these courses would you like to see more demonstrations? How would additional demonstrations make it easier for you to learn? Discuss your answers with your classmates.

5. Long ago, Heraclitus claimed, "Eyes are more accurate witnesses than ears." First discuss the meaning of this quotation. Then discuss how it relates to the need to include demonstrations in your process speech.

ACTIVITIES

1. Identifying and Analyzing Applied Uses of Demonstrations

A. Prepare a list of twenty jobs that would require you to demonstrate something. For example, a vacuum-cleaner salesperson would likely be required to demonstrate how a vacuum cleaner works. Share your list with your classmates.

B. Survey several teachers who teach classes in different subject areas in your school. Find out how many give demonstrations with lessons, how often they give demonstrations, and what kinds of demonstrations they give. Share your findings with your class.

2. Giving a Process Speech on How to Do Something

Write a list of five processes that you know how to do well. Think through each process. Which one can you explain completely in less than five minutes? Jot down the steps of the process that you think you can best explain within the time limit. Using only your brief list of steps, deliver an extemporaneous speech explaining the process. If necessary, use audiovisual aids in your speech. Ask your classmates to use the "Evaluation Checklist for Process Speeches" (page 368) to evaluate your presentation. Ask for feedback especially on your nonverbal behavior, your attention to your listeners' familiarity with your topic, your use of visual aids, and your organization (the completeness and the clarity of your presentation).

3. Giving a Process Speech on How to Make Something

Think back to a project you have completed in which you made something, such as a special meal, a birdhouse, a garden, a skirt, a computer program, a video, or a piece of art. Review the steps in the process and write them down in order. Also list all the materials you needed. Organize your lists into an outline that you can use to present a speech giving complete directions for following the process. Deliver your speech to your classmates. Try to use notes as little as possible, but be careful not to leave out any steps or materials. Ask your listeners to use the guidelines for an oral critique of a process speech on page 367 to give you an evaluation of your presentation.

4. Giving a Process Speech on How Something Works

Think of the many simple tools and devices you commonly use, for example, a pencil sharpener, a nail file, a can opener, an eraser, a necklace clasp, or a bicycle pump. Read two or three short explanations of how one of these common tools or devices works. Taking what you think is the best information from your sources, write a two- or three-page explanation of your own. Present your explanation in a speech to your class. Use audiovisual aids to demonstrate the item that you are explaining. Conduct a question-and-answer session following your speech and respond to your audience's feedback. Ask your listeners to use the "Evaluation Checklist for Process Speeches" (page 368) to critique your presentation.

5. Preparing a Written Critique of a Process Speech

Watch a television program, a video tape, or a movie in which a speaker presents a process—either how to do something, how to make something, or how something works. Prepare a short written critique of the presentation. Consult the "Evaluation Checklist for Process Speeches" (page 368) to ensure that you do not overlook important features of the speaker's verbal and nonverbal behavior.

1. Can you drive a car? Can you operate a sewing machine, power tools, or a food processor? Quite likely, you know how to use a number of machines to make your life more comfortable and more productive. You learned how to operate these machines through written instructions, personal direction, or probably a combination of both. In turn, you have probably helped others learn how to operate equipment, too. How effective have you been at giving such lessons? Imagine that you have been asked to teach a classmate, a co-worker, or someone else how to operate a particular machine. How will you go about doing so? First, identify the person you will teach. Then, identify a specific machine you could teach someone to operate. List the steps that have to be followed to operate this piece of equipment, along with any other details that would be helpful to a learner. Be prepared to present your lesson in class and to respond to feedback on how well you have explained the process of operating the equipment.

2. Training is a continual process in most skilled occupations. Each year thousands of teachers return to school to learn new instructional methods and to brush up on developments in their subject areas. Salespeople need to be trained in the uses and features of new products and then go on to train their customers. Most organizations either have special training personnel or hire consultants to give this instruction. In addition, managers and workers are often called upon to train newcomers and to retrain experienced staff. Imagine that you have been called upon to give a training session. Begin by identifying your audience. Are they newcomers or experienced hands? Next, identify your setting. Are you in business, education, military service, or some other organization? Then, identify the process you will teach. Choose a process you know well—perhaps changing a tire, giving first aid, or preparing a recipe or a formula. List the steps of the process, and decide the best way to present them clearly and completely. Consider making a visual aid or two. Be prepared to give your training session in class. Ask for feedback from your classmates on the effectiveness of your presentation.

VOTE
GABRIEL
STUDENT
COUNCIL

16

THE PERSUASIVE SPEECH

OBJECTIVES:

After studying this chapter, you should be able to

1. Define persuasive speaking.

2. Use logical reasoning to support points in your speech.

3. Appeal to emotions.

4. Establish your credibility.

5. List ethical standards.

6. Select a persuasive speech topic.

7. Write the specific purpose for a persuasive speech.

8. Explain and use six methods of organizing persuasive speeches.

9. Determine your audience's attitude toward your topic.

10. Analyze and evaluate a persuasive speech.

And so I remind you that (1) Ann Welch has proven leadership experience and (2) Ann Welch is a hard worker who will work for each of you. Tomorrow when you go to the polls, think about these two reasons and then vote for Ann Welch for Senior Class president.

Gloria Marcus had just finished her persuasive speech. As she walked to her seat, she felt that the audience was impressed with her material and would vote for Ann Welch.

What is a persuasive speech? How does it differ from an informative speech? How do you prepare your speech so that you can return to your seat with the kind of confidence that Gloria Marcus felt? In this chapter you will find the answers to these and other key questions about the persuasive speech.

WHAT IS A PERSUASIVE SPEECH?

A **persuasive speech** is one that establishes a fact, changes a belief, or moves an audience to act on a policy. A persuasive speech that establishes a *fact* proves that something is true or false. Consider the following two specific purposes:

I want to persuade the class that Carson is guilty of robbing the grocery store.
I want to persuade the class that certain types of tests discriminate against minorities.

In both cases, the statements are either true or false. However, simply offering proof that supports a statement of fact does not mean that everyone in the audience will be willing to accept that statement as true. In many cases, what a speaker is trying to prove is very complex or is open to question. It is always up to the audience to determine whether a speaker has convincingly proved that a statement of fact is true.

A persuasive speech that establishes or changes a *belief* is one that focuses on what is right or wrong, good or bad, best or worst, moral or immoral. A belief cannot be proven to be either true or false. Consider the following two specific purposes:

I want to prove that small schools are better for most students than large schools are.
I want to prove that *M*A*S*H* was the best television comedy series ever produced.

Both of these specific purposes are for speeches that attempt to establish or change a belief. While you cannot prove that a belief is true or false, you can supply convincing information to justify a belief. For the two specific purposes stated above, you would try to show what in particular makes one school better than another or makes one specific television comedy the best ever produced.

A persuasive speech that changes a *policy* is one that focuses on a particular action. When you give a speech on a policy, you try to convince the audience to act on some policy or to agree that some policy should be changed. Consider the following two specific purposes:

I want to prove that the budget for space exploration should be increased.
I want to persuade the class to vote for Ann Welch.

When you are giving a persuasive speech, remember that what convinces one listener will not necessarily convince everyone.

The first specific purpose attempts to get an audience to agree that a policy should be changed. The second attempts to get an audience to act in a particular way.

ACTIVITY: Analyzing Specific Purposes for Persuasive Speeches

Identify the following specific purposes as establishing a fact, establishing or changing a belief, or changing a policy.

1. I want to persuade the class that social security benefits should be reduced.

2. I want to persuade the class that the United States should abolish the electoral college.

3. I want to persuade the class that South High has a better basketball team than North High.

4. I want to persuade the class to watch a documentary on television tonight.

5. I want to persuade the class that funding for programs combating illiteracy should be increased.

PREPARING TO SPEAK

To get ready to give a persuasive speech, you need to choose a topic, decide on your speech objective, gather supporting information, and consider the techniques of persuasion.

Choosing Your Topic

As with any other type of speech, you should choose a topic that interests you and that you already know something about. For a persuasive speech, these guidelines mean that you will look for a topic that you are concerned about or a topic that you believe in. Attempts to speak on topics that do not interest you or that you have insufficient information about will lead to disaster in persuasive speeches.

Are you concerned about censorship, crime, political tension, the arms race? If so, these are topics you can use for a persuasive speech. Since Gloria Marcus was concerned with getting Ann Welch elected, that was the topic Gloria talked about.

Deciding on Your Speech Objective

As soon as you have a topic in mind, you need to write a clear specific purpose, often called a **proposition.** A persuasive speech proposition is a complete sentence that states either (1) the fact you are trying to establish, (2) the belief you are trying to establish or change, or (3) the policy you are trying to get your audience to support or act on. Almost any topic can be phrased to accomplish any of these goals. For example, imagine that you have decided to give a speech on taxes. You might write one of the propositions of fact, belief, or policy given at the bottom of this page.

How you write a proposition is based on what you want to accomplish. With the first proposition, your only goal is to prove that income taxes are

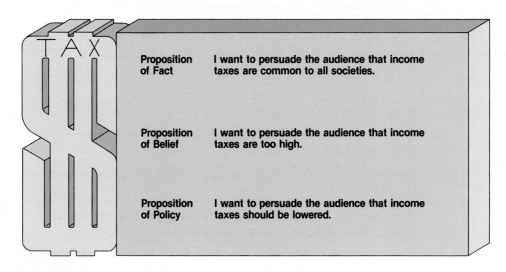

Proposition of Fact	I want to persuade the audience that income taxes are common to all societies.
Proposition of Belief	I want to persuade the audience that income taxes are too high.
Proposition of Policy	I want to persuade the audience that income taxes should be lowered.

common to all societies, a statement of fact that is or is not true. With the second, your emphasis is on getting your audience to accept a value judgment—that taxes are too high. With the third, your emphasis is on what should be done—reduce taxes.

Gloria Marcus might have written any of the following propositions for her speech on Ann Welch.

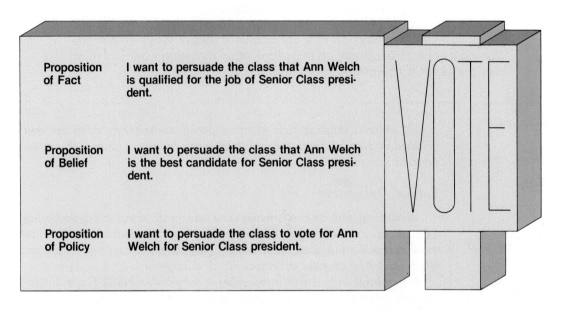

Proposition of Fact	I want to persuade the class that Ann Welch is qualified for the job of Senior Class president.
Proposition of Belief	I want to persuade the class that Ann Welch is the best candidate for Senior Class president.
Proposition of Policy	I want to persuade the class to vote for Ann Welch for Senior Class president.

Gathering Supporting Information

In Chapter 10 you looked at sources of material for your speech. For your persuasive speech you will want to examine those same potential sources: your own information, information from others (interviews and surveys), and reading material. For her speech supporting Ann Welch for Senior Class president, Gloria Marcus gathered information from her own experience, from talks with people who knew Ann and who had worked with her (including her teachers), from school records that were public information, and from reports in the school paper of Ann's accomplishments. For a speech on taxes, you would likely find the best supporting information from reading published material.

TECHNIQUES OF PERSUASION

How do you get people to think, to believe, or to act the way you want them to? One way is to use logical reasoning—to convince the audience by using rational argument. Another way is to appeal to the audience's emotions—to affect the way members of the audience feel so that they will agree with you. A third way is to establish your credibility—to make the audience believe in you and like you. Since each of these methods makes a different appeal within a single speech, effective persuasive speakers often use one or more of these techniques to reach as many members of an audience as possible.

Logical Reasoning

People may well choose to think, to believe, or to do something according to what appears most logical to them. When **logical reasoning** is used to develop a persuasive speech, the specific purpose is supported with reasons, which are based on valid evidence.

A **reason** is a statement that justifies an action or a belief. For example, suppose you wanted to persuade the members of the class to see the Drama Club's upcoming production of *Grease*. You would give your audience reasons to do so. You could try to persuade your classmates with such statements as (1) *Grease* is one of the most popular musicals of all time; (2) the songs and dancing are excellent; (3) the acting is great. Each of these statements is a reason.

Evidence is all the material that proves the truth of the reasons. For instance, the first reason, "*Grease* is one of the most popular musicals of all time," must be proven. If you can show that the *World Almanac* lists *Grease* as one of the longest-running Broadway shows ever, the *Almanac* statement

PEANUTS●
By Charles M. Schulz

Even when you *are* right, your argument will not "sound right" unless you are able to present valid reasons that logically support it.

would be evidence. Think of the two elements of logical reasoning this way: Reasons answer the question "Why?" Evidence provides specific examples for reasons.

Finding Reasons. Where can you find good reasons? For some speeches, you can look to yourself. Reasons often become obvious once you start thinking about your topic. For example, consider Gloria Marcus's speech. Gloria Marcus is one of Ann Welch's supporters. She believes that Ann is qualified, and she wants members of the class to recognize Ann's qualifications. Therefore, Gloria asks herself, "What are the qualifications for a Senior Class president?" For answers she thinks of such traits as leadership experience, intelligence, personality, and hard work. After considering what she knows about Ann, Gloria decides to focus on Ann's experience and her hard work as reasons that Ann is qualified to be Senior Class president.

A second source for reasons is other people. Gloria asked various people—students, teachers, and school officials—to comment on Ann's qualifications. Some of these people gave testimonials—statements attesting to Ann's worth—that Gloria used in her speech.

A third source for reasons includes written material such as books, magazines, and newspapers. Gloria could not find a book about Ann Welch, of course, but she did find some school newspaper articles about her. In addition, Gloria found books and articles on the subject of leadership. In their explanations of qualifications for leadership, these sources discussed many criteria, including the importance of experience and hard work.

Which reasons should you use in your speech? First, select the reasons that have the best support. For example, look at the first reason Gloria gave in support of Ann Welch for Senior Class president: Ann Welch has leadership experience. If Gloria discovered that although Ann had such experience it was very limited, then leadership experience would not be a good reason to present. Ann may still be an excellent candidate for the office but not because she has had a great deal of leadership experience. Gloria would need to look for other reasons that had stronger support.

Second, consider whether the audience will accept the reason and will regard the reason as important. For example, Gloria had to decide whether her audience would believe that leadership experience and hard work are important considerations when selecting a class officer.

Supporting Reasons with Evidence. In your speech you will support your reasons with evidence. Evidence consists of facts and expert opinions. For example, when Gloria argues that Ann Welch has the experience necessary to ensure Ann's success as class president, Gloria needs to be able to prove her point. As evidence of Ann's experience, Gloria cited two facts: that Ann was vice-president of her Sophomore Class and that Ann is editor of the school paper.

A **fact** is an item or a statement that can be verified by testing, by observing, or by consulting reference material. For example, the statement "iron is heavier than tin" is a fact. First, the information can be checked in reference books that give the specific gravity of elements. Second, the statement can be verified by weighing equally sized samples of iron and tin.

Gloria's supporting reason that Ann Welch is editor of the student paper is also a fact because it too can be verified.

During the American Booksellers Association Convention on May 26, 1985, Jonathan Kozol gave a persuasive speech on the need to work to reduce illiteracy. In the following passage from that speech, notice the facts he used to support his reasoning.

> Sixty million U.S. adults—one third of our adult population—cannot read a daily paper, a book, a welfare form, the Bill of Rights, a housing lease, a road map, the antidote instructions on a can of kitchen cleanser, the word of God within the Bible, or the word of man within the verse of Milton or the tales of Tolstoy or the United States Constitution. Twenty-two percent of adults cannot write a check that will be processed by their bank. The same number can't address an envelope to reach its destination. Forty-ninth out of 158 members of the UN in our literacy levels, we are also twenty-fourth in books produced per capita. The Soviet Union ranks fifth from the top in literacy.
>
> Of the 45 percent of U.S. adults who do not read newspapers, only 10 percent abstain by choice. The rest can't understand them. Four in ten Bostonians can't read the Boston *Globe;* four in ten New Yorkers cannot read the New York *Times.* In the state of Utah, where the population is almost entirely white and native-born, 200,000—that's more than one in five adults—can't read a daily paper.
>
> Forty percent of recent military recruits read between the fifth- and eighth-grade levels. Forty percent! The army has been forced to issue comic books to serve as instruction manuals; indeed, a five-page comic book is needed to explain how to release the hood of a jeep. You may wonder about the length of the comic books that tell a soldier what to do with a cruise missile . . .
>
> Sixty percent of prison inmates and 85 percent of juveniles who come before the courts are unable to read. Forty-seven percent of young black adults are illiterate. That figure will rise to 50 percent within the next four years. One million teenage kids read at third-grade level.
>
> Illiteracy costs the government and taxpayers approximately $120 billion a year, $14 billion alone for prison costs and welfare maintenance directly tied to the unemployability of illiterate adults, over $100 billion more in lowered GNP. That's the bottom line, as they say in Washington. There is, however, another loss which is not reflected in the GNP: the insult to democracy. It is the compromise of all that is suggested by our wistful reference to "a Jeffersonian ideal" that rests upon the full, informed participation of the people. Whether a nation so divided can prevail for long without erosion of its democratic dreams becomes a question with disturbing implications.

An **expert opinion** is a statement of belief about a subject from a person who is recognized as an authority on that subject. Statements of belief contain information that cannot be proved true or false. They express beliefs, opinions, attitudes, and other types of personal value judgments.

Although expert opinion is not always as strong as factual evidence, expert opinions are as important as facts in some matters. For example, consider the statement that Ann Welch is a hard worker. Gloria can support that statement by showing what jobs Ann has held and the number of hours she has worked at them. Still, the concept of "hard worker" involves an opinion about how much work a person has to do to qualify as a "hard worker." If the teacher serving as advisor to the school paper said that Ann Welch is a hard worker, that teacher's statement would stand as expert opinion though it would still not be a statement of fact. The teacher's experience with other editors over the years and with other students currently working on the paper would establish the teacher as qualified to express an opinion on whether or not Ann truly is a "hard worker."

To help you organize your thoughts on the information covered so far, here is an outline of the reasons and evidence compiled by Gloria Marcus for her persuasive speech.

Proposition: I want to persuade the Senior Class to vote for Ann Welch for president. [Why?]

    I. Ann Welch has a great deal of leadership experience. [First reason]
        A. Ann was vice-president of her Sophomore Class. [Evidence]
        B. Ann is editor of the school paper. [Evidence]
    II. Ann Welch is a hard worker. [Second reason]
        A. When she was vice-president, she organized the Sophomore Class fund-raising efforts. [Evidence]
        B. As editor of the paper, she not only writes the editorials that appear but also edits most of the copy. [Evidence]

Emotional Appeals

A second technique for persuading an audience is using emotional appeals. An **emotional appeal** is a statement used to arouse such feelings as anger, joy, or sadness in an audience. Emotional appeals can convince an

Even though an audience may be convinced, they may not be motivated to *act* on their beliefs unless the speaker appeals to their emotions as well as their intellect.

audience that an argument is right and can also persuade the audience to act in the way the speaker wants.

One of the frustrating aspects of human nature is that an audience may well agree with a speaker but may never translate that agreement into action. For example, some of Gloria Marcus's classmates might believe that Ann Welch would make a good Senior Class president, but they might not take the time to vote for Ann. Why not? Many people will not do anything about their beliefs until their emotions become involved. Speakers, therefore, often need to get an audience to feel excitement, responsibility, anger, satisfaction, joy, sadness, or some other emotion that will spur its members to follow through with action.

Building emotional appeals begins with careful use of specific words and details. The more specifics you name, the more vivid a picture you are likely to create. For example, notice how Gloria develops the following statement with specifics to create a vivid picture of one of Ann's qualifications.

> *General statement:* Ann Welch has been known to work hard.
> *Specific statement:* When Ann Welch thought that students weren't being rewarded for their efforts to clean up the schoolyard, she went to the principal's office, waited until he was free, and then took him on a tour of the grounds and pointed out exactly what the students had done.

The words *work hard* are not likely to stir Gloria's audience to action or to arouse strong feelings. However, by specifying how Ann Welch took the time to show the principal how much work students had done, Gloria appeals to feelings of responsibility and pride in her audience. She begins to get her listeners emotionally involved. By showing exactly how Ann works hard on her own to support student projects, Gloria persuades her audience of fellow students that Ann should be their leader.

Emotional appeals are further developed by selecting vivid words. The stronger the impression a word leaves, the better the chance for arousing emotions. Consider Gloria's use of vivid words to develop the following general statement:

> *Statement:* Ann Welch is cool in an emergency.
> *Vivid development:* Ann Welch was outside school enjoying the fresh air with hundreds of other students. Suddenly, coal black clouds began building rapidly. The wind steadily picked up force—papers began to swirl in the air, the sky crackled with thunder and lightning. Ann recognized the threat of a tornado and sensed the danger of students panicking. Quickly, she got a few friends together and worked out a plan to lead the students calmly to the basement of the school. As a result of her swift action, not a single person was injured in the move to safety.

Finally, emotional appeals are heightened by the use of personal references. Make the members of the audience feel that they have a personal stake in the matter. The more the material relates specifically to each member of the audience, the more likely that the entire audience will become emotionally involved.

Too impersonal: Ann Welch is planning to do some things that will make graduation better.

Personal reference to audience: You've worked hard for your diploma. You deserve to have your achievement recognized. Ann Welch is suggesting a graduation policy that calls for *every* one of you to receive your diploma in person. This policy will guarantee you the individual recognition you deserve.

Establishing Credibility

A third way that people are persuaded is through the credibility of the speaker. **Credibility** is the quality of being worthy of belief or trust. You probably rely on certain people you consider believable or trustworthy to help you make decisions. You follow the advice of your parents, teachers, or friends. Why? Usually you trust these people because you see them as competent, sincere, and dynamic. Since audience belief in a speaker is vitally important to the speaker's ability to influence, you need to take special care to build your credibility when delivering a persuasive speech.

Competence. **Competence** is the state of being well qualified. Competence comes from depth and breadth of knowledge about a subject. To establish your competence, you not only have to *be* competent, you have to *show* your audience that you are competent. The more you know about a topic and the better you can display your knowledge, the more likely that your audience will believe in you.

For example, imagine that you are trying to convince your classmates to buy a certain brand of running shoes. You could establish your competence by demonstrating how much you know about the construction of the shoe and the anatomy of the human foot. It stands to reason that if you could show why a particular running shoe improves the protection of runners' feet, your explanation would be more likely to persuade the audience than if you could only say that the particular shoe looks good or is popular. Regardless of the subject, listeners will look for signs of competence in a speaker. Unless members of the audience have already been "sold" before the speech begins, they will not "buy" from someone who is not knowledgeable.

In her speech boosting Ann Welch's candidacy, Gloria Marcus established her own competence by convincing the audience that she knew Ann Welch's record of service and could recognize the qualities of leadership.

Sincerity. **Sincerity** is a sign of a speaker's truly caring about his or her topic and audience. People who are sincere speak in a tone of voice that reflects that sincerity. Sincerity can rarely be faked successfully. To establish their sincerity, speakers must have a true interest in both their subject and their audience. If Gloria really thinks that Ann Welch is the best candidate for president and if Gloria is truly interested in the welfare of the Senior Class, she is likely to sound sincere in her speech. If, on the other hand, Gloria does not really care about Ann Welch's qualifications or actually thinks that the Senior Class elections are unimportant, then her delivery will lack the sincerity necessary to persuade her audience.

One of the most effective ways for a speaker to establish credibility is to demonstrate competence in the subject he or she is presenting.

Dynamism. Dynamism is the energy, enthusiasm, and excitement that a speaker shows for the topic in the speech. Audiences are more likely to be persuaded by speakers who have a lively personality. If a speaker is enthusiastic, friendly, and cheerful, audiences will be inspired by that dynamism, will pay attention, and will be more open to the speaker's message. Enthusiasm is infectious. The more excited you are about what you are saying, the more likely that your audience will be affected by your message.

Ethical Standards

Ethical standards are the guidelines that a society sets for right, just, and moral behavior. Violating ethical standards can destroy a speaker's credibility. It is unethical for public speakers to lie, to distort, to deceive, to engage in name-calling, to attack a person or an idea without giving evidence to support the attack, and to deny the opposition the right to reply.

Your goal in your speech is to persuade the members of your audience, not to manipulate them. What is the difference? **Persuasion** involves convincing the members of an audience to agree with you of their own free will. **Manipulation** involves shrewd or devious management of facts for your own purpose. Whereas persuasion relies on the ethical use of logical reasoning, manipulation is based on the unethical distortion of information.

What can happen to you if you try to manipulate your audience or follow any other unethical practices? Maybe nothing. However, it is more likely that you will fail to achieve your goal. People may be fooled for a time. However, as soon as they discover that a speaker has been deceiving them, the speaker loses all credibility on that topic and on other topics as well. When speakers are no longer believable, they become totally ineffective.

Some speakers believe that unethical behavior is all right if it is for a just cause. However, in public speaking the end (what you want to achieve) never justifies unethical means.

Analyzing Reasons, Emotional Appeal, Credibility, and Sincerity for a Persuasive Speech

List at least five reasons that you can use to support the speech proposition you chose for the Activity on page 382. Which of the five are the best reasons? Why? Then list at least two items of evidence that support each of these reasons.

Next, identify one method that you can use to develop your speech proposition by appealing to your audience's emotions. Why do you think this method will be effective? Finally, indicate the best method you can use to establish your credibility on your proposition. What information can you give to show your competence to discuss your topic? What can you do to establish your sincerity?

ADAPTING YOUR SPEECH TO YOUR AUDIENCE

Before you decide how to organize your material, you must consider the likely makeup of your audience and how best to adapt your speech to that particular audience. With the persuasive speech more than with any other, adapting your speech so that it both reaches and moves your audience is crucial to its success.

Although the people in any audience will have many different attitudes about a topic, an entire audience can be classified as mostly favorable, mostly neutral, mostly apathetic or lacking information, or mostly hostile. (Review Chapter 9 for details on gathering information about your audience.) To be

Knowing whether your audience is mostly favorable, mostly neutral, mostly apathetic, or mostly hostile to your point of view will help you tailor your speech to persuade that particular group of listeners.

sure of your audience's attitude toward your topic, you may want to conduct a poll. For example, a few days before delivering her speech, Gloria gave each person in class the following questionnaire.

**QUESTIONNAIRE
FOR STUDENT ELECTIONS**

1. If student elections were held today, who would you vote for?
   _____

2. For each candidate, indicate the letter of the phrase that best summarizes your feelings about that person:

   Bill Garver   _____
   Ann Welch   _____
   Jack Phillips   _____
   Laura Simpson   _____

   A. I am strongly in favor of his/her candidacy.
   B. I am somewhat in favor of his/her candidacy.
   C. I have no strong feelings one way or the other about his/her candidacy.
   D. I don't know much about him/her, or I am not interested in the election.
   E. I am somewhat opposed to his/her candidacy.
   F. I am strongly opposed to his/her candidacy.

Sometimes you will not be able to circulate a questionnaire among the members of the audience you plan to address. In such cases, you have to make guesses based on your knowledge of your listeners' thoughts and feelings about your topic.

Favorable Audience

A **favorable audience** is one in which the majority of listeners agree from slightly to very much with the speaker's proposition. For instance, by using her questionnaire, Gloria Marcus discovered that most of the class already seemed to favor Ann Welch. In fact, only a few responses showed much support for other candidates. Yet, in an election no one can ever be sure of what voters will do. Therefore, Gloria's goal in her speech to this audience was to arouse their interest and to try to motivate them to act. When facing a favorable audience, a speaker must not only strengthen the listeners' initial feelings but also motivate them to act on those feelings.

Neutral Audience

A **neutral audience** is one that has not reached a decision one way or another about the speaker's proposition. Neutral audiences are not inclined to take any side in the matter and will give all sides an equal hearing. Members of a neutral audience need information to persuade them to take a stand. If, as a result of her questionnaire, Gloria had learned that her audience was neutral, she would have faced a special task. She would have had to supply her listeners with such a wealth of information supporting Ann's candidacy that they would be convinced that the best choice of action was to vote for Ann.

Apathetic Audience

An **apathetic audience** is an audience in which a majority of members do not have any interest in the speaker's proposition. With some topics a speaker can assume that most members of the audience do not care much about the whole issue. For example, from her questionnaire results, Gloria might have discovered that most members of the Senior Class did not show a great deal of interest in the election. In this case Gloria's goal in her speech would be to help the audience recognize Ann's strengths and to show why voting is important. In other words, Gloria would have to make her listeners care.

Hostile Audience

A **hostile audience** is one in which the majority of listeners are opposed to the speaker's proposition. With some topics, especially highly controversial

---

ACTIVITY: **Using a Questionnaire to Identify an Audience's Attitudes**

Make up a questionnaire similar to the one on page 390 to help you determine the attitudes that members of your audience have toward the proposition you began developing in the Activity on page 382. Hand out your questionnaire to every person in your audience; then collect the questionnaires and tabulate your responses. Fill in the chart below, indicating the number of students who voted for each attitude.

—Strongly in favor   —Apathetic or uninformed
—Slightly in favor   —Slightly against
—Neutral   —Strongly against

On the basis of your questionnaire, what is the attitude of the majority of the audience? As a result of your audience's general attitude about your proposition, what do you see as the major obstacle you will have to overcome when you deliver your speech?

ones, you may notice that many people in a hostile audience are either very much against your proposal or very much in favor of a different one. For example, from the questionnaire results, Gloria might have found that class members were very much against Ann Welch's candidacy. Gloria's goal in her speech then would be to lay the groundwork for a change of opinion. In this case Gloria first would have to establish her own credibility. Then she might decide to approach the issue indirectly, or she might choose to present favorable information about Ann, hoping that such information would out-weigh her listeners' objections. Gloria would be unlikely to sway her listeners completely in one speech, but she might open their minds a little so that they would begin to regard Ann's candidacy more favorably.

ORGANIZING YOUR INFORMATION

To a large extent, your chances of succeeding with your speech will depend on how you organize your information. For the most part your organization will be guided by your impression of your audience's attitude and by the nature of the material you are presenting. Speeches are organized according to two approaches: deductive and inductive.

Deductive Approach

A **deductive approach** is one in which the goal is stated first and then reasons are presented to support it. If Gloria took a deductive approach to organizing her speech in support of Ann Welch for president, her basic outline might look like this.

Proposition: You should support Ann Welch for Senior Class president.
I. Ann Welch has proven leadership experience.
II. Ann Welch is a hard worker who will work for you.

For your persuasive speech, you should consider three types of deductive approaches: the statement-of-reasons method, the problem-solution method, and the comparative-advantage method.

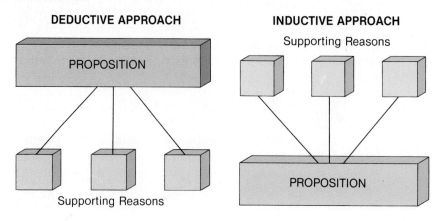

DEDUCTIVE APPROACH

PROPOSITION

Supporting Reasons

INDUCTIVE APPROACH

Supporting Reasons

PROPOSITION

Statement-of-Reasons Method. The **statement-of-reasons method** is the classic deductive approach in which the proposition is stated directly, followed by reasons supporting it. As you examine your material, you may decide that two or three reasons alone are strong enough to convince an audience to agree with your proposition. In addition, you may decide that the audience is not so opposed to your ideas that they will be turned off by this direct approach. In such a case, you would organize your speech by stating your objective first and then giving your reasons.

Notice in the following example that Gloria's statement-of-reasons organization in support of Ann Welch is the same as the deductive organization outlined on page 392.

> *Proposition:* You should support Ann Welch for Senior Class president.
> I. Ann Welch has proven leadership experience.
> II. Ann Welch is a hard worker who will work for you.

Problem-Solution Method. The **problem-solution method** is a deductive approach in which the speaker first presents the problem and then offers at least one possible solution for that problem. The following example shows how Gloria could use the problem-solution method to organize her speech in support of Ann Welch.

> *Proposition:* I want to persuade the class to support Ann Welch for Senior Class president.
> I. The Senior Class officers face several problems. [Problem]
>   A. Students are apathetic.
>   B. Teachers don't respect student opinion.
> II. Ann Welch can solve these problems. [Solution]
>   A. Ann Welch can generate student interest in the class.
>   B. Ann Welch is respected by the faculty.

Comparative-Advantage Method. The **comparative-advantage method** is a deductive approach in which each of the reasons is presented as a benefit to the audience. Sometimes the benefit of each reason is stated in comparison form; at other times the comparative advantage is simply implied. The following outline shows how Gloria could organize her speech by using the comparative-advantage method. (Notice that the comparative terms *more* and *harder* are used to state the advantages of voting for Ann Welch.)

> *Proposition:* I want to persuade the class to support Ann Welch for Senior Class president.
> I. Ann Welch has more experience than any other candidate.
> II. Ann Welch has shown the ability to work harder than any other candidate.

Inductive Approach

An **inductive approach** is one that begins with a statement of reasons and builds to the statement of the proposition. When you organize your

Scientific knowledge is established by inductive reasoning. A
conclusion is drawn only after much evidence has been gathered, and
every piece of evidence must support the conclusion.

material inductively, try to get your audience to agree with your information
before you present your goal. An inductive approach often works well with
a hostile audience.

If Gloria took an inductive approach to her speech in support of Ann
Welch for president, her outline might take the following form.

Proposition: I want to persuade the class to support Ann Welch for Senior
Class president.
   I. Ann Welch is a proven leader.
   II. Ann Welch is a hard worker who will work for you.
   III. You should support Ann Welch for Senior Class president.

When organizing a persuasive speech, consider three inductive approaches: the criteria-satisfaction method, the negative method, and the
Monroe motivated sequence.

Criteria-Satisfaction Method. The **criteria-satisfaction method**
is especially useful when you think that your audience will likely be hostile
toward the subject. In the first part of the speech, you get the audience to
agree to the soundness of certain criteria. Then in the rest of the speech,
you show how your proposal satisfies those criteria. For instance, Gloria
Marcus could organize her speech according to the criteria-satisfaction
method shown in the following outline.

Proposition: I want to persuade the class to support Ann Welch for Senior
Class president.

I. Most of us are likely to agree on the same criteria.
   A. A class president should have experience.
   B. A class president should have a record as a hard worker.
II. Ann Welch meets both of these criteria.
   A. Ann Welch has considerable leadership experience.
   B. Ann Welch has proven to be a hard worker.
III. You should support Ann Welch for Senior Class president.

Negative Method. In the **negative method,** the speaker shows that no other option except the option proposed by the speaker will be acceptable. The negative method is another organizational plan that works well with a hostile audience. Here is an example of how Gloria Marcus could use the negative method to organize her speech.

Proposition: I want to persuade the class to support Ann Welch for Senior Class president.
   I. Bill Garver has no real leadership experience.
   II. Laura Simpson has no real leadership experience.
   III. Jack Phillips has a little experience but has not shown an inclination to be willing to pitch in with the work.
   IV. Ann Welch has leadership experience and has proven herself to be a hard worker.
   V. You should support Ann Welch for Senior Class president.

Monroe Motivated Sequence. The **Monroe motivated sequence** was first suggested by Professor Alan H. Monroe. It is based on the premise that in order to convince an audience to act, a speaker needs to accomplish at least five steps: (1) draw *attention* to the problem; (2) show a *need* for some action; (3) outline a plan that will *satisfy* that need; (4) help the audience *visualize* the benefits of that plan of action; and (5) suggest a specific *action* that puts the plan into practice.

If Gloria were to organize her speech using the Monroe motivated sequence, her outline might take the following form.

Proposition: I want to persuade the class to support Ann Welch for Senior Class president.
   I. We have all seen Senior Classes flounder for lack of leadership. [Attention]
   II. Yet, the Senior Class is the class with the greatest expectations in high school. [Need]
   III. Experiences at other schools have shown that a strong leader can restore class spirit and can help a class accomplish its goals. [Satisfaction]
   IV. Led by a president with a clear vision of this class's possibilities and a commitment to hard work, this class can go down in history. [Visualization]
   V. Vote for Ann Welch, a hard-working, proven leader with a vision. [Action]

Organizing Information for a Persuasive Speech

Review the information that you have gathered in completing the previous activities concerning your proposition for a persuasive speech. Then select your method of organization (statement-of-reasons, problem-solution, comparative-advantage, criteria-satisfaction, negative, or Monroe motivated sequence). Be prepared to explain why you believe this method is the best one to use in your speech. Finally, outline the main points of your speech, following the order you selected.

DELIVERING YOUR SPEECH CONVINCINGLY

As you learned earlier in this chapter, dynamism is a major element of credibility. One of the keys to dynamism is delivery. Although delivery is important in any speech, anything less than your most enthusiastic delivery is likely to diminish your chances of persuading your audience.

Rehearse your speech for your family or for a few good friends. Choose people who will be honest with you. Their feedback will help you perfect your delivery.

Using Audiovisual Aids

Because an audience can get a better grasp of information by seeing it as well as hearing it, you will want to look for opportunities to use visual aids in your persuasive speech.

For a persuasive speech, photographs are often good motivational tools. A particularly vivid photograph can stir an audience to action. For example, when giving a speech seeking to persuade the audience to support hunger relief efforts in Ethiopia, a speaker can convince the audience of the need for such relief by showing photographs of starving Ethiopian children.

Films, slides, and photographs can also help an audience visualize a need. However, if you use these devices, you must make sure that the presentation of them does not go on for so long that the audience loses attention. No doubt you have had the experience of sitting in a darkened room with a speaker showing slides. Perhaps the first few slides aroused your interest. The next few may have held it. However, if the speaker went on showing slide after slide, you were probably more ready to go to sleep than to take action on the speaker's propositions.

Responding to Feedback

While you speak, your audience will be giving you subtle, and at times not-so-subtle, feedback that will help you determine how you are doing. If your audience shows signs of boredom, you will need to boost the energy level of your delivery. If your audience seems to be doubtful, you will need to spend more time presenting information that supports your proposition.

Do not treat your speech as though it were engraved in stone. Feel free to add to a point, shorten a point, speed up, slow down, or even insert some humor if you feel the situation demands it.

ACTIVITY: **Rehearsing a Persuasive Speech and Preparing Audiovisual Aids**

Using the outline you developed for the Activity on page 396, rehearse your persuasive speech carefully. Mark the ideas that you feel should be given special vocal emphasis. Work to achieve this emphasis. Then decide what kinds of audiovisual aids, if any, you will use to help make your speech more effective. Gather or prepare these aids. Be prepared to give your persuasive speech in class.

ANALYZING AND EVALUATING A PERSUASIVE SPEECH

Both oral and written critiques are as essential for persuasive speeches as they are for informative speeches. However, while an informative speech critique focuses on the speaker's efforts to help the audience understand and remember the information, the persuasive speech critique focuses on the speaker's efforts to motivate the audience to believe the proposition or to act upon it.

The Oral Critique

When preparing an oral critique for a persuasive speech, keep the following guidelines in mind:

1. *Praise one or two things that were well done in the speech*. Focus on what the speaker did to heighten the persuasive effect of the speech. For example, imagine you were preparing an oral critique of Gloria's speech in support of Ann Welch's candidacy. If you thought that the quality of Gloria's evidence made her speech particularly persuasive, you would want to focus on that point.

2. *Include only one or two negative comments*. Focus your comments on what you consider to be the greatest hindrances to achieving the speaker's purpose. For example, regardless of how many minor points you might be able to cite, if you thought that the greatest weakness in Gloria's speech was her inability to relate material directly to you and other members of the audience, you would want to focus on that weakness.

3. *Indicate what the speaker could have done to improve the presentation*. For example, if you had made the negative comment given in the second item above, you would want to show Gloria what she might have done to relate the speech more directly to you and the class.

4. *Be specific*. Tell the speaker exactly what he or she did right and did wrong.

When giving an oral critique, recall critiques you have received. What feedback was most helpful? Offer this same kind of feedback in your critiques.

Evaluation Checklist for Persuasive Speeches

Organization:
Was the purpose of the speech clear?
Did the introduction gain attention? Did it clarify the purpose?
Was each of the main points clearly identifiable?
Did the main points follow a consistent pattern?
Did the speaker make good use of transitions?
Did the conclusion summarize the key points? Did it
leave the speech on a high point?

Content:
Did the speaker appear to understand the topic fully?
Did the speaker appear to consider the audience's
interest, knowledge, and attitude?
Was enough specific information given to make the key
points of the speech understandable?
Were materials selected that would help the audience
remember the key ideas?
Were reasons presented to support the purpose?
Did the supporting material provide sufficient evidence
to support the reasons presented?
Did the speaker use any emotional appeals to motivate
the audience?
Did the speaker present the speech ethically?
Did the speaker build or maintain credibility?

Language:
Was the language precise?
Were the words specific and concrete?
Did the speaker use words that the audience could understand?
Did the speaker emphasize key ideas?
Was the tone appropriate for the audience and the occasion?

Delivery:
Did the speaker seem confident?
Was the speaker dressed appropriately?
Did the speaker show enthusiasm?
Did the speaker look at the audience during the speech?
Were the speaker's facial expressions, gestures, and
movements natural?
Were the speaker's articulation, enunciation, and
pronunciation correct?

Additional comments:

Evaluation:

The Written Critique

The written critique of a persuasive speech closely analyzes the speaker's argument and presentation. Use the checklist on page 399 as the basis for your critique.

This checklist can be used as a basis for evaluating the speech Susan B. Anthony made after being fined for voting in the 1872 presidential election (see pages 603-604 for the complete text of this speech).

Organization. Begin by analyzing the organization. Ms. Anthony first arouses the audience's interest by stating that she has been indicted of a crime. Then she clearly states her purpose: "It shall be my work this evening to prove to you that in thus voting, I not only committed no crime, but instead, simply exercised my citizen's rights, guaranteed to me and all United States citizens by the national Constitution, beyond the power of any state to deny." She then proceeds to show how the Constitution guaranteed these rights. Once the audience accepts that these rights are guaranteed, she proceeds to show that any state that denies these rights violates the supreme law of the land. The only way a state could be justified in denying women rights, she claims, is if women are not persons. Therefore, she asks her final question: "Are women persons?" to which the resounding answer must be *yes*. Finally, she ends with what to her can be the only logical conclusion drawn from these facts: "Being persons, then, women are citizens; and no State has a right to make any law, or to enforce any old law, that shall abridge their privileges or immunities. Hence, every discrimination against women in the constitutions and laws of the several States is today null and void."

Content. Examine the quality of the material and the way it is used to build a logical case and to motivate the audience. Ms. Anthony uses the Constitution as the basis of her argument and quotes from it to make her points. Perhaps in a longer speech she could have included more facts and specific details to support her argument. For example, she might have given examples of laws she found particularly unjust. She presents her material in a way that stirs the audience's emotions. For example, in speaking of disenfranchised women, she says,

> To them this government is not a democracy. It is not a republic. It is an odious aristocracy; a hateful oligarchy of sex; the most hateful aristocracy ever established on the face of the globe. An oligarchy of wealth, where the rich govern the poor, or an oligarchy of learning, where the educated govern the ignorant, might be endured; but this oligarchy of sex, which makes father, brothers, husbands, sons, the oligarchs over the mother and sisters, the wife and daughters of every household—which ordains all men sovereigns, all women subjects, carries dissension, discord, and rebellion into every home of the nation.

Language. Examine the language of the speech. Susan B. Anthony uses vivid language to make her points, and she uses parallel structure to make her points memorable. For example, "And we formed it, not to give the blessings of liberty, but to secure them; not to the half of ourselves and

the half of our posterity, but to the whole people, women as well as men."
In addition, she makes her topic a concern of every American, not just of women, since dissension, discord, and rebellion hurt us all.

Delivery. You need to hear a speech, of course, to be able to examine the speaker's delivery. When you read a speech, you must limit your analysis and evaluation to its organization, content, and structure.

ACTIVITY: **Giving an Oral Critique of a Persuasive Speech**

Look through an issue of *Vital Speeches of the Day* to find a persuasive speech you think is especially effective. Prepare an oral critique of this speech. Deliver it to your class.

GUIDELINES FOR DELIVERING A PERSUASIVE SPEECH

- Is my specific purpose (speech objective) clear?
- Can I provide good reasons for my proposition?
- Can I provide evidence in support of each reason?
- Can I discuss each reason in a way that is likely to motivate the audience?
- Can I establish my credibility on my topic?
- Have I analyzed my audience?
- Have I organized my material to meet audience attitudes?
- Can I use verbal and nonverbal skills to present my speech convincingly?

Profiles in Communication

Bob Bartholomew

As a consistent leader in real estate sales and, since 1980, the sales manager of a branch office for Grady Realtors, Bob Bartholomew has learned how to put a wide variety of communication skills to practical use.

In his role as sales manager, he writes advertisements, conducts seminars for his staff of seventeen salespeople, and motivates them to meet the goals he sets for the office. Each of these tasks requires Mr. Bartholomew to carefully analyze his topic, purpose, and audience. Before advertising a property, he must identify its key selling features. Then he must present these features in language that is both informative and appealing to prospective buyers.

Conducting seminars calls upon similar communication skills. To prepare a seminar, Mr. Bartholomew must become thoroughly familiar with his subject. Next, he needs to organize his knowledge into a complete, concise lesson that will make the information clear to his busy sales staff in a minimum of time. Finally, he must use his verbal and nonverbal skills to deliver the information and respond to feedback. Motivating his staff and setting goals for his office further test Mr. Bartholomew's persuasive and analytic abilities.

In selling, Mr. Bartholomew emphasizes what he calls "the art of gentle persuasion." Trying to pressure a client into buying is not in the client's or the salesperson's best interest. According to Mr. Bartholomew, a good real estate agent strives to learn what a client is seeking and then introduces the client to properties that fill the bill. What makes this task challenging is that many clients are unfamiliar with the real estate market and often have inaccurate or mistaken notions of their wants and needs.

To identify a client's true wants and needs, an agent must be able to read the verbal and nonverbal clues given by the client. Only by asking questions and listening carefully to the client's responses and comments can an agent accurately interpret these clues and find the right property for the client.

To accomplish the many tasks that face a real estate agent, the most important skills to have, according to Mr. Bartholomew, are good communication skills. Successful agents are not only effective speakers but also attentive listeners, organized planners, and accurate interpreters of human behavior. Mastering these skills has helped Bob Bartholomew succeed at what he feels is a very satisfying profession: "helping families find a house that they will call home."

SUMMARY

A persuasive speech establishes a fact, strengthens or changes a person's attitudes or beliefs, or moves a person to action. Although there is no sure way to guarantee that your speech will be effective, you can increase your chances of persuading your audience if you adhere to the following guidelines.

Have a clear persuasive purpose. The purpose should be stated to establish a fact, to strengthen or to change a belief, or to move an audience to act.

Find the best information possible on the topic. Consider your experience, interview and survey others, and read relevant sources.

One way to persuade an audience is to present good reasons supported by valid evidence. Reasons are statements that justify a specific purpose. They answer the question "Why?" about the proposition. Good reasons come from your experience and your reading. Reasons are selected on the basis of how well they can be supported and how they relate to the audience.

Any reason needs to be supported with evidence. Evidence consists of facts and expert opinions. Facts are statements that can be verified. Expert opinions are opinions from people who have gained experience in particular fields.

A second way to persuade an audience is by appealing to the listeners' emotions. Emotional appeals begin with careful attention to specifics, are furthered by vivid word selection, and are heightened with audience references.

A third way to persuade an audience is by establishing credibility. Credibility is the faith the audience has in the speaker and the speaker's knowledge. Credibility is built on competence, knowledge of the topic, sincerity and good will toward the audience, and dynamism—the speaker's enthusiasm.

All persuasion must meet ethical standards. Lying, distorting, and name-calling have no place in persuasive speaking.

Organize your speech so that it takes into account your audience's attitude toward your topic. Audiences can be labeled as favorable, neutral or undecided, apathetic, or hostile. Which method of organization you choose will depend on how you read your audience's attitude.

Organize your speech using either deductive or inductive patterns to present your reasons. More specifically, reasons can be organized in any of the following patterns: statement-of-reasons, problem-solution, comparative-advantage, criteria-satisfaction, negative, and Monroe motivated sequence.

Deliver your speech as convincingly as possible. Use audiovisual aids and respond to audience feedback.

A critique of a persuasive speech focuses on the speaker's ability to motivate the audience to believe the proposition or to act upon it. An oral critique consists of comments made directly to the speaker. Begin by praising one or two things that were done well. Then criticize one or two things that could have been done better. Show the speaker what he or she could have done to make the speech better, and in all cases, be specific. Focus on the use of reasons and evidence, the ways the speaker established credibility, the use of emotional appeals, and the ethics of the presentation.

A written critique is often based on a checklist of questions directed toward the organization, content, language, and delivery of the speech.

CHAPTER VOCABULARY

Look back through this chapter to find the meaning of each of the following terms. Write each term and its meaning in your communication journal.

apathetic audience
comparative-advantage
   method
competence
credibility
criteria-satisfaction
   method
deductive approach
dynamism
emotional appeal

ethical standards
evidence
expert opinion
fact
favorable audience
hostile audience
inductive approach
logical reasoning
manipulation
Monroe motivated
   sequence

negative method
neutral audience
persuasion
persuasive speech
problem-solution
   method
proposition
reason
sincerity
statement-of-reasons
   method

REVIEW QUESTIONS

1. Both an informative and a persuasive speech provide information. What makes a persuasive speech different from an informative speech?

2. One kind of persuasive speech establishes a fact. What do two other kinds do?

3. You should support your proposition with reasons. What two types of evidence should you use to support your reasons?

4. Using logical reasoning is one technique of persuasion. What are two other techniques?

5. One way of appealing to emotions is to use specific words and details. What are two others?

6. To give your speech effectively, you must establish your credibility. What are the three elements of speaker credibility?

7. In your speech, you should try to persuade, not to manipulate, your audience. What is the difference between persuasion and manipulation?

8. When you use deductive organization, you state your proposition first and then give your reasons. What are three types of deductive organization?

9. When you use inductive organization, you state your reasons first and lead up to your proposition. What are three types of inductive organization?

10. An informative speech critique focuses on the speaker's ability to help the audience understand and remember the material. On what does a persuasive speech critique focus?

1. Audience analysis is extremely important for effective persuasive speaking. Discuss why a speaker needs to approach each audience differently.

2. Suppose you were giving a speech to three different audiences. First identify these audiences. Then discuss what you would do differently to adapt your speech to each of them.

3. All of us have encountered unethical speakers at one time or another. First discuss the question, "Does the end ever justify the means in public speaking?" Then discuss the methods used by unethical speakers to manipulate their audiences.

4. Blaise Pascal once wrote, "People are generally better persuaded by the reasons which they have themselves discovered than by those which have come into the minds of others." First discuss the meaning of this quotation. Then discuss how it relates to the persuasive speech.

5. Public relations specialists are people whose business it is to make the public think a certain way. Alan Harrington once wrote, "Public-relations specialists make flower arrangements of the facts, placing them so that the wilted and less attractive petals are hidden by sturdy blossoms." First discuss the meaning of the quotation. Then discuss whether it describes persuasion or manipulation.

ACTIVITIES

1. Examining Techniques of Persuasion

A. Find five different advertisements. Label each one according to its primary audience appeal. Is its appeal based on reasons and evidence? emotion? source credibility? Explain your answers.

B. Select a persuasive speech from an issue of *Vital Speeches of the Day*. Identify portions of the speech that contain logical reasoning, make emotional appeals, and establish credibility. Be prepared to read these portions to the class and to discuss the techniques of persuasion used in them.

2. Analyzing a Persuasive Speech

Briefly outline the main points of a persuasive speech from *Vital Speeches of the Day*. What kind of organization did the speaker use? Was it statement-of-reasons, problem-solution, comparative-advantage, criteria-satisfaction, negative, or Monroe motivated sequence? How effective was the speaker's argument? What were its strengths and weaknesses? Be prepared to discuss the main points you outlined and your analysis of the speech in class.

3. Giving a Persuasive Speech That Establishes a Fact

Think of a situation that concerns you and that can be proven true or false—for example, paragraphs written in black or blue ink are easier to read than paragraphs written in red ink, people usually are (or are not) quick to adopt safety devices, homework does (or does not) help students learn a subject thoroughly. First, state your specific purpose; then write a proposition of fact. Organize your information and identify whether you use a deductive or inductive approach. Deliver your speech to your class. Ask your classmates to use the "Evaluation Checklist for Persuasive Speeches" (page 399) to give you an oral critique of your speech.

4. Giving a Persuasive Speech That Establishes or Changes a Belief

Undoubtedly, you know of a situation that you would like to see improved. State the improvement that could be made and write it as a proposition of belief. Develop a logical argument for making the improvement and write a short list of notes outlining this argument. Present your argument in an extemporaneous speech to your class. Leave time for a question-and-answer session following your speech. Finally, ask your classmates to use the guidelines for an oral critique of a persuasive speech on page 398 to give you an oral critique of your speech.

5. Giving a Persuasive Speech That Changes a Policy

Actions taken by administrators, teachers, and student groups and committees at your school are generally governed by established policies. Think of a policy you would like to see changed at your school. Clearly identify the policy and the change you would like to see made. Then state this change as a specific purpose for your speech and write a proposition of policy. Organize your supporting facts and other information in a brief outline that will fit easily on a 3- by 5-inch card. Using only the outline on your card, deliver your speech to your class. Following your speech, conduct a question-and-answer session in which you and your classmates first discuss the policy change you presented in your speech and then discuss the strengths and weaknesses of the speech itself.

1. Think of the many discussions you have had during the past week. You can probably recall several in which others were trying to convince you of something or you were trying to persuade others. Later, after the discussion was over, did you think of what you should have said to present your position more effectively? Here is your chance to relive that discussion and bring your later ideas into play. Begin by outlining the original discussion. Who was involved? Who said what? What was the outcome of the discussion? Study your outline, and decide exactly when and how you should have presented the ideas you had later. Write a three- or four-page dialogue of the discussion, inserting your later ideas where they will have the greatest effect. Be prepared to present your dialogue in class and to explain the differences between your dialogue and the actual discussion that took place. Ask for feedback from your classmates on how effectively you presented your opinions in the two situations.

2. People who work in sales need strong persuasive skills to overcome all kinds of customer resistance. Potential buyers may object to price, may not believe that they need the product or service, may prefer a competing brand, or may simply be wary of sales pitches. Nevertheless, few successful salespeople take no for a final answer. Instead, they analyze the customer's resistance and find a way to overcome it. Imagine that you have just taken a job selling a product or service you believe in. Write a 3- to 4-minute sales talk to present to your first customer tomorrow. Begin by identifying your product or service. Choose one that you use and regard as the best of its kind. Next, identify your customer. Will you sell to shoppers in a mall? mechanics in service stations? buyers for retail stores? Try to anticipate your customer's resistance. List the ten strongest objections you think your customer might have. In your sales talk, make sure you address these objections. Be prepared to present your sales talk in class. Don't forget to use visual aids, if possible. Ask your classmates to give you feedback on the persuasiveness of your sales talk.

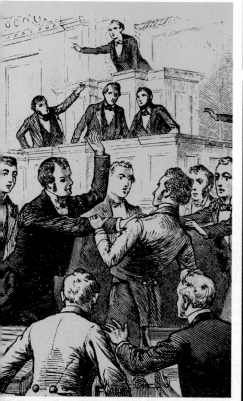

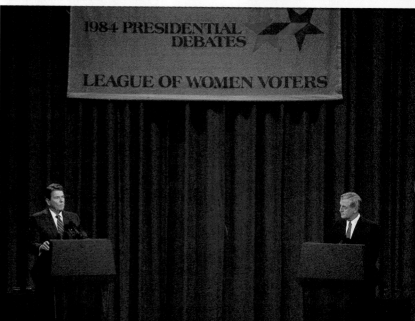

1984 PRESIDENTIAL DEBATES

LEAGUE OF WOMEN VOTERS

UNIT FIVE
DEMOCRATIC PROCESSES

GROUP DISCUSSION

OBJECTIVES:

After studying this chapter, you should be able to

1. Define discussion.

2. List and explain types of discussion.

3. Choose the correct wording for a discussion question.

4. Identify types of questions.

5. Suggest an organization for each type of discussion question.

6. Participate in discussion.

7. Identify styles of leadership.

8. List responsibilities of a leader.

9. Lead a discussion.

10. Identify and manage conflict in a group discussion.

11. Use group discussion to find acceptable solutions to problems, to arrive at decisions, and to enlighten an audience.

12. Evaluate a group discussion.

"Tom, do you know that the legislature is talking about passing a bill to raise the minimum age for getting a driver's license from sixteen to eighteen?"
"I haven't heard anything about that."

"You know, that would be a good topic for our Public Forum in November."

"I think you might have something there, Yvonne. Would you be willing to organize a committee to look into whether raising the minimum age for getting a driver's license would be a good issue for our Public Forum Series? If your committee decides that it is, do you think you could go ahead and suggest who would be on the panel, when it would meet, and things like that?"

"Sure," answered Yvonne. "We've been looking for a good idea for the November Forum. If the legislature is serious about this change, I'm sure that a lot of people here at school will want to know more about it."

Yvonne thinks that she has identified a topic that will definitely interest the other students in her school. However, Yvonne will not be relying solely on her own judgment. She is going to work within a group—a committee that will determine whether or not the topic truly will interest other students. In group discussions, such as Yvonne's committee meeting, individuals work together to share ideas, to find solutions to problems, and to arrive at decisions.

WHAT IS GROUP DISCUSSION?

Group discussion is a goal-directed form of communication. This means that it differs from group conversation in that it has a specific purpose

These committee members engaged in group discussion are sharing information and ideas to achieve a specific purpose.

and follows a specific format. In other words, in group discussion a small group of people do not get together just to "shoot the breeze." Instead, they meet in a group for the purpose of sharing information, solving a problem, or arriving at a workable decision.

An effective group contains a manageable number of people. Ordinarily, groups work best with five to seven people. Many people who work in groups say that five is a good number. A group of five contains enough people to stir up a lively discussion but not so many that members feel unable to talk easily and freely. Also, if a group has an even number of members, it may reach a split decision, with 50 percent of the members backing one choice and the other 50 percent backing another. Having an odd number prevents a deadlock, or tie.

To carry on an effective discussion, the group must have a good working environment. The group should work in a well-lit room and should be seated in a circular pattern. When working in private, the group should sit in a full circle, since this seating arrangement gives everyone equal status. In addition, it allows each member to see every other member and to exchange ideas directly and freely.

When working in public, the group should sit in a semicircle with the opening of the semicircle facing the audience. This seating arrangement allows members to exchange ideas freely and gives the audience a clear view of the proceedings.

Groups are likely to work most effectively when they are well rested. Expecting a group to work effectively late at night or after several taxing classes can often be unrealistic. In addition, groups generally work best for relatively short time periods. After a group has met for an hour or more, it is likely to lose much of its effectiveness. Rather than try to work when everyone is tired, the group should bring the discussion to a close and arrange to meet another day.

An effective group is **cohesive,** which means that its members work together as a unit. A group works best when its members feel comfortable with each other. They do not have to be best friends, but they do have to respect each other and be willing to cooperate. When a group contains people who already know each other and who have worked well together in the past, the group will likely become cohesive in little time. When a group contains people who do not know each other and who come from different backgrounds, the members may take a while to learn how to work well together.

The Purpose of Group Discussion

The purpose of group discussion is to share information, to arrive at the best possible solution to a problem, and to make the best possible decision. Why is group discussion an effective means of achieving these purposes? First, the people in a group will usually offer varied points of view. With several people offering ideas, a group can provide a broader range of information and can generate a larger choice of solutions and decisions than one person can. Second, a person working alone has only his or her own resources to draw upon. Even if that person is willing to work long hours, he or she will not be able to amass the amount of information that a group of people can. Third, a group can offer more expertise, or specialized knowledge, on a particular subject. Even if one person knows a great deal about a topic, other members of a group can usually contribute information that will provide additional insight. The old saying "two heads are better than one" especially applies to group discussions, which contain several minds all working on a single topic.

Types of Group Discussions

Group discussions may be public or private. A **public group discussion** is held in front of an audience to share information and to stimulate thinking. Meeting in public offers a group an opportunity to publicize the topic of the discussion. A **private group discussion** is held in closed session so that group members can share information among themselves to solve a problem or to make a decision. Then the group either can carry out the solution or decision itself or can make a recommendation to a larger group.

Private Group Discussion. In business, in government, and in most situations in which a group of people are gathered to accomplish a task, private group discussions are the most common means for solving problems and for making decisions. Private group discussion usually takes the form of a committee meeting, a round-table discussion, or a progressive discussion. Two types of committees are the standing committee and the ad hoc committee.

Decisions on many of the nation's weightiest problems are reached in formal group settings, such as this Congressional committee meeting.

A **standing committee** is a semipermanent group that is part of a larger group. Many organizations have such standing committees as a social committee, a membership committee, or a budget committee. These small groups study problems that fall within their province, or scope of duties or functions. Their goal is to make recommendations to the organization of which they are a part. For example, an organization would turn a problem related to dues over to the budget committee for consideration. The members of the budget committee would discuss the problem in a private meeting and would then present the committee's proposed solution to the organization's leaders or perhaps to the entire organization.

An **ad hoc committee** is a group that is formed to study a single issue. The opening story of this chapter tells of the formation of an ad hoc committee to consider whether the issue of raising the age for getting a driver's license would be a good one to discuss in the Public Forum Series that the class sponsors. An ad hoc committee is disbanded when it has completed its task.

A **round-table discussion** is used to share information on a specific issue. Each member in a round-table discussion gives a brief report to the entire group on the issue; then the group discusses the separate reports. For example, teachers in your school might have a round-table discussion to share information about the effect that a new board of education ruling will have on each of the school's programs. A teacher from the English department might start with a report on how the ruling would affect English instruction. Then a coach from the physical education department might give a report on how it would affect school sports. After all the reports had been given, the group might discuss the effects that bear on all departments.

A **progressive discussion** is a group discussion in which a large group is divided into small groups that each discuss a different aspect of a topic. For example, one group might discuss the causes of a problem while another might devise possible solutions. The assumption of a progressive discussion is that everybody is not prepared to discuss the entire question. A progressive discussion gives group members an opportunity to work on one particular part of an issue rather than the entire issue.

Public Group Discussion. Two common types of public group discussions are the panel and the symposium. Both can be opened up to questions and comments from the audience, thus turning them into public forums.

A **panel** is a group that discusses a topic of common interest to its members and to a listening audience. A panel is usually composed of four to six experts on a particular topic who are brought together to share information and opinions. For example, a local community might sponsor a panel discussion on the role of state government in financing public elementary and secondary education. The community might bring together a member of the state legislature, someone from the education department at a local college, members of the local board of education, and others who are leaders in state government and in public education. As a panel discusses a topic, the audience can hear various points of view on it. Very seldom will a panel solve a problem or arrive at a decision. Yet, a panel may very well provide the information that another group can use to reach a solution or a decision.

A **symposium** is a form of public group discussion in which four to six people present short, prepared speeches. If the speeches are effective, the symposium can be very informative and stimulating. At the end of the prepared speeches, the members of the symposium discuss among themselves the ideas that have been presented.

Occasionally, the listening audience has a chance to ask questions or make comments at the end of a panel discussion or a symposium. When this is the case, the panel or the symposium becomes a **forum,** an opportunity for open discussion of ideas.

ACTIVITY: **Identifying Topics and Choosing a Discussion Format for Group Discussion**

Form a discussion group containing five to seven students. Brainstorm, tossing ideas back and forth among yourselves, to come up with a list of ten topics that you would like to discuss as a group. For example, you might list pass/fail grading as one topic, and movie or music censorship as another, along with eight additional topics that interest the members of the group. Then decide within your group which discussion format would be the best one to use for each topic.

DESIGN FOR ORDERLY GROUP DISCUSSION

In this section you will look at the elements of an orderly discussion, but keep in mind that a real discussion will not always perfectly conform to this order. Nevertheless, if the group has strong leadership and concerned members, a group discussion can be reasonably well organized.

Choose a Topic

The first step in orderly discussion is to choose a topic. Often the topic is chosen for the group. For example, a private discussion group is usually formed to solve a particular problem, such as litter in the cafeteria or overcrowded student parking. Even a public discussion group is likely to be assigned a topic, such as opening school playgounds for weekend use or adding a wing to the public library.

Occasionally a group is asked to select its own topic. When a group has this opportunity, it should choose a topic that its members find interesting. In the case of a public discussion, the topic also needs to interest the audience. In addition the group should select a topic that is significant or worth the time needed to discuss it. For example, raising the age requirement for a driver's license would probably be a significant topic for high-school students. Finally, the group should choose a topic it can cover effectively in the discussion period. A topic such as the effects of the Vietnam War might be significant, but it is too broad for a group to cover well in one discussion period.

Phrase a Discussion Question

The next step in orderly discussion is to phrase the topic as a discussion question. Why a question? First, well-phrased questions stimulate objective discussion. Second, they stimulate careful thinking. Suppose a group of club members decided to discuss the topic of dues. In the first meeting, the group would need to phrase a specific question related to that topic, such as "Should dues be raised?" or "What are the criteria for determining the best dues level?" The goal of the discussion would be to answer the question that had been asked. Based on the discussion, the group might eventually decide that dues should be lowered or that dues should be determined on the basis of needs.

A well-phrased discussion question should meet the following guidelines:

1. *The question's wording should be clear and concise.* When the wording is vague, the group will be unsure about how to proceed. Consider the wording of the following two questions.

What should high schools be doing to get the job done?
Should the curriculum be looked into?

The Greek philosopher Plato (427?–347 B.C.) understood the wisdom of beginning a group discussion with a carefully formulated question. In many of his most famous writings, several characters engage in lively debate on an issue raised by an opening question.

Wording such as *get the job done* and *be looked into* is vague. Notice how these questions can be revised to make them more specific and clearer.

What should high schools be doing to ensure that students who graduate have achieved at least minimum levels of competency?
Should each course in the high-school's curriculum be re-evaluated to make sure that it meets the goals set by the state board of education?

The revised wording of these two questions helps the group know exactly what it is trying to achieve in the discussion.

2. *The question's wording should promote objective discussion.* The wording of a question should be neutral and should not sway the group one way or another. For example, consider the phrasing of the following question: "Should our ridiculously low standards for high-school athletic eligibility be raised?" The wording of this question would sway a group at the start to assume that standards are too low. However, whether or not standards are too low is one of the issues that the group should be deciding during the discussion. A better phrasing would be "Should North High School's minimum standards for athletic eligibility be revised?"

3. *The question should include only one topic.* The question "What should North High do to improve its football and basketball teams?" involves two separate questions. Although both deal with athletics, what might improve the football team might not necessarily improve the basketball team. If both questions need to be considered, then they should be phrased as two separate questions: "What should be done to improve North High's football team?" and "What should be done to improve North High's basketball team?"

4. *Consider rewording a question that is phrased to allow for only a yes or a no answer.* For example, the question "Should a student who cheats on a test receive an F?" might be better phrased as "What should the policy be for dealing with students who cheat on tests?"

Although it is preferable to phrase questions so that they cannot be answered *yes* or *no*, sometimes it is not practical to do so. For example, suppose a group has been formed to consider the question "Should all students be required to take four years of English?" Trying to rephrase this question to avoid a *yes* or a *no* answer may introduce other issues that the group was not expected to consider. In such cases, a group should stick with the original question and, ignoring simple *yes* and *no* answers, should go on to discuss the topic fully.

Types of Questions

The discussion question should be identifiable as a question of fact, a question of evaluation, or a question of policy. In addition to clarifying the question, phrasing it according to one of these three categories helps the group determine an effective organization for dealing with the topic.

Questions of Fact. Questions of fact determine what is true. For example:

Is pollution from aerosol cans destroying the ozone in our atmosphere?
Do vocational schools provide the training necessary for students to obtain good jobs?
Was Columbus the first European explorer to reach the New World?

Questions of Evaluation. Questions of evaluation test the relative value of a person, a place, a thing, or an idea. Answering such questions requires the group to make judgments. Questions of evaluation are characterized by evaluative words such as *effective, good, worthy, better,* or their opposites. Although criteria can be chosen for such things as "best" and "smartest" and subjects can be measured against those criteria, there is no way to verify the findings. The results are still a matter of judgment, not a matter of fact. Notice the evaluative terms used in the following three questions of evaluation.

What was the funniest movie produced last year?
Who is the best swimming instructor?
Which science course is more difficult: chemistry or biology?

Questions of Policy. Questions of policy consider what action should be taken. Often they include the word *should.* By far the greatest number of questions examined by discussion groups in everyday situations are questions of policy. Here are three examples of questions of policy.

Should funding for solar energy research and development be increased?
Should all nuclear arms be dismantled?
Should people be prevented from smoking in public places?

At this business meeting, a *question of policy* is the basis for discussion. The participants are deciding what the firm should do.

Prepare a Discussion Outline

The next step in orderly discussion is the preparation of a discussion outline. The discussion outline contains the key questions that must be answered in any sensible discussion of the topic question. These key questions, often called issues, differ depending on whether the discussion question is one of fact, of evaluation, or of policy.

Outlining Questions of Fact. The outline for most questions of fact involves defining and classifying. The main points of an outline are questions that will (1) define key words, (2) find information that satisfies the definitions or that fits the classifications, and (3) determine whether any other circumstances might affect the decision. This organization is illustrated by the following outline for a discussion question.

Discussion Question: What are the goals of secondary education?
I. What do we mean by *goals?* [Defining key words]
II. What material determines each of these goals? [Finding information that sets up each classification]
III. What current conditions must be considered when selecting goals? [Determining what circumstances affect the decision]

Outlining Questions of Evaluation. The outline for most questions of evaluation involves finding the standards upon which to make the judgment. The main points include questions that (1) determine the criteria for making the judgment, (2) determine the information related to the discussion question, (3) match the information with the criteria, and (4) consider whether any other circumstances affect the evaluation. Note how these questions are handled in the following sample outline for a question of evaluation.

Discussion Question: Is North High the best high school in the area?
I. What are the criteria for determining the "best" high school? [Determining the criteria for making the judgment]
II. What facts need to be considered in comparing North High to other high schools in the area? [Determining information related to the discussion question]
III. Do the facts show that North High meets all criteria or more criteria than other high schools in the area? [Matching facts with criteria]
IV. Are there any other circumstances that affect the evaluation? [Considering circumstances that affect the decision]

Outlining Questions of Policy. The main points for an outline of a question of policy include questions that are based on John Dewey's steps of reflective thinking. His five steps are (1) defining the problem, (2) analyzing the problem, (3) suggesting possible solutions, (4) selecting the best solution, and (5) suggesting ways of carrying out the solution. To define the problem, begin by stating it as a question. The other four steps are stated in the following questions: (1) What is the nature of the problem (its size and scope)? (2) What are the possible solutions to the problem? (3) Which is the best solution? (4) How can this solution be implemented, or carried out?

John Dewey (1859-1952), an American educator and philosopher, developed the five steps of reflective thinking that we use in outlining questions of policy.

The following example of an outline for a question of policy uses these questions.

Discussion Question: What should be done to lower student absenteeism at North High School? [Stating the problem]

   I. What is the nature of the student absenteeism problem? [Analyzing the problem]
      A. How many students are absent each day?
      B. What is the effect of absenteeism on student morale?
   II. What are possible solutions to the absenteeism problem? [Giving all possible solutions]
  III. Which is the best solution? [Identifying which solution will do the best job of making the problem smaller and limiting its effect]
  IV. How can the solution be implemented? [Suggesting ways to carry out the solution]

Using the Outline. Early in the discussion, members of the group should decide on specific wording for the outline they will follow. Will discussion always follow these steps exactly? No, probably not. How closely a group follows an outline depends on the direction of its leadership and on the commitment of its members to adhere to the outline. Very few groups stay on track throughout. However, if the group follows an outline, everyone will be working to accomplish the same goals in the discussion. In short, following an outline helps a group avoid straying from the question under discussion.

Identifying Types of Discussion Questions and Writing an Outline for a Group Discussion

First, turn the topics you listed in the activity on page 416 into discussion questions. Identify each question as a question of fact, of evaluation, or of policy. Then read the following numbered questions and identify each as a question of fact, a question of evaluation, or a question of policy. Finally, select five questions and develop an outline for each one. Share your outlines with your classmates.

1. Is ComputerPal the best computer training school in the city?

2. What should be done to raise SAT scores in this school?

3. What are my goals in attending high school?

4. Should North High raise its minimum grade point requirement for participating in interscholastic sports?

5. To what extent should parents be responsible for their children's actions?

TAKING PART IN GROUP DISCUSSIONS

Too often, people mistakenly think that group discussions are much like the informal rap sessions they get into with friends and acquaintances. Although it is true that rap sessions and group discussions both involve talking with others about a single topic, participation in a group discussion requires a great deal more commitment, energy, and just plain hard work. A group's goal is to arrive at the very best decision possible. A group can arrive at the best decision only if every participant is willing to shoulder several necessary responsibilities.

Be Prepared

Good decisions are reached by discussing the best information available. Before you sit down with your group to discuss the question, prepare yourself fully. Review Chapter 10 if you need to brush up on methods of researching topics for speeches. In this section, you will be briefly introduced to several additional steps for finding information for discussion.

1. *Read available information carefully.* In some situations another group or individual may have gathered information that is made available to your group. For example, if you are on a committee to select a class gift for your high school, you may receive a packet of information that tells about the gifts given by the previous ten classes, the methods used to raise money, the amount of money spent on each gift, and other related details. Obviously,

you and your group will want to take advantage of this information. Before your group meets, be sure that you take time to read and study any information that has been made available to you.

2. *Consider your own experiences.* Think through any experiences you have had with the question. While you may not have been on a committee for purchasing a gift for the school before, you may have worked with other groups to raise money. If you think about your methods and procedures—about what worked and what did not in the other groups—you may discover information that can help your new group.

3. *Ask others for information and opinions.* For example, before the school gift committee has its first meeting, members might interview teachers or the principal to find out what the school needs. In addition, the group could poll fellow classmates to get additional ideas about what gift to buy.

4. *Use library sources.* Especially when you are discussing a question that you know has been discussed by others, you are likely to find books, magazine articles, and other useful sources of information on it in the library. Talk with the librarian and explain your needs so that the librarian can help you locate available material.

Test Your Preparedness

Before taking part in a discussion, test your preparedness. Before the meeting, take time to strengthen any area in which you are weak. You are reasonably well prepared if you are able to answer *yes* to the following questions:

Are you able to *define* the problem? Do you know exactly what it is that you need to find out?

Can you *analyze* the problem? Are you able to break it down into its parts? These subdivisions will lead you to questions that will help you determine the kinds of information you need to arrive at a solution.

Can you *evaluate* your facts? Can you separate facts from opinions? Can you determine whether or not your facts truly support the ideas being considered?

Have you *arranged* the facts under appropriate headings? Can you put them in a logical order that leads to their conclusions?

Can you *select* the important facts? Can you tell which of your facts are most important in relation to the various issues?

Can you *spot the inadequacy* of data? Can you see where the holes are? Do you know where you and the group will need more information?

Can you *suspend judgment* until you have all the facts? Can you look for material that will support more than one position?

Are you able to *draw conclusions*? Can you decide what kinds of conclusions are warranted after you have examined all of your factual material?

Meet Responsibilities of Participation

The members of a discussion group have several responsibilities. Make sure that you are familiar with the following guidelines for meeting your responsibilities when you take part in a group discussion.

1. *Share information.* As you gather information, be sure that you pass it along to the other members in your group. For example, if you are on the class gift committee and have gotten opinions from twenty classmates about what gift to get, relate these opinions to your group. In addition, tell the group how you got your information and about any other pertinent details you learned.

2. *Ask questions.* Good discussion is built on good questioning. Well-phrased questions help ensure that important information gets covered. For example, if your group is wondering how much money to collect for a class gift, you can ask, "How much did the previous three classes spend for their gifts?" If the information is available, this question will lead you to it. If the information is not available, other members of your group may suggest ways of finding out. If your group does not think the question is important, either you can show why it is or you can drop the subject and focus on other information that the group decides will be more useful.

3. *Help the group stay on track.* Helping a group stay on track is vital to its success, since people often find group discussion an opportunity for talking about everything but the topic. When a group gets off track, one of its members needs to remind and encourage the others to get back to the topic. For example, you might say to fellow members of the gift committee, "I think we're straying from how much other classes spent on their gift" or "Let's see, aren't we still trying to decide how much money we want to raise?"

Productive group discussion depends upon the active participation of every member of the group.

4. *Listen critically.* In a group discussion speakers often concentrate so hard on what they want to say that they do not listen closely to what is going on. Yet, some of the best group participants are not those who have a great deal of information to present. Instead, they concentrate on understanding what is being said so that they are able to ask the right questions, find the right examples, and give the right explanations. By being good listeners, they help the group understand and agree on points of the discussion.

5. *Weigh and evaluate ideas, facts, and opinions.* The main point of group discussion is to take advantage of many people's thoughts. However, a group will get nowhere if at least one of its members is not able to evaluate the information presented. Someone needs to ask questions such as

> What was the source of the information presented?
> What were the bases for conclusions?
> Was the information true?
> Are any facts or ideas contradictory?
> Does the conclusion logically follow from the information presented?

6. *Be considerate.* Although this point may seem obvious, it is often ignored in the heat of discussion. Let others finish what they are saying before you break in. Resist giving in to your emotions. You may think that someone's point is poorly supported, and you may be right, but do not become abusive or short-tempered toward the person making the point. Never make personal remarks. Focus your comments on facts and issues.

7. *Cooperate with others.* Do not act as if the material you present is yours alone. Once presented, it belongs to the group. Encourage others to comment on the information. Do not take negative comments personally.

8. *Speak clearly and loudly enough to be heard.* Even in private discussion, speaking clearly and distinctly is important. In panels and symposiums, doing so is vital.

ACTIVITY: Preparing for a Group Discussion

Imagine that you are going to take part in a group discussion on the question "Are standardized tests a valid measure of a person's ability to do college-level work?" Tell what you would do to prepare yourself for such a discussion. For the question being discussed, which steps of preparation do you think would be most important? Why?

LEADING GROUP DISCUSSIONS

Leadership is the ability to guide the group toward its goal. Being appointed or elected leader does not mean that a person will automatically be a good leader. Effective leaders earn their right to lead, exercise their leadership responsibly, and know what needs to be done.

Earn the Right to Lead

Good leaders earn the right to lead by being prepared. Being a good leader is often a matter of setting an example. If you are group leader and expect group members to be well prepared, you must be well prepared yourself. You will find that groups are not likely to accept leaders who do not know what they are talking about and who expect everyone else to do the work.

Good leaders earn the right to lead by showing their own willingness to work hard. Not only will group members work harder if their leader is willing to work, but they will maintain their support for that leader.

Good leaders earn the right to lead by demonstrating good speaking skills. People expect leaders to be clear and precise. If you are hesitant and fill sentences with "uh" and "ah," people will likely question your ability to lead. If, however, you are confident, enthusiastic, and decisive, people will be more likely to support you.

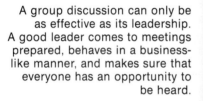

A group discussion can only be as effective as its leadership. A good leader comes to meetings prepared, behaves in a business-like manner, and makes sure that everyone has an opportunity to be heard.

Exercise Leadership Responsibly

When people are appointed leaders, they behave in many different ways. Most leaders adopt one of the following styles.

Laissez-faire Leadership. Laissez-faire leadership is a style that puts the responsibility for procedure in the hands of the group. This style, sometimes called *nondirective,* can work well if several members of the group assume the leadership role. However, since most people define leadership as giving direction, this style is often considered *nonleadership.* Unless everyone in your group knows exactly what to do in a discussion and can proceed *without* direction, members of the group are likely to find that laissez-faire leadership provides insufficient guidance.

Authoritarian Leadership. Authoritarian leadership is a style that places *all* responsibility in the hands of an authoritarian leader. This style, sometimes called *directive*, can work well if time is short and if all members want and need total direction. However, some leaders direct the group so strictly that they become tyrants. Tyrannical leaders soon lose the support of group members. Once members begin to resent the group leader, they cease to be effective. If they believe that their ideas are not going to be heard or regarded, they quit discussing them.

Democratic Leadership. Democratic leadership is a style in which the leader offers suggestions for procedures but asks the other members of the group for their ideas about organization, about the roles that members should play, and about the tasks that should be accomplished. This style is sometimes called *supportive,* because the leader asks for ideas and supports those who give them. The democratic leader guides the group in finding a direction but does not rule with an iron hand.

Notice the difference in these three styles of leadership as expressed in the following statements.

"Well, we're supposed to make a decision about the class gift. What do all of you think we should do?" [Laissez-faire leadership]

"We're gathered to make a decision about the class gift. The way we're going to reach this decision is by each of you doing the following tasks exactly as I assign them." [Authoritarian leadership]

"We're gathered to make a decision about the class gift. I think that we should begin by finding out what classes have done in the past—how they collected money, how they decided what to get, and how much they spent. How does this sound as a procedure? Is there anything else we should be looking at?" [Democratic leadership]

Get the Discussion Started

An effective leader gets the discussion started on the right track. The leader is responsible for gathering group members together, selecting a time and a place to meet, making sure that the place is set up properly, and introducing the task to the group.

An effective leader suggests an **agenda,** or outline for discussion. Although anyone in the group has the right to suggest how to proceed, it is up to the leader to propose at least a tentative outline. The group may change the outline, may suggest throwing it out and starting over, or may elect to follow it closely.

Keep the Discussion Moving

An effective leader keeps the discussion moving toward the group's goal. To do this, a leader should have a series of questions related to the agenda. By asking questions, the leader encourages others to start contributing their ideas, facts, and opinions. For example, on the topic of a class gift the leader might ask, "What gifts have previous classes given in the past few years?"

If no one answered, the leader might ask, "Where can we get this information?"

Of equal importance to asking questions is seeing to it that everybody has an equal chance to participate. Though all members of the group will not take equal amounts of time, each one should be given an equal opportunity to talk. If one person seems to be doing most of the talking, the leader is responsible for seeing to it that other members have opportunities to contribute their ideas, information, and comments. Likewise, if one or two people do not say much, it is up to the leader to try to draw them out.

An effective leader keeps the discussion moving by summarizing whenever the group has decided on a point. During a discussion, a group will make decisions. When the group appears to be in agreement, the leader should stop and clearly state the point that everyone seems to be agreeing on. By summarizing points, the leader makes sure that all members are agreeing to the same thing.

An effective leader keeps the discussion moving by calming tension. Group members are likely to pursue their points aggressively in any good discussion. An effective leader breaks in before individuals begin to become angry. For example, when one person will not let another person finish before taking issue, the leader might say, "Bill, I don't think you are letting Harriet make her point. Would you go over that again, Harriet?" When two members appear to be building up to an argument, the leader might say, "Hold it a second. I know you two are on opposite sides of this, but let's see where you might have some points of agreement."

"And now at this point in the meeting I'd like to shift the blame away from me and onto someone else."

This group leader is attempting to keep the discussion moving—away from himself. How would you react if you were a member of this group?

Keep Records

An effective leader sees to it that someone is recording points of agreement. Sometimes a discussion group will have agreed on six or eight points along the way, and a week later either no one can accurately remember what the group decided, or members will differ on the wording of the decisions.

A good written record can help eliminate confusion and prevent disagreement. Keeping accurate records involves writing down each of the points that the leader summarizes and receives group agreement on.

Close the Discussion

An effective leader closes the discussion when a decision has been reached about the main discussion question. There is no need for a group to continue once it has achieved its goal. To close the discussion, the leader summarizes all the agreed-upon points and gives the members a chance to comment on them and make any final modifications.

ACTIVITY: **Analyzing Leadership of a Group Discussion**

Listen to a group discussion. What kind of leadership style does the leader use: laissez-faire, authoritarian, or democratic? How can you tell? What are some examples that illustrate that kind of style? How effective is the leader? How do you account for the leader's effectiveness or ineffectiveness? If you had been the leader, what would you have done differently? Share your findings with your classmates.

Identify and Manage Conflict

In any group discussion, conflicts may arise between members of the group. **Conflict** is a form of disagreement. In group discussion an ordinary disagreement becomes conflict when two or more people struggle to win recognition of one idea or point of view over another. As the word *struggle* implies, neither party involved in a conflict is likely to give in or compromise easily.

On first appearance all conflict may seem to be undesirable. In reality a measure of conflict is healthy in group discussion because conflict tests ideas, thereby helping the group to arrive at the best solution possible. However, conflict can get out of hand to the point where constructive discussion becomes impossible. To prevent conflict from disrupting group discussion, the leader needs to be able to recognize when a conflict is developing, to diagnose the nature of the conflict, and to provide a method for helping the group manage the conflict.

The four guidelines for managing disagreement in conversation were covered in Chapter 7. The following discussion will focus on recognizing conflict, diagnosing the cause of conflict, and dealing with conflict in group discussion.

1. *Recognize the presence of conflict.* During discussion, someone, usually the leader, should recognize when a conflict is developing. If a conflict is not identified as it develops, it may escalate until it disrupts the entire group and prevents constructive discussion.

For instance, if the group is discussing the Senior Class gift, Don may be in favor of a permanent announcement board to be built in front of the school entrance. Carol, on the other hand, may be in favor of a new scoreboard for the gymnasium. At first, their disagreement may proceed as a healthy exchange of the pros and cons of the two choices. However, as the discussion goes on, Don and Carol may become involved in a struggle that goes beyond an objective weighing and contrasting of positions. If this occurs, someone—preferably the group leader—needs to recognize that a disruptive conflict has developed.

Sure signs of disruptive conflict are the unwillingness of one group member to hear out another member's point of view, the use of derogatory remarks rather than logical argument by a group member when discussing opposing points of view, and the inability or unwillingness of one group member to recognize the worth and reasonableness of another person's ideas and statements.

When it becomes apparent that an interpersonal conflict is developing, the group leader should redirect attention to the issue at hand.

2. *Determine the basis of the conflict.* Group members are likely to come into conflict over procedures, facts, definitions, values, interpretations of facts, or almost any facet of a topic under discussion.

When members of a group disagree, the disagreement often tends to spread beyond the specific issue at hand and into other areas. When this occurs, the disagreement needs to be dealt with at once before it becomes a disruptive conflict.

For instance, Don may say to Carol, "We've worked on five committees together, and you have never agreed with any of my ideas." If the group tries to ignore Don's statement, the conflict may intensify and prevent productive discussion. At the time such a comment is made, the group leader or another member of the group should halt the spread of the conflict by saying something like "Now, just a minute. The issue is not whether Carol always disagrees with you; the issue is the merits of an announcement board versus the merits of a scoreboard."

3. *Resolve the conflict.* Since conflict often spreads beyond the issue under discussion, the leader needs to keep the group focused on dealing with that issue. On the issue of the class gift, for example, the leader may say, "We all seem to agree on the importance of a valuable gift. However, there is some disagreement on whether our money would be better spent on an announcement board or a scoreboard. Assuming for a moment that these are our best choices, let's start listing the information that can help us decide between them. Then we can move into the advantages and disadvantages of each choice. Let's start our list with information about how much each of the two boards costs."

If the leader is successful, he or she can keep the disagreement from becoming a battle of egos. Remember: people often become argumentative and defensive not because they believe strongly in their idea but because they do not see any way of giving up the idea without losing face. Every member of the group can help avoid disruptive conflict by recognizing when a disagreement is becoming a struggle of egos and by offering suggestions that will bring all members back to a cooperative discussion of the issue at hand.

ACTIVITY: Analyzing Conflict in Group Discussion

Recall a group discussion in which you participated and in which conflicts developed between group members. What were the conflicts about? What part did the group leader play in resolving the conflicts? How effective were the group leader and the other members of the group in dealing with the conflicts? Share your experiences and your views with your classmates, and discuss ways that conflicts can be managed effectively in group discussions.

MANAGING GROUP CONFLICT

Problem	Cause	Solution
Group members arguing about what to do next	Lack of clarification of goals	Identify goals of discussion
Group members arguing about a point that has been discussed	Conflict over differences in recall and interpretation	Read record of discussion and review facts and reasoning
Group members arguing about whether something is true	Conflict concerning factual information	Analyze and evaluate information; if necessary, find additional supporting information
Group members arguing over the meaning or significance of facts or other points of discussion	Conflict over interpretation	Analyze facts or points of discussion and their relationships to each other and to topic of discussion
Group members arguing over what is "more important" or "better"	Conflict over values	Identify and establish criteria for determining value
Group members arguing about solution to issue	Conflict over goals, methods, or results of discussion	1. Review goals of discussion to determine specific criteria for meeting goals 2. Review and evaluate methods, especially logical reasoning, used to reach solutions 3. Analyze solutions to determine which solution best meets criteria
Group members interrupting and being inconsiderate of one another	Ego conflict	Remind group of purpose and goal of discussion and call upon all members to show tolerance and respect for one another's views
Group members trying to defeat one another's ideas rather than discussing possible solutions	Ego conflict	Focus attention on the ideas being disputed and on the advantages and disadvantages of each idea

REACHING A GROUP DECISION

The goal of a group discussion is to reach a decision. Groups generally arrive at their decisions in three common ways. One way is by **decree,** in which the leader dictates the group's decision. Especially when a group is being run in a directive, authoritarian style, the leader will listen to group comments and then state a decision. If the leader has enough power over the group, if the leader is manipulative, or if the leader is very persuasive, group members will let the leader dictate the group's decision. However, the decree method of decision making is likely to destroy group morale. If group members do not take part in making a decision, they are unlikely to work to carry out that decision. Although there are times when this kind of decision-making is appropriate, it is not the most effective method for reaching a decision in most circumstances.

A second way of reaching a decision is by **voting,** in which the opinion held by most members of a group is adopted as the decision of the entire group. There are times when the group just cannot seem to agree on key points. Yet, the group must arrive at a decision. Under these conditions the group should take a vote. As in any democratically run organization, a majority wins. A **majority** means that over half the members favor one decision. The problem with voting is that those on the losing side are likely to be disgruntled and may not work to carry out the decision.

By far the best way of arriving at a decision is by consensus. **Consensus** means that the group's decision is worded in such a way that the entire group agrees on it. If the members of a group cannot agree on a point, the group should reword that point until consensus is reached before moving to vote on it. Of course, there is potential for **false consensus,** that is, acting as if there is agreement when there really is not. Avoiding false consensus is the responsibility of every group member. When participating in a group discussion, be sure that you know what you think and feel, and that you express your views clearly.

Drawing by C. Barsotti. © 1985 by the New Yorker Magazine, Inc.

"Then, gentlemen, it is the consensus of this meeting that we say nothing, do nothing, and hope it all blows over before our next meeting."

Although the members of this group have reached a decision through consensus, their discussion does not seem to have been very productive.

Analyzing Decision-Making

Think about the last group you worked in. Were the decisions made by decree, by vote, or by consensus? What effect did the method of arriving at decisions have on the group's morale? Discuss your views with your classmates.

EVALUATING GROUP DISCUSSION

How much you improve your discussion skills will depend on how you take advantage of criticism. Group discussions are evaluated by observers. Each observer takes careful notes of what happens. Since you are likely to

EVALUATION FORM FOR GROUP DISCUSSION

Name	Information contributed	Questions asked	Followed plan	Listening	Courtesy

Evaluate each person on each criterion: 1 (poor) to 5 (superior)

work as both an observer and a participant, you should know how group discussions are evaluated.

One way to evaluate a group discussion is to concentrate on what each person in the group is doing. Each speaker can be rated on a 1–5 scale on the characteristics that have been discussed. The evaluation shows the observer's reactions to each group member's performance. In the sample "Evaluation Form for Group Discussion" shown on page 434, each person can earn up to twenty-five points.

A second way to evaluate a group discussion is to focus on the discussion process. To do this, you should have some record of who is talking and to whom he or she is speaking. Then after the discussion, you can make your judgment about the balance of participation. An effective method for keeping this record is to diagram the discussion process. Write the letter G, which stands for *group,* in a square on a piece of paper. Then, in a circular pattern around the G, write the participant's initials within squares. Place the leader's initials at the top. Each time a person talks, place a slash by that person's initials and draw an arrow from that person's initials to the initials of the

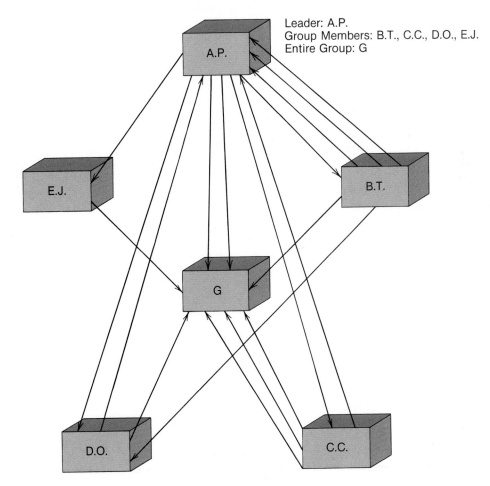

Leader: A.P.
Group Members: B.T., C.C., D.O., E.J.
Entire Group: G

other group member to whom the person is speaking. If the comment seems intended for the entire group, draw the arrow to the center square containing the letter G. A sample diagram of this method is shown on page 435. Note in the diagram that A.P., the leader, talked most and that E.J. talked least. B.T. talked mostly to A.P., and C.C. talked mostly to the entire group.

A third way to evaluate a discussion is to focus on the quality of the discussion. To do so, you should answer the following questions.

Was the group goal clearly stated as a question of fact, of evaluation, or of policy?

Did the group have a discussion outline?

Were conclusions that were drawn based on information presented in the discussion?

Was the decision defensible?

ACTIVITY: Evaluating Group Discussion

Listen to a group discussion, either a live discussion or a radio or television program. Choose a method of evaluation and evaluate the discussion. Share your evaluation with your classmates.

GUIDELINES FOR PARTICIPATING IN GROUP DISCUSSION

- Am I prepared?
- Do I share information objectively?
- Do I ask questions?
- Do I try to help the group stay on track?
- Do I examine information that is presented?
- Am I considerate of others' views?
- Do I cooperate?
- Do I speak loudly and clearly enough for everyone to understand?
- As a leader, have I earned the right to lead?
- Do I understand and carry out the responsibilities of leadership?
- Am I able to identify and help manage conflict?

Profiles in Communication

"When the client is paying the bill, the client expects results," says architect Gary Hoyt about the business meetings he regularly attends. As a self-employed businessman with professional interests in both architecture and computer software, Mr. Hoyt often needs to take part in group discussions with clients, with other professionals such as engineers and bankers, and with a variety of businesspeople and government officials.

The main value of such discussions, according to Mr. Hoyt, is that they "help in reaching sounder decisions because ideas are tested by many points of view." Bringing together a variety of perspectives also creates the right environment for discovering new ideas.

"The first thing to do in a meeting is to break the ice," Mr. Hoyt states. "It's very important to introduce people. Too often discussion leaders don't do enough to make participants comfortable." Mr. Hoyt has found that humor and a relaxed but professional atmosphere can help put everyone in the right frame of mind to engage in productive discussion.

Mr. Hoyt notes that the focus of discussion changes as a project progresses. "Early discussions," he says, "involve a lot of brainstorming and help define the direction of a project. Later discussion zeroes in on specific issues as they develop." He warns that bad decisions and weak planning at any stage of discussion "can make subsequent meetings a waste."

Mr. Hoyt gives the following advice for holding successful group discussions. First, "put together a good group of people" to approach the matter at hand with a variety of skills and perspectives. Second, "be organized—have a specific goal in each meeting. Know what you want to accomplish, but don't be too rigid." Third, help participants to feel at ease. Fourth, "don't let the discussion bog down." Here again, humor is useful—"humor can help shake out mental 'cobwebs' and get discussion moving." Fifth, "always follow up an outstanding meeting with phone calls and notes to let participants know that things went well. People like going to meetings in which things get done." Finally, be sure to keep records of the proceedings.

Group discussions cannot solve every problem, but Gary Hoyt has found good discussions vital in achieving the successes he has had in his business ventures.

SUMMARY

Group discussion is a formal way of communicating in which a small number of people interact face-to-face to share information, to solve a problem, or to arrive at a decision. Although some problems are best handled by an individual, a group can provide many advantages for problem solving.

Group discussions may be public or private. The two most common types of public group discussions are the panel and the symposium. The most common types of private group discussions are the committee, the round table, and the progressive discussion.

Having an effective discussion involves gathering a workable number of people, developing cohesiveness, formulating a clear question, having clear organization, and drawing conclusion.

Having a well-organized discussion involves several steps. A group begins by wording a discussion question that is clear and objective, that is limited to one topic, and that is phrased as a question of fact, of evaluation, or of policy. The group then composes a discussion outline based on the type of question.

Taking part in a group discussion involves being well prepared and meeting the responsibilities of a participant. Leading A group discussion requires earning the right to lead and exercising leadership responsibly. a group leader is responsible for getting the discussion started, suggesting an agenda, keeping the discussion moving, summarizing points on which the group has agreed, seeing to it that someone is recording conclusions, and closing the discussion effectively.

Conflicts can arise during group discussion. Identifying and managing conflict involves recognizing the presence of conflict, determining the basis of the conflict, and resolving the conflict.

The goal of a group discussion is to arrive at a decision. A leader can dictate a decision, a group can vote on a decision, or a group can reach a decision by consensus. The consensus method is best for group morale.

A group discussion can be evaluated. The evaluation can concentrate on what each participant is doing, on the discussion process, or on the quality of the discussion.

CHAPTER VOCABULARY

Look back through this chapter to find the meaning of each of the following terms. Write each term and its meaning in your communication journal.

ad hoc committee	forum	questions of evaluation
agenda	group discussion	questions of fact
authoritarian leadership	laissez-faire leadership	questions of policy
cohesive	leadership	round-table discussion
conflict	majority	standing committee
consensus	panel	symposium
decree	private group discussion	voting
democratic leadership	progressive discussion	
false consensus	public discussion	

1. For what three reasons is a group better suited to making a decision than an individual is?

2. A panel is a group of four to six people who discuss a topic of mutual interest to them and to their audience. In what way does a panel differ from a symposium?

3. The committee meeting is a form of private discussion. How does an ad hoc committee differ from a standing committee?

4. A discussion topic should always be phrased as a question. Why?

5. One type of discussion question is a discussion of fact. What are two other types?

6. The outline for a question of evaluation includes four main points. What are they?

7. One major responsibility of a participant is to share information. What are three others?

8. One style of leadership is laissez-faire. What are two other styles?

9. Disagreements between group members can turn into disruptive conflicts. What steps should a group leader take to manage such conflicts?

10. A decision can be reached by decree, by voting, or by consensus. Why is consensus the most effective method?

DISCUSSION QUESTIONS

1. Discuss with your classmates why discussion groups are a necessary part of a democratic society. How do discussion groups help participants voice their opinions? How do group members keep the power of leaders in check?

2. Some people feel too shy to express their opinions in group discussions. Discuss ways in which a person can overcome shyness. Then discuss ways in which an effective leader can help and encourage a shy group member.

3. Conflict is likely to arise in group discussions. Discuss ways for determining that a conflict is building before it becomes a serious disagreement. Then discuss ways in which a good leader can manage the conflict.

4. The Bible says, "If the blind lead the blind, both shall fall into the ditch." First, discuss the meaning of this quotation. Then discuss how it relates to the qualities needed by an effective leader.

5. In relation to committees, *Vogue* magazine once offered the following definition of a camel: "a horse planned by a committee." First, discuss the meaning of this quotation. Then discuss how the quotation illuminates the weaknesses of the group decision-making process. Finally, discuss whether the strengths of the group decision-making process outweigh its weaknesses.

1. Identifying Topics and Participants for Group Discussion

Think about your school. List five issues facing your school that would be suitable for group discussion. For example, you might list pass/fail grading, the need for new gym equipment, changes in graduation requirements, or the dress code. Then turn each of these topics into a discussion question. Identify groups of students and teachers who would be interested in each topic.

2. Analyzing Public Group Discussion

Study your daily newspaper. Look for reports of meetings of Congress, of the state legislature, of the city council, and of local clubs. Then prepare a list of eight or ten topics that are being resolved through public group discussion. Classify the level of interest of each topic as local, state, national, or international; then identify specific groups that would be concerned with these topics.

3. Analyzing a Public Meeting

Attend a public forum, a city council meeting, or a school board meeting. Report afterward on such items as the number of people in attendance, the number of participants, the way the meeting was conducted, the topics discussed, and the action taken.

4. Preparing an Outline for Group Discussion

Read each of the following questions:

a. What are the advantages and the disadvantages of a liberal arts education?

b. What role should the federal government play in supporting the arts in this country?

c. In what ways are young children influenced by television?

d. Should all high-school students be required to take at least one year of a foreign language?

Prepare an outline for a group discussion of each of these questions.

5. Conducting Group Discussion

A. Select a topic suitable for a panel discussion. Elect a leader. Hold at least one meeting in which the panel plans the general outline of the discussion. Study the subject before the discussion takes place. Then conduct the panel discussion in front of the class. At the end of the panel discussion, open the discussion to the other members of the class.

B. As a class, choose a topic for discussion. Then turn this topic into a question. Conduct a progressive discussion. Choose five issues for your question. Divide the class into five groups and assign each group to discuss one issue. Then have the leader of each group report to the entire class on the discussion or the conclusion that group reached.

Real-Life Speaking Situations

1. Before making important decisions, many families hold a meeting to discuss possible courses of action. These meetings may deal with vacation plans, household chores, family projects, or any of the many issues that families face. If your family has such conferences, you may likely have wished at one time or another that you were the discussion leader. Picture yourself as head of your own family, with your own husband or wife and your own children. Your family needs to make a decision, and you have called a conference to discuss it. First, identify the members of your family. Next, identify the issue that your family needs to discuss. Write an informative speech, two or three minutes long, on how you would lead the discussion. Be sure to cover your leadership style, the method your family uses to arrive at a decision, the part that each family member plays in the discussion, and the decision reached through the discussion. Be prepared to present your speech in class. Invite feedback from your classmates on the effectiveness of your leadership.

2. Think of the businesses that you deal with frequently. Many of them are probably small businesses run by the owner with a handful of employees. To succeed, the owner must be skilled not only at providing a particular product or service but also at running the business itself. One way that owners of small businesses meet the many demands that face them is by calling their employees together to discuss how the business can best meet the wants and needs of customers. Imagine that you run your own small business. You have had a good year, but lately business has begun to slip. To help you decide how to deal with this decline, you gather your employees for a group meeting. How will you handle the meeting? Begin by identifying the business you are running. Next, specify who your employees are and what each of them could likely contribute to the discussion. Write a three- or four-page dialogue of your group discussion, ending with a conclusion about what has caused your business decline and a decision on what can be done to reverse the decline. Be prepared to present your dialogue in class and to respond to feedback on the effectiveness of your discussion.

DEBATE

OBJECTIVES:

After studying this chapter, you should be able to

1. Define debate.

2. Write and test a debate proposition.

3. Identify three kinds of propositions.

4. Write the major issues of a proposition recommending a policy.

5. Identify two kinds of affirmative cases.

6. Identify three kinds of negative cases.

7. Define refutation.

8. List the four most common types of arguments used in debate.

9. List the four steps of refutation.

10. List the five steps of rebuttal.

11. Prepare a flow sheet.

12. Judge a debate.

Don Benson was concerned. His opponent, Toni Hamilton, was strong, and her attack was all that Don had heard it would be. Only two minutes had passed, and Don had felt the sting of Toni's thrusts. Don knew he was down—but he knew he wasn't out. He would fight back.

Don Benson is not wrestling, or boxing. Instead, he is doing something just as exciting and even more important to him as a student leader. Don is debating.

Debate as a means of decision-making has its origins in the governmental assemblies and law courts of ancient Greece and Rome.

WHAT IS DEBATE?

Debate is formalized public speaking in which participants prepare and present speeches on opposite sides of an issue to determine which side has the stronger arguments. Debate is one of the major ways people in a democratic society make decisions.

The tradition of debate as a means of decision making goes all the way back to the ancient Greeks. However, debate continues to be an essential element of the democratic process in the United States today. Debates in legislative assemblies, in courtrooms, and in other public forums have led to decisions on personal freedom, civil rights, and war and peace. In addition, in the past thirty years presidential debates have played a prominent role in elections. Keep in mind, though, that not only is learning to debate important to decision making, it is also fun. No form of public speaking is more satisfying than proving the strength of your position and defending it against the attacks of others.

This chapter will focus on formal debate, the kind that high-school and college students use in debate contests all over the country. Formal debate has a number of specialized terms and procedures that make it a distinctive form of public speaking. Even if you do not plan on participating in competitive debate, familiarizing yourself with its principles will help you in many speaking situations.

Controversy

Formal debate begins with a controversy expressed as a proposition. A **proposition** is a persuasive specific purpose that establishes a fact, establishes or changes a belief, or recommends a policy. For debate, a proposition must be controversial; that is, a proposition must deal with a question that has valid evidence for at least two solutions that divide public opinion relatively evenly. In the opening situation, Don Benson and Toni Hamilton were debating the proposition "*Resolved,* That the minimum age for obtaining a driver's license should be raised to 18."

Two Sides

The two sides in a debate are called the *affirmative* and the *negative*. The affirmative side supports the wording of the debate proposition. The negative side opposes it. If, for instance, the proposition were "*Resolved,* That the minimum age for obtaining a driver's license should be raised to 18," then the affirmative would give speeches in support of the increase, and the negative would give speeches opposing the increase. The affirmative side begins the debate, since it is seeking a change in belief or policy.

Speakers

Each side has at least two speakers, except in Lincoln-Douglas debate, in which each side has only one speaker. Although legislative debate may have any number of speakers on a side, formal debate usually has two speakers on each side. To help you learn how to debate, you may be asked to argue a proposition with just one person on each side.

The speakers on opposing sides take turns presenting their arguments. In some debate formats, speakers are also given opportunities to question, or to cross-examine, the speaker who has just finished.

Status Quo

The existing state of affairs—currently held beliefs and currently followed courses of action—is called the **status quo.** Debate begins with the assumption that the status quo is satisfactory until proven otherwise. For instance, the minimum age for a person to obtain a driver's license in most states is sixteen. Sixteen is neither the only age that could be considered nor necessarily the best age. However, because sixteen is the legal age in most states, it is the status quo and will continue to be the law until enough evidence is presented to change it.

Since it is the affirmative side that seeks a change from the status quo, the speakers on that side have the burden of proof. The **burden of proof** is the obligation of the affirmative team to present sufficient reason for changing the existing system. Until this burden of proof is met, the negative side has nothing to do. Therefore, it is up to the affirmative to go first and to present a strong enough argument in favor of the change to force the negative to reply.

Constructive and Rebuttal Speeches

Each speaker has a chance to speak twice. During a formal debate each speaker presents two speeches: a constructive speech and a rebuttal speech. A *constructive speech* builds an argument; a *rebuttal speech* rebuilds it.

In theory, during the first round of speeches the affirmative and negative teams attempt to establish reasons for the superiority of their side. During the second round of speeches, the two opposing teams attempt to rebuild arguments that have been questioned or attacked. In practice, however, speakers on each side spend at least some of their time in *refutation*—denying or attacking an argument raised by the other side. Refutation leads to clashes that make debate exciting. During both their constructive speeches and their rebuttal speeches, debaters reserve a portion of their time to refute the arguments of their opponents.

In the courtroom a defendant is innocent until proven guilty; likewise in debate, the status quo is satisfactory until proven otherwise.

ACTIVITY: Identifying Affirmative and Negative Positions in Debate

Imagine that you will participate in a debate on the proposition *"Resolved,* That public schools should remain open eleven months of the year." (1) What will be the affirmative side? (2) What will be the negative side? (3) Which side will go first?

THE PROPOSITION

Debaters attempt to support or to defeat a topic stated as a proposition. Propositions are grouped under three main types according to purpose.

Because of its importance in determining the scope of the debate, a proposition must be carefully worded.

Types of Propositions

As you listen to different kinds of political, legal, and social debates, you will see that debates differ depending on their propositions. Propositions are grouped into three types according to purpose: (1) to establish a fact, (2) to establish or change a belief, or (3) to recommend a policy.

Propositions Affirming a Fact. Propositions that affirm a fact determine what is true or false. This type of proposition is most common in courts of law where the prosecution tries to prove such propositions as "Anita Jones is not legally bound by the terms of the contract"; "Chris Smith is guilty of shoplifting clothes from the Plaza Department Store"; or "Tom Green is the legal owner of the 1987 automobile in question." Debaters of a proposition of fact search out reasons and evidence to prove or disprove the proposition.

Propositions Establishing or Changing a Belief. Propositions that seek to establish or to change a belief state the relative merit of a person, place, or thing. Propositions of belief always include evaluative words such as *effective, good, worthy, better,* or their opposites. "*Resolved,* That Parker High has the best football team in the state"; "*Resolved,* That Mrs. George is an effective leader"; and "*Resolved,* That computer language is easier to master than Latin" are examples of propositions of belief. Although the debaters can set up criteria for "best," "effective," or "easier" and can measure the subjects against those criteria, there is no way of verifying the findings—the result is a matter of judgment, not a matter of fact.

Propositions Recommending a Policy. Propositions that recommend a policy determine what action should be taken. "*Resolved,* That solar energy research should be significantly increased"; "*Resolved,* That the United States should adopt a national health insurance program for all citizens"; and "*Resolved,* That unemployment benefits should not continue indefinitely for people out of work" all focus on a specific plan of action that is to be considered by the debaters. The inclusion of the word *should* in propositions of policy makes this type of proposition the easiest to recognize and the easiest to phrase. By far the greatest number of propositions facing debaters in real world settings are propositions of policy.

Wording Propositions

Well-worded debate propositions meet three tests.

Burden of Proof. The proposition must be worded to give the "burden of proof" to the affirmative. State the proposition in a way that forces those in favor of changing an idea, an institution, or a current policy to speak first. For example, the proposition "*Resolved,* That the federal income tax should be abolished" is stated correctly because abolishing the tax would be a change from current policy. If, on the other hand, the proposition were worded "*Resolved,* That the federal income tax should be continued," it would be incorrect. The burden of proof would be on the wrong side.

"We are certainly not sending them two dollars for a transcript of that!"

When a formal debate deteriorates into a shouting match, it is apparent to everyone that the participants have run out of logical arguments.

Suppose you wanted to debate the issue of whether to maintain your high-school football program. How would you word the proposition for this issue? The following wording would be incorrect: *"Resolved,* That Murray High School should maintain its football program." This wording does not propose a change. However, if you said, *"Resolved,* That the Murray High School football program should be abolished" (or some similar word for *abolished*), then you would be placing the burden of proof properly on the side favoring change. Placing the burden of proof on the affirmative is by far the most important criterion for a successful debate proposition.

One Topic. The proposition should contain only one topic. The proposition *"Resolved,* That the Murray High School football and basketball programs should be abolished" is incorrect because it contains two topics. Either topic (the football program or the basketball program) is debatable—but both cannot be debated at the same time.

Clarity. The meaning of the words used in the proposition should be clear to debaters and listeners alike. Very often debaters come up with wordings that are vague or difficult to understand. For instance, the proposition *"Resolved,* That qualifications for welfare recipients should be reevaluated" is not clearly stated. The words "should be reevaluated" give no idea of what the affirmative side has in mind. The word "reevaluated" needs to be replaced with a term that specifies the reevaluation, such as "broadened" or "more restrictive."

PREPARING YOURSELF FOR DEBATE

Once your team has a well-worded proposition, you will need to gather information to support your position (see Chapter 10 for more on gathering information). In addition to finding information, your preparation will include discovering the key issues and finding reasons and evidence.

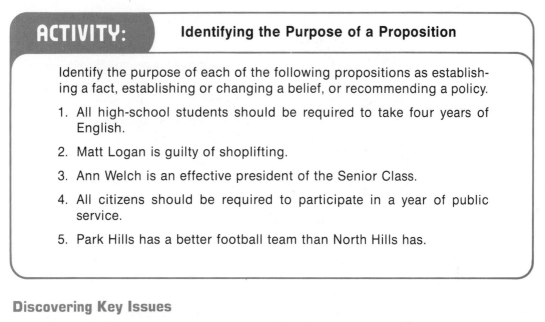

Identify the purpose of each of the following propositions as establishing a fact, establishing or changing a belief, or recommending a policy.

1. All high-school students should be required to take four years of English.

2. Matt Logan is guilty of shoplifting.

3. Ann Welch is an effective president of the Senior Class.

4. All citizens should be required to participate in a year of public service.

5. Park Hills has a better football team than North Hills has.

Discovering Key Issues

In debate, **issues** are key questions that must be answered to determine who wins the debate. Issues take the form of questions, because issues are themselves neither affirmative nor negative. For example, suppose you were planning to debate the proposition of policy *"Resolved, That law enforcement agencies should be given greater freedom in investigation and prosecution of crime."* Since a proposition of policy implies both a problem and

Here, team members are preparing for a debate by discussing their proposition and gathering reasons that justify their position.

a solution, the two key issues could be worded as follows: (1) Do present conditions create significant problems that cannot be solved under the status quo? and (2) Will the suggested policy (giving law enforcement agencies greater freedom to investigate and prosecute crime) solve the problems?

The following example shows how these two broad issues might be broken down into a series of more specific issues (questions).

Proposition: Resolved, That law enforcement agencies should be given greater freedom in the investigation and prosecution of crime.

I. Do present conditions create significant problems?
   A. To what extent are law enforcement agencies hampered in their investigation and prosecution of crime?
   B. What potential harms come from current restrictions?
   C. What are the limits of an individual's rights?
   D. What criteria are used to determine when current restrictions are too strict?
   E. Can these problems be solved under the status quo?
II. Would greater freedom for law enforcement agencies solve the problems?
   A. Would the plan for greater freedom be practical?
   B. Would greater freedom be the best way of solving the problems?

The Proof

In a debate, proof consists of the reasons and evidence given to answer the questions that make up the key issues.

Reasons. **Reasons** are statements that justify the proposition. As you conduct your research, you should find both affirmative and negative reasons, regardless of which side you are on. You will find that knowing the reasons for the opposition's point of view will help you strengthen your own case by making you aware of the evidence that may be used against your argument. For example, if you were debating the proposition that greater freedom should be given to law enforcement agencies, you would likely end up with many of the following reasons for and against the issues.

Issue: Is there a problem?

Affirmative Reasons:
1. Law enforcement agencies are hampered because recent Supreme Court decisions have unduly restricted them in their investigation and prosecution of crime.
2. Law enforcement agencies should be given greater freedom because judicial restrictions have caused much of the increase in crime.
3. Law enforcement agencies should be given greater freedom because criminal suspects are able to take advantage of technicalities in the present law to escape trial and judgment by a jury of their peers.

Negative Reasons:
1. Law enforcement agencies are not unduly restricted in their investigation and prosecution of crime.
2. Judicial restrictions have very little to do with the crime rate.
3. Suspects and defendants who profit are taking advantage of rights guaranteed by the Constitution.

Issue: Would greater freedom solve the problems?

Affirmative Reasons:
1. Greater freedom would solve many problems by allowing more evidence to be gathered and put before juries.
2. Greater freedom would solve the problems because it would lead to more convictions, which in turn would reverse the alarmingly high crime rate.
3. Greater freedom would solve the problems without creating new problems.

Negative Reasons:
1. Those who commit crimes can be convicted within the framework of the present system if law enforcement agencies respect the law in collecting evidence.
2. Greater freedom would have little effect on crime.
3. Greater freedom would give law enforcement agencies too much power, which some officials would be tempted to abuse.

    Evidence. Although you need good reasons, reasons alone are not enough to prepare you to debate. You also need good evidence. **Evidence** includes the facts and opinions given to support each reason. While you are gathering information, look for examples, statistics, and quotations that support the reasons you have listed.

    When you find material that you believe can be useful as evidence, write it on note cards following the guidelines discussed on pages 227–28 in Chapter 10. For example, you might create the following note card for a debate on giving greater freedom to law enforcement agencies.

UNDUE RESTRICTIONS

    According to William Long, Superior Court Judge, King County, Washington, the question of unlawful searches and seizures "has become so highly technical that an officer who goes into a hotel room with a search warrant for one piece of evidence and finds something else can't use that other evidence. It's suppressed, so the criminal can go free."

                    "How Much Crime Can America Take?"
                    U.S. News and World Report,
                    April 10, 1964, p. 66.

Before using this quotation as evidence, you would make sure that it meets the following tests:

1. *Is the evidence recent enough to be relevant to today's problems?* The more out of date the evidence is, the more irrelevant it is likely to be to a current debate. For instance, the quotation in *U.S. News and World Report* is dated 1964. In the many years since this quotation was made, a number of changes have occurred in the field of criminal law.

2. *Is the evidence well documented?* You need to know where the evidence came from and who said it. The quotation from *U.S. News and World Report* is well documented.

3. *Is the source reliable?* You need to know whether the source can be believed. *U.S. News and World Report,* the source of the article, is a widely quoted, reliable national magazine. Because the source of the quotation is a Superior Court Judge of Washington, he is a reliable source of information on matters of law.

4. *Is the evidence objective?* You need to determine whether the evidence is inclined to be partial to one side or another of an issue. For the quotation given in the example, you would need to determine whether William Long had an objective viewpoint on the issue.

ACTIVITY: Writing a Proposition for a Debate

Write a proposition for a debate.

1. List potential issues (subquestions) under the two key issues of problem and solution that are relevant to your debate proposition.

2. List four affirmative and four negative reasons under your proposition. (These reasons are likely to relate to one or the other of the issues—see pages 450–451 for examples.)

3. Prepare fifteen evidence cards to be turned in to your teacher. Record your information according to the guidelines suggested in this chapter.

THE CONSTRUCTIVE SPEECH

Your next step in preparing for debate is working with members of your team to establish your **constructive speech,** which builds an argument for an affirmative or a negative case. A **case** is made up of the arguments and evidence on which a team bases its stand on a given proposition.

Affirmative Case

The **affirmative case** presents reasons and evidence that indicate a problem with the present system and that show why the action stated in the

The affirmative side begins the debate. Only if the affirmative presents a *prima facie* case, giving valid reasons for changing the status quo, can the debate continue.

proposition offers the best solution to that problem. Because the affirmative always has the burden of proof, the affirmative argument needs to present a *prima facie* case. A **prima facie case** is one that contains sufficient evidence to win a debate if the other side presented no argument. In other words, a *prima facie* case convinces a judge that the affirmative argument is valid. If the affirmative side cannot build a *prima facie* case, that is, if the affirmative argument does not provide enough reasons for changing the status quo, then there is no need for negative argument and consequently no reason for debate.

Will you be able to use all the reasons and evidence you find in your research? Probably not. In formal debate, the first affirmative speech is limited to eight or ten minutes, depending upon the format used. When you subtract the minute or two necessary for an introduction and conclusion, you will have only about six to eight minutes left to state and prove your points, enough time for thorough presentation of only two to four reasons. For practice debates in class, your time limits are likely to be even shorter.

After you have gathered reasons and evidence, you will want to consider two of the major patterns of organization debaters use: the traditional problem-solution pattern and the comparative-advantages pattern.

Problem-Solution Pattern. The **problem-solution pattern** (also called "need-plan pattern") organizes information to demonstrate that the problem cannot be solved by the status quo and to show that the proposal stated in the proposition will solve the problem practically and beneficially. The problem-solution pattern has at least three parts that attempt to prove (1) that a significant problem exists, (2) that adopting the proposal will help solve the problem, and (3) that adopting the proposal is the best way of solving the problem. Such an organization might look like this:

Resolved, That law enforcement agencies should be given greater freedom in investigation and prosecution of crime.

I. Restrictive Supreme Court rulings on law enforcement agencies have resulted in an increase in the crime rate.
II. Our plan for greater freedom would work to solve this problem.
III. Our plan for greater freedom would be the best way to solve this problem.

Comparative-Advantages Pattern. The **comparative-advantages pattern** organizes information to demonstrate that the proposal would have significant advantages over the status quo. When you see no harm resulting from current actions, you may support a proposition solely on the basis of its superiority to the status quo. For example, if you are able to show your friend who takes the long route to school that another route is shorter, has fewer traffic lights, and will enable him to get to school faster, your friend may be inclined to try the route because it is comparatively advantageous. The question then is not whether something is wrong with the long route, but whether the suggested route is really significantly better.

The comparative-advantages pattern does not relieve you of the burden of considering whether a problem exists. However, instead of identifying a "need for a change" (a serious problem that cannot be solved by the status quo) and then giving a solution, you would suggest a new proposal whose benefits would be so significant that the plan should be adopted whether a problem exists or not. For example, "giving significantly greater freedom to crime-fighting agencies" may contribute to the protection of all citizens (a comparative advantage) even if restrictions on these agencies are not considered a serious problem.

The comparative-advantages pattern differs from the problem-solution pattern in two important ways. In the comparative-advantages pattern, (1) the plan is always presented and discussed in detail immediately, and (2) the plan focuses on the two, three, or four advantages of the proposition over the status quo. Here is a typical organization that follows the comparative-advantages pattern.

Resolved, That law enforcement agencies should be given greater freedom in the investigation and prosecution of crime.
I. [Detailed explanation of the specific points of the proposal are given here.]
II. The proposal would be comparatively advantageous to the status quo for the following reasons:
   A. Greater freedom would contribute to protection of all citizens by lowering the crime rate.
   B. Greater freedom would create more effective deterrence to crime, thereby helping to prevent young people from pursuing criminal activities.

The comparative-advantages pattern allows you to place emphasis where emphasis is needed: on what the plan will do, on how much better than the status quo it will be, and on whether it can or will create problems as well as advantages. In arguing comparative advantages, you must remember that you will have to prove that the advantages you cite will be significant. For example, your friend is not likely to try to develop a whole new set of habits in order to save fifteen seconds on his thirty-minute drive to school. Fifteen seconds is not enough of a time savings to call for that change.

The organization you select will always be based on the reasons and evidence you have gathered.

Negative Case

The negative side's main goals are to prove the negative constructive case and to show the weakness of the affirmative's argument. The **negative case** gives reasons and evidence that (1) act as straight refutation of the affirmative case, (2) defend the status quo, or (3) present a counterplan. The organization of negative speeches depends on which of these three courses the speech will take. Although you may decide to change your approach if the affirmative side presents an argument that differs from what you had expected, most of the time you will make your choice before the debate begins, depending on the evidence you have discovered.

Straight-Refutation Approach. **Straight refutation** means that the entire negative case will be a denial of each affirmative argument stated. In other words, the negative side denies whatever reasons the affirmative team presents.

In arguing against the affirmative case, the negative side can refute the affirmative argument, defend the status quo, or present a counterplan.

For example, study the following two outlines, both of which would be suitable for a debate on the proposition of giving greater freedom to law enforcement agencies. The first outline presents the affirmative case. The second presents the negative case using the straight-refutation approach.

Affirmative Case:
  I. Restrictive Supreme Court rulings on law enforcement agencies have resulted in a continued increase in the crime rate.
  II. Our plan for greater freedom would work to solve this problem.
  III. Our plan for greater freedom would be the best way to solve this problem.

Negative Case Using Straight Refutation:
  I. Supreme Court rulings have not been the cause of the increase in the crime rate.
  II. Giving greater freedom to law enforcement agencies would not work to solve this problem.
  III. Giving greater freedom to law enforcement agencies would create more problems.

Defense of the Status Quo. The negative team that elects to defend the status quo will explain it and will show either how it is already meeting the alleged problems or how it could meet them. The negative side's defense of the status quo against the affirmative case for giving more freedom to law enforcement agencies could be organized in the following way.

Negative Case Defending the Status Quo:
  I. Under the present system police have the tools to enable them to cope with the increase in the crime rate.
  II. The present system works better than would giving greater freedom to law enforcement agencies.
  III. The present system has more benefits and fewer disadvantages than would giving greater freedom to law enforcement agencies.

The defense of the status quo has a major advantage. The negative team takes a positive stance and therefore stands for something rather than simply being against whatever the affirmative says. When the negative side defends the status quo, the affirmative is often forced to go on the defensive. Instead of supporting its own case, the affirmative side must attack the constructive arguments of the negative side.

The major disadvantage of defending the status quo is that doing so calls for more skill on the part of the negative side. This approach requires the negative side to construct an affirmative argument for the status quo, as well as a negative argument against the proposition for change.

Counterplan. A **counterplan** is the presentation of a different solution. Ordinarily, only the solution suggested in the proposition is debated. However, if the negative side agrees that a problem exists, it has the option of presenting a solution that differs substantially from the affirmative's proposition. The debate then becomes a clash between the relative merits of the

Rather than refute the affirmative side's proposition, the negative side may choose to present an alternative proposition, or *counterplan*.

two solutions rather than between whether or not a need for a change exists. The first negative argument usually presents the counterplan and shows how it will meet the need identified by the affirmative.

Negative Case Counterplan:
I. The negative side agrees that there is an increase in the crime rate.
II. The best solution to this problem would be to involve more citizens in crime prevention programs.
III. Increased citizen participation in crime prevention would work better to lower the crime rate than would giving law enforcement agencies greater freedom.
IV. Increased citizen participation in crime prevention would provide more benefits and fewer disadvantages than would giving law enforcement agencies greater freedom.

The advantage of the counterplan is that it may catch the affirmative side off guard. In effect, when the negative side proposes a counterplan, the first affirmative speech has been wasted. Although neutralizing the opening affirmative reason may look like a big advantage to inexperienced debaters, it often is not, because this approach reduces the debate to the issues of which plan works best and has fewest disadvantages. Because the affirmative side determines the needs, the affirmative argument is usually better suited to those needs. Despite this weakness, however, once in a while the negative side does elect to use the counterplan. More often than not, if the negative team members believe that the status quo has weaknesses, they are better off presenting a minor repair than defending the superiority of the status quo.

Your choice of approach will depend on the material you have. Most of the time, you will use either straight refutation or defense of the status quo.

Selecting Reasons Suited to Different Patterns of Argument

Suppose you are on the affirmative side debating the proposition:

"*Resolved,* That the United States should substantially reduce its foreign policy commitments." In your research you have discovered the numbered reasons listed after these directions. First, select the reasons you would choose if you were going to use a problem-solution pattern. Then select the reasons you would choose if you were going to use a comparative-advantages pattern. Finally, imagine that you are on the negative side and that you are using the straight-refutation pattern. List the reasons you would use against the reasons you selected for the comparative-advantages pattern.

1. Our foreign policy commitments have led to the loss of valuable friendships and prestige.

2. Our foreign policy commitments have weakened our nation's defense.

3. Our foreign policy commitments have not significantly aided under-developed nations.

4. Our foreign policy commitments have not deterred aggression.

5. Our foreign policy commitments have weakened regional alliances.

6. Reducing commitments would better enable us to meet the goals of our foreign policy as set forth by the administration.

7. Reducing commitments would allow us to strengthen ties with traditional allies.

8. Reducing commitments would result in fewer problems than present policy causes.

REFUTATION AND REBUTTAL

Refutation means attacking the ideas of the opposition. **Rebuttal** means rebuilding your ideas after they have been attacked.

What Can Be Refuted?

No matter which side you have taken in a debate, you may refute your opposition's quantity of evidence, quality of evidence, and reasoning from the evidence.

Quantity of Evidence. Any reason that is presented by either side in a debate must be supported with evidence. Sometimes debaters give very little or even no supporting evidence. In such cases, the opposing team may simply refute an argument on that basis—lack of evidence. For example, imagine that a debater gives little or no evidence to support the following reason: "Supreme Court decisions have unduly restricted law enforcement agencies." An opposing debater could refute that reason by saying "The affirmative has asserted that Supreme Court decisions have unduly restricted law enforcement agencies. We remind the affirmative that they have the burden of proof and until we hear evidence to support the assertion, we need not reply to it."

Quality of Evidence. A better method of refutation is to attack the quality of the evidence presented. If sheer number of evidence cards were the most important consideration, the team with the greater number of cards would win every time. A judge would need only to count cards and would not have to weigh arguments. In fact, though, there is often no direct relationship between the number of evidence cards and the quality of proof. One statement by a law enforcement officer about the effect of court decisions on crime could be worth far more than interviews with a dozen citizens gathered at random.

Reasoning from the Evidence. The most effective form of refutation is to attack the opposition's reasoning from the evidence. Each argument presented in a debate is composed of at least three elements: (1) evidence or data from which a conclusion is drawn, (2) the conclusion itself, and (3) the reasoning that links the evidence and the conclusion. Most debates involve four common types of reasoning: generalization, causation, analogy, and sign.

Building an argument, like building a house, means providing strong support. Each of your reasons must be upheld by sound evidence.

1. **Generalization.** A **generalization** is a conclusion based on one or more specific instances. For example, imagine that you noticed in math class that Heather had a pocket calculator, Tim had a pocket calculator, and Tanya had a pocket calculator. If you drew the conclusion that all your classmates had pocket calculators, you would be reasoning by generalization.

In debating the proposition about giving law enforcement agencies more freedom, your opponent might argue that for the past twenty-five years most Supreme Court decisions related to investigation and prosecution of crime have restricted law enforcement agencies. To support the statement, your opponent might cite three examples: the Mapp decision, the Mallory decision, and the Miranda decision. Thus, your opponent would be generalizing, using specific instances—the specific cases—as the basis for a conclusion—that most Supreme Court decisions have restricted law enforcement agencies.

You refute such a generalization by asking three questions.

1. *Are enough instances cited?* Two or three examples are seldom enough to draw a generalization.
2. *Are the specific instances typical of all possible instances?* If examples are not typical, they do not provide a sound basis for a generalization.
3. *Are there any negative instances, instances that prove the opposite?* If negative instances can be found, they may disprove the generalization.

2. **Causation.** A **causation** argument provides a conclusion that is a direct result (effect) of one or more given sources or conditions. For example, imagine that your friend Heather told you that she studies math at least one hour a night. If you drew the conclusion that Heather will surely get a good grade in math, you would be reasoning by causation. Your reasoning may likely be sound because studying at least one hour a night often helps to produce good grades.

In another instance, your opponent might argue that the crime rate has risen dramatically *as a result* of Supreme Court decisions restricting law enforcement agencies. Thus, your opponent would be presuming a causal relationship between Supreme Court actions and the crime rate. However, a rise in the crime rate does not necessarily mean that there is a causal relationship between that rise and the Supreme Court decisions.

To refute a causal relationship, ask the following two questions.

1. *Are the items of evidence important enough to cause the conclusion?* If the effect can occur without the information being cited as evidence, then that information is not an important cause.
2. *Do other factors really cause the effect?* If other sources or conditions seem more important in bringing about the effect, then you can question the causal relationship of the information presented as evidence.

3. **Analogy.** An argument can be based on an **analogy,** which is a comparison of something with a similar event, state, or set of circumstances. For example, imagine that a classmate, Tim, has been elected to the National Honor Society. As you think about Tim's background, you recall that he is a junior, has a B average, and is active both in Glee Club and on the school

newspaper. If you drew the conclusion that another classmate, Tanya, ought to have been elected to the National Honor Society because her background is similar to Tim's, you would be reasoning by analogy.

During a debate on crime, your opponent might argue that when law enforcement agencies in another country similar to ours (perhaps England or Canada) were given increased freedom, the crime rate there went down. If your opponent reasoned that the United States should give increased freedom to law enforcement agencies because the crime rate decreased when England or Canada relaxed controls over their law enforcement agencies, your opponent would be reasoning by analogy.

To refute an analogy, ask the following two questions.

1. *Are the subjects that are being compared similar in all important ways?* In this case, are criminal activity and the legal system in the United States similar to criminal activity and the legal system found in England or Canada? If subjects do not have significant similarities, then they are not really comparable.

2. *Are any of the differences between the subjects important to the conclusion?* Do the crime rate and legal system in the United States differ in important ways from the crime rate and legal system in England or Canada? If so, then an analogy drawn between the United States and either of the other two countries may not be sound.

4. **Sign.** A **sign argument** draws a conclusion based on certain signs or indicators. For example, imagine that you see that your brother's eyes are watering and that his nose is running. If you drew the conclusion that he has a cold, you would be reasoning by sign. In a debate on crime rate, your opponent might argue using signs by saying that the increase in the percentage of unsolved crimes is a sign of undue restrictions on law enforcement agencies.

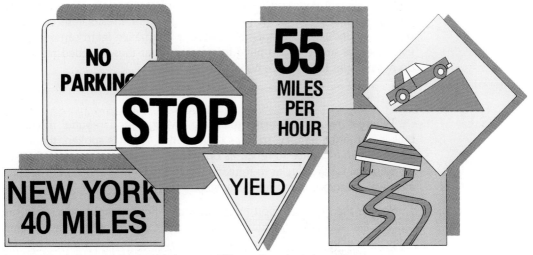

Just as road signs indicate driving conditions, the signs in a *sign argument* indicate specific conclusions.

To refute a sign argument, ask the following questions.

1. *Do the signs given as evidence always indicate the conclusion?* Do watering eyes and a running nose always indicate a cold? If not, they are not reliable indicators of the conclusion.

2. *Are enough signs present?* Are the two signs, watering eyes and a running nose, enough to predict a cold? If not, the presence of the signs does not necessarily imply the conclusion.

3. *Are there contradictory signs?* Is your brother alert and energetic? If so, he may not have a cold.

How to Refute

Refutation means attacking an argument. In a debate, your refutation must be as organized as your planned speeches. Think of refutation as units of argument that are organized according to the following four steps.

1. *State clearly and concisely the argument you are going to refute.* For example, you might say, "The affirmative has argued that Supreme Court decisions have unduly restricted law enforcement agencies in the investigation of crime."

2. *State what you will prove.* You must tell the audience how you plan to proceed so that they will be able to follow your thinking. For example, you might say, "We on the negative side are going to argue that although law enforcement agencies are indeed restricted, there is no reason to believe that the restrictions are either undue or unnecessary."

3. *Present the proof completely with documented evidence.* For example, you might present facts, statistics, and quotations to back up your assertion that the restrictions are neither undue nor unnecessary.

4. *Draw a conclusion.* You cannot rely on the audience or the judge to draw the proper conclusion for you. Do not go on to another argument before you have drawn your conclusion. For example, you might say, "Therefore, we can see that although the police are restricted, the restrictions can hardly be labeled undue or unnecessary. Until the affirmative team can offer more evidence, we are going to have to conclude that these needed restrictions do not hamper law enforcement agencies."

Rebuttal

Whereas *refutation* means attacking an argument, *rebuttal* means rebuilding an argument. As soon as the negative side has spoken, the affirmative is given a chance to repair its original points that were attacked.

Rebuttal is very similar to refutation in form. To help make your rebuttal effective, present it in the following steps.

1. *Restate the argument you made originally.* For example, you might say, "In our first speech we argued that Supreme Court decisions have unduly restricted law enforcement agencies in the investigation of crime."

2. *State what your opponent said against your original point.* For example, you might say, "The negative argued that although law enforcement agencies

The other team's job is to *refute*, or tear down, your argument; then your team's job is to *rebut*, or rebuild, it.

are indeed restricted, there is no reason to believe that the restrictions are either undue or unnecessary."

3. *State your position on your opponent's attack.* For example, you might say, "I think you will see that the evidence the negative side has presented is far outweighed by evidence from all over the country."

4. *Present the proof completely with documented evidence.* Use facts, statistics, examples, details, and quotations to support statements you make in rebuttal. For example, you might give a recent quotation from a police commissioner stating that court decisions have hampered efforts to indict and prosecute felons.

5. *Draw a conclusion.* For example, you might say, "Therefore, we can see that even though the negative was able to present some isolated evidence in support of their attack, the bulk of the evidence supports our point that court decisions have unduly restricted law enforcement agencies."

THE FLOW SHEET

Listening is a critical debate skill. Your ability to debate effectively depends greatly on your immediate understanding of each speech. Take notes on what each speaker says, and in parentheses, remind yourself of what you will say in reference to each point the opposition makes.

Make careful outline notes of each speech on what is called a **flow sheet.** Get an 8½" by 14" legal-sized pad and turn the pad sideways. Draw eight columns on the page. Then take notes on each speech as it is given. Using complete or nearly complete sentences to eliminate the possibility of misquoting, write each of the reasons presented, and include a sketch of the evidence in abbreviated form. You will find that getting each speech down on paper in a separate column will help you see what has happened to each of the major arguments throughout the debate.

SAMPLE FLOW SHEET

PROPOSITION: *Resolved,* That law enforcement agencies should be given greater freedom in investigation and prosecution of crime.

1st Aff. Constructive	1st Neg. Constructive	2nd Aff. Constructive	2nd Neg. Constructive
I. Restrictive Supr. Court rulings on law enforcement have resulted in continued increase of major crime.	Status quo is okay.	Supr. Court rulings show status quo not effective.	Aff. plan is not effective. Disadvantages: 1. Reduce individual freedom.
A. Violent crime up 200% since 1961.	1. Rise in crime rate not linked to Supr. Court rulings.	1. Supr. Court rulings linked directly to 200% increase.	2. Threat to civil liberties. 3. Increase court backlog. Disadvantages 1, 2 and 3 outweigh the possible decrease in street crime.
B. Crime up 25% in past 5 years.	2. Rise in crime rate due to increase in population.	2. Crime rate has grown 8 times faster than population.	
II. Giving greater freedom would solve these problems. A. Police can work more effectively with fewer restrictions.	1. Police will be tempted to abuse authority.	1. Police work better without Supr. Court rulings.	
B. Crime rate will decrease.	2. Crime rate will increase due to more arrests for minor crimes.	2. Crime rate will fall: no link with number of arrests.	
III. Giving greater freedom would be the best solution to the problem. A. It would reduce street crime.	Citizens crime watch would be better solution.	1. Crime watch is not enough.	
B. It would reduce the number of victims.	∅	2. Argument for reduced number of victims — dropped.	

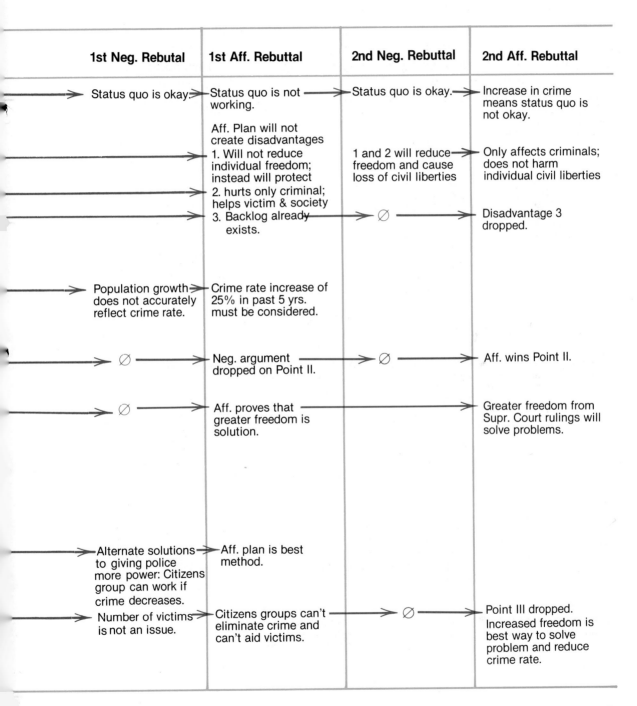

1st Neg. Rebutal	1st Aff. Rebuttal	2nd Neg. Rebuttal	2nd Aff. Rebuttal
Status quo is okay.	Status quo is not working.	Status quo is okay.	Increase in crime means status quo is not okay.
	Aff. Plan will not create disadvantages 1. Will not reduce individual freedom; instead will protect	1 and 2 will reduce freedom and cause loss of civil liberties	Only affects criminals; does not harm individual civil liberties
	2. hurts only criminal; helps victim & society		
	3. Backlog already exists.	∅	Disadvantage 3 dropped.
Population growth does not accurately reflect crime rate.	Crime rate increase of 25% in past 5 yrs. must be considered.		
∅	Neg. argument dropped on Point II.	∅	Aff. wins Point II.
∅	Aff. proves that greater freedom is solution.		Greater freedom from Supr. Court rulings will solve problems.
Alternate solutions to giving police more power: Citizens group can work if crime decreases.	Aff. plan is best method.		
Number of victims is not an issue.	Citizens groups can't eliminate crime and can't aid victims.	∅	Point III dropped. Increased freedom is best way to solve problem and reduce crime rate.

Identifying Arguments and Questioning Their Reasoning

Identify the following arguments as generalization, causation, analogy, or sign. Then, for each of the four arguments, write two questions that you need to ask about that kind of reasoning.

1. After our neighbor painted his house, the leaves on the tree in front of our house started to turn brown. The paint must have had some poison in it.

2. Most of us got our lowest golf scores on the fifth hole. The fifth hole must be the easiest.

3. We think it's the measles. He has a fever and has broken out in a rash.

4. The plan worked well for North High's junior class. It will probably work for our junior class.

DEBATE FORMATS

Although a debate can follow any format, there are three that should be mentioned. These are traditional debate, cross-examination debate, and Lincoln-Douglas debate.

Traditional Debate. Traditional debate involves two affirmative speakers and two negative speakers, who deliver prepared speeches within set time limits, such as those in the following typical schedule.

Constructive Speeches		*Rebuttal Speeches*	
1st Affirmative	10 min.	1st Negative	5 min.
1st Negative	10 min.	1st Affirmative	5 min.
2nd Affirmative	10 min.	2nd Negative	5 min.
2nd Negative	10 min.	2nd Affirmative	5 min.

Cross-Examination Debate. Cross-examination debate takes place between two affirmative speakers and two negative speakers. This form of debate is more direct than traditional debate, because it gives the participants the opportunity to question their opponents. In addition, the give and take between speakers provides an enjoyable, lively exchange of ideas. Although time limits may vary, the following format is frequently used.

1st Affirmative	8-minute constructive speech
2nd Negative	3-minute questioning of 1st Affirmative
1st Negative	8-minute constructive speech
1st Affirmative	3-minute questioning of 1st Negative
2nd Affirmative	8-minute constructive speech

1st Negative	3-minute questioning of 2nd Affirmative
2nd Negative	8-minute constructive speech
2nd Affirmative	3-minute questioning of 2nd negative
1st Negative	4-minute rebuttal speech and summary
1st Affirmative	4-minute rebuttal speech and summary
2nd Negative	4-minute rebuttal speech and summary
2nd Affirmative	4-minute rebuttal speech and summary

Lincoln-Douglas Debate. **Lincoln-Douglas debate** is a form of debate in which only one speaker represents each of the opposing sides and only values propositions are debated. The name of this style of debating comes from a series of oratorical clashes that took place between Abraham Lincoln and Stephen A. Douglas in the Illinois senatorial race in 1858. Because the Lincoln-Douglas format focuses on the skills of individual debaters and takes a shorter period of time than formal debate, it is well suited to classroom practice.

Although Lincoln-Douglas debate takes much less time than traditional debate or cross-examination debate, it includes all the elements of argument, refutation, and rebuttal practiced in the longer formats. Here is the time schedule of a typical Lincoln-Douglas debate.

Affirmative	6-minute constructive speech
Negative	3-minute questioning of the Affirmative
Negative	7-minute constructive speech and refutation
Affirmative	3-minute questioning of the Negative
Affirmative	4-minute rebuttal speech
Negative	6-minute rebuttal speech and summary
Affirmative	3-minute rebuttal speech and summary

In this schedule each speaker has thirteen minutes of speaking time and a cross-examination period to ask and to answer questions on the constructive speeches.

Time schedules and even some of the elements of Lincoln-Douglas debate differ slightly from situation to situation. In some cases no rebuttal speeches are given; in others the audience is permitted to question the speakers. One of the most positive features of the Lincoln-Douglas debate is its adaptability to varied circumstances and requirements.

Lincoln-Douglas debate deals with values debate, not policy. The word *should* never appears in a values resolution, because the affirmative side is not called upon to prove the need for a change in the status quo. Values debate simply calls upon the affirmative side to argue the truth of its proposition and the negative side to argue the falsity of that proposition. While the arguments in formal debate rely heavily on large amounts of factual evidence, the arguments in Lincoln-Douglas debate place more emphasis on evidence consisting of the logical analysis of philosophical issues.

There are four basic types of values argued in Lincoln-Douglas debate: moral, utilitarian, social, and aesthetic. Any combination of these values may be used in either defending or denying a values resolution. For example, in the proposition "*Resolved*, That war is a moral way to settle disputes between nations," the debaters may wish to argue the morality of war, the utility of war, or the societal necessity of war. In the proposition "*Resolved, That protection of the environment is more desirable than economic development*," the debaters may wish to argue the morality of endangering the environment, the usefulness of the environment as opposed to the usefulness of development, society's need to grow economically, and the aesthetic values of preserving nature.

Though Lincoln-Douglas debate is values debate, it has several similarities to policy debate. Lincoln-Douglas debate includes argument, refutation, rebuttal, and cross-examination. Also, arguments must be proven by establishing logical connections between reasons and evidence.

In the original Lincoln-Douglas debates, Abraham Lincoln's reliance on logic, quick wit, and sharp questioning made him a formidable opponent.

While similar in some ways, Lincoln-Douglas debate and policy debate have significant differences. One chief difference lies in the underlying philosophy of the two forms of debate. The appeal of the Lincoln-Douglas form lies in its philosophical approach to debating. Because values are argued rather than proven (what is moral is always debatable and cannot be proven), the debaters are not seeking solutions or new policies to enact. Instead, they test the truth of questions concerning values. Such testing promotes exploration and increased understanding of our values systems and beliefs.

The Debate Brief

The **debate brief** is a complete outline of the affirmative and the negative cases. It is written prior to the debate and includes all the reasons each side can present and an outline of the evidence that can be cited for each reason. Each of the items in the outline is written as a complete sentence.

ACTIVITY: Writing a Debate Brief

Choose a format for a debate. Decide on a proposition. Establish the affirmative and negative sides; then write a debate brief that identifies the specific arguments each side would present.

JUDGING DEBATES

The very nature of the debate process makes judging difficult. Debate is not like a basketball game in which a player gets two points for a field goal and one point for a foul shot and the team with the higher total wins. Debate is more like swimming, skating, and gymnastics, in which a panel of judges gives points indicating each judge's estimation of how well each performer met a standard. Criteria for judgment are fairly standard, but applying the criteria is difficult, and two or more judges may disagree in their decisions. In a debate that has only one judge, that judge may rule that the affirmative case wins, whereas another judge might have ruled that the negative side had the stronger arguments.

Ordinarily, traditional debates are judged by determining which team won the key issues. Let's first look at a traditional debate in which the affirmative team uses a problem-solution pattern. For the affirmative team to win, it will have to prove the following points.

1. That there is a significant problem
2. That the affirmative side's proposition will solve the problem
3. That the proposition offers the best solution

For the negative team to win, it needs to defeat only one of the affirmative side's three issues. The negative side can win by presenting one of the following arguments.

1. That no problem exists
2. That the affirmative side's proposition would not solve the problem
3. That the affirmative side's proposition is either not the best way to solve the problem or will cause new problems

Now, look at a traditional debate in which the affirmative side uses a comparative-advantages pattern. For the affirmative team to win, it must make the following points.

1. That its proposition offers significant advantages over the status quo
2. That its proposition will not create significant problems when implemented

For the negative team to win, it needs to defeat only one of the affirmative side's two issues. The negative team can win by presenting one of the arguments on the following page.

1. That the advantages are not significant
2. That significant disadvantages will result

Because the debate focuses on these two issues, the final speakers especially need to concentrate on the issues, making sure that a judge can see their position clearly. In many close debates, neither side actually wins an issue. Instead, the debate is decided by determining which side demonstrated superior skill in debating.

On most ballots each judge is asked to give each debater points for how effective the debater was in regard to each of six criteria: analysis, evidence, reasoning, organization, refutation, and presentation. If no issues are decisively won or lost, the team with the greater number of speaker's points is judged the winner of the debate.

For each debate, the judge or judges will complete a ballot. A ballot usually provides a place to insert speaker's points. It also contains sufficient space for comments about each speaker, and of course, it has a place to indicate who won. No one standard ballot exists for all high-school debates. However, the American Forensic Association ballot shown on page 471 is used quite often and provides a representative model of the ballots used in judging most traditional debates in high-school competition.

Lincoln-Douglas debates are judged much the same way traditional debates are. The winner in a Lincoln-Douglas debate is the speaker who earns more points in organization, reasoning, delivery, supporting evidence, and persuasive argumentation of values. The ballot shown at the bottom of page 471 indicates the guidelines and format that judges generally follow in evaluating Lincoln-Douglas debate.

Listening carefully to this debater's rebuttal speech, the judges assess her skills and mark their ballots accordingly.

American Forensic Association Debate Ballot

FORM C

Division _____ Round _____ Room _____ Date _____ Judge _____

Affirmative _____ Negative _____

Check the column on each item which, on the following scale, best describes your evaluation of the speaker's effectiveness:

1—poor	2—fair	3—average	4—excellent	5—superior

1st Affirmative	2nd Affirmative		1st Negative	2nd Negative
1 2 3 4 5	1 2 3 4 5	Analysis Reasoning Evidence Organization Refutation Delivery	1 2 3 4 5	1 2 3 4 5

Total _____ Total _____ Total _____ Total _____

Team Ratings:
AFFIRMATIVE: poor fair average excellent superior
NEGATIVE: poor fair average excellent superior

Rank each debater in order of excellence (1st for best, 2nd for next best, etc.).

COMMENTS:

1st Aff. (name) _____ Rank ( )

_____

_____

2nd Aff. (name) _____ Rank ( )

_____

_____

COMMENTS:

1st Neg. (name) _____ Rank ( )

_____

_____

2nd Neg. (name) _____ Rank ( )

_____

_____

REASONS FOR DECISION

In my opinion, the better debating was done by the _____ (AFFIRMATIVE OR NEGATIVE)

JUDGE'S SIGNATURE _____ SCHOOL _____

Florida Forensics Program
LINCOLN-DOUGLAS DEBATE BALLOT

Round_____ Room _____ Time _____ Date _____ Judge _____

Affirmative (name & code) _____

Negative (name & code) _____

Instructions to Judges

1. Unlike team debate, the resolution to be debated will be a proposition of value, rather than a proposition of policy. Thus, the debaters are encouraged to develop argumentation on conflicting underlying principles to support their positions. To that end, they are *not* responsible for practical applications. There is no *need* for a plan (or for plan attacks).

2. In making your decision, you might ask yourself the following questions:
   a. Which debater persuaded you that his position was more valid? (Which debater communicated more effectively?)
   b. Did the debater support his position appropriately, using logical argumentation throughout, and evidence where necessary?

3. Rate each debater's performance by assigning points to each on the following scale of 0-30.

Poor	Fair	Good	Excellent
0-15	16-20	21-25	26-30

   The points you award must correlate with your decision.

4. Remember, this is debate and not unrelated individual oration.

5. The debate will follow these time limits:

Affirmative constructive	6 minutes
Cross examination by negative	3 minutes
Negative constructive	7 minutes
Affirmative cross-examination	3 minutes
Affirmative rebuttal	4 minutes
Negative rebuttal	6 minutes
Affirmative rebuttal	3 minutes

1 2 3 4 5 (AFFIRMATIVE)		1 2 3 4 5 (NEGATIVE)
	---------- Organization and Development of Ideas ----------	
	-------------- Reasoning and Analysis --------------	
	---------- Delivery (Style and Persuasiveness) ----------	
	Support of ideas (through example, authoritative opinion and/or fact)	
	---------- Clash with opponent's arguments ----------	
	-------------- Argumentation of Values --------------	

AFFIRMATIVE   COMMENTS AND REASONS FOR DECISION   **NEGATIVE**

Total _____ Total _____

In my opinion, the debate was won by _____ upholding (aff) (neg)

Signature of judge _____

Profiles in Communication

Since launching his political career in 1960, Ohio state senator Stanley Aronoff has worked his way up to president pro tempore and floor leader of the majority party. Building such a successful career takes dedication, hard work, and, according to Sen. Aronoff, effective communication skills.

Sen. Aronoff began developing his public speaking skills in high school. Encouraged by his favorite teacher, he participated in school drama productions and student government, both of which helped him develop the confidence to deliver public speeches. He further credits much of his success in politics to his knowledge of debate and his mastery of persuasive speaking techniques—two more areas of expertise that he began developing in high school.

One of the most important speech lessons he has learned is the need to adapt his statements to the audience at hand. "Speaking for television is different from speaking to print journalists or to other politicians during floor debates," Sen. Aronoff reports. For television, short, encapsulated statements are best, he says, because "you can talk for fifteen minutes, but all that will ever get on the air is a twenty-six-second segment." In contrast, when speaking to print journalists, "you can take the time to explain the issues in some detail, knowing that many of your ideas will be reported."

High-school students need not wait to become active in politics. New volunteers may begin by posting signs or doing research. Some may find themselves in speaking situations, such as making phone calls and knocking on doors to campaign for candidates and issues. To develop speaking skills that will help them in these and future political activities, students are advised to take part in student government, speaking competitions, and forensic programs.

Sen. Aronoff believes that "the art of politics is taking complex issues and reducing them to their simplest form." This art, of course, is also a primary communication skill that applies to a number of speaking tasks, such as focusing a discussion on a specific topic, providing clear explanations, and creating logical arguments. Through his public speaking and his many other commitments, Sen. Aronoff pursues "the most gratifying part of being a public servant—accomplishing tasks that are meaningful and are an asset to society."

Judging a Debate

First, imagine that you are judging a debate. What issues would the affirmative side have to win to win the debate? What issues would the negative side have to win? Then listen to a classroom debate and give a decision based on who won the issues. Also, give your evaluation of how each speaker performed according to the six criteria on which speakers are rated: analysis, evidence, reasoning, organization, refutation, and presentation.

GUIDELINES FOR PARTICIPATING IN DEBATE

- Has the proposition been clearly stated?
- Have I researched the topic carefully?
- Have I determined the key issues for the debate?
- Have I developed a case that is consistent with the material?
- Have I prepared a brief of my case?
- Have I anticipated the arguments of my opponent?
- Am I prepared to refute the arguments of my opponent?
- Am I prepared to rebuild the arguments my opponent attacks?
- Have I practiced?

SUMMARY

Debate is a form of decision making in which two or more people prepare and present speeches on opposite sides of a public issue.

The specific purpose of a debate is called a proposition, which clearly states a position on a specific topic. The proposition is phrased to affirm a fact, to create or to change a belief, or to recommend an action that should be taken.

Propositions are worded to give the burden of proof to the affirmative side. Propositions should be clearly worded and should deal with only one topic, which should be controversial.

Issues are the questions whose answers provide information that is vital to resolving the proposition. From the issues, speakers can determine the key reasons for and against the proposition and can form a case. A case consists of the arguments and evidence that a team uses as a foundation for its position.

For the affirmative side, a case may follow a problem-solution pattern or a comparative-advantages pattern. A problem-solution pattern shows the nature and extent of a problem that cannot be solved by the status quo and presents a proposition that will solve the problem in a practical, beneficial way. A comparative-advantages pattern shows that the proposal would be a significant improvement over the status quo.

For the negative side, the case may be straight refutation, denying the truth of what the affirmative side has said; a defense of the status quo, showing that the status quo can solve the problem; or a counterplan, presenting another answer in a plan that differs from that offered by the proposition.

Refutation is the attacking of ideas. Refutation may be based on the amount of evidence, the quality of the evidence, or the reasoning from the evidence. Good refutation follows four steps: stating the argument clearly, stating your position on the argument, presenting proof, and drawing a conclusion.

Rebuttal is the rebuilding of an argument. Good rebuttal follows five steps: restating the original argument, stating the opponent's position, stating your position on your opponent's attack, presenting proof, and drawing a conclusion.

A debate brief is a complete outline of the affirmative case or the negative case or both. The debate brief includes all the reasons given for the case and excerpts of all key evidence in support of the reasons.

Notes for debate are taken in the form of a flow sheet. The outline of each speech should show what the arguments were, what attacks were made against the arguments, what was rebuilt, and what the effects of the attacks and rebuilding were.

Debate can follow any number of formats. The most common formats are traditional, cross-examination, and Lincoln-Douglas.

Debates are judged on the basis of which side gave the best argument concerning the issues and of which side did the better job of debating.

CHAPTER VOCABULARY

Look back through this chapter to find the meaning of each of the following terms. Write each term and its meaning in your communication journal.

- affirmative case
- analogy
- burden of proof
- case
- causation
- comparative-advantages pattern
- constructive speech
- counterplan
- cross-examination
- debate
- debate brief
- evidence
- flow sheet
- generalization
- issues
- Lincoln-Douglas debate
- negative case
  prima facie case
- problem-solution pattern
- proposition
- reasons
- rebuttal
- refutation
- sign argument
- status quo
- straight refutation
- traditional debate

1. What are the three tests for the wording of a debate proposition?

2. The three types of debate propositions are propositions affirming a fact, propositions establishing or changing a belief, and propositions recommending a policy. What is an example of each?

3. What are the two key issues for a proposition recommending a policy?

4. One way an affirmative case can be organized is by the problem-solution pattern. What is another way?

5. One way a negative case can be organized is by the straight-refutation approach. What are two other ways?

6. What is a weakness of the straight-refutation approach?

7. What is the difference between refutation and rebuttal?

8. One method of rebuttal is to criticize the quantity of the evidence. What are two other methods?

9. One common type of reasoning is generalization. What are three other types?

10. What are the five steps of rebuttal?

DISCUSSION QUESTIONS

1. Discuss the reasons why the affirmative goes first in a debate.

2. Discuss the major differences between a traditional case and a comparative-advantages case. When is one superior to the other?

3. Discuss why "defense of the status quo" is likely to be a stronger case than "straight refutation."

4. Discuss why the affirmative must win all issues to win a debate.

5. Thomas Fuller wrote, "Argument seldom convinces anyone contrary to his inclinations." First discuss the meaning of this quotation. Then discuss how it relates to debate.

ACTIVITIES

1. Choosing Topics and Propositions for Debate

A. List three topics that you believe are worthy of debate. Then write three debate propositions for each. List each set of propositions in the order of your preference for debate, giving the one you most prefer first.

B. Choose a topic for debate. For this topic, write a proposition affirming a fact. Then write a proposition establishing or changing a belief. Finally, write a proposition recommending a policy.

2. Explaining How to Word a Proposition

Prepare a process speech explaining how to word a proposition. Present your speech to your classmates. As you cover the three tests that a well-worded proposition must meet, use a visual aid to give at least one example of each test.

3. Revising the Wording of Propositions

Rewrite the following propositions to meet the three tests of wording a proposition.

a. Domestic auto makers should be required to install air bags and front-wheel drive on all cars.
b. The system of funding public elementary education through property taxes should be reconsidered.
c. An equal rights amendment should not be adopted.
d. The current method for responding to stated complaints by customers interacting with retail sales personnel and with customer service personnel should be altered in favor of customer satisfaction.
e. Motorcycle manufacturers should be permitted to produce for private ownership motorcycles that can exceed the legal speed limit by more than ten miles an hour.

4. Organizing Support for an Issue

A. Select an issue to support a proposal of your own choice. Write the affirmative and the negative reasons that make up the proof for this issue. Then find evidence to support each of the reasons. Be prepared to discuss why your evidence provides convincing support for the affirmative and negative positions.

B. Use a problem-solution or comparative-advantages pattern to organize the reasons and evidence you gathered for part A. Identify the status quo clearly, and be specific about how your reasons and evidence resolve the issue.

5. Preparing for a Debate

A. Select one of the following propositions or a proposition of your own choice for debate. Then list the key issues for the proposition that you select.

1. *Resolved,* That the minimum age to obtain a driver's license should be raised to 18.
2. *Resolved,* That all fifty states should follow the same yearly schedule for public schooling.
3. *Resolved,* That all cat owners should be required to keep their pets on a leash.

B. Select a partner, choose a side, and prepare to debate the proposition you chose for part A. Make sure that your issues can be supported by specific reasons. Prepare a file of evidence cards that you could use in developing your case for the proposition you chose for part A. Identify the pattern or approach you use to organize your evidence. Predict your opposition's arguments for the debate itself and for rebuttal and refutation. Be prepared to discuss why your position is sound and convincing.

Real-Life Speaking Situations

1. Debate is often used by decision-makers in a democratic society to resolve opposing views. You may have seen debates involving presidential candidates, members of Congress, local leaders, or other influential speakers. Many controversial topics that have a direct bearing on your life are discussed in these debates. Think of a debate that you have heard or read concerning a controversial topic. Recall the debate as clearly as you can, and chart it on a flow sheet. Now, imagine that you are a judge who must decide who won the debate. (As a matter of fact, you will be a judge when you become a voter and cast your ballot on debated issues.) Write a two- or three-page report on the main features of the debate—the proposition, the affirmative and negative cases, the issues, any refutation or rebuttal, and the outcome. Finally, give your evaluation of the debate. Who won? Why? What were the strong points and weak points of the opposing arguments? Be prepared to give your report in class and to conduct a question-and-answer session afterward.

2. Attorneys practice debate as a profession. Laws and regulations establish the legal status quo. Cases involving these laws and regulations test them through debate. Opposing attorneys present affirmative and negative arguments concerning how legal standards are applied in the specific situation of each case. A judge or jury then evaluates the attorneys' arguments and decides which is stronger. Imagine that you are an attorney preparing the argument for your next case. Begin by defining your position and the specifics of the case. Will you present the affirmative or the negative side—that is, are you the defense or the prosecution? What legal issues will you debate? Who is your client? What arguments will you offer to support your position? Write a two- or three-page informative speech presenting your case. Be prepared to deliver your speech in class and to conduct a question-and-answer session in which you defend your position against issues and arguments offered by your classmates. Ask your teacher or a classmate to judge whether or not you won the case.

PARLIAMENTARY PROCEDURE

OBJECTIVES:

After studying this chapter, you should be able to

1. List five principles upon which parliamentary procedure is built.

2. Explain the procedures for running a meeting.

3. List privileged motions in order of precedence.

4. List subsidiary motions in order of precedence.

5. Explain the purpose of incidental motions.

6. Explain the purpose of renewal motions.

7. Follow the form for getting a motion on the floor.

8. Explain how to amend and vote upon a motion.

9. Explain ways of delaying discussion of motions.

10. List the major officers of a parliamentary group.

Ann Welch, newly elected president of the Senior Class, was holding her first meeting. During discussion of the motion, *"Resolved,* That the Senior Class hold the Spring Dance at the Topper Club, Saturday, June 4," Gary moved to amend the motion by striking "Topper Club" and inserting "Morris Hall." From the other side of the room, Stephanie suggested that the entire question be returned to the social committee; at the same time León said, "I move to lay this on the table."

Ann sputtered, "I'm not sure whether this is . . ."

Cal interrupted and said, "I move we adjourn."

Scratching her head, Ann mumbled, "Well, there's another motion. Now let's see . . ."

A voice from the back called, "Let's impeach Ann. She doesn't know what she's doing!"

All at once voices from *everywhere* began shouting, "Impeach Ann! Impeach Ann!"

Suddenly, Ann bolted upright in her chair. The book on parliamentary procedure that she had been studying fell to the floor. "Thank goodness," Ann thought, "it was only a dream."

Ann's fear that she would not be able to conduct a meeting had caused her nightmare. She thought of parliamentary procedure as a difficult subject rather than as a tool that would enable her to hold orderly meetings. If you are willing to put in just a little time, you not only can master the rules but can learn to use them effectively.

Parliamentary procedure, which is a set of rules for conducting orderly meetings, serves three major functions. *First,* it helps make meetings run more smoothly. *Second,* it helps a group focus on the issues that are most important to the entire membership. *Third,* it ensures that meetings are run according to democratic principles.

THE PRINCIPLES OF PARLIAMENTARY PROCEDURE

Many groups conduct their business at meetings to which all members are invited. To maintain order, these meetings are generally conducted according to five principles of parliamentary procedure.

The set of rules for conducting meetings is called *parliamentary procedure* because it is based on the rules and customs of the British Parliament.

Only One Item at a Time

Only one item of business may be considered at a time. This principle enables a group to focus its energies on one topic. Only after that one topic has been debated and then passed, defeated, or delayed may the group move on to another topic.

Open Discussion

Everyone has a right to express an opinion, and each opinion is treated as valuable. Democratic principles recognize that any idea, policy, or belief can be looked at in several ways. Parliamentary procedure establishes a forum where all sides can express their views on a question. Open discussion of all opinions enables the group to arrive at the best decision.

Equality of Voting Rights

Every member has the right to vote, and each vote is counted as equal. Any decision reached by the group must be based on the collective judgment of the group's membership.

The Majority Rules

The group always follows the decision of the majority. Most votes require a **simple majority,** which consists of at least one more than half the number of people voting. Special situations take two thirds of those voting to pass an issue under debate.

Protection of Minority Rights

When any motion concerns an infringement of personal rights, at least two thirds of those present and voting must affirm that motion for it to pass. Of course, minority rights are also protected by rules giving minority opinion an equal right to be heard on all motions. When minority opinion is strong enough, it can and often does change enough minds within the original majority to prevent passage of a motion that the minority opposes.

ACTIVITY: Analyzing a Group Meeting

Observe a meeting of a formal group, such as a town council, a service club, or your school's debating society. In what ways are the rights of individuals in the group protected? What benefits do the members derive from observing the five principles covered in the beginning of this chapter? What benefit does the public derive from the fact that proceedings are a matter of public record? Discuss these questions with your classmates.

Public Record

In addition to the five principles given on page 481, policy demands that all proceedings be a matter of public record. The group's secretary takes minutes of every meeting, and these minutes are kept on file.

RULES FOR RUNNING MEETINGS

Every meeting can be run according to one set of rules covering almost all situations. Most of the rules used by governmental, business, educational, and social groups in the United States have been adapted from procedures established in the British Parliament. Many parliamentary authorities have written down these sets of rules in books that groups can use to help organize their meetings. By far the most influential of these books is *Robert's Rules of Order, Newly Revised.*

Of course, an organization has the option of creating its own set of rules. These rules would then be included in the organization's constitution and bylaws.

Rules of parliamentary procedure cover the writing of the constitution and bylaws, the duties of officers, and the specific rules governing debate. Although all of these rules and procedures are important, the ones that are most vital to you in your role as a potential leader or member of an organization are those that deal directly with running a meeting.

Have a standard handbook on parliamentary procedure available at meetings to answer procedural questions as they arise.

Calling Meetings

When a meeting is planned, members of the group should be informed by written notice, usually at least ten days in advance. Written notice for a meeting should always include the date, the time, and the place of the meeting.

Advance notice is especially important when officers plan to hold a special meeting or a meeting for a group that does not meet on a regular schedule. Many organizations, though, do schedule regular meeting times (the first Tuesday of each month, for example). For regular meetings, officers send members written notice of the meeting, along with a short list of items that will be discussed at that meeting. This list of items is called an **agenda.**

What happens if officers fail to give members advance notice? Any business that is conducted at such a meeting can be nullified. In addition, if it can be proved that officers deliberately did not give notice of a meeting, that they planned to hold a secret meeting, they can be removed from office.

The Quorum

At the beginning of a meeting, the chairperson must always make sure that a quorum is present. A **quorum** is the number of members that must be present for the group to conduct business. A quorum can be set at any number. For very large assemblies, 20 percent of the membership often constitutes a quorum. For most groups, the quorum is set at 40 to 60 percent of the membership. If no number is set by an organization, then the quorum is one person more than 50 percent of the membership.

The quorum should be high enough so that the business conducted represents the thinking of the organization. However, it must be low enough so that it can be met without difficulty at meetings that are reasonably well attended.

Order of Business

The order of business for a meeting involves the sequence of items on the agenda. Most formal organizations use the following standard items, which are suggested in *Robert's Rules of Order.*

Call to order
Reading and approval of the minutes of the previous meeting
Officers' reports
Standing committee reports
Special committee reports
Old business
New business
Announcements
Adjournment

Any group can set its order of business in its bylaws. Even when an order is set, items can be shifted with the consent of the group.

Suppose that your class were going to function as an organization. What number would you suggest as a quorum? Why? At the first meeting of your class, the primary new business might likely be to elect officers. Write an agenda that could be used for that meeting. Make sure that you include the standard items listed under "Order of Business" on page 483. Then share your agenda with your classmates and respond to feedback from them.

MOTIONS

All of the business in a meeting conducted according to parliamentary procedure is handled through motions. **Motions** are proposals for action made by members of a parliamentary organization. In this section you will look at very short definitions of each type of motion. Later in this chapter, you will study more complete explanations so that you will be able to use motions effectively.

Business in a formal parliamentary body, large or small, is conducted through *motions*.

Classification of Motions

In most groups you will use five classifications of motions: privileged, main, subsidiary, incidental, and renewal.

Privileged Motions. Privileged motions concern the running of the meeting itself. There are four privileged motions that you need to know.

1. **Adjourn.** The motion to **adjourn** calls for the meeting to close.
2. **Recess.** The motion to **recess** calls for a short break during the meeting itself.
3. **Question of Privilege.** The motion **question of privilege** calls for immediate action on such things as heating, lighting, ventilation, and disturbances.
4. **Call for the Orders of the Day.** The motion **call for the orders of the day** alerts the chairperson that a scheduled event has been overlooked.

Main Motions. Main motions are those that set forth the items of business that will be considered. For example:

"I move that club members actively participate in the drive to eradicate illiteracy."
"I move that we hold a Valentine's dance on February 14th."
"I move that club members volunteer to work one hour a week at the local day-care center."

Subsidiary Motions. Subsidiary motions relate to the treating or disposing of a motion being discussed. There are eight subsidiary motions that you need to know.

1. **Lay on the Table.** The motion to **lay on the table** calls for a postponement of action until someone makes a motion to remove the original motion from the table.
2. **Previous Question.** The motion to move the **previous question** calls for a vote to stop discussion on a motion.
3. **Limit or Extend Debate.** The motion to **limit debate** or to **extend debate** calls for setting a time limit for individual speeches or for the entire debate.
4. **Postpone to a Definite Time.** The motion to **postpone to a definite time** calls for a postponement of action until a particular time set by the person making the motion.
5. **Refer to a Committee.** The motion to **refer to a committee** calls for shifting discussion of the matter at hand to a smaller group meeting at some other time.
6. **Amend.** The motion to **amend** calls for an alteration in the wording of a motion.
7. **Postpone Indefinitely.** The motion to **postpone indefinitely** calls for a postponement of discussion for that session and thus prevents the main motion from coming to a vote.

Incidental Motions. Incidental motions relate to questions of procedure arising out of the discussion. There are a number of incidental motions that are commonly used.

1. **Appeal.** The motion to **appeal** is used to force the chairperson to submit a disputed ruling made by the chairperson to a vote by the entire group.
2. **Close Nominations.** The motion to **close nominations** calls for an end to the process of nominating persons for offices.
3. **Division of Assembly.** The motion **division of assembly** requires the chairperson to call for a second vote, which will preferably be conducted by a method other than the method used to conduct the first vote.
4. **Division of Question.** The motion **division of question** requires the chairperson to divide a motion with more than one part into its various parts. Dividing a question allows each part to be discussed and voted on separately.
5. **Parliamentary Inquiry.** The motion to raise a question of **parliamentary inquiry** is made to request information about whether making a motion would be in order. This motion is always addressed to the chair.
6. **Point of Order.** The motion **point of order** calls attention to a violation of parliamentary procedure.
7. **Object to Consideration.** The motion **object to consideration** allows the group to dismiss a main motion that is irrelevant, inappropriate, or for some other reason undesirable. Objections to consideration must be made before any debate of the main motion begins and before any subsidiary motions are made.
8. **Reopen Nominations.** A motion to **reopen nominations** is made to allow more nominations to be made after nominations have been closed.
9. **Suspend the Rules.** A motion to **suspend the rules** calls for the suspension of any standing rule that the organization may have for that particular meeting. Such suspensions allow members to do something not normally allowed by the rules.
10. **Voting.** A motion concerning the method of voting calls for the chairperson to take the vote in the manner stated in the motion (by secret ballot, for instance).
11. **Withdraw a Motion.** A move to **withdraw a motion** gives the person who made the motion permission to remove it from consideration.

Renewal Motions. Renewal motions get discussion reopened on decisions that have already been made. There are three renewal motions that you will use.

1. **Reconsider.** The motion to **reconsider** calls for discussion of a motion that has already been passed.
2. **Rescind.** The motion to **rescind** calls for cancellation of action taken on a previous motion.

3. **Take from the Table.** The motion to **take from the table** calls for reopening discussion of a motion that had earlier been moved to lay on the table.

Precedence

Precedence refers to the ranking of motions. Privileged and subsidiary motions are ranked above main motions in the following order:

1. Adjourn
2. Recess
3. Question of Privilege
4. Call for the Orders of the Day
5. Lay on the Table
6. Previous Question
7. Limit Debate or Extend Debate
8. Postpone to a Definite Time
9. Refer to a Committee
10. Amend
11. Postpone Indefinitely
12. Main Motion

A motion of higher precedence (1 is highest, 2 is next, and so forth) is in order when a motion of lower precedence is on the floor. For example, suppose that the main motion before a student council meeting is "to hold a dance in the school gym on Saturday, March 15, beginning at 9 P.M." If while the motion is being debated someone moves "to lay the motion on the table" (number 5 in precedence), this motion takes precedence over the main motion (number 12). If after the motion "to lay on the table" is seconded, someone else moves "to postpone discussion of the main motion until the next meeting" (number 8), this motion is out of order because "lay on the table" (number 5) is of higher precedence than "postpone to a definite time" (number 8).

Incidental motions and renewal motions are not ranked in order of precedence because they are made in direct response to motions and circumstances currently taking place in the meeting. Consequently, these two types of motions are dealt with as they are made rather than in a sequential order of precedence.

Table of Parliamentary Motions

The table on page 488 gives a concise overview of the rules governing motions. Requiring a **second** means that a person other than the person making the motion must indicate that he or she is willing to have the group consider that motion. *Amendable* refers to whether any changes in the motion are allowed. *Debatable* refers to whether that motion can be discussed by the group before it is voted upon. The first column, labeled "Rank," in the first section of the table gives the order of precedence of privileged, subsidiary, and main motions.

Table of Parliamentary Motions

Privileged, Subsidiary, and Main Motions

Rank	Name of Motion	Interrupt a Speaker?	Need a Second?	Debatable?	Amendable?	Vote
1.	Adjourn	no	yes	no	no	maj.
2.	Recess	no	yes	yes*	yes*	maj.
3.	Question of privilege	yes	no	no	no	none
4.	Call for the orders of the day	yes	no	no	no	none
5.	Lay on the table	no	yes	no	no	maj.
6.	Previous question	no	yes	no	no	⅔
7.	Limit or extend debate	no	yes	yes*	yes*	⅔
8.	Postpone to a definite time	no	yes	yes*	yes*	maj.
9.	Refer to a committee	no	yes	yes*	yes*	maj.
10.	Amend	no	yes	yes	yes	maj.
11.	Postpone indefinitely	no	yes	yes	no	maj.
12.	Main motion	no	yes	yes	yes	maj.

* Consult an authority, such as *Robert's Rules of Order*, for restrictions placed on these motions.

Incidental Motions

Name of Motion	Interrupt a Speaker?	Need a Second?	Debatable?	Amendable?	Vote
Appeal	yes	yes	yes	no	maj.
Close nominations	no	yes	no	yes	⅔
Division of assembly	yes	no	no	no	none
Division of question	yes	no	no	yes	none
Parliamentary inquiry	yes	no	no	no	none
Point of order	yes	no	no	no	none
Object to consideration	yes	no	no	no	⅔
Reopen nominations	no	yes	no	yes	maj.
Suspend the rules	no	yes	no	no	⅔
Voting, motions relating to	no	yes	no	yes	maj.
Withdraw a motion, leave to	yes	no	no	no	maj.

Renewal Motions

Name of Motion	Interrupt a Speaker?	Need a Second?	Debatable?	Amendable?	Vote
Reconsider	no	yes	yes	no	maj.
Rescind	no	yes	yes	yes	⅔
Take from the table	no	yes	no	no	maj.

Understanding Motions

The key to understanding and using motions is to know when a motion is in order, whether it is debatable or amendable, and what vote it requires to pass. Use the table on page 488 to help you complete the following activities.

1. For each of the following situations, indicate whether the second motion is in order.
   a. Tom moves to have a party. Paul moves to amend the motion.
   b. Ella moves to take a recess. May moves to lay on the table the motion about having a party.
   c. Heather moves to postpone the motion until the next meeting. Tyrone moves to adjourn.
   d. Juan moves to redecorate the meeting room. Joan moves to refer the motion to a committee.
   e. Tanya moves to amend the motion. Sylvia moves the previous question.
2. Indicate whether each of the following motions is amendable.
   a. Take a recess
   b. Main motion
   c. Lay on the table
   d. Postpone to a definite time
   e. Adjourn
3. Indicate what vote (no vote, simple majority, or two-thirds majority) each of the following motions requires to pass.
   a. Call for the orders of the day
   b. Close nominations
   c. Take from the table
   d. Previous question
   e. Amend

USING MOTIONS

Each parliamentary motion has its own specific characteristics and uses. This section answers key questions about how motions are used in parliamentary proceedings.

Getting a Motion on the Floor

When new business is called for, how can members get a motion on the floor? According to the rules of parliamentary procedure, no discussion is in order unless a motion is on the floor. Thus, one of the first concerns is making sure that you understand how to make a main motion. The procedure for making a motion involves the following five steps.

"You can't move we adjourn, Wilson. We just started."

Inappropriate motions waste the group's time. Become familiar with the proper procedure and precedence for making motions.

1. The chairperson grants the floor by stating the member's name, for example, "Tom" or "Mr. Lopez."
2. The person makes a motion, such as "I move that the annual dance be held at 8 P.M. Saturday, June 4, at the Topper Club."
3. Another member of the group seconds the motion by calling out, "I second the motion," or simply "Second." The member who seconds need not be recognized. Since seconding only indicates willingness to have the motion discussed, the seconder need not be in favor of the motion. If no one calls out a second, the chair asks, "Is there a second?"
4. If the chair does not hear a second, he or she says, "The motion fails for lack of a second. Is there any further business?" If the chair does hear a second, he or she states the motion and calls for discussion. If the motion to hold the annual dance at the Topper Club has been seconded, the chair says, "It has been moved and seconded that the annual dance be held at 8 P.M. Saturday, June 4, at the Topper Club. Is there any discussion?"
5. After discussion of a main motion (or immediately in cases where no discussion is allowed), the chair calls for a vote.

The purpose of holding discussion is to allow members to express their views on the main motion at hand before voting on it. Ultimately, the main motion will have to be passed, defeated, or delayed before another main motion can be made. Main motions require a second, are amendable and debatable, and require a majority vote for passage.

Voting

After discussion of a main motion (or immediately in cases where no discussion is allowed), the chair calls for a vote: "Those in favor of the motion say 'aye'; those opposed say 'no.' " After the vote the chair says either "The ayes have it, and the motion is passed" or "The nos have it, and the motion is lost." The chair then goes on with the meeting by saying, "Is there any further business?"

How are motions voted upon? Ordinarily an oral vote is taken, with members saying either "aye" or "no" aloud. If a member of the group wishes to vote by some other method, a motion about how to vote is always in order. Except when a two-thirds majority is required, all motions require a simple majority vote. Votes are counted by the chairperson or the secretary or sometimes by both.

When a vote is taken and the outcome is too close to call, what should be done? The group always has the right to assure itself that the votes are counted correctly. By using the motion "Division of assembly" (or by just calling out "Division"), a member can indicate his or her opinion that the vote is close enough to require a recount. If the first vote was by voice, the second count will be by show of hands or by standing.

Before a vote is taken, does a member have the right to move that the vote be by roll call or by secret ballot? Yes. However, a motion on voting needs a second and is carried by a majority vote. A **roll call vote** is one in which the secretary calls the name of everyone assembled, and each person votes by saying "aye," "no," or "abstain." A vote to **abstain** indicates that the member does not wish to support or to oppose a motion that is being voted upon. If the voting is by secret ballot, each member of the group submits his or her vote anonymously in writing.

Votes can be taken in various ways, including by voice, by standing, by written ballot—or by raising hands, as this group is doing.

When can and should the chairperson vote? There is often a great deal of confusion about when the chair votes. One of the chair's most important rights is the right to vote to break a tie. Therefore, if a motion requiring a majority has fifteen aye votes and fifteen no votes, the chair may vote. However, the chair can never be forced to vote. If the chair refuses to vote when there is a tie, the motion fails for lack of a majority.

Breaking a tie, though, is not the chair's only opportunity to vote. The chair has the right to vote any time the chair's vote will affect the decision. For example, suppose that sixteen members vote yes on a motion and fifteen vote no. If the chair does not vote, the motion will carry. If, however, the chair votes no, the vote will be a tie and will fail for lack of a majority. Likewise, if a motion requires a two-thirds vote, and nineteen members vote aye and ten vote no, the chair may vote. If the chair votes aye, the results will be twenty aye and ten no (a two-thirds majority), and the motion will pass.

After a motion has been voted on, can anything be done to change the outcome? Yes. There are two major options. First, any time after a motion has been passed, a member of the group may move to rescind it. To *rescind* means to cancel the action taken on a previous motion. Suppose that your group has voted to allow eating at meetings. At any time, a member has the right to say, "I move to rescind the motion allowing eating at our meetings." This motion needs a second, is debatable, is amendable, and requires a two-thirds vote for passage. If a member has given advance notice of a motion (for instance, if the motion to rescind has appeared on an agenda distributed to members ten days in advance of the meeting), the motion can be passed with a simple majority.

Second, within the same meeting or at the next meeting, a member may move to reconsider a motion. Parliamentary procedure allows for people to change their minds on an issue. Suppose you just voted in favor of a motion to have a banquet on Saturday evening, March 14, and the motion passed. If, later in the meeting, you begin to think you made a mistake, you can move to reconsider. This motion means that you are asking the group for permission to reopen discussion on the question. If your motion to reconsider passes, then discussion on the banquet is reopened and eventually another vote will be taken. If your motion to reconsider fails, then the group moves on to other business.

You can see that reconsidering a motion can be used to delay the proceedings of a meeting or to obstruct the will of the majority. To prevent members of a group from abusing the motion to reconsider, a very important parliamentary qualification is attached. When a member moves to reconsider a motion, the chair will ask whether that member voted on the winning side. If the member did not vote with the majority, then that member cannot make a motion to reconsider. For instance, if you move to reconsider the vote on the banquet, the chair will ask whether you voted in favor of the banquet in the first place. If you did not, you would not be permitted to make a motion to reconsider. Only if you voted with the majority on a motion can you move to reconsider that motion.

If discussion is becoming repetitive, what can be done to bring about a vote? There are two ways to bring a motion to a vote. The first is very informal and carries no parliamentary authority, but it may still achieve the goal of bringing about a vote. A member simply calls out "Question." Although anyone who wishes to discuss the motion further has the right to do so, the knowledge that at least one person wants to get on to the vote may lead others to show a similar feeling. Also, a chairperson may say, "It sounds as if some of you believe we have exhausted meaningful discussion. Are we ready to get on to the vote?" Keep in mind that if someone still wants to talk, shouting out "Question" does not require that a vote be taken.

The second way to bring about a vote is more formal. When a member is ready to vote, he or she raises one hand to be recognized, and when called upon by the chair, makes the motion to move the previous question. By making a motion to move the previous question, a member says that he or she wants a vote taken to see whether the group wants to stop discussion and vote on the motion. A positive vote on this motion means that no further discussion of the motion be allowed. The chair then calls for a vote on the main motion before the group. Because this motion limits the freedom of speech, it requires a two-thirds vote for passage. Note that after getting a second, the main motion is neither debatable nor amendable.

Changing the Main Motion

Can the wording of a main motion be changed? Yes. A main motion can be changed in several ways. First, if a motion is so poorly phrased that it is difficult to understand, the person who made the motion can ask to withdraw that motion. Usually, the motion is withdrawn if the person who originally seconded it gives permission. However, the chair must get the consent of the group. The chair will usually ask, "May we give Tom leave to withdraw his motion?" If someone objects, a vote is taken. If a majority favors withdrawing, Tom is able to withdraw his motion. To avoid poorly worded motions, the maker of a motion should put it in writing and have several people check the wording before the motion is presented.

Second, a member can move to amend. At any time during discussion of a motion, any member can move to amend that motion. To *amend* a motion means to take official parliamentary action to change the wording of that motion. Of all motions, amending is one of the most often used and most often misused.

The first rule governing amendments is that an amendment must be specific when it is put before the group. An amendment may be put before the group in any of five ways. To illustrate, suppose that someone has moved "to hold the annual Spring Dance at 8 P.M. Saturday, June 4, at the Topper Club." The five ways to amend this motion are

1. By inserting: "I move to amend the motion by inserting the word *formal* after *Spring*."
2. By adding: "I move to amend the motion by adding the words *Lower Pavilion* after *Club*."

During the discussion of a motion, any member may move to amend it. Amendments must always state exactly what changes are desired.

3. By striking out: "I move to amend the motion by striking out the word *annual.*"
4. By striking out and inserting: "I move to amend the motion by striking out *8* and inserting *9.*"
5. By substituting: "I move to amend the motion by substituting for it the following: *To hold a picnic at 2 p.m. June 4, at Parker Field.*"

People often make the mistake of trying to amend without indicating the specific changes they wish to make. Why is it so important to state the changes specifically? As soon as an amendment is made and seconded, discussion shifts to the amendment. Before carrying on additional discussion of the main motion, the amendment must be passed or defeated. If the wording of the amendment is not specific, confusion arises and a great deal of time is wasted.

The second rule concerning amendments is that only one primary amendment and one secondary amendment may be considered at a time. A **primary amendment** is an amendment of the main motion. A **secondary amendment** is an amendment of a primary amendment. After each secondary amendment is voted upon, the chair reopens discussion of the primary amendment, and another secondary amendment can be proposed. After the primary amendment is voted upon, the chair reopens discussion on the main motion, and another primary amendment can be proposed. After all moved amendments have been voted upon, the main motion may be voted upon.

The third rule concerning amendments is that an amendment must be germane to a motion. To be **germane** means that the amendment must in some way involve the same question that is raised by the motion to which it is applied. If a member moved to amend the annual dance motion by adding "and that eating shall be allowed at group meetings," the amendment would not be germane.

The fourth rule is that an amendment cannot be made by inserting the word *not* into the main motion. Although an amendment may change the intention of the motion, the amendment cannot be merely a negative expression of the main motion. For instance, if a member made a motion "to donate money to the Orchard Retirement Home," another member would be out of order in trying to revise the motion by inserting *not* before *to donate*. On the other hand, a motion to amend by "striking out *money* and inserting *furniture*" would be in order.

Putting Off Discussion

Are any parliamentary procedures available for delaying discussion of a motion either temporarily or permanently? Yes. Each of the following ways can be used to delay discussion.

First, if a motion seems inappropriate for the group's consideration, a member can "object to consideration." This motion is in order before any debate on the motion occurs. For example, if at the meeting of the Junior Class one student moved "to ask the principal to purchase supplies for Mrs. Kwan's tenth-grade homeroom," another student could object to consideration of the question on the grounds that it is irrelevant to the ordinary business of the group since that business is supposed to pertain to eleventh-grade issues. Objection to consideration does not require a second, is not debatable, and is not amendable. It requires a two-thirds vote to pass.

Second, if a member believes that discussion of a subject would be more appropriate either later in the meeting or at a different meeting, he or she can move "to postpone to a definite time." This is a motion to defer action temporarily. For example, if a motion requiring data about finances is before the group and the class treasurer has not yet arrived, a member can move to delay consideration of the subject until the treasurer gets to the meeting.

The motion for temporary postponement provides a convenient and efficient way to handle business because as soon as the time indicated in the motion to postpone arrives, the main motion is brought back before the group automatically. For instance, using the example in the previous paragraph, as soon as the treasurer gets to the meeting, the bill is again open for discussion. If another motion is being discussed, the chair will wait until that motion has been dispensed with and then move immediately to the postponed motion. If a motion is postponed until the next meeting, the agenda for the next meeting will show that motion under old business. A motion to postpone requires a second, is debatable, is amendable, and takes a majority vote.

Third, if a member believes that a motion should be delayed but is not sure exactly when would be the best time to return to it, he or she can move to "lay the motion on the table." This motion places the main motion on the secretary's table where it stays until someone moves to take it from the table.

"To lay on the table" is probably the best known of the delaying motions, but it is also the most abused. The most frequent misuse is in specifying a time. For example, the wording "I move to lay the motion on the table until next week" is improper since the motion to lay on the table cannot specify any time limit. If a member wants the motion set aside at this meeting but brought up at the next meeting, then he or she should move to postpone it, not to lay it on the table.

The motion to lay on the table is not debatable or amendable. In addition, it requires a second and takes a majority vote.

Expressing Disagreement

What can a member do if he or she thinks something is out of order? Depending on the situation, there are two choices. First, a member can rise to a point of order. Rising to a point of order is proper at any time. When someone stands and says "Point of order," the chair will ask that person to

Even in the most organized and formal groups, disagreements can become conflicts. Be sure that your organization knows how to restore order.

state the point (even if doing so interrupts another speaker). If the speaker is correct, the chair will change the procedure accordingly. Asking the chair to consider a point of order is neither debatable nor amendable, and it does not require a vote.

Second, a member can appeal the decision of the chair. If a member believes that the chair has made a judgmental decision that does not seem in keeping with the parliamentary rules used by the group, that member can appeal the decision. With this motion a member calls upon the chair to open discussion on the merits of the judgment and then to put the question to a vote. If a majority of those voting support the person making the appeal, then the chair's decision is reversed. A chairperson has a great deal of power and authority; however, any time that a member appeals a decision, the chair must call for discussion and for a vote on the motion. In this way, motions to appeal provide members with at least one means for seeing to it that the chair does not misuse authority.

Dealing with Complicated or Time-Consuming Subjects

What should a member do if he or she thinks that the subject is too complicated or too time consuming for the group to consider? In these circumstances, a member can refer the motion to a committee. The purpose of this motion is to have a smaller group consider a matter in detail in order to save time for the larger group. Many organizations run almost entirely under a committee structure, requiring that every motion come through a committee before it can be debated on the floor. Most organizations have at least a few standing committees, each considering a certain type of question, so that most business is reviewed by a committee before being sent to the entire organization for consideration.

A member who makes a motion to refer to committee may wish to designate the makeup of the committee and its authority. For example, someone might say, "I move to refer the motion to a committee of three members appointed by the chair with instructions to report back to this group at our next regular meeting." The major purpose of the committee is to determine what information about the subject will be needed, to gather that information, and to make a recommendation to the group. The group then has the right to debate and, if it wishes, to make the changes that the committee suggests.

Controlling Length

Is there anything that can be done to affect the length of either individual speeches or of the entire debate? Yes. Before debate begins on any issue, or even during the debate itself, a member can move to limit or to extend debate. Notice how this motion works. Let's say that within a certain group speakers are ordinarily allowed to talk as long as they wish. However, for today's debate you fear that everyone may want to speak at great length. You may say, "I move to limit speeches to three minutes each." If you are concerned about the total length of the discussion, you may say, "I move to limit the total discussion to one hour." This motion may be debated briefly, and it is amendable so far as the time is concerned. In addition, because it is an infringement on the right of free speech, it requires a two-thirds vote.

Is there anything that a member can do to stop a meeting? Yes. A member can stop a meeting in either of two ways. First, any member can move to recess, which will stop the meeting for a few minutes. For example, someone might say, "I move we take a fifteen-minute recess." Second, anyone who believes that the group has finished for the day can move to adjourn. Neither of these motions is debatable. A motion to recess is amendable as to time. Both motions require a majority vote for passage.

ACTIVITY: **Making Motions According to Parliamentary Procedure**

First, suppose you belong to an organization and want to propose buying a lectern for the meeting room. Write down the steps you will follow to get the motion before the group. Practice saying the steps aloud.

Next, amend the motion to buy a lectern. Suppose you decide that the group should buy a gavel instead of a lectern. Write how you will make such an amendment. Practice the wording aloud.

Finally, imagine that a vote has been taken on the amendment but that you think the voice vote is too close to call a winner. Tell your class what you will say.

OFFICERS

Parliamentary organizations have at least three key officers. The chairperson presides over meetings of the organization. The vice-chairperson presides when the chairperson is absent. The secretary keeps an accurate record of each meeting.

The Role of the Chairperson

The **chairperson**, or chair, is responsible for running pleasant, efficient meetings and for protecting the rights of everyone at the meeting. To do this, the chairperson must have a mastery of parliamentary procedure.

First, the chairperson should govern the group according to parliamentary procedure. Parliamentary procedure provides an established organizational pattern that all members can agree upon. Following parliamentary procedure helps ensure that meetings are run efficiently, fairly, and effectively.

Second, the chairperson should educate the members of the organization. The chair should explain procedures whenever necessary, so that everyone understands what is taking place and why it is taking place.

The chairperson of a group presides over the meetings and is responsible for conducting them according to parliamentary procedure.

For example, suppose that one member moves "to lay on the table the motion before the group," and someone else shouts "Second." Then the chairperson says in a curt manner, "It's been moved and seconded to lay the motion on the table. All those in favor say 'aye.'" Even though the chairperson has observed parliamentary procedure, many members of the group may think that something is wrong. The fact is that most people do not fully understand what *to lay on the table* and other common parliamentary motions mean. Likewise, many people may not be sure which motions are debatable, which are amendable, and what votes are required. A much better procedure would be for the chairperson to make the following statement:

"It's been moved and seconded to lay the motion on the table. If this motion is passed, the matter will be set aside until someone moves formally to take it from the table. Because this motion is neither debatable nor amendable, we will move directly to the vote. All those in favor of deferring this matter for some indefinite period, please say 'aye.'"

The chair needs only a few moments to explain what is happening, but the time invested in explanation will likely save time in the long run and will help prevent some members from feeling confused and anxious. In addition, such a method serves as an educational device for the membership. Over the course of several meetings, the chair can give enough instruction so that the majority of the members can painlessly learn most of the essentials of key motions.

Third, the chairperson should be sensitive to the method that he or she uses to recognize members. Procedure calls for a member to raise one hand (or at large meetings to stand) to be recognized. In small groups, people may just speak out. Some chairpersons unfairly allow certain individuals the right to speak at any time regardless of who else wishes to speak. Effective chairpersons use the following guidelines to maintain fair speaking order.

1. The person who made the motion has the right to speak first.
2. The chair should call on each person by name.
3. The chair should, if possible, try to alternate speakers so that the different sides of an issue are presented in a balanced discussion.
4. Everyone should have a chance to speak once before anyone gets the chance to speak for a second time.
5. The chair should not always look at the same section of the group or to the same person at the start of debate.

Fourth, the chair should maintain order. To maintain order the chair should insist that all members follow parliamentary procedure during meetings. By using this agreed-upon procedure, all members receive equal treatment and have an equal chance to participate. If a meeting becomes unruly, the chair should call for order and for a return to procedure. If this action fails, the meeting should either be adjourned or be recessed until order can be regained.

The chairperson at this meeting obviously needs to invest some time in educating members in the use of parliamentary procedure.

The Role of the Vice-Chairperson

The **vice-chairperson** assumes the duties of the chair when the chair is unable to do so. The vice-chair also assumes the duties of the chair when the chair steps down to debate a motion. Once a chair steps down, he or she cannot resume the role of chair until that particular motion is voted upon.

The Role of the Secretary

The **secretary** is the major recording officer and keeper of records. As such, the secretary must be trustworthy and accurate.

The primary role of the secretary during a meeting is to take the minutes. A record of minutes should include the following information:

1. The kind of meeting (regular or special)
2. The name of the organization
3. The date, hour, and place of the meeting
4. The name of the presiding officer
5. The number of members present and the names of absentees
6. The action taken on minutes of the previous meeting
7. Committee reports
8. Each main motion, the name of the person introducing it, and the action taken
9. Points of order and appeals
10. Any material that in the future may be helpful in explaining what was done at the meeting
11. The program, if any
12. The time of adjournment

ACTIVITY: **Holding a Meeting According to Parliamentary Procedure**

Imagine that your class is a parliamentary organization. Select one person to act as chairperson. Then have that person hold a meeting. During the meeting members of the class should practice using various parliamentary motions. When someone in class does not understand what has happened, or if someone makes a mistake in procedure, the class should stop and discuss the point. Keep minutes of the meeting. Compare your minutes with those of your classmates.

GUIDELINES FOR USING PARLIAMENTARY PROCEDURE

- Do I know the meanings and uses of parliamentary motions?
- Do I understand when a motion is in order?
- Do I know how to make commonly used motions?
- Do I know what motions relate to voting?
- Do I know how to change a motion?
- Do I know the duties of the chairperson, the vice-chairperson, and the secretary?

Patricia Paulsen-Mathewson

Patricia Paulsen-Mathewson first learned of parliamentary procedure in a high-school speech course. Now, as president of a Midwest chapter of Jaycees, a national community service organization, Ms. Paulsen-Mathewson considers parliamentary procedure indispensable in conducting meetings.

One advantage she finds in parliamentary procedure is that it takes the "emotion" out of disagreements. Because the rules require that all discussion must pertain to the issue at hand, personal comments and side issues are not permitted to distract the group. She notes from experience that "parliamentary procedure is fair to everyone involved."

In addition to ensuring objectivity in discussion, parliamentary procedure helps knowledgeable members accomplish their goals. Ms. Paulsen-Mathewson recalls winning a contested point in one group discussion by presenting a motion that brought the opposition up short because they were not as well schooled in using *Robert's Rules of Order.* "Motions are turning points" in the proceedings, she comments. She emphasizes that a group member must be able to use motions effectively in order to have a say in group decisions.

Of course, not all members, particularly new ones, are adept in parliamentary procedure. For this reason, Ms. Paulsen-Mathewson suggests that people in leadership positions such as hers coach the general membership at key times in a meeting. For example, when the discussion of an idea seems complete but no motion is heard, she might say, "I'd like to entertain a motion to . . ."

To know when this coaching is needed, Ms. Paulsen-Mathewson watches for nonverbal cues from members. If a member's facial expression indicates that he or she is confused or uncertain, Ms. Paulsen-Mathewson attempts to clarify the current order of business, perhaps by offering a summary statement. She also paraphrases what members say to be sure their ideas are clear to all.

Experience gained through regular use of parliamentary procedure is the best teacher, according to Ms. Paulsen-Mathewson. "You want the rules to serve you," she says. "You need not be a slave to the rules." Through her own mastery of parliamentary procedure, Ms. Paulsen-Mathewson has achieved a leadership position that brings her a great deal of personal enjoyment and satisfaction in serving her community.

Following parliamentary procedure helps a group organize meetings so that they run smoothly, helps a group focus on issues that are important to the entire membership, and helps a group ensure that its decisions can stand up under public scrutiny. Parliamentary procedure is based on five principles: that everyone has a right to express his or her opinion, that every member has a right to vote, that the majority rules, that minority rights should be protected, and that only one item of business may be considered at a time. All proceedings are a matter of public record.

Parliamentary motions are grouped under five headings: privileged, main, subsidiary, incidental, and renewal. Privileged motions apply to the running of a meeting itself. Subsidiary motions relate to the treating or disposing of a main motion being discussed. Incidental motions relate to questions of procedure arising out of discussion of a main motion. Renewal motions reopen discussion on decisions that have already been made.

All group members need to know how motions are made: The chair recognizes a member; the member states a motion; the chair calls for a second; the chair states the question. After discussion (if discussion is allowed), the motion is voted on.

The wording of a motion can be changed by requesting leave to withdraw and by amending. An amendment can be adopted to insert, add, strike, strike and insert, or substitute part of a motion.

Voting is usually done by voice or by hand, but it can be done by ballot or roll call if a motion to do so is made and passed. Discussion is brought to a vote by calling "question" or by moving the previous question. After a vote, a motion can, under certain circumstances, be reconsidered or rescinded.

Motions can be delayed or set aside by objecting to consideration, by postponing to a definite time, or by laying on the table. If a motion seems to be out of order, a member can rise to a point of order or can appeal the decision of the chair. If a motion is too complicated, it can be referred to a committee. If a debate is too long, a member can move to limit it. If a member feels debate has been cut short, he or she can move to extend it. Someone who wants to stop a meeting can move to recess or to adjourn.

Key officers are chair, vice-chair, and secretary. The chairperson knows parliamentary procedure, explains what is happening during the meeting, is sensitive to recognizing members, and keeps order. The vice-chair presides when the chair is unable to do so or when the chair steps down. The secretary is responsible for keeping the minutes.

CHAPTER VOCABULARY

Look back through this chapter to find the meaning of each of the following terms. Write each term and its meaning in your communication journal.

abstain
adjourn
agenda
amend
appeal
call for the orders of the day
chairperson
close nominations
division of assembly
division of question
germane
incidental motions
lay on the table
limit or extend debate
main motion

motions
object to consideration
parliamentary inquiry
parliamentary procedure
point of order
postpone indefinitely
postpone to a definite time
precedence
previous question
primary amendment
privileged motions
question of privilege
quorum
recess
reconsider

refer to a committee
renewal motions
reopen nominations
rescind
roll call vote
second
secondary amendment
secretary
simple majority
subsidiary motions
suspend the rules
take from the table
vice-chairperson
withdraw a motion

REVIEW QUESTIONS

1. Parliamentary procedure serves several purposes. What are they?

2. Parliamentary procedure is based on five principles. What are they?

3. Privileged motions have to do with the conduct of meetings. With what are subsidiary motions concerned?

4. Incidental motions relate to questions of procedure that arise from debate. What is the purpose of renewal motions?

5. Precedence refers to the ordering or ranking of motions. First, list privileged motions in order of precedence. Then list subsidiary motions in order of precedence.

6. The procedure for getting a motion on the floor involves five steps. What are they?

7. After a main motion has been discussed, the chair calls for a vote. How may a motion be voted on?

8. One way of changing the wording of a motion is by amendment. In what five ways may an amendment be put before a group?

9. What are the ways of delaying a discussion or a vote on a motion?

10. What are the duties of the chair, the vice-chair, and the secretary?

DISCUSSION QUESTIONS

1. Discuss parliamentary procedure as a democratic process. To what extent are the rights of the minority protected? To what extent are the rights of the majority protected? What are the pros and cons of majority rule? In addition to voting, what other aspects of parliamentary procedure promote democratic processes?

2. Discuss whether parliamentary procedure can be used at every kind of meeting. For what types of meetings is it most appropriate? Are there any types of meetings in which parliamentary procedure is not appropriate?

3. Discuss the circumstances under which it is better to postpone a motion to a definite time rather than to lay it on the table.

4. Discuss the reasons why some motions take a two-thirds vote to pass, while others take only a simple majority.

5. James Reston wrote, "A resolute minority has usually prevailed over an easygoing or wobbly majority whose prime purpose was to be left alone." First discuss the meaning of the quotation. Can you think of any historical instances in which Reston's quote proved true? How can a minority gain power over a majority? Then discuss what the chair can do in situations where a small minority dominates the meeting.

ACTIVITIES

1. Analyzing a Public Meeting

Attend an official public meeting such as those held by a city council or a school board. Report to the class on the business transacted, the various motions presented, the nature of the discussion, the actions of the chair, the tactics that the chair used to settle conflicts, and the participation of the members.

2. Explaining How and Why Parliamentary Procedure Is Used

A. Prepare a process speech explaining parliamentary procedure to your class. After your speech, ask for and respond to feedback from your classmates.

B. Prepare a short informative speech explaining the rules governing the precedence of motions. After your speech, ask your classmates for oral critiques of your speech.

C. Prepare a persuasive speech telling why meetings should be held according to the rules of parliamentary procedure.

3. Running a Meeting According to Parliamentary Procedure

A. Run a meeting according to parliamentary procedure. Plan to have each member of the class submit a motion (such as, "I move that *Oklahoma!* be selected as the Junior Class musical this year"). Before the meeting, have an agenda committee composed of three members of the class word the motions and set up an agenda. Have a second committee of three members set up rules to govern discussion. Make sure that these rules cover maximum length of speeches, number of times a person may speak on one motion, and method of determining the chairperson for each debate.

Each member of the class should be prepared to present a short speech supporting the motion he or she submits. Discuss each motion until it is passed, defeated, or delayed.

B. Have each member of the class act as chair in a discussion of a motion. Other class members should contribute to the discussion by making privileged, subsidiary, or incidental motions. The chair will rule on each motion and will conduct the discussion until the motion is passed, defeated, or delayed by passage of some other motion. First, have a short practice round in which mistakes are called to the chair's attention so that the chair can correct them. In a second round, have the chair step down when he or she makes a mistake, and have another student take over as chair. The goal is for the chair to get through an entire motion without making a procedural mistake.

C. Practice voting by voice, by show of hands, by rising, by roll call, and by written ballot on such things as appointing a committee, changing the time or place meetings will be held, and other actions that might be proposed as motions in a meeting.

4. Dealing with Disagreement in a Meeting

Working with a group of classmates, improvise a situation that involves a meeting in which a serious disagreement arises between two members. In turn have each member of the group act as chairperson and settle the conflict.

Real-Life Speaking Situations

1. Neighbors often form homeowners or renters associations, crime-watch commit-tees, and community councils to deal with local issues. Rarely do all people in such groups think alike, yet they must be able to function as a unified body. To achieve this unity, the group usually establishes guidelines for conducting busi-ness. In many cases these guidelines adhere to parliamentary procedure. Imagine that you have recently moved into your first house or apartment. You read in a newsletter from the homeowners or renters association that a regulation you oppose will be discussed at the next meeting, so you decide to attend in order to express your opinion. Assuming that the meeting is conducted according to parliamentary procedure, how will you present your views? Begin by defining the regulation. How will it affect you? Why do you oppose it? Next, identify how others at the meeting feel about the regulation. How many are for it? How many are opposed? Would you be more willing to support the regulation if it were amended? Write a two- or three-page informative speech narrating what you would do in this situation. Be prepared to present your speech in class and to respond to feedback from your classmates.

2. All businesses in our country are subject to government regulation. In many cases government agencies hold open meetings in which businesspeople and others can present their views on these regulations. Such meetings generally follow parliamentary procedure; consequently, speakers familiar with parliamentary pro-cedure stand a better chance of making their points than do speakers who are not. Imagine that you are in business and are attending a meeting of a govern-mental body in order to oppose a regulation that affects your company. How will you present your views? Begin by defining your company and the governmental body. Do you work for a large corporation, for a regional firm, or for yourself? Are you addressing a federal, state, or local municipal agency? Next, identify the regulation. What will it govern? Why is it being enacted? Finally, specify your arguments against the regulation. Why exactly do you oppose it? Write a three- or four-page dialogue of an open meeting in which you present your views, using at least three parliamentary motions. Be prepared to present your dialogue in class and to conduct a question-and-answer session on your use of parliamentary procedure.

UNIT SIX
PERFORMING ARTS

CHAPTER 20

ORAL INTERPRETATION

OBJECTIVES:

After studying this chapter, you should be able to

1. Define oral interpretation.

2. Explain the value of oral interpretation.

3. List three different types of literature available for oral interpretation.

4. Choose material to read.

5. Analyze material for reading.

6. Prepare an introduction to the reading.

7. Practice your reading.

Jack was puzzling over the meaning of Robert Frost's poem "Stopping by Woods on a Snowy Evening," which he was assigned to read for his English class. As he was discussing his difficulty with Karen, she said, "Here, let me read you the lines you're having trouble with." As Karen read out loud, she brought the ideas and feelings of the lines to life.

Jack listened carefully. When she finished, he said, "From the way you said those lines, I think I can see now what Frost meant—thanks, Karen."

WHAT IS ORAL INTERPRETATION?

Karen's reading was a good example of oral interpretation. **Oral interpretation** is the art of verbally communicating the ideas, feelings, and

Visit your local library at storytime to see how enjoyable oral interpretation can be—for reader and listener alike.

basic scheme or structure of a work of literature to one or more people. The oral interpreter's use of voice, facial expression, and gesture to communicate meaning from the printed page is an art form in itself. The art of oral interpretation provides benefits for both the reader and the listener.

The reader benefits by getting a strong sense of enjoyment in entertaining listeners with a reading that presents a rich interpretation of the work. Through the act of preparing a piece to present it to others, readers clarify meanings for themselves as well as for others and gain insights that go beyond any they can get by reading the work silently.

For the listener the benefit may be even greater. Performance brings a work to life. As a rule, people enjoy a play much more when they see it

ACTIVITY: Finding Examples of Contemporary Storytellers

Before books were printed, stories and tales were passed on to others orally. The storyteller, who relayed the history and lore of a tribe, played a vital role in tribal life. During the Middle Ages, bards and minstrels carried stories from one village to another. Brainstorm with your class-mates to form a list of storytellers in the modern world. Be specific. Think of different kinds of stories that you hear, such as historical, humorous, science fiction, and sports. Where do you hear them? Who tells these stories?

acted out than when they simply read it to themselves. Likewise, many people enjoy a poem, a short story, or an excerpt from a novel much more when it is interpreted aloud than when it is read silently. The library reading hour during which children cluster about the reader and give every ounce of attention to the story is a classic example of the excitement of oral interpretation.

CHOOSING MATERIAL

The success of your oral interpretation will depend on your choice of material. To choose material, you need to recognize the kinds of literature best suited for oral interpretation.

Types of Literature

What is literature? **Literature** consists of writings expressing ideas of permanent or universal interest. It is characterized by excellence of form or expression. Usually, literature can be categorized as prose, poetry, or drama.

Prose. Writing that corresponds to usual patterns of speech is called **prose.** Newspaper and magazine articles, novels, short stories, and this textbook are all examples of prose. Prose is usually subdivided into the categories of nonfiction and fiction.

Nonfiction deals with factual information, which is true or at least is supposed to be true. Nonfiction tells about real people and actual events.

Biography and autobiography are popular forms of nonfiction. Biography is the story of a person's life written by another person. Autobiography is the story of a person's life written by that person.

Another popular form of nonfiction is the essay, which is a composition that presents an author's thoughts or feelings on a subject. An essay can be defined by its purpose. The purpose of a narrative essay is to tell a story, while the purpose of a descriptive essay is to describe, or give an impression of, a topic. An expository essay either gives information, explains something, or defines something. A persuasive essay is designed to influence people's thinking or behavior. Many literary essays combine elements of two or more of these four types.

Fiction, on the other hand, presents material that is imagined or invented by the author. Fiction may be based on real happenings or events, but the dialogue, plot, and characters are created out of the author's imagination. In other words, fiction may be based on truth, but it is not truth. In literature, fiction refers to the novel or the short story.

Poetry. **Poetry** is the communication of an idea, experience, or emotion through the creative arrangement of words according to their meaning, sound, and rhythm. Poetry is often identified as either traditional or nontraditional. **Traditional poetry** is language arranged in lines with a regular rhythm and often with a definite rhyme scheme. Much **nontraditional poetry** does away with regular rhythm and rhyme, but it is still arranged in lines. Both traditional and nontraditional poetry are marked by the use of *imagery* (language that appeals to the senses), *figurative language* (language that is not meant to be interpreted in a literal sense), and *rhythm* (the arrangement of stressed and unstressed syllables). Two of the most popular types of poetry are the *narrative* and the *lyric*.

Narrative poetry is poetry that tells a story. A narrative poem can be short, like a ballad (a story told in verse that is usually meant to be sung) or long, like an epic (a long poem that relates the deeds of a hero).

Lyric poetry is verse, usually brief, that expresses the poet's emotions or personal thoughts. In ancient Greece certain poems were recited to the strumming of a lyre (a guitarlike instrument), hence the term *lyric poetry*. Lyric poetry is likely to express a single or primary emotion, which usually is implied rather than stated.

Drama. A **drama** is a story written to be acted out on a stage. A drama may be written in either prose or poetry. A playwright usually emphasizes character, conflict, and action, which are developed by the use of dialogue. Stage directions are provided to help the actors and the director bring the characters and action to life.

Finding a Selection

How do you choose a suitable selection to read? To help you make your choice, here are several criteria for evaluating selections.

Universal Appeal. Universal appeal means that a work has at least some relevance to the experience of all human beings. Having universal appeal does not mean that everyone will automatically like that selection. However, if a work has universal appeal, very likely it will be of interest to most people.

One example of a work with universal appeal is Robert Frost's poem "The Road Not Taken":

Two roads diverged[1] in a yellow wood,
And sorry I could not travel both
And be one traveler, long I stood
And looked down one as far as I could
To where it bent in the undergrowth;

Then took the other, as just as fair,
And having perhaps the better claim,
Because it was grassy and wanted wear;
Though as for that the passing there
Had worn them really about the same,

And both that morning equally lay
In leaves no step had trodden black.
Oh, I kept the first for another day!
Yet knowing how way leads on to way,
I doubted if I should ever come back.

[1] **diverged** [dĭ-vurj′d]: *v.* branched off.

I shall be telling this with a sigh
Somewhere ages and ages hence:
Two roads diverged in a wood, and I—
I took the one less traveled by,
And that has made all the difference.

In this poem Frost is considering the universal experience of making life choices. Don't we all face making such choices? Since the poem deals with a subject that is relevant to all human experience, it is said to have universal appeal.

Insight. Most good literature offers readers an insight into life. **Insight** is a view or an understanding that reveals an inner truth about something. For example, consider the messages of "The Road Not Taken." In this poem Robert Frost uses the word *road* as a symbol (a word standing for something else) of life. The fork in the road stands for a choice the speaker has to make. By presenting the speaker's thoughts about making the choice, Frost's poem gives insight into what happens as a result of making one life choice over another.

Lucy is looking in the wrong place for insights. They are found not "between the lines" but in our own reflections about a work. A sensitive oral interpretation can guide us to these inner truths.

Feelings. Most good literature has a special power that stirs readers' feelings. Sometimes the reader's **feelings,** or emotional reactions, are a result of the ideas that are expressed. Sometimes they are a result of the language used to express the ideas. In his poem "Annabel Lee," Edgar Allan Poe paints a picture of a man's intense feeling of loss at the death of his young bride.

It was many and many a year ago,
    In a kingdom by the sea,
That a maiden there lived whom you may know
    By the name of Annabel Lee;
And this maiden she lived with no other thought
    Than to love and be loved by me.

I was a child and *she* was a child,
    In this kindgom by the sea,
But we loved with a love that was more than love—
    I and my Annabel Lee;
With a love that the winged seraphs[1] of heaven
    Coveted[2] her and me.

And this was the reason that, long ago,
    In this kingdom by the sea,
A wind blew out of a cloud, chilling
    My beautiful Annabel Lee;
So that her highborn kinsmen came
    And bore her away from me.
To shut her up in a sepulcher[3]
    In this kingdom by the sea.

The angels, not half so happy in Heaven,
    Went envying her and me:
Yes!—that was the reason (as all men know,
    In this kingdom by the sea)
That the wind came out of the cloud by night,
    Chilling and killing my Annabel Lee.

But our love it was stronger by far than the love
    Of those who were older than we—
    Of many far wiser than we—
And neither the angels in Heaven above,
    Nor the demons down under the sea,
Can ever dissever[4] my soul from the soul
    Of the beautiful Annabel Lee;

For the moon never beams, without bringing me dreams
    Of the beautiful Annabel Lee;
And the stars never rise, but I feel the bright eyes
    Of the beautiful Annabel Lee:
And so, all the nighttide,[5] I lie down by the side
Of my darling—my darling—my life and my bride,
    In the sepulcher there by the sea—
    In her tomb by the sounding sea.

---

[1] **seraphs** [sĕr'əfs]: angels.
[2] **Coveted** [kŭv'ĭ-tĭd]: envied.
[3] **sepulcher** [sĕp'əl-kər]: a tomb or burial place.
[4] **dissever** [dĭ-sĕv'ər]: separate.
[5] **nighttide:** nighttime.

The speaker in the poem was so deeply in love with Annabel Lee that he felt their lives were intertwined. When Annabel Lee died, the speaker began to believe that the power of their love would keep their spirits together. The depth of the love and the sense of loss expressed in the poem stir the emotions of many readers, creating feelings of sadness and melancholy.

Potential for Interpretation. Some literature has only one meaning, which can be captured with a quick silent reading. However, much good literature is more complicated, revealing additional meaning and insight with each reading. The richer the material, the greater chance it offers for a successful oral interpretation.

Quality. Quality refers to the excellence of the selection. Choose a work that is constructed well. Look at the way language is used. Does the writer use vivid words? Are the sentences or lines skillfully crafted? As a rule, the better a work is written, the easier it is to read orally.

Occasion. Choose a work that suits the occasion. For example, if the occasion is the celebration of your grandmother's sixtieth birthday, you will most likely choose a selection that praises a grandmother. If the occasion is a graduation ceremony, you will want to choose a work that deals with hope, the future, or some other suitable topic.

The time limit should also enter into your choice of a selection. If you have only five minutes for your reading, make sure that your selection does not take ten minutes to read. Although longer works of prose and drama can be condensed, poetry is difficult to cut without destroying the meaning of the work. For your first assignment at least, you should try to find a selection that you can read in its entirety in the time available. For instance, "The Road Not Taken" requires between sixty and ninety seconds to read; "Annabel Lee" takes about two minutes.

Reading a carefully chosen selection to a relative or someone else who is special can bring extra joy to almost any occasion.

Choosing Selections for Oral Interpretation

Bring to class a list of fifteen of your favorite works of literature. Your list should include titles of stories, poems, and plays. Take a vote to see how many students would like to hear readings of each of the selections on your list.

UNDERSTANDING YOUR SELECTION

How well you can interpret meaning for others depends on how well you understand the work yourself. The following six guidelines apply to any form of literature—prose, poetry, or drama.

Meaning

Meaning is the idea or feeling that is communicated by a work. After you have chosen a selection, you must study it to make sure that you understand both its total meaning and the meaning of its individual words. To discover meaning you must be concerned with both *denotation*—the dictionary definition of words—and *connotation*—the feelings aroused by the words. A dictionary can help you check word denotations. Literature, especially poetry, uses words in ways that are not always common. Consequently, to make sure that you have the sense of a particular word within its context, you may want to look up even the words that you believe you already understand. Since some selections make specific references to times, places, and events, you may want to check these allusions by reading sections from encyclopedias, biographies, and history books. Alfred, Lord Tennyson's popular poem "The Charge of the Light Brigade" illustrates the importance of understanding total context. Study the following excerpt from this poem.

> Theirs not to make reply,
> Theirs not to reason why,
> Theirs but to do and die:
> Into the valley of Death
>   Rode the six hundred.
>
> Cannon to right of them,
> Cannon to left of them,
> Cannon in front of them
>   Volleyed and thundered;
> Stormed at with shot and shell,
> Boldly they rode and well,
> Into the jaws of Death,
> Into the mouth of Hell
>   Rode the six hundred.

To read this poem effectively, first you must understand specific historic references. This narrative tells the story of a group of soldiers referred to as "the light brigade," which was a cavalry unit with only small arms and swords for weapons. During the Crimean War this group was mistakenly sent into battle against overwhelming Turkish forces. Although the brigade fought bravely, it was totally wiped out.

Second, you must understand the dictionary meanings of individual words and terms. For example, the word *volley* refers to the simultaneous firing of the guns that were on all sides of the brigade as they rode into the valley.

Third, you must understand the connotation of such words and terms as "valley of Death," "jaws of Death," and "mouth of Hell." All three of these are different ways of expressing the fate that faced the entire brigade. Each phrase expresses the inevitability of death for every single person.

How do you know whether you fully understand the meaning of a selection? A good way to test your understanding is to write a paraphrase of the work. *Paraphrasing* means putting the selection into your own words. When you can write the idea of a work in your own words, you can feel confident that you really understand it.

Arrangement

Arrangement is the organization of a work. Like a speech, a work of literature has a beginning, a middle, and an end. Most fiction and drama begin with details that set the stage. The opening is usually followed by rising action. Suspense builds to a climax, which is the high point of conflict or the

It is not necessary to start your reading at a high level of excitement. Most stories begin quietly and build to a climax.

turning point in a story. Following the climax comes the falling action, which continues until the end of the work.

Consider the arrangement of a typical detective story. The story opens with details of a crime. Then comes the rising action. A detective is called in, and he or she begins to question witnesses. The detective finds clues and slowly fits them into a pattern. The suspense builds until the climax, that moment when the detective solves the crime. Then in the last few minutes the detective explains how he or she put the clues together, and the story ends.

The Speaker

Who is speaking? All literature is told by someone. In some literature the speaker is a clearly defined **narrator,** a person who is actually telling the story. The narrator may be the person whom the story is about or a person telling a story about someone else.

To interpret literature successfully, you must stand in the speaker's shoes and read the piece as though you were speaking your own thoughts. In the opening of Edgar Allan Poe's "The Cask of Amontillado," the speaker is Montresor. To interpret this selection successfully, you would have to become Montresor, who in his controlled madness is anticipating his revenge on Fortunato.

> The thousand injuries of Fortunato I had borne as I best could; but when he ventured upon insult, I vowed revenge. You, who so well know the nature of my soul, will not suppose, however, that I gave utterance to a threat. *At length* I would be avenged; this was a point definitively settled—but the very definitiveness with which it was resolved precluded the idea of risk. I must not only punish, but punish with impunity. A wrong is unredressed when retribution overtakes its redresser. It is equally unredressed when the avenger fails to make himself felt as such to him who has done the wrong.
>
> It must be understood that neither by word nor deed had I given Fortunato cause to doubt my good will. I continued, as was my wont, to smile in his face, and he did not perceive that my smile *now* was at the thought of his immolation.

Audience

To interpret successfully, you must know to whom the work is directed. Most works are directed to a specific person or to a general audience. For example, in the opening of Robert Browning's monologue "My Last Duchess," the Duke of Ferrara, the speaker, is showing a painting of his first wife to an envoy who has been sent to arrange the details of the Duke's second marriage.

> That's my last Duchess painted on the wall,
> Looking as if she were alive. I call
> That piece a wonder, now: Frà Pandolf's[1] hands
> Worked busily a day, and there she stands.
> Will't please you sit and look at her?

[1] **Frà Pandolf:** an imaginary monk and painter of the Italian Renaissance period. *Frà* means "Brother."

Mood

Mood refers to the emotional tone that predominates in a selection. Although a mood may appear to be neutral, more often than not it conveys a particular feeling, such as happy or sad, angry or pleasant, dreamy or serious. For instance, the mood of "Annabel Lee" is somber, sad, and haunting. In a longer work, the mood can change as the work moves along.

Punctuation and Word Grouping

In silent reading, punctuation serves as a guideline to accurate understanding. In oral reading, a speaker uses voice, articulation, pauses, and gestures to punctuate words and to group ideas.

Stops in thought (commas, semicolons, colons, dashes, and periods) are shown by pauses of varying lengths. Parentheses are shown by changes in volume. As you read a poem, keep in mind that capitalization at the start of a line does not necessarily indicate a pause at that point. Look again at a portion of "Annabel Lee."

The angels, not half so happy in Heaven,
    Went envying her and me:
Yes!—that was the reason (as all men know,
    In this kingdom by the sea)
That the wind came out of the cloud by night,
    Chilling and killing my Annabel Lee.

When reading this selection aloud, you would take short pauses at the commas in the first and fifth lines and longer pauses at the colon in line two, the exclamation mark and dash combination in line three, and the period at the end of the stanza. You would change expression—probably lower your voice—with the parenthetical section in lines three and four.

Italicized or underscored words are read in a louder volume. Quotation marks are expressed by shifts in vocal characteristics. Question marks are indicated by rising inflections. In some cases groups of words in a sentence have a particularly strong meaning or significance. These word groups can be main clauses, subordinate clauses, and phrases. To indicate the importance of such word groups the speaker must use vocal variation, such as increased loudness or rate, when reading them. For example, look at the following section of "Thank You, M'am" by Langston Hughes.

The woman said, "Um-hum! You thought I was going to say *but,* didn't you? You thought I was going to say, *but I didn't snatch people's pocketbooks.*

The first sentence would be read in a loud voice with emphasis on *"but"* and upward inflection on "didn't you?" The first seven words in the second sentence are one grouping of words, which would be read slowly. The final six words—*"but I didn't snatch people's pocketbooks"*—are a second grouping. Because these words are italicized, they would be read in a louder volume.

Analyzing a Poem for Oral Interpretation

Read the following poem carefully and answer the questions that come after it. Then read the work aloud.

The Day Is Done

Henry Wadsworth Longfellow

The day is done, and the darkness
    Falls from the wings of Night,
As a feather is wafted downward
    From an eagle in his flight.

I see the lights of the village
    Gleam through the rain and the mist,
And a feeling of sadness comes o'er me
    That my soul cannot resist:

A feeling of sadness and longing,
    That is not akin to pain,
And resembles sorrow only
    As the mist resembles the rain.

1. What impression do you form of the speaker?
2. To whom is the speaker speaking?
3. What is the mood of the poem?
4. Where would short pauses and long pauses occur?
5. What is the meaning of the poem? Write a short paraphrase.

PRESENTING YOUR INTERPRETATION

Just as a speech can be presented in different ways, so too can an oral reading. Currently, two methods of presentation are popular. In one, the interpreter memorizes the selection. In the second, the interpreter has the selection in view, which lets the audience know that the interpreter is not the source of the material being presented. No matter which method you choose, you will need to practice your selection until you are thoroughly familiar with it.

Practicing

The key to successful oral interpretation is practice. Although there are some individuals who can sight-read satisfactorily, even professionals usually require careful practice to prepare for a reading so that the audience will be able to understand the work fully.

Practice your selection exactly as you plan to give it. Your practice sessions will not help you if you sit in a chair and read the selection silently. Silent reading will not prepare you for an oral presentation. Of course, you must read the selection over several times silently to familiarize yourself with the material. However, not until you practice orally will you be able to use the techniques that make the difference between successful and unsuccessful oral interpretations.

Using a Manuscript

Even if you are planning to interpret a selection from memory, you will still be wise to have the manuscript in view. In almost all cases, the manuscript should be typed (double-spaced) and marked in ways that will help you with your reading. You may place the manuscript on a lectern, or you may hold it in your hands. Some interpreters prefer sitting on a high stool; some prefer to stand.

Although you may want to mark words for special emphasis, you should have such a strong feeling for their meaning that your voice will convey the proper emphasis naturally. Still, in practice you may want to try a given passage several different ways until you are convinced that you are presenting the idea or feeling most effectively.

Preparing Your Delivery

Adjust your speaking rate to suit your selection. Heavy, serious material should be read slowly. Light, humorous material can usually be read more quickly.

The best way to prepare for your performance is to read your selection aloud, many times, until you are comfortable with it.

Of special importance is clear articulation and correct pronunciation. Articulation in oral interpretation should be precise. Remember, you are reading for the entertainment of your audience. They must hear every sound clearly in order to appreciate the material completely. Also, there is no excuse for mispronunciation in oral interpretation. Difficult words can be marked in any way you find effective to help you pronounce them correctly.

The effectiveness of your interpretation will be strengthened by your nonverbal behavior. Gestures, movements, and facial expressions should be natural and should accent the meaning of the material. You may want to tape-record one or more of your rehearsals. Then you can play the tape back to make sure that each section sounds the way you intend.

Giving an Introduction

To help your listeners understand and enjoy your presentation, you will often want to provide them with introductory information about it. For example, you may want to tell your audience why you have chosen the particular selection you are presenting. Is the selection one of your favorites? Do you think that it will particularly appeal to your listeners? Does it relate to a poem, story, or play that is familiar to your listeners? By briefly mentioning what you enjoy about the selection or what makes it suitable for your audience, you direct your listeners' attention to elements that will increase their enjoyment of your interpretation.

Other information that you may want to give in an introduction includes background details about the selection and its author. Knowing the time period, culture, and other circumstances that influenced the creation of your selection will help your listeners understand the words, images, and subject matter it contains.

When you present a selection from a play or a story, be sure that you review the action that preceded the passage and that you identify the characters involved in it. Also explain any special features of the setting or the plot that will affect your audience's appreciation or enjoyment of your presentation.

Keep your introduction brief. Give only the information your audience needs or can use to gain further enjoyment and understanding of your presentation. Make sure that the main focus of your interpretation is always on your delivery of the selection itself.

ACTIVITY: Preparing a Manuscript for Oral Interpretation

Choose one of the selections from the list you compiled for the Activity on page 518. Prepare a manuscript of this selection for practice in oral interpretation. Type it double-spaced. Mark the copy in ways that will help you with your reading.

INTERPRETING PROSE

Prose presents special concerns for interpretation. Among these concerns are point of view, time available, and condensing.

Point of View

Point of view refers to who is telling the story. It is the angle of vision from which the audience sees the events in the story unfold. For example, a story may be told in the first person, using the pronoun *I* to identify the narrator, or it may be told in the third person. It may be limited to one character, or it may be omniscient, seeing into the minds of all the characters. The focus may be consistent, or it may shift from character to character. To identify point of view, you must first identify who is telling the story.

First Person. When the point of view is first person, a character identified by the pronoun *I* tells the story. Sometimes this character is the main character. For example, "The Cask of Amontillado" (see page 520 for an excerpt) opens with Montresor telling you, the reader, "The thousand injuries of Fortunato I had borne as best I could; but when he ventured upon insult, I vowed revenge."

Sometimes the character telling the story is an observer who relates events that happened to others. For example, notice the point of view in the following passage from "The Inexperienced Ghost" by H. G. Wells:

> The scene amidst which Clayton told his last story comes back very vividly to my mind. There he sat, for the greater part of the time, in the corner of the authentic settle by the spacious open fire, and Sanderson sat beside him smoking the Broseley clay that bore his name. There was Evans, and that marvel among actors, Wish, who is also a modest man. We had all come down to the Mermaid Club that Saturday morning, except Clayton, who had slept there overnight—which indeed gave him the opening of this story. We had golfed until golfing was invisible; we had dined, and we were in that mood of tranquil kindliness when men will suffer a story. When Clayton began to tell one, we naturally supposed he was lying. It may be that indeed he was lying—of that the reader will speedily be able to judge as well as I. He began, it is true, with an air of matter-of-fact anecdote, but that we thought was only the incurable artifice of the man.

Third Person. When the point of view is third person, the focus may be limited to one person. For example, the point of view in "Before the End of Summer" by Grant Moss, Jr. is limited to the point of view of Bennie, a ten-year-old boy. The following passage shows Bennie's lack of understanding of the mourners' grief at a funeral when they are told that Miss May is in heaven, a land flowing with milk and honey.

> The Reverend Isaiah Jones was certain that Miss May Mathis was there, resting in the arms of Jesus, done with the sins and sorrows of this world. Bennie wondered why Mr. John covered his face with his hands, and why Miss May's sister Ethel, who had come all the way from St.

Louis, cried out, and why people cried, if Miss May was so happy in this land. It seemed that they would be glad for her, so glad they would not cry. Or did they cry because they were glad? He could not understand.

A very common device of prose is the use of an observer who appears to be ever-present and all-knowing. This observer may tell what the characters say and do and at times may include what the characters think. For example, examine the following short lines from *My Friend Flicka* by Mary O'Hara:

McLaughlin was somewhat taken aback, but his wife concealed a smile. . . . Kennie found himself the most important personage on the ranch.

In these sentences, some unknown person is able to explain both Mc-Laughlin's and Kennie's feelings. This unknown person is an example of an ever-present observer.

Recognizing point of view will help you determine the voice to use when reading aloud. The third-person point of view calls for you to read in your own voice. For a story written in first person, however, you may want to take on the vocal qualities of the person telling the story.

Time Available

Most prose, especially fiction, is likely to take a while to read aloud. When you are allotted only five minutes for a reading, you must either find a short

DENNIS THE MENACE

"READ IT AGAIN, DAD. I COULD LISTEN TO THE THREE LITTLE BEARS ALL NIGHT."

Choosing the right selection is the first step in presenting an oral reading that your audience can enjoy "all night," or as long as the time available.

enough selection, read only a portion of the selection, or condense the selection.

In some longer works you can find a part that stands on its own well enough to be read by itself. For example, you may find a description, a bit of dialogue, or a subplot that can be handled within your time limit. At other times you may want to condense the piece to make it short enough to read in the time available.

Condensing

Condensing, or cutting a work to make it more concise, may be necessary for any one of a number of reasons. For example, the work may be too long for the time allotted; portions of it may be inappropriate for a particular audience; or the style of some sections may not lend itself to oral presentation.

However, because authors carefully create their works to produce a specific overall literary effect, it is best to avoid condensing unless you can retain the text's original meaning and mood.

Here are several guidelines you can follow when you condense prose.

1. Cut descriptive and narrative passages that are not essential to the story line.
2. Cut or condense flashbacks.
3. Cut quotation tags, such as "he said" or "Mary replied," and references to manner of speaking.
4. Cut references to the way a character gestures or moves.
5. Cut references to events that happened earlier in the story or to events that relate to portions of the story not included in your reading.

ACTIVITY: **Giving an Oral Interpretation of a Prose Selection**

Choose a work of prose you would like to share with your classmates. Study it carefully, making sure you understand the point of view. Then give an oral interpretation of it.

INTERPRETING POETRY

Poetry is highly charged language. Usually, a poem is arranged in lines with a regular rhythm and often with a definite rhyme scheme. In addition, to heighten feeling and to provide unique insights, poets often use figurative language and imagery.

When giving an oral interpretation of a poem, always try to capture the feelings expressed by the poem. These feelings are conveyed through rhythm, meter, rhyme, imagery, and figurative language.

In comparing prose and poetry, British poet Samuel Taylor Coleridge (1772-1834) said, "Prose, —words in their best order; poetry, —the best words in their best order." When you read a poem aloud, keep in mind that the poet has chosen and placed each word with great care.

Rhythm

Rhythm is the flow of stressed and unstressed syllables in a poem. Rhythm, which occurs in all speech, gives a musical quality to poetry. Rhythm can be described in a number of ways, such as fast, slow, soothing, disturbing, or exciting. When you read a poem, make sure that you capture the music of its lines.

Meter

Poetry gains its rhythm through meter. **Meter** is the pattern of stressed and unstressed syllables in a line of verse. Meter is developed within each line of a poem and is measured by the foot. A **foot** is a group of syllables arranged according to a definite pattern. Most poetry follows one of four metrical patterns.

1. **Iambic**—two syllables with accent on the second (unstressed + stressed)

> To him who in the love of Nature holds
> Communion with her visible forms, she speaks
> (from "Thanatopsis" by William Cullen Bryant)

2. **Trochaic**—two syllables with accent on the first (stressed + unstressed)

> Once upon a midnight dreary, while I pondered, weak and weary,
> (from "The Raven" by Edgar Allan Poe)

3. **Anapestic**—three syllables with accent on the third (unstressed + unstressed + stressed)

> And the sleep in the dried river-channel where bulrushes tell
> That the water was wont to go warbling so softly and well.
> (from "Saul" by Robert Browning)

4. **Dactylic**—three syllables with accent on the first (stressed + unstressed + unstressed)

> Cannon to right of them,
> Cannon to left of them,
> (from "The Charge of the Light Brigade" by Alfred, Lord Tennyson)

By determining the meter of a poem, you are able to decide which words should be emphasized. Suppose that you were reading the following line from "The Charge of the Light Brigade"

Cannon to left of them

Do you stress the word *cannon*? *left*? *them*? Do you stress all three? Since the meter is dactylic, you stress the first syllable of *cannon* and the word *left:*

Cannon to **left** of them

Meter also affects rhythm. Quick, regular meter creates a rhythm of excitement; slower meter creates a rhythm of peace, contentment, or sadness. In some cases meter will even determine how words are pronounced.

Rhyme

Traditional poems are likely to have a rhyming pattern. **Rhyme** is a pattern of similar sounds that gives a poem a melodic quality that is pleasing to the ear. Letters of the alphabet are used to signify the rhyming pattern: *a* denotes the first line and all other lines with the same rhyme; *b* denotes the next line with a different pattern; and *c* denotes the third pattern. For instance, Ralph Waldo Emerson's "Music" would be marked as follows:

It is not only in the rose,	*a*
It is not only in the bird,	*b*
Not only where the rainbow glows,	*a*
Nor in the song of woman heard,	*b*
But in the darkest, meanest things	*c*
There alway, alway something sings.	*c*

Although this poem has a clear rhyming pattern, the rhyme should not affect vocal punctuation. For example, in the next-to-last line there is no punctuation after the word *things*. Therefore, when this line is read, the *things/sings* rhyme should not be emphasized by a pause after *things*.

Figurative Language

In reading poetry, you must be able to interpret **figurative language,** the use of words and phrases that are not meant to be interpreted in their literal sense but instead are used to create new meanings and vivid images. Figurative language includes such figures of speech as metaphors (Bob is a rat), similes (Debbie runs like the wind), and alliteration (Sam stared silently), which abound in poetry. Carl Sandburg's short poem "Fog" illustrates the power of figurative language in poetry.

> The fog comes
> on little cat feet.
>
> It sits looking
> over harbor and city
> on silent haunches
> and then moves on.

This short poem is built on the metaphor of fog moving the same way that a cat does. The fog comes in "on little cat feet"; it sits for a while; and then it moves silently away. By likening the movement of fog to the movement of a cat, the poet uses figurative language to create a unique and insightful image.

Imagery is the use of words and phrases to describe something in a way that creates mental pictures for the reader. Poets, as well as other writers, use images to help readers participate in sensory experiences. Although the images created are often visual, writers also use words that suggest other sensory impressions as well: the way that things sound, smell, taste, or feel to the touch.

The following lines from Edna St. Vincent Millay's poem "Recuerdo" (a word meaning *remembrance* in Spanish) illustrate the use of imagery. As you read these lines, notice how the words help you imagine the sensations of the experience that the poet is describing.

> We were very tired, we were very merry—
> We had gone back and forth all night on the ferry;
> And you ate an apple, and I ate a pear,
> From a dozen of each we had bought somewhere;
> And the sky went wan, and the wind came cold,
> And the sun rose dripping, a bucketful of gold.

Choral Speaking

Poetry is often performed for an audience through choral speaking. **Choral speaking** refers to an oral interpretation performance in which several voices speak together in groups. Often, these groups are divided in the same way that a vocal chorus is—according to pitch. If the chorus has enough members it is divided into the four singing groups: soprano, alto, tenor, and bass. Then the different groupings are put into various combinations to achieve special effects. For instance, the soprano and tenor voices together will give an effect different from the effect of alto and bass voices together.

The goal in choral work is to maintain a coordinated ensemble sound. Care is taken to match pitch patterns, to consider harmony, and to develop tempo and rhythm. Just as singing groups require a good director, so do vocal choruses. A good choral group will add a dimension to a reading that an individual cannot approach.

Choral speaking is used in many ways. One use is to heighten the effect of ritualistic presentations. Prayers, statements of faith, and patriotic rituals may all customarily be carried out and enhanced by choral speaking. A second use of choral speaking is to heighten the dramatic force of a work. Early Greek drama relied heavily on the chorus to perform narrative, transition, and commentary. Today in plays, a chorus can represent an entire group of characters or can symbolically represent some nonhuman force. A third use of choral speaking is to give a new dimension to poetry. Many poems, such as Carl Sandburg's "Chicago," offer a special auditory experience. Through the power of the chorus every aspect of the poem can be interpreted.

Choral speaking creates much of the power in a live performance of ancient Greek drama.

Work with a group of eight students whose voices can be divided into four groups: two sopranos, two tenors, two altos, and two basses. Prepare a reading of Carl Sandburg's poem "Chicago."

First, analyze the material as you would any poem. Then, assign various passages to each vocal group. For example, for the five lines that open the poem, you might assign altos to read the first line, tenors the second, sopranos the third, basses the fourth, and have them all read together on the fifth. Finally, practice with the group.

> Hog Butcher for the World,
> Toolmaker, Stacker of Wheat,
> Player with Railroads and the Nation's Freight Handler;
> Stormy, husky, brawling
> City of the Big Shoulders:

They tell me you are wicked and I believe them, for I have seen your
    painted women under the gas lamps luring the farm boys.
And they tell me you are crooked and I answer: Yes, it is true I have
    seen the gunman kill and go free to kill again.
And they tell me you are brutal and my reply is: On the faces of women
    and children I have seen the marks of wanton hunger.
And having answered so I turn once more to those who sneer at this my
    city, and I give them back the sneer and say to them:
Come and show me another city with lifted head singing so proud to be
    alive and coarse and strong and cunning.
Flinging magnetic curses amid the toil of piling job on job, here is a tall
    bold slugger set vivid against the little soft cities;
Fierce as a dog with tongue lapping for action, cunning as a savage
    pitted against the wilderness,
> Bareheaded,
> Shoveling,
> Wrecking,
> Planning,
> Building, breaking, rebuilding,

Under the smoke, dust all over his mouth, laughing with white teeth,
Under the terrible burden of destiny laughing as a young man laughs,
Laughing even as an ignorant fighter laughs who has never lost a battle,
Bragging and laughing that under his wrist is the pulse, and under his
    ribs the heart of the people,
> Laughing!

Laughing the stormy, husky, brawling laughter of Youth, half-naked,
    sweating, proud to be Hog Butcher, Toolmaker, Stacker of Wheat,
    Player with Railroads and Freight Handler to the Nation.

The arrival of a traveler who could spin a good yarn brightened the austere lives of the pioneers.

INTERPRETING DRAMA

Since dramas are meant to be performed on stage, they usually make excellent material for oral interpretation. The keys to effective interpretation of drama are characterization, use of physical action, placement of characters, distinguishing characters, and condensing.

Characterization

Characterization refers to what the people in the drama are like. Physical characteristics include such things as height, weight, sex, color of eyes, and color of hair. Internal characteristics refer to such things as thoughts and feelings. Physical and internal characteristics are revealed by both what is said and what is done.

Use of Physical Action

While performers in a play are free to use their entire bodies and the entire stage to play a part, you must restrict your actions when giving an oral interpretation. Your goal is to suggest movement. If action is important to a scene, you may describe the action briefly in your introduction.

Preparing an Oral Interpretation of a Dramatic Passage

Prepare an oral interpretation of the following passage from *The Sound of Music,* written by Howard Lindsay and Russell Crouse with music by Richard Rodgers and lyrics by Oscar Hammerstein II.

The play is the story of the Von Trapp Family Singers and takes place in Austria before World War II. In this scene, Liesl, sixteen, the oldest daughter, is secretly meeting Rolf, a young village boy who has a strong pro-German attitude. Although by the end of the play Rolf has become a strong Nazi, his feelings for Liesl lead him to help the Von Trapp family escape from Austria at the time of Nazi occupation at the beginning of World War II.

Liesl. Good night, Rolf.

Rolf *(Walking on with his bicycle).* Liesl!

Liesl *(Going to him).* Yes?

Rolf. You don't have to say good night this early just because your father's home—

Liesl. How did you know my father was home?

Rolf. Oh, I have a way of knowing things.

Liesl. You're wonderful.

Rolf *(Resting the bicycle on its stand).* Oh, no, I'm not—really.

Liesl. Oh, yes you are. I mean—how did you know two days ago that you would be here at just this time tonight with a telegram for Franz?

Rolf. Every year on this date he always gets a birthday telegram from his sister.

Liesl. You see—you *are* wonderful.

Rolf. Can I come again tomorrow night?

Liesl *(Sitting on the bench).* Rolf, you can't be sure you're going to have a telegram to deliver here tomorrow night.

Rolf *(Sitting beside her).* I could come here by mistake—with a telegram for Colonel Schneider. He's here from Berlin. He's staying with the Gauleiter but I—*(Suddenly concerned)* No one's supposed to know he's here. Don't tell your father.

Liesl. Why not?

Rolf. Well, your father's pretty Austrian.

Liesl. We're all Austrian.

Rolf. Some people think we ought to be German. They're pretty mad at those who don't think so. They're getting ready to—well, let's hope your father doesn't get into any trouble. *(He goes to his bicycle.)*

Liesl *(Rising).* Don't worry about Father. He was decorated for bravery.

Rolf. I know. I don't worry about him. The only one I worry about is his daughter.

Liesl *(Standing behind the bench).* Me? Why? *(Rolf gestures to her to stand on the bench. She does and he studies her.)*

Rolf. How old are you, Liesl?

Liesl. Sixteen—What's wrong with that?

(They kiss, break away in confusion and Rolf jumps on his bicycle and rides off. Liesl shouts with joy and runs off in the opposite direction.)

Placement of Characters

In a play actors talk to each other. In a reading you must suggest the interaction, but you cannot show it because you are reading all the parts. By directing your attention to different locations, you can indicate where various characters are.

Distinguishing Characters

You can use your voice and body to distinguish between characters. For example, when two males are talking, you might read one part with a slightly faster rate and a slightly lower pitch than you read the other. Avoid exaggerating these differences, however, or your characters will become *caricatures*—comic distortions of themselves.

Condensing

In addition to the guidelines given on page 527 for cutting prose, you can also use the following guidelines when condensing drama.

1. Cut characters that are not essential to the major action of the play.
2. Cut material that repeats earlier action.
3. Cut parts that involve a great deal of stage action.

GUIDELINES FOR GIVING AN ORAL INTERPRETATION

- Do I use the manuscript properly?
- Do I use my voice well for emphasis?
- Do I use sufficient variety and emphasis to maintain interest?
- Is my rate appropriate to the material?
- Is my articulation clear?
- Is my pronunciation correct?
- Are my gestures, movements, and facial expressions natural?
- Does my selection have characteristics of good literature?
- Have I researched the piece I have selected?
- Have I prepared an introduction for the reading?
- Do I know the mood of the work?
- Have I practiced my reading thoroughly?

Profiles in Communication

Edward A. Newhouse

For some people oral interpretation is an art. For others it is a pleasurable way to entertain listeners by bringing a written text to life. For Navy Chaplain Edward Newhouse oral interpretation is both of these and much more—it is a sacred trust.

Each week Chaplain Newhouse reads a selection from the Bible as part of the worship service. A year at Princeton University studying communication skills convinced him of "how important effective reading techniques can be," the chaplain reports. "Accurately reading the text to my congregation helps them experience the Word itself—helps them really feel it."

Giving such readings exercises a number of Chaplain Newhouse's communication skills. For example, by varying his rate, pitch, and volume, he adds emphasis to words and phrases. He also uses pauses to emphasize important points. He adds that pauses can be tricky, though, because "pauses seem longer to an audience than to a speaker, and if they are too long, listeners get the impression that the speaker is lost or confused."

Oral interpretation also plays a key role in the religious rituals Chaplain Newhouse performs. He always strives for "a certain amount of drama in performing a ceremony." As Chaplain, he is both a participant and a director; consequently, he must set the scene for others' roles as well as perform his own. For example, he always has a bride and groom face one another rather than face him so that they share the words and gestures of the ceremony rather than simply deliver them to the chaplain.

Chaplain Newhouse gives the following advice for creating effective oral interpretations: (1) Practice your reading with someone else—preferably a good speech coach, but anyone will usually do; (2) "Connecting words such as *and* and *but* are often more important than you think, and they often call for emphasis"; (3) "Emphasis is the key to good interpretation"—master the use of pauses, gestures, and other methods of achieving emphasis; (4) "React to feedback from your audience"—look for signs of boredom, enthusiasm, and other audience responses and adapt your delivery accordingly; (5) "Don't get caught up in punctuation"—read the piece to express your interpretation of it; and, most important, (6) "Practice, practice, practice," he repeats for emphasis.

Oral interpretation is the art of communicating the ideas, feelings, and basic scheme or structure of a work of literary art to one or more people.

Oral interpretations usually present prose, poetry, or drama. Prose, ordinary language captured in writing, is divided into fiction and nonfiction. Poetry, language arranged in lines with regular rhythm and often with a definite rhyme scheme, is divided into several types. The most common types are narrative—poetry that tells a story—and lyric—poetry that focuses on emotions or thoughts. Drama is a story written to be acted out on a stage. To find a selection, look in a literature book or in other anthologies (collections of literary works).

Material for oral interpretation should have universal appeal, should show insight into the human condition, should show feelings, should have potential for interpretation, and should fit the time available.

There are several guidelines for interpreting material. Make sure that you understand the meaning of the piece. Identify who is speaking. Know to whom the work is directed. Consider the mood and the method of characterization. Understand the arrangement, punctuation, and grouping.

The key to successful oral delivery of a work is practice. Practice the selection exactly as you plan to give it. Keep the manuscript in view. Work on flexibility of voice, on speaking rate, on articulation and pronunciation, and on nonverbal expression.

Giving an introduction to your presentation can increase your listeners' understanding and enjoyment. Information often given in an introduction includes reasons why you enjoy the work; background details about the selection and its author; relationships between the selection and other works known by your audience; and a review of the characters, the preceding action, the setting, or the plot of a story or drama.

For prose, determine the point of view and identify the characters. If time for presenting the selection is short, either choose a short selection or condense the selection. For poetry, be conscious of figurative language and examine the work's structure to find the meter and rhyme pattern.

For drama, determine how you will show physical action, how you will develop characterization, and how you will present material to reflect placement of characters and to distinguish characters.

CHAPTER VOCABULARY

Look back through this chapter to find the meaning of each of the following terms. Write each term and its meaning in your communication journal.

anapestic	condensing	feelings
arrangement	dactylic	fiction
choral speaking	drama	figurative language

(continued on page 538)

foot	mood	prose
iambic	narrative poetry	rhyme
imagery	narrator	rhythm
insight	nonfiction	traditional poetry
literature	nontraditional poetry	trochaic
lyric poetry	oral interpretation	universal appeal
meaning	poetry	
meter	point of view	

REVIEW QUESTIONS

1. What is oral interpretation?

2. List three kinds of literature that are appropriate for an oral reading.

3. "Universal appeal" is one guideline for selecting a reading. What are four others?

4. "Understanding meaning" is one guideline for understanding a work. What are five others?

5. What is the difference between first-person and third-person narration?

6. What distinguishes poetry from prose?

7. What is the pattern of stressed and unstressed syllables in each of the four kinds of meter—iambic, trochaic, anapestic, and dactylic?

8. How is choral speaking different from an individual interpretation?

9. In an oral reading of drama, how would you show the placement of characters?

10. What are five guidelines for condensing prose?

DISCUSSION QUESTIONS

1. Discuss the ways in which preparation for an oral reading differs from preparation for a speech.

2. Discuss the circumstances under which choral speaking should be considered for oral interpretation.

3. Three things contribute to a successful oral interpretation—the material, the interpreter, and the audience. Discuss the role of each.

4. Thornton Wilder once wrote, "The less seen, the more heard." First, discuss the meaning of this quotation. Then explain how it relates to oral interpretation.

5. A. E. Housman once wrote, "Perfect understanding will sometimes almost extinguish pleasure." First, discuss the meaning of this quotation. Then discuss how it relates to oral interpretation.

1. Choosing Selections for Oral Interpretation

A. Working in a group, make a list of types of literature and specific selections that are enjoyed most by each person in the group. Then identify which selections would be well-suited to oral interpretation.

B. Using your literature book (or any anthology of literature), choose at least one example of each of the major kinds of literature (prose, poetry, drama) that you think would be a good selection for an oral reading. Be prepared to discuss why you made each selection.

2. Analyzing Oral Reading

Think about the times during the past few days that someone in person or on television has read material to you.

Would any of these readings be called "oral interpretation"? Why? Why not?

3. Using Vocal Techniques to Communicate Meaning and Mood

A. Select a short work. Read it aloud, showing how vocal punctuation can be used to change the meanings of words and ideas. Be prepared to discuss your reading with your classmates after you have finished.

B. Select two poems that are totally different in mood. Explain how you would read each poem to show the differences in mood between them.

4. Reading and Analyzing Poetry

A. First, identify the meter of the following two selections. Then read each poem aloud and discuss with your classmates the poet's use of figurative language in each poem.

Iambic—unstressed + stressed
Trochaic—stressed + unstressed
Anapestic—unstressed + unstressed + stressed
Dactylic—stressed + unstressed + unstressed

1. For the Angel of Death spread his wings on the blast,
   And breathed in the face of the foe as he pass'd;
   And the eyes of the sleepers wax'd deadly and chill,
   And their hearts but once heaved, and for ever grew still!

   (from "The Destruction of Sennacherib" by Lord Byron)

2. I wandered lonely as a cloud
    That floats on high o'er vales and hills,
    When all at once I saw a crowd,
    A host, of golden daffodils;
    (from "I Wandered Lonely as a Cloud" by William Wordsworth)

B. Identify the rhyme patterns in each of the following poems. Then read the poems aloud and discuss with your classmates how reading aloud helps communicate the meanings of specific words and the meaning of the total poem.

1. It is blue-butterfly day here in spring,
    And with these sky-flakes down in flurry on flurry
    There is more unmixed color on the wing
    Than flowers will show for days unless they hurry.

    But these are flowers that fly and all but sing:
    And now from having ridden out desire
    They lie closed over in the wind and cling
    Where wheels have freshly sliced the April mire.
    ("Blue-Butterfly Day" by Robert Frost)

2. The tusks that clashed in mighty brawls
    Of mastodons, are billiard balls.

    The sword of Charlemagne the Just
    Is ferric oxide, known as rust.

    The grizzly bear whose potent hug
    Was feared by all, is now a rug.

    Great Caesar's bust is on the shelf,
    And I don't feel so well myself.
    ("On the Vanity of Earthly Greatness" by Arthur Guiterman)

5. Reading a Prose Selection Aloud

Bring a favorite story to class and read it (or a condensation of it) aloud. Before you begin reading, identify the point of view and the main character(s) in the story. Use your vocal skills to express punctuation and mood. When you finish your reading, briefly discuss the story's meaning and conduct a question-and-answer session.

Real-Life Speaking Situations

1. At some time in your life, you will likely find yourself taking care of a small child—perhaps your brother or sister, son or daughter, or niece or nephew. Children have short attention spans. No matter how many toys they have or how much they enjoy playing games, children still get bored. One age-old method for entertaining children is telling stories. Imagine that you are taking care of two children, a boy and a girl, and that they have promised to take their nap if you will tell them a story. What story will you tell? How will you tell it? What nonverbal behavior will you use? First, identify the children. How old are they? How do they behave? What is their relationship to you? Next, identify the circumstances. What time is it? Where are you going to tell the story? Finally, identify the story. Pick a specific story that you can tell in three to four minutes. Be prepared to tell the class your information about your audience and the setting and then to present the story as if you were telling it to the children.

2. At one time books were available only in print. With the advent of phonograph records and especially tape recordings, however, books have gone audio. Confidence-building courses, diet plans, and other popular nonfiction—as well as texts in science, economics, and a wide range of subjects—are widely available on cassette tapes. In addition, spoken versions of written material are widely used in training and teaching. Cassette tapes offer instruction in nearly all topics from acting and automotive mechanics to Zen and zoology. Imagine that you need to create an audio teaching aid. How will you present your lesson to make it as instructive as possible? Prepare a three- to four-minute reading of any written instructional material—a how-to book, a set of directions for assembling something, a scout manual, a critical analysis of a story. Pay special attention to how you use your voice to help your listeners understand the information. When do you vary your rate? your tone? your pitch? your volume? Be prepared to present your reading in class and to explain briefly how you used verbal and nonverbal skills to make your reading instructive.

THEATER

OBJECTIVES:

After studying this chapter, you should be able to

1. Understand and explain the elements of drama.

2. Tell the difference between informal and formal theater.

3. Trace the historical development of drama.

4. Prepare a pantomime performance.

5. Prepare an improvisation.

6. Explain and use the criteria for selecting a play.

7. List and explain the duties of six nonacting roles in theater production.

8. Cast a play.

9. Prepare yourself to act in a play.

The house lights dimmed, the orchestra struck up the overture, the cast assembled on stage waiting for the curtains to open. Paul Lehman was nervous—no doubt about it. But he was also excited. It was opening night of the High School Mummers' production of *Grease*, and he was one of the stars.

Regardless of the number of shows you have seen or performed in, opening night is always something special. Today, movies and television are our primary sources of dramatic art, but as great as the electronic media are, they cannot match the excitement of experiencing live theater.

DRAMA

Drama is an artistic form of communication in which a story dealing with human conflict is acted out on a stage. Drama has five essential features, or elements.

First, drama tells a story. Usually the story is written out in full in a script; however, sometimes the story is made up by the actors as they go along. Second, the story is presented by live performers through dialogue. Third, drama usually has some overall meaning, or theme. Fourth, drama is performed in some designated area. Most productions are performed in a room that contains a stage and seats for an audience. Fifth, drama is meant to be seen by a live audience. The excitement of theater involves the interaction of performers playing their parts and an audience reacting to them.

Drama may be informal theater or formal theater. Informal theater relies on the actor's imagination to generate the action. In actor training, informal theater exercises are used to help performers become more aware of their senses. Two types of informal theater that you will study are pantomime and improvisation.

In formal theater the actors follow a complete script, which provides both the dialogue and directions for the action in the play. Most of the plays performed in schools are examples of formal drama.

Formal plays are classified as either comedy or tragedy. These two forms are often defined by how they end—comedies have happy endings and tragedies have sad or disastrous endings. **Comedy** is often based on exaggerated or eccentric behavior. Its goal is to give people joy or to make them laugh. Comedy can be both humorous and scornful. **Tragedy** tells stories of people who are brought down by circumstances. **Classical tragedy** presents highborn people who fall to ruin as a result of some "tragic flaw."

In ancient Greece, some amphitheaters were gigantic. Actors had to wear exaggerated masks to let distant spectators know which character was which. Today, our symbol for "theater" is a pair of Greek masks, one smiling and one frowning.

ACTIVITY: Listing Favorite Comedies and Tragedies

Work with a group of your classmates. First, make a list of comedies you have seen and enjoyed. Then make a list of tragedies you have seen and enjoyed. Share your lists with your classmates.

A SHORT HISTORY OF THEATER

The roots of theater are deep. It is likely that in prehistoric times, people acted out various scenes to explain meanings to others, to relive adventures, or perhaps even to entertain. For example, picture the hunter returning to the cave with his catch and then acting out the events of the hunt to tell others exactly what he had done. In fact, given our knowledge of human nature, we can even speculate that the hunter may have exaggerated a little to make the story more exciting.

Formal theater began in ancient Greece as religious celebrations associated with the worship of Dionysus, the god of wine. These festivals lasted five or six days. The final three days were devoted to dramas that competed for annual prizes. In these dramas the stories were told by a **chorus,** a group of people who narrated the events. Records dating from about 534 B.C. show that the actor and dramatist Thespis won the first contest. The word **thespian,** for "actor," comes from his name.

The first great formal theater was founded in Athens in the fifth century B.C. The four greatest Greek playwrights were Aeschylus, Sophocles, Euripides, and Aristophanes. Many of their plays are still performed today. Among the most popular are *Oedipus Rex* by Sophocles, *Medea* by Euripides, and *Lysistrata* by Aristophanes.

Greek plays were presented with one, two, or three actors playing all the parts and with a chorus that narrated the greatest portion of the action. All participants wore masks, and all parts were played by men.

Greek drama followed certain principles. First, the drama was designed to bring about a *catharsis,* or releasing of emotions, in the audience. Second, the main characters in the drama were of noble birth. Third, the main character in a tragedy suffered a fall as a result of a tragic flaw in his or her nature. Fourth, the drama was written in poetic language.

Greek dramas were presented in an amphitheater setting that had a round or rectangular playing area with an altar, a booth or hut used for changing, and seats all around the playing area. There was no raised stage as we know it.

About 200 B.C., the focus of drama shifted to Rome. The surviving Roman dramas are considered inferior to the Greek dramas, which they imitated. However, the Romans made major contributions to the physical setting of the theater by developing a more modern type of theater building with an elevated stage. Plautus and Terence are the two most renowned Roman playwrights.

With the decline and fall of Rome, formal theater also declined. During the Middle Ages (A.D. 500–1450), presentations dealing with Biblical events and parables were staged by the Church. In England groups of players constructed pageant wagons and set each separate scene of their dramas at a different place in town. This period was known for **miracle plays,** which dramatized events from the Bible and from the lives of saints, and for **morality plays,** which presented allegorical stories in which all characters personified religious or moral abstractions.

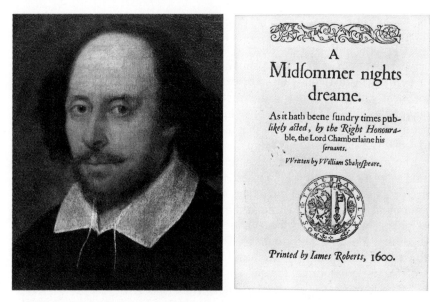

From the Elizabethan era to the present, William Shakespeare has been one of the most popular playwrights in the English language. The comedy *A Midsummer Night's Dream,* which for a 1600 printing bore the fashionably ornate frontispiece pictured on the right, continues to be popular today.

From 1350 to 1650, a period called the **Renaissance** (literally, "rebirth") brought renewed interest in Greek and Roman plays. In addition, original comedies, tragedies, and **pastoral plays** (love stories in idealized woodland settings) were created and performed. A major contribution was Italy's **commedia dell'arte,** popular comedy in which professional actors improvised (meaning "made up") their roles as stock characters in humorous, standardized situations.

English Renaissance drama flourished between 1590 and 1630. This period is notable for the development of secular (nonreligious) themes, the rise of professionalism in both acting and play writing, and the performance of plays in English rather than in Latin. This series of theatrical events brought about the development of the great Elizabethan theater.

The Elizabethan theater era was named for Elizabeth I, who ruled as queen of England from 1558 to 1603. William Shakespeare (1564–1616), regarded as one of the world's greatest playwrights, wrote and performed during this age. His plays include tragedies, comedies, and histories (chronicles of historical events).

The French theater blossomed at the end of the Renaissance (1622–1673) with the works of Molière, who was a comic genius. His plays ridiculing people, ideas, hypocrisy, medicine, and forced marriages were the high point of the period and are still popular today.

After 1660, a new era of drama began in England. This period, called the **Restoration** after the restoration of the royal family of Stuart to the throne in 1660, continued until 1700. Restoration drama, which is also called **comedy of manners,** is characterized by satire that makes fun of social customs. A significant development of the Restoration period was that women were allowed to appear on stage for the first time.

During the nineteenth century, **romanticism** flourished throughout Europe. In general, during the Romantic Period, the belief in the reliance on reason was replaced by the belief that human beings should be guided by feelings and emotions. The drama of this period took on a greater variety as playwrights experimented with new themes and characterizations.

Late in the nineteenth century, modern drama was born with the works of such dramatists as Ibsen in Norway, Strindberg in Sweden, Chekhov in Russia, and Galsworthy and Shaw in Great Britain. This early modern period was marked by **realism,** a movement to portray people and situations as they really are in everyday life.

During the past few decades playwrights have experimented with many styles of theater. One of the most interesting styles to emerge has been the theater of the absurd. In this style, life is viewed as meaningless and people's strivings as absurd, since they cannot do anything to improve the human lot.

Today, many different styles of theater coexist, with no one style dominating. Revivals provide opportunities to see the styles of the past, while experimental theater presentations allow us to watch new theatrical styles emerging.

ACTIVITY: Studying Quotations from Great Dramas

The following quotations are taken from dramas written by several of the greatest leaders of the theater. Practice reading the quotations aloud. Analyze each quotation. What idea or feeling is being expressed? Read the quotations aloud in class and discuss their meaning.

1. Destiny waits for the free man as well as for him enslaved by another's might. *The Libation Bearers*—Aeschylus

2. How dreadful knowledge of the truth can be / When there's no help in truth! *Oedipus Rex*—Sophocles

3. Did my heart love till now? Forswear it, sight! / For I ne'er saw true beauty till this night. *Romeo and Juliet*—William Shakespeare

4. The more we love our friends, the less we flatter them; it is by excusing nothing that pure love shows itself. *Le Misanthrope*—Molière

5. To crave for happiness in this world is simply to be possessed by a spirit of revolt. What right have we to happiness? *Ghosts*—Henrik Ibsen

INFORMAL THEATER

Informal theater is the spontaneous theater of the imagination. Participating in informal theater allows a performer to develop theatrical experience without being involved in a formal production. Informal theater provides learning exercises that can help you develop acting skills by making you more aware of ways to communicate ideas and feelings. Two specific types of informal theater are pantomime and improvisation.

Pantomime

Pantomime is dramatic communication performed entirely without words. Remember times when you silently mimicked the way a person put on makeup or answered the telephone? Such mimicry is an example of pantomime. Today, Marcel Marceau is probably the most famous professional **mime** (pantomimist). Audiences are amazed at how he can communicate so well using no words at all. He relies entirely on gesture, facial expression, and movement. Every action performed by a mime—even the smallest movement of a finger or the slightest change of expression—is designed to carry meaning.

Pantomiming is especially good practice for learning to express physical and mental states. Trying to pantomime such actions as picking a flower, meeting a girl, or digging a ditch can help you develop a heightened awareness of the feelings associated with those actions. You can work on using your facial expression and bodily movement to express the happiness, sad-

If you have ever played charades, you are acquainted with pantomime and with the challenge of communicating without words.

ness, guilt, anxiety, or exertion that is involved in a particular activity or situation.

Preparation. Preparation for pantomiming involves using your powers of observation. Suppose you want to pantomime a person getting angry. As a model for your behavior, you would select a person you know well. To prepare, you would try to picture the facial expression, gestures, and other body movements that the person exhibits when angry. (Keep in mind that pantomime is silent; for example, the person may yell when angry, but yelling is not suitable for pantomime.) Then you would try to imagine yourself in a situation that usually makes this person angry. As you act out the situation, remember that you are playing the part of a specific person and are trying to imitate everything the person does. You may often find it helpful to work with a mirror so that you can observe how well you are doing.

Most likely you will not remember all of the person's behaviors. In that case, you will need to make additional observations to perfect your pantomime. The next time the person gets angry, observe his or her exact behavior very closely. Start with the person's face. What kind of look enters the eyes? Notice the mouth. Do the lips pucker, or do the corners of the mouth turn down? Does the person's face change color? Are there any other distinctive facial changes? Now check the person's body. What does this person do with his or her hands and arms? Perhaps this person clenches the hands into fists, or maybe he or she waves the arms. Once you feel that you have mastered particular behaviors, concentrate on the entire sequence. Is there a building of emotion? How long does the anger last? Be concerned with accuracy of detail. Think of the cause of the person's anger. Can this be shown? How might you recreate the details or incidents that lead the person to become angry?

Pantomime, like any drama, is accurate in detail. It is also slightly exaggerated. Stage gestures must be broader, more sweeping than reality, so that the audience can see them and can recognize what they mean. Preserve accuracy of detail, but show some slight exaggeration to communicate a pantomimed message clearly.

Practice. To become a better pantomimist, you must practice. Suppose you are trying to pantomime a child's attempts at tying a shoelace and have carefully observed children's behavior. Now you must practice going through the entire routine. This is the point where you need to use your own imagination. When would a child be tying a shoe—under what circumstances? What can you do to show those circumstances? As you think about possibilities, practice the action. What can you do to make your pantomime more dramatic? Perhaps just as you have finally succeeded in forming a bow, you tug on the laces to tighten the knot and the lace breaks. Or perhaps you grin with success at tying the lace only to have the bow come undone just when you thought you had finished.

Eventually you may want to work with others in class to create more complicated scenes. Suppose, for example, you wanted to pantomime a crowd reacting to a football play that resulted in the winning touchdown being scored in a tense, hotly contested game. You and one, two, or three others could sit on a bench facing an audience of classmates. Then each of you would imitate various kinds of behavior, such as jumping up and down or hugging each other.

Sound Effects. Although pantomime is nonverbal, you can still use sound effects. Squeaks, squawks, squeals, and other sounds may play an important part in creating the action. For instance, when acting as if you are lifting a heavy box, you may grunt or groan.

Improvisation

Improvisation is a form of drama that portrays spontaneous reactions to a situation. One important difference between improvisation and pantomime is that improvisation includes speech as well as action. For a classroom exercise, your teacher may outline an opening situation such as the following one for you and a partner to play out.

> You had a date for the evening. However, at the last minute your date calls to say that the next-door neighbor has fallen down the stairs and needs someone to take her to the doctor. Your date asks you to cancel your plans because someone must take the neighbor to the hospital and stay to determine the situation.

As soon as you understand the situation, the two of you can play out the scene. Your dramatization of the event is an improvisation. The situation provides a starting point. The improvisation plays out the scene. Like any drama, improvisation includes at least the following three basics: a dramatic point, dialogue, and characterization.

A Dramatic Point. Although life itself may be viewed as drama, just showing life as it occurs would not be very effective on stage. For drama, whether you are doing improvisation or creating a play, your situation must have a dramatic point, or climax. The **climax** is the moment of highest intensity in a play. Sometimes the dramatic point is simple—sometimes it is very complicated.

Without a dramatic point, an improvisation is unlikely to hold an audience's interest. For example, an audience would soon lose interest in a dialogue between you and your partner in which the two of you chatted aimlessly about the weather. If, on the other hand, you and your partner were trying to figure out how to get a wealthy friend to invite you both to a pool party so that you could escape the hot weather, your solution to this problem could provide a dramatic point. Your audience's enjoyment will greatly depend on the creativity and skill you show in building up to your dramatic point.

Dialogue. Dialogue is conversation between two or more characters. Although dialogue originally applied to conversation between just two people (as opposed to **monologue,** which refers to a speech given by a person alone on stage), today all the conversation in a play is called dialogue. The purpose of dialogue is to help an audience understand the characters and the situation. Therefore, if you and your partner were devising an improvisation for the dating situation outlined above, your dialogue would reveal

"Alas, poor Yorick!" These words begin a famous *soliloquy* from Shakespeare's play *Hamlet*. A soliloquy is one kind of monologue in which a character expresses his or her inner thoughts aloud.

the feelings and thoughts of two people caught in such circumstances and would show how the situation built to a climax and was resolved.

Characterization. Characterization means the portrayal of the physical, intellectual, and emotional traits of each character. For example, in the improvisation assignment outlined on the previous page, you and your partner may decide to portray the woman as a nervous, excitable person who has trouble thinking under tension and the man as a spoiled brat who loses his temper quickly whenever he is crossed. On the other hand, you could portray the woman as an egotist who, though she performs charitable actions, is really insensitive to others' needs and the man as a meek person who always does what he is told, no matter how unjust it is. These two "dramas" would differ tremendously because of the differences between the characters.

During an improvisation you may not have enough time to think of ways to develop a character very much. Still, the nature of the situation will help you determine what you will say. For example, if you were portraying the man as a spoiled brat, you would want to exhibit the kinds of behavior that you would expect from such a person in such circumstances. You would be quick to anger. Perhaps you would whine and cry.

Whatever type of character you decide to develop, be consistent throughout the improvisation, whether it is supposed to last for one minute or ten minutes. In addition, never break up—that is, never start laughing—in the middle of an improvisation. Keep in mind that you are creating an illusion. To do so, you must be consistent and stay in character.

Performing a Pantomime and an Improvisation

First, pantomime one of the following situations. Then, working with a partner, develop one of the other situations into an improvisation.

1. You walk by a pet shop, see a dog in the window, go into the shop to ask about the dog, and get so taken with it that you buy it.

2. You order a sandwich and a glass of milk, and you get a bowl of soup and a glass of soda water.

3. You ask a person you don't know very well out on a date for the first time.

4. You walk into a china shop carrying a large package.

5. You are watching a sporting event on television, and your favorite team is losing.

SELECTING A PLAY FOR FORMAL THEATER

Formal theater involves the acting out of a complete script that includes both dialogue and action. A successful theatrical production starts with the selection of the right play. Selecting the play is usually the job of the director. If you are responsible for selecting a play, you will want the answers to several questions.

Has the play been released? A **release** is a formal permission from the owner of a play's production rights to allow someone to produce that play. For example, the popularity of *A Chorus Line, Annie,* or *Amadeus* might lead you to consider selecting one of these plays. Your first question would be whether you are allowed to do the show. While a show is on Broadway, it is protected by contract from being performed by any group until it is released.

How much is the royalty? For almost any show you select, you will have to pay a **royalty,** which is a payment of money for the right to produce the show. Just as the author of a book gets a small amount of money for each new book sold, so the author of a play receives a small amount of money each time that play is produced. The more recent or popular the show, the higher the royalty is likely to be.

How large is the cast? A **cast** is the group of actors in a play. The cast is not the same as the number of characters. Sometimes in plays with many characters, one actor will play several parts. Therefore, a show with thirty characters may require a cast of only fifteen or twenty people.

Both the size and composition of the cast are important considerations in selecting a play. For example, *A Chorus Line* is a musical that requires about sixteen characters, men and women. All must be able to dance. A

At the end of well-performed play, the audience usually requests a *curtain call* by applauding until the cast reappears on stage.

few must be capable singers and actors as well. *Death Trap,* on the other hand, is a mystery that has only three major characters, two men and a woman. To make your selection, you have to know how many actors you will need, how many will have major parts, and how many will need to have special skills, such as the ability to sing or dance.

What are the technical requirements? **Technical requirements** are the items such as the sets, props, lighting, and costumes that are needed to create the physical environment within the play. To determine the technical requirements for the sets in a play, you would ask such questions as how many sets will be needed and how large the stage must be. *A Chorus Line,* for example, has a very simple set. *Annie,* on the other hand, requires many different sets. Identifying all the technical requirements for a play will require you to read the play several times, analyzing it closely for items needed in each scene.

Do you have the space and machinery to build sets? Do you have the room and the equipment to create the different settings in the play? Again, answering this question will require you to study the play closely.

Is the play worth doing? After all is said and done, this is the key question. The following criteria are some of the most important considerations for determining whether you should select a particular play.

Current relevance. Some dramas become very quickly dated. Yet plays like *Hamlet* by Shakespeare and *The Sea Gull* by Anton Chekhov have ideas that still speak to us even though they were written in other time periods and other countries.

Appropriateness for your particular audience. Some plays may be all right for neighborhood theaters, dinner theaters, or Broadway and yet not necessarily be right for a high-school production. Think about the kinds of shows your classmates are likely to appreciate. If you are unsure about which play to select, you might try surveying your classmates or whoever will be in your audience.

Emotional and intellectual stimulation. It should cause the audience to think, to ponder. Some plays may be entertaining while having little intellectual or emotional value. Although there are times when such a play is appropriate, for the most part you should choose a play that will stir your audience's thoughts and emotions.

You might ask, "Where can I find titles of plays to choose from?" Although your school or city library will have drama anthologies that may be helpful, you are more likely to come up with suitable titles by going through publications that list and review shows. One such publication is *Dramatics.* Each issue has a new play and articles about various aspects of producing plays.

The following plays are among those that have been popular over the years.

Musicals: *The Music Man, Little Mary Sunshine, Carousel, Oliver, The Wiz, The King and I, West Side Story*

Comedies: *Auntie Mame, The Boy Friend, Charley's Aunt, Arsenic and Old Lace, Harvey, Life with Father, Blithe Spirit*

Dramas: *Our Town, A Streetcar Named Desire, A Raisin in the Sun, Dark of the Moon, The Madwoman of Chaillot, I Remember Mama, The Diary of Anne Frank*

Costumes and sets, whether minimal or elaborate, help to create the emotional stimulation the audience will receive from the play.

AUDITIONS

Most high-school and college plays are cast through open auditions. An **audition** is a formal tryout in which people have a chance to show their abilities. Usually these auditions are open to anyone in school who wishes to try out for a part. A director who has a particular person in mind for a part may give that person an audition before the open auditions. Many professional shows are cast in this way. At times, auditions are closed, which means that only those who meet specific conditions are allowed to try out. For example, tryouts may be open only to those with singing or dancing experience in shows or only to those in the junior class.

Holding Auditions

A director will announce when auditions will be held. Auditions are likely to be held right after school for two or three days. Sometimes a separate audition is held for each type of part. For example, auditions for singers may be held one day, auditions for lead speaking parts a second day, and auditions for all other parts a third day.

Sometimes you are expected to be familiar with the part you are auditioning for. In this case, you will be asked to prepare a short piece from the role in which you are interested. For such auditions, the director usually puts copies of the play in the school library a week or two before auditions are scheduled. Those who plan to audition can then read the play and practice a portion of it. At other times, you are asked to read a part "cold," that is, without having practiced. To audition for a musical, you may be asked to bring any ballad or show tune you are familiar with. Sometimes at auditions you are given a situation and asked to improvise.

Casting

Ordinarily, the director decides who will be in the cast after he or she has heard everyone. The turnout of students at auditions is usually two or three times the number of parts in a play.

During auditions the director looks for such things as experience, physical build, vocal qualities, and attitudes that are needed to portray each particular character. To be cast at all is exciting. Keep in mind the old saying "There are no small parts, only small actors."

Suppose that you are directing a play. Create an audition form that you could use to help you make decisions about each person trying out.

REHEARSALS

From the day a play is cast until its first performance, the participants go through a series of rehearsals. **Rehearsals** are practice sessions. It is during rehearsal that the play takes shape. Rehearsals may be conducted for a period of from two or three weeks to eight or ten weeks, depending upon the experience of the cast and the complexity of the play.

Once you accept a part in a play, you have a verbal contract stating that you will attend all rehearsals and all performances. Although someone may need to miss a rehearsal, even people with the smallest parts are expected to be at all rehearsals unless excused by the director.

Early in the rehearsal schedule, the performers usually practice the play scene by scene. For example, one entire rehearsal might be devoted to a single complicated scene. As performance time nears, more of the play is covered at every rehearsal. During the last week or ten days, the entire play may be rehearsed at each practice session. At all stages of the rehearsal, the director may make suggestions to the actors as they are working. At the end of each rehearsal the director gives the cast feedback about how that portion of the show is going.

During the last week of rehearsal, all the technical aspects are added. Scenery is finished and lighting is coordinated. The last two or three rehearsals are called *dress rehearsals;* in these, every aspect of the show is rehearsed just as it will be done at the time of performance.

During rehearsals the actors have many chances to practice their lines and their movements under the director's guidance.

Gathering Information About Rehearsals

Meet with the teacher in your school who is directing the next play, and ask the following questions concerning auditions and the rehearsal schedule:

1. How many parts are in the play and what are they?

2. Will those who try out need to be familiar with the play?

3. Will those who try out need any special skills, such as singing ability?

4. How long a period is scheduled for rehearsals?

5. How long will each rehearsal be?

6. When will all actors need to know all their lines?

7. When are dress rehearsals scheduled?

Report your findings to your classmates.

THE ROLE OF NONACTORS

There are many nonacting roles that are essential to a successful production. These roles, which include such tasks as directing the play, setting up the stage, and costuming the characters, are not only necessary to the theatrical production, but are also fun to accomplish.

Producer

As head administrator of a dramatic production, the **producer** is the person responsible for bringing together the script, the theater, the director, and in the case of professional theater, the financing for a show. Although the producer is a major role separate from the director in professional theater, in high-school theater the producer is also usually the director.

Director

The **director** is in charge of selecting the play, casting, coaching the actors, and coordinating the work of the set designer and the costumer. In short, the director has the ultimate responsibility for the production. Although the teacher in charge of drama will most likely direct the major productions, students often are able to gain experience in directing scenes, one-act plays, and other short productions. If you are interested in directing, you may be assigned also to assist the teacher or the director in carrying out the many tasks a director must do.

Technical Director

The **technical director** is in charge of constructing sets, positioning and operating lights, managing the curtain, and tearing down the set. Technical directors work closely with directors. In effect, the director tells the technical director what he or she is trying to accomplish, and the technical director constructs a set and arranges lighting that will meet those goals. To assist in the work that needs to be done backstage, a technical director will often appoint a stage manager to be in charge of particular tasks.

Stage Manager

The **stage manager** is in charge of the entire backstage. The stage manager's goal is to see to it that the performance follows the exact pattern the director has set in rehearsals. This job involves making sure that actors are in their proper places to go on stage, cuing actors (helping them learn when they go on and when they speak), prompting when necessary, and in general helping rehearsals run smoothly. The stage manager records all of the director's instructions about blocking, cues, and sound effects in a master prompt book so that anyone at any time can see the movement of a scene. Once the production begins, the stage manager takes over many of the director's chores managing the actors and the overall production of the show.

Set Designer

The **set designer** is responsible for designing all visual elements, including stage sets and lighting, that will be used for the production. The set designer works closely with the director in order to design a set and lighting that will create the proper atmosphere for the play. A successful set will supplement the play's lines and action to create a mood that will help the audience better understand the meaning and intent of the show. For instance,

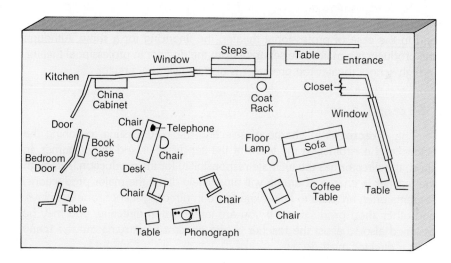

ORGANIZATIONAL CHART OF PERSONNEL IN A THEATRICAL PRODUCTION

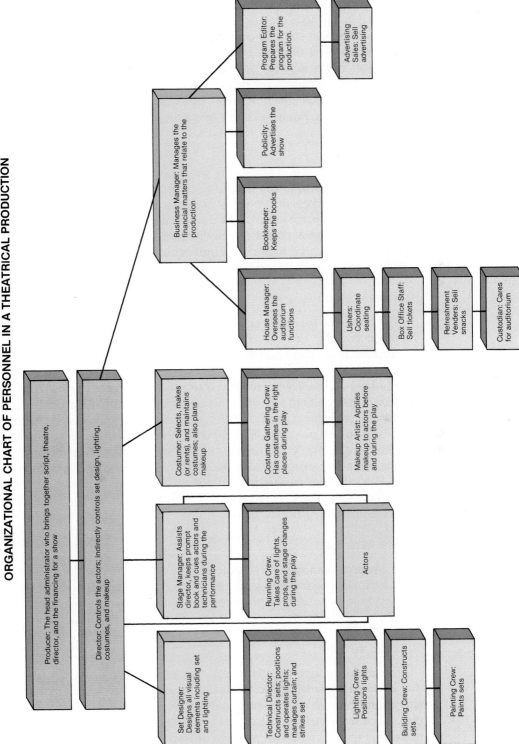

Producer: The head administrator who brings together script, theatre, director, and the financing for a show

Director: Controls the actors; indirectly controls set design, lighting, costumes, and makeup

Business Manager: Manages the financial matters that relate to the production

Program Editor: Prepares the program for the production.

Advertising Sales: Sell advertising

Publicity: Advertises the show

Bookkeeper: Keeps the books

House Manager: Oversees the auditorium functions

Ushers: Coordinate seating

Box Office Staff: Sell tickets

Refreshment Venders: Sell snacks

Custodian: Cares for auditorium

Costumer: Selects, makes (or rents), and maintains costumes; also plans makeup

Costume Gathering Crew: Has costumes in the right places during play

Makeup Artist: Applies makeup to actors before and during the play

Stage Manager: Assists director, keeps prompt book and cues actors and technicians during the performance

Running Crew: Takes care of lights, props, and stage changes during the play

Actors

Set Designer: Designs all visual elements including set and lighting

Technical Director: Constructs sets; positions and operates lights; manages curtain; and strikes set

Lighting Crew: Positions lights

Building Crew: Constructs sets

Painting Crew: Paints sets

a comedy or a musical generally requires sets and lighting different from those used in a serious drama.

The set designer starts by creating a **floor plan,** which is a diagram that shows the positions of walls, entrances, and furnishings on the stage. The set designer draws separate designs for each of the different settings in a particular play. Although some plays, such as *The Diary of Anne Frank,* have only one set for the entire production, other plays have two, three, or even more different sets. For an example of a floor plan, see page 558.

Costumer

The **costumer** is in charge of the performers' attire. The costumer takes his or her lead from what the director is trying to accomplish and then helps to coordinate the dress of the actors. For contemporary plays, the costumer may limit his or her role to simply offering ideas on what actors should wear. However, for historical drama or other presentations that require unique or specifically designed costumes, the costumer will be in charge of renting or making appropriate clothing and certain props.

Business Manager

The **business manager** takes care of the financial matters that relate to the production. For example, the business manager works with the director to pay bills, issue and keep track of tickets, file receipts, and keep good records.

The business manager may also be responsible for printing programs. A program includes listings of the cast in order of appearance, of the production staff, and of committees and crews. Programs also carry ''acknowledgments'' for those who lent assistance. For example, if a florist donated the plants for a wedding scene, the florist's name would be acknowledged on the program.

The business manager is also likely to be in charge of publicity for the show. Publicity may involve making posters, submitting articles about the show to the school or local newspaper, writing press releases for local radio or television stations, and distributing tickets.

House Manager

The **house manager** is in charge of the ushers, who seat the audience. Being house manager involves selecting the ushers, coordinating their dress, and supplying them with the programs. The house manager is also in charge of checking house lighting, air conditioning, heating, and ventilation.

Makeup Artist

The **makeup artist** (or in a larger production, *makeup crew*) applies the performers' cosmetics, such as base coat, eye shadow, and so forth, and also creates beards, mustaches, and other special effects for the roles in a play. Since stage makeup requirements are different from those for regular makeup, a special committee needs to be formed to see to it that actors are properly made up. Sometimes actors do their own makeup, but usually applying makeup is the task of the makeup artist or makeup crew.

ACTIVITY: **Choosing Nonacting Roles**

Working in groups, have each person list the various nonacting roles in order of personal preference. Then share your lists and discuss specific reasons why you would or would not want particular nonacting roles.

PREPARING TO ACT IN A PLAY

Suppose you have been cast in a play. You have been given a script, and your first rehearsal is next week. What should you do to prepare yourself?

Study the Play

First, of course, you should read the play thoroughly. If you are unfamiliar with the play as a whole, your first reading (sometimes done with the entire cast on the first day of rehearsal) is solely to get you acquainted with the play. During the second reading, you begin to examine organization, style, mood, and character relationships. It is during this reading that you begin to understand the play's theme, which is what the author is trying to say through the dramatic events, and the play's particular style.

This cast is in the midst of its second reading of the script and is beginning to examine the relationships between characters.

Analyze Characters and Their Motivations

Rehearsals help you learn about the character you are playing. By studying the script carefully, you begin to get a feel for why the character acts as he or she does. When the author does not make motivations clear in the script or in notes, you will want to work with your director to identify motivations that will help you to play the role believably.

After you understand why your character behaves as he or she does, you can begin to explore how you will portray that behavior. Studying your role will bring up decisions that you will need to make about the character's physical presence and voice. You will look for answers to questions about how the character walks (quickly or slowly), stands (upright, stooped, slouched), sounds (soft-spoken, abrasive, boisterous), and acts in various situations. To find answers to your questions, consider any comments the author makes in notes, read closely what other characters say about your character in their dialogue, and analyze the actions that the author has your character take.

Of course, any of the decisions you make during the first few rehearsals may be changed as you practice your part and get more information. As rehearsals progress, you may think and feel differently about your character, and you or your director may wish to alter your portrayal. Moreover, as a show develops, it begins to take on its own personality, which also may affect the way you play your role.

Another way of getting insight into your character is to observe how real people behave when they are in situations like those being portrayed. An accomplished actor is an excellent observer of human nature. Although the author may have captured everything necessary for the role, it is likely that a performer will draw upon his or her personal experience, which will help bring the character to life for an audience.

Learn Lines

Some people have more trouble than others in learning lines. Nevertheless, at some point midway in the rehearsal schedule, all performers are supposed to have mastered their lines so that they can concentrate on character development. Most performers learn their lines in one of the following ways.

1. *Actors learn lines through constant repetition.* If you read through your part enough times, you will probably learn the lines eventually. Some people are "quick studies," which means that after just a few readings they have a part virtually memorized. Others may have to go over a part countless times. The repetition method of memorizing works best with those who have good visual memory.

2. *Actors learn lines through visualization of the scene.* Most plays are composed of a series of scenes. Each scene has its own special features. Some people learn their lines best one scene at a time after they have thoroughly digested every aspect of that scene. For example, if you get a firm enough understanding of a scene, you may learn the lines almost

Cast members often pair off to help each other learn lines. An actor might also ask a friend or family member to provide cues.

automatically, since they seem to be the most logical and natural expression to accompany what happens in that scene. If you are having a great deal of trouble with a scene, your director may suggest that you rework a line to fit your impression of the setting. With some plays you are permitted less latitude for rewriting than with others. For example, directors have difficulty with beginning actors who want to rewrite Shakespeare so that they can learn the lines better.

3. *Actors learn lines through association with a cue word, gesture, or action.*
After a play is underway, an actor can associate dialogue with a cue word, gesture, or action of another character. Although making such associations may work very well, an actor that depends on such cuing can get in trouble when another performer forgets or changes a cue. Still, using cues may help you remember specific words and phrases that give you difficulty.

Learn Movement—Blocking

One of the major questions that beginning performers have is what to do while on stage. Most play scripts provide each actor with general directions, which are often enclosed in parentheses. For example, the script will specify when to come on stage and when to leave. However, stage directions may be less specific about telling a performer how and where to move while on stage. The job of planning movement is up to the director. During early rehearsals directors give specific directions for how movement will occur. The overall plan for actor movement is called **blocking.**

A theatrical stage is divided into nine parts (see the diagram on page 564). *Upstage* means farthest from the audience; *downstage* means closest to the audience. In old theaters the stage floor was actually slanted downward

AREAS OF A STAGE

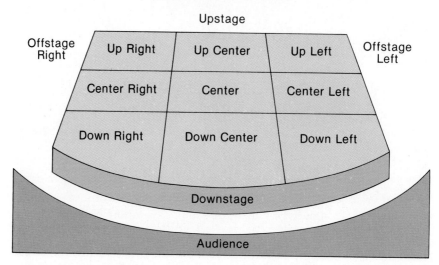

so that people sitting in the audience could see better. In modern theaters the stage is flat, and the auditorium seating is slanted.

Stage directions are given in terms of the actor as he or she faces the audience. Thus, *stage right* refers to the actor's right, not the audience's right. During early rehearsals the director will go over the blocking with each actor. For example, as another performer delivers a line, you may need to move from a chair at downstage left, walk behind a sofa at center stage, and then stand behind that sofa for several additional lines. You, as a participant in the scene, would draw that movement at that particular place in your copy of the script. Then while that line is being rehearsed, you would practice your movement.

Stage movement always has a purpose. Sometimes it is simply to get the actor from one place to another. However, movement may also occur for dramatic effect. Although movement will be diagramed early in the rehearsal period, it may be changed as rehearsals proceed. Both the director and the actors have a chance to discuss what movement seems appropriate to the action that is taking place.

At every point in a play, the stage should be balanced. A good director will maintain such balance throughout the play by coordinating the actors' movements so that the actors are in complementary areas of the stage.

Learn Business

Business refers to the actions that performers use to establish the atmosphere or the particular situation in a scene or to identify an individual character. For example, if one character were forever rubbing his nose, that action would be business that the actor uses to identify the character. Business helps actors create a scene and stay in character even when they are not "on." In this way business helps to create the total illusion of reality within the play.

ABBREVIATIONS FOR STAGE DIRECTIONS

UR	Upper Right	**¼ L**	Turn ¼ away from center front toward stage left
UC	Upper Center		
UL	Upper Left	**¼ R**	Turn ¼ away from center front toward stage right
CR	Center Right		
C	Center	**PSL**	Stand in profile towards stage left
CL	Center Left		
LR	Lower Right	**PSR**	Stand in profile towards stage right
LC	Lower Center		
LL	Lower Left	**¾ USL**	Turn ¾ away from facing center front toward upper stage left
D	Downstage		
U	Upstage	**¾ USR**	Turn ¾ away from facing center front toward upper stage right
XC	Cross Center Stage		
XSL	Cross Stage Left	_____	Underline words which are to be emphasized
XSR	Cross Stage Right		
XDR	Cross Down Right	✂	Cut
XUR	Cross Up Right		
XDL	Cross Down Left		
XUL	Cross Up Left		
X̑	Cross on curved line		
↑	Voice up		
↓	Voice down		

Sample of Scripts Marked with Stage Directions
Scene from Act I of *THE DIARY OF ANNE FRANK*

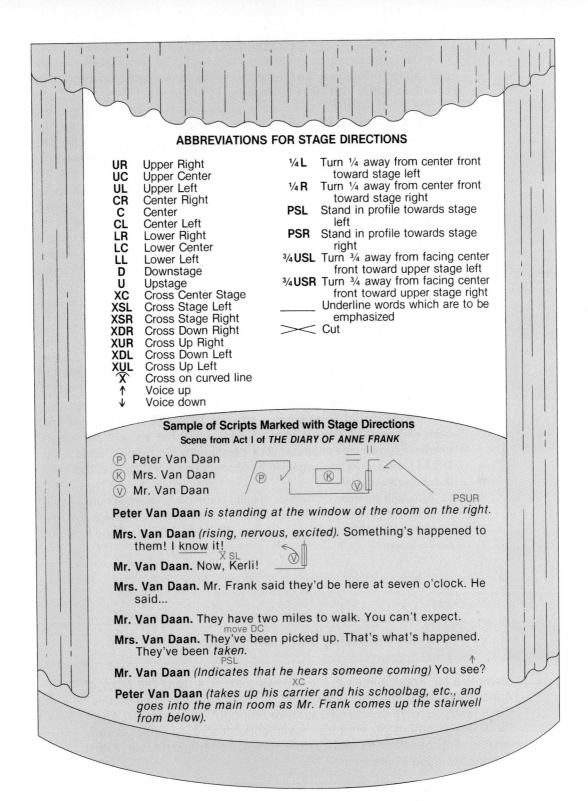

Ⓟ Peter Van Daan
Ⓚ Mrs. Van Daan
Ⓥ Mr. Van Daan

PSUR

Peter Van Daan *is standing at the window of the room on the right.*

Mrs. Van Daan *(rising, nervous, excited).* Something's happened to them! I <u>know</u> it!

X̑ SL

Mr. Van Daan. Now, Kerli!

Mrs. Van Daan. Mr. Frank said they'd be here at seven o'clock. He said...

Mr. Van Daan. They have two miles to walk. You can't expect.

move DC

Mrs. Van Daan. They've been picked up. That's what's happened. They've been *taken.*

PSL

Mr. Van Daan *(Indicates that he hears someone coming)* You see? ↑

XC

Peter Van Daan *(takes up his carrier and his schoolbag, etc., and goes into the main room as Mr. Frank comes up the stairwell from below).*

Some beginning actors perform quite well when they are saying their lines but fail miserably by contributing nothing to the drama when they are not speaking. To create an illusion of real life, every actor on stage must contribute to this total effect by engaging in appropriate business.

On the other hand, some actors develop such overpowering business that they are constantly calling attention to themselves, even when the audience's attention is supposed to be focused elsewhere. In the play *The Diary of Anne Frank*, almost all characters are on stage at the same time, but each is in a different location. As the play proceeds, attention may be focused on Anne and her mother at center stage and then shift to a character on the other side of the stage. However, all the actors are busy at all times. If while attention is supposed to be on Anne and her mother one of the other actor's business is so dramatic that it calls attention to itself, then it would be inappropriate. Sometimes only a fine line exists between portraying a well-defined character with fully integrated business and stealing the show.

Avoid Stereotypes

Acting is creative. Although some behavior is virtually universal, a good actor goes beyond trite, conventional responses. For example, Anne Frank is a thirteen-year-old girl. An actress could play the part simply by thinking of how any girl that age behaves. However, to portray Anne successfully, a performer must be sensitive to the girl's peculiar situation. In other words, an actress would need to get beyond the stereotype and uncover what makes Anne special. Playing her as a typical thirteen-year-old girl would not work well because Anne's circumstances made her life and her actions unique. Even when a character lives a fairly normal life, unlike Anne's, you should always work on portraying those special traits and features that make the character special.

Although stereotypes help us identify common or average human traits, the effective performer must go beyond the stereotypes. Perhaps the most important task the actor faces in playing a role is creating a unique individual on the stage.

ACTIVITY: Practicing a Speaking Role

Memorize Mr. Frank's lines in the following excerpt from *The Diary of Anne Frank*. How long did it take you to memorize them completely? Did it take you more or less time than you thought it would take? Then, for Scene 2, outline Mr. Frank's movements on stage. Finally, identify what kind of business the performers should use to portray Mr. Frank and the situation in the scene.

The Diary of Anne Frank

by Frances Goodrich and Albert Hackett

Act One

The scene remains the same throughout the play. It is the top floor of a warehouse and office building in Amsterdam, Holland. The three rooms of the top floor and a small attic space above are exposed to our view. The largest of the rooms is in the center with two small rooms, slightly raised, on either side. On the right is a bathroom, out of sight. A narrow, steep flight of stairs at the back leads up to the attic. The rooms are sparsely furnished with a few chairs, cots, and a table or two. The windows are painted over. In the main room there is a sink, a gas ring for cooking, and a wood-burning stove for warmth.

The room on the left is closet size. There is a skylight in the sloping ceiling. Directly under this room is a small steep stairwell, with steps leading down to a door. This is the only entrance from the building below. When the door is opened, we see that it has been concealed on the outer side by a bookcase attached to it.

Scene 2

It is early morning, July, 1942.

Mr. Van Daan, a tall, portly man in his late forties, is in the main room, pacing up and down, nervously smoking a cigarette. His clothes and overcoat are expensive and well cut.

Mrs. Van Daan sits on the couch, clutching her possessions—a hatbox, bags, etc. She is a pretty woman in her early forties. She wears a fur coat over her other clothes.

Peter Van Daan is standing at the window of the room on the right, looking down at the street below. He is a shy, awkward boy of sixteen. He wears a cap, a raincoat, and long Dutch trousers, like "plus fours."[1] At his feet is a black case, a carrier for his cat.

The yellow Star of David[2] is conspicuous on all of their clothes.

Mrs. Van Daan *(rising, nervous, excited)*. Something's happened to them! I know it!

Mr. Van Daan. Now, Kerli!

Mrs. Van Daan. Mr. Frank said they'd be here at seven o'clock. He said . . .

Mr. Van Daan. They have two miles to walk. You can't expect . . .

Mrs. Van Daan. They've been picked up. That's what's happened. They've been taken . . .

[Mr. Van Daan *indicates that he hears someone coming.*]

Mr. Van Daan. You see?

---

[1] **"plus fours":** baggy trousers gathered under the knee; also called *knickers.*
[2] **Star of David:** a six-pointed star, a symbol of Judaism that Nazis required Jews to sew on all their clothing for identification as Jews.

[Peter *takes up his carrier and his schoolbag, etc., and goes into the main room as* Mr. Frank *comes up the stairwell from below. His movements are brisk, his manner confident. He wears an overcoat and carries his hat and a small cardboard box. He crosses to the* Van Daans, *shaking hands with each of them.*]

Mr. Frank. Mrs. Van Daan, Mr. Van Daan, Peter. [*Then in explanation of their lateness*] There were too many of the Green Police[3] on the streets . . . we had to take the long way around.

[*Up the steps come* Margot Frank, Mrs. Frank, Miep *(not pregnant now), and* Mr. Kraler. *All of them carry bags, packages, and so forth. The Star of David is conspicuous on all of the* Franks' *clothing.* Margot *is eighteen, beautiful, quiet, shy.* Mrs. Frank *is a young mother, gently bred, reserved. She, like* Mr. Frank, *has a slight German accent.* Mr. Kraler *is a Dutchman, dependable, kindly.*

  As Mr. Kraler *and* Miep *go upstage to put down their parcels,* Mrs. Frank *turns back to call* Anne.]

Mrs. Frank. Anne?

[Anne *comes running up the stairs. She is thirteen, quick in her movements, interested in everything, mercurial[4] in her emotions. She wears a cape, long wool socks, and carries a schoolbag.*]

Mr. Frank (*introducing them*). My wife, Edith. Mr. and Mrs. Van Daan [Mrs. Frank *hurries over, shaking hands with them.*] . . . their son, Peter . . . my daughters, Margot and Anne. [Anne *gives a polite little curtsy as she shakes* Mr. Van Daan's *hand. Then she immediately starts off on a tour of investigation of her new home, going upstairs to the attic room.*

  Miep *and* Mr. Kraler *are putting the various things they have bought on shelves.*]

ACTING IN A PLAY

After what may appear to be an endless succession of rehearsals, the time will finally arrive when the curtain goes up and you are on stage in front of the audience for the first time. All that you have practiced must come through in your performance. In addition to all that you have studied about preparing for a role, there are at least three guidelines for bringing the role to life on stage.

Variation

Variation means changes in pitch, rate, and volume of voice. Many young actors turn the spontaneous vocal variety and emphasis they showed in rehearsals into flat, meaningless vocal variation during the actual performance. In a sense, every performance is different, for each time you say

[3] **Green Police:** Nazi police who wore green uniforms.
[4] **mercurial:** quickly changeable.

your lines, you will make minor variations that will, or should, bring a freshness to the performance.

Intensity

Intensity is the depth of feeling a performer has for a part. An actor must be in character when the curtain rises. There are actors who stumble through their last rehearsals, striking fear into the hearts of their directors, but who on the night of performance come alive. However, most actors do not rely on such last-minute tactics.

Whether or not you have been able to bring a character to life at every rehearsal, you must do it during the show. When the curtain goes up, you must have in your mind that the dramatic action is happening for the very first time. You must bring every bit of force to the performance that a real person would bring to the experience if he or she were in the character's circumstances in real life. In fact, you must be larger—in a way, more real—than life.

To achieve this intensity, you need to be well rested, well fed, and in good health. The energy a performer expends during a performance is tremendous. If you have never been in a play before, you may be surprised at just how tired you are at the final curtain.

Truth

A character in a play has a **truth,** a validity that is consistent with the play. Sometimes as rehearsals proceed, an actor finds that he or she can get a greater reaction from the audience with only a slight distortion of character. Then with each following rehearsal or performance, the distortion grows until at some point the character is no longer true. You must bring intensity, and you must have variation, but you must also bring truth to the character. Once your efforts begin to create distortions, you have destroyed the character you are trying to portray.

ACTIVITY: Analyzing a Scene

Look again at the excerpt from *The Diary of Anne Frank* on pages 567–68. The various stage directions give you clues about the way the scene should be played. Draw a diagram of the stage. Then indicate the movements of the characters.

Finally, analyze the excerpt. Be prepared to explain your answers to the following questions: (1) Where does the scene take place? (2) How many characters are involved? (3) What are the characteristics of Anne? (4) What is the mood of the scene?

Profiles in Communication

Today's theater patrons expect high-quality sound in every seat in the house. Meeting these expectations is the job of Burton E. Dikelsky, general manager of a regional theater that offers a range of dramatic, musical, and dance productions. He sees this emphasis on audio fidelity as fallout from high-tech electronics. "People can get quality sound right in the home and even in the car they drive. They don't want to buy a ticket and hear less."

In addition to advancements in audio reproduction, progress in electronics has produced improved devices for technicians and performers to use in sound transmission. For example, cordless microphones can not only amplify the human voice but also project it without the slightest distortion. Concealed microphones can save the day in theaters where dated architecture and mediocre acoustics complicate the sound crew's job of projecting voices and music.

The production of a show is not the only area in which electronics has had an impact on live performances. Theater managers use television advertising to attract audiences. "We can present all the quality entertainment we want, but the public has to know about it or we don't sell tickets," Mr. Dikelsky states.

While he has a master's degree in theater, he sounds like a marketing specialist when he describes his efforts in promoting shows. He recalls one situation in which only 500 tickets of the 1,886 available had been sold with only a week left before show time. He arranged for the star to be interviewed on a televised talk show on the Friday evening prior to the opening performance the following Wednesday. When the curtain went up, over 1,600 seats were filled. While advertising via the electronic media is not the only form of promotion that theater managers use, Mr. Dikelsky calls it a key factor in his theater's ticket sales.

Despite the assistance that electronic equipment provides in theatrical productions, Mr. Dikelsky sees no substitute for the performer's continual effort to perfect vocal communication skills. Having been a director himself, he says, "There will always be the demand from directors for performers to learn impeccable articulation, controlled breathing, vocal variety—the basic skills of vocalization that an effective oral communicator develops."

GUIDELINES FOR TAKING PART IN A PLAY

- Have I analyzed the play completely?
- Do I understand the motivations behind my character?
- Do I understand the other characters in the play?
- Have I chosen the gestures, movements, and voice that best serve my character?
- Have I taken advantage of my own powers of observation to bring truth to the character?
- Have I relied on stereotyped reactions, or have I really created appropriate, fully rounded human responses for my character?
- Have I memorized my lines?
- Can I bring intensity to the performance?
- Do I play the role with enough diversity?
- Is my portrayal true to the character?

SUMMARY

In drama, a story is acted out on a stage before an audience. Drama may be informal or formal theater. Although informal theater has probably existed for as long as human beings have, the first formal theater appeared in Athens in the fifth century B.C. Greek theater contributed the concepts of an actor and a formal playing area. Theater has evolved through the Middle Ages, the Renaissance, the Restoration, the Romantic Age, down to us today.

Pantomime is nonverbal dramatic communication. A pantomimist is a keen observer. Skill in pantomime is developed through constant practice.

Improvisation is based on spontaneous reaction. It involves pantomime and voice. All improvisation has dialogue, characterization, and a dramatic point.

Producing a play involves several steps. Play selection is based on availability, amount of royalty (if any), size of cast, type of theater available, and value of the selection.

Theater includes many nonacting parts. The director is in charge of selecting the play, casting, blocking, and coaching actors. A technical director is in charge of constructing sets, positioning and operating lights, managing the curtain, and tearing down the set. A costumer coordinates the dress of the actors. A business manager takes care of financial matters that relate to the production. The house manager is in charge of ushers, house lighting, air conditioning, heating, and ventilation.

To obtain a role in a play, people usually audition. A director will announce when auditions will be held. Each person usually prepares a short part from the role in which he or she is interested. After the director hears all auditions, he or she selects the cast.

If you are cast in a play, you must prepare for your part. You study the play, analyze the characters and their motivations, learn your lines, learn the movement, and develop the business appropriate to your character in different situations.

Acting in a play requires intensity, variation in presentation, and development of the truth of a character.

CHAPTER VOCABULARY

Look back through this chapter to find the meaning of each of the following terms. Write each term and its meaning in your communication journal.

audition	English Renaissance	realism
blocking	drama	rehearsals
business	floor plan	release
business manager	formal theater	Renaissance
cast	house manager	Restoration
characterization	improvisation	romanticism
chorus	informal theater	royalty
classical tragedy	intensity	set designer
climax	makeup artist	stage manager
comedy	mime	technical director
comedy of manners	miracle plays	technical requirements
commedia dell'arte	monologue	thespian
costumer	morality plays	tragedy
dialogue	pantomime	truth
director	pastoral plays	variation
drama	producer	

REVIEW QUESTIONS

1. What are the five essential elements of drama?

2. Formal drama began as part of religious ceremony. Who was Thespis?

3. Pantomime and improvisation are both types of informal theater. How does improvisation differ from pantomime?

4. One factor to consider when deciding whether a play is worth doing is the interest of your audience. What are two other factors?

5. Opening night is preceded by many rehearsals. What is the purpose of a dress rehearsal?

6. Stage directions tell the actors where and how to move on the stage. What is meant by "stage right"?

7. How does blocking help the actors determine their movements on the stage?

8. One way an actor contributes to a scene and makes a character come alive is through business. What is meant by "business"?

9. What are the responsibilities of a director?

10. What are the responsibilities of a stage manager?

DISCUSSION QUESTIONS

1. Prepare a three- to five-minute oral report on one of the following periods of drama: Greek, Roman, Medieval, Renaissance, Elizabethan, Restoration, Romantic, Realistic. Then discuss each of these periods with your classmates.

2. Discuss the role of the director in bringing a play to the stage.

3. Discuss the effect of sets, lighting, props, costumes, and makeup on acting and the actor.

4. T. S. Eliot wrote, "A play should give you something to think about. When I see a play and understand it the first time, then I know it can't be much good." First discuss the meaning of this quotation. Then discuss whether or not you agree with it.

5. Cervantes wrote, "The most difficult character in comedy is that of the fool, and he must be no simpleton that plays that part." Discuss the meaning of this quotation with your classmates.

ACTIVITIES

1. Reporting on Nonacting Features of a Production

Watch a community theater or professional theater production. Give an extemporaneous oral report discussing the costumes, scenery, and lighting for the play. How appropriate were they to the action of the play? Can you think of any changes that would have made them better?

2. Presenting a Dramatic Selection

A. Select a two- to four-minute excerpt from a play that your class might consider doing this year. Present this selection to your class as if you were performing it for an audition. Ask for and respond to feedback from your classmates.

B. Select a monologue. Rehearse it and then perform it in front of your class. Ask for and respond to feedback from your classmates.

3. Communicating with Pantomime

A. Working in a group, identify the kinds of actions you would need to make to pantomime the following situations:

1. Dealing with a vending machine that has taken your money without giving you the merchandise you wanted

2. Trying to keep a kite in the air

3. Walking barefoot across hot sand or a hot street

4. Carrying a large box down a flight of stairs

5. Planting a garden

B. Pantomime actions that would be characteristic of

1. A photocopy machine making a copy

2. A dog begging for a treat

3. A tree in a spring breeze

4. A computer running a program or a video game

5. A bird preening itself

4. Creating an Improvisation

Working with a partner, improvise one of the following situations:

a. A parent teaching a teenager to drive

b. A person haggling over the price of a vase at a flea market

c. Two teenagers on a blind date

d. A salesperson making his or her first call

e. A babysitter trying to calm down an unruly child

5. Reporting on an Audition

Attend an audition for a play—a school play, a neighborhood play, or a little theater play. Be prepared to tell the class how the audition was held. Where did the audition take place? Who was there? What did those who were auditioning have to do? Did the director indicate how he or she would decide whom to cast for specific roles?

Real-Life Speaking Situations

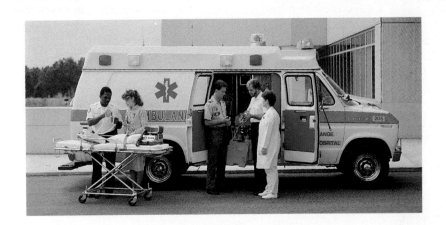

1. In his famous line "All the world's a stage," Shakespeare was referring to the universal experience of role-playing. Most people star in their own dramas and also play parts in those of others. Sometimes a script is provided, but more often lines must be improvised to suit the circumstances. A quick glance at practically any crowd reveals the variety of costumes, makeup, props, and other facets of appearance that people adopt to play their roles. What roles do you play? Are you a baseball player? scout? babysitter? salesclerk? How much script are you given for each role? Do you need to wear a special costume? Which roles involve props? Does anyone give you direction? In some cases you are probably expected to help direct others in playing a particular role. Imagine that you are going to teach someone how to play one of your roles. Write a three- or four-page instructive speech on how to play a role that you know well. Be prepared to deliver your speech in class and to conduct a question-and-answer session on the theatrical features of the role you present in your speech.

2. Some jobs involve role-playing that has all the elements of theater. For example, in many restaurants employees are required to wear special costumes and are given specific direction on how to act. In many cases, retail clerks, parking valets, and others who greet the public are even given particular lines to say. Other occupations, such as construction worker, accountant, teacher, and computer programmer, generally allow for more improvisation in costume and dialogue. Imagine that you are going to hire someone to do a specific job that involves wearing a uniform, acting in a particular way toward others, saying at least a few scripted lines, and using some required props. Create a two- or three-minute lesson teaching someone how to do this job. Begin by identifying the job. Choose one that is familiar to you either through your own experience or through what friends or relatives have told you about a job of theirs. Analyze the job to determine its theatrical features. In your lesson, identify these features and give specific instruction concerning them. Be prepared to give your lesson in class and to conduct a short question-and-answer session on how elements of the theater apply to the job you present.

RADIO AND TELEVISION

OBJECTIVES:

After studying this chapter, you should be able to

1. Give a brief history of radio.

2. Explain briefly how radio works.

3. Explain the major role of radio today.

4. Give a brief history of television.

5. Explain briefly how television works.

6. Explain the major role of television today.

7. List three major effects of television viewing on people.

8. Outline a plan for viewing television wisely.

9. List circumstances under which you might be on radio or television.

10. List three different types of microphones and the advantages of each.

Cynthia was excited, but she was also nervous. She had won a contest, and the prize was an appearance on a national television variety show. Since she was a talented performer, she was eager for the chance to present one or two of her routines. Although she had performed for large audiences before, never had she dreamed of reaching so many people at one time. The network estimated that the variety program was seen by about eight million people each week.

The play *A Chorus Line* holds the record as the longest-running Broadway show. It has had more than 3,500 consecutive performances! If the theater where it appears held as many as 1,000 people (and few Broadway theaters hold more than 500), then a maximum of 3,500,000 people could have seen this play in its many years on Broadway. In contrast, an average situation comedy on television will have more viewers in a single night than *A Chorus Line* has had during its entire run. The size of the audience for a popular television show can be mind-boggling. For example, an estimated eighty million people, roughly one third of the entire population of the United States, saw the final installment of the series *M*A*S*H* in February of 1983. These numbers alone give an idea of the potential power of the electronic media—radio and television—to influence attitudes and behaviors.

A BRIEF HISTORY OF RADIO AND TELEVISION

Can you imagine life without radio and television? Although radio and television are a firmly established part of the American way of life, more than 25 percent of our entire population were at least eighteen years old before they ever saw a television program. In addition, many people living in the United States can well remember the days before radio.

How Was Radio Developed?

In the late 1800's, people had two means of long-distance communication—telegraph and telephone (and both of these were in their infancy). In 1895, Guglielmo Marconi, an Italian inventor, created the first radio communication. By 1901, Marconi's equipment was sending signals across the Atlantic Ocean.

Experiments in radio broadcasting began in about 1910, when Lee De Forest produced a program starring the famous tenor Enrico Caruso singing from the Metropolitan Opera House in New York. Radio's first experimental programs began in 1916. KDKA earned its reputation as the first professional station with its broadcast of the results of the 1920 presidential election.

Within a few years, stations had sprouted up in all parts of the country. NBC, which began in 1926, was the first national network. Between about 1925 and 1950, radio had its "golden age." During that time soap operas (so named because many were sponsored by soap companies), afternoon children's serials, and nighttime comedy and dramas became popular. You may still hear your parents and grandparents talking about such radio shows as *Amos 'n' Andy, Fred Allen, Jack Benny, George Burns and Gracie Allen, Gangbusters, The Shadow, Inner Sanctum, Stella Dallas, Ma Perkins, Grand Central Station,* and *The Mercury Theater on the Air.*

However, during the 1950's the rise of television completely changed radio's role. For a while, some people even thought that television would make radio obsolete. Today, even though television broadcasts the types of shows for which radio was once famous, radio's audience is larger than ever. Statistics show that the average home may contain as many as six radios.

Can you guess what these people are going? They are creating the sound effects for a 1926 radio performance of ''Rip Van Winkle.''

Of course, many cars, trucks, and even motorcycles are equipped with radios, and portable radios come in all sizes, shapes, and styles. Every major city has anywhere from ten to thirty radio stations. In order to grow, or even just to survive, radio has had to change its goals. Instead of presenting the comedies, dramas, soap operas, and variety shows that once made up most of its programming, radio now concentrates on music, news, and conversation.

Whereas television must attempt to appeal to a mass audience, radio stations make money by appealing to a specific market. Any reasonably large city contains a number of radio stations that specialize in broadcasting a particular kind of music, such as classical music, contemporary top-forty hits, country and western music, religious music, music of the past, ethnic music, or soft music. Other stations feature continuous news programs and talk shows. Although many cities still have a station that tries for mass appeal, such stations are becoming fewer and fewer. Nevertheless, while most radio focuses on music and news, some stations still broadcast dramas, comedies, and variety shows.

ACTIVITY: Giving an Oral Report on Radio History

Prepare an oral report on the ''golden age'' of radio or on some other phase of radio history, such as early developments, a specific kind of programming, current trends, or the future of radio programming. Present your report to your classmates.

How Does Radio Work?

Radio is a form of electronic communication in which sound waves are converted into electronic signals that are transmitted and received. Sound consists of vibrations that travel through the air by sound waves. When sound is being broadcast, a **microphone** is used to pick up sound waves. As the sound waves enter the microphone, they disturb the electrical current in it, creating electronic vibrations that match the sound waves. The microphone then sends these electronic vibrations to a control board where they are relayed to a transmitter. The **transmitter** produces carrier waves that are combined with the electrical waves to become a radio signal. The signal is then sent from the transmitter to an **antenna,** which broadcasts the signal into the air as **air waves.**

The air waves may be transmitted as **AM** (amplitude modulation) or **FM** (frequency modulation). Both AM and FM waves spread out horizontally and vertically. However, the vertical waves of FM signals are not reflected back to earth as AM waves are. Consequently, AM signals are received at greater distances than FM signals.

Moreover, transmitters vary in power. Strong stations transmit at 50,000 watts (the maximum allowed). Stations can transmit any wattage below this number with 250 watts being about the minimum. In most communities, various stations transmit at different strengths. A 50,000-watt station can be heard for 1,000 miles when reception is good. A 250-watt station can be heard only in its hometown, or at most in other towns very near to it. FM transmitters vary from 100 watts to 100,000 (from about 15 miles to about 65 miles).

Most radio receivers are equipped to receive AM, FM, or both. A radio receiver includes an antenna, a tuner, amplifiers, and at least one speaker. The **antenna** is a wire or a metal rod that picks up radio waves. As you probably recall from the first paragraph of this discussion, antennas are also used to send signals. Antennas play a major role in both sending and receiving radio and television transmissions. The **tuner** selects a specific radio wave from the great number that are striking the antenna at the same

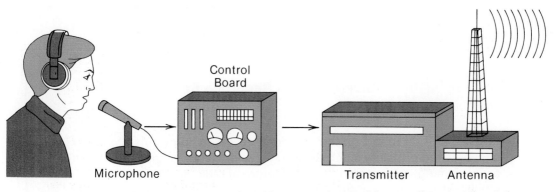

Microphone Control Board Transmitter Antenna

Have you ever wondered how sounds travel from a distant radio station to your radio's speaker?

time. **Amplifiers** strengthen the signal, while the **speaker** changes the electrical signal back into the sounds that were broadcast.

How Was Television Developed?

The groundwork for television was laid in the 1870's when it was discovered that there was a way to transform light variations into electrical signals. In 1878, Sir William Crookes invented the cathode ray tube, the heart of the television receiver. Both a mechanical scanning disc and the first photoelectric cells were designed just a few years later. However, it wasn't until 1923 when V. K. Zworykin applied for a patent on the iconoscope, an all-electric television tube, that the development of television broadcasting became possible. Other major contributions during the 1920's came from Philo Farnsworth, who invented the electric camera, and Allen B. Dumont, who developed the first home television receivers.

By May of 1928, television was far enough advanced in the United States that WGY in Schenectady, New York, began regularly scheduled experimental telecasts three afternoons a week. Still, progress was rather slow. NBC and CBS, the two major radio networks in the United States at that time (ABC was part of NBC), experimented with television broadcasting

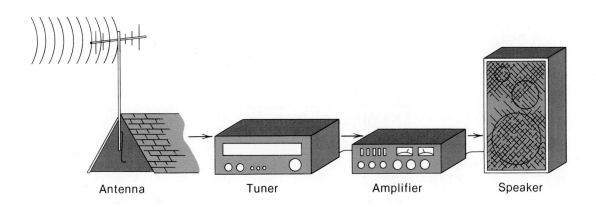

Antenna   Tuner   Amplifier   Speaker

throughout the 1930's. Yet, a full decade passed before NBC introduced television as a regular service in 1939. A year later, in 1940, a coaxial cable between New York and Philadelphia made it possible for programs to be originated in one city and shown in the other. However, the depression of the 1930's, the growing anticipation of war, and the actual outbreak of World War II slowed television's development.

When the first postwar television sets went on sale in the United States in 1946, all predictions were for television to become a boom industry. Sales of sets multiplied, and stations popped up as fast as the FCC (Federal Communications Commission) would license them. Finally, in 1951 coast-to-coast television became a reality. By the 1960's television had become a fixed part of our lives. Today, 98 percent of all homes have at least one television set, and in 83 percent of those homes at least one set is color.

Despite television's continued success, or maybe because of it, the face of television is changing. For thirty years three networks (NBC, CBS, and ABC) have dominated television. However, several technological changes have threatened the networks' hold on television broadcasting. One of the most important changes is the rise of cable television. By the early 1980's most of the major cities in the United States were wired for cable, and major companies like Warner Amex were able to provide programming that began to eat into network shares. In addition, technological advancements like video tape recorders and video disks freed viewers from having to be at home at a certain hour to watch a particular program.

The first television sets seemed almost magical. The shrewd owner of this diner used one to draw business during the 1950 World Series.

How Does Television Work?

Television is a form of electronic communication in which sound waves and light waves are converted into electronic signals that are transmitted and received. The sound, or **audio,** portion of a television program is transmitted in essentially the same way as a radio transmission. The major difference between television and radio, of course, is in the transmission of the picture, or **video,** signals. Although you see what appears to be a complete picture on your screen, a television transmitter cannot send a complete picture at once. Instead, it sends tiny parts of the picture that follow one another so quickly that your eyes perceive all the parts as a complete picture. A television camera scans the picture it sees and divides it into several hundred thousand tiny parts. While doing this scanning, the camera also converts the light waves that make up the picture into electronic signals for each of these parts. These signals for the picture and the sound are then transmitted to receivers (television sets) that convert the signals back into light waves and sound waves that can be seen and heard.

The process of transmitting a television program begins when light from a scene enters a television camera. The camera tube captures the image and changes the light image into video signals, which are beams of electrons encoded for transmission. Black-and-white cameras have only one tube; color cameras have at least three tubes, one for each primary color.

Next, an electron gun shoots the beams of electrons across a target in lines arranged much the way that you read, from left to right and from top to bottom. In the United States, television cameras use a scanning pattern of 525 lines. One frame is completed when an electron gun fills in the 525 lines. An electron beam moves so fast that it produces 30 frames in a second! Simultaneously, each of the three camera tubes, also called *vidicon tubes,* converts its color to a video signal. When the signals from the vidicon tubes reach a television set, the set separates the color information so that you see a full-color picture that is much the same as the picture that entered the camera.

Most television signals are sent through the air by a transmitter that produces separate audio and video signals. The combined audio and video signal is carried by wire to an antenna and is then broadcast. Although waves travel at the speed of light, the curvature of the earth prevents them from being picked up by receivers more than 150 miles or so from the transmitter. In addition, television signals are not reflected back to earth. Therefore, when television pictures are sent long distances, they must go by cable or must be relayed by satellites. In addition to being used for reaching remote places, cables are used by networks to send their programs to their affiliates.

A television receiver (often called a *set*) is composed of an antenna, a tuner, amplifiers, separators, and a picture tube. The antenna collects signals. Like a radio tuner, a television tuner selects the signal the viewer wants to receive. Complicated electronic circuits amplify the signal and separate the audio from the video. The audio portions go to the speaker; the video signals go to the picture tube. The neck of a color tube holds three electron guns, one for each of the primary colors; a black-and-white set has but one gun. These guns shoot the beams of light onto the screen just as the electron guns in the camera shoot the beams onto a target. In this way the picture tube re-creates the image that was captured by the cameras.

ACTIVITY: Explaining How Television Works

Prepare an extemporaneous process speech summarizing how television works. Be prepared to use audiovisual materials—perhaps drawings, diagrams, or sketches on the chalkboard—to explain equipment and steps in the process. Rehearse your speech. Then deliver it to your classmates.

EFFECTS OF TELEVISION

Television is a powerful tool for communicating. It creates and reinforces attitudes, beliefs, and values. In many ways, television teaches us how to behave. Traditionally, human beings have adopted their value systems from their families, friends, schools, and religious organizations. Children observe that their parents, brothers, sisters, grandparents, and close friends behave a certain way and then behave accordingly. As children grow to adulthood, schools, religious organizations, and other social institutions reinforce the teachings of family and friends.

With the mass production of newspapers, magazines, and books in the nineteenth century, people came to be influenced by what they read as well as by those around them. As a result, the printed word took its place as a molder of public opinion and a creator of societal norms. In the twentieth century, movies and radio and, more recently, television have taken a prominent place alongside print as molders of public opinion.

Of all these mass media, television has by far the greatest potential for influence. On an average, people spend more than twenty-five hours a week watching it. In fact, perhaps as much as 20 percent of the population watches television forty hours each week.

Television appeals to so many viewers for several reasons. People can read print and look at pictures, and they can listen to radio. However, television can be both seen and heard. While movies give the same sensory impact as television, they are not nearly as convenient as television nor can they provide as much entertainment as inexpensively as television can.

Unfortunately, the values that television teaches may not always be in the best interests of society. For example, television has been criticized for presenting a view of the world in which happiness seems to be a result of what people have and what they can buy. Television has also been criticized for the amount of violence it brings into the home and for the stereotypic manner in which it portrays both women and minorities. Consequently, when you watch television, you must watch it critically. In other words, you need to be aware of when the message it sends conflicts with the standards of your home and community.

This family watches television actively, not passively. Discussing what they see helps them keep television's messages in perspective.

ACTIVITY: Analyzing Television Programming

Brainstorm with your classmates to identify ways in which television's portrayal of American life differs from life as you know it. Discuss why these differences exist and what effects they may have on viewers of different ages. Be prepared to give specific examples to back up each of your points.

USING, NOT ABUSING, TELEVISION

How can you get the most out of television? To use television to your advantage, you must put yourself and your family in charge of what you watch. If you are like a majority of people, you turn on the television either because you want to watch a particular program or because you are tired, frustrated, or bored. Then when the show you are watching ends, you automatically watch whatever comes on next. Gaining control of your viewing habits will take some effort and commitment.

Think of television as food. You cannot eat everything in sight. For your body to work properly, you need to balance the foods you eat. If you fill up on candy and desserts and do not eat a balance of healthful foods, you will become sick. Of course, everyone does not eat a perfectly balanced diet at all times, but most people do try to eat a variety of nutritious foods. Much television programming is like candy or dessert: consuming controlled amounts of it may be fine, but making it a steady diet can prove unhealthy. Do you or your family have a television diet problem? The only way to know is to take stock of what you and your family watch.

Take inventory of your viewing habits. For a two-week period, make a record of your own and your family's viewing. Keep a piece of paper by the television. Every time you or any member of your family turns on the television, whether for five or ten minutes or for several hours, write down who was watching, what programs were watched, and how long they were watched. For this two-week period, try to maintain your normal viewing habits so that you will have an honest analysis.

Begin your analysis by taking a careful look at how many hours each member of your family watches television for the two-week period. Compare your averages to the national average of twenty-five hours a week. If you watch television this much or more, you may be consuming too much television.

Determine the balance of television programs you watch. Keep a record of what kinds of shows you and your family watch during the test period.

FRED BASSET   **BY ALEX GRAHAM**

Avoid making the same mistake that Fred's owners have. Gain control over your television viewing by making a plan and sticking to it.

The kinds of shows you watch may be even more important than the total number of hours spent watching television. Compute the amount of time each member of your family spends watching specific kinds of programs, such as news broadcasts, documentaries, sporting events, game shows, music videos, situation comedies, and movies.

Establish criteria for worthwhile viewing. Individual tastes vary, of course, and what one family decides is worthwhile may not seem worthwhile to another family. Therefore, you and your family need to discuss what makes for worthwhile viewing within given categories.

Take control of your viewing schedule. Consult a weekly television guide. Most newspapers include a weekly television guide with their Saturday or Sunday edition. Using this schedule, the whole family can sit down and circle those shows that they plan to watch that week. Then the family can evaluate the schedule in terms of both total hours and kinds of programming. Naturally, for one reason or another, you may not watch some of the programs that you select. In addition, you may decide to substitute a show later on in the week. However, the point is that you are exerting control over your viewing habits by planning the majority of your viewing. Such a plan can help you prevent spending excessive time watching television when you do not really want or need to, and it should help you develop a balance that is good for you.

ACTIVITY: Taking Inventory of Your Television Viewing

Follow the two-week plan discussed above for taking an inventory of your own and your family's viewing habits. At the end of the two-week period, report your findings to your classmates and discuss the advantages of taking control of your television viewing.

COMMUNICATING ON RADIO OR TELEVISION

Perhaps you are interested in a career in radio or television. Both the technical and the performing sides of broadcasting require years of training and experience. However, even if you do not work in broadcasting, you may very well have an opportunity at some time to appear on radio or television in one of the following situations.

Panel Discussions

You may be asked to participate in a panel discussion on a local radio or cable television station. As a member of almost any business, religious, or educational group, you may become involved in issues facing the group or the community at large. Especially with the rise of cable television and its mission of providing citizens with access to local broadcast media, more and more of these kinds of panel discussions are being carried on radio and television.

Interviews

All radio and television stations are sensitive to those who are "in the news." Every day, individuals who have achieved major accomplishments, who are experts in a field, or who have popularized certain positions are being interviewed on local stations.

Talk Shows

People who become well known are likely to be asked to appear on local, regional, and national talk shows. Talk-show hosts are constantly on the lookout for people who have unusual occupations or fresh approaches to issues, or who have recently written an article or a book, won an award, or for some other reason caught the public eye.

Opinion Statements

Occasionally, local stations allow responsible individuals equal time at the end of daily newscasts to state their views on particular issues. If you have a strong idea on a public issue and if you have well-documented support for your position, you may likely get an opportunity to broadcast your view.

ACTIVITY: Exploring Opportunities to Be on Radio and Television

Watch a local talk show, magazine format show, or news show. Under what circumstances are "average people"—those who are not celebrities—likely to make appearances on these programs? Do you know anyone who has been on radio or television? (Don't forget commercials, fund drives, and other promotional spots.) Be prepared to take part in a group discussion about the possibilities for an "average" person to be on the broadcast media.

HOW TO PERFORM ON RADIO AND TELEVISION

Before appearing on radio or television, you will want to become familiar with some basic information about radio and television production.

Dealing with Microphones

Although many microphones receive sound from only one direction, most studio microphones can pick up sound from any direction. There are three types of microphones commonly used on radio and television: hand mikes, lavaliere mikes, and stationary mikes. Each has its advantages and disadvantages, which you can learn to handle effectively.

Funky Winkerbean by Tom Batiuk. © 1986 by News America Syndicate. Reprinted by permission of News America Syndicate.

Even experienced broadcasters occasionally find themselves in this embarrassing situation. Learn how to tell when the mike is "live."

Hand Microphone. As the name implies, a **hand microphone** is meant to be held in the hand. Although most hand mikes receive sound from any direction, their quality is not as good as that of stationary mikes. To get the best quality, you should hold a hand mike about one foot below and slightly in front of your mouth. Speak across the end of the microphone and not into it.

You have to be very careful in handling a hand mike. Do not swing it around or drop it; put it down gently. Keep in mind that the cable keeps you within a limited radius. Before the telecast, make sure that the cable is long enough to give you freedom of movement.

Lavaliere Microphone. A **lavaliere microphone,** which is about the size of a finger, is hung on a cord across your chest or is clipped to your clothing. For the best sound quality, the mike should be placed about six inches below the chin. The lavaliere mike gives you greater freedom of hand movement than the hand mike does. However, since the mike can receive sound from any direction, outside noises are picked up easily. In addition, unless you hide it, you cannot use it for dramatic scenes.

Stationary Microphone. **Stationary microphones** are identified according to their placement: hanging microphones, standing microphones, and hidden microphones. With any of these, you must stay in range or let the engineer know when you will move so that the engineer can adjust the microphone to your range. Desk and stationary mikes give you the same problems as hand mikes: They limit your movement. If you have a good sound engineer, the hanging mike will give you the greatest freedom.

Mastering the Camera

During rehearsal, the director will experiment with various camera angles and distances. In general, you should always look into whatever camera is on. The on-camera is indicated by a red light.

When you are supposed to be speaking directly to the audience, hold eye contact with the lens of the camera that is on. When different cameras are used, move your head slowly until you make eye contact with that camera. If you are conversing with another person, maintain eye contact with that person, not with the camera.

Handling the Script

On radio, you will speak from a script. Be sure not to rattle the pages of the script, since the mikes will pick up this noise. In addition, take care to keep the pages in order and do not lose your place.

Working with a Teleprompter

The **teleprompter** is a machine that pulls paper from one roller to another at a speed adjusted to your reading pace. The lettering on the teleprompter is magnified, and the teleprompter is mounted right above the camera lens so that you can maintain eye contact with the lens while reading. Still, when you use a teleprompter, you should avoid keeping your eyes glued to it. The biggest disadvantage of the teleprompter is its cost.

Reading Cue Cards

Cue cards are large sheets of cardboard with notes or an entire script written on them in felt-tip pen. The cards are held as near to the lens as possible while remaining out of sight of the viewing audience. You, of course, must depend on the cards being in the right order and being shifted as you need them. If the cards are not handled properly, you must do your best without them until the handler gets them in order.

Receiving Instructions from the Director

The director watches the performance on several television monitors that show different scenes and camera angles. Using a headset with a microphone, the director sends instructions to a person next to the camera. That person relays the director's instructions to the actors by giving hand signals for time cues, directional cues, and audio cues.

⋅ACTIVITY: Reporting on a Television Production

Visit a local television station and watch a show being produced. Notice the following details.

1. What kinds of microphones are used?

2. Are any performers prompted by a teleprompter, cue cards, or some other means?

3. Who seems to be in charge of giving hand signals?

4. What hand signals are given, and how often are they used?

Report your findings to your classmates.

Common Time Cues and Their Meanings

Cues	Meanings
Pointing to camera	show on the air
Touching nose with forefinger	go ahead as planned
Rotating hands	speed up
Stretching imaginary rubber band	slow down
Pulling index finger across throat	cut
1, 2, 3, 4, or 5 fingers	time left in minutes
Showing fist	15 seconds left
Showing two fists held out straight	cut for a station break
Cupping hand to look like a C	commercial coming up

Common Directional Cues and Their Meanings

Cues	Meanings
Moving hand toward self	come closer
Using a pushing motion	go back
Using a walking motion with fingers	walk
Extending hands palms out	stop

Common Audition Cues and Their Meanings

Cues	Meanings
Cupping hands around ears	louder
Pushing hands toward floor	softer
Moving hands toward mouth	closer
Holding thumb and forefinger horizontal like the beak of a bird and moving them	keep talking

Profiles in Communication

Wendy Brenon

Wendy Brenon's workday as morning newscaster at KEMM FM in Greenville, Texas, begins before 6:00 A.M. as she checks the "sheriff and police calls." She comments, "A newsperson's worst nightmare is to come in one morning, and absolutely nothing worth reporting has happened."

After a quick briefing from the night disk jockey, Ms. Brenon reviews the Associated Press wire service printout, marking stories she will use on the air. This task is fairly simple because the stories are listed in order of importance; however, she also checks closely for any story that might be of local interest.

After that, she rapidly thumbs through the stack of city and county news articles the afternoon newscaster has written. By then it is after 6:00 A.M., almost time for her to rehearse the "Farm Report" at 6:30 and the news broadcast at 7:00. She has just long enough to look over the urgent items posted on her office wall and to "cheat a little" by glancing over the local newspaper.

To rehearse for the "Farm Report," as for all her broadcasts, Wendy Brenon first reads through the copy silently one time. Then she reads through it one time aloud, with a pencil held between her teeth. "It sound silly," she says, "but it works. It's a trick I learned when I first came to KEMM. Right after you read out loud holding a pencil—it works best with a pencil, not a pen—in your teeth, you articulate more clearly. That's important in radio since the listeners can't see your expressions or gestures."

Other skills Wendy Brenon believes a radio newsperson needs to cultivate are interviewing with open questions, meeting and talking to all types of people easily, and acting. She says, "My training in acting makes me able to appear excited about everything and interested in everyone, even under pressure."

However, Ms. Brenon believes the most important quality of a good newscaster is the ability to "stay on top of everything." A radio newscaster is always on call, talking to people, looking for stories. "It can get hectic. Last year when a tornado hit Greenville, we were the only station on the air. I was literally reading from notes written on my sleeves and hands." Ms. Brenon admits that radio newswork isn't always quite that hectic, but it is usually a challenge to anyone's communication skills.

GUIDELINES FOR APPEARING ON A BROADCAST

- Can I use the microphone properly?
- Am I familiar enough with the script to use it well?
- Have I considered time constraints?
- Do I look at the camera at appropriate times?
- Should I use a prompting device, and if so, which one?
- Am I familiar with hand signals?

SUMMARY

Radio and television are firmly established in American life. The first radio programs were broadcast in the 1920's. The "golden age" of radio occurred in the 1930's and 1940's. Today radio primarily broadcasts music, news, and talk shows.

A radio works by repeating sound vibrations originated in a studio and transmitted through the air to a receiver. Radio waves are transmitted as AM or FM. AM transmitters can reach greater distances than FM transmitters because vertical AM radio waves are reflected back to earth and vertical FM radio waves are not.

Although television was first developed in the late 1920's, it did not have much impact as a mass communication medium until after World War II. By the 1950's television had already surpassed radio as the major medium for entertainment programming. Today 98 percent of American homes have at least one television set. With the advent of cable and the use of video recorders, the field of television is changing rapidly.

Television is more complicated than radio because television transmissions include both pictures and sound. A television set contains an antenna, a tuner, an amplifier, separators, and a picture tube. Audio portions go to the speakers, and video signals to the picture tube.

The major effect of television is its force in creating and reinforcing attitudes, beliefs, and values. Television has such a tremendous potential for influence because of the great number of hours people spend watching it, because it can be both seen and heard, and because it inexpensively provides a large amount of varied entertainment.

It is important to learn to use and not abuse television. There are five steps you can take toward establishing a reasonable viewing schedule: (1) Take an inventory of your own and your family's viewing habits. (2) Determine how many hours you spend viewing television. (3) Determine the balance of television programs you watch. (4) Establish criteria for worthwhile viewing. (5) Set up a balanced schedule.

Someday, you may be asked to appear on radio or television. People who are not celebrities are sometimes asked to participate in panel discussions, to be interviewed, to appear on a talk show, or to give an opinion at the end of a newscast.

To present yourself well on radio and television, you must understand how to deal with microphones and cameras. You must also know how to handle your script, how to work with a teleprompter and with cue cards, and how to understand the director's hand signals.

CHAPTER VOCABULARY

Look back through this chapter to find the meaning of each of the following terms. Write each term and its meaning in your communication journal.

air waves	FM	stationary microphones
AM	hand microphone	teleprompter
amplifier	lavaliere microphone	television
antenna	microphone	transmitter
audio	radio	tuner
cue cards	speaker	video

REVIEW QUESTIONS

1. What are the steps in the transmission of a radio broadcast?

2. What is meant by the "golden age" of radio?

3. A radio receiver includes an antenna. What are three other essential parts?

4. Station WGY is important to the history of television. In what year did WGY in Schenectady, New York, begin regularly scheduled telecasts three afternoons a week?

5. For television to work, an image must be transmitted from the place where it originates to your television screen. What are the steps in this process?

6. Television possesses great potential to influence people. What are three reasons for this?

7. Taking an inventory of your viewing habits is one step toward controlling your television habits. What are three other steps?

8. You may find yourself called upon to be on television. What are four common television opportunities that may arise?

9. A hand mike is one kind of microphone. What are two other kinds?

10. Both teleprompters and cue cards help a speaker follow a script. How are teleprompters different from cue cards?

1. Discuss the difference in the relationship a speaker has with an audience when giving a public speech and when giving a speech on television.

2. Discuss the ways in which television affects our perception of social reality. Give examples that show where television and real life are at odds.

3. The famed architect Frank Lloyd Wright once called television "chewing gum for the mind." Discuss whether or not you agree with his assessment.

4. Erwin Canham once wrote, "The day of the printed word is far from ended. Swift as is the delivery of the radio bulletin, graphic as is television's eye-witness picture, the task of adding meaning and clarity remains urgent. People cannot and need not absorb meaning at the speed of light." First, discuss the meaning of the quotation. Then discuss whether or not you agree with it.

5. Newton Minow wrote, "Children will watch anything, and when a broadcaster uses crime and violence and other shoddy devices to monopolize a child's attention it's worse than taking candy from a baby. It is taking precious time from the process of growing up." First, discuss the meaning of the quotation. Then discuss whether or not you agree with it.

ACTIVITIES

1. Reporting on How Radio and Television Work

A. Prepare a three- to five-minute process speech on how a specific piece of equipment, an operating procedure, or some other facet of radio contributes to broadcasting a message. Prepare at least one visual aid to accompany your explanation. Rehearse the speech and present it to your class. Leave time for a short question-and-answer session after your speech.

B. Prepare a three- to five-minute process speech on how a specific piece of equipment, an operating procedure, or some other facet of television contributes to broadcasting a message. Prepare at least one visual aid to accompany your explanation. Rehearse the speech and present it to your class. Leave time for a short question-and-answer session after your speech.

2. Reporting on the History of Radio and Television

A. Find an article or a book that covers an interesting and important development in radio history not discussed in this chapter. Prepare a three- to five-minute informative speech on this development. Rehearse your speech and present it to your class. Leave time for a short question-and-answer session after your speech.

B. Find an article or a book that covers a development that has taken place within the past five years in television broadcasting. Prepare a three- to five-minute speech on this development and the changes that you think it will make in the future of television. Rehearse your speech and present it to your class. Leave time for a short question-and-answer session after your speech.

3. Exploring the Uses and Misuses of Television

A. Some people feel that Americans, particularly young people, spend too much time watching television. What do you think? Join with four or five other students in a group and discuss your views. Give a three- to five-minute report to the rest of your class on your group's conclusions.

B. Do you feel that television has had a favorable or an unfavorable effect on our lives? Prepare a three- to five-minute persuasive speech presenting your views. Rehearse your speech and deliver it to your class. Encourage feedback from your classmates after your speech.

C. Television can be an effective educational tool. However, it can be equally as effective in teaching misinformation and negative values as in teaching accurate, true information and positive values. Do you think that television is being used properly or improperly in educating teenagers? in educating children under twelve years old? in educating Americans in general? Prepare a three- to five-minute persuasive speech presenting your views. Rehearse your speech and deliver it to your class. Encourage feedback from your classmates after your speech.

4. Analyzing Television Viewing Habits

Survey the students in your school to find out their average television-viewing habits. Analyze your findings to discover trends concerning average number of viewing hours, preferred programming, parental guidance, differences between weekday and weekend viewing, and other viewing-habit information. Based on your information, identify what you see as the most interesting and important results of your survey. What do you think the results indicate about future viewing habits or about other facets of television viewing? Share your findings and views in class discussion with your classmates.

5. Preparing for an Appearance on Radio or Television

Have you ever been on radio or television? If not, think of a situation in which you may appear on radio or television someday. How did or how would you prepare yourself for your appearance? Did or would you practice what to say? If appearing on television, what did or would you wear? If you have already appeared on radio or television, give an oral report to your class on your experience and tell what you plan to do differently if you appear again. If you have not appeared on radio or television, give an oral report to your class on what you would do or say if you were to appear on a specific program or in a specific situation, such as a commercial, a promotional spot for public television, or an instructional videotape.

Real-Life Speaking Situations

1. Children's programming is often criticized for the amount of violence it contains, for the kinds of commercial appeals it makes, for the role models it presents, and for other faults that many parents also see in regular broadcasts. Of course, children can often watch these regular broadcasts as well. If you had a child, how would you handle his or her television viewing? Would you set restrictions? Why, or why not? Imagine that you and a friend each have young children who are the same age, say six to eight years old. Your friend is concerned about the quality of children's shows aired on Saturday morning. Write a two- or three-minute dialogue between you and your friend discussing your children's television viewing. Begin by identifying your friend's objections to Saturday morning children's programs. Then present your responses to these objections. Do you agree or disagree? Why? Finally, offer your own views and your policy on monitoring your child's television viewing. Be prepared to read your dialogue aloud in class and to respond to feedback on the views you present.

2. By selling just a few minutes of advertising time on the air waves, television networks can pay for running several times that many minutes of programming. Opportunities to advertise on television range from a single spot a few seconds long on a local broadcast to regular sponsorship of a nationally syndicated series. Imagine that you have a small business and want to advertise on television. Write a two- or three-minute informative speech on the advertisement you would run. First, identify your product or service and determine who buys it. Next, think of a station whose programming might interest an audience of your prospective customers. For example, if your business provides a local service, you will need only local coverage; while if you sell a special-interest product or service, you will want to run your ad on a station that appeals to that special interest, such as a sports or music station. Finally, describe a thirty- to sixty-second television advertisement you would run, and discuss how your ad takes advantage of television's combined audio and video delivery. Include visual aids to show what would appear on the television screen. After your speech, ask your classmates for feedback on the effectiveness of your ad.

APPENDIX OF SPEECHES

Note to the student: Keep in mind that speeches are created to be spoken. As you read the following speeches, try to say them aloud. Often, an oral reading will reveal facets of a speech, such as rhyme, alliteration, rhythm, and emphasis, that may go unnoticed in a silent reading.

INFORMATIVE SPEECH

"A Profile of the Successful High-Tech Salesperson"

Jeanne Greenberg, Chairman of Personality Dynamics, Inc.

Jeanne Greenberg, Chairman of Personality Dynamics, Inc., presented this speech to The Sales Executives Club of New York. In her speech, Ms. Greenberg defines high-tech salespeople as those who sell "micro and macro computers, telecommunications and office automation, a computer time-sharing network, application software, medical equipment, and satellite systems." She states that successful salespeople of such high-tech products are "a rare breed" possessing a unique set of characteristics that enable them to succeed. A good informative speech presents new information to an audience in an interesting way. How well does this speech meet these criteria? What kinds of specific facts and details does Ms. Greenberg give to support her statements about the defining characteristics of a high-tech salesperson?

I would like to share with you a few of the things we have learned through working closely with a number of high-tech firms. They are confronting some special problems in selecting top-level salespeople. After analyzing their unique needs, and comparing them to other industries, we have been able to identify a new breed of salesperson.

This new definition of what it takes to succeed in sales has specific and direct applications in the high-tech field. But I think there is also much that the sales profession at large can learn from those who are succeeding on the frontier of new developments.

High-technology is quickly permeating every aspect of our lives . . . and changing the way we do things—from paying our phone bills to preparing a marketing strategy.

As we shift from an industrial to an information society, those changes are bound to affect the way we think . . . and, therefore, the way we sell.

So, I hope that by taking out a psychological pen and drawing a profile for you of this new breed of successful high-tech salesperson, that all of you, regardless of the product or service you are selling, will be able to assimilate some aspect of these findings into your sales management experience.

A recent story in *Computerworld* placed the intensely competitive and extremely volatile nature of high-tech sales into perspective. The lead paragraph read: "Bankruptcies, layoffs and liquidations have intensified among high-technology firms in recent months . . . but at the same time, more new firms than ever before are showing a spectacular growth performance in earnings and revenues."

Competition in high-technology is quickly sorted out. Only the best emerge. The rest are left behind. Casualties can have the timing of a cobra . . . success can be fleeting . . . and a product's life-cycle can be as short as two years.

What is occurring in high-tech is compressed . . . condensed into a shorter period of time than any other development in history. If nothing else, this makes the lessons easier to study.

All of this is occurring at head-spinning rates. These new technological developments allow us to do more than the same old things faster . . . what are being created are new approaches and new opportunities.

Before describing our findings, let me take a minute to define high-technology. I think my favorite definition comes from a magazine specializing in the field, which has a detailed, two-page, double-spaced definition . . . all of which begins with the phrase: "We do not have a clear-cut definition of high-technology."

In point of fact, high-tech has become a buzzword, which some have used to describe everything from the space shuttle to the electronic typewriter.

Let me try to be a little more specific.

We consider something to be high-tech when it offers a significant departure from the past.

Often this is a matter of degrees, rather than an absolute.

In the beginning, a high-tech product is characterized by its capability of doing or measuring something intangible.

Then, as its possibilities become better understood, and its uses become more defined . . . it becomes accepted in the marketplace.

So, the first salesperson of an abacus had a more difficult task than those around him who were peddling sandals. His marketplace was limited, its uses difficult to comprehend at first, and the need had to be explained—if not created.

Centuries later, the pocket calculator posed a similar dilemma. They were initially expensive, really too large to fit into anyone's pocket, and only used by a rare few. Now, banks give them away along with toasters as incentives for opening an account.

So, today's high-technology quickly becomes tomorrow's state-of-the-art, and the day after is merely commonplace.

Along the way, our future is reshaped.

What these new technologies do is create or realign markets and demands. And that affects all of us.

For the purposes of our study, we took a look at companies selling micro and macro computers, telecommunications and office automation, a computer time sharing network, application software, medical equipment and satellite systems.

Among successful salespeople of such high-tech products, and they are a rare breed, we found they possess some striking differences from salespeople who thrive in almost every other field.

John Hoffman, vice president of sales for Computer Sciences Corporation, an international computer-based services firm, went so far as to say, "When it comes to high-tech sales, the old rules of selling no longer apply."

This is because successful high-tech salespeople are not really selling products or services. What they actually sell are solutions . . . solutions which must be customized to meet the unique needs of each client.

In most sales situations, success is the result of a salesperson's ability—and inner need— to persuade. Nearly a quarter of a century ago, we termed this inner need "ego drive." Someone who is ego driven has to convince other people to see things their way. For a top salesperson, closing a sale is the ultimate means of persuasion, providing enormous ego enhancement. His or her self-picture improves dramatically with a conquest and diminishes with failure.

In most sales situations, enough ego drive is never too much.

However, for someone selling high-tech products, we have found that if the need to persuade is too intense, it can be a hindrance—rather than the asset it is in most sales situations.

Why is this?

The reason involves the very nature of most high-tech sales. High-tech salespeople must be willing to build a sale in a slow, step-by-step process.

The intensely ego-driven individual who wants the sale immediately will have difficulty delaying gratification long enough to succeed in a high-tech sale.

It is also very difficult to project the image of a concerned consultant when the need to close a sale is overpowering.

I want to be clear here: Successful high-tech salespeople must have some ego drive, or else they will never close a sale—but their drive must be tempered.

Ultimately, a high-tech sale takes time—which means it takes patience, follow through, persistence, empathy and the ability not to take rejection too personally.

What evolves is an individual who is extremely attentive to a client's needs, and totally intent upon seeking an ideal solution to each client's unique problems.

While some motivation to persuade is still needed to sell high-tech products effectively, our research shows that too much is not a good thing.

Because the nature of high-tech sales is distinct from typical sales situations, it takes a different breed of salesperson to succeed.

According to Don Walker, vice president of sales for Comshare, Inc., a firm providing computer time-sharing services, "There is no one widget for each problem, which distinguishes high-tech from any other kind of sale."

Since each client has unique needs, each high-tech product or service must be tailored to meet those needs completely—or else the sale will be lost to a competitor.

A high-tech salesperson, then, should be perceived by clients as technically knowledgeable, sincere and competent professional—with a strong sense of personal integrity.

Clients are looking for a salesperson who has a consultant's demeanor—because once the system is installed, the salesperson's responsibility does not end. The sale forms the basis for a continuing, long-lasting relationship in which the salesperson serves as a consultant—troubleshooting any problems that might arise and implementing new facets of the system as needs expand.

Clients are keenly aware that they are not simply buying another piece of equipment. In fact, in many ways they are acquiring an ancillary employee.

So the ability to develop a trusting, long-lasting relationship is essential to success in high-tech sales—since additional products and services will be expected by a client for a long time to come.

To service clients in an extremely professional and responsive manner, our research shows that successful high-tech salespeople must project a solid, stable and reliable image.

It is not the type of situation where you can simply drop a few glossy brochures on a client's lap, recite a prepared speech, follow-up with a few persistent phone calls, and hope to make a sale.

Clients ask informed questions, and the salesperson who does not know his or her product and understand the client's needs inside-out is going to be perceived as being poorly prepared—reflecting negatively on their product and company.

We have found that most productive high-tech salespeople are also extremely well organized. They have to be able to handle details well and organize their work effectively. This personal organization gives them the capacity to keep many things in mind simultaneously—including the technical aspects and capabilities of a wide spectrum of products and services.

High-tech salespeople also need to be bright, articulate and confident enough to deal with key executives in major corporations. Since the purchases are substantial and the products will have tremendous impact on the overall effectiveness of the entire company, the sale is generally made at the highest level of an organization.

To excel, high-tech salespeople must have the ability to get their points across strongly and confidently—without appearing pushy or overly aggressive. Such an individual should also be unpretentious, because of the diversity of people encountered. There is a precarious balance between presenting a professional consultant's image, while simultaneously being open to meeting with people in all types of corporate situations.

As Bob Latavik, a manager for Prime Computer, one of the first manufacturers of minicomputers, put it, "High-tech salespeople do not have to convince just one individual, such as a purchasing agent, within a firm." They have to convincingly speak the language of programmers, system analysts, directors of information, managers of research, financial controllers, vice presidents of marketing, presidents and chief executive officers.

Our research findings underscore that people who excel in high-tech sales are excellent communicators—both verbally and in writing. They must have the ability to compose letters, proposals and reports clearly, concisely and convincingly. This is distinct from salespeople in almost every other field, who, for the most part, view paperwork as drudgery and an obstacle to closing additional sales.

Over time in this kind of selling, one has to be technically-oriented to succeed. The problem is that not all people who are technically-oriented can sell. In fact, from the point of basic personality characteristics, the successful salesperson and the successful technician are almost polar opposites.

So, simply moving people from the technical side to the sales side would be corporate suicide.

Still, a technical background is a necessary starting point, as is pointed out by Marty Sanfelter, IBM's recently-promoted marketing manager for Southeast Asia. He describes a scenario where one's "technical credibility" is being challenged all along the way:

Innocently enough, a high-tech salesperson starts out by asking, "What kind of collection basis are you using?" But if the prospect responds with a curt "Ten bit BCD's," the sale could come to a grinding halt—unless the salesperson could say something like, "Our binary code decimal base ranges from point one to point zero, zero one—which could significantly increase your capabilities." But what does the salesperson say when the technician responds, "The floating exponent range of my calibration is more than your system can handle."?

At this point, most salespeople would have to excuse themselves, saying something like, "Well, that is a very good question . . . let me get back to my technical people and I'll have an answer for you first thing in the morning." But, of course, the next morning the prospect may be hard to find.

You can see why the successful high-tech salesperson is a rare breed.

The individual must be a long-timer, because the firm's investment will not be recovered in six months or even a year. He or she must have enormous perseverance. Attention must be paid to the slightest detail or solutions will not be complete. And such an individual must be thoroughly knowledgeable about their products as well as the business world. Meanwhile, the high-tech salesperson needs persuasive ability—but it must be tempered.

Where do you find this new breed of salesperson?

Short of hiring twins, it is difficult to come across someone who can stand out in both the technical and sales ends of the business world.

Most good people are not looking—and even if they were, there are not enough of them to go around.

So, where do you look for those who are not looking?

First of all, we suggest you determine the degree of technical knowledge that is needed for the particular sales position. This will depend on the sophistication of your product, your clients and your marketplace. Keep in mind that *high*-technology is a matter of *degrees*.

One of the most overlooked places for finding high-tech salespeople is right under your own feet. A potential record-breaking salesperson might be working in your company—doing something completely different, wasting his or her natural ability.

A recent study by Source Edp shows that nearly 90 percent of scientific programmers and analysts are interested in exploring new computer jobs. Certainly not all of these—but some of these individuals with the needed technical expertise have the untapped, innate ability to sell.

What is needed is a program to uncover and assess this hidden sales talent. Once such individuals with the requisite technical background and the desire and ability to sell are identified, the rest is in the capable hands of a sales trainer.

Now, I have just described a unique individual for you . . . the successful high-tech salesperson . . . and from the start, I told you that by getting a clearer understanding of what it takes to succeed on the leading edge of new developments, there would be lessons for all of us in sales.

What are those lessons, and how can you translate them into your own situations?

The common thread winding throughout the field of high-tech sales is that the client is becoming increasingly sophisticated and knowledgeable before making purchases.

We have conducted studies in numerous other industries, which show that this trend in consumer awareness is having far-reaching consequences throughout the entire sales profession. Well thought-out and researched questions are being asked before even the most minor acquisitions are made. And there is little patience, let alone sales, for the salesperson who tries to gloss over any concerns or objections.

We are all being propelled into the information society. Even today it has been estimated that 75 percent of all jobs involve computers in some way. "Our awareness is finally catching up with the development pace of high-technology," as Peter Drucker said.

It has been said that the restructuring of America from an industrial to an information society will easily be as profound as the shift from an agricultural society to an industrial society.

And that restructuring will have enormous implications for those who will continue to succeed in sales.

The solution-oriented salesperson with a consultant's demeanor, substantial service motivation, thorough product knowledge and tempered persuasive ability may be considered specialized now. But I think we can all learn from those who are succeeding on the frontier of new developments.

One thing we have certainly learned is that change will not occur slowly.

PROCESS SPEECH

"The Half-Time Show"

Monica Seebohm, student speaker

In this speech, student Monica Seebohm presents the steps involved in putting on a half-time show at a football game. The effectiveness of a process speech depends upon how clearly the steps of the process are presented and how well each of the steps is explained. After hearing a process speech, members of the audience should be able to list the steps of the process and either perform them to carry out the process or understand each of them clearly and thereby gain an understanding of the full process. How clearly has Ms. Seebohm stated the five steps of putting on a half-time show? Is her speech aimed at enabling her audience to perform or to understand the process she is presenting? Note how the introduction and the conclusion of the speech are tied together. How does linking the beginning and the ending of the speech in this way contribute to the effectiveness of the speech?

Football is an American tradition. But when the half-time whistle blows, the spectators who rush out to get a snack are missing a second American tradition. This tradition is the half-time show. Millions of American high-school and college students are involved in marching band programs. But many of the fans don't appreciate or understand the time, the work, and the effort that goes into putting a half-time show on the field. For the next four minutes, I want to familiarize you with the steps involved in putting on a half-time show.

The first step in putting on a half-time show is for the leader to plan the routines that the band will execute. Half-time shows are planned in the summertime, weeks before the first practice. The band director thinks of the various routines and sets them up on paper on grids like this one. This grid resembles a football field with each instrumental section of the band denoted by a different symbol [visual aid 1]. Suppose that as a part of the show the director wanted the band to move in unison onto the field and then break into four blocks. He would draw the following grid [visual aid 2]. A complete half-time show might require twenty or thirty such grids, each indicating the number of steps and the direction.

The second step in putting on a half-time show is for the band leader to familiarize the section leaders with the formations he has planned. Section leaders meet with the band director once a week to discuss the drill. Each section leader is in charge of four or eight band members on the field, so if the band consists of eighty band members, the director would meet with ten to twenty section leaders. It is in these discussions that problems members may encounter are worked out. It's a lot easier to remedy a collision on paper than it is to remedy a collision on the football field. When the section leaders understand the movements of their units, they are ready to show members of their sections the various movements involved in each of the formations.

The third step in putting on a half-time show is for section leaders to work with their band members so that they can follow their various assignments.

There are six contemporary concepts of marching maneuvers: unison band, follow-the-leader, movable block, squad-four, step-two, and circular. Members of the band might learn some or all of these in order to carry out various maneuvers. This one example of a formation that might be used at the very beginning of the show illustrates a "movable block," a concept in which the band divides into symmetrical or asymmetrical units with each unit moving through the routine as a unit [visual aid 2 again].

The movements of a band are orchestrated to musical beats. And each move is organized to a count of eight. For example, it takes eight steps, or beats, to move five yards. This is what is referred to as marching "eight to five." When you watch a band on the football field and they march in straight lines, it is because all band members are taking the same size steps and are marching eight steps for each five-yard line [visual aid 3]. During a routine, squad members move to the command of military-like instructions from each squad leader. Key commands include "About face," which means you have to turn directly around; "Left face," which means you have to do a sharp turn to the left; and "Drag turn right," which means making a slow marching turn to the right [speaker demonstrates each command as she speaks].

As you march, you follow field markings to give you directions [visual aid 2 again]. Yard lines are your most important signposts; they let you know where you are as you march across the field. Hash marks are also very important, because they let you know how far off the sideline you are and how far from the middle of the field you are. And the press box can also be very important for you if you get mixed up and you are not quite sure of which side is the home side.

The next step in putting on a half-time show is to practice the drill. The entire band meets to work on drill together. The routine should flow as it did on the grid. The various squads should fit together to form the entire marching band. For instance, suppose at the start of the show, all the band is lined up on the sideline between the forty-yard lines, facing the playing field. To get started, the squad leader yells, "Forward march." Everyone in the band then marches out toward the sideline on the other side of the field. The first line members move "eight to five" until they reach their stopping point. Each of the next lines takes slightly shorter steps, being sure to stay in a straight line, until the band is properly spaced on the field [visual aid 4]. As soon as that point is reached, the squad leader says, "Left face." While members in Section C left face and march left as they learned in practice, section D marches right, and sections A and B continue forward. At that point the leader says, "Continue for eight, about face and return for eight." At this time sections A and B move right face and left space respectively for sixteen steps [visual aid 5]. If every member of the band has moved properly, the entire band will have completed the first stage of a formation.

The final step in putting on a half-time show is completion of the show itself. Early the day of the game all the members assemble in uniform to polish each step. Five minutes before half-time, the band assembles on the sideline. The half-time whistle blows and it's showtime. For the next ten minutes it is the band's responsibility to entertain that crowd.

At the end of the show, as band members march off the football field with pride in a job well done, they may forget the steps of planning, teaching leaders, teaching members, coordinating, and practice; but they will certainly remember the fun of the show itself. Next time you're at a football game and the half-time whistle blows, skip the snack and enjoy the performance.

PERSUASIVE SPEECH

"Woman's Right to the Suffrage"

Susan B. Anthony

Susan B. Anthony, a leader in the women's rights movement during the late 1800's, was arrested and fined in Rochester, New York, for trying to vote in the 1872 presidential election (nearly fifty years before the passage of the women's suffrage amendment). This persuasive speech is her defense of her action. Notice how tightly she packages her argument

Friends and Fellow Citizens: I stand before you tonight under indictment for the alleged crime of having voted at the last Presidential election, without having a lawful right to vote. It shall be my work this evening to prove to you that, in thus voting, I not only committed no crime, but instead, simply exercised my citizen's rights, guaranteed to me and all United States citizens by the national Constitution, beyond the power of any state to deny.

"We, the people of the United States, in order to form a more perfect union, establish justice, insure domestic tranquility, provide for the common defense, promote the general welfare, and secure the blessings of liberty to ourselves and our posterity, do ordain and establish this Constitution for the United States of America."*

It was we, the people, not we; the white male citizens; nor yet we, the male citizens; but we, the whole people who formed the Union. And we formed it, not to give the blessings of liberty, but to secure them; not to the half of ourselves and the half of our posterity, but to the whole people, women as well as men. And it is a downright mockery to talk to women of their enjoyment of the blessings of liberty while they are denied the use of the only means of securing them provided by this democratic-republican government—the ballot.

For any state to make sex qualification that must ever result in the disfranchisement of one entire half of the people is to pass a bill of attainder, or an *ex post facto* law, and is therefore a violation of the supreme law of the land. By it the blessings of liberty are forever withheld from women and their female posterity. To them this government has no just powers derived from the consent of the governed. To them this government is not a democracy. It is not a republic. It is an odious aristocracy; a hateful oligarchy of sex; the most hateful aristocracy ever established on the face of the globe. An oligarchy of wealth, where the rich govern the poor, or an oligarchy of learning, where the educated govern the ignorant, might be endured; but this oligarchy of sex, which makes father, brothers, husband, sons, the oligarchs over the mother and sisters, the wife and daughters of every household—which ordains all men sovereigns, all women subjects, carries dissension, discord, and rebellion into every home of the nation.

Webster, Worcester, and Bouvier all define a citizen to be a person in the United States, entitled to vote and hold office.

The only question left to be settled now is: Are women persons? And I hardly believe any of our opponents will have the hardihood to say they are not. Being persons, then, women are citizens; and no State has a right to make any law, or to enforce any old law, that shall abridge their privileges or immunities. Hence, every discrimination against women in the constitutions and laws of the several States is today null and void.

SPEECH OF INTRODUCTION

Introduction of Gertrude Lawrence to the New York Advertising Club

G. Lynn Sumner, President of the New York Advertising Club

The purpose of an introduction is to present someone, often a main speaker, to an audience. The essentials of a speech of introduction are to name the speaker; to emphasize the speaker's authority, expertise, or importance; to show the introducer's enthusiasm for the speaker or the speaker's message; to identify the speaker's topic; and in some cases, to mention the occasion. Often, the most difficult task in an introduction is to praise the speaker without embarrassing him or her or setting expectations so high that they cannot possibly be met. In this introduction, G. Lynn Sumner does an excellent job of praising Gertrude Lawrence and

* The preamble to the Constitution.

getting the audience ready to listen to her speech. What means does Ms. Sumner use to build her credibility? What does she do to set the tone for her speech? In what ways does Ms. Sumner praise Gertrude Lawrence and build the audience's enthusiasm? If you had been in the audience, what would your reaction have been to this speech?

It is a traditional example of the busman's holiday that when a sailor gets a day's shore leave, he goes rowing in Central Park. And if you would know what advertising men are doing these autumn nights—well, they are flocking to the Morosco Theatre, where some aspects of the advertising business have been cleverly put into a play called *Skylark*. The scintillating star of that play—Miss Gertrude Lawrence—is our special guest of honor today. That is the reason why we had no trouble whatever getting a complete set of our vice presidents at the head table.

In *Skylark*, Miss Lawrence plays a familiar part—the neglected wife of an advertising agency executive who is so busy with his clients and his speculative plans for prospective clients that he too often forgets to come home. Of course this is just a play—just a comedy—all in fun— for I am very sure that if Miss Lawrence were *really* the wife of an advertising executive, his chief problem would be to keep his mind on his work.

From observation of her theatre audiences, supplemented by observations of this audience, Miss Lawrence has some observations of her own to make about advertising and advertising men. I hope she doesn't pull her punches. It is a great pleasure to present one of the most charming and talented actresses of the English and American stage—Miss Gertrude Lawrence.

KEYNOTE SPEECH

Keynote Address to the Democratic National Convention (1976)

Barbara Jordan, Congresswoman from Texas

A keynote speech presents the issues that are of primary interest to an assembly (in this speech, a political convention) for the purpose of establishing unity and generating enthusiasm. Such a speech sets a tone, or key note, for the assembly. On July 12, 1976, Barbara Jordan, Congresswoman from Texas, delivered the following keynote address to the Democratic National Convention. In her speech, Representative Jordan stresses unity and challenge. Note that throughout the speech she uses such phrases as "common spirit," "common ties," and "one nation" to help develop the theme of unity. Also note that unlike many speeches of this kind, she does not overdo her praise for her party. One of the strengths of the speech is the way she recognizes mistakes that have been made but uses them to suggest that her party has learned from those mistakes. What specific methods does Representative Jordan use to arouse enthusiasm for the goals of the Party? In the latter part of the speech, what does she identify as the needs of the Democratic Party in winning national support? How effective do you think this speech is in creating unity and enthusiasm?

One hundred and forty-four years ago, members of the Democratic Party first met in convention to select a Presidential candidate. Since that time, Democrats have continued to convene once every four years and draft a party platform and nominate a Presidential candidate. And our meeting this week is a continuation of that tradition.

But there is something different about tonight. There is something special about tonight. What is different? What is special? I, Barbara Jordan, am a keynote speaker.

A lot of years passed since 1832, and during that time it would have been most unusual for any national political party to ask that a Barbara Jordan deliver a keynote address . . . but tonight here I am. And I feel that notwithstanding the past that my presence here is one additional bit of evidence that the American Dream need not forever be deferred.

Now that I have this grand distinction what in the world am I supposed to say?

I could easily spend this time praising the accomplishments of this party and attacking the Republicans but I don't choose to do that.

I could list the many problems which Americans have. I could list the problems which cause people to feel cynical, angry, frustrated: problems which include lack of integrity in government; the feeling that the individual no longer counts; the reality of material and spiritual poverty; the feeling that the grand American experiment is failing or has failed. I could recite these problems and then I could sit down and offer no solutions. But I don't choose to do that either.

The citizens of American expect more. They deserve and they want more than a recital of problems.

We are a people in a quandary about the present. We are a people in search of our future. We are a people in search of a national community.

We are a people trying not only to solve the problems of the present: unemployment, inflation . . . but we are attempting on a larger scale to fulfill the promise of America. We are attempting to fulfill our national purpose; to create and sustain a society in which all of us are equal.

Throughout our history, when people have looked for new ways to solve their problems, and to uphold the principles of this nation, many times they have turned to political parties. They have often turned to the Democratic Party.

What is it, what is it about the Democratic Party that makes it the instrument that people use when they search for ways to shape their future? Well I believe the answer to that question lies in our concept of governing. Our concept of governing is derived from our view of people. It is a concept deeply rooted in a set of beliefs firmly etched in the national conscience, of all of us.

Now what are these beliefs?

First, we believe in equality for all and privileges for none. This is a belief that each American regardless of background has equal standing in the public forum, all of us. Because we believe this idea so firmly, we are an inclusive rather than an exclusive party. Let everybody come.

I think it no accident that most of those emigrating to America in the 19th century identified with the Democratic Party. We are a heterogeneous party made up of Americans of diverse backgrounds.

We believe that the people are the source of all governmental power; that the authority of the people is to be extended, not restricted. This can be accomplished only by providing each citizen with every opportunity to participate in the management of the government. They must have that.

We believe that the government which represents the authority of all the people, not just one interest group, but all the people, has an obligation to actively underscore, actively seek to remove those obstacles which would block individual achievement . . . obstacles emanating from race, sex, economic condition. The government must seek to remove them.

We are a party of innovation. We do not reject our traditions, but we are willing to adapt to changing circumstances, when change we must. We are willing to suffer the discomfort of change in order to achieve a better future.

We have a positive vision of the future founded on the belief that the gap between the promise and reality of America can one day be finally closed. We believe that.

This my friends, is the bedrock of our concept of governing. This is a part of the reason why Americans have turned to the Democratic Party. These are the foundations upon which a national community can be built.

Let's all understand that these guiding principles cannot be discarded for short-term political gains. They represent what this country is all about. They are indigenous to the American idea. And these are principles which are not negotiable.

In other times, I could stand here and give this kind of exposition on the beliefs of the Democratic Party and that would be enough. But today that is not enough. People want more. That is not sufficient reason for the majority of the people of this country to vote Democratic. We have made mistakes. In our haste to do all things for all people, we did not foresee the full consequences of our actions. And when the people raised their voices, we didn't hear. But our deafness was only a temporary condition, and not an irreversible condition.

Even as I stand here and admit that we have made mistakes I still believe that as the people of America sit in judgment on each party, they will recognize that our mistakes were mistakes of the heart. They'll recognize that.

And now we must look to the future. Let us heed the voice of the people and recognize their common sense. If we do not, we not only blaspheme our political heritage, we ignore the common ties that bind all Americans.

Many fear the future. Many are distrustful of their leaders, and believe that their voices are never heard. Many seek only to satisfy their private work wants. To satisfy private interests.

But this is the great danger America faces. That we will cease to be one nation and become instead a collection of interest groups: city against suburb, region against region, individual against individual. Each seeking to satisfy private wants.

If that happens, who then will speak for America?

Who then will speak for the common good?

This is the question which must be answered in 1976.

Are we to be one people bound together by common spirit sharing in a common endeavor or will we become a divided nation?

For all of its uncertainty, we cannot flee the future. We must not become the new puritans and reject our society. We must address and master the future together. It can be done if we restore the belief that we share a sense of national community, that we share a common national endeavor. It can be done.

There is no executive order; there is no law that can require the American people to form a national community. This we must do as individuals and if we do it as individuals, there is no President of the United States who can veto that decision.

As a first step, we must restore our belief in ourselves. We are a generous people so why can't we be generous with each other? We need to take to heart the words spoken by Thomas Jefferson:

Let us restore to social intercourse that harmony and that affection without which liberty and even life are but dreary things.

A nation is formed by the willingness of each of us to share in the responsibility for upholding the common good.

A government is invigorated when each of us is willing to participate in shaping the future of this nation.

In this election year we must define the common good and begin again to shape a common good and begin again to shape a common future. Let each person do his or her part. If one citizen is unwilling to participate, all of us are going to suffer. For the American idea, though it is shared by all of us, is realized in each one of us.

And now, what are those of us who are elected public officials supposed to do? We call ourselves public servants but I'll tell you this: we as public servants must set an example for the rest of the nation. It is hypocritical for the public official to admonish and exhort the people to uphold the common good if we are derelict in upholding the common good. More is required of public officials than slogans and handshakes and press releases. More is required. We must hold ourselves strictly accountable. We must provide the people with a vision of the future.

If we promise as public officials, we must deliver. If we as public officials propose, we must produce. If we say to the American people it is time for you to be sacrificial; sacrifice. If the public official says that, we (public officials) must be the first to give. We must be. And again, if we make mistakes, we must be willing to admit them. We have to do that. What we have to do is strike a balance between the idea that government should do everything and the idea, the belief, that government ought to do nothing. Strike a balance.

Let there be no illusions about the difficulty of forming this kind of a national community. It's tough, difficult, not easy. But a spirit of harmony will survive in America only if each of us remembers that we share a common destiny. If each of us remembers when self-interest and bitterness seem to prevail, that we share a common destiny.

I have confidence that we can form this kind of national community. I have confidence that the Democratic Party can lead the way. I have that confidence. We cannot improve on the system of government handed down to us by the founders of the Republic, there is no way to improve upon that. But what we can do is to find new ways to implement that system and realize our destiny.

Now, I began this speech by commenting to you on the uniqueness of a Barbara Jordan making the keynote address. Well I am going to close my speech by quoting a Republican President and I ask you that as you listen to these words of Abraham Lincoln, relate them to the concept of a national community in which every last one of us participates: As I would not be a slave, so I would not be a master. This expresses my idea of Democracy. Whatever differs from this, to the extent of the difference is no Democracy.

INSPIRATIONAL SPEECH

"I Have a Dream"

Dr. Martin Luther King, Jr.

In August 1963, more than 200,000 people attended a rally in Washington, D.C. to focus attention on demands for equality in jobs and civil rights. For many people the high point of the day was the delivery of the famous inspirational speech "I Have a Dream" by Dr. Martin Luther King, Jr. An inspirational speech usually stresses the importance of the work of the group being addressed, outlines the challenges the group faces, and uses language to stimulate sustained group effort. In his speech Dr. King meets these goals. Throughout, he stresses the time has come to pursue the group's goal of making racial justice a reality. In stirring language, he identifies the trials and tribulations of many in his audience; however, rather than allowing his audience "to wallow in the valley of despair," he outlines the challenge of the future—his dream for the people. The power, motivation, and inspiration of Dr. King's speech are developed through his skillful use of repetition, parallelism, and metaphor. Beginning in the fourth paragraph with his reference to "cashing a check," how does Dr. King use metaphor to heighten the impact of his message on his audience? What is the effect of repetition and parallelism in the "I have a dream" section in the latter part of the speech? In your opinion, what is the most inspirational passage in Dr. King's speech? How does Dr. King's use of language make this passage powerful?

I am happy to join with you today in what will go down in history as the greatest demonstration for freedom in the history of our nation.

Five score years ago, a great American, in whose symbolic shadow we stand today, signed the Emancipation Proclamation. This momentous decree came as a great beacon light of hope to millions of Negro slaves, who had been seared in the flames of withering injustice. It came as a joyous daybreak to end the long night of their captivity.

But one hundred years later, the Negro is still not free. One hundred years later, the life of the Negro is still sadly crippled by the manacles of segregation and the chains of discrimination. One hundred years later, the Negro lives on a lonely island of poverty in the midst of a vast ocean of material prosperity. One hundred years later, the Negro is still languished in the corners of American society and finds himself an exile in his own land. So we have come here today to dramatize a shameful condition.

In a sense we've come to our nation's Capitol to cash a check. When the architects of our republic wrote the magnificent words of the Constitution and the Declaration of Independence, they were signing a promissory note to which every American was to fall heir. This note was a promise that all men—yes, black men as well as white men—would be guaranteed the unalienable rights of life, liberty, and the pursuit of happiness.

It is obvious today that America has defaulted on this promissory note insofar as her citizens of color are concerned. Instead of honoring this sacred obligation, America has given the Negro people a bad check; a check which has come back marked "insufficient funds." But we refuse to believe that the bank of justice is bankrupt. We refuse to believe that there are insufficient funds in the great vaults of opportunity of this nation. So we've come to cash this check—a check that will give us upon demand the riches of freedom and the security of justice. We have also come to this hallowed spot to remind America of the fierce urgency of *now*. This is no time to engage in the luxury of cooling off or to take the tranquilizing drug of gradualism. *Now is the time* to make real the promises of Democracy. *Now is the time* to rise from the dark and desolate valley of segregation to the sunlight of racial justice. *Now is the time* to lift our nation from the quicksands of racial injustice to the solid rock of brotherhood. *Now is the time* to make justice a reality for all of God's children.

It would be fatal for the nation to overlook the urgency of the moment. This sweltering summer of the Negro's legitimate discontent will not pass until there is an invigorating autumn of freedom and equality. Nineteen sixty-three is not an end, but a beginning. Those who hope that the Negro needed to blow off steam and will now be content will have a rude awakening if the nation returns to business as usual. There will be neither rest nor tranquility in America until the Negro is granted his citizenship rights. The whirlwinds of revolt will continue to shake the foundations of our nation until the bright day of justice emerges.

But there is something that I must say to my people who stand on the warm threshold which leads into the palace of justice. In the process of gaining our rightful place we must not be guilty of wrongful deeds. Let us not seek to satisfy our thirst for freedom by drinking from the cup of bitterness and hatred.

We must forever conduct our struggle on the high plane of dignity and discipline. We must not allow our creative protest to degenerate into physical violence. Again and again we must rise to the majestic heights of meeting physical force with soul force. The marvelous new militancy which has engulfed the Negro community must not lead us to a distrust of all white people, for many of our white brothers, as evidenced by their presence here today, have come to realize that their destiny is tied up with our destiny. And they have come to realize that their freedom is inextricably bound to our freedom. We cannot walk alone.

And as we walk we must make the pledge that we shall always march ahead. We cannot turn back. There are those who ask the devotees of civil rights, "When will you be satisfied?" We can never be satisfied as long as the Negro is the victim of the unspeakable horrors of police brutality. We can never be satisfied as long as our bodies, heavy with the fatigue of travel, cannot gain lodging in the motels of the highways and the hotels of the cities. We cannot be satisfied as long as the Negro's basic mobility is from a smaller ghetto to a larger one. We can never be satisfied as long as our children are stripped of their selfhood and robbed of their dignity by signs stating "For Whites Only." We cannot be satisfied as long as a Negro in Mississippi cannot vote and a Negro in New York believes he has nothing for which to vote. No, no, we are not satisfied, and we will not be satisfied until justice rolls down like waters and righteousness like a mighty stream.

I am not unmindful that some of you have come here out of great trials and tribulations. Some of you have come fresh from narrow jail cells. Some of you have come from areas where your quest for freedom left you battered by the storms of persecution and staggered by the winds of police brutality. You have been the veterans of creative suffering. Continue to work with the faith that unearned suffering is redemptive.

Go back to Mississippi, go back to Alabama, go back to South Carolina, go back to Georgia, go back to Louisiana, go back to the slums and ghettos of our Northern cities knowing that somehow this situation can and will be changed. Let us not wallow in the valley of despair.

I say to you today, my friends, so even though we face the difficulties of today and tomorrow, I still have a dream. It is a dream deeply rooted in the American dream.

I have a dream that one day this nation will rise up and live out the true meaning of its creed: "We hold these truths to be self-evident; that all men are created equal."

I have a dream that one day on the red hills of Georgia the sons of former slaves and the sons of former slaveowners will be able to sit down together at the table of brotherhood; I have a dream—

That one day even the state of Mississippi, a state sweltering with the heat of injustice, sweltering with the heat of oppression, will be transformed into an oasis of freedom and justice; I have a dream—

That my four little children will one day live in a nation where they will not be judged by the color of their skin but by the content of their character; I have a dream today.

I have a dream that one day down in Alabama, with its vicious racists, with its governor having his lips dripping with the words of interposition and nullification, one day right there in Alabama little black boys and black girls will be able to join hands with little white boys and white girls as sisters and brothers; I have a dream today.

I have a dream that one day every valley shall be exalted, every hill and mountain shall be made low, and rough places will be made plane and crooked places will be made straight, and the glory of the Lord shall be revealed, and all flesh shall see it together.

This is our hope. This is the faith that I go back to the South with. With this faith we will be able to hew out of the mountain of despair a stone of hope. With this faith we will be able to transform the jangling discords of our nation into a beautiful symphony of brotherhood. With this faith we will be able to work together, to pray together, to struggle together, to go to jail together, to stand up for freedom together, knowing that we will be free one day.

This will be the day . . . This will be the day when all of God's children will be able to sing with new meaning. "My country 'tis of thee, sweet land of liberty, of thee I sing. Land where my fathers died, land of the pilgrim's pride, from every mountainside, let freedom ring," and if America is to be a great nation—this must become true.

So let freedom ring—from the prodigious hilltops of New Hampshire, let freedom ring; from the mighty mountains of New York, let freedom ring—from the heightening Alleghenies of Pennsylvania!

Let freedom ring from the snowcapped Rockies of Colorado!

Let freedom ring from the curvaceous slopes of California!

But not only that; let freedom ring from Stone Mountain of Georgia!

Let freedom ring from Lookout Mountain of Tennessee!

Let freedom ring from every hill and molehill of Mississippi. From every mountainside, let freedom ring, and when this happens . . .

When we allow freedom to ring, when we let it ring from every village and every hamlet, from every state and every city, we will be able to speed up that day when all of God's children, black men and white men, Jews and Gentiles, Protestants and Catholics, will be able to join hands and sing in the words of the old Negro spiritual, "Free at last! free at last! thank God almighty, we are free at last!"

DEDICATION SPEECH

"The Gettysburg Address"

President Abraham Lincoln

A dedication speech is given to commemorate the official unveiling or opening of a memorial, park, building, or some other place or thing for a particular purpose. On November 19, 1863, Abraham Lincoln presented a speech to dedicate the National Soldiers' Cemetery at Gettysburg, Pennsylvania. Prior to President Lincoln's speech, Edward Everett, president of Harvard, senator, and orator of the day, had delivered a two-hour analysis of the battles at Gettysburg. Following this lengthy tribute, President Lincoln presented his three-minute dedication that has been hailed as the finest example of its kind—and certainly the most widely quoted of American speeches. What does Lincoln do in the speech to build force behind the word dedicated? *In your opinion, what qualities in the speech have caused it to endure as one of the world's great statements?*

Fourscore and seven years ago our fathers brought forth on this continent a new nation, conceived in liberty, and dedicated to the proposition that all men are created equal.

Now we are engaged in a great civil war, testing whether that nation, or any nation so conceived and so dedicated, can long endure. We are met on a great battlefield of that war. We have come to dedicate a portion of that field as a final resting-place for those who here gave their lives that that nation might live. It is altogether fitting and proper that we should do this.

But, in a larger sense, we cannot dedicate—we cannot consecrate—we cannot hallow—this ground. The brave men, living and dead, who struggled here, have consecrated it far above our poor power to add or detract. The world will little note nor long remember what we say here, but it can never forget what they did here. It is for us, the living, rather, to be dedicated here to the unfinished work which they who fought here have thus far so nobly advanced. It is rather for us to be here dedicated to the great task remaining before us—that from these honored dead we take increased devotion to that cause for which they gave the last full measure of devotion; that we here highly resolve that these dead shall not have died in vain; that this nation, under God, shall have a new birth of freedom; and that government of the people, by the people, for the people, shall not perish from the earth.

PRESENTATION SPEECH

Presentation of Honorary Citizenship to Sir Winston Churchill

President John F. Kennedy

A presentation speech is often given at a ceremony in which an honor, an award, a prize, or a gift is bestowed upon someone. Although a presentation speech sometimes includes a long tribute to the recipient, for the most part it is a fairly short, formal statement of why the person is being recognized. At the very least, the presentation speech should discuss the nature or importance of the award or gift and the accomplishments of the individual. In the following short speech, note how President Kennedy highlights why Winston Churchill had earned the honor he is being given. Why is this occasion a unique one in United States history? How does Kennedy justify bestowing this honor on Churchill?

Ladies and gentlemen, Members of Congress, Members of the Cabinet, His Excellency the British Ambassador, Ambassadors of the Commonwealth, old friends of Sir Winston led by Mr. Baruch, ladies and gentlemen: We gather today at a moment unique in the history of the United States.

This is the first time that the United States Congress has solemnly resolved that the President of the United States shall proclaim an honorary citizenship for the citizen of another country, and in joining me to perform this happy duty the Congress gives Sir Winston Churchill a distinction shared only with the Marquis de Lafayette.

In naming him an honorary citizen, I only propose a formal recognition of the place he has long since won in the history of freedom and in the affections of my, and now his, fellow countrymen.

Whenever and wherever tyranny threatened, he has always championed liberty. Facing firmly toward the future, he has never forgotten the past. Serving six monarchs of his native Great Britain, he has served all men's freedom and dignity.

In the dark days and darker nights when Britain stood alone—and most men save Englishmen despaired of England's life—he mobilized the English language and sent it into battle. The incandescent quality of his words illuminated the courage of his countrymen.

Indifferent himself to danger, he wept over the sorrows of others. A child of the House of Commons, he became in time its father. Accustomed to the hardships of battle, he has no distaste for pleasure.

Now his stately ship of life, having weathered the severest storms of a troubled century, is anchored in tranquil waters, proof that courage and faith and the zest for freedom are truly indestructible. The record of his triumphant passage will inspire free hearts all over the globe.

By adding his name to our rolls, we mean to honor him, but his acceptance honors us far more. For no statement or proclamation can enrich his name now; the name Sir Winston Churchill is already legend.

Acceptance Speech of the 1950 Nobel Prize for Literature

William Faulkner, author

The purpose of an acceptance speech is to give thanks for receiving an award. Most acceptance speeches include a brief thanks to those responsible for giving the award and, if the recipient was helped by others, thanks to those who share in the honor. In the following speech, note how William Faulkner moves from acceptance of the award in the first paragraph to the problems facing writers in an age of uncertainty. The power of the speech rests in his faith that humanity will not only endure but prevail. By the end of the speech, the reader recognizes that Faulkner is praising the spirit and importance of writing as an inseparable part of mankind's efforts to rise above despair. On what basis does Faulkner place his faith in the endurance of the human race? How does Faulkner's statement of this faith relate to the purpose of his speech—to express thanks for receiving the Nobel Prize for Literature?

I feel that this award was not made to me as a man, but to my work—a life's work in the agony and sweat of the human spirit, not for glory and least of all for profit, but to create out of the materials of the human spirit something which did not exist before. So this award is only mine in trust.

It will not be difficult to find a dedication for the money part of it commensurate with the purpose and significance of its origin. But I would like to do the same with the acclaim, too, by using this moment as a pinnacle from which I might be listened to by the young men and women already dedicated to the same anguish and travail, among whom is already that one who will some day stand where I am standing.

Our tragedy today is a general and universal physical fear so long sustained by now that we can even bear it. There are no longer problems of the spirit. There is only the question: When will I be blown up? Because of this, the young man or woman writing today has forgotten the problems of the human heart in conflict with itself which alone can make good writing because only that is worth writing about, worth the agony and the sweat.

He must learn them again. He must teach himself that the basest of all things is to be afraid: and, teaching himself that, forget it forever, leaving no room in his workshop for anything but the old verities and truths of the heart, the universal truths lacking which any story is ephemeral and doomed—love and honor and pity and pride and compassion and sacrifice. Until he does, he labors under a curse. He writes not of love but of lust, of defeats in which nobody loses anything of value, of victories without hope and, worst of all, without pity or compassion. His griefs grieve on no universal bones, leaving no scars. He writes not of the heart but of the glands.

Until he learns these things, he will write as though he stood among and watched the end of man. I decline to accept the end of man. It is easy enough to say that man is immortal simply because he will endure; that when the last ding-dong of doom has clanged and faded from the last worthless rock hanging tideless in the last red and dying evening, that even there will still be one more sound; that of his puny inexhaustible voice, still talking. I refuse to accept this.

I believe that man will not merely endure; he will prevail. He is immortal, not because he alone among creatures has an inexhaustible voice, but because he has a soul, a spirit capable of compassion and sacrifice and endurance. The poet's, the writer's, duty is to write about these things. It is his privilege to help man endure by lifting his heart, by reminding him of the courage and honor and hope and pride and compassion and pity and sacrifice which have been the glory of his past. The poet's voice need not merely be the record of man, it can be one of the props, the pillars to help him endure and prevail.

CONTEST SPEECH

"The Quest for Convenience"

Charles T. Lukaszewski, student speaker at Minnesota State
Class A Speech Tournament

In this speech Charles Lukaszewski analyzes the relationship between convenience and human values. He cites both positive and negative facets of this relationship but sees an overall harmful dominance of convenience over values in America. He contends that the failure of our value system to keep pace with "the quest for convenience" has "left basic human values neglected." However, he does not suggest that we abandon this "quest," but instead, he simply advocates "updating our values . . . to temper it." What kind of material does he use to support his statements about convenience and values? Do you find his discussion informative and convincing? Why, or why not?

America is on a quest for convenience. We spend thousands and thousands of hours looking for the fastest and easiest ways to get our work done. Every aspect of our society has been reshaped by technological progress. However, by putting every ounce of energy into convenience, we've left nothing to help our society grow. New conveniences intensify the relevance of values in society, but they demand those values be cast in modern terms. Our thirst for convenience is overpowering the value growth in America and creating urgent problems that must be solved.

That Americans want convenience is no secret. In fact, we're made aware of it each and every day. Advertisements bombard us with the "user-friendly," the "high-tech," "wash-and-wear," and the "new and improved." The self-cleaning oven saves mom scrubbing time, while "Dawn" takes the grease out of her way. The "24 hour drive-thru" and the Instant Cash Machine also make life that "little bit easier." Convenience, it seems, is everywhere.

Nor can we ever get enough of it. How many times a day does the thought, "There's got to be a better way to do this," cross your mind? Everybody thinks it, and you can often safely bet that someone's already found that better way, for American history is a history of invention. The United States Patent Office is flooded by an average 325 new applications each day. When the Office was first established, it took a few weeks to get a patent, but it is now so deluged that, even with the aid of large computers, the process takes 25 months or more. Inventors know America constantly wants a better way to do things. They know we're on a quest for convenience.

The technological changes wrought by this quest affect our values in important ways. A study on the subject conducted by Harvard University concluded, "technology has a direct impact on values by bringing about new opportunities." We can see the truth of this statement if we look around our country today. Convenience technologies have not only changed every aspect of the way we live, but also opened more avenues to more people than ever before. Unfortunately, we are finding it difficult, if not impossible to take advantage of them because our value system has not kept pace with technology.

I have already touched on the direct nature of the relationship between convenience and values. The fact that conveniences can't satisfy every human need is a simple way to demonstrate that they coexist. Technology takes us conveniently from New York to London in just three hours aboard a supersonic transport, but technology can't blend a good cup of coffee. It takes a human taste tester to find the perfect beans. And technology can whiz my SAT scores to the college of my choice, but it can't write the essay that will gain me admission. Values are just as necessary with convenience because people are just as necessary.

Given that convenience and values coexist, we should ask how they affect one another. It's obvious that the values we hold result in convenience. We cherish life, liberty and the pursuit of happiness, all three of which are enhanced by conveniences. For instance, American Democracy has been immeasurably strengthened by computers and television. The joining of these two tools has made it possible for every American to participate in the political process.

This is just one way in which an important value can be enhanced by conveniences.

However, those same conveniences can upset the value system. The television that brings us into politics brings other pictures from around the world: hunger and racism in Africa, the arms race between superpowers, and bad news in one's home town. Children, who do not fully understand values, grow up to these pictures on TV every day. They are not prepared to interpret what they see, and psychologists believe this may harm their personal value systems later. Convenience and values are tied together because they affect one another in important ways.

Unfortunately, America's value system has not kept pace with convenience, and this has created urgent problems while strangling value growth. Two examples symbolize America's "social slip." First, we've found it almost impossible to answer moral questions raised by new conveniences, questions like: who should get expensive new medical treatments, is television too violent, what are we to do with our nuclear arsenal? Baby Jane Doe is a case in point. Modern technology could have sustained her life if her parents chose to, but in making that decision they had no precedents to guide them, no established right or wrong. Moral and ethical dilemmas like this are becoming commonplace, because we've gotten so far ahead of ourselves that convenience can't stimulate our values fast enough.

A second example lies in the failure of institutions in urban America. Professor Richard Rosenbloom conducted a study on the subject in the sixties. He found that traditional institutions and values were incapable of coming to grips with the new problems of America's cities. The things he saw persist today: cities unable to deal with education, crime control and public welfare problems; businesses unable to bring their know-how to bear on urban projects; and economic and political interests getting in the way of housing for the poor. We face problems today that 20 years ago were considered the fault of value decay. This says little of our social progress in that time.

I've explained that convenience and values are intimately related. But in America today these two forces are no longer working in tandem. The serious problems this is causing *must* move us to update our value system. For, if we do not, the danger of conveniences being used inappropriately, and potentially harmfully, becomes a certainty. Our exclusive focus on finding easier ways of living is responsible, because it's left basic social values neglected. The culprit, therefore, is not the quest for convenience itself, but rather the importance we have placed on it.

The point I'm making is best expressed by economist Robert Heilbroner: "Advances in technology must be compatible with an existing society." Conveniences are very important, but we've seen the problems and dangers of neglected value growth. We can solve our problem by putting a little less energy into easier lifestyles and a little more into updating our values. We know convenience and values stimulate one another. If we reorder our priorities to take advantage of this, we can have convenience and value growth at the same time. The quest for convenience can continue to better the lives of all Americans. We need only our values to temper it.

CONTEST SPEECH

"The Value of Silence"

Brigitte Viellieu, student speaker who placed sixth in the 1986 National Forensic League Finals

Brigitte Viellieu uses a problem-solution approach to develop a convincing persuasive argument for the "value of silence." Following a discussion of ways in which quiet is beneficial and noise is harmful, she presents a counterpoint that "some people want and even need noise." Then she returns to her argument for the value of silence, asserting that silence provides opportunities for reflection. In her conclusion she dramatically emphasizes her main point by asking her audience to remain silent rather than applaud at the close of her speech. What methods does she use in the opening of her speech to set the tone for her message? What types of information does she use to support her statements? How convincing do you find Ms. Viellieu's argument? Which points do you find most convincing or memorable? Do any of her points seem weak, over-drawn, or unnecessary? How would you develop a counterargument to Ms. Viellieu's proposition that people need more silence in their lives?

Poets have long sung the praises of silence—the awesome silence of a clear starry night, the peaceful silence of a midwinter snowfall, the welcome silence of a well-earned rest at the end of a busy day.

Now, for just one moment, I would like you to listen to this. (pause) That is silence. And most of us are uncomfortable with it. We've lost its charm, its value. Now, while we were all silent, I noticed what an intensive audience this is. And I noticed that this audience is somewhat larger than yesterday's.*

Noticing these things like I did might seem unimportant. What does it matter if you notice the size of a crowd or how attentive someone is?* But this observation means a great deal in our world, or at least it should. In silence, we can appreciate our surroundings and understand better what they mean to us. We can look into ourselves and search our souls.

We need silent time for understanding—silence to evaluate ourselves, our advantages, our disadvantages, our past experiences, our goals, and our friends. And this evaluation has more depth than silence. Now, I realize some of us do appreciate silence, but too often we don't provide it in our world. I know I don't. I simply eliminate it spontaneously.

For example, my mother was very angry at me the other day. She was right for being angry. I said something terrible, and I hurt her feelings. But, I couldn't handle that, so when I got home, I went straight to my room, put on my headphones and listened to the music. If things got too quiet I would have had to take a closer look, a painful look at the fact that I really hurt someone that I love. And when I went to bed that night, I made sure that I left my headphones on—no silence for me, no silence for thinking, no silence for learning. And in learning we should have silence as our rule; however, too often this rule is broken.

According to *U.S. News and World Report,* students in schools near JFK Airport lose a total of one hour of learning time each day. Now, I'm not talking about one hour per month, or one hour per week, but one hour every day. And when these same students get home from school, they probably drown out any silence with blaring headsets.

Foreseeing some of these problems with noise, Thomas Edison predicted that if noise continued to increase as it was doing when he lived, man might evolve into a creature that would be eventually born deaf. Have you ever thought that maybe your grandchildren wouldn't be able to hear the sounds of a robin in the springtime, or the music from *My Fair Lady,* or even your words to them, "I Love You."

Doctor Louis Freeman, a medical researcher, said it is very possible that they may not hear any of those sounds, for he stated, "If noise continues to rise as it has been rising, which is at a rate of 1 or more decibels per year, everyone would be stone deaf by the year 2000." So, at the rate we are going, in another fourteen years hundreds of speech coaches could be waiting on the unemployment line.

Despite these facts I have just given about noise, some people want and even need noise. Take yourself for instance. When you come home from work or school, what's the first thing you do if no one is home? Turn on the TV in the family room, maybe the stereo in your bedroom? Have you ever left the house totally quiet, snuggled down in your most comfortable chair to think about what happened that day?

We talk about the rat race of the Western man, versus the inner peace and discipline of the Eastern guru. But he is truly not different from us; he has simply learned the security of silent art and meditation. In contrast, we feel safer in noise because it is easier to have the radio and the TV think for us, then we don't have to think for ourselves.

Maybe if I lived in silence, I could see some of my flaws more clearly. Perhaps I was rude to someone at work or school, without thinking about it. And I never took that quiet moment to realize that I needed to apologize—to my mom. Maybe I lost a friend. Not only can we learn more, but we can enjoy more. Maybe I could just enjoy the human harmony of this room.

---

* Observations varied from room to room and audience to audience.

TVs and radios and stereos are sound barriers that we must break. And, like the pilot who soars beyond the sound barrier, we can let our minds soar beyond all that superficial noise that constricts us. We are all capable of sensitive and creative thinking. How can we constantly choose noise over silence? Most of us do. Edward Depolviere, a national noise control official, states that noise is the only pollutant some people actually want. Truck drivers want the meanest sounding rigs, and teenagers want the loudest woofers and tweeters. To prove this point, a company tried to sell a quiet vacuum cleaner a number of years ago, but it didn't sell. Why? Well, who wants a quiet appliance? If it doesn't make some roar, it must not be getting the job done. We are so accustomed to noise that if noise isn't present something must be wrong.

The book *Stories Behind Everyday Things* explains how one Virginia housewife handles the dreaded silence. She couldn't even tolerate it at bedtime and found it necessary to switch on her hairdryer so she could fall asleep to its hum. I don't know who switched it off.

And if you can't stand silence, for $29.95 you can buy a record entitled "White Sound," which produces sounds that are a cross between a convention of babbling seagulls, and the love calls of mating whales.

Why are we afraid of silence? Are we afraid if we turn off our noise that we will be able to see what an unthinking, unfeeling, and uncaring world we've become? In a study on human behavior, L.K. Cannon and K.E. Matthews show that when noise is present we are less likely to help a person who has dropped a stack of books and needs help. And perhaps even more tragic is the fact that as the noise level ascends, aggressive behavior increases. Barren and Burre's book *Understanding Human Interaction* says that it is reasonable to assume that the amount of noise in our cities contributes to the amount of violence that occurs there.

Can such a tense world learn that there is beauty in silence? Are we capable of experiencing the silences of a starry night, a snowfall, and a well-earned rest? Now obviously silence isn't just noticing how attentive someone is, or the size of a crowd. Silence is observing and learning about ourselves and the people and things around us. Without silence I can never measure your worth. I can't see your pain if all I'm doing is babbling about my new outfit and how someone glanced at it. I can't perceive your loneliness if I'm always wearing my headphones. I can't even see your love for me if I am never willing to quietly think about your devotion.

We all need to grasp and learn the value of silence, for it can charm us into knowing ourselves.

I once went to a college Christmas concert, and before the last song the concert master asked the audience not to applaud at the end. He felt that the beauty of this song could better live in silence than in applause, and likewise, I ask you not to applaud at the end of my speech. Not that I don't like the sound of hands clapping for me, it's just that I truly believe that you can better absorb what I have said in the silence that follows. After all, if you don't understand my silence, you haven't understood my words.

CONTEST SPEECH

"The Green Mountain Boys"

W. Benson Chiles, student speaker who placed first in the 1986 Texas state competition

In this contest-winning speech, W. Benson Chiles sings the praises of patriotic Americans who went by the name of the Green Mountain Boys. The goal of his speech is to paint a vivid picture of the role that the Green Mountain Boys played during the Revolutionary era. By outlining their valor and accomplishments, Mr. Chiles presents them as examples of all the heroes that have answered the call to defend their country. What does Chiles do to show that the acts of the Green Mountain Boys are the

Ethan Allen, Seth Warner, Stephen Fay, Zadock Remington, Colonel James Easton, Major Brown, Captain Edward Mott, Captain Samuel Herrick. Gentlemen, our basic freedoms are in peril. The time has come to fight.

Almost ten years prior to the Revolutionary War, these men answered a roll call when they banded together in an effort to protect local property rights from royal decrees. Named after area mountains, the Green Mountain Boys played a substantial role in the American Revolution. Men like the Green Mountain Boys were the backbone for America during the Revolutionary era. Untrained and ununiformed, these men had a divine sense of righteousness and freedom when they volunteered for demanding military campaigns. This individualism and independence, which became so prevalent in the American militia of the time, provided the desire and commitment necessary to defeat such a world power as Britain. Nonconformity had grown in individuals from the necessity to survive and the opportunity to prosper in the new land, America. The acts of the Green Mountain Boys are the epitome of the boldness of spirit which brought freedom to our land.

At the outset of the War when battles were fought at Lexington and Concord, Ethan Allen, the original leader of the Green Mountain Boys began collaborating with other area leaders to find ways to assist America in the War with their mother country. With some discussion, they agreed on an attack of Fort Ticonderoga, a vital British stronghold which contained many needed weapons. This fort was the main barrier between American and British Canadian colonies because of its strategic location on Lake Champlain. On the night of May 9, 1775, after marching sixty miles and recruiting over two hundred Green Mountain Boys from cities along the way, Allen and his men stood at Hands Cove ready to cross the lake and attack the fort. With some difficulty they procured enough boats to make the crossing and just before dawn they stormed the fort and forced the British to surrender their valuable asset.

Americans gained three beneficial results from this victory. First, the Americans now controlled the route to Canada, allowing General Richard Montgomery's army to capture Montreal in the winter of 1775-1776. Second, it gave Americans confidence and courage to continue in the War. Third, the weapons confiscated from the fort were very instrumental in driving the British from the city of Boston later in the War.

But things did not continue to turn out so well for the Green Mountain Boys. Ethan Allen, being his usual brash self, made a premature attack on Montreal and was captured in the process, eliminating himself from the remainder of the War. Fortunately though, Seth Warner provided very capable leadership for the Green Mountain Boys who became a well-trained, disciplined fighting force.

When the British began sending reinforcements to Canada for full scale attack on America, the Green Mountain Boys again rose to the call and helped defend Fort Ticonderoga and added a decisive victory at Longueuil. But the most exciting and important victory for the Green Mountain Boys came at the Battle of Bennington, where they marched to the rescue of retreating American troops and defeated the army of Johnny Burgoyne.

The Green Mountain Boys, with their flaming spirit, gave America the winning edge over their red-coated foes of Britain by clearing a path to Canada. These men risked their lives for the freedoms which they held true, stated by Thomas Jefferson in the Declaration of Independence. The Green Mountain Boys, in their quest for freedom, began the spark and the fire which has historically remained as an ember capable of being rekindled during our country's time of need. As we know, this ember was rekindled in World War I when our young men left their farms to answer an overseas call to stop a wave of oppression that had developed in Europe. And again our patriots rekindled the fire in the early 1940's by openly enlisting in World War II to halt the onslaught of Hitler and his army. Even today, the flame of patriotism is there to be rekindled when called upon because of that small band of men, whose rough disposition and independent spirit helped lead us to victory and freedom.

So, when we think of the Green Mountain Boys' roll call, we will remember the heroes who answered roll in World War I and World War II and know that the future holds many more heroes who will also risk their lives to answer the roll call of freedom.

GLOSSARY

A

abstain a vote made by a member of a parliamentary meeting who does not wish to support or to oppose a motion that is being voted upon

abstract words words that name things, such as ideas, values, and beliefs, that cannot be perceived by the five senses

ad hoc committee a group that is formed to study a single issue

adjourn a privileged motion calling for the close of a meeting

affirmative case in debate, the reasons and evidence presented to indicate a problem with the present system and to show why the action stated in the proposition offers the best solution to that problem

agenda an outline for a group discussion; a list of items that will be discussed at a group meeting

air waves radio and television signals that are broadcast into the air

AM amplitude modulation; air waves that are transmitted using amplitude modulation

amend a subsidiary motion callling for an alteration in the wording of a motion

amplifier a device used to strengthen a radio or television signal

analogy a form of reasoning by comparison

anapestic a poetic metrical pattern having three syllables with the accent on the third

anecdote a brief, often amusing, story

announcement a statement of a speaker's feelings about a point, given to emphasize that point

antenna a wire or metal rod used to send and receive radio and television transmissions

apathetic audience an audience in which a majority of members do not have any interest in the speaker's proposition

appeal an incidental motion used to force the chairperson to submit a disputed ruling made by the chairperson to a vote by the entire group

arrangement the organization of a work

articulation the shaping of speech sounds into recognizable oral symbols that go together to make up a word

association the process of tying a behavior to some vivid mental image

attention sustained regard, or interest

audience the listeners or spectators attending a presentation or performance; the people who hear a speech

audio the sound portion of a television broadcast

audiovisual aids materials that a speaker uses to clarify or to add to the verbal presentation of a speech

audition a formal tryout in which people have a chance to show their abilities

authoritarian leadership a style of leadership that places all responsibility in the hands of an authoritarian leader; also called *directive*

B

bandwagon a propaganda technique that encourages people to act because "everyone else is doing it"

begging the question assuming the truth of a statement before it is proven

blocking the overall plan for actor movement

body the portion of a speech in which the main points are developed

body language the use of facial expression, eye contact, gesture, posture, and movement to communicate

brainstorming making a list of whatever comes to mind as you think about a subject

breathiness a quality of voice that results from too much unvoiced air escaping through the vocal folds as a person is speaking

burden of proof the obligation of the affirmative team in a debate to present sufficient reason for changing the existing system

business the actions that performers use to establish the atmosphere or the particular situation in a scene or to identify an individual character

business call a telephone call made to conduct business, to request information from a business or an organization, or to pursue some other official matter

business manager the person in charge of financial matters relating to a dramatic production

C

call for the orders of the day a privileged motion that alerts the chairperson that a scheduled event has been overlooked

call numbers the number, sometimes including letters, used to organize books in a library

card catalog a collection of cards arranged by subject, author, and title, listing all the books in a particular library

card-stacking a propaganda technique in which only partial information is presented so as to leave an inaccurate impression

case the arguments and evidence on which a debate team bases its stand on a given proposition

cast the group of actors in a play

causation an argument in which the conclusion is a direct result of one or more given sources or conditions

cause-and-effect order a pattern of organization in which information is arranged to show causes or conditions and the effects or results of those causes or conditions

cavity a partially enclosed area

chairperson the officer in a parliamentary organization who is responsible for running pleasant, efficient meetings and for protecting the rights of everyone at the meetings

channels the means used to send messages

characterization the portrayal of the physical, intellectual, and emotional traits of each character in a drama

chart a visual aid that gives information in word or tabular form

choral speaking an oral interpretation performance in which several voices speak together in groups

chorus a group of people who narrate the events in a play

chronological order a pattern for arranging details or events according to the order in which they happen in time

circumflex an up-and-down inflection

citation a statement that gives credit to the source of quoted material

clarity the clearness of language that results from choosing the right words

classical tragedy tragedy that presents highborn people who fall to ruin as the result of some "tragic flaw"

cliché a figurative expression that has been used so often that it has lost its power or effect

climactic order a pattern of organization in which items of information are arranged according to their order of importance

climax the moment of highest intensity in a play

closed questions questions that can be answered with *yes* or *no* or with only one or two words

close nominations an incidental motion that calls for an end to the process of nominating persons for office

cohesive able to work together as a unit; cooperative

college interview an interview conducted by a representative of a college to help determine whether or not to select an applicant for admission

comedy a drama that usually has a happy ending and is often based on exaggerated or eccentric behavior

comedy of manners a form of drama that was popular in England during the Restoration and that is characterized by satire that makes fun of social customs

commedia dell'arte popular Italian Renaissance comedies in which professional actors improvised their roles as stock characters in humorous, standardized situations

communication the process of sharing information by using symbols to send and receive messages

comparative-advantage method a deductive approach for presenting information in which each of the reasons is presented as a benefit to the audience

comparative-advantages pattern in debate, a pattern for organizing information in a case to demonstrate that the proposal stated in the proposition would have significant advantages over the status quo

comparison a statement that shows the similarities between objects, people, or ideas

comparison-and-contrast order a pattern of organization in which items of information are arranged to show similarities and differences between them

competence the state of being well qualified

conclusion a short ending that reemphasizes the key ideas of a speech and leaves the attention of the audience on a high note

concrete words words that name things that can be perceived by the five senses

condensing cutting a work to make it more concise

conflict in group discusion, a form of disagreement in which two or more people struggle to win recognition of one idea or point of view over another

conflicting expression a facial appearance that does not agree with a speaker's words or feelings

connotation the feelings and associations aroused by a word; the "hidden" meaning of a word determined by experiences a person has had with the concept the word symbolizes

consensus a group decision that is worded in such a way that the entire group agrees on it

constructive speech the speech given during a debate that builds an argument

context clues information contained within a sentence or within surrounding sentences that helps a reader figure out the meaning of an unfamiliar word

contrast a statement that shows the differences between two things

conventional accepted by a large number of people

conversation the informal exchange of thoughts and feelings by two or more people

costumer the person in charge of the performers' attire in a theatrical production

counterplan in debate, the negative side's presentation of a different solution from the solution proposed in the affirmative case

credibility the quality of being worthy of belief or trust

criteria-satisfaction method an inductive method for organizing information in which a speaker first gets the audience to agree with the soundness of certain criteria and then shows how the speaker's proposal will satisfy those criteria

critical listening trying to understand what is being said and testing the strength of the ideas presented

critique an analysis and evaluation of something, such as a speech

cross-examination debate a debate format that, like traditional debate, involves two affirmative and two negative speakers, but that allows greater opportunity than does traditional debate for participants to question their opponents

cue cards large sheets of cardboard with notes or with an entire script written on them in felt-tip pen

D

dactylic a poetic metrical pattern having three syllables with the accent on the first

deadpan an expressionless facial appearance that never changes, regardless of what is being said

debate a form of public speaking in which participants prepare and present speeches on opposite sides of an issue to determine which side has the stronger arguments

debate brief a complete outline of the affirmative and the negative cases in a debate

decoding finding the meaning of verbal and nonverbal signals

decree a decision dictated by the leader of a group discussion

deductive approach a method for organizing information in which the goal is stated first and then reasons are presented to support it

definition an explanation of what a word or concept means

democratic leadership a style of leadership in group discussion in which the leader offers suggestions for procedures but asks the other members of the group for their ideas about organization, about the roles the members should play, and about the tasks that should be accomplished; also called *supportive*

demographic data information about the characteristics of a population

demonstration a procedure in which a speaker goes through the actual steps of a process in order to help an audience understand that process

denotation the dictionary meaning that most people in a culture give to a word

description a word picture of a person, place, thing, or event

diagram a visual representation of details and ideas

dialect a regional or cultural variety of language differing from standard English in pronunciation, sentence structure, and use of words

dialogue a conversation between two or more characters in a drama

diaphragm a dome-shaped muscle at the base of the lungs that plays a key role in the breathing process

diction the words chosen to send messages

directions the instructions for finding a particular place

director the person in charge of selecting a play, casting, blocking, coaching the actors, and coordinating the work of the set designer and the costumer

disagreements situations in which two or more people do not share the same view or opinion on something

discussion the process of talking through a disagreement by identifying the problem, determining its nature and causes, talking about possible ways to solve the problem, and selecting the best choice

division of assembly an incidental motion requiring the chairperson to call for a second vote, which will preferably be conducted by another method than the method used to conduct the first vote

division of question an incidental motion requiring the chairperson to divide a motion with more than one part into its various parts so that each part can be discussed and voted on separately

drama an artistic form of communication in which a story dealing with human conflict is acted out on a stage; a story written to be acted out on a stage

dynamism the energy, enthusiasm, and excitement that a speaker shows for the topic in a speech

E

emotional appeals statements used to arouse an emotional reaction, such as anger, joy, or sadness, in an audience

empathizing being sensitive to the feelings of others

emphasis the force or special attention given to a particular word or point

encoding the process of turning ideas and feelings into verbal and nonverbal symbols

English Renaissance drama drama that flourished in England between 1590 and 1630 and that is notable for having nonreligious themes and for giving rise to professionalism in both acting and playwriting

entertain to amuse an audience

enunciation the distinctness of speech sounds

environment immediate surroundings, including color, lighting, sound, and space

ethical standards the guidelines that a society sets for right, just, and moral behavior

ethos the distinguishing character, attitudes, beliefs, and nature of a particular person or group of people

etiquette good manners; a pattern of behavior that should be observed in social and public life

euphemism a word or phrase that is not very expressive or vivid but is used in place of words that are thought to be unpleasant or distasteful

evidence a fact, an opinion, or other information given to support a reason

exaggeration a form of figurative language when it is used to emphasize or to enlarge, but not to deceive

example a single instance that supports or develops a statement

expert opinion a statement of belief about a subject from a person who is recognized as an authority on that subject

extemporaneous speech a speech that is fully prepared but not memorized, giving the speaker both control over the speech and opportunity for adaptation and last-minute changes

extend debate (See *limit or extend debate*.)

eye contact a nonverbal means of communication that involves the way a speaker looks at the audience and the way the audience looks at the speaker

F

fact information that can be proved, or verified, by testing, by observing, or by consulting reference material

false analogy an analogy that draws invalid conclusions from weak or often farfetched comparisons

false consensus a group decision in which the members of the group act as if there is agreement on the decision when there really is none

false premise a premise that is untrue or distorted

faulty reasoning a mistake in the reasoning process

favorable audience an audience in which the majority of listeners agree from slightly to very much with the speaker's propositions

feedback verbal and nonverbal reactions that indicate to a sender that a message has been received and understood

feelings emotional reactions

fiction prose that presents material that is imagined or invented by the author

figurative comparison a statement that shows the similarities between things that are essentially unalike

figurative language words or phrases that are not meant to be interpreted in their literal sense, but instead are used to create new meanings and vivid images

floor plan a diagram that shows the positions of walls, entrances, and furnishings on a stage

flow sheet outline notes of each speech given in a debate

FM frequency modulation; air waves that are transmitted using frequency modulation

follow-up questions questions that are related to the subject matter of an earlier question

foot a group of syllables arranged according to a definite pattern in a poem

formal outline a brief skeleton of a speech

formal settings situations in which senders and receivers can prepare for their communication beforehand; such as interviews, group discussions, and debates

formal theater a dramatic production that involves the acting out of a complete script, including both dialogue and action

forum a panel discussion or symposium in which the audience is permitted to ask questions and make comments, providing an opportunity for open discussion of ideas

fricatives the consonant sounds that make a frictionlike noise: [f], [v], [θ], [ð], [s], [z], [ʃ], [ʒ], and [j]

G

generalizations general conclusions or opinions drawn from particular observations

general purpose the overall intent of a speech

general words words that refer to an entire category of items

germane   to be relevant; a requirement in parliamentary procedure that an amendment must in some way involve the same question that is raised by the motion to which it is applied

gestures   the movements people make with their arms, hands, and fingers to communicate

glides   the sounds that result from the gliding movement of the articulators: [l], [r], [w], and [j]

goal   a speaker's reason for speaking

good will   an audience's respect or positive feeling for a speaker

grammar   the rules and conventions for speaking and writing English

graph   a special type of drawing that shows comparative information

group discussion   a goal-directed form of communication in which people meet in a group for the purpose of sharing information, solving a problem, or arriving at a workable decision

H

hand microphone   a microphone that is meant to be held in the hand

harshness   a quality of voice characterized by an unpleasant, grating sound that may also be hard or metallic

hasty generalizations   general conclusions or opinions drawn from very few observations

hearing   being able to detect sounds

heckler   a person who tries purposely to disturb a speaker

hoarseness   a quality of voice characterized by a thickness of sound or a muffled or rasping sound

hostile audience   an audience in which the majority of the listeners are opposed to the speaker's proposition

house manager   the person in charge of the ushers in a theater and of conditions in the theater building itself, such as the temperature control, house lighting, and ventilation

hyperbole   (See *exaggeration.*)

I

iambic   a poetic metrical pattern having two syllables with an accent on the second

illustration   a detailed example

imagery   the use of words and phrases to describe something in a way that creates mental pictures for the reader

impromptu speech   a speech delivered on the spur of the moment with no direct preparation

improvisation   a form of drama that portrays spontaneous reactions to a situation

incidental motions   proposals made in a parliamentary meeting that relate to questions of procedure arising out of the discussion

inductive approach   a method for organizing information, beginning with the statement of reasons and building to the statement of the proposition

inflection   the upward or downward glide of pitch as a person speaks

inform   to present new information to an audience or to give new insights into information the audience already has

informal settings   the casual, unstructured situations in which most communication occurs

informal theater   the spontaneous theater of the imagination, including pantomime and improvisation

informative speech   a speech that provides information

insight   a view or an understanding that reveals an inner truth about something

intensity   the depth of feeling a performer has for a part

interest   the involvement, or concern, an audience shows in a topic

interference   anything that interferes with, or gets in the way of, clear communication

interpersonal communication   communication between two or more people

interview   a form of communication in which people obtain information by asking questions

interviewee   a person being interviewed

interviewer   a person who conducts an interview

intimate space   the distance—up to eighteen inches between those communicating—at which conversations take place between family members and people who know each other well

introduction   the several sentences that make up the beginning of a speech; the presentation of one person to another or to a group

irony   the use of words to imply that something is considerably different, perhaps even the opposite, from what is actually said

irrelevant evidence   information that has nothing to do with the argument being made

issues   key questions that must be answered to determine who wins a debate

J

jargon   language that is understood by people in a particular group or field but is not necessarily understood by those outside the group

job interview   an interview in which an employer and a job applicant exchange information about one another

K

key the average pitch at which a person speaks

knowledgeable source a person who is likely to have knowledge on a particular subject

L

laissez-faire leadership a style of leadership that puts the responsibility for procedure in the hands of the group; also called *nondirective*

language a system of sounds and symbols used to communicate ideas and feelings

larynx the voice box

lavaliere microphone a portable microphone, about the size of a finger, that hangs on a cord around the neck or is clipped to an article of clothing

lay on the table a subsidiary motion calling for a postponement of action until someone makes a motion to remove the original motion from the table

leadership the ability to guide a group toward its goal

leading questions questions that suggest the answer that is expected or desired

lectern (See *speaker's stand.*)

limit or extend debate a subsidiary motion that calls for setting a time limit for individual speeches or for the entire debate

Lincoln-Douglas debate a form of debate in which only one speaker represents each of the opposing sides and only values propositions are debated

listening getting meaning from sounds that are heard

literal comparison a statement that shows the similarities between things that are essentially alike

literature writing that expresses ideas of permanent or universal interest and that is characterized by excellence of form and expression

loaded words words that evoke a very strong positive or negative attitude toward a particular person or group

logical reasoning the use of reasons supported by valid evidence to develop the specific purpose of a speech

loudness the intensity of sound

lyric poetry verse that is usually brief and that expresses the poet's emotions or personal thoughts

M

main ideas the most important points that a speaker presents

main motions proposals made in a parliamentary meeting that set forth the items of business that will be considered

main points (See *main ideas.*)

majority more than half of a total number; in voting, the side that wins because over half of the number of those voting support that position

makeup artist the person in a theatrical production who applies the performers' cosmetics, as well as creating beards, mustaches, and other special effects; in large productions the makeup artist is assisted by a crew

manipulation shrewd or devious management of facts for one's own purposes

manuscript speech a speech that is written out completely and read to an audience

masking purposely using a facial expression normally associated with one feeling to disguise other, true feelings

meaning the idea or feeling communicated by a work

melody the variations in pitch that help to give expression to a person's voice

memorized speech a speech that is written out completely and remembered word for word so that a speaker can deliver it exactly as it was written without reading from the manuscript

messages ideas and feelings that make up the content of communication

metaphor a comparison between essentially unlike things without using the words *like* or *as*

meter the pattern of stressed and unstressed syllables developed within each line of verse

microphone an electronic device that broadcasts sound by picking up sound waves and sending them to a control board where they are then sent to a transmitter

mime a pantomimist

miracle plays plays that dramatize events from the Bible and from the lives of saints

mnemonic devices rhymes, acronyms, and other verbal forms that are created to help people remember information

monologue a dramatic speech given by a character who is alone on stage

monotone a melody pattern that consists of only one tone

Monroe motivated sequence an inductive method for presenting information, including five steps: drawing attention to a problem, showing a need for action, outlining a plan to satisfy that need, visualizing benefits, and suggesting action

mood the emotional tone that predominates in a selection

morality plays medieval plays that present allegorical stories in which all characters personify religious or moral abstractions

motions   proposals for action made by members of a parliamentary organization

movement   the way a person moves

N

name-calling   a form of labeling in which words are used in a manner intended to arouse powerful negative feelings

narration   an account of the details of a story or an event

narrative poetry   poetry that tells a story

narrator   a person who is telling a story

nasal cavity   the nose

nasality   a quality of voice characterized by too much nasal resonance

nasals   sounds resonated in the nasal cavity: [m], [n], [ŋ]

negative case   in debate, the reasons and evidence given to refute the affirmative case, to defend the status quo, or to present a counterplan

negative method   an inductive method for organizing information in which the speaker shows that other options are not as acceptable as the option proposed by the speaker

neutral audience   an audience that has not reached a decision one way or another about a speaker's propostion

neutral questions   questions that give the interviewee no hint of what particular answer the interviewer desires

nonfiction   prose that deals with factual information which is true or at least is supposed to be true

nonstandard English   language that is not totally in keeping with, and in some cases even violates, established rules and conventions of English

nontraditional poetry   poetry that does not have a regular rhythm and rhyme, but is arranged in lines

nonverbal communication   a method of communicating that consists of all the elements of communciation other than words

nonverbal symbols   any means used to communicate without words, including tone of voice, facial expressions, and body movements

note cards   cards created during research to record information (or a summary of it) along with the source of that information

O

object to consideration   an incidental motion allowing the group to dismiss a main motion that is irrelevant, inappropriate, or for some other reason undesirable

occasion   the time, the place, and various other conditions that help define the setting in which a speech is given

open questions   questions that must be answered with an explanation

opinion   personal beliefs or attitudes

optimum pitch   the pitch at which a person speaks with the least strain and with the very best resonance, usually approximately four notes above the lowest note a person can speak comfortably

oral cavity   the mouth

oral interpretation   the art of verbally communicating the ideas, feelings, and basic scheme or structure of a work of literature to one or more people

P

panel   a group that discusses a topic of common interest to its members and to a listening audience

pantomime   dramatic communication performed entirely without words

paralanguage   the use of voice variation and extraneous sounds to communicate

parallelism   the repetition of the same word or phrase to emphasize an idea, a mood, or some other feature in a work

paraphrasing   putting into your own words your understanding of another person's ideas

parliamentary inquiry   an incidental motion made to request information about whether making a motion would be in order

parliamentary procedure   a set of rules for conducting orderly meetings

partial demonstration   a demonstration in which either some of the parts are already completed or the size of items is exaggerated so that the audience will be able to see them clearly

pastoral plays   Renaissance plays that present love stories in idealized woodland settings

perception check   a verbal response stating one person's understanding of someone else's nonverbal behavior

personal reference   a speech introduction in which the speaker relates the topic of the speech to the audience's experience

personal space   the distance—consisting of eighteen inches to four feet of space between those communicating—at which conversations occur between acquaintances

persuade   to stimulate interest in a topic, to change an attitude or belief, or to move an audience to action

persuasion   the attempt to convince others to do something or to change a personal conviction or belief of their own free will

persuasive speech   a speech that establishes a fact, changes a belief, or moves an audience to act on a policy

pharyngeal cavity   the throat

physical noise   sounds that prevent a person from being heard

pitch   the highness or lowness of a sound

plosives   the consonant sounds that make an explosive sound when spoken: [p], [b], [t], [d], [k], and [g]

poetry   the communication of an idea, experience, or emotion through the creative arrangement of words according to their meaning, sound, and rhythm

point of order   an incidental motion calling attention to a violation of parliamentary procedure

point of view   the angle of vision from which the audience sees the events in a story unfold; refers to who is telling the story

poise   a person's composure, assurance of manner, and confidence in handling situations

postpone indefinitely   a subsidiary motion that calls for postponement of discussion for the remainder of a meeting and thus prevents the main motion from coming to a vote

postpone to a definite time   a subsidiary motion that calls for a postponement of action until a particular time set by the person making the motion

posture   the position of a person's body

precedence   the ranking of motions in parliamentary procedure

precise words   words that express a person's thoughts or feelings accurately or exactly

premise   in an argument, a stated or implied starting point that is assumed to be true

previous question   a subsidiary motion calling for a vote to stop discussion on a motion

prima facie **case**   a case that contains sufficient evidence to win a debate if the other side presented no argument

primary amendment   an amendment of a main motion

primary source   a source that can provide firsthand information

private group discussion   a group discussion held in closed session so that group members can share information among themselves to solve a problem or make a decision

privileged motions   proposals made in a parliamentary meeting that concern the running of the meeting itself; adjournment, recess, questions of privilege, or call for the orders of the day

problem-solution method   a deductive approach for presenting information in which the speaker first presents the problem and then offers at least one possible solution for that problem

problem-solution pattern   in debate, a pattern for organizing information in a case to demonstrate that a problem cannot be solved by maintaining the status quo and that the proposal stated in the proposition will solve the problem practically and beneficially; also called *need-plan pattern*

problem-solving method   a four-part method for resolving disagreements: identifying the problem, determining its nature and causes, talking about possible ways to solve the problem, and selecting the best choice

process speech   an informative speech that explains how to do something, how to make something, or how something works

producer   the head administrator of a dramatic production, who is responsible for bringing together the script, the director, the theater, and in the case of professional productions, the financing for a show

progressive discussion   a form of group discussion often used as a classroom assignment in which the class is divided into small groups and each group discusses a different aspect of a topic

pronunciation   the grouping and accenting of speech sounds

propaganda   a form of persuasion that tries to convince people to accept an idea or belief without thinking for themselves

proposition   in a persuasive speech and in debate, a specific purpose that establishes a fact, establishes or changes a belief, or recommends a policy

prose   writing that corresponds to usual patterns of speech

psychological noise   the thoughts and feelings people have that interfere with their paying attention to what is being said

public discussion   a form of group discussion that is held in front of an audience to share information and to stimulate thinking

public space   the distance—consisting of more than twelve feet of space between speaker and audience—at which impersonal communication, such as public speaking or oral reading, takes place

public speaking   a formal speaking situation in which one person speaks to an audience of many individuals to entertain, inform, or persuade them

purpose   what a speaker intends to achieve in a speech

Q

quality   the tone of a person's voice

question of evaluation   a discussion question concerning the relative value of a person, a place, a thing, or an idea

question of fact a discussion question aimed at determining what is true

question of policy a discussion question that considers what action should be taken

question of privilege a privileged motion that calls for immediate action on such things as ventilation, heating, lighting, and disturbances

quorum the number of members that must be present for a group to conduct business

quotation a statement of the exact words of another person

R

radio a form of electronic communication in which sound waves are converted into electronic signals that are transmitted and received

random sample a sample in which, in theory, every member of a group has the same chance of being selected

range the spread between the lowest note and the highest note that a person can speak comfortably

rate the speed at which a person talks

realism a movement in drama to portray people and situations as they really are in everyday life

reason a statement that justifies an action, a belief, or a proposition

rebuttal the speech given during a debate that summarizes and rebuilds an argument that has been attacked

receiver the person who receives a message

recess a privileged motion calling for a short break during a meeting

recommendation a short statement that tells an audience what specific behavior the speaker wants the audience to follow

reconsider a renewal motion calling for discussion of a motion that has already been passed

refer to a committee a subsidiary motion that calls for shifting discussion of the matter at hand to a smaller group meeting at some other time

refutation a denial of or an attack on the ideas of the opposition in a debate

rehearsals practice sessions

release a formal permission from the owner of a play's production rights to allow someone to produce that play

reliable source a person who can be depended upon to give accurate information

Renaissance the period of European history (from 1350 to 1650) which brought a rebirth of interest in Greek and Roman drama

renewal motions motions made in a parliamentary meeting that get discussion reopened on decisions that have already been made

reopen nominations an incidental motion made to allow more nominations to be made after nominations have been closed

repetition a method for achieving emphasis by saying the same thing again

report a detailed factual account based on research

rescind a renewal motion calling for cancellation of action taken on a previous motion

resonance reinforcement of sound produced by the vibration of bone and cavity resonators

resonators the bones in the chest, the neck, and the head and the cavities of the throat, the nose, and the mouth, which reinforce sound

restatement the repetition of an idea but not necessarily in the same words

Restoration the period of British history, from 1660–1700, during which the comedy of manners was the most popular form of drama

résumé a brief account of personal data

rhetorical question a question that is not meant to be answered, but instead is asked in order to involve an audience in a speech

rhyme a pattern of similar sounds that gives a poem a melodic quality that is pleasing to the ear

rhythm the arrangement, or flow, of stressed and unstressed syllables that gives a musical quality to poetry

roll call vote a vote in which the secretary calls the name of everyone assembled, and each person votes by saying "aye", "no," or "abstain"

romanticism the belief that human beings should be guided by feelings and emotions

round-table discussion a form of group discussion used to share information about a specific issue

royalty a fee paid for the right to produce a show

S

sarcasm cutting or bitter irony

second an indication that a person other than the person making a motion is willing to have the group consider the motion

secondary amendment an amendment of a primary amendment

secondary source a source that can provide information gained from other sources

secretary the major recording officer and keeper of records in a parliamentary organization

self-introduction the presentation of oneself to another person or to a group

semantic noise interference caused by words that lead to misunderstanding by triggering strong negative feelings against the speaker or the content of the speech

sender   a person who sends a message

sensory words   words that appeal to one or more of the five senses

set designer   the person responsible for designing all visual elements, including stage sets and lighting, that will be used in a production

sign argument   an argument that draws a conclusion based on certain signs or indicators

simile   a comparison using the word *like* or *as* to relate essentially unlike things

simple majority   a majority that consists of at least one more than half the number of people voting

simple words   familiar words, usually of one or two syllables

sincerity   a sign of a speaker's truly caring about his or her topic and audience

slang   highly informal language made up of newly coined words or figures of speech or old words used in new ways

social call   a telephone call made for pleasure or for help in solving a personal problem

social space   the distance—consisting of four to twelve feet of space between those communicating—at which formal conversations occur

spatial order   a pattern of organization in which items are arranged according to their position in space

speaker   in electronic communication, a device that changes an electrical signal back into the sounds that were broadcast; a person who speaks

speaker's stand   a piece of furniture designed to hold a speaker's materials

specific purpose   in a speech, the specific goal stated in one complete sentence

specific words   words that focus on particular items within a category

stage fright   the nervousness that speakers or performers feel before and during a presentation

stage manager   the person who is in charge of the entire backstage and makes sure that the production follows the exact pattern the director has set in rehearsals

standard English   language that is in keeping with established rules and conventions of English

standing committee   a semipermanent group that is part of a larger group; studies problems within its scope of duties or functions and makes recommendations concerning those problems to the larger group

standing microphone   a microphone that stands on the floor or is attached to a lectern

startling statement   a one- to three-sentence speech introduction that catches an audience's attention

statement-of-reasons method   the classic deductive method for presenting information in which the proposition is stated directly, followed by reasons supporting it

stationary microphones   microphones that remain in one place and are not intended for portable use

statistics   numerical facts

status quo   the existing state of affairs; currently held beliefs and currently followed courses of action

step   an abrupt change in pitch

stereotype   a biased belief or attitude about a whole group of people based upon insufficient or irrelevant evidence

stirring ending   a speech conclusion that helps intensify the emotion, or feeling, that the speaker wants the audience to experience

straight refutation   an approach used in building a negative debate argument in which the entire negative case is a denial of each affirmative argument stated

subject area   a general area that is too broad to be used as a topic

sublanguage   a subsystem of an established language that provides a group of people with convenient words for ideas and objects that are of great importance to that group and that are spoken about frequently within that group; for example, slang, dialect, and jargon

subsidiary motions   proposals made in a parliamentary meeting that relate to the treating or disposing of a motion being discussed

summary   a short restatement of the key ideas in a longer work, such as a speech

supporting details   the items, such as facts, examples, statistics, reasons, or incidents, that a speaker uses to back up main ideas

survey   a method of gathering information by questioning or canvassing people selected at random or by quota

suspend the rules   an incidental motion calling for suspension of any standing rule that the organization may have for that particular meeting

symbol   something that stands for something else

symposium   a form of public discussion in which four to six people present short, prepared speeches and then, following the speeches, discuss among themselves the ideas that have been presented

system   a group of elements that work together

T

take from the table   a renewal motion that calls for reopening discussion of a motion that had earlier been moved to lay on the table

technical director the person in a theatrical production who is in charge of constructing sets, positioning and operating lights, managing the curtain, and tearing down the set

technical requirements the items such as the sets, props, lighting, and costumes that are needed to create the physical environment within the play

teleprompter a mechanical prompting device that is set up to pull a sheet of paper from one roller to another at a speed adjusted to the reader's reading pace

television a form of electronic communication in which sound waves and light waves are converted into electronic signals that are transmitted and received

thesis statement a statement that expresses the overall concern of a speech

thespian an actor

timing the controlled pacing of a speech so that it fits within a time limit and achieves maximum effect

tone the speaker's attitude toward a subject and an audience, which is expressed primarily through the sound of the speaker's voice and the speaker's choice of words

topic a specific category within a subject area

topical order a pattern of organization in which a topic is broken down into parts that are rearranged in an order determined by the speaker and stated in the specific purpose of the speech

trachea the windpipe

traditional debate a debate format that involves two affirmative speakers and two negative speakers

traditional poetry language arranged in lines with a regular rhythm and often with a definite rhyme scheme

tragedy drama that usually has a sad or disastrous ending and that tells the story of someone who is brought down by circumstances

transfer a method of building a connection between things that are not logically connected

transitional devices words or phrases that connect ideas and parts of speech in order to help a speaker organize and emphasize information

transmitter an electronic device that produces carrier waves that are combined with electrical waves to become a radio or television signal

trochaic a poetic metrical pattern having two syllables with an accent on the first

truth a validity in characterization that is consistent throughout the play

tuner an electronic device that selects a specific signal from the great number that are striking the antenna at the same time

U

understatement the opposite of exaggeration; the statement of an idea in terms that are less than what could have been used

unity the organization of a speech so that all parts of the speech relate to its specific purpose stated in the thesis statement

universal appeal relevance to the experience of all human beings

V

variation changes in pitch, rate, and volume of voice that bring freshness to a dramatic production

verbal symbols words

vice-chairperson an officer of a parliamentary organization who assumes the duties of the chair when the chair is unable to do so

video the picture portion of a television broadcast

vividness the quality of being full of life, vigorous, or exciting

vocal folds the muscles of the larynx; also called *vocal cords*

vocalized pauses the meaningless speech sounds that speakers use to fill time

voiced describes sounds made by vibrations of the vocal folds

voiceless describes sounds made when the vocal folds are open so that air breathed out does not vibrate them

volume (See *loudness*.)

voting a method for reaching a group decision in which the opinion held by the majority of the members of a group is adopted as the decision of the entire group; an incidental motion concerning the manner in which the chairperson is to take a vote, such as secret ballot or show of hands

W

withdrawal the physical or psychological removal of yourself from a disagreement

withdraw a motion an incidental motion giving the person who made the motion permission to remove it from consideration

INDEX

Body of speech, 238-242 (See also Informative speech; Persuasive speech; Process speech.)
determining main points, 239-40
developing main points, 241-42
organizational patterns, 240-41
Body language, 44-49, 147 (See also Nonverbal behavior)
facial expressions, 46-47
gestures, 47-48
movement, 48
posture, 48
Boileau, Nicholas, 259
Bones as resonators, 69
Bourne Identity, 223
Brainstorming, 186-87 (See also Ideas for speech topics.)
Braley, Berton, 199
Breathing and vocal sound, 66-68
Breathy quality of voice, 79
Brenon, Wendy, 592
Brief, debate, 466-69
Broadway, 552
Brown, Sundai, 312
Browning, Robert, 520
"Business," in acting, 564-65
character's mannerisms, 564-65
inappropriate, 566
Business manager, for theater, 560
Business self-introductions, 117
Business telephone call, 127-29
"Butterflies" when speaking, 295
Burden of proof, 445, 447 (See also Affirmative side.)

C

Cable television, 582, 587
Call numbers, 223
Calls, telephone, 125-29
business, making, 127-29
social, making, 125-26
social, receiving, 126-27
Camera, electric television, 581
Camera, television, working with, 589-90
eye contact and, 589-90
Canham, Erwin, 595
Card catalog, 222-23
Cards, note, 226-27
Card-stacking, propaganda technique, 102
Careers in television and radio, 587
Caricatures, 535
Caruso, Enrico, 578
"Cask of Amontillado, The," 520
Casting a play, 555
Catharsis, 545
Cathode ray tube, 581

Causation, 460
Cause-and-effect order, 331
Cavities as resonators, 69-71
nasal cavity (nose), 70
oral cavity (mouth), 70-71
pharyngeal cavity (throat), 69-70
Cervantes, Miguel de, 573
Chairperson, duties of, 498-500 (See also Parliamentary procedure.)
Chaney, Lynda, 152
Channels, communication, 7
Character, being in, 569
Character, understanding, 562
Character development, 551
Characters, in oral reading, 535
Charades, 548
"Charge of the Light Brigade," 518-19, 529
Chart, 335, 338 (See also Audiovisual aids.)
Chekhov, Anton, 547, 553
"Chicago," 531, 532
Chiles, W. Benson, 616-17
Choral speaking, 530-32
Chorus, Greek, 545
history of, 545
vocal, 530-31
Chorus Line, A, 552, 553, 578
Chronological order, 329
Churchill, Sir Winston, 284
Cicero, 35
Circumflex, 75
Citation of source, 228
Classification, 326
Clichés, 279
Climactic order, 330
Climax, 325, 519-20, 550 (See also Oral interpretation.)
in narration, 325
Clothing, appropriate, 296-97 (See also Appearance.)
Coaxial cable, 582
Cohesiveness, in group, 413
"Cold" reading, 555
Coleridge, Samuel Taylor, 528
College interview, 11, 161-79
Color, environmental, 52-53
Comedy, type of play, 544, 546, 554
of manners, 546-47
Commedia dell'arte, 546
Communication, 3-18 (See also Conversation; Discussion; Speech.)
caring about, 16
channels of, 7
feedback during, 5, 7-8
finding ideas for, 13
interference in, 15-16
need for, 8-10
nonverbal, 43-46, 57-58
people's roles in, 5-6

steps in, 12-18
Communicator, how to be an effective, 16-18
Comparative-advantages pattern, 393, 454
Comparison-and-contrast order, 331
Comparisons as support, 198-99
contrast, phrased as, 199
figurative, 198
literal, 198
Competence, establishing, 387
Complexity, in literature, 517
Conclusion of a speech, 246-47 (See also Informative speech; Persuasive speech; Process speech.)
recommendation, 246
stirring ending, 246-47
summary, 246
Concrete, 268-69
Condensing material, 527, 535
Conflict, 519-20
Conflict in group discussion, 429-32 (See also Disagreement.)
identifying it, 429-30
managing it, 429-32
Conflicting facial expression, 297-98 (See also Nonverbal communication.)
Connotation, 30-32, 280, 518-19
negative, 31
neutral, 31
positive, 31
Consensus, decision by, 433
Consonants, IPA symbols for, 72
Construction of a speech, 237-61 (See also Informative speech; Persuasive speech; Process speech.)
Context clues, listening technique, 96
Contrast, comparison phrased as, 199
Conversation, 137-57
body language in, 147
defined, 138
feelings, verbalization of, 151
good habits in, 142-48
guidelines for, 151
handling disagreement in, 148-51
influencing others through, 140
misunderstanding in, avoiding, 144
nonverbal cues in, 146
paralanguage in, 147
paraphrasing in, 144-45, 151
pleasure in, 138
practicing, 147-48
questions, asking good, 143
reasons for, 138-40
relationships and, 138-39
word pictures, creating, 145-46

PHOTO CREDITS

COVER, James A. Sugar/Black Star;
Title Page, HBJ Photo/Earl Kogler; page ii, (tl), Mark Peters/
Black Star; (cl), T. M. Green/West Stock, (bl), Granger Collection,
(tr), Granger Collection, (cr), Charles Gupton/Stock, Boston,
(br), Rick Friedman/Black Star; 1, Freda Leinwand; 2, James A.
Sugar/Black Star; 4, Billy E. Barnes/The Southern Light Agency;
8, John Coletti/Stock, Boston; 9, Billy E. Barnes/Jeroboam; 11,
(tl), Ken Karp/OMNI-Photo Communications, (tc), Bonnie Freer/
Peter Arnold, (tr), Mark Godfrey/Archive Pictures, (bl), Granger
Collection, (bc), Ann Hagen Griffiths/OMNI-Photo Communi-
cations; (br), Granger Collection; 14, (l), Freda Leinwand, (r),
HBJ Photo; 17, Roy King/After Image; 19, HBJ Photo/Judy
Allen-Newberry; 23, (l), Sandy Macys/Taurus Photos, (r), Brent
Jones; 24, Robert Frerck/Odyssey Productions; 26, (all 4), North
Wind; 28, Pam Hasegawa/Taurus Photos; 35, Granger Collec-
tion; 36, Communispond, Inc.; 41, (l), HBJ Photo/Sam Joosten,
(r), Jim Pickerell/Black Star; 42, HBJ Photo; 46, Hugh Rogers/
Monkmeyer Press Photo Service; 48, Robert McElroy/Woodfin
Camp & Assoc.; 51, Paul Conklin/Monkmeyer Press Photo Ser-
vice; 54, (tl), Arthur Grace/Stock, Boston; 55, (tr), David R.

Frazier, (bl), Rich Vogel/Leo deWys, Inc., (br), Tom Tracy/Photophile; 57, Granger Collection; 59, HBJ Photo/Peter A. Burg; 63, (l), Louis Fernandez/Black Star, (r), Jim Pickerell/Black Star; 64, HBJ Photo/Sam Joosten; 74, Gregg Mancuso/After Image; 76, Spectrogram aligned by Lori F. Lamel and Hong C. Leung, courtesy of Prof. Victor W. Zue, Massachusetts Institute of Technology; 79, Andrew Sacks/Art Resource; 83, HBJ Photo/Mark Pokempner/Click, Chicago; 87, (l), HBJ Photo, (r), Ellis Herwig/The Picture Cube; 88, James A. Sugar/Black Star; 91, Frank Siteman/The Picture Cube; 94, Farrell Grehan/Alpha, FPG; 96, Richard Howard/Black Star; 99, Scala/Art Resource; 101, Eastfoto; 105, B. Bartholomew/Black Star; 106, HBJ Photo/Peter A. Burg; 111, (l), Vincent Serbin/Leo deWys, Inc., (r), Richard Pasley Stock, Boston; 112, (tl), Teri Gilman/After Image, (cl), Nancy Pierce/Black Star, (bl), Frank Fisher/After Image, (tr), Glen Cloyd/Taurus Photos, (br), Granger Collection; 113, Frank Siteman/The Picture Cube; 114, Jeff Lowenthal/Woodfin Camp & Assoc.; 118, HBJ Photo/Courtesy Destiny Properties; 120, Brent Jones; 122, Joseph A. DiChello, Jr.; 123, Cary Wolinsky/Stock, Boston; 127, Michal Heron/Woodfin Camp & Assoc.; 131, HBJ Photo/Judy Allen-Newberry; 135 (l), HBJ Photo, (r), Michal Heron/Woodfin Camp & Assoc.; 136, Brent Jones; 138, Granger Collection; 140, Ellan Young/Photo Researchers; 145, Michal Heron/Woodfin Camp & Assoc.; 146, Richard Hutchings; 152, HBJ Photo/Judy Allen-Newberry; 157, (l & r), HBJ Photo/Sam Joosten; 158, Frank Fisher/After Image; 160, Michael Grecco/Stock, Boston; 162, Jeff Cadge/The Image Bank; 170, Gregg Mancuso/Stock, Boston; 172, (l), Louis Fernandez/Black Star, (r), Alex Webb/Magnum Photos; 175, HBJ Photo/Judy Allen-Newberry; 179, HBJ Photo/Sam Joosten; 180, (tl), Granger Collection, (cl), David R. Frazier, (bl), Richard Hutchings, (tr), Joe Skymba/Berg & Assoc., (cr), Wynn Miller/After Image, (br), Granger Collection; 181, David R. Frazier; 182, John Coletti/Stock, Boston; 184, Richard Hutchings; 188, (l), David R. Frazier, (c), Michal Heron/Woodfin Camp & Assoc., (r), Ellis Herwig/The Picture Cube; 190, Joseph A. DiChello, Jr.; 193, Patrick L. Pfister/Stock, Boston; 195, Paul Conklin/Monkmeyer Press Photo Service; 200, HBJ Photo/Peter A. Burg; 207, (l), John Lei/Stock, Boston, (r), Carlos Vergara/Nawrocki Stock Photo; 208, Mimi Forsyth/Monkmeyer Press Photo Service; 210, Michal Heron/Monkmeyer Press Photo Service; 213, HBJ Photo; 215, Robert H. Glaze/Artstreet; 217, Bohdan Hrynewych/The Southern Light Agency; 219, Barbara Barnes/Photo Researchers; 221, Dawson Jones, Inc./After Image; 224, HBJ Photo; 227, Timothy Eagan/Woodfin Camp & Assoc.; 229, HBJ Photo/Lodder Photography; 235, (l & r), HBJ Photo; 236, Brent Jones; 240, Dave Schaefer/The Picture Cube; 243, Owen Franken/Stock, Boston; 244, Monroe Leung/ROTHCO Cartoons; 247, Paul Kennedy/Leo deWys, Inc.; 249, Charles Gordon/West Stock; 253, Ann Hagen Griffiths/OMNI-Photo Communications; 256, HBJ Photo/Marc Pokempner/Click, Chicago; 261, (l), Billy E. Barnes/Jeroboam, (r), George Contorakes/The Stock Market; 262, Michael Philip Manheim/West Stock; 264, Granger Collection; 273, Lynn Johnson/Black Star; 275, Mary Evans Picture Library/Photo Researchers; 277, (l), Cary Wolinsky/Stock, Boston, (c), Joseph Nettis/Photo Researchers, (r), Ellis Herwig/The Picture Cube; 279, Robert H. Glaze/Artstreet; 281, Daniel F. Wilson; 287, (l), HBJ Photo/Sam Joosten, (r), HBJ Photo; 288, Ben Marra/West Stock; 291, Steve Meltzer/West Stock; 298, Ron Sherman/After Image; 302, Joseph A. DiChello, Jr.; 306, Jeff Dunn/The Picture Cube; 308, (l), Culver Pictures, (r), UPI/Bettmann Newsphotos; 310, J. Barry O'Rourke/The Stock Market; 312, HBJ Photo; 317, (l & r), HBJ Photo/Sam Joosten; 318, (tl), Charles Gupton/Stock, Boston, (cl), Chuck Keeler, Jr./After Image, (bl), Granger Collection, (tr), Scala/Art Resource, (br), Joseph Traver/Gamma-Liason; 319, HBJ Photo; 320, Michael Hayman/Stock, Boston; 322, Peter Menzel/Stock, Boston; 324, Judy White/Berg & Assoc.; 330, Brownie Harris/The Stock Market; 333, Michael Grecco/Stock, Boston; 341, David R. Frazier; 343, Paul J. Satton/Duomo; 347, Judy Allen-Newberry/HBJ Photo; 353, (l), Sam Joosten/HBJ Photo, (r), Edith G. Haun/Stock, Boston; 354, Tom Tracy/After Image; 360, Frank Siteman/The Picture Cube; 362, Donald Dietz/Stock, Boston; 364, Brent Jones; 366, Patrick Ward/Stock, Boston; 369, HBJ Photo; 371, HBJ Photo/Peter A. Burg; 375, Burk Uzzle/Woodfin Camp & Assoc.; 376, G. Cloyd/Taurus Photos; 379, Paul Fusco/Magnum Photos; 385, Bruce Kliewe/Jeroboam; 388, Ted Spiegel/Black Star; 389, Lester Sloan/Woodfin Camp & Assoc.; 394, Erich Hartmann/Magnum Photos; 396, Richard Hutchings; 398, Pam Hasegawa/Taurus Photos; 402, HBJ Photo/Lodder Photography, 407, (l), Michael Philip Manheim/West Stock; (r), Walter Hodges/West Stock; 408, (tl), Peter Vilms/Jeroboam, (cl), Bettmann Archive, (bl), James A. Sugar/Black Star, (tr), Steve Liss/Gamma-Liason, (cr), Diana Walker/Gamma-Liason, (br), British Information Service; 409, Ted Spiegel/Black Star; 410, Rick Friedman/The Picture Cube; 412, Michal Heron/Woodfin Camp & Assoc.; 414, Bruce Hoertel/Gamma-Liason; 417, Culver Pictures; 419, Billy E. Barnes; 421, The Bettmann Archive/Bettmann; 424, Jerry Markatos/The Southern Light Agency; 426, Sepp Seitz/Woodfin Camp & Assoc.; 430, Tom Tracy/After Image; 437, HBJ Photo; 441, (l), HBJ Photo, (r), Rhoda Sidney/Leo deWys, Inc; 442, Sybil Shelton/Peter Arnold, Inc.; 444, The Bettmann Archive; 446, Culver Pictures; 449, Rick Friedman/Black Star; 453, HBJ Photo; 455, HBJ Photo; 457, Rick Friedman/Black Star; 459, Joseph A. DiChello, Jr.; 468, Myron H. Davis/Nawrocki Stock Photo; 470, HBJ Photo/Sam Joosten; 472, Office of Senator Stanley Aronoff; 477, (l), HBJ Photo, (r), Frank Fisher/After Image; 478, Paul Seaman/Photo Researchers; 480, Granger Collection; 482, HBJ Photo; 484, Eric Kroll/Taurus Photos; 491, David R. Frazier; 494, Peter Byron/Black Star; 496, The Bettmann Archive; 499, HBJ Photo; 502, HBJ Photo/Marc Pokempner/Click, Chicago; 507, Ellis Herwig/Stock, Boston; 508, (tl), Roy Morsch/The Stock Market, (cl), Phylane Norman/Nawrocki Stock Photo, (bl), The Bettmann Archive, (tr), James H. Karales/Peter Arnold, Inc., (cr), Boulton-Wilson/Jeroboam, (br), Paul Light/Lightwave; 509, Joseph A. DiChello, Jr.; 510, Paul Merideth/Click, Chicago; 512, Ellis Herwig/The Picture Cube; 517, HBJ Photo; 519, Brian Payne/West Stock; 523, Ann Hagen Griffiths/OMNI-Photo Communications; 528, Granger Collection; 531, Martha Swope Photography; 533, Art Resource; 536, HBJ Photo; 541, (l), Michal Heron/Monkmeyer Press Photo Service; (r), HBJ Photo; 542, HBJ Photo/Earl Kogler, courtesy University of Central Florida Theatre Dept.; 546, (l), Granger Collection; (r), by permission of Folger Skakespeare Library; 548, Billy E. Barnes/Jeroboam; 551, Martha Swope Photography; 553, Martha Swope Photography; 555, R. Touchstone, Stockphotos, Inc./The Image Bank; 556, Paul Fusco/Magnum Photos; 561, Will/Deni McIntyre/Photo Researchers; 563, Michael Hayman/Click, Chicago; 570, HBJ Photo/Paul Merideth/Click, Chicago; 575, HBJ Photo/Sam Joosten; 576, Richard Pasley/Stock, Boston; 579, Frederic Lewis Photographs; 582, AP/Wide World Photos; 585, Billy E. Barnes/The Southern Light Agency; 592, HBJ Photo/Judy Allen-Newberry; 597, (l), HBJ Photo, (r), HBJ Photo, courtesy Strasberg Companies.

A 7
B 8
C 9
D 0
E 1
F 2
G 3
H 4
I 5
J 6